PREPARATION FOR THE

GRADUATE
RECORD
EXAMINATION
(GRE)

3 hour test

PREPARATION FOR THE
GRADUATE RECORD EXAMINATION (GRE)

by Jerry Bobrow, M.A.

Consultants:
William A. Covino, M.A.
David L. Becker, M.A.
Merritt L. Weisinger, J.D.

Contemporary Books, Inc., regrets the omission of the consultants' names from the first printing of *Preparation for the Graduate Record Examination*.

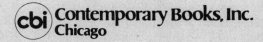

cbi Contemporary Books, Inc.
Chicago

Published by Contemporary Books, Inc.
180 North Michigan Avenue, Chicago, Illinois 60601
Manufactured in the United States of America
Library of Congress Catalog Card Number: 78-60504
International Standard Book Number: 0-8092-7671-2

Published simultaneously in Canada by
Beaverbooks
953 Dillingham Road
Pickering, Ontario L1W 1Z7
Canada

Contents

PREPARATION FOR THE

GRADUATE RECORD EXAMINATION (GRE)

PREFACE

Test-taking is *no fun!* And unless you are one of the select few who enjoy taking tests, then you probably have feelings of apprehension, anxiety, worry, or even outright panic at the thought of taking the Graduate Record Examination.

Regardless of the reason, you are now faced with a three-hour exam that tests some abilities that you may not have used since high school. However, with the proper materials and techniques, you can certainly *prepare yourself* for this exam.

The techniques explained in this book are the outcome of the five years of successful GRE prep sessions at California State University, Northridge, which I have organized, directed, and instructed. This book is geared to the student who needs thorough study materials for complete preparation; it has been based on the carefully tested educational principles and techniques used in the prep sessions.

Many special features make this book a *unique* study tool for the GRE.

These special features are:

1. A careful analysis of each exam area (including the new areas on analytical ability and quantitative comparison). A highly detailed section introduces each exam area, explaining "What is measured," "What is required," and "What you should know"—and provides samples, techniques, and important strategies.

2. A self-pacing checklist. This is provided so that the individual student has a systematic process with which to attack each area of the exam. This sequential learning process will allow them successively to gain testing insight, practice techniques, build confidence, and relieve test anxiety. Returning students will find this approach tremendously helpful, especially if they have not taken classes for some time.

3. Three full-length new-format practice tests. The candidate can simulate taking the actual examination by taking the three full-length practice exams. The student marks his/her answers on the answer sheet in much the same way that the machine-graded answer sheet is marked for the actual GRE. Next, the candidate can evaluate his/her own aptitude by correcting the answers and comparing his/her score with the GRE Score Approximator. All problems are completely explained.

4. A positive systematic approach. This is a complete section on an overall test-taking method that has been proven successful.

1

5. A question-answer section.   This section answers the most common questions about the newly restructured GRE.

Additional features include:

6. An introductory mini-exam.   This exam is designed to quickly familiarize the student with the exam areas and enable him to detect any test-taking weaknesses.

7. Basic skills diagnostic self-tests and review areas.   A section of diagnostic self-tests on basic arithmetic, algebra, and geometry, keyed to the review section, aids students in pinpointing weak areas quickly.

8. Extra practice and review section.   A section of extra practice problems is included for the Verbal and Quantitative areas of the exam.

9. Etymologies and word list.   A short list of basic word etymologies, stressing prefixes and suffixes, and a graduate word list of 2,300 common words, are provided for review.

Thus the book combines up-to-date coverage of new areas, study approaches, and test-taking techniques with full length practice test sections and thorough review.

I have found this approach highly effective in my work of assisting over 5,000 graduate students to prepare for the GRE and I firmly believe that by using this book and carefully following this study sequence, you will receive the best test preparation possible.

FORMAT OF THE RESTRUCTURED 1977-1978 GRE APTITUDE TEST

Section I	**Verbal Ability**	**80 Questions**
	Sentence Completion	15-20 Questions
	Analogies	15-20 Questions
50 minutes	Antonyms	15-20 Questions
	Reading Comprehension	20-25 Questions
	(2 long passages and	
	3 short passages)	

Section II	**Quantitative Ability**	**55 Questions**
	Quantitative Comparison	30 Questions
	(Suggested time—	
	20 minutes)	
50 minutes	Math Ability	25 Questions
	(Suggested time—	
	30 minutes)	

Section III	**Analytical Ability**	**40 Questions**
25 minutes	Analysis of Explanations	

Section IV	**Analytical Ability**	**30 Questions**
	Logical Diagrams	15 Questions
	(Suggested time—	
	6 minutes)	
25 minutes	Analytical Reasoning	15 Questions
	(Suggested time—	
	19 minutes)	

Section V	**Either Quantitative Ability,**	
	Verbal Ability, Analytical	
	Ability or Experimental	
25 minutes	**Section**	**About 25 Questions**

Total Testing Time: 175 Minutes =   Approximately
     2 hours, 55 minutes   230 Questions

SELF-PACING STUDY CHART—CHECKLIST

Week #1

_____ 1. Read the GRE bulletin carefully

_____ 2. Check with graduate departments to find out the scores you need (a total of 1,000 on the Verbal and Quantitative sections is considered about average)

_____ 3. Read Chapter 1, "Questions Commonly Asked About the Restructured GRE"

_____ 4. Take the Mini-Exam; correct, score, compare, and analyze

_____ 5. _READ CHAPTER 3 VERY CAREFULLY,_ "A Closer Look at Each Exam Area"

Week #2

_____ 6. Familiarize yourself with Testing-Strategies—A Positive Systematic Approach

_____ 7. Take Math Review Diagnostic Self-Tests; correct and review weak areas

_____ Arithmetic

_____ Algebra

_____ Geometry

Week #3

_____ 8. Review section on word problems and graph reading

_____ 9. Take Practice Test 1 (you may wish to take this first test slowly, not for time, but more for technique); correct and analyze

_____ 10. Review explanations to Practice Test 1

_____ 11. Look over etymology and word list

Week #4

_____ 12. Take Practice Test 2 (timed); correct and analyze

_____ 13. Review explanations to Practice Test 2

_____ 14. Extra Verbal or Quantitative practice (if necessary)

Week #5

_____15. Take Practice Test 3 (timed); correct and analyze
_____16. Review explanations to Practice Test 3
_____17. Extra Verbal or Quantitative practice (if necessary)

Week #6

_____18. Review "A Closer Look at Each Exam Area" (chapter 3)
_____19. Read "A Few Final Tips" on testing
_____20. Reread *GRE information bulletin*

Questions Commonly Asked About the Restructured GRE

Who Administers the GRE and What Is Its Purpose?

The GRE is administered by the Educational Testing Service (ETS) of Princeton, New Jersey. It is used for several purposes: (1) to help undergraduate and graduate schools appraise their students' achievements; (2) to give graduate schools information concerning the educational background and general scholastic ability of their applicants; and (3) to help fellowship sponsors in their selection of recipients.

How Is the GRE Used?

Your scores on the GRE provide one common denominator by which you and applicants from other institutions can be compared. This does not mean, however, that the scores on the GRE are more important for admission than your scholastic standing, letters of recommendation, reports of committees that interview you, or your personal qualities and characteristics. Each college or university system—and often the individual department—sets up its score standards for admission to its specific programs.

What Is the Difference between the Aptitude Test and the Advanced Test?

The Aptitude Test, usually taken by all candidates, provides a measure of general scholastic ability at the level required for graduate study. The Advanced Test taken only when specifically required, measures the candidate's mastery of materials needed for success in his intended graduate major. This test deals with specific subject matter.

What Subjects Are Covered by Advanced Tests?

There are advanced tests in the following areas: Biology, Chemistry, Computer Science, Economics, Education, Engineering, French, Geography, Geology, German, History, Literature in English, Mathematics, Music, Philosophy, Physics, Political Science, Psychology, Sociology, and Spanish. Subscores are reported for the tests in Biology, Engineering, French, Geography, Geology, History, Music, Psychology, and Spanish.

When Are the GRE's Administered?

There are six nationwide administrations of the examinations during each school year—in October, December, January, February, April, and June. The administrations are on Saturday, with the Aptitude Test given at 8:30 in the morning and the Advanced Tests given at 1:30 in the afternoon. (Special summer administrations are given in July, August, and September in limited locations.)

Where Are the GRE's Administered?

The examinations are administered at hundreds of examination centers located at schools and colleges in every state of the United States and many other countries. Check with your local college or university testing and placement officer for local administrations. A list of testing centers is provided in the GRE information bulletin.

What If You Cannot Take a Saturday Test or Need Special Arrangements?

If you prefer a Monday administration for religious reasons, it probably can be arranged. The ETS also can provide special arrangements for handicapped students and special arrangements for persons who have to travel more than seventy-five miles to a regular testing center.

When and How Should I Register?

Every candidate should file a registration form with ETS in advance of the test date and pay an examination fee of $13 for the Aptitude Test and $13 for the Advanced Test. This registration should be done about seven weeks prior to your selected exam date. A $4 late registration fee is charged after their deadlines.

What About Walk-In Registration?

In the case of an emergency, walk-in testing will be allowed, but only if sufficient space and test materials are available after all normally registered students are admitted. You must take a completed registration form to the center and you will be billed for the test fee plus a $10 walk-in service fee.

How Many Times Can You Take the GRE?

You can take the GRE several times during your college career. If you wish, you can apply for the test at any time in order to take it for practice, but keep in mind that the scores of each testing appear on the transcript sent to the schools you designate.

What Materials Do I Need or Can I Use on the GRE?

You should have a watch and three or four sharpened number-2 pencils with which to mark your answer sheet. No books, notes, slide rules, calculators, scratch paper, or other aids are allowed in the testing room. All figuring is to be done in the margins of the test booklet.

How Long Is the GRE?

The GRE Aptitude Test is 2 hours and 55 minutes in length; the Advanced Tests are about 2 hours and 45 minutes in length.

What Is the Structure of the Restructured GRE?

The restructured GRE consists of three major exam areas: Verbal Ability, Quantitative Ability, and Analytical Ability. The Verbal Ability section consists of questions dealing with analogies, antonyms, sentence completion, and reading comprehension. The Quantitative Ability section consists of math ability problems and quantitative comparison problems. The new Analytical Ability section is composed of three different types of questions: analysis of explanations, logical diagrams, and analytical reasoning. The chapter entitled "A Closer Look at Each Exam Area" gives a complete breakdown and explanation of each area.

How Is the New GRE Different from the Old GRE?

The old GRE consisted of four sections; Verbal Ability, Reading Comprehension, Quantitative Ability, and either Verbal or Quantitative Ability. The restructured test is described above. The major differences are: the new Analytical section, time allotment, and the inclusion of quantitative comparison problems.

How Is the New GRE Scored?

The restructured GRE will generate 3 scores: Verbal, Quantitative, and Analytical, all on a scale from 200 to 900. The Verbal and Quantitative scores can be interpreted in the same way as on previous tests. Since norms have been long established for these two areas, a percentile ranking will be included as usual. The new Analytical section scores will appear in a shaded box indicating the introductory nature of the section and will have no percentile rankings, until some have been established.

How Will the Colleges Use the New Section?

Because the Analytical score is new, the colleges will be using it to determine an empirical relationship between that score and one's performance in graduate study. The use of this new section will be flexible, varying from college to college.

What About the Question Structure and Value?

All questions on the GRE are multiple choice questions with either four or five possible choices. All questions in any one section are of equal value.

Should I Guess on the GRE?

The GRE is scored in such a way that there is a penalty for wrong answers to discourage wild guessing. One point is earned for every right answer, one-fourth of a point (or one-third of a point for a four-answer question) is deducted for every answer marked incorrectly, and no points are considered if the answer is left blank. If you can definitely eliminate one or more choices, you have a greater chance of choosing the right answer and you should probably guess.

Can I Prepare for the GRE? How?

Subject matter review for the mathematical questions on the GRE is of the most benefit, since many students have not been confronted with algebra or geometry for some time. Success in the Verbal and Analytical sections depends most heavily on *process* review, testing strategies, and practice, rather than subject matter review. The maximum amount of preparation for the GRE can be achieved by carefully working through this book and following the important strategies and techniques outlined here.

How Can I Get More Information?

This GRE preparation book gives intensive practice in the areas of ability tested on the Aptitude Test and a sampling of kinds of questions that may appear on the Advanced Test in each area. If you need more information, however, you should get the GRE information bulletin at your undergraduate institution, or write to the Educational Testing Service at one of the addresses given below. The GRE information bulletin contains a registration form and gives the times and locations for the current year's tests. You may also request a booklet describing the Advanced Tests that interest you. Otherwise, the appropriate booklet will be sent when you register for the Advanced Test.

If you live in Alaska, Arizona, Arkansas, California, Colorado, Hawaii, Idaho, Montana, Nevada, New Mexico, Oklahoma, Oregon, Texas, Utah, Washington, or Wyoming, write to:

Educational Testing Service
Box 1502
Berkeley, California 94701

If you live in any other state or in Puerto Rico, write to:

Educational Testing Service
Box 955
Princeton, New Jersey 08540

2

Sampling Test-Type Problems—
Mini-Exam

The best way to familiarize yourself with the newly restructured GRE and its requirements is to take a sampling of the typical problems in each area. The mini-exam that follows will give you an excellent perspective of the test structure. It is designed as an introduction to the testing areas. The actual practice tests found later in this book will give you a much more complete scope of the range of problem types and difficulties.

Take the mini-exam under strict test conditions with each section timed accurately as follows:

Section I   20 minutes
Section II   20 minutes
Section III   10 minutes
Section IV   10 minutes
Section V   (NOT INCLUDED IN MINI-EXAM)

The actual GRE is approximately 2½ times as long (175 minutes), with normal fatigue and anxiety factors affecting your score. Taking the full-length practice tests will aid you in these areas.

After correcting the mini-exam and comparing your score, carefully read the explanations and strategies in Section III.

Now turn to the next page, remove the answer sheet to record your answers, and begin the mini-exam.

Mini-Exam

Tear out Answer Sheet for Mini-Exam, page ix.

SECTION I: VERBAL ABILITY

SENTENCE COMPLETION

Directions: Each question in this test consists of a sentence in which one or two words are missing. Beneath the sentence are five words or word sets. Choose the word or word set that *best* completes the sentence. Then mark the appropriate space in the answer column.

1. Since she felt that the tragedy was _____, she ascribed its cause to fate.
   (A) poignant
   (B) justified
   (C) unavoidable
   (D) unnecessary
   (E) necessary

2. William Seward was _____ as a _____ because he sought the purchase of Alaska, which had been labeled "Seward's Folly."
   (A) prescribed—nut
   (B) lampooned—warmonger
   (C) inscribed—traveler
   (D) condemned—fool
   (E) proscribed—gambler

3. A certain television actor amuses his audience because of the _____ of his _____. His audience laughs hysterically when he seems "to put his foot in his mouth."
   (A) impartiality—actions
   (B) malapropisms—speech
   (C) animation—face
   (D) clumsiness—movement
   (E) sting—satire

4. Despite the many bribes they offered the player, the "fixers" did not succeed in _____ his integrity.
   - (A) undermining
   - (B) discouraging
   - (C) discovering
   - (D) reducing
   - (E) enhancing

5. Such _____ habits of dress would not be imitated by a _____ person.
   - (A) peculiar—erratic
   - (B) intolerable—effusive
   - (C) careless—fastidious
   - (D) ornate—garish
   - (E) meticulous—energetic

6. A wise person will not _____ sectional habits or customs; he will _____ those practices or actions which he enjoys.
   - (A) deprecate—participate in
   - (B) countenance—join in
   - (C) disapprove—depreciate
   - (D) question—denounce
   - (E) enjoy—find pleasure in

7. A fortunate but small number of people work at jobs which are in themselves _____ and are not performed chiefly for the return which they bring.
   - (A) painful
   - (B) useful
   - (C) wearisome
   - (D) necessary
   - (E) pleasurable

8. This author may be considered a cheerful and kindly sage; his writings are characterized by _____ but not by _____.
   - (A) warmth—frustration
   - (B) laconicism—zeal
   - (C) levity—sincerity
   - (D) moderation—consideration
   - (E) insipidity—verbosity

ANALOGIES

Directions: In each of the following questions select the lettered pair which best expresses a relationship similar to that expressed in the original pair.

---

9. LOOM : DISASTER : :
   - (A) impend : catastrophe
   - (B) howl : storm
   - (C) question : puzzle
   - (D) hurt : penalty
   - (E) imminent : eminent

10. STUDY : GRANT : :
    - (A) honor : medal
    - (B) matrimony : dowry
    - (C) merit : scholarship
    - (D) research : fellowship
    - (E) student : bonus

11. BURGLAR : ALARM : :
    - (A) snake : hiss
    - (B) air raid : siren
    - (C) trespasser : bark
    - (D) ship : buoy
    - (E) crossing : bell

12. HEART : MAN : :
    - (A) tail : dog
    - (B) lungs : child
    - (C) computer : jet
    - (D) well : pump
    - (E) engine : car

13. REMORSELESS : COMPASSION : :
    - (A) unscrupulous : qualms
    - (B) opportunist : opportunity
    - (C) impenitent : sin
    - (D) intrepid : rashness
    - (E) querulous : lamentation

14.   FIGURATIVE : METAPHORICAL : :
   (A)   slang : speech
   (B)   autonomasia : literal
   (C)   irony : meaningless
   (D)   colloquial : allegorical
   (E)   probity : improbity

15.   POSTERIOR : SIMULTANEOUS : :
   (A)   posthumous : following
   (B)   concurrent : ensuing
   (C)   prolonged : before
   (D)   synchronous : contemporaneous
   (E)   subsequent : coincidental

16.   SCALENE : EQUILATERAL : :
   (A)   obtuse : acute
   (B)   unity : coherence
   (C)   irregular : regular
   (D)   chemistry : alchemy
   (E)   quantifier : qualifier

ANTONYMS

Directions: Each question in this test consists of a word printed in capital letters followed by five words lettered (A) through (E). Choose the word that has most nearly the OPPOSITE meaning from the word in capital letters. Mark the appropriate space in the answer column. Consider all choices before deciding which one is best, since some choices are very close in meaning.

---

17.   FLEXIBLE:
   (A)   unable
   (B)   obdurate
   (C)   rational
   (D)   easy
   (E)   likable

18.   PERPETUATE:
   (A)   concretize
   (B)   delay
   (C)   abrogate
   (D)   collate
   (E)   derive

19.   OBSTINATE:
   (A)   resolved
   (B)   stained
   (C)   complaisant
   (D)   resourceful
   (E)   mindful

20.   EUPHONY:
   (A)   tune
   (B)   harmony
   (C)   note
   (D)   chord
   (E)   cacophony

21. PROLIX:
   (A) open
   (B) parting
   (C) arrogant
   (D) pithy
   (E) long

22. PEACEABLE:
   (A) broken
   (B) delicate
   (C) fractious
   (D) soft
   (E) quiet

23. SESSILE:
   (A) ceasing
   (B) mobile
   (C) steady
   (D) solvent
   (E) searing

24. AVERSION:
   (A) proclivity
   (B) ease
   (C) state
   (D) revision
   (E) suasion

READING COMPREHENSION

Directions: Each passage is followed by a group of questions. Read each passage and choose the *best* answer to each question. Then mark the appropriate space in the answer column. Answers should be chosen on the basis of what is stated and implied.

A glance at the five leading causes of death in 1900, 1910, and 1945, years representing in some measure the early and late practice of physicians still active, shows a significant trend. In 1900 these causes were (1) tuberculosis, (2) pneumonia, (3) enteritis, typhoid fever, and other acute intestinal diseases, (4) heart diseases, and (5) cerebral hemorrhage and thrombosis. Ten years later the only change was that heart disease had moved from fourth to first place, tuberculosis now being second, and pneumonia third. In 1945, however, the list had changed profoundly. Heart diseases were far out in front; cancer, which had come up from eighth place, was second; and cerebral hemorrhage and thrombosis, third. Fatal accidents, which had been well down the list, were now fourth, and nephritis was fifth. All of these are, of course, composites rather than single diseases, and it is significant that, except for accidents, they are characteristic of the advanced rather than the early or middle years of life.

25. On the basis of the paragraph, which of the following statements is most tenable?
   (A) a cure for cancer will be found within this decade.
   (B) many of the medical problems of today are problems of the gerontologist (specialist in medical problems of old age).
   (C) older persons are more accident-prone than are younger persons.
   (D) tuberculosis has been all but eliminated.
   (E) heart disease has never been a real threat to the aged.

26. Which of the following trends is LEAST indicated in the paragraph?
    (A)   as one grows older he is more subject to disease.
    (B)   pneumonia has become less common.
    (C)   relative to mortality rates for acute intestinal diseases, the mortality rate for cancer has increased.
    (D)   the incident of heart disease has increased.
    (E)   fatal accidents claim more lives today than ever.

27. Which of the following statements is most nearly correct?
    (A)   such mortality trends are caused by decreased infant mortality.
    (B)   the data reported are a function of improved diagnosis and reporting.
    (C)   the mortality data are based on the records of physicians who practiced continuously from 1900 to 1945.
    (D)   there appears to be a greater change in the mortality patterns from 1910 to 1945 than in the decade ending in 1910.
    (E)   pneumonia was the chief cause of death in 1945.

28. In 1945, what was the leading cause of death?
    (A)   fatal accidents
    (B)   cerebral hemorrhage
    (C)   heart diseases
    (D)   cancer
    (E)   whooping cough

Poor discipline has three principal roots: the pupils, the teacher, and external factors. Often a combination of all three elements or of any two actuates a high degree of disorder.

In a few classrooms, there are some pupils who are so emotionally ill that the best teacher working in the most favorable setting cannot easily achieve control of the class. Even three or four such children can infect the entire group unless these troublemakers are taken care of.

Sometimes the acoustics, the length, the shape and the age of a room make for unrest and confusion. Teaching can be difficult if the classroom is too big, too small, too difficult to supervise, or too drafty. If the room has an alcove, unruly atmosphere though the entire class can make the individual teacher's plight a sad one indeed.

But the chief reason children cooperate or fail to cooperate is the teacher herself. She may have a weak personality, thus emboldening normally adjusted children to become mischievous or lazy. Consciously or subconsciously, they will seek to dominate her. And, as part of her personality, her voice may be the source of the trouble; perhaps it lacks resonance; perhaps it is harsh; perhaps it is pitched too high or too low.

As adjuncts of a teacher's personality we should consider her methods, her planning, her attention to routines, her appearance, her concern for neatness and her attitude toward children. If she does not rank high on these counts, she will probably be unable to control the class.

Therefore, any teacher whose class is misbehaving should first do some self-evaluation. Literally and figuratively (and, above all, objectively!), she should view herself in a mirror and seek to determine the extent to which she is or is not to blame for the undesirable situation. After this honest appraisal, she may look beyond herself to less easily alterable factors, such as the pupils, the school, the principal, and the community.

29. Of the following titles, the one which best suggests the central idea of the passage is
(A) Personality Plus
(B) How to Improve Discipline
(C) Adjusting Instruction
(D) The Causes of Poor Discipline
(E) Teacher, Know Thy Weaknesses

30. Of the following, the one which is among the three principal sources of poor discipline mentioned by the author is
(A) poor planning
(B) the teacher's voice
(C) the pupils
(D) the teacher's methods and routines
(E) failure to practice self-evaluation

31. The subject of the third paragraph can be summed up as
(A) why pupils misbehave
(B) room problems contributing to poor discipline
(C) external factors contributing to poor discipline
(D) aggravations of the problem
(E) the teacher's problems in discipline

32. Of the following statements, the one that the author does not make or imply is
(A) it is easier for a teacher to change her own practices than her principal's
(B) one of the reasons for poor discipline may be the teacher's lack of attention to room decoration
(C) if a teacher is really competent and objectively tries to improve, she should have no discipline problems
(D) deeply disturbed pupils may need special placement
(E) the chief cause of poor discipline is the teacher herself

33. Of the following statements, the one that the author does not make or imply is
    (A) a small group of disturbed children may upset an entire class
    (B) L-shaped rooms are less conducive to good discipline than ordinary rectangular rooms
    (C) children who ordinarily cooperate may become disorderly if their teacher's personality lacks force
    (D) a teacher should always keep her voice moderately low; she should never shout
    (E) self-evaluation is an important duty for the teacher

34. All of the following are mentioned by the author as possible causes of disciplinary trouble except
    (A) the teacher's unpleasant voice
    (B) the teacher's authoritarian attitude
    (C) the classroom's poor state of repair
    (D) the school's poor emotional climate
    (E) emotionally unstable children

S T O P
IF YOU FINISH BEFORE TIME IS CALLED, CHECK YOUR
WORK ON THIS SECTION ONLY. DO NOT WORK
ON ANY OTHER SECTION IN THE TEST.

SECTION II: QUANTITATIVE ABILITY

TIME—20 MINUTES
22 QUESTIONS

QUANTITATIVE COMPARISON

(SUGGESTED TIME—8 MINUTES)
12 QUESTIONS

Directions: Each question in this section consists of two quantities, one in Column A and one in Column B. You are to compare the two quantities and on the answer sheet blacken space

A if the quantity in Column A is the greater;
B if the quantity in Column B is the greater;
C if the two quantities are equal;
D if the relationship cannot be determined from the information given.

All numbers used are real numbers.
Figures are not necessarily drawn to scale.

	Column A	Column B
1.	$\dfrac{2}{5} \times \dfrac{1}{3} \times \dfrac{7}{12}$	$\dfrac{7}{8} \times \dfrac{7}{12} \times \dfrac{1}{3}$
2.	$x > 0$ $x + y$	$x - y$
3.	$x > 0$ $x\sqrt{.25} = .7$ x	$\dfrac{4}{3}$
4.	$r = 2$ $s = 2r$ $\dfrac{r^2 + s^2}{r}$	$\dfrac{s^3}{r + s}$

Problems 5–7 refer to the following diagram:

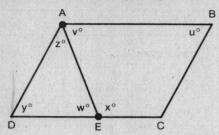

AD = AE = BC   ABCD is a parallelogram

	Column A	**Column B**
5.	$x°$	$z°$
6.	$v°$	$y°$
7.	AE	EC

$$a < b$$

8.	$(a + b)^2$	$(a - b)^2$
9.	$\dfrac{7}{\sqrt{7}}$	$\sqrt{7}$

Problems 10–12 refer to the following graphs:

EXPENDITURES FOR 2 YEARS

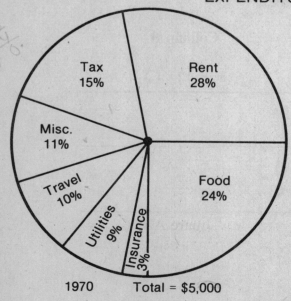

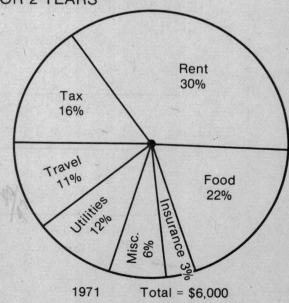

	Column A	Column B
10.	1970 Insurance expenditures	$180
11.	% increase in expenditures from 1970 to 1971	25%
12.	1971 food expenditure	1970 food expenditure

MATH ABILITY

(SUGGESTED TIME—12 MINUTES)
10 QUESTIONS

Directions: Solve each of the following problems and mark the *best* answer on your answer sheet. All scratch work should be done in the available space. All numbers used belong to the real number system. Diagrams are not necessarily drawn to scale.

13. Which one of the following fractions is greater than $\frac{2}{5}$?

(A) $\frac{2}{7}$

(B) $\frac{3}{8}$

(C) $\frac{9}{25}$

(D) $\frac{1}{4}$

(E) $\frac{5}{12}$

14.

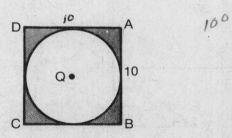

Side AB measures 10 cm. Circle Q intersects square ABCD at 4 points. The shaded area is approximately how many square cm.?

(A) 94

(B) 24

(C) 5

(D) 6

(E) 74

15. If $x = 2y + 3$ and $y = 4$ then $\dfrac{x - 2}{y} =$

   (A) 11
   (B) $\dfrac{13}{4}$
   (C) $\dfrac{11}{4}$
   (D) $\dfrac{9}{4}$
   (E) $\dfrac{1}{2}$

16. Given that $x^6 + 4x + 6 = x^6 + 7$, what is the value of x?
   (A) 4
   (B) $\dfrac{1}{4}$
   (C) $\dfrac{4}{7}$
   (D) $\dfrac{7}{4}$
   (E) $\dfrac{13}{4}$

17. If the ratio of men to women to children at a play was 5 : 3 : 1 which of the following could not be the number of adults at the play?
   I.   9
   II. 15
   III. 24
   IV. 36
   (A) I only
   (B) III only
   (C) I and IV
   (D) II and III
   (E) I, II, IV

18.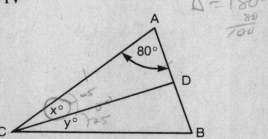

CD is an angle bisector. AC = AB. $\angle A = 80°$. Find $\angle x$.
   (A) 75
   (B) 25
   (C) 50
   (D) 20
   (E) cannot be determined.

19. The net price of a $25 item after successive discounts of 20%
and 30% is

(A) $12.50
(B) $11.00
(C) $14.50
(D) $21.00
(E) $14.00

20.

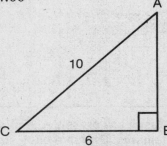

The area of right triangle ABC is:

(A) 30
(B) 20
(C) 48
(D) 24
(E) cannot be determined.

21. The approximate value of $\sqrt{\dfrac{7231}{221}}$ is:

(A) 12
(B) 60
(C) 6
(D) 36
(E) 4

22. Bob can do a job in 8 hours. If Tom works with him, the job
will be completed in 3 hours. How long would it take Tom to
do the job alone?

(A) 7 hours
(B) 4 hours
(C) $4\frac{4}{5}$ hours
(D) $3\frac{3}{5}$ hours
(E) 8 hours

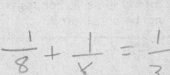

S T O P
**IF YOU FINISH BEFORE TIME IS CALLED, CHECK YOUR
WORK ON THIS SECTION ONLY. DO NOT WORK
ON ANY OTHER SECTION IN THE TEST.**

SECTION III: ANALYTICAL ABILITY

ANALYSIS OF EXPLANATIONS

TIME—10 MINUTES
16 QUESTIONS

Directions: A fact situation and a result are presented. Following the result are several numbered statements. Evaluate each statement in relation to the fact situation and the result.

Each statement is to be considered separately from the other statements. The following sequence of A, B, C, D, and E is to be examined *in order* following each statement. The first choice that cannot be eliminated is the correct choice.

Choose A if the statement is inconsistent with, or contradictory to, something in the fact situation, the result, or both together.

Choose B if the statement presents a possible adequate explanation of the result.

Choose C if the statement is deducible from something in the fact situation, the result, or both together.

Choose D if the statement either support or weakens a possible explanation of the result. It is then relevant to an explanation.

Choose E if the statement is irrelevant to an explanation of the result.

Use common sense to make all decisions; no background in formal logic is necessary. Unlikely or remote possibilities should not be considered.

SITUATION: With the smuggling of drugs becoming an ever-increasing problem, the Border Patrol initiated a strict program of systematically checking every person, his or her belongings, and the vehicle used for crossing. Three shifts of ten men and women inspectors were used in this around-the-clock, time-consuming, but effective system. Unfortunately, the new system was very expensive and was scrapped for a simpler, less effective system of random inspection after only one year of operation.

RESULT: Smuggling of drugs increased sharply after the new system was scrapped.

1. More smuggling of drugs was done during the new system.

2. The smugglers circumvented the new system easily by using different routes.

3. Smuggling of other contraband decreased during the new system.

4. Smugglers were aware of the changing systems.

5. The random system is a very poor system.

6. The Border Patrol could not afford the new system.

7. More smugglers were being caught after they were already in the country.

8. During the new system, three men passed the Border Patrol without being inspected the first day.

SITUATION: Mr. and Mrs. Fisher wanted to buy a three-bedroom house. Their realty broker had taken them to six places before they spotted what they wanted. Mrs. Fisher's brother, a contractor, came out to inspect the house and gave his approval. A number of the Fishers' friends also took a look at the house and were quite impressed. The location was also perfect. Deciding that this was the right place for them, they signed a legal contract and left a check for a deposit.

RESULT: The Fishers did not buy the house, but rented it instead.

9. The house had a small kitchen.

10. The Fishers' check bounced.

11. The house was in poor condition.

12. The people selling the house wanted more money.

13. The rent payment was much less than the house payment.

14. The Fishers liked the house.

15. The lot was smaller than it first appeared.

16. One of the Fishers' relatives did not like the house.

STOP

**IF YOU FINISH BEFORE TIME IS CALLED, CHECK YOUR
WORK ON THIS SECTION ONLY. DO NOT WORK
ON ANY OTHER SECTION IN THE TEST.**

SECTION IV: ANALYTICAL ABILITY

TIME—10 MINUTES
12 QUESTIONS

LOGICAL DIAGRAMS

(SUGGESTED TIME—2 MINUTES)
6 QUESTIONS

Directions: In this section, five diagrams are presented that illustrate the relationship among three classes. You are to choose the one diagram that best illustrates the relationship among three given classes. There are three possible relationships between any *two* different classes:

One class completely within another class, but not vice versa, is represented by

When two classes have some, but not all members in common, the relationship is represented by

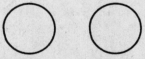

When two classes have no members in common, the relationship is represented by

Note: The relative size of the circles does not represent the size of the class.

The following five possible choices refer to questions 1, 2, and 3.

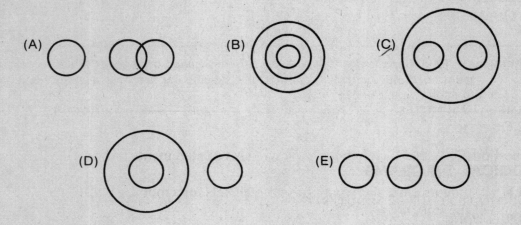

1. Cats, dogs, animals

2. Tall men, thin men, women

3. Tables, coffee tables, chairs

The following five possible choices refer to questions 4, 5, and 6.

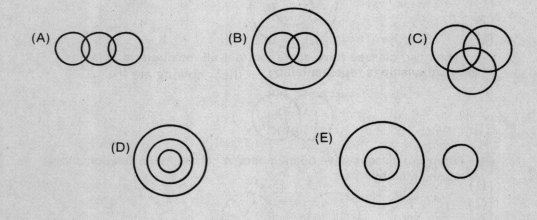

4. Cars, motor vehicles, Cadillacs

5. Friendly people, healthy people, wealthy people

6. Athletes, scholars, people

ANALYTICAL REASONING

(SUGGESTED TIME—8 MINUTES)
6 QUESTIONS

Directions: Each question or group of questions is based on a set of statements or a passage. You are required to choose the *best* answer to each question.

Questions 7, 8, and 9 refer to the following set of statements.

(1) 12 students are standing in line to buy tickets for a movie.
(2) 5 of the students are girls.
(3) Each girl is next to a boy.
(4) Each boy is not necessarily next to a girl.
(5) A boy is at the front of the line.
(6) 4 girls are in the first half of the line.
(7) 2 boys are at the end of the line.
(8) A girl is 10th in line.

7. The first four students in line are composed of:
   (A) 1 Boy, 3 Girls
   (B) 4 Boys
   (C) 1 Girl, 3 Boys
   (D) 2 Girls, 2 Boys
   (E) Cannot be determined

8. In the second half of the line, which of the following are true:
   I. 2 girls are next to each other
   II. 3 boys are next to each other
   III. 4 boys are next to each other
   IV. There are 5 boys
   (A) II & III
   (B) I & IV
   (C) I & III
   (D) II & IV
   (E) III & IV

9. After the first 3 students buy their tickets and are admitted:
   (A) The next 3 students are boys.
   (B) The next 3 students are girls.
   (C) The next 3 students are 1 boy and 2 girls.
   (D) The next 3 students are 1 girl and 2 boys.
   (E) There are still 5 girls in line.

Questions 10–12

The fruits of modern technology have reduced the need for manpower, causing widespread unemployment. Therefore, modern technology is more of a curse than a blessing.

10. The argument above is based on which of the following assumptions:

   I.   modern technology does not create new jobs.

   II.   modern technology is a necessary evil.

   III.   widespread unemployment is bad.

(A) I

(B) I & III

(C) I & II

(D) II

(E) III

11. This argument would be strengthened by pointing out that

   I.   a job shortage already exists.

   II.   even computers need operators.

   III.   man is basically lazy.

(A) I

(B) II

(C) III

(D) I & II

(E) II & III

12. The argument would be weakened *most* by pointing out that

(A) man has created these machines.

(B) most workers are supporting families.

(C) some companies are overstaffed.

(D) cures for many diseases can be attributed to modern technology.

(E) industry shows a recent decline in manufacturing.

STOP

IF YOU FINISH BEFORE TIME IS CALLED, CHECK YOUR
WORK ON THIS SECTION ONLY. DO NOT WORK
ON ANY OTHER SECTION IN THE TEST.

SECTION V OF THE ACTUAL TEST IS EITHER
QUANTITATIVE, VERBAL, ANALYTICAL—OR AN
EXPERIMENTAL SECTION THAT DOES NOT
AFFECT YOUR SCORE.

MINI-EXAM ANSWERS

SECTION I: VERBAL ABILITY

SENTENCE COMPLETION

1.	C	4.	A	7.	E
2.	D	5.	C	8.	A
3.	B	6.	A		

ANALOGIES

9.	A	12.	E	15.	E
10.	D	13.	A	16.	C
11.	C	14.	D		

ANTONYMS

17.	B	20.	E	23.	B
18.	C	21.	D	24.	A
19.	C	22.	C		

READING COMPREHENSION

25.	B	29.	D	33.	D
26.	A	30.	C	34.	B
27.	C	31.	C		
28.	D	32.	C		

SECTION II: QUANTITATIVE ABILITY

QUANTITATIVE COMPARISON

1.	B	5.	A	9.	C
2.	D	6.	C	10.	B
3.	A	7.	D	11.	B
4.	B	8.	D	12.	A

MATH ABILITY

13.	E	17.	E	21.	C
14.	B	18.	B	22.	C
15.	D	19.	E		
16.	B	20.	D		

SECTIONS III & IV: ANALYTICAL ABILITY

ANALYSIS OF EXPLANATIONS

1.	A	7.	D	13.	B
2.	A	8.	A	14.	C
3.	E	9.	E	15.	D
4.	B	10.	D	16.	A
5.	C	11.	A		
6.	C	12.	A		

LOGICAL DIAGRAMS

1.	C	3.	D	5.	C
2.	A	4.	D	6.	B

ANALYTICAL REASONING

7.	D	9.	C	11.	A
8.	D	10.	B	12.	D

SCORING YOUR MINI-EXAM

After carefully correcting your answer sheet, compute your raw score as follows:

1. Total the number correct for the specific area (verbal, quantitative, or analytical).

2. Total the number of problems in that area that you attempted but missed.

3. Take the total in step 2 and multiply it by $\frac{1}{4}$ (or divide by 4).

4. Take the number that you got in the step above and subtract it from the total correct in step 1.

5. You now have your raw score. Raw score = number right — $\frac{1}{4}$ (number attempted but missed).

6. Repeat these steps for each area.

EXAMPLE:
1. Let's say that on the Verbal Ability section you got 20 correct.
2. You attempted 12 others, but missed them.
3. Multiplying 12 by $\frac{1}{4}$ equals 3.
4. Subtracting 20 — 3 = 17.
5. 17 is your raw score.
The actual formula:

$$20 - \frac{1}{4}(12)$$
$$20 - 3$$
$$17$$

Now that you have computed your raw scores for each area, compare them on the chart below:

	Excellent	Good	Fair	Poor
Verbal Ability	34–30	29–23	22–16	15–1
Quantitative Ability	22–19	18–14	13–10	9–1
Analytical Ability	28–26	25–20	19–13	12–1

For a closer analysis of your mini-exam, fill in the analysis sheet that follows. Then compare your individual area scores on the following page.

MINI-EXAM ANALYSIS SHEET

SECTION I

VERBAL ABILITY

	Possible	Completed	Right	Wrong
Sentence Completion	8			
Analogies	8			
Antonyms	8			
Reading Comprehension	10			
OVERALL VERBAL	34			

SECTION II

QUANTITATIVE ABILITY

	Possible	Completed	Right	Wrong
Quantitative Comparison	12			
Math Ability	10			
OVERALL QUANTITATIVE	22			

SECTIONS III & IV

ANALYTICAL ABILITY

	Possible	Completed	Right	Wrong
Analysis of Explanations	16			
Logical Diagrams	6			
Analytical Reasoning	6			
OVERALL ANALYTICAL	28			

SECTION V (not included)

RAW SCORE = NUMBER RIGHT $- \frac{1}{4}$ (number attempted but missed)

OVERALL SCORES SHOULD BE RAW SCORES

COMPARE YOUR SCORE—MINI-EXAM RATING SHEET

SECTION I

	(Use Broken-Down Raw Scores)			
	Excellent	*Good*	*Fair*	*Poor*
VERBAL ABILITY				
Sentence Completion	8	7–6	5–4	3–1
Analogies	8	7–6	5–4	3–1
Antonyms	8–7	6–5	4	3–1
Reading Comprehension	10–9	8–7	6–5	4–1
OVERALL VERBAL	34–30	29–23	22–16	15–1

SECTION II

QUANTITATIVE ABILITY

	Excellent	Good	Fair	Poor
Quantitative Comparison	12–11	10–8	7–6	5–1
Math Ability	10–9	8–7	6–5	4–1
OVERALL QUANTITATIVE	22–20	19–14	13–10	9–1

SECTIONS III & IV

ANALYTICAL ABILITY

	Excellent	Good	Fair	Poor
Analysis of Explanations	16–15	14–11	10–6	5–1
Logical Diagrams	6	5	4	3–1
Analytical Reasoning	6	5	4	3–1
OVERALL ANALYTICAL	28–26	25–20	19–13	12–1

RAW SCORE = NUMBER RIGHT $-\frac{1}{4}$ (number attempted but missed)

OVERALL SCORES SHOULD BE RAW SCORES

After you have given yourself a general rating in each specific exam area, you should check the following:

1. Did I complete each area? (Did I work too slowly?)
2. Did I get more answers right than wrong in each area?
3. In what areas am I weak?

After carefully reading the explanations to each problem, you should answer the following:

4. Did I make simple mistakes? (Did I work too quickly? Did I miss problems that I knew how to do?)
5. Did I guess carelessly?
6. Did I spend time on problems that were much too difficult for me?

Each problem should be categorized, either mentally or on paper, as "within my knowledge" or "beyond my knowledge." Knowing your limitations is important for budgeting time on the exam.

The whole process of analyzing each area and individual problem should be completed for *each* Practice Test to assure *maximum* benefit.

NOW THAT YOU HAVE COMPLETED THE MINI-EXAM AND CAREFULLY ANALYZED AND COMPARED YOUR PERFORMANCE, PLEASE CONTINUE READING. THIS NEXT SECTION IS OF *MOST* IMPORTANCE TO *YOU!*

3

A Closer Look: Each Exam Area
Explained and Analyzed

This section is designed to give you important *insight, familiarity,* and *testing strategies* for each exam area.

Each exam area will be explained in three important categories:

What Is Measured: What ability is being tested.
What Is Required: What you will be asked to do.
What You Should Know: Test-taking strategies and techniques.

After the in-depth analysis of each testing area, the mini-exam problems are explained carefully. The emphasis in explaining each practice problem is on *technique for further application.*

INTRODUCTION TO VERBAL ABILITY

The Verbal Ability Section consists of four types of questions:

Sentence Completion—15-20 questions
Analogies—15-20 questions
Antonyms—15-20 questions
Reading Comprehension—20-25 questions (2 long passages and 3 short passages)

They are generally designed to discover your knowledge of word meanings, your vocabulary level, your ability to reason logically, and your skill at understanding what you read.

This section contains about 80 questions and has a 50-minute time limit.

A detailed analysis and explanation of each verbal exam area follows.

SENTENCE COMPLETION

What Is Measured

Sentence completion measures one aspect of reading comprehension. This aspect deals with your ability to select a word or words that are consistent in logic and style with the other parts of the sentence. A broad range of general knowledge is reflected in these sentences.

What Is Required

Sentence completion questions consist of a sentence in which one word or two words are missing. It is your job to fill in the missing words from among a number of choices given. To do so, you have to read and understand the section of the sentence given, and then choose the word or words that *best* complete the thought expressed in the sentence. The answer you choose must be idiomatically suited to the rest of the sentence. It also must be grammatically correct and in keeping with the mood of the sentence.

What You Should Know—Technique and Strategies

1. Try to understand the complete thought or thoughts of the sentence. Remember: The correct choice *must* be consistent with the main idea of the sentence. Think of words you would insert before looking at the choices.

2. Consider three things when choosing a fill-in for a sentence completion question: First, the answer you choose must make sense in the sentence. Second, the answer must help carry out the meaning of the sentence. Third, the answer must be idiomatic and grammatically correct.

3. Carefully examine the parts of the sentence around the blank space or spaces. Usually, these words will immediately eliminate some of the choices.

4. Certain words in the sentence will always tip off the correct choice. Underline these SIGNAL WORDS as you spot them. Sometimes they will actually define the word or words you need.

5. These SIGNAL WORDS will often give the sentence a strong positive or negative connotation. The correct word or words must carry the same connotation.

6. Some sentences will change connotations from positive to negative or negative to positive. Some of the signal words for such changes are: "but," "although," "except," "in contrast," and "despite." The correct choice in a two-word fill-in would then require words of opposite connotation.

7. If you do not spot the correct answer immediately, then read each of the five choices into the complete sentence. Check the requirements quickly for each. You will be able to eliminate some choices because they "just don't sound right." But don't spend too much time on any one question of this type. Put a check by your answer and return if time permits.

8. Keep in mind that in a two-word fill-in, *both words* must fit well structurally, as well as contextually. Usually more than one choice will have a *first* word that fits. In such a case, the second word will be easier. But don't be afraid to work from the second word first.

9. Always test your final choice by inserting the word or words in the complete sentence.

10. If you can eliminate *more than one choice,* the odds are in your favor for an educated guess.

SENTENCE COMPLETION: ANSWERS AND EXPLANATIONS

Directions: Each question in this test consists of a sentence in which one or two words are missing. Beneath the sentence are five words or word sets. Choose the word or word set that *best* completes the sentence. Then mark the appropriate space in the answer column.

1. Since she felt that the tragedy was _____, she ascribed its cause to fate.
    (A) poignant
    (B) justified
    (C) unavoidable
    (D) unnecessary
    (E) necessary

The correct answer is (C) unavoidable. Signal words: *since, tragedy,* and *ascribed to fate.* The word *since* signals a cause-effect relationship between the first half and the second half of the sentence. We tend to ascribe to fate things which cannot be helped or avoided. Choice A is not applicable, since it would not explain the conclusion of the sentence. Choices (B) and (E) are incorrect since they are not proper adjectives for the word *tragedy.* Choice D could apply to a tragedy but would tend to conflict with the concept of fate.

2. William Seward was _____ as a _____
because he sought the purchase of Alaska, which had been labeled
"Seward's Folly."
(A)   prescribed—nut
(B)   lampooned—warmonger
(C)   inscribed—traveler
(D)   condemned—fool
(E)   proscribed—gambler

The correct choice here is (D) condemned—fool. We are looking
for a two-word combination containing a verb and a noun with negative connotations. The signal words are: "Seward's Folly." Choice (A)
is the only other answer which might be considered since it contains the
word *nut,* but the word *prescribed* is not appropriate.

3. A certain television actor amuses his audience because of the
_____ of his _____. His audience laughs
hysterically when he seems "to put his foot in his mouth."
(A)   impartiality—actions
(B)   malapropisms—speech
(C)   animation—face
(D)   clumsiness—movement
(E)   sting—satire

The correct answer is (B) malapropisms—speech. The signal
words are: *laughs hysterically,* and *foot in his mouth.* The expression
"putting your foot in your mouth" means saying something you
shouldn't, something that might be taken the wrong way. Choices A,
C, and D can be eliminated immediately because they do not relate to
speaking. Choice E is incorrect because stinging satire would not cause
hysterical laughter.

4. Despite the many bribes they offered the player, the "fixers" did
not succeed in _____ his integrity.
(A)   undermining
(B)   discouraging
(C)   discovering
(D)   reducing
(E)   enhancing

The answer here is (A) undermining. The signal word *despite*
indicates a contrast between the first and last parts of the sentence. The
words *bribes, did not succeed,* and *integrity* are key words. We are
looking for a negative word that describes what the bribes were meant
to accomplish—what they would do to the player's integrity. Only
answers A, B, and D are negative; and both B and D are too mild.

5. Such _____ habits of dress would not be imitated
    by a _____ person.
    (A) peculiar—erratic
    (B) intolerable—effusive
    (C) careless—fastidious
    (D) ornate—garish
    (E) meticulous—energetic

The answer is (C) careless—fastidious. *Habits of dress* and *not
be imitated* are the signal words. We are looking for a pair of words
that are antonyms. The first will refer to dress habits, the second will
describe a *person*. Only answer C fits both of these requirements.

6. A wise person will not _____ sectional habits or cus-
    toms; he will _____ those practices or actions which
    he enjoys.
    (A) deprecate—participate in
    (B) countenance—join in
    (C) disapprove—depreciate
    (D) question—denounce
    (E) enjoy—find pleasure in

The correct choice is (A) deprecate-participate in. Signal words:
wise person will not—actions he enjoys. We are looking for a negative-
positive pair of words that describe responses to actions. Only choice
(A) is relevant.

7. A fortunate but small number of people work at jobs which are
    in themselves _____ and are not performed chiefly for
    the return which they bring.
    (A) painful
    (B) useful
    (C) wearisome
    (D) necessary
    (E) pleasurable

The answer is (E) pleasurable. The signal words *fortunate* and
not performed for return define the answer. We are looking for a word
with a strong positive connotation. Choices B, D, and E are positive,
but only choice E fits our definition.

8. This author may be considered a cheerful and kindly sage: his writings are characterized by _____ but not by _____.

    (A)   warmth—frustration
    (B)   laconicism—zeal
    (C)   levity—sincerity
    (D)   moderation—consideration
    (E)   insipidity—verbosity

The best answer is (A) warmth—frustration. Signal words are *cheerful* and *kindly*. The second part of this sentence is going to clarify or support the first. The words *but not by* signal that we want the first word to be positive, but the second must be negative. The only other combination containing a negative second word is (E) insipidity—verbosity. However, the first of the pair is not positive and neither word supports our signal words.

ANALOGIES

What Is Measured

This type of question tests your ability to understand logical relationships among words and ideas. It can also test your vocabulary.

What Is Required

Each analogy expresses a relationship between two things. It is this relationship that you must figure as you look for the correct two-word fill-in to complete the analogy. You are required to select the pair of words which best expresses a relationship similar to that in the original pair of words.

What You Should Know

1. Always try to determine the *relationship* expressed in the pair of given words. For example, two words may express a cause-effect, part-whole, or place-inhabitant relationship.

2. The formula "A:B::C:D" is read "A *is to* B *in the same way as* C *is to* D." Try to think of an *explanation* for the A:B relationship. Use the obvious, but try to be as exact as possible in looking for similarities and differences. Watch for connotations, or hidden feelings associated with words.

3. After carefully determining the relationship between the given words, examine the *relationships* between words in the Choice A. You are looking for the *same* or most nearly the same *relationship*.

4. Remember that the *order* of the answer words must be in the *same sequence* as the order of the question words. For example, the analogy INAUGURATION : PRESIDENT : : ORDINATION : PRIEST is correct. But INAUGURATION : PRESIDENT : : PRIEST : ORDINATION is incorrect because the order in the second pair of words is the reverse of the order in the first pair of words.

5. Check to see that the parts of speech used in the two sections of an analogy are consistent and follow in the same sequence. For example, if the first pair of words contains a noun and an adjective in that order, the second pair of words should contain a noun and an adjective in that order. Thus, GOD : GOOD : : DEVIL : BAD is correct. But GOD : GOOD : : DEVIL : BADLY is incorrect.

6. Understand that the second pair of words in an analogy does not have to be from the same context, class, type, or species as the first pair of words. For example, in the analogy PUPPY : DOG : : SAPLING : TREE, the first pair of words refers to an animal and the second pair refers to a plant. But the relationship between the words in both pairs is the same—a puppy is a young dog in the same way as a sapling is a young tree.

7. In some instances the words used in the analogies may be very difficult. Try to put the words in a sentence to determine meaning and part of speech. Breaking the words up into prefixes, suffixes, and roots can also be helpful. (See list of prefixes, suffixes, roots on page 571.)

8. Look at all of the choices before choosing an answer, but do not spend *too much* time on any of the questions.

9. Usually you can eliminate two or three of the choices fairly easily. The two or three choices left may all be very close and possibly all good answers. You are looking for the *best* answer—exactly the same relationship, if possible. (Reminder: Order is important.)

10. Since $\frac{1}{4}$ point is subtracted for each incorrect answer, guessing blindly will not help. If you can eliminate a few choices (two at least), then *guess*. (The odds are in your favor.)

A LITTLE EXTRA ON ANALOGIES

For the most part, the analogies that appear on the GRE can be classified into specific categories. You will find it helpful to be able to recognize some of these categories and the common relationships immediately. Do not try necessarily to memorize these categories or to classify the analogies you are given on the exam. Instead, reason out the relationships shown in the first pair of analogies and then carefully choose a second pair that has a corresponding relationship.

Following are BASIC TYPES of analogies:

CLASSIFICATIONS—sorts, kinds, general to specific, specific to general, thing to quality or characteristic, opposites, degree, etc.

A broad category is compared to a narrower category
Example—RODENT : SQUIRREL :: fish : flounder
    (broad   (narrower   (broad   (narrower
  category)   category)   category) category)

A person is compared to a characteristic
Example—GIANT : BIGNESS :: baby : helplessness
  (person)   (characteristic) (person) (characteristic)

The general is compared to the specific
Example—PERSON : BOY :: vehicle : bus
  (general)   (specific)   (general) (specific)

A word is compared to a synonym of itself
Example—VACUOUS : EMPTY :: seemly : fit
    (word)   (synonym)   (word) (synonym)

A word is compared to an antonym of itself
Example—SLAVE : FREEMAN :: desolate : joyous
   (word)   (antonym)   (word)   (antonym)

A word is compared to a definition of itself
Example—ASSEVERATE : AFFIRM ::
     (word)   (definition)
   segregate : separate
   (word)   (definition)

A male is compared to a female
Example—COLT : FILLY :: buck : doe
  (male)   (female)   (male) (female)

A family relationship is compared to a similar family relationship
Example—FATHER : SON :: uncle : nephew
  (family relationship)   (family relationship)

A virtue is compared to a failing
Example—FORTITUDE : COWARDICE : :
            (virtue)   (failing)
        honesty : dishonesty
        (virtue)   (failing)

An element is compared to an extreme of itself
Example—WIND : TORNADO : : water : flood
        (element)   (extreme)   (element) (extreme)

A lesser degree is compared to a greater degree
Example—HAPPY : ECSTATIC : : warm : hot
        (lesser   (greater   (lesser   (greater
        degree)   degree)   degree)   degree)

The plural is compared to the singular
Example— WE : I : : they : he
        (plural) (singular)   (plural)   (singular)

STRUCTURALS—part to whole, whole to part, part to part, etc.

A part is compared to a whole
Example—LEG : BODY : : wheel : car
        (part)   (whole)   (part)   (whole)

A whole is compared to a part
Example—TABLE : LEGS : : building : foundations
        (whole)   (part)   (whole)   (part)

OPERATIONALS—time sequence, operations, stages, phases, beginning to ending, before to after, etc.

One element of time is compared to another element of time
Example—DAY : NIGHT : : sunrise : sunset
        (time   (time   (time   (time
        element)   element)   element)   element)

A time sequence relationship is expressed
Example—START : FINISH : : birth : death
        (beginning) (ending)   (beginning) (ending)

A complete operation is compared to a stage
Example—FOOTBALL GAME : QUARTER : :
            (operation)   (stage)
        baseball game : inning
        (operation)   (stage)

MANY ANALOGIES WILL OVERLAP INTO MORE THAN ONE OF THE ABOVE
BASIC TYPES AND WILL HAVE TO BE ANALYZED BY THEIR PURPOSE,
USE, CAUSE-EFFECT RELATIONSHIP, ETC.

A user is compared to his tool
Example—FARMER : HOE : :   dentist : drill
        (user)   (tool)   (user)   (tool)

A creator is compared to a creation
Example—ARTIST : PICTURE : :   poet : poem
     (creator)   (creation)   (creator) (creation)

A cause is compared to its effect
Example—CLOUD : RAIN : :   sun : heat
      (cause)   (effect)   (cause) (effect)

A person is compared to his profession
Example—TEACHER : EDUCATION : :
       (person)   (profession)
      doctor : medicine
     (person)   (profession)

An instrument is compared to a function it performs
Example—CAMERA : PHOTOGRAPHY : :
     (instrument)   (function)
     yardstick : measurement
   (instrument)   (function)

A symbol is compared to an institution
Example—FLAG : GOVERNMENT : : cross : Christianity
    (symbol)   (institution)   (symbol) (institution)

A reward is compared to an action
Example—MEDAL : BRAVERY : : trophy : championship
    (reward)   (action)   (reward)   (action)

An object is compared to an obstacle that hinders it
Example— AIRPLANE : FOG : : car : rut
     (object)   (obstacle)   (object) (obstacle)

Something is compared to a need that it satisfies
Example—WATER : THIRST : : food : hunger
     (thing)   (need)   (thing)   (need)

Something is compared to its natural medium
Example— SHIP : WATER : : airplane : air
     (thing)   (natural   (thing)   (natural
           medium)   medium)

Something is compared to something else that can operate it
Example—DOOR : KEY : : safe : combination

An object is compared to the material of which it is made
Example—COAT : WOOL : : dress : cotton
    (object)   (material)   (object) (material)

ANALOGIES: ANSWERS AND EXPLANATIONS

Directions: In each of the following questions select the lettered pair which best expresses a relationship similar to that expressed in the original pair.

9. LOOM : DISASTER : :
    (A)   impend : catastrophe
    (B)   howl : storm
    (C)   question : puzzle
    (D)   hurt : penalty
    (E)   imminent : eminent

(A) *Loom* is to *disaster* in the same way as *impend* is to *catastrophe.*

The relationship expressed here is that of a *verb* that threatens or predicts an occurrence and a *noun* which represents the actual event. Notice the negative connotations. Choice (A) is the best answer, as *impend* : *catastrophe* is a verb-noun combination that has the same relationship. This choice is especially simple as both words are synonymous with the given pair.

10. STUDY : GRANT : :
    (A)   honor : medal
    (B)   matrimony : dowry
    (C)   merit : scholarship
    (D)   research : fellowship
    (E)   student : bonus

(D) *Study* is to *grant* in the same way as *research* is to *fellowship.*

There is a relationship of *dependence* here, as a study is the reason for a grant and the grant makes the study possible by financing it. The best choice in this case is (D) *research : fellowship,* as a fellowship finances research in the same way that a grant finances a study. Another possible choice might be (B) matrimony : dowry, since a dowry does finance matrimony, but the synonymous meaning of the words in choice (D) makes the relationship more exactly the same.

11. BURGLAR : ALARM : :
(A)   snake : hiss
(B)   air raid : siren
(C)   trespasser : bark
(D)   ship : buoy
(E)   crossing : bell

(C) *Burglar* is to *alarm* in the same way as *trespasser* is to *bark*.
The analogy here is one of a *person* being frightened or deterred by a *sound*. The best answer is clearly (C), as a trespasser would be frightened or deterred by a bark in the same way. No other choice suggests this antagonistic relationship.

12. HEART : MAN : :
(A)   tail : dog
(B)   lungs : child
(C)   computer : jet
(D)   well : pump
(E)   engine : car

(E) *Heart* is to *man* in the same way as *engine* is to *car*.
This analogy expresses a *part-to-whole* relationship, but more specifically the heart is the essential, life-giving part of a man. If his heart stops, he dies. Therefore, the best answer is choice (E), since the *engine* is the "life-giving" part of the *car*. When the engine breaks down the car "dies" also.

13. REMORSELESS : COMPASSION : :
(A)   unscrupulous : qualms
(B)   opportunist : opportunity
(C)   impenitent : sin
(D)   intrepid : rashness
(E)   querulous : lamentation

(A) *Remorseless* is to *compassion* in the same way as *unscrupulous* is to *qualms*.
The relationship expressed here is one of exact opposites, since *remorseless* means ruthless without pity and *compassion* is the quality of tenderness or mercy. Note the parts of speech—adjective : noun. The correct choice is (A) *unscrupulous : qualms,* which expresses the same opposite relationship. All other choices are easily eliminated, as they are pairs of synonyms, not antonyms.

14.   FIGURATIVE : METAPHORICAL : :
- (A)   slang : speech
- (B)   autonomasia : literal
- (C)   irony : meaningless
- (D)   colloquial : allegorical
- (E)   probity : improbity

(D) *Figurative* is to *metaphorical* in the same way as *colloquial* is to *allegorical*.

Figurative and *metaphorical* both mean symbolic, not to be taken literally. The relationship between them is one of *synonyms*. The only choice that meets this requirement is (D) *colloquial : allegorical.* This is the *best* of the choices given.

15.   POSTERIOR : SIMULTANEOUS : :
- (A)   posthumous : following
- (B)   concurrent : ensuing
- (C)   prolonged : before
- (D)   synchronous : contemporaneous
- (E)   subsequent : coincidental

(E) *Posterior* is to *simultaneous* in the same way as *subsequent* is to *coincidental.*

The relationship here is one of *position in time. Posterior* means coming later in time, whereas *simultaneous* means happening at the same time. While choice (B) *concurrent : ensuing* expresses the proper relationship, the words are in reversed order and therefore we must eliminate it. The correct choice is then (E) *subsequent : coincidental,* with *subsequent* meaning following and *coincidental* meaning coinciding or occurring at the same time.

16.   SCALENE : EQUILATERAL : :
- (A)   obtuse : acute
- (B)   unity : coherence
- (C)   irregular : regular
- (D)   chemistry : alchemy
- (E)   quantifier : qualifier

(C) *Scalene* is to *equilateral* in the same way as *irregular* is to *regular.*

The relationship here is one of measurement—all different to all the same. *Scalene* refers to a figure with all sides of a different length whereas *equilateral* refers to a figure with all sides equal. *Irregular* refers to different and *regular* means the same.

ANTONYMS

What Is Measured

This type of question tests your vocabulary as well as your sensitivity to the exactness of the meanings of the choices.

What Is Required

You are required to choose a word that has the opposite or nearly opposite meaning of the given word.

What You Should Know—Strategies and Techniques

1. Choose the most nearly correct word from among the choices given. Sometimes the antonym given might not be the exact word you would use yourself. But if it is the *best* of the choices, it is the correct answer.

2. Work as quickly as you can. Scan the possible answers and decide immediately on the correct one. Take time out to study each individual choice only if the words are unfamiliar or especially difficult for you.

3. Although the words used should not be technical or obscure, they may be long and/or difficult. Break these words up into prefixes, suffixes, and roots to help in deriving the meaning. (Check the list of prefixes, suffixes, and roots on page 571.)

4. Use the given word in a short, clear sentence. This will give you a context to work from and should help you in understanding the meaning. Next, substitute the choices into the original sentence and check to see which choice gives you the most nearly opposite meaning.

5. Beware of choosing an antonym that has a *much broader* or a much *more limited* meaning than the given word. Suppose you had to choose an antonym for this example:

ECONOMICAL:
- (A) deistic
- (B) liberal
- (C) lavish
- (D) frugal
- (E) amicable

The correct answer would be (C) lavish, not (B) liberal. The reason is that while the word "liberal" opposes the word "economical," "liberal" is too narrow in scope. The word "lavish" is more nearly at the opposite end of the word-pole from "economical."

6. The voice and tense of the given word can be a clue. If the given word is in the passive voice, the answer should be in the passive voice. If the question word is in the past tense, the answer should be, too. Suppose you had to choose an antonym for this example:

TERMINATE:

    (A)   praise
    (B)   begin
    (C)   started
    (D)   cheer
    (E)   full

The correct answer would be (B) begin, not (C) started, because the given word is in the present tense and the answer must be in the same tense.

7. Be alert to the part of speech used in the question word and in the answer choices. The correct answer should be the *same* part of speech as the given word. So, for example, if the question word is a noun, the correct answer would also be a noun.

8. Many words carry a strong connotation with them. If the connotation of the given word is positive, then your choice should have a negative connotation.

9. You should not expect to find literal definitions on exactly opposite meanings on these tests. Your ability to think and reason is tested by your ability to choose the *best* answer. Remember, you are looking for *antonyms;* don't make the common error of picking a synonym.

10. If you can eliminate a few of the choices, guessing is then to your advantage. Usually your first choice is your best educated guess.

ANTONYMS: ANSWERS AND EXPLANATIONS

Directions: Each question in this test consists of a word printed in capital letters followed by five words lettered (A) through (E). Choose the word that has most nearly the OPPOSITE meaning from the word in capital letters. Mark the appropriate space in the answer column. Consider all choices before deciding which one is best, since some choices are very close in meaning.

17. FLEXIBLE:
    (A) unable
    (B) obdurate
    (C) rational
    (D) easy
    (E) likable

Answer: (B) obdurate

Explanation: The word *flexible* is defined as "capable of being easily bent, susceptible to modification." The correct choice here is *obdurate,* meaning "hardened against persuasions." None of the other four choices is applicable.

18. PERPETUATE:
    (A) concretize
    (B) delay
    (C) abrogate
    (D) collate
    (E) derive

Answer: (C) abrogate

Explanation: *Perpetuate* means "to make continuous or everlasting." The best choice in this case would be *abrogate,* which means "to abolish promptly." Choices (A), (D), and (E) may be eliminated, as they have no relation to the word. Choice (B) is the only other choice that may be considered, but it is not the *best* choice because *delay* implies only a temporary postponement or hindrance to action, not a definite end.

19. OBSTINATE:
  (A) resolved
  (B) stained
  (C) complaisant
  (D) resourceful
  (E) mindful

Answer: (C) complaisant

Explanation: The word *obstinate* means "firmly sticking to one's purpose or opinion; not yielding to persuasion; stubborn." Choices (B), (D), and (E) may be eliminated, as they are unrelated in meaning to our key word. Choice (A) *resolved*, meaning "determined, firm in purpose," is a synonym of *obstinate*. Therefore, the word most nearly opposite is (C) *complaisant*, meaning "obliging, agreeable, or yielding."

20. EUPHONY:
  (A) tune
  (B) harmony
  (C) note
  (D) chord
  (E) cacophony

Answer: (E) cacophony

Explanation: *Euphony* is defined as "agreeableness of sound; pleasing effect to the ear." The correct antonym would be (E) *cacophony*, which is the quality of having a harsh sound or dissonance. Notice that both words contain the root "phone" meaning sound. The key here is positive and negative connotation. We are looking for a *negative* word to contrast with our key word. Choices (A), (C), and (D) have no value connotation at all, while choice (B), *harmony*, is positive.

21. PROLIX:
  (A) open
  (B) parting
  (C) arrogant
  (D) pithy
  (E) long

Answer: (D) pithy

Explanation: *Prolix* is an adjective meaning "extended or very long and wordy." Choice (E) may be eliminated immediately as it is a synonym. Choices (A), (B), and (C) have no relation to our key word. The answer is choice (D) *pithy*, which means "brief, concise, and to the point."

22. PEACEABLE:
   (A)   broken
   (B)   delicate
   (C)   fractious
   (D)   soft
   (E)   quiet

Answer: (C) Fractious

Explanation: The word *peaceable,* meaning "disposed to peace or inclined to avoid conflict," carries a positive connotation. We are looking for a word with negative meaning for our answer. Immediately we can eliminate choices (B), (D), and (E). Choice (A) *broken,* has no relation to our word. Therefore, the answer is (C) *fractious,* meaning "cross, cranky, or irritable."

23. SESSILE:
   (A)   ceasing
   (B)   mobile
   (C)   steady
   (D)   solvent
   (E)   searing

Answer: (B) mobile

Explanation: We are looking for the opposite of *sessile,* which means "permanently attached." Choices (A), (D), and (E) are not applicable. Choice (C) may be eliminated, as it is a synonym of the key word. The correct choice is (B) *mobile,* meaning "moveable."

24. AVERSION:
   (A)   proclivity
   (B)   ease
   (C)   state
   (D)   revision
   (E)   suasion

Answer: (A) proclivity

Explanation: The word *aversion* implies an extreme dislike, an avoidance. In contrast to this heavily negative connotation we are looking for a positive word implying attraction. Choices (B), (C), and (D) are not related to our key choice. (E) *suasion,* meaning "the act of urging or trying to persuade" is positive, but implies an effort to elicit a response. The correct answer, (A) *proclivity,* means a natural inclination toward something. This is clearly the *best* choice.

READING COMPREHENSION

What Is Measured

The Reading Comprehension section measures your ability to read and understand passages that are typical of the kinds of materials you would read at your level of education. The questions on these exams test nine (9) major skills. These are the ability to (1) understand what is stated, (2) perceive what is implied, (3) draw conclusions from information given, (4) develop generalizations, (5) search out hidden meanings, (6) find errors in logic, (7) form value judgments, (8) detect bias in writing, and (9) think critically.

What Is Required

In the Reading Comprehension section will be given five (5) passages. Two are long and three are short. Each passage is followed by questions based on its content. You are required to choose the *best* answer to each question.

The reading materials given and the types of questions asked throughout the examination vary in difficulty.

The easiest kind of question simply tests your understanding of what you have read by asking you to list facts or explain the meaning of words.

At the next stage of difficulty, the questions call for you to interpret materials by giving the central thought of the passage or noting contradictions.

The third stage of difficulty consists of questions in which you must apply principles or opinions expressed in the reading passage to other situations.

The final and most difficult kind of question asks you to evaluate what you have read and to agree or differ with the point of view of the author.

What You Should Know

Follow these five steps in beginning a reading comprehension test: First, look at the first three or four *questions* (not the choices) following the passage to see what type of *question* you will be answering. Second, skim the passage quickly to get the general idea. Third, read the passage carefully and critically, *underlining leading phrases and ideas*. Fourth, determine what conclusions are reached and why. Finally, read each question carefully, then look for the answer in the text.

1. Be sure to answer the questions only on the basis of the information given to you in the passage, and *not from outside information* you may happen to know.

2. Notice whether a question refers to a specific line, sentence, or quotation from the reading passage. The answer to such a question is almost certain to be found in or near this reference in the passage.

3. Work as quickly as you can. Your time is limited, so don't waste it. Make good use of it by reading the passage critically and marking where main ideas, arguments, and related facts begin. Then, answer the questions in a systematic and organized way.

4. Be suspicious of words such as "never," "always," "wholly," and "forever" in the answer choices. Usually, answers that use such categorical terms are incorrect.

5. Choose the *most appropriate* answer to the question. Often more than one answer seems correct. You must choose the *best* one.

6. The answers do not usually follow the order of the text. In most cases, you have to skip from one part of the passage to another to find an answer.

7. Some of the passages may be very technical and sophisticated. Even if you have no familiarity with the subject matter in a passage, you should be able to read through it and work out the answers.

8. Although not all the material in the passage will be useful in answering the questions, you should read the passage thoroughly at least once. Don't skip any sections.

9. Leave the more difficult questions for last. Try to answer the easier ones first so that you have time to spend thinking about the harder ones.

10. If you get stuck on a question, put a check by it and return later if time permits. Remember: If you can eliminate more than one choice, an educated guess is in your favor.

READING COMPREHENSION: ANSWERS
AND EXPLANATIONS

Directions: Each passage is followed by a group of questions. Read each passage and choose the *best* answer to each question. Then mark the appropriate space in the answer column. Answers should be chosen on the basis of what is stated and implied.

A glance at the five leading causes of death in 1900, 1910, and 1945, years representing in some measure the early and late practice of physicians still active, shows a significant trend. In 1900 these causes were (1) tuberculosis, (2) pneumonia, (3) enteritis, typhoid fever, and other acute intestinal diseases, (4) heart diseases, and (5) cerebral hemorrhage and thrombosis. Ten years later the only change was that heart disease had moved from fourth to first place, tuberculosis now being second, and pneumonia third. In 1945, however, the list had changed profoundly. Heart diseases were far out in front; cancer, which had come up from eighth place, was second; and cerebral hemorrhage and thrombosis, third. Fatal accidents, which had been well down the list, were now fourth, and nephritis was fifth. All of these are, of course, composites rather than single diseases, and it is significant that, except for accidents, they are characteristic of the advanced rather than the early or middle years of life.

The first sentence indicates that three lists are to be compared; the result will be a "significant trend." A repeat of the word "significant" clues the location of the trend-statement. Modifiers like "significant," "in some measure," and "profoundly" are worth noting because they signal the most important or least important information.

25.   On the basis of the paragraph, which of the following statements is most tenable?
   (A)   a cure for cancer will be found within this decade.
   (B)   many of the medical problems of today are problems of the gerontologist (specialist in medical problems of old age).
   (C)   older persons are more accident-prone than are younger persons.
   (D)   tuberculosis has been all but eliminated.
   (E)   heart disease has never been a real threat to the aged.

(B). The information in (B) directly corresponds to the "significant" conclusion in the paragraph's final sentence. (A) is beyond the time scope of the paragraph; (C) is untenable because the final sentence states that accidents are not characteristic of advanced years. There is no evidence in the paragraph which supports (D) or (E).

26. Which of the following trends is <u>LEAST</u> indicated in the paragraph?
- (A)   as one grows older he is more subject to disease.
- (B)   pneumonia has become less common.
- (C)   relative to mortality rates for acute intestinal diseases, the mortality rate for cancer has increased.
- (D)   the incidence of heart disease has increased.
- (E)   fatal accidents claim more lives today than ever.

(A). All of the statements except (A) are solidly supported by a comparison of the "cause lists" for 1900, 1910, and 1945. (A) is a conclusion implied by the paragraph but not directly stated.

27. In 1945, what was the <u>leading cause</u> of death?
- (A)   fatal accidents
- (B)   cerebral hemorrhage
- (C)   heart diseases
- (D)   cancer
- (E)   whooping cough

(C) is the correct answer.

28. Which of the following statements is <u>most nearly correct</u>?
- (A)   such mortality trends are caused by decreased infant mortality.
- (B)   the data reported are a function of improved diagnosis and reporting.
- (C)   the mortality data are based on the records of physicians who practiced continuously from 1900 to 1945.
- (D)   there appears to be a greater change in the mortality patterns from 1910 to 1945 than in the decade ending in 1910.
- (E)   pneumonia was the chief cause of death in 1945.

(D). (A) and (B) are merely speculative, and (E) is false. Although (C) corresponds to information in the paragraph's first sentence, the words "in some measure" label that information as partial. We are told that in 1945 the list changed "profoundly"; thus (D) is recognized to be completely correct.

<u>Poor discipline</u> has <u>three principal roots</u>: the <u>pupils</u>, the <u>teacher</u>, and <u>external factors</u>. Often a <u>combination</u> of all three <u>elements</u> or of any two actuates a high degree of disorder.
In a few classrooms, there are <u>some pupils</u> who are <u>so emotionally ill</u> that the <u>best teacher</u> working in the most favorable setting <u>cannot</u> easily <u>achieve control</u> of the class. Even three or four <u>such children can infect</u> the entire group unless these troublemakers are taken care of.

Sometimes the acoustics, the length, the shape and the age of a room make for unrest and confusion. Teaching can be difficult if the classroom is too big, too small, too difficult to supervise, or too drafty. If the room has an alcove, unruly atmosphere through the entire class can make the individual teacher's plight a sad one indeed.

But the chief reason children cooperate or fail to cooperate is the teacher herself. She may have a weak personality, thus emboldening normally adjusted children to become mischievous or lazy. Consciously or subconsciously, they will seek to dominate her. And, as part of her personality, her voice may be the source of the trouble; perhaps it lacks resonance; perhaps it is harsh; perhaps it is pitched too high or too low.

As adjuncts of a teacher's personality we should consider her methods, her planning, her attention to routines, her appearance, her concern for neatness and her attitude toward children. If she does not rank high on these counts, she will probably be unable to control the class.

Therefore, any teacher whose class is misbehaving should first do some self-evaluation. Literally and figuratively, (and, above all, objectively!) she should view herself in a mirror and seek to determine the extent to which she is or is not to blame for the undesirable situation. After this honest appraisal, she may look beyond herself to less easily alterable factors, such as the pupils, the school, the principal, and the community.

This passage is easily divided into three main sections. This division process is clued by the first sentence, which lists the main elements, thus signaling that they will be discussed sequentially. But, it is important to label the subject of each paragraph in the margin to avoid any confusion, because the subjects are not discussed in the order they are presented in the first sentence.

29. Of the following titles, the one which best suggests the central idea of the passage is
(A) Personality Plus
(B) How to Improve Discipline
(C) Adjusting Instruction
(D) The Causes of Poor Discipline
(E) Teacher, Know Thy Weaknesses

(D). The first sentence of the passage emphasizes the "roots" or "elements" (both synonymous to "cause") of poor discipline, and the passage elaborates upon these. (B) is incorrect because, although the passage suggests how teaching may be improved, it does not speak much about "less easily alterable factors." (A), (C), and (E) are incorrect because they suggest that the teacher or teaching is the central idea, rather than an element of it.

30. Of the following, the one which is among the <u>three principal</u> sources of poor discipline <u>mentioned by the author</u> is
(A)   poor planning
(B)   the teacher's voice
(C)   the pupils
(D)   the teacher's methods and routines
(E)   failure to practice self-evaluation

(C). All of the other chioces are sources of poor teaching, not poor discipline.

31. The subject of the third paragraph can be summed up as
(A)   why pupils misbehave
(B)   room problems contributing to poor discipline
(C)   external factors contributing to poor discipline
(D)   aggravations of the problem
(E)   the teacher's problems in discipline

(C). (A) is incorrect because it is the subject of the whole passage. (B), (D), and (E) are each touched upon in the third paragraph, but no one is general enough to include the rest, as (C) does.

32. Of the following statements, the one that the author <u>does not</u> make or imply is
(A)   it is easier for a teacher to change her own practices than her principal's
(B)   one of the reasons for poor discipline may be the teacher's lack of attention to room decoration
(C)   if a teacher is really competent and objectively tries to improve, she should have no discipline problems
(D)   deeply disturbed pupils may need special placement
(E)   the chief cause of poor discipline is the teacher herself

(C). The teacher is only one of three causes of poor discipline; therefore, her improvement alone will not necessarily solve the problem.

33. Of the following statements, the one that the author <u>does not</u> make or imply is

(A) a small group of disturbed children may upset an entire class

(B) L-shaped rooms are less conducive to good discipline than ordinary rectangular rooms

(C) children who ordinarily cooperate may become disorderly if their teacher's personality lacks force

(D) a teacher should always keep her voice moderately low; she should never shout

(E) self-evaluation is an important duty for the teacher

(D). The author writes about every voice characteristic but volume, and implies by his encouragement of a "strong" teacher personality that the teacher *should* speak loudly.

34. All of the following are mentioned by the author as possible causes of disciplinary trouble <u>except</u>

(A) the teacher's unpleasant voice

(B) the teacher's authoritarian attitude

(C) the classroom's poor state of repair

(D) the school's poor emotional climate

(E) emotionally unstable children

(B). (A), (C), (D), and (E) are all causal factors directly addressed by the author. (B) is not stated as a cause of poor discipline, but is rather implied as a cure. The teacher is advised not to embolden children through a weak personality; in other words, she is encouraged to become *more* authoritarian.

INTRODUCTION TO QUANTITATIVE ABILITY

The second 50-minute section of the GRE is usually Quantitative Ability, consisting of 55 problems.

Two types of multiple-choice questions appear in the Quantitative Ability section:

1. Quantitative Comparison questions with 4 possible choices (about 30 questions),

AND

2. Standard multiple-choice Math Ability questions with 5 possible choices (about 25 questions).

NOTE:

All scratch work must be done on the space provided on the actual test booklet.

Diagrams are not necessarily drawn to scale.

All numbers used are in the real number system.

All diagrams are on a plane or flat surface.

Since both types may include graph reading, special instruction, strategies, and techniques are included separately for graphs.

An understanding of higher math is not necessary, only algebra and geometry.

A detailed analysis and explanation of each quantitative exam area follows.

QUANTITATIVE COMPARISON

What Is Measured

Quantitative Comparison measures the ability to make quick and precise decisions involving the comparison of two given quantities. This section tests your ability to use insight, short-cut computations, approximations, and simplified mathematical techniques.

What Is Required

This section requires you to compare two quantities as >, <, =, or not comparable.

Each question in this part consists of two quantities, one in Column A and one in Column B. You are to compare the two quantities and mark answer

A if the quantity in Column A is the greater;
B if the quantity in Column B is the greater;
C if the two quantities are equal;
D if the comparison cannot be determined from the information given.

NOTE: Figures, equations, or graphs given for reference may appear. If given, these are the bases for the comparison.

What You Should Know

1. All problems in this section are of equal value. They emphasize the use of short, quick techniques. You should *never* spend more than about a minute on any one problem. Check the troublesome problems and return to them if time permits.

2. Performing the complete computation is often a waste of time. You do not necessarily have to solve each column of the given problem, just do whatever is necessary to *make the comparison*.

3. If no *variables* are involved, then answer D is *never* a possible choice. You can always compare actual values.

4. After establishing one answer, such as A > B, try to establish another, contradictory, answer, such as A < B or A = B. *If you can establish more than one answer, immediately choose answer D.*

EXAMPLE: Compare X and Y if X = 2 and Y = 1. Answer is A, but if X = 1 and Y = 2, then B is the answer. If both are possible, the correct answer is D.

5. When substituting into a problem, remember that 0 and 1 behave uniquely. *Try* them first.

6. Replacing with a simple positive and then negative number is also effective. Don't forget the negatives and positives. Remember that —1 is greater than —2.

7. Remember that fractions between 0 and 1, and between 0 and −1, behave uniquely in problems dealing with powers and roots. Try them first or second.

8. You should *always* mark diagrams where possible, as geometric figures are not necessarily drawn to scale. (Sketching a more accurate figure is also helpful if time permits.)

9. Always choose simple numbers as replacements first. You are the one who has to do the computations.

10. If you can eliminate one choice, then take your educated guess.

GRAPH AND CHART READING

Since graphs and charts may appear in either Math Ability or Quantitative Comparison, here is some important additional information.

What You Should Know

1. Familiarize yourself with the graph and all information presented. Be sure you understand what is being presented. Read the labels carefully.

2. Written descriptions accompanying the graph are usually important. Read them carefully.

3. The graph is there for reference; attempting to memorize data is a waste of time.

4. Use *only* the data presented on the graph or accompanying it. Even if the graphic data seems incorrect, do not use your outside knowledge of the subjects.

5. Look for *trends* or the *obvious* on the graph.

6. Sometimes the printed pictures and labels on graphs or charts are small and difficult to read. Be as accurate as possible.

7. A graph may have insufficient grid lines to answer a question with desired accuracy. Use the edge of your answer sheet to either line up the answer or draw in the line.

8. The unit of measure used in the graph may be large and burdensome. Use scaled units or short abbreviations, but don't waste time on large units.

EXAMPLE: $2,000,000 + 3,000,000 = 5,000,000$
SIMPLER: 2 mil + 3 mil = 5 mil OR 2 units + 3 units = 5 units. (1 unit = 1 million.)

9. Graphs usually have anywhere from two to eight problems related to them. Even if the graph appears very difficult, you can usually get a few points by merely being able to read data from it.

10. You should not spend too much time on any one problem. If you have trouble with a problem, place a check by it and return to it for a moment before leaving the graph-related questions. If you can eliminate one or two choices, you should take your educated guess.

QUANTITATIVE COMPARISON: ANSWERS AND EXPLANATIONS

Directions: Each question in this section consists of two quantities, one in Column A and one in Column B. You are to compare the two quantities and on the answer sheet blacken space

      A if the quantity in Column A is the greater;
      B if the quantity in Column B is the greater;
      C if the two quantities are equal;
      D if the relationship cannot be determined from the information given.

	Column A	Column B

1. $\frac{2}{5} \times \frac{1}{3} \times \frac{7}{12}$ $\frac{7}{8} \times \frac{7}{12} \times \frac{1}{3}$

The correct answer is (B). Since both sides are being multiplied by $\frac{7}{12}$ and $\frac{1}{3}$, these may be eliminated from both columns.

$$\frac{2}{5} \times \frac{1}{3} \times \frac{7}{12} \qquad\qquad \frac{7}{8} \times \frac{7}{12} \times \frac{1}{3}$$

Now you need only to compare $\frac{2}{5}$ and $\frac{7}{8}$. Simple observation or the cross-multiplication method will prove that $\frac{2}{5} < \frac{7}{8}$.

$$x > 0$$

2. $x + y$ $x - y$

The correct answer is (D). Trying some small values is required here, remembering that x must be greater than 0. Let $x = 1$ and $y = 0$:

          (1) + (0)   (1) − (0)
            1   =   1

In this case, the columns are equal. Now you should try two other values, keeping in mind that you are trying to get a $>$ or $<$.

Let $x = 2$ and $y = 1$

          (2) + (1)   (2) − (1)
           3   =   1

In this case Column A is greater than Column B. Since there are two different answers depending on your choice of values, the correct answer is (D) *cannot be determined.*

	Column A	**Column B**

$$x > 0$$
$$x\sqrt{.25} = .7$$

3. $\qquad x \qquad\qquad\qquad\qquad \dfrac{4}{3}$

The correct answer is (A). You must first solve the equation $x\sqrt{.25} = .7$. The square root of .25 is .5. Simplifying the equation to

$$x(.5) = .7 \text{ or } .5x = .7$$

and then multiplying through by 10 gives: $5x = 7$.

Dividing through by 5 leaves $x = \dfrac{7}{5}$. Now you must compare $\dfrac{7}{5}$ and $\dfrac{4}{3}$. Using the method of cross-multiplication, you get:

Since 21 is greater than 20, $\dfrac{7}{5}$ is greater than $\dfrac{4}{3}$.

$$r = 2$$
$$s = 2r$$

4. $\qquad \dfrac{r^2 + s^2}{r} \qquad\qquad\qquad \dfrac{s^3}{r + s}$

The correct answer is (B). Since $r = 2$, you can solve for s by replacing as follows: $s = 2(2)$, $s = 4$. Now, substituting for r and s, you get

$$\dfrac{(2)^2 + (4)^2}{2} \qquad\qquad\qquad \dfrac{(4)^3}{(2) + (4)}$$

Simplifying:

$$\dfrac{4 + 16}{2} \qquad\qquad\qquad \dfrac{64}{2 + 4}$$

$$\dfrac{20}{2} \qquad\qquad\qquad \dfrac{64}{6}$$

Finally:

$$10 \qquad\qquad < \qquad\qquad 10\tfrac{4}{6}$$

Problems 5–7 refer to the following diagram:

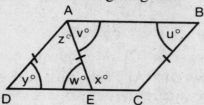

ABCD is a parallelogram.   AD = AE = BC.
Notice how you should mark the diagram. $y° = w°$, because angles
opposite equal sides in a triangle are equal. ABCE is an isosceles
trapezoid, therefore $v° = u°$. Since $y°$ and $u°$ are opposite angles
in a parallelogram, they are equal and logically $y° = w° = v° = u°$.

Column A	Column B
$x°$	$z°$

5.

The correct answer is (A). $x°$ is an exterior angle of triangle
AED, therefore $x° = z° + y°$ and $x°$ must be greater than
$z°$ because $y°$ cannot be 0. (An exterior angle of a triangle
equals the sum of the opposite angles.)

6. $v°$ $y°$

The correct answer is (C). Marking this diagram properly would
immediately give you the correct answer by observation. Notice,
once again, how the diagram was marked.

7.   AE   EC

The correct answer is (D). You are not given sufficient information to make a comparison.

$$a < b$$

8. $(a + b)^2$ $(a - b)^2$

The correct answer is (D). You should substitute small numbers
following the condition $a < b$. Let $a = 0$ and $b = 1$, therefore:

$$(0 + 1)^2 \qquad\qquad (0 - 1)^2$$
$$(1)^2 \qquad\qquad (-1)^2$$

Finally: 1   =   1

Now you should try two different values for a and b.
Let $a = 1$ and $b = 2$.
Then:

$$(1 + 2)^2 \qquad\qquad (1 - 2)^2$$
$$(3)^2 \qquad\qquad (-1)^2$$
$$9 \qquad\qquad 1$$

In one case columns A and B are equal, in the second case
Column A is greater than B. Since different answers occur,
depending on the values chosen, the correct answer is (D)
cannot be determined.

Column A	Column B

9. $\dfrac{7}{\sqrt{7}}$ $\sqrt{7}$

The correct answer is (C). Multiplying both columns by $\sqrt{7}$ produces the following:

$$\sqrt{7} \times \frac{7}{\sqrt{7}} \qquad\qquad \sqrt{7} \times \sqrt{7} = \sqrt{49} = 7$$

and 7 $=$ 7

Problems 10–12 refer to the following graphs:

EXPENDITURES FOR 2 YEARS

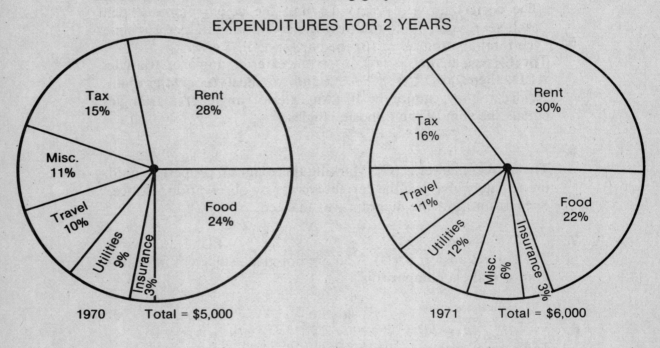

1970   Total = $5,000   1971   Total = $6,000

---

10.   1970 Insurance expenditures $180

The correct answer is (B). 3% of $5,000 is $150.

$$\begin{array}{r} 5{,}000 \\ \times \quad .03 \\ \hline \$150.00 \end{array}$$

and $150 is less than $180.

Column A	Column B

11. % increase in expenditures   25%
from 1970 to 1971

The correct answer is (B). To compute percent increase, put the amount for the first year at the bottom of the fraction and the difference between the two years at the top.

$$\frac{6,000 - 5,000}{5,000} = \frac{1,000}{5,000} = \frac{1}{5}$$

Changed to a percent is 20%.
20% is less than 25%, therefore answer (B) is correct.

12.   1971 food expenditure   1970 food expenditure

The correct answer is (A). To find the actual amount spent each year, you should multiply the corresponding percent times the total amount spent for the corresponding year.
In this case:

$6,000 × 22% $5,000 × 24%

Thus: $1,320   > $1,200

MATH ABILITY

What Is Measured

The Math Ability section measures your ability to solve math problems by using insight, logic, and an application of the concepts and skills of arithmetic, algebra, geometry, and graph reading. They also test your ability to think quickly and to grasp the meaning of a problem.

What Is Required

In this section you are required to solve problems by using information given and mathematical calculations. All scratch work should be done on the page. Mark the *best* answer of the *five* choices on your answer sheet.

What You Should Know

1. All problems in this section are of equal value. You should never spend more than a few minutes on any one problem. Check the troublesome problems and return to them if time permits.

2. Work carefully, but quickly. Simple mistakes will often give you an incorrect answer that *is* one of the choices.

3. Make sure that you are answering the right question. *Underline* what you are asked to solve for.

4. Check to see if your answer *is reasonable*. Many times you will be able to eliminate two or three choices because they are ridiculous answers. This could save you the mistake of marking an answer 3 when the correct answer is 30.

5. Look for the key words "approximate" or "the answer *is about* _____." Estimating is a valuable *tool* in many problems. Often you can estimate the answer even if an approximation is not requested. Take a quick glance at the choices to see how close the numbers are to each other. This will tip you off as to how accurate you must be.

6. Marking in diagrams can be very helpful and save you valuable time. Always mark diagrams when possible. EXAMPLE: In triangle ABC, AB = BC.

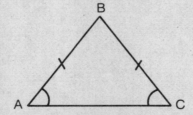

The angles opposite the equal sides are also equal. Notice that identical markings denote equals.

7. Some problems can be worked more easily by working from the given choices. First try to solve the problems regularly. If you encounter trouble, plugging the choices into the problem can be very effective.

8. Simplify the problem if possible. Some problems have been complicated by data that have no bearing on correct choice selection. Line out irrelevant material.

9. Sometimes algebraic expressions, explanations, or formulas can be more easily understood by substituting numbers for the variables. Don't be afraid to replace the letters with numbers to give you a clearer understanding if necessary.

10. If you can eliminate one or two choices, an educated guess is in your favor. Don't guess blindly.

MATH ABILITY: ANSWERS AND EXPLANATIONS

Directions: Solve each of the following problems and mark the *best* answer on your answer sheet. All scratch work should be done in the available space. All numbers used belong to the real number system.

13.   Which of the following fractions is greater than $\frac{2}{5}$?

(A) $\frac{2}{7}$

(B) $\frac{3}{8}$

(C) $\frac{9}{25}$

(D) $\frac{1}{4}$

(E) $\frac{5}{12}$

The correct answer is (E). $\frac{5}{12}$ is greater than $\frac{2}{5}$. When comparing fractions, the fastest method in most cases is by simply putting the fractions next to each other and cross-multiplying upwards.

The fraction with the greater number at the top is the greater fraction.

EXAMPLE:

Since 25 is greater than 24 , $\frac{5}{12} > \frac{2}{5}$. (This is really just finding a common denominator.)

Another method of comparing fractions is changing them all to a percent or decimal. This method may be faster in some cases.

Notice the words underlined in the question, are *greater than* $\frac{2}{5}$.

It is a good practice to underline what you're looking for in each question. This would be considered an easy question.

14.

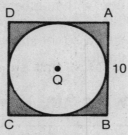

Side AB measures 10 cm. Circle Q is inscribed in square ABCD, intersecting at 4 points.

The shaded area is approximately how many square cm.?

(A)   94
(B)   24
(C)   5
(D)   6
(E)   74

The correct answer is **(B)**. 24 is the only reasonable answer; therefore this problem could be answered correctly with merely simple insight. To actually work the problem, you must first find the area of the square and then subtract the area of the circle. The area of the square is 100 sq. cm. from the formula Area = side × side. The area of the circle is a little more difficult to figure out, as the radius of the circle is not given. You must discover that the diameter is 10 (side of the sq.) and the radius is therefore 5. Using the formula for area of a circle $A = \pi r^2$:

$$A = \pi(5)^2$$
$$A = \pi(25)$$
(π is approximately 3)

therefore area of circle is about 3 × 25, or 75. Subtracting 75 from 100 leaves 25. 24 is the best answer.

Shaded area and *approximately* are important words here.

15. If $x = 2y + 3$ and $y = 4$, then $\dfrac{x - 2}{y} =$

   (A) 11

   (B) $\dfrac{13}{4}$

   (C) $\dfrac{11}{4}$

   (D) $\dfrac{9}{4}$

   (E) $\dfrac{1}{2}$

The correct choice is (D) $\dfrac{9}{4}$.

In this problem you must first substitute 4 for y in the first equation to get

$$x = 2(4) + 3$$

Next, solve for x and you get $x = 11$. Finally substitute 11 for x and 4 for y in the given phrase and you get $\dfrac{(11) - 2}{4}$. Simplified, this is $\dfrac{9}{4}$.

The key to this problem is remembering that you are solving for $\dfrac{x - 2}{y}$. Be aware of the fact that simple mathematical mistakes would have probably given you answers (B) or (C). Not substituting into the phrase would give answer (A). This problem is of medium difficulty.

16.   Given that $x^6 + 4x + 6 = x^6 + 7$, what is the *value of x*?

(A)   4

(B) $\frac{1}{4}$

(C) $\frac{4}{7}$

(D) $\frac{7}{4}$

(E) $\frac{13}{4}$

The correct answer is (B) $\frac{1}{4}$.

This problem is fairly simple if you can spot the irrelevant material that can be eliminated. Since x^6 is on both sides of the equation it cancels itself out and you are left with simply $4x + 6 = 7$.

Subtracting a 6 from both sides

$$
\begin{array}{rl}
4x + 6 &= 7 \\
-\,6 &-6 \\
\hline
4x &= 1
\end{array}
$$

leaves the equation $4x = 1$. Dividing both sides by 4,

$$\frac{4x}{4} = \frac{1}{4}$$

gives the correct answer of $\frac{1}{4}$.

17. If the ratio of men to women to children at a play was 5:3:1, which of the following <u>could not be</u> the number of <u>adults</u> at the play?

I.   9
II.   15
III.   24
IV.   36
(A)   I only
(B)   III only
(C)   I and IV
(D)   II and III
(E)   I, II, IV

The correct answer is (E). Since you are asked to find the number that could not be adults, you must first find the numbers that *could be* adults. The adult ratio of men to women is 5:3. This means that there can be either 8 adults at the play, or multiples of 8: 16, 24, 32, 40. . . . Therefore 9, 15, and 36 could not be the number of adults. This multiple-multiple choice type of problem lends itself well to eliminating possible choices. When you realize that 9 is not a possible number of adults, then choices (B) and (D) can be eliminated, as neither includes I. Once you know that I and II must be in the answer, immediately mark (E) as the only choice that contains I and II.

Notice the underlined words, *could not be* and *adults*. This question is of average difficulty.

18.

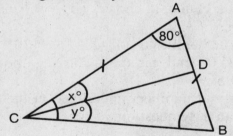

CD is an angle bisector. AC = AB. $\angle A = 80°$. Find $\angle x$.
(A)   75
(B)   25
(C)   50
(D)   20
(E)   cannot be determined.

The correct answer is (B) 25°. The important technique in this problem is the clear markings. Notice that segments AC and AB are marked similarly. $\angle C$ and $\angle B$ are also marked the same because angles opposite equal sides are equal. $\angle x$ and $\angle y$ are also marked similarly because the angle bisector CD, forms equal angles. Angle A is marked 80°. With the diagram properly marked, insight into the problem-solving technique becomes much simpler. The interior angles of a triangle total 180°. Since $\angle A$ is 80°, 100° are left to be divided equally between $\angle C$ and $\angle B$. Therefore, $\angle C$ and $\angle B$ are 50° each. $\angle x$ is half of $\angle C$ and is therefore 25°.

19. The net price of a <u>$25</u> item after <u>successive discounts</u> of <u>20%</u> and <u>30%</u> is:
- (A) $12.50
- (B) $11.00
- (C) $14.50
- (D) $21.00
- (E) $14.00

The correct answer is (E). $14.00 is the net price after the discounts. Solving successive discount problems involves being careful with arithmetic. First take 20% of the original $25.00:

$$
\begin{array}{r}
25.00 \\
\times\ .20 \\
\hline
5.0000
\end{array}
$$

This comes to $5.00. Then subtract the $5.00 from the $25.00. You are left with $20.00. Now take 30% of the $20.00:

$$
\begin{array}{r}
20.00 \\
\times\ .30 \\
\hline
6.0000
\end{array}
$$

This comes to $6.00. Subtract the $6.00 from the $20.00 and you are left with the correct answer of $14.00. A second look at the choices would help you eliminate choices (B) $11.00 and (D) $21.00 as ridiculous answers.

The common error here is to add 20% and 30% together and then take 50% of $25.00 and get the incorrect amount of $12.50, which is one of the choices.

Notice the words and numbers underlined in the question. This would be considered an easy question.

20.

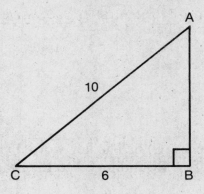

The area of <u>right triangle</u> ABC is
(A)   30
(B)   20
(C)   48
(D)   24
(E)   cannot be determined.

The correct answer is (D) 24. To solve this problem you need to be familiar with the Pythagorean Theorem, $a^2 + b^2 = c^2$. This lets you find the third side of a right triangle when two sides are known. (C) must refer to the side opposite the right angle. In this instance you need to find the height of the triangle (third side) to be able to use the area formula $A = \frac{1}{2}$ (base $\times$ height). Using the Pythagorean Theorem:

$$a^2 + (6)^2 = (10)^2$$
$$a^2 + 36 = 100$$
$$a^2 = 64$$
$$a = 8$$

Now using the area formula

$$A = \frac{1}{2}(6)(8)$$

$$A = \frac{1}{2}(48)$$

$$A = 24$$

A simpler technique involving some insight could be used if you identified triangle ABC as a $3 - 4 - 5$ triangle. Using this ratio you know that the height is 8, since one side is 6 and the other is 10. From here you could immediately substitute into the area formula.
Note the underlined key terms.

21.   The <u>approximate</u> value of $\sqrt{\dfrac{7231}{221}}$ is:

(A)   12
(B)   60
(C)   6
(D)   36
(E)   4

The correct answer is (C) 6. The key word *approximate* tells you to round off each number. Rounding off to the nearest hundred gives you $\sqrt{\dfrac{7200}{200}}$. Simplifying and dividing leaves $\sqrt{36}$, which is 6.

22.   Bob can do a job in 8 hours. If Tom works with him, the job will be completed in 3 hours. How long would it take Tom to do the job alone?

(A)   7 hours
(B)   4 hours
(C) $4\dfrac{4}{5}$ hours
(D) $3\dfrac{3}{5}$ hours
(E)   8 hours

The correct answer is (C) $4\dfrac{4}{5}$ hours. This type of problem involves a very uncommon method of setting up an equation with one variable. Since Bob can do the job in 8 hours, in 1 hour he could do $\dfrac{1}{8}$ of the job. You don't know how long it would take Tom, so in 1 hour he could do $\dfrac{1}{x}$ of the job. In 3 hours, they will have finished the job; therefore in 1 hour they will finish $\dfrac{1}{3}$ of the job.

This leaves the working equation:

$$\underset{\text{(Bob's rate)}}{\dfrac{1}{8}} \quad + \quad \underset{\text{(Tom's rate unknown)}}{\dfrac{1}{x}} \quad = \quad \underset{\text{(together)}}{\dfrac{1}{3}}$$

Multiplying both sides of the equation by the common denominator $24x$ gives $(24x)\dfrac{1}{8} + (24x)\dfrac{1}{x} = (24x)\dfrac{1}{3}$.

Simplifies to: $3x + 24 = 8x$
Subtracting $3x$ from both sides leaves $24 = 5x$
Dividing by 5 gives the solution $\dfrac{24}{5} = x$ or $4\dfrac{4}{5}$

This is a difficult problem. Eliminating choices (D) and (E) as ridiculous answers would have increased your odds in guessing.

INTRODUCTION TO ANALYTICAL ABILITY

This *new* area of the GRE consists of two separately timed sections of 25 minutes each:

Analysis of Explanations—40 problems (25 minutes)

Logical Diagrams—15 problems
Analytical Reasoning—15 problems   (25 minutes for both)

These two sections will be scaled together from 200 to 900 to make up your Analytical Ability score.

ANALYSIS OF EXPLANATIONS

What Is Measured

This new type of question measures your ability to: (1) recognize and understand logical relationships; (2) judge the agreement and coherence of interrelated statements; and (3) reach a conclusion by using a sequential procedure to eliminate incorrect choices.

What Is Required

Each set of questions presents a fact situation and a result. Several numbered statements follow the result. You are required to evaluate each statement in relation to the fact situation and the result.

NOTE: Each statement should be considered separately from the other statements. The following sequence of A, B, C, D, and E is to be examined *in order,* following each statement. *The first choice that cannot be eliminated is the correct choice.*

> *Choose A*   if the statement is inconsistent with, or contradictory to, something in the fact situation, the result, or both together.
>
> *Choose B*   if the statement presents a possible adequate explanation of the result.
>
> *Choose C*   if the statement is deducible from something in the fact situation, the result, or both together.
>
> *Choose D*   if the statement either supports or weakens a possible explanation of the result. It is then relevant to an explanation.
>
> *Choose E*   if the statement is irrelevant to an explanation of the result.

Use common sense to make all decisions; no background in formal logic is necessary. Unlikely or remote possibilities should not be considered.

What You Should Know

1. Choices must be read in *order* and selected on that basis.
2. Underline the main idea and related arguments.
3. Make sure you understand the main purpose of the passage and how it relates to the result.
4. Read the given statement carefully, trying to find its relationship to the fact situation and the result.
5. Remember that choices A and C refer to the fact situation, the result, or both together.
6. B, D, and E refer only to the result.

7. Keep in mind that you must detect an *inconsistency* or *contradiction* before selecting choice A.

8. There is a fine line between choices B (a possible adequate explanation) and choice D (either supports or weakens a possible explanation). Remember, B has to be adequate *by itself,* whereas D either supports or weakens a *partial explanation.*

9. Choice C may be chosen *only* if the statement is deducible and therefore *must* be true.

10. Treat each statement separately. *Do not* use actual knowledge from the previous question, but *do* use the answers for a guideline for your choices.

11. Look for the obvious possibility, result, or reaction. Avoid the obscure or uncommon situation. Use common sense in looking for the most straightforward explanation.

12. If you are not sure of an answer, keep in mind that you MUST take the FIRST one that you cannot eliminate. Any guessing that you do for this type of problem should therefore automatically be at least partially an educated guess.

ANALYSIS OF EXPLANATIONS: ANSWERS AND EXPLANATIONS

Fact Situation 1

1. A

This statement contradicts the fact that the new system was an *effective* system.

2. A

The effectiveness of the new system, coupled with its time-consuming multiple shifts, which checked everyone, contradicts this statement.

3. E

Since the fact situation and the result do not mention other contraband at all, this statement is not contradictory, explanatory, or deducible, and does not support or weaken any possible explanation of the result. Unrelated as it is, the statement is clearly irrelevant.

4. B

This statement does not contradict the fact situation or the result, and does provide a good explanation for the renewed surge of drug smuggling after the stricter program ended.

5. C

This statement does not contradict anything in the fact situation or result, and does not *directly* explain the *sharp* increase in smuggling.

6. C

This statement does not contradict anything in the fact situation or result, and does not at all explain the increase in smuggling. But the statement is *deducible* from the stated fact that the new system was scrapped because it was very expensive.

7. D

The fact situation and result do not mention captures away from the border, so this statement does not contradict anything. Neither does it explain increased smuggling; in fact, more captures might tend to decrease smuggling. Since the statement doesn't point back to any solid information in the fact situation, it is not deducible. However, because increased captures would *decrease* smuggling, the statement *weakens* a possible explanation of the result, so (D) is the correct choice.

8. A

We are told that no one skipped inspection during the new system.

Fact Situation 2

9. E

The fact situation and result do not mention the kitchen or room size, so this statement does not *contradict* anything. Neither does it *explain* the result, since the Fishers did accept the house as a rental, small kitchen and all. There is no information from which it might be relevant to an explanation. With all these choices eliminated, the statement remains *irrelevant*.

10. D

This statement does not contradict the fact that the Fishers left a check; nor does it directly explain why they finally did not buy it. No information in the fact situation or result allows you to deduce further information about the check. However, the statement is relevant to a possible explanation, since a bounced check would disqualify the Fishers' credit and discourage the homeowner from selling to them, perhaps even from renting to them.

11. A

The many people who approved the house, especially the contractor, are an indication that it was in good condition.

12. A

This change-of-mind is inconsistent with the fact that a legal contract had been signed.

13. B

This statement does not contradict anything in the fact situation or result, and is a possible explanation for the Fishers' attraction to renting instead of buying.

14. C

This statement is not at all contradictory, but neither does it explain the Fishers' change of mind. However, it is deducible from their decision that it was the "right place for them."

15. D

This statement does not contradict the Fishers' approval and decision based on their first impression, but it does not adequately explain why they still decided to live there despite the small lot. There is no information from which you can deduce the statement, but the statement is *relevant* to the explanation; it *weakens* the result that they still decided to live on a lot which finally seemed too small.

16. A

This statement is inconsistent with the fact situation. The only relative that visited the house was Mr. Fisher's brother and he gave it his approval.

INTRODUCTION TO ANALYTICAL ABILITY

LOGICAL DIAGRAMS

What Is Measured

This new section measures your ability to determine relationships between independent or interdependent sets or categories.

What Is Required

In this section, five diagrams are presented that illustrate the relationship among three classes. You are to choose the one diagram that best illustrates the relationship among three given classes. There are three possible relationships between any *two* different classes:

One class completely within another class, but not vice versa, is represented by

When two classes have some, but not all members in common, the relationship is represented by

When two classes have no members in common, the relationship is represented by

NOTE: The relative size of the circles does not represent the size of the class.

What You Should Know

1. Understand the three possible relationships between any two different classes or sets.

2. Decide on the *most inclusive* or *general* category explaining the relationships.

3. *Sketch* your own diagram as you read the classes or sets.

4. Compare your diagram with the given choices and select the most similar diagram.

5. If your answer is [diagram], then A is completely within B and B is completely within C.

6. If you choose [diagram], then two of the sets have something in common and one set does not.

7. If you choose [diagram], then all of the sets have no members in common.

8. If you choose [diagram], then two sets have nothing in common, but are both within a greater set.

9. If you choose [diagram], then two sets have some members in common and are both within a greater set.

10. If you choose [diagram], then all three sets have one or more members in common, but not all.

11. If you choose [diagram], then two sets have some members in common, and the third set is within the intersection or overlap.

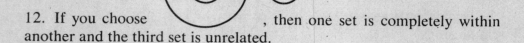

12. If you choose ⬭, then one set is completely within another and the third set is unrelated.

13. If you choose ⬭, then two sets have one or more members in common and the third set is exclusively within one set.

14. If you choose ⬭, then set A has some members in common with set B, and set B has some different members in common with set C. Set A and set C have no members in common.

15. If you choose ⬭, then one set (A) is completely within another set (B), and a third set (C) has something in common with both sets. The third set is not completely within either or both sets.

16. The relative size of the circles has no relationship to the size of the respective sets.

17. If you can eliminate one or more of the choices, then take an educated guess. You should be able to eliminate some choices if you can determine the relationship between any two of the sets or classes.

EXPLANATION OF MINI-EXAM LOGICAL DIAGRAMS

1. Cats, dogs, animals

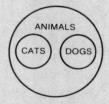

The correct answer is (C). Cats and dogs have no members in common but are both within the greater, more general, set of animals.

2. Tall men, thin men, women

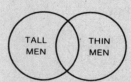

The correct answer is (A). Tall men and thin men can have members in common as a man can be tall and thin. Women are unrelated to these two sets.

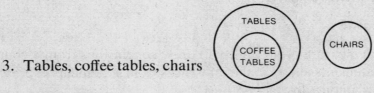

3. Tables, coffee tables, chairs

The correct answer is (D). Coffee tables are within the greater set of tables, and chairs are unrelated to these two sets.

4. Cars, motor vehicles, Cadillacs

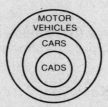

The correct answer is (D). Cadillacs are a specific kind of car, and cars are less specific types of motor vehicles.

5. Friendly people, healthy people, wealthy people

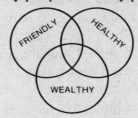

The correct answer is (C). All three sets, friendly, healthy, and wealthy people can have members in common as a person can be friendly, healthy and wealthy, all at the same time.

6. Athletes, scholars, people

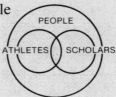

The correct answer is (B). Athletes and scholars can have members in common as someone can be an athlete and a scholar. Both of these sets are within the larger set of people.

ANALYTICAL REASONING

What Is Measured

This new section measures your ability to draw conclusions from a complex series of statements and to make inferences from statements expressing relationships among abstract entities.

What Is Required

Each question or group of questions is based on a set of statements or a passage. You are required to choose the *best* answer to each question.

What You Should Know

1. If you are given a list of statements, number the statements or use markings to clarify the relationships.

2. Draw diagrams or make charts, if possible, as visual problems lend themselves to sight solutions and elimination of possible answers.

3. Learn how to use an elimination-of-possibility chart.

EXAMPLE: (1) Tom, Bob, and Fred are a butcher, a baker, and a tailor, but not necessarily in that order.

(2) Tom is not the baker.

(3) Fred is the butcher.

Notice how the chart is constructed (you will probably want to abbreviate to save time):

	Butcher	*Baker*	*Tailor*
Tom			
Bob			
Fred			

Mark an X for NO and an O for YES.
Statement (2) yields the first marking: Tom is not the baker.

	Butcher	*Baker*	*Tailor*
Tom		x	
Bob			
Fred			

Statement (3) tells you that Fred is the butcher, but this also tells you that Fred *cannot* be the baker or the tailor, and Bob and Tom *cannot* be the butcher.

	Butcher	*Baker*	*Tailor*
Tom	x	x	
Bob	x		
Fred	o	x	x

Now by looking at the chart, it is evident that Tom must be the tailor; therefore Bob is the baker.

The fully completed chart is as follows:

	Butcher	*Baker*	*Tailor*
Tom	x	x	o
Bob	x	o	x
Fred	o	x	x

4. Cross out contradictory statements or mark them as such.
5. Make a list of elements given in the proper sequence.

EXAMPLE: (1) Ed is taller than Jim.
              (2) Hank is shorter than Chris.
              (3) Chris is shorter than Jim.

List these in order: 1. Ed
                       2. Jim
                       3. Chris
                       4. Hank

Now questions from this information can be easily answered.

6. Look for a "tip-off" word or sentence to solve the problem or complete the relationship. This "tip-off" word or sentence can give you the needed connection.

7. Read the statements and rules given carefully as they are the boundaries for your selection.

8. If an argument, statement, or paragraph is given, underline important words or phrases.

9. If drawing a diagram, completing a chart, or ordering a group appears appropriate for the problem, try that for only a few minutes, as in many cases a partial chart or simple deduction can give you the correct answer. Complete the chart as need arises in the questions if you are unable to do so at the very beginning.

10. If you can eliminate one or more answers, then guessing is to your advantage. In this type of problem, Analytical Reasoning, you can often make a good intuitive guess.

Questions 7–9 refer to eight statements that can be used to make a diagram as follows:

1.	B
2.	G
3.	G
4.	B
5.	G
6.	G
7.	B
8.	B
9.	B
10.	G
11.	B
12.	B

In this set of questions, the diagram is almost a necessity to answer the questions. Although this is not always the case, it is usually helpful to diagram or chart the information. The statements can be used to complete the diagram by carefully filling in the positive statement first.

(5) A boy is at the front of the line.

(7) 2 boys are at the end of the line.

(8) A girl is 10th in line.

1.	B
2.	
3.	
4.	
5.	
6.	
7.	
8.	
9.	
10.	G
11.	B
12.	B

Now splitting the line in half by placing a mark after the first 6 students accommodates the statement that 4 girls are in the first half of the line. Since statement (2) says that 5 of the students are girls, then the second half of the line is composed of 5 boys and 1 girl.

<pre>
     1. B
     2.
     3.
     4.
     5.
     6. _____
     7. B
     8. B
     9. B
    10. G
    11. B
    12. B
</pre>

Now to arrange the 4 remaining girls and 1 boy in the front half of the line, statement (3) *Each girl is next to a boy,* and (4) *Each boy is not necessarily next to a girl,* must be considered. The only possible arrangement, following these rules and using a little "trial and error," is the complete line shown at the beginning of this explanation.

7. D 2 Girls, 2 Boys
By inspection of the diagram.

8. D II & IV
3 boys are next to each other and there are 5 boys. By inspection of the diagram.

9. C
The next 3 students are 1 boy and 2 girls. By removing the first three students from the diagram.

10. B I & III
Modern technology does not create new jobs and widespread unemployment is bad. These are two very evident assumptions since the argument states that modern technology reduces the need for manpower and that this is a curse.

11. A I

A job shortage already exists. Answer I is the only one that strengthens or supports the argument. If a job shortage already exists, then anything causing more unemployment would be bad.

12. D

Cures for many diseases can be attributed to modern technology. This is the strongest statement of the group that supports modern technology.

AT THIS POINT, YOU SHOULD DECIDE WHETHER YOU NEED SOME BASIC REFRESHER PRACTICE AND REVIEW IN ARITHMETIC, ALGEBRA, OR GEOMETRY. TURN TO PAGES 380, 425, 456 AND TAKE THE SHORT DIAGNOSTIC SELF-TESTS IN EACH AREA AND REVIEW THE APPROPRIATE SECTION.

4

Test-Taking: A Positive Systematic Approach

TEST-TAKING STRATEGIES: THE POSITIVE SYSTEMATIC APPROACH

Good scores on most important exams depend on two factors: (1) your knowledge of the subject matter and (2) your test-taking ability. Your knowledge of subject matter is reviewed in the practice tests and extra practice sections. It is that second important factor—test-taking ability—which this section discusses.

Even outstanding knowledge of subject matter may be minimized by poor test-taking ability. This general ability includes such skills as answering the *right* question (knowing precisely what is being asked), budgeting your time wisely, eliminating ridiculous answers, and avoiding "traps." Using what you know in these areas is VERY IMPORTANT for success on the GRE.

Five years of research with graduate students taking the GRE and other major tests has yielded a positive systematic approach known as the "one-check, two-check" system.

Use the "one-check, two-check" system to mark your answer sheet and/or test booklet. The procedure is as follows:

1. Answer easy questions immediately.
2. Place one check next to any problem you attempt and find to be difficult or time-consuming.
3. Place two checks next to problems that are beyond your knowledge or otherwise impossible for you.

     √√Impossible for you
     √Possible but difficult

Make this judgment quickly. Decide whether you can work the problem quickly, or might be able to work it ($\checkmark$), or cannot work it ($\checkmark$ $\checkmark$). After working all the problems you can do immediately, return to work those with one check. If you complete them, try the two-check problems.

FOR EXAMPLE:

1 Ⓐ ● Ⓒ Ⓓ Ⓔ
$\checkmark$ 2 Ⓐ Ⓑ Ⓒ ● Ⓔ
$\checkmark\checkmark$ 3 Ⓐ Ⓑ Ⓒ Ⓓ Ⓔ
4 Ⓐ Ⓑ Ⓒ ● Ⓔ
5 ● Ⓑ Ⓒ Ⓓ Ⓔ
$\checkmark$ 6 Ⓐ ● Ⓒ Ⓓ Ⓔ
$\checkmark\checkmark$ 7 Ⓐ Ⓑ Ⓒ Ⓓ Ⓔ

Notice the markings to the left of the simulated answer form. Make these markings lightly on the answer sheet, and erase them thoroughly before the end of the time period for each section.

The test taker in this example worked problem #1 quickly and marked it accordingly. He tried problem #2, but could not come up with one of the choices so he put a $\checkmark$ by the problem, deciding to come back to it. Problem #3 dealt with a formula and process completely unfamiliar to the student, so after reading the question he immediately marked $\checkmark$ $\checkmark$ and went to #4, realizing that any time spent on #3 would be wasted. He solved and marked #s 4 and 5 within a few minutes. On #6 he saw two possible answers but felt B was best and marked it. Because he was unsure of this answer, he checked it for a possible second look. #7 contained material which he had seen before and could not work; realizing his limitation he gave a $\checkmark$ $\checkmark$ to this problem.

If you complete all the easy and "one-check" problems in a section by the end of your time, you will have at least worked all the problems you can positively do and some you thought were possible. These are the problems that usually make or break your score, so *getting the correct answer to the problems you know how to work is most important.*

This "one-check, two-check" system helps you avoid:

(1) Spending too much time on any one problem.
(2) Wasting time on problems beyond your knowledge.
(3) "Getting stuck."

At the same time, you become accustomed to the problems by first working the ones you know and build confidence as you work them.

Those test-takers who put this Positive Systematic Approach to work are bound to achieve higher scores than those who take the test haphazardly.

5

Three Full-Length Simulation Practice Tests

THIS SECTION CONTAINS THREE (3) NEW-FORMAT GRE PRACTICE APTITUDE TESTS WITH ANSWERS AND COMPLETE EXPLANATIONS. THE PRACTICE-TEST FORMAT, QUESTION STRUCTURE, NUMBER OF QUESTIONS, LEVELS OF DIFFICULTY, AND TIME ALLOTMENTS ARE *EQUIVALENT* TO THOSE ON THE ACTUAL GRE (THE ACTUAL GRE MAY NOT BE DUPLICATED AND THESE QUESTIONS ARE NOT TAKEN DIRECTLY FROM THE TEST).
FOLLOW THESE TIME ALLOTMENTS:

SECTION I	50 minutes
SECTION II	50 minutes
SECTION III	25 minutes
SECTION IV	25 minutes
SECTION V	25 minutes

PRACTICE TEST 1

Tear out Answer Sheet for Practice Test I, pages xi and xii.

SECTION I: VERBAL ABILITY

TIME—50 MINUTES
80 QUESTIONS

Directions: Each question in this test consists of a sentence in which one or two words are missing. Beneath the sentence are five words or word sets. Choose the word or word set that *best* completes the sentence. Then mark the appropriate space in the answer column.

---

1. Progress in government, science, art, literature, philosophy, and religion _____ great civilizations from mere groups of communities.
   - (A)   describes
   - (B)   extols
   - (C)   extricates
   - (D)   distinguishes
   - (E)   relinquishes

2. Although a tenet may be _____ in nature, it cannot be considered a _____.
   - (A)   colored—miniature
   - (B)   ceremonial—relic
   - (C)   incorrect—lie
   - (D)   simple—rite
   - (E)   ridiculous—doctrine

3. The closet _____ a reprehensible odor from _____ fumes.
   - (A)   enclosed—noxious
   - (B)   exuded—stifling
   - (C)   developed—aromatic
   - (D)   convened—herbivorous
   - (E)   grimaced—foul

4. There are stories and highly _____ suppositions that the Hyksos built a considerable empire in Egypt, although there are few written records or definite evidences of their conquests.
   - (A)   plausible
   - (B)   peculiar
   - (C)   challenging
   - (D)   improbable
   - (E)   historical

5. The frontier settlements cut across colonial boundary lines, breaking down local customs and laying the basis for a truly _____ point of view.
- (A) democratic
- (B) national
- (C) agrarian
- (D) sectional
- (E) military

6. In accordance with the _____, the restrictions against freedom of worship were _____.
- (A) will—abrogated
- (B) morality—lifted
- (C) movement—developed
- (D) formula—aggravated
- (E) ukase—rescinded

7. Students who display a(n) _____ attitude toward their teachers cannot expect to receive _____ for their efforts.
- (A) receptive—rewards
- (B) stubborn—plaudits
- (C) deceptive—failure
- (D) intransigent—grades
- (E) abysmal—punishment

8. His success in converting the people to his way of thinking was largely a result of his _____ criticisms of the existing order.
- (A) substantial
- (B) emotional
- (C) indiscreet
- (D) persuasive
- (E) unbridled

Directions: In each of the following questions select the lettered pair which best expresses a relationship similar to that expressed in the original pair.

---

9. PROSPEROUS : PRODIGAL ::
- (A) rich : gorgeous
- (B) poor : frugal
- (C) wealth : prosperous
- (D) lachrymose : indolent
- (E) well-to-do : heedless

10. CONDONE : ERROR : :
   (A)   extenuate : crime
   (B)   moderate : tone
   (C)   placate : pardon
   (D)   reprisal : retaliation
   (E)   expiate : sin

11. TERSE : TURGID : :
   (A)   cow : pig
   (B)   tremendous : prodigious
   (C)   state : nation
   (D)   slim : obese
   (E)   mountain : sea

12. FAILURE : TIMOROUSNESS : :
   (A)   sagacity : experience
   (B)   smarting : ointment
   (C)   study : mastery
   (D)   experiment : hypothesis
   (E)   heredity : wisdom

13. SINGLE : PROTEAN : :
   (A)   cursed : hallowed
   (B)   reasonableness : sensibility
   (C)   inexorable : austere
   (D)   varying : steadfast
   (E)   unvarying : transient

14. ACID : CARBOY : :
   (A)   disillusionment : life
   (B)   solution : mineral
   (C)   water : jug
   (D)   discipline : army
   (E)   destructiveness : railway

15. PEREMPTORY : POSITIVE : :
   (A)   demented : vexed
   (B)   celibate : without relatives
   (C)   ancient : old
   (D)   generosity : parsimony
   (E)   ineluctable : indefeasible

16. ZEAL : ASSIDUOUSLY : :
    (A)   determination : flatteringly
    (B)   ardor : elusively
    (C)   error : not thoroughly
    (D)   perfunctory : diligently
    (E)   indolence : cursorily

17. VIRTUOSO : TYRO : :
    (A)   sophistication : ingenuity
    (B)   end : beginning
    (C)   bellicosity : ingenuousness
    (D)   knowledge : rudiments
    (E)   complexity : elementary

Directions: Each question in this test consists of a word printed in capital letters followed by five words lettered (A) through (E). Choose the word that has most nearly the OPPOSITE meaning from the word in capital letters. Mark the appropriate space in the answer column. Consider all choices before deciding which one is best, since some choices are very close in meaning.

---

18. SALUBRIOUS
    (A)   pernicious
    (B)   apt
    (C)   peripheral
    (D)   intact
    (E)   saline

19. FAMINE
    (A)   fasting
    (B)   satiety
    (C)   family
    (D)   hunger
    (E)   canine

20. WARY
    (A)   weary
    (B)   lorn
    (C)   audacious
    (D)   cautious
    (E)   lost

21. MELANCHOLY
    (A)   mixed
    (B)   medial
    (C)   mental
    (D)   debonair
    (E)   ailing

22. DISAVOW
    (A)   offer
    (B)   display
    (C)   asseverate
    (D)   refute
    (E)   lose

23. CONTENTIOUS
    (A)   with
    (B)   warlike
    (C)   amicable
    (D)   against
    (E)   menial

24. IGNOMINY
- (A) shame
- (B) nobility
- (C) tally
- (D) ignorance
- (E) mind

25. GERMANE
- (A) non-German
- (B) irrelevant
- (C) penitent
- (D) biological
- (E) gruesome

26. QUERULOUS
- (A) fickle
- (B) bibulous
- (C) ill
- (D) nasty
- (E) amenable

27. EXIGUOUS
- (A) copious
- (B) exacting
- (C) exigent
- (D) ilk
- (E) brazen

Directions: Each passage is followed by a group of questions. Read each passage and choose the *best* answer to each question. Then mark the appropriate space in the answer column. Answers should be chosen on the basis of what is stated and implied.

---

harder passage

The objection likely to be made to this argument would probably take some such form as the following. There is no greater assumption of infallibility in forbidding the propagation of error, than in any other thing which is done by public authority on its own judgment and responsibility. Judgment is given to men that they may use it. Because it may be used erroneously, are men to be told that they ought not to use it at all? To prohibit what they think pernicious, is not claiming exemption from error, but fulfilling the duty incumbent on them, although fallible, of acting on their conscientious conviction. If we were never to act on our opinions, because those opinions may be wrong, we should leave all our interests uncared for, and all our duties unperformed. An objection which applies to all conduct, can be no valid objection to any conduct in particular. It is the duty of governments, and of individuals, to form the truest opinions they can; to form them carefully, and never impose them upon others unless they are quite sure of being right. But when they are sure (such reasoners may say), it is not conscientiousness but cowardice to shrink from acting on their opinions, and allow doctrines which they honestly think dangerous to the welfare of mankind, either in this life or in another, to be scattered abroad without restraint, because other people, in less enlightened times, have persecuted opinions now believed to be true. Let us take care, it may be said, not to make the same mistake: but governments and nations have made mistakes in other things, which are not denied to be fit subjects for the exercise of authority: they have laid on bad taxes, made unjust wars. Ought we therefore to lay on no taxes, and, under whatever provocation, make no wars? Men, and governments, must act to the best of their ability. There is no such thing as absolute certainty, but there is assurance sufficient for the purposes of human life. We may, and must, assume our opinion to be true for the guidance of our own conduct: and it is assuming no more when we forbid bad men to pervert society by the propagation of opinions which we regard as false and pernicious.

I answer, that it is assuming very much more. There is the greatest difference between presuming an opinion to be true, because, with every opportunity for contesting it, it has not been refuted, and assuming its truth for the purpose of not permitting its refutation. Complete liberty of contradicting and disproving our opinion, is the very condition which justifies us in assuming its truth for purposes of action; and on no other terms can a being with human faculties have assurance of being right.

28. We may assume that it is the writer's contention that
- (A) one must not publish doctrines inimical to the welfare of mankind
- (B) one must permit every doctrine, false or true, to be published
- (C) it is the duty of governments and of individuals to form the truest opinion possible, then to act upon it
- (D) because government may, on occasion, exercise its powers injudiciously, it should not therefore be forbidden of such powers
- (E) we assume infallibility in forbidding the propagation of error

29. The meaning of the second sentence is
- (A) nothing is more erroneous than the thought that anything done by public authority is infallible
- (B) believing that things may be done by public authority on its own authority, without recourse to any other sanction, is a prime error
- (C) government has no more opportunity for error in censorship than in its other exercises of power
- (D) there is no such thing as absolute certainty
- (E) the government is infallible and may forbid the propagation of error

30. The case for censorship is in part justified by
- (A) syllogism: deduction from a major hypothesis and a minor hypothesis
- (B) inductive reasoning: reasoning to a conclusion from relevant instances
- (C) analogy: reasoning by comparison with similar situations
- (D) experience: citing of instances of successful censorship
- (E) rhetoric: persuasive skill in the use of language

31. The argument given against censorship runs as follows:

   (A)   censorship is a form of cowardice—a refusal to obey the promptings of one's conscience

   (B)   censorship is, in effect, a begging of the question. It assumes what it should prove—namely, that an opinion is wrong

   (C)   on no other terms than complete liberty of contradicting and disproving an opinion can a being with human faculties have the sense of being a rational, complete individual

   (D)   we may not prohibit the free play of mind on the pretext that it may be used erroneously; that is the risk a free society takes

   (E)   truth is good; censorship is bad

1   Schiller was the first to ring a change on this state of things by
2 addressing himself courageously to the entire population of his coun-
3 try in all its social strata at one time. He was the great popularizer
4 of our theatre, and remained for almost a century the guiding spirit
5 of the German drama of which Schiller's matchless tragedies are still
6 regarded by many people as the surpassing manifestos. Schiller's
7 position, while it demonstrates a whole people's gratitude to those
8 who respond to its desires, does not however furnish a weapon of
9 self-defense to the "popularizers" of drama, or rather its diluters.
10 Schiller's case rather proves that the power of popular influence
11 wrought upon a poet may be vastly inferior to the strength that radi-
12 ates from his own personality. Indeed, whereas the secret of ephem-
13 eral power is only too often found in paltriness or mediocrity, an
14 influence of enduring force such as Schiller exerts on the Germans
15 can only emanate from a strong and self-assertive character. No poet
16 lives beyond his day who does not exceed the average in mental
17 stature, or who, through a selfish sense of fear of the general, allows
18 himself to be ground down to the conventional size and shape.
19 Schiller, no less than Ibsen, forced his moral demands tyrannically
20 upon his contemporaries. And in the long run your moral despot,
21 provided he be high-minded, vigorous, and able, has a better chance
22 of fame than the pliant time-saver. However, there is a great differ-
23 ence between the two cases. For quite apart from the striking dis-
24 similarities between the poets themselves, the public, through the
25 gradual growth of social organization, has become greatly altered.

32. Schiller's lasting popularity may be attributed to

   (A) his meeting the desires of a whole people, not just a segment of the people

   (B) his abiding by his inmost convictions

   (C) his mediocrity and paltriness

   (D) his courageous facing up to the problems of his day

   (E) his ability to popularize the unknown

33.   In line 1, "on this state of things" refers to
    (A)   romantic drama
    (B)   the French play of contrived construction
    (C)   drama directed to the rich and well-born
    (D)   the popularizers of the theatre of today
    (E)   the ruling class

34.   In line 23, "the two cases" refer to
    (A)   pliant time-server and moral despot
    (B)   the one who exceeds the average in mental stature and the one who allows himself to be ground down to conventional size
    (C)   the popularizer and the poet of enduring fame
    (D)   Ibsen and Schiller
    (E)   the man of character and the man of wealth

35.   We may assume that the author
    (A)   is no believer in the democratic process
    (B)   has no high opinion of the "compact majority"
    (C)   regards popularity with the people as a measure of enduring success
    (D)   is opposed to the aristocracy
    (E)   has no fixed opinions

36.   A word used in an ambiguous sense (having 2 or more possible meanings) in this passage is
    (A)   "poet" (lines 11, 15, 24)
    (B)   "people" (lines 6, 7)
    (C)   "power" (lines 10, 13)
    (D)   "popularizer" (lines 3, 9)
    (E)   "moral" (lines 19, 20)

    Freudian psychoanalysis introduced the term Pleasure Principle to psychological research. It refers to the will-to-pleasure as one of life's motivating factors. Alfred Adler, on the other hand, introduced the term Power Principle, and his theory of psychology stresses the will-to-power. Latterly, Viktor Frankl, also of Vienna, has been writing about the Meaning Principle or will-to-meaning. He states that man's deepest striving is for a higher and ultimate meaning to existence. Each person, he maintains, should make as his mission in life the meaning of the relationship of the unique personality to the universe and to every other unique personality; education needs a concept of man in steady search of meaning.

The most serious threat to modern man, it would seem, is not physical annihilation but the alleged meaninglessness of life. This latent vacuum becomes manifest in a state of boredom. Automation will lead to more and more free time and many will not know how to use their leisure hours. This is evidenced today by what Dr. Frankl refers to as Sunday Neurosis, the depression which afflicts people who become conscious of the lack of content in their lives when the rush of the busy week stops. Nothing in the world helps man to keep healthy so much as the knowledge of a life task. Nietzsche wisely said, "He who knows a Why of living surmounts every How."

37. a. "The Search for Meaning" aptly states the central theme of this passage.
     b. According to the passage, Freud's Pleasure Principle is regarded as unimportant by Dr. Frankl.
     (A)   both a and b are correct
     (B)   a is correct; b is incorrect
     (C)   a is incorrect; b is correct
     (D)   both a and b are incorrect

38. a. Adler's Power Principle implies a struggle among individuals to achieve dominion over others.
     b. Implicit in the passage is the fact that education needs to deal with personal concerns rather than with social concerns.
     (A)   both a and b are correct
     (B)   a is correct; b is incorrect
     (C)   a is incorrect; b is correct
     (D)   both a and b are incorrect

39. a. According to the author, people who keep busy are never bored.
     b. The passage implies that man should ask himself "What is the meaning of life?" as well as "What is the meaning of my life?"
     (A)   both a and b are correct
     (B)   a is correct; b is incorrect
     (C)   a is incorrect; b is correct
     (D)   both a and b are incorrect

40. a. According to the author, people spend their lives striving to eradicate life's meaninglessness.
     b. According to the passage, Sunday Neurosis affects most people who find that they have nothing to do on Sundays.
     (A)   both a and b are correct
     (B)   a is correct; b is incorrect
     (C)   a is incorrect; b is correct
     (D)   both a and b are incorrect

41.   a. According to Nietzsche, as quoted in the selection, people who have a philosophy of life will automatically know how to get along in the world.

   b. According to the passage, people would be better off with more rather than with fewer working hours.

   (A)   both a and b are correct

   (B)   both a and b are incorrect

   (C)   a is correct; b is incorrect

   (D)   a is incorrect; b is correct

The post-Sputnik publicity given to education has served to point up many new and controversial ideas being tried in elementary schools. Science from the kindergarten up is being stressed in some school systems. Others are giving foreign languages in the primary grades. Individualized reading is winning friends in New York City, whereas in Joplin the trend is toward departmentalization of reading.

Some of these experiments will probably prove valuable in whole or in part. Under the test of time, others will be revealed as more meretricious than meritorious. But no matter what vogues may find temporary favor, it can probably be predicted that the experience-curriculum will be employed more intensively and extensively in our land. Based on sound philosophical and psychological principles, this approach has already been demonstrated to be superior to any based on the idea that the elementary school is a place for abstract cogitation, rote learning, and passive acceptance of the written and the spoken word.

"Experience teaches" is an adage born in antiquity and respected thenceforward. However, teachers must be aware that the learning which stems from the experience increases in proportion to the depth of one's participation in it. Finally, the experience is of greatest value when it is derived from a previous experience or leads to one in which the accrued knowledge can be reapplied. If the application comes in an out-of-school situation, so much the better, for schoolwork thus becomes more meaningful to the child and simultaneously enriches his life.

Critics of and those who misunderstand the experience-curriculum picture school children running helter-skelter and all but climbing the walls. This is a gross exaggeration. They are permitted to handle objects freely, get together in groups, and move about when necessary in the course of their studies; but the fundamental approach is oriented in concepts of mental, rather than physical, activity. Each child, whatever his I.Q., is given a chance to "think through" problems, make judgments, and arrive at conclusions after analyzing pertinent facts.

Correctly interpreted and implemented, therefore, the experience-curriculum seems to be stable and enduring. Whatever educational fashions may come and go, it will, in all likelihood, serve as the keystone for the best methods and practices in the future.

42. a. The central idea in the above passage is that many people misunderstand the purposes and practices of the experience-curriculum.
     b. The author implies that the experience-curriculum is one of several new experiments of great value in education.
     (A)   both a and b are correct
     (B)   a is correct; b is incorrect
     (C)   a is incorrect; b is correct
     (D)   both a and b are incorrect

43. a. A procedure referred to in the passage is that of breaking up heterogeneous classes daily and re-forming them into homogeneous classes for reading period.
     b. The suggestion that gifted children may be allowed to skip a grade is NOT mentioned or implied in the passage.
     (A)   both a and b are correct
     (B)   a is correct; b is incorrect
     (C)   a is incorrect; b is correct
     (D)   both a and b are incorrect

44. a. The author states that the launching of Sputnik I caused American educators to try out many new ideas in elementary schools.
     b. The author of the above passage states that when experiences are continuous, rather than disparate, they are most worth while.
     (A)   both a and b are correct
     (B)   a is correct; b is incorrect
     (C)   a is incorrect; b is correct
     (D)   both a and b are incorrect

45. a. The author of the above passage implies that experience should proceed gradually from the concrete to the abstract.
     b. The author of the above passage implies that questions calling for critical thinking are not important aspects of the experience-curriculum.
     (A)   both a and b are correct
     (B)   a is correct; b is incorrect
     (C)   a is incorrect; b is correct
     (D)   both a and b are incorrect

46. a. The author of the above passage clearly implies that children should be taught to respect the written word.
     b. It can be inferred from the passage that special programs for slow learners are a definite part of the experience-curriculum.
     (A)   both a and b are correct
     (B)   a is correct; b is incorrect
     (C)   a is incorrect; b is correct
     (D)   both a and b are incorrect

Because money is the metamorphosed shape of all other commodities, the result of their general alienation, for this reason it is alienable itself without restriction or condition. It reads all prices backwards, and thus, so to say, depicts itself in the bodies of all other commodities which offer to it the material for the realization of its own use-value. At the same time the prices, wooing glances cast at money by commodities, define the limits of its convertibility, by pointing to its quantity. Since every commodity, on becoming money, disappears as a commodity, it is impossible to tell from the money itself, how it got into the hands of its possessor, or what article has been changed into it. *Non olet* from whatever source it may come. Representing on the one hand a sold commodity, it represents on the other a commodity to be bought.

47. One characteristic of money is that
     (A) it bears no trace of its source.
     (B) it is tainted.
     (C) it is based upon some precious metal as a standard.
     (D) it has a constant use-value.
     (E) it depicts the value of commodities.

48. The statement that money is alienable means
     (A) it is easily taken away from someone.
     (B) it can be exchanged for something else.
     (C) it is the cause of much dissension.
     (D) its small size makes it a convenience in trading.
     (E) it can be used when trading with foreigners.

49. The author is thinking of money as
     (A) the basis of finance.
     (B) something different from commodities.
     (C) of fixed value.
     (D) a token.
     (E) a convenience.

50. Prices may be thought of as
     (A) another expression of money.
     (B) enticements to the purchaser.
     (C) the realization of money.
     (D) entirely convertible.
     (E) a measure of the value of money.

51. The value of money depends upon
     (A) whether or not the market is glutted.
     (B) the use to which it is put.
     (C) the amount to which it is alienable.
     (D) its exchange value in terms of goods.
     (E) the realization of its own use-value.

52. The subject of the paragraph is
    (A) money and commodities.
    (B) money as a medium of exchange.
    (C) price determination.
    (D) the value of money in terms of price.
    (E) the metamorphosed shape of money.

Select the word or word set which *best* completes each of the following sentences.

53. It is not easy to _____ a story. One must exercise real judgment and knowledge in determining where to _____ it.
    (A) augment—digest
    (B) shorten—aggravate
    (C) analyze—expose
    (D) abridge—modify
    (E) expurgate—enhance

54. One who _____ to excess may correctly be called _____.
    (A) curses—immoral
    (B) grumbles—querulous
    (C) drinks—teetotaler
    (D) gambles—lecher
    (E) speaks—laconic

55. The witness told his story apparently with indifference, yet with _____ enough to fix the words in the juror's memory.
    (A) emphasis
    (B) mannerism
    (C) garrulousness
    (D) literacy
    (E) authority

56. Let them perish! I shall take my _____ for all the humiliation I suffered in my youth.
    (A) reprisal
    (B) condemnation
    (C) vengeance
    (D) opportunity
    (E) punishment

57. The lawyer attempted to _____ the gravity of his client's offense by ascribing it to a condition of _____.

   (A)   condone—premeditation
   (B)   mitigate—temporary insanity
   (C)   minimize—malevolence
   (D)   aggravate—unawareness
   (E)   soften—intolerance

58. A good axiom to remember, to serve as a source of consolation, is that a single _____ does not constitute _____.

   (A)   apple—a meal
   (B)   winter—old age
   (C)   misfortune—victory
   (D)   idea—story
   (E)   flower—spring

59. The _____ base of the giant tree is _____ evidence of its antiquity.

   (A)   red—vivid
   (B)   round—tacit
   (C)   concrete—definite
   (D)   complete—striking
   (E)   gnarled—mute

60. Liberty and slavery differ only in the nature of the controlling authority. As a result, freedom can be easily perverted into _____.

   (A)   servitude
   (B)   humility
   (C)   arrogance
   (D)   defeat
   (E)   liberty

61. Certain community groups on the East Side have opposed plans to _____ its slums and replace them with modern "projects."

   (A)   reconstruct
   (B)   resurrect
   (C)   raze
   (D)   alleviate
   (E)   alter

Select the lettered pair which best expresses a relationship similar to that expressed in the original pair.

62. GOSSIP : HAMLET : :
   (A) village : reputation
   (B) truth : story
   (C) press : nation
   (D) chapter : book
   (E) gossip : newspaper

63. CHARACTER : DISSIPATION : :
   (A) signature : forgery
   (B) rock : erosion
   (C) landscape : flatness
   (D) task : fatigue
   (E) food : fasting

64. PILOT : SEXTANT : :
   (A) mason : awl
   (B) teacher : quadrant
   (C) reader : novel
   (D) woodman : axe
   (E) ploughman : scythe

65. LAGOON : BAY : :
   (A) island : peninsula
   (B) ocean : gulf
   (C) cove : bay
   (D) stream : outlet
   (E) brook : river

66. CARICATURE : PORTRAIT : :
   (A) imitate : lampoon
   (B) similarity : likeness
   (C) quotation : allusion
   (D) likeness : sketch
   (E) paraphrase : verbatim

67. PHLEGMATIC : STOLIDITY : :
   (A) dry : moderation
   (B) accident : recklessness
   (C) degenerate : perversity
   (D) headlong : impetuosity
   (E) quiet : tacit

68. CONTIGUOUS : CLOSE : :
- (A) wit : approach
- (B) warmth : glow
- (C) off : from
- (D) adjacent : sequence
- (E) next : by

69. MARTIAL : HALCYON : :
- (A) belligerent : growling
- (B) Mars : sun
- (C) warlike : peaceful
- (D) worried : soothed
- (E) warlike : mournful

70. WHEAT : CHAFF : :
- (A) wine : dregs
- (B) humanity : dregs
- (C) dross : ore
- (D) wisdom : cunning
- (E) lead : gold

The *opposite* of:

71. PARSIMONIOUS
- (A) frugal
- (B) preying
- (C) partial
- (D) open-handed
- (E) silly

72. MELLIFLUOUS
- (A) smear
- (B) polite
- (C) raucous
- (D) noxious
- (E) mending

73. PARIAH
- (A) trustful
- (B) cynosure
- (C) exile
- (D) omen
- (E) iniquitous

74. INTRANSIGENT
- (A) resentful
- (B) negating
- (C) be determined
- (D) acquiescent
- (E) unruly

75. PROFLIGATE
- (A) prodigious
- (B) costly
- (C) luxurious
- (D) prodigal
- (E) parsimonious

76. PERSPICACIOUS
- (A) erudite
- (B) dull
- (C) tactful
- (D) persistent
- (E) wise

77. RECONDITE
   (A) ill
   (B) obscure
   (C) concise
   (D) abstract
   (E) verbose

78. AVERSION
   (A) foible
   (B) flagrant
   (C) sign
   (D) penchant
   (E) hatred

79. DISCLOSE
   (A) open
   (B) imitate
   (C) express
   (D) dissimulate
   (E) invade

80. EQUANIMITY
   (A) identity
   (B) anonymity
   (C) disproportion
   (D) perturbation
   (E) compensation

S T O P
IF YOU FINISH BEFORE TIME IS CALLED, CHECK YOUR
WORK ON THIS SECTION ONLY. DO NOT WORK
ON ANY OTHER SECTION IN THE TEST.

SECTION II: QUANTITATIVE ABILITY

TIME—50 MINUTES
55 QUESTIONS

Quantitative Comparison

(SUGGESTED TIME—20 MINUTES)
30 QUESTIONS

Directions: Each question in this section consists of two quantities, one in Column A and one in Column B. You are to compare the two quantities and on the answer sheet blacken space

A if the quantity in Column A is the greater;
B if the quantity in Column B is the greater;
C if the two quantities are equal;
D if the relationship cannot be determined from the information given.

All numbers used are real numbers.
Diagrams are not necessarily drawn to scale.

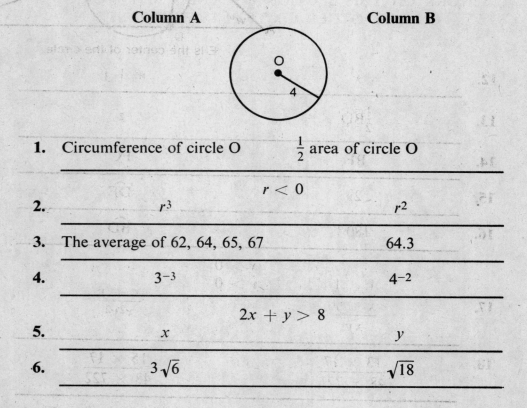

	Column A	**Column B**

1. Circumference of circle O $\frac{1}{2}$ area of circle O

$$r < 0$$

2. r^3 r^2

---

3. The average of 62, 64, 65, 67   64.3

---

4. 3^{-3} 4^{-2}

$$2x + y > 8$$

5. x y

---

6. $3\sqrt{6}$ $\sqrt{18}$

Questions 7–8 refer to this diagram.

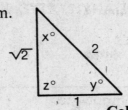

	Column A	Column B
7.	$x + y$	z
8.	x	y

$$m^3 = -1$$

9.	m	-2
10.	$\dfrac{5}{\sqrt{5}} \times \dfrac{1}{3} \times \dfrac{4}{7}$	$\dfrac{1}{3} \times \sqrt{5} \times \dfrac{4}{7}$
11.	$x - y$	$y - x$

Questions 12–16 refer to this diagram.

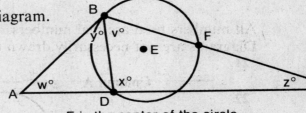

E is the center of the circle.

12.	x	$w + y$
13.	$\frac{1}{2}\widehat{BD}$	z
14.	BF	FC
15.	$2v$	$\widehat{DF}$
16.	$180°$	$\widehat{BD}$

$$x > 0$$
$$y > 0$$

17.	$\dfrac{\frac{1}{x} + \frac{1}{y}}{xy}$	$\dfrac{x + y}{x^2 y^2}$
18.	$\dfrac{13 \times 17}{48 \times 721}$	$\dfrac{15 \times 17}{48 \times 722}$

$$x^2 + 2x + 1 = 0 \qquad 4y^2 + 4y + 1 = 0$$

19.	x	y

Column A	Column B

$$5 \leq p \leq 7$$
$$3 < q < 11$$

20. p q

Questions 21–24 refer to this diagram.

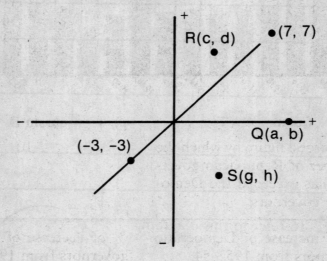

21. g h

22. d c

23. b d

24. $-h$ -3

$$2x + 3y = 11$$
$$5x + 2y = 22$$

25. x y

Questions 26–29 refer to this graph.

Governorship Trend

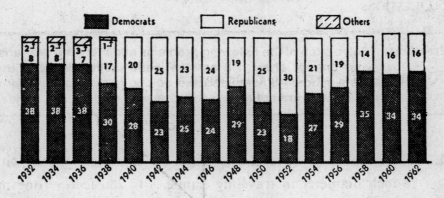

	Column A	Column B
26.	The largest figure by which the number of Republican governors has exceeded the Democratic governors.	10
27.	% of increase of Democratic governors from 1952–54	% of decrease of Republican governors from 1952–54
28.	The ratio of Democratic governors to Republican governors in 1940	The ratio of Democratic governors to Republican governors in 1956
29.	Republican governors in 1960	Re-elected Democratic governors in 1938

$$a \neq b$$
$$a > 0$$
$$b > 0$$

| **30.** | $a \times b$ | $a + b$ |

Math Ability

(SUGGESTED TIME—30 MINUTES)
25 QUESTIONS

Directions: Solve each of the following problems and mark the *best* answer on your answer sheet. All scratch work should be done in the available space. All numbers used belong to the real number system. Diagrams are not necessarily drawn to scale.

---

31. The number of revolutions made by a bicycle wheel with a 28-inch diameter in traveling $\frac{1}{2}$ mile is (5,280 feet = one mile) ($\pi = \frac{22}{7}$)

    (A) 720
    (B) 180
    (C) 360
    (D) 120
    (E) 90

32. Of the following, the value closest to that of $\dfrac{42.10 \times .0003}{.002}$ is

    (A) .063
    (B) .63
    (C) 6.3
    (D) 63
    (E) 630

33. If a man travels r miles an hour for h hours and s miles an hour for t hours, what is his average rate in miles per hour for the entire distance traveled?

    (A) $rh + st$

    (B) $\dfrac{rh + st}{2}$

    (C) $\dfrac{r}{h} + \dfrac{s}{t}$

    (D) $\dfrac{rh + st}{h + t}$

    (E) $\dfrac{rh + st}{h - t}$

34. If $a = \frac{1}{2}$, $b = \frac{2}{3}$ and $c = \frac{3}{4}$, what is the value of $\dfrac{2a + 3b}{c}$?

    (A) $\frac{1}{4}$

    (B) $2\frac{1}{4}$

    (C) 3

    (D) 4

    (E) 6

35. The accompanying figure consists of squares and isosceles right triangles. What percent of the entire figure is the area of the shaded part?

    (A) 50%

    (B) 56%

    (C) 60%

    (D) 69%

    (E) 75%

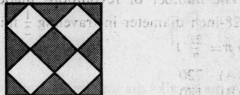

36. Assuming that the series will continue in the same pattern, the next number in the series 3, 5, 11, 29 . . . is

    (A) 41

    (B) 47

    (C) 65

    (D) 57

    (E) 83

37. A storekeeper purchased an article for $36. In order to include 10 percent of cost for overhead and to provide $9 of net profit, the markup should be

    (A) 25%

    (B) 35%

    (C) $37\frac{1}{2}$%

    (D) 40%

    (E) 45%

38. A rectangular carton has twice the height, one-third the length, and four times the width of a second carton. The ratio of the volume of the first carton to that of the second is

    (A) 16 : 3

    (B) 3 : 1

    (C) 8 : 3

    (D) 3 : 8

    (E) 8 : 5

39. If $d = m - \dfrac{50}{m}$, and m is a positive number which increases in value, d
(A) increases in value
(B) remains unchanged
(C) decreases in value
(D) fluctuates up and down in value
(E) none of these

40. If $9x + 5 = 23$, the numerical value of $18x + 5$ is
(A) 46
(B) 51
(C) 2
(D) $23 + 9x$
(E) 41

41. A man walks diagonally from one corner of a rectangular lot to the opposite corner. If he walks at the rate of 5 feet a second, and the lot is 50 feet by 120 feet, how many seconds will he save by walking diagonally instead of walking along the perimeter of the lot?
(A) 8 seconds
(B) 10 seconds
(C) 17 seconds
(D) 34 seconds
(E) 25 seconds

42. What is the number of feet traversed in 1 second by an automobile that is traveling 30 miles an hour?
(A) 176
(B) 2
(C) 2,640
(D) 44
(E) 22

43. In which, if any, of the following can the 2s be cancelled out without changing the value of the expression?
(A) $2x - 2m$

(B) $\dfrac{\dfrac{x}{2}}{\dfrac{2}{m}}$

(C) $\dfrac{2x - m}{2}$

(D) $\dfrac{x^2}{m^2}$

(E) none of these

44. In which of the following equations does y vary inversely as x?

    (A) $y = \dfrac{x}{12}$

    (B) $x = 32y$

    (C) $xy = 5$

    (D) $\dfrac{y}{x} = 9$

    (E) $x = y$

Questions 45–48 refer to this graph.

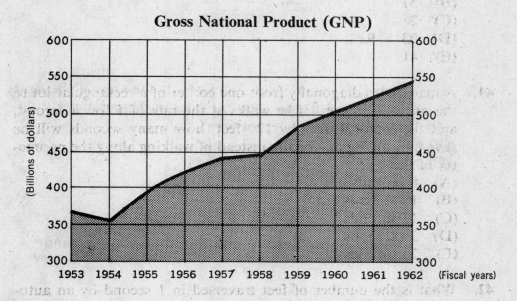

Gross National Product (GNP)

45. Between 1953 and 1961, how many times did the gross national product decline from one year to the next?

    (A) 1
    (B) 2
    (C) 3
    (D) 4
    (E) 5

46. How long did it take the gross national product to rise approximately one hundred billion dollars from 1955?

    (A) 1 year
    (B) 2 years
    (C) 3 years
    (D) 4 years
    (E) 5 years

47. Between which two years was the rise in gross national product the greatest?
- (A)   1958–1959
- (B)   1957–1958
- (C)   1960–1961
- (D)   1959–1960
- (E)   1953–1954

48. By approximately what percentage did gross national product rise between 1958 and 1960?
- (A)   eight percent
- (B)   twenty-five percent
- (C)   fifteen percent
- (D)   eleven percent
- (E)   nineteen percent

49. This figure consists of 5 equal squares. If the area of the figure is 180 sq. in., find the number of inches in the perimeter.
- (A)   36 inches
- (B)   45 inches
- (C)   72 inches
- (D)   900 inches
- (E)   144 inches

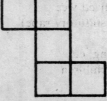

50. Express as a single fraction the sum of the fractions $\dfrac{r}{s}$ and $\dfrac{x}{y}$.

- (A) $\dfrac{rx}{sy}$

- (B) $\dfrac{r + x}{s + y}$

- (C) $\dfrac{r}{s} + \dfrac{x}{y}$

- (D) $\dfrac{r + y}{s + y}$

- (E) $\dfrac{ry + sx}{sy}$

Questions 51–55 refer to this chart.

City Arrests, Distribution by Sex, 1961

(Data in this table are from reports furnished the FBI by 2,776 cities over 2,500 in population. This represents a total population of 85,158,360.)

Offense charged	Males	Females	Total
Criminal homicide:			
Murder and nonnegligent manslaughter	3,791	834	4,625
Manslaughter by negligence	1,458	160	1,618
Forcible rape	7,143	—	7,143
Robbery	31,563	1,612	33,175
Aggravated assault	46,951	8,404	55,355
Burglary—breaking or entering	122,400	4,077	126,477
Larceny—theft	186,999	41,068	228,067
Auto theft	56,409	2,138	58,547
Other assaults	126,817	14,967	141,784
Embezzlement and fraud	28,548	5,738	34,286
Stolen property; buying, receiving, etc.	9,808	937	10,745
Forgery and counterfeiting	17,821	3,792	21,613
Prostitution and commercialized vice	7,563	19,280	26,843
Other sex offenses (includes statutory rape)	37,652	8,552	46,204
Narcotic drug laws	21,227	3,853	25,080
Weapons; carrying, possessing, etc.	33,746	2,239	35,985
Offenses against family and children	31,099	3,918	35,017
Liquor laws	84,790	14,258	99,048
Driving while intoxicated	153,462	10,760	164,222
Disorderly conduct	373,760	61,126	434,886
Drunkenness	1,286,309	112,984	1,399,293
Vagrancy	134,569	12,957	147,526
Gambling	99,529	9,042	108,571
All other offenses	403,757	76,342	480,099
Suspicion	110,692	14,924	125,616
TOTAL ARRESTS, 1961	3,417,863	433,962	3,851,825

Source: Federal Bureau of Investigation

51. Approximately how many times more men than women were arrested in American cities in 1961?

(A) 2
(B) 4
(C) 6
(D) 8
(E) 10

52. Which of the following statements is false?
  (A) More men than women were arrested for burglary in American cities in 1961.
  (B) No women were arrested for forcible rape in American cities in 1961.
  (C) About fourteen times as many men as women were arrested for drunken driving in American cities in 1961.
  (D) More men than women were arrested for each classification of crime in American cities in 1961.
  (E) More women were arrested for drunkenness in American cities in 1961 than for any other offense.

53. For which of the following offenses were the most men arrested in American cities in 1961?
  (A) murder and manslaughter
  (B) larceny
  (C) forgery and counterfeiting
  (D) auto theft
  (E) disorderly conduct

54. Which of the following offenses accounted for a larger percentage of the total female arrests than of the total male arrests in American cities in 1961?
  (A) auto theft
  (B) disorderly conduct
  (C) drunkenness
  (D) burglary
  (E) carrying and possessing weapons

55. Which of the following offenses accounted for a percentage of the total female arrests in American cities in 1961 which most closely approximates the percentage of the total male arrests for the same offense?
  (A) offenses against family and children
  (B) prostitution and commercialized vice
  (C) drunken driving
  (D) auto theft
  (E) carrying and possessing weapons

STOP
IF YOU FINISH BEFORE TIME IS CALLED, CHECK YOUR WORK ON THIS SECTION ONLY. DO NOT WORK ON ANY OTHER SECTION IN THE TEST.

SECTION III: ANALYTICAL ABILITY

Analysis of Explanations

TIME—25 MINUTES
40 QUESTIONS

Directions: A fact situation and a result are presented. Following the result are several numbered statements. Evaluate each statement in relation to the fact situation and the result.

Each statement is to be considered separately from the other statements. The following sequence of A, B, C, D, and E is to be examined *in order* following each statement. The first choice that cannot be eliminated is the correct choice.

> *Choose A*   if the statement is inconsistent with, or contradictory to, something in the fact situation, the result, or both together.
>
> *Choose B*   if the statement presents a possible adequate explanation of the result.
>
> *Choose C*   if the statement is deducible from something in the fact situation, the result, or both together.
>
> *Choose D*   if the statement either supports or weakens a possible explanation of the result. It is then relevant to an explanation.
>
> *Choose E*   if the statement is irrelevant to an explanation of the result.

Use common sense to make all decisions. No background in formal logic is necessary. Unlikely or remote possibilities should not be considered.

Set I.

FACT SITUATION: Tom Stone, a high school honor student, could not decide where he wanted to go to college. At the recommendation of his counselor, Mrs. Snyder, he applied to a number of different colleges and universities. Most of these were in Southern California, but two were in Oregon and one was in Colorado. Tom was accepted by each school to which he applied, on the basis of his high grade-point average and aptitude test scores. About half of these schools offered Tom at least partial scholarships, and three of the colleges offered him full scholarships. Tom visited the out-of-state colleges and a few of the local colleges before making his final decision.

RESULT: Tom decided to attend a local college.

1. Tom wanted to commute to school from home.

2. The out-of-state schools were appealing to Tom.

3. Tom's older brother was attending a local college.

4. The Stone family could not afford to send Tom to college.

5. Tom did not have enough information about the out-of-state colleges.

6. Local colleges have tough entrance requirements.

7. Most of the colleges in the country would probably have accepted Tom.

8. Local colleges offered Tom a better selection of courses.

9. Mrs. Snyder wanted Tom to go to a local junior college.

10. Tom was not athletic.

Set II.

FACT SITUATION: Mr. Bell, a TV network president, was not in favor of trying out a new comedy series. He enjoyed the pilot program, but felt that it dealt with too many controversial issues. His vice-president, Mr. Dinkle, not only was in favor of trying the program, but urged him to do so. After carefully discussing the new program with the rest of his staff, Mr. Bell decided to go ahead and try it.

RESULT: The program was never aired on TV.

11. The TV network president was fired before the new season.

12. The network president reluctantly agreed to put the program on TV.

13. The sponsors disliked the pilot.

14. The staff was in agreement with the network president.

15. The network ratings were on a steady decline.

16. Mr. Dinkle's cousin wrote the new program.

17. The new program was not approved by the censors.

18. The comedy series featured a well-known star.

19. Controversial issues were of no concern to Mr. Bell.

20. Mrs. Bell never watched TV.

Set III.

FACT SITUATION: Workers at the Stiller Steel Mill went on strike on August 5 because of a wage dispute. The union representatives felt that the company was not bargaining in good faith and ordered the strike. Contract negotiations were proceeding smoothly until the last week of July, when company representatives could not agree to the union's wage proposals and broke off negotiations. None of the 2,000 employees showed up for work the morning of August 5, but about 400 picketers were at the company's front gate vowing not to return without the wage increase. Union funds were apportioned to the strikers to meet living expenses while on strike, but would only be sufficient until September 1. The company's loss of business would force bankruptcy by about the same time.

RESULT: The strikers returned to work on August 29th.

21. The company conceded to the strikers.

22. The Stiller Steel Mill was closed down on August 29.

23. The workers' strike was not successful.

24. The wage proposal was unreasonable.

25. Stiller Steel Mill has the highest base wage for employees in the country.

26. Negotiations resumed before August 29th.

27. This was the first union strike at this mill.

28. Steel manufacturing costs have risen sharply in the past few years.

29. Fringe benefits were a major factor in the strike.

30. Neither party in the dispute gave in easily.

Set IV.

FACT SITUATION: While shopping at a local supermarket, Mrs. Mendez bumped into an old friend, Mrs. Tucker, whom she had not seen in 10 years. After a little reminiscing, Mrs. Mendez invited Mrs. Tucker and her husband to dinner that evening to meet her family and finish reminiscing. Mrs. Tucker accepted the invitation for 6 P.M.

When Mrs. Mendez arrived home, her older daughter greeted her with a message from Mr. Mendez. Mr. Mendez had accepted a dinner invitation for the evening at Mr. and Mrs. Handler's house for him and his wife. Mrs. Mendez was very upset about the whole situation as she had not gotten the Tuckers' phone number. She immediately called her husband at work and explained the situation.

RESULT: Mr. and Mrs. Mendez had dinner with the Handlers.

31. Mr. Mendez insisted on going to the Handlers' house for dinner.

32. Mrs. Mendez didn't like the Tuckers.

33. The Tuckers arrived at 6 P.M. for dinner but were greeted by the Mendez's children.

34. Mrs. Mendez could not get a baby sitter on such short notice.

35. Mr. Handler was Mr. Mendez's employer.

36. Mrs. Mendez contacted the Tuckers and made another date.

37. All 3 couples had dinner together at the Mendez home.

38. Mrs. Mendez's daughter had a date that night.

39. The Handlers were moving away the next day.

40. Mrs. Mendez called Directory Assistance and got Mrs. Tucker's phone number.

STOP
IF YOU FINISH BEFORE TIME IS CALLED, CHECK YOUR WORK ON THIS SECTION ONLY. DO NOT WORK ON ANY OTHER SECTION IN THE TEST.

SECTION IV: ANALYTICAL ABILITY

TIME—25 MINUTES
30 QUESTIONS

Logical Diagrams

(SUGGESTED TIME—6 MINUTES)
15 QUESTIONS

Directions: In this section, five diagrams are presented that illustrate the relationship among three classes. You are to choose the one diagram that best illustrates the relationship among the three given classes. There are three possible relationships between any *two* different classes:

One class completely within another class, but not vice versa, is represented by

When two classes have some, but not all, members in common, the relationship is represented by

When two classes have no members in common, the relationship is represented by

Note: The relative size of the circles does not represent the size of the class.

Questions 1–7 are based on the following diagrams:

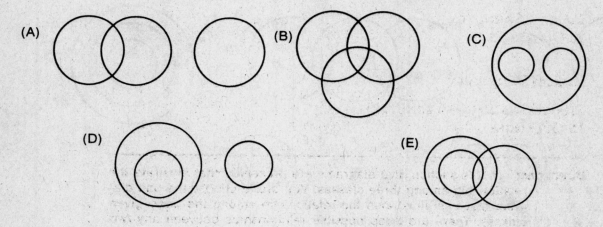

1. Roses, flowers, cats

2. Plumbers, electricians, people

3. Bowlers, trumpet players, doctors

4. Housewives, tall women, slender women

5. Adults, smokers, women

6. People who dance, dancers, men

7. Sportswriters, television watchers, bluejays

Questions 8–15 are based on the following diagrams:

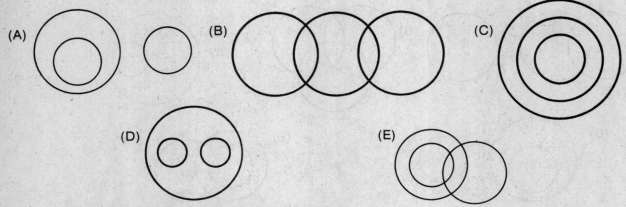

8.   Carrots, lettuce, salad ingredients

9.   Waiters, aunts, song lovers

10. money, paper, metal

11. Joggers, males, boys

12. Alcoholic beverages, wines, soaps

13. Glue, gum, sticky substances

14. Timex, watch, timepieces

15. Felines, cats, birds

Analytical Reasoning

(SUGGESTED TIME—19 MINUTES)
15 QUESTIONS

Directions: Each question or group of questions is based on a set of statements or a passage. You are required to choose the *best* answer to each question.

Questions 16, 17, and 18 refer to the following set of statements.

(1)   10 men and women are seated around a rectangular table.
(2)   A man has to be seated next to a woman.
(3)   Only one person can be seated at each end of the table.
(4)   Two men cannot be seated next to each other.
(5)   Half of the people are women.

16. Which of the following *cannot* be deduced from the above: *what is false*
    (A) There are 5 males at the table.
    (B) Men will never be at both ends of the table.
    (C) Women are seated across from men all around the table.
    (D) Women will never be at both ends of the table.
    (E) Three men cannot be on one side of the table.

17. If one more man wishes to sit at the table, considering the conditions:
    (A) He must sit at one end.
    (B) He must sit on the side.
    (C) Two others must switch places to accommodate him.
    (D) He cannot be seated.
    (E) He can sit anywhere.

changing situation

18. If two more people wish to be seated at the table:
    I.   They can both be women.
    II.   They can both be men.
    III. They can be one man and one woman.
    (A) I & III
    (B) I & II
    (C) II & III
    (D) III
    (E) I, II, & III

only workul what you have

Questions 19–22

In order to prepare for her daughter's wedding, Mrs. Stewart hired a
    florist, a caterer, a dressmaker, and a printer.
Mrs. Stewart wanted to meet with each to discuss preparations.
She had time to see only three of them per day.
The florist was available all day Monday and on Tuesday morning.
The caterer was available on Monday afternoon and all day on Tuesday.
The dressmaker was available all day on Monday and on Thursday.
The printer was available on Monday evening, on Wednesday morning,
    and on Friday afternoon.

19. If Mrs. Stewart could only use the car in the mornings, then
    (A) she could not complete preparations in one week.
    (B) she would have to see the caterer on Tuesday and the printer
         on Wednesday.
    (C) she would have to see the dressmaker on Tuesday.
    (D) she could complete preparations before Thursday.
    (E) she would have to see the florist on Tuesday and the caterer
         on Monday.

20. Which of the following could *not* occur?

    I.   She could meet with the caterer and the printer at the same time.

   II. She could meet with the florist and the dressmaker at the same time.

 III. She could meet with the florist, the dressmaker, and the printer at the same time.

   (A) I

   (B) II

   (C) III

   (D) I & II

   (E) II & III

21. If Mrs. Stewart wanted to have all preparations completed before Wednesday, then

   (A) she would have to meet with three of them on Monday.

   (B) she would have to meet with at least two of them on Tuesday.

   (C) she would have to see either the florist or caterer on Tuesday.

   (D) she would have to see either the dressmaker or printer on Tuesday.

   (E) special arrangements would have to be made.

22. If the printer changed his schedule and could only meet with Mrs. Stewart on Tuesday morning, how could she have preparation completed before Wednesday?

   (A) Meet with the florist on Monday morning, the caterer on Tuesday morning, and the dressmaker on Tuesday afternoon.

   (B) Meet with the florist on Tuesday afternoon, the caterer on Monday afternoon, and the dressmaker on Monday morning.

   (C) Meet with the florist on Monday morning, the caterer on Tuesday afternoon, and the dressmaker on Monday afternoon.

   (D) Meet with the florist on Monday afternoon, the caterer on Monday evening, and the dressmaker on Tuesday afternoon.

   (E) Preparations could not be completed before Wednesday.

Questions 23–25

Recent studies indicate that at the present rate of increase, within two years a single-family dwelling will be unaffordable by the average family. Therefore, apartment living will increase noticeably in the near future.

23. The argument presented assumes that
  I.   the present rate of price increase will continue.
  II. families will turn to renting instead of buying.
  III. construction of apartments will double within the next two years.
  (A) I
  (B) II
  (C) III
  (D) I & II
  (E) II & III

24. This argument would be weakened by the fact(s) that
  I.   many inexpensive single-family dwellings are presently being built.
  II. bank loan interest rates have increased.
  III. apartment living is also becoming very expensive.
  (A) I
  (B) II
  (C) III
  (D) I & III
  (E) II & III

25. Which of the following statements is deducible from the argument?
  (A) The recent studies were for a five-year period.
  (B) Condominiums are expensive, but plentiful.
  (C) The average family income will decrease in the next two years.
  (D) Home costs are increasing more rapidly than average family incomes.
  (E) The average family will increase within the next two years.

Questions 26–30

(1)   Morton, Hiller, Nelson, and Wood are three athletes and one sportswriter. Wood is not necessarily the sportswriter.

(2)   The three athletes are a football player, a baseball player, and a basketball player.

(3)   Morton and Hiller were spectators when the baseball player pitched his first game.

(4)   Both Wood and the football player have been interviewed by the writer at the same time.

(5)   The writer has written articles on Morton and Wood after separate interviews.

(6)   Wood doesn't know Nelson.

(7)   The basketball player has never been interviewed.

26.   Which of the following statements is true?
(A)   Morton is the baseball player.
(B)   Wood is the football player.
(C)   Wood and Nelson are best friends.
(D)   Nelson is not the football player.
(E)   Morton and Hiller are both basketball players.

27.   Which of the following must be true?
  I.   Wood knows the writer.
 II.   Nelson knows the writer.
III.   Hiller knows Nelson.
(A)   I
(B)   II
(C)   I & II
(D)   I & III
(E)   II & III

28.   If the writer wanted to interview someone new, he would have to interview:
(A)   Morton
(B)   Hiller
(C)   Nelson
(D)   Wood
(E)   Hiller or Wood

29. Which of the following statements is *FALSE?*
   - I. Morton is the football player.
   - II. Hiller is the sportswriter.
   - III. Nelson is the basketball player.
   - (A) I & II
   - (B) II & III
   - (C) I & III
   - (D) All of the above.
   - (E) None of the above.

30. If the sportswriter interviews Morton, then which of the following must be true?
   - I. Morton will have been interviewed at least twice.
   - II. Wood will never have been interviewed.
   - III. The basketball player will never have been interviewed.
   - (A) I
   - (B) II
   - (C) III
   - (D) I & III
   - (E) II & III

S T O P
IF YOU FINISH BEFORE TIME IS CALLED, CHECK YOUR
WORK ON THIS SECTION ONLY. DO NOT WORK
ON ANY OTHER SECTION IN THE TEST.

SECTION V: MATH ABILITY

TIME—25 MINUTES
25 QUESTIONS

Directions: Solve each of the following problems and mark the *best* answer on your answer sheet. All scratch work should be done in the available space. All numbers used belong to the real number system. Diagrams are not necessarily drawn to scale.

---

1. A boy walks m miles in h hours. At the same rate, how many miles will he walk in b hours?

    (A) $b = \dfrac{m}{h}$

    (B) $\dfrac{mh}{b}$

    (C) mb

    (D) $\dfrac{mb}{h}$

    (E) hbm

2. A baseball team won 4 games and lost 20. What fraction of its games did the team win?

    (A) $\dfrac{1}{5}$

    (B) $\dfrac{1}{4}$

    (C) $\dfrac{4}{5}$

    (D) $\dfrac{5}{6}$

    (E) $\dfrac{1}{6}$

    $\dfrac{4}{24}$

3. In a barrel there are 60 pints of a solution that is 20 percent alcohol. How many pints of pure alcohol must be added to produce a solution that is 40 percent alcohol?
    (A)   12 pints
    (B)   20 pints
    (C)   24 pints
    (D)   120 pints
    (E)   none of these

    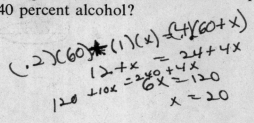

4. John can mow a lawn in 20 minutes and Frank can mow the same lawn in 30 minutes. How long will it take them working together to mow the lawn?

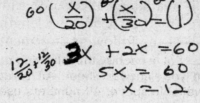

(A) 10 minutes
(B) $12\frac{1}{2}$ minutes
(C) 15 minutes
(D) 25 minutes
(E) 12 minutes

5. A group of n persons in an automobile crosses the Hudson River on a ferry. What is the formula for the total cost, T, if the charge is 50 cents for the car and driver and c cents for each additional person?

(A) $T = 50 + (n - 1)c$
(B) $T = n + c$
(C) $T = 50 + cn$
(D) $T = nc$
(E) none of these

6. A cylindrical vessel whose diameter is 4 inches is filled with a liquid to a depth of 6 inches. An irregular solid is placed in the vessel, thus causing the liquid to rise 1 inch, as shown in the figure. The volume of the solid

(A) can not be determined from these data
(B) depends upon the shape of the solid
(C) depends upon the density of the liquid
(D) is approximately 4 cubic inches
(E) is approximately $12\frac{1}{2}$ cubic inches

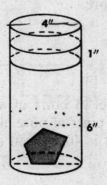

7. A man is planning to build a rectangular enclosure at the rear of a building and to fence it in on three sides as shown in the figure. There is available 60 feet of fencing. The width of the enclosure is represented by x and the length by y.

    All of the following statements are true EXCEPT
    (A) $2x + y = 60$
    (B)   The area of the enclosure is xy
    (C)   The area of the enclosure is $60x - 2x^2$
    (D)   When $x = 15$, the enclosed area is 450 sq. ft.
    (E)   The enclosed area is greatest when $x = y$

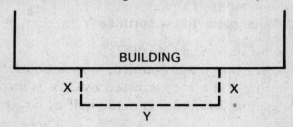

8. A salesman receives a salary of $50 a month and a commission of 4 percent on all sales. What amount of sales each month must he make to bring his total monthly income to $200?
    (A) $150
    (B) $600
    (C) $3,750
    (D) $5,000
    (E) $7,500

9. The algebraic expression $(a + b)^2$, in which a and b are two unequal positive numbers, can be represented by a single square composed of two squares and two rectangles as shown in the figure below. If the expression $(a + b + c)^2$ were represented by a figure of this kind, it would be composed of 3 squares and
    (A)   no rectangles
    (B)   2 rectangles
    (C)   3 rectangles
    (D)   4 rectangles
    (E)   6 rectangles

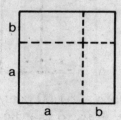

10. If, after successive discounts of 15 percent and 10 percent have been allowed on the marked price, the net price of a certain article is $306, the marked price is
   (A) $234.09
   (B) $382.50
   (C) $400.00
   (D) $408.00
   (E) $450.00

11. The volume, V, of a circular cone whose radius is r and whose altitude is h is given by the formula $V = \dfrac{\pi r^2 h}{3}$. Which, if any of the following statements is true?
   (A) If both r and h are doubled, V is doubled.
   (B) If both r and h are increased by 2, V is increased by 8.
   (C) If r is doubled and h is made half as large, V remains the same.
   (D) If r is divided by 3 and h is multiplied by 9, V remains the same.
   (E) none of these

12. Of the following, the pair that is NOT a set of equivalents is
   (A) .021%, .00021
   (B) 1.5%, 3/200
   (C) $\frac{1}{4}$%, .0025
   (D) 225%, .225
   (E) 475%, 4.75

13. A rectangle is revolved through 360° about its longer side as an axis. If the longer side is a units and the shorter side is b units, the volume of the resulting solid in cubic units is
   (A) πab^2
   (B) $\pi a^2 b$
   (C) $2\pi ab$
   (D) $2\pi ab^2$
   (E) none of these

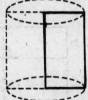

14. A merchant buys cloth at $1.60 per yard. At what price per yard should he mark the cloth so that he may sell it at a discount of 20 percent from the marked price and still make a profit of 20 percent of the selling price?
   (A) $2.00
   (B) $2.40
   (C) $2.50
   (D) $2.60
   (E) $5.00

Questions 15–19 refer to this graph.

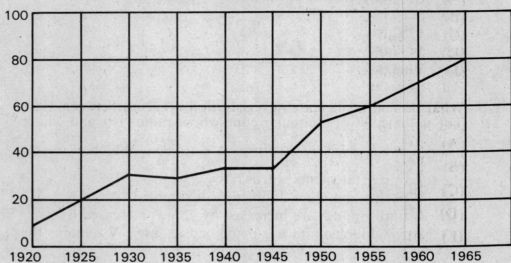

Growth in Motor Vehicle Registration Since 1920

The graph above shows the growth in motor vehicle registration since 1920.

15. Approximately how many motor vehicles were registered in 1930?
    (A) 10 million
    (B) 20 million
    (C) 40 million
    (D) 25 million
    (E) none of these

16. Approximately how many motor vehicles were registered in 1955?
    (A) 80 million
    (B) 70 million
    (C) 20 million
    (D) 60 million
    (E) 40 million

17. Approximately how many times as many motor vehicles were registered in 1955 as in 1925?
    (A) 40
    (B) 3
    (C) 2
    (D) 4
    (E) 8

18. Approximately how many more motor vehicles were registered in 1965 than in 1955?
(A) 10 million
(B) 15 million
(C) 20 million
(D) 25 million
(E) 30 million

19. What percent of increase in registration occurred between 1955 and 1965?
(A) 10%
(B) $\frac{1}{3}$%
(C) 20%
(D) $33\frac{1}{3}$%
(E) 40%

20. Three contractors supplied laborers for a job. The first supplied 7 men for 3 days; the second, 4 men for 5 days; and the third, 5 men for 9 days. The contractors paid their men a total of $774 in wages. If each laborer received the same daily wage, how much did the group of men working for the second contractor receive for the job?
(A) $56.80
(B) $180.00
(C) $193.50
(D) $227.65
(E) none of these

21. A man walks for 4 hours at the rate of y miles an hour. He stops an hour for lunch and then returns to the starting point by a route which is twice as long, but he travels in an auto whose speed is 5 times that of his walking rate. Find the number of hours spent on the entire trip.
(A) $5\frac{3}{5}$ hours
(B) 6 hours
(C) $6\frac{3}{5}$ hours
(D) 7 hours
(E) 8 hours

22. A rectangular piece of cardboard 9 inches by 12 inches is made into an open box by cutting a $2\frac{1}{2}$ inch square from each corner and bending up the sides. Find the volume of the box if no allowance is made for overlapping of the edges.
   (A) 70 cubic inches
   (B) 270 cubic inches
   (C) $154\frac{3}{8}$ cubic inches
   (D) 195 cubic inches
   (E) 40 cubic inches

23. If the angles of a triangle are in the ratio 2:3:5, the triangle is
   (A) acute
   (B) isosceles
   (C) obtuse
   (D) right
   (E) none of these

24. Five equal squares are placed side by side to make a single rectangle whose perimeter is 360 inches. Find the number of square inches in the area of one of these squares.
   (A) 72 sq. in.
   (B) 324 sq. in.
   (C) 900 sq. in.
   (D) 5,184 sq. in.
   (E) 9,000 sq. in.

25. When $a = 2$, $c = 1$ and $d = 0$, what is the value of the expression $4a + 2c^2 - 3d^2$?
   (A) 7
   (B) 9
   (C) 12
   (D) 15
   (E) 10

PRACTICE TEST I: ANSWERS

SECTION I: VERBAL ABILITY

SENTENCE COMPLETION

1.	D	4.	A	7.	B
2.	C	5.	B	8.	D
3.	B	6.	E		

ANALOGIES

9.	B	12.	A	15.	C
10.	A	13.	E	16.	E
11.	D	14.	C	17.	D

ANTONYMS

18.	A	22.	C	26.	E
19.	B	23.	C	27.	A
20.	C	24.	B		
21.	D	25.	B		

READING COMPREHENSION

28.	B	37.	B	46.	D
29.	C	38.	B	47.	A
30.	C	39.	C	48.	B
31.	B	40.	D	49.	D
32.	B	41.	C	50.	A
33.	C	42.	D	51.	E
34.	D	43.	A	52.	E
35.	B	44.	C		
36.	D	45.	D		

SENTENCE COMPLETION

53. D	56. C	59. E
54. B	57. B	60. A
55. A	58. B	61. C

ANALOGIES

62. C	65. E	68. E
63. B	66. E	69. C
64. D	67. D	70. A

ANTONYMS

71. D	75. E	79. D
72. C	76. B	80. D
73. B	77. C	
74. D	78. D	

SECTION II: QUANTITATIVE ABILITY

QUANTITATIVE COMPARISON

1. C	11. D	21. A
2. B	12. C	22. A
3. A	13. A	23. B
4. B	14. D	24. A
5. D	15. C	25. A
6. A	16. A	26. A
7. B	17. C	27. A
8. B	18. B	28. B
9. A	19. B	29. D
10. C	20. D	30. D

MATH ABILITY

31. C	40. E	49. C
32. C	41. A	50. E
33. D	42. D	51. D
34. D	43. E	52. D
35. A	44. C	53. E
36. E	45. A	54. B
37. B	46. E	55. A
38. C	47. A	
39. A	48. D	

SECTION III: ANALYTICAL ABILITY

ANALYSIS OF EXPLANATIONS

1.	B	15.	D	29.	A
2.	D	16.	D	30.	C
3.	B	17.	B	31.	B
4.	A	18.	D	32.	A
5.	A	19.	A	33.	C
6.	E	20.	E	34.	D
7.	C	21.	B	35.	B
8.	B	22.	A	36.	B
9.	A	23.	B	37.	C
10.	E	24.	D	38.	E
11.	B	25.	D	39.	B
12.	C	26.	C	40.	B
13.	B	27.	E		
14.	A	28.	D		

SECTION IV: ANALYTICAL ABILITY

LOGICAL DIAGRAMS

1.	D	6.	E	11.	E
2.	C	7.	A	12.	A
3.	B	8.	D	13.	D
4.	B	9.	B	14.	C
5.	B	10.	B	15.	A

ANALYTICAL REASONING

16.	C	21.	C	26.	D
17.	D	22.	C	27.	A
18.	D	23.	D	28.	C
19.	B	24.	D	29.	E
20.	A	25.	D	30.	D

SECTION V: MATH ABILITY

1.	D	10.	C	19.	D
2.	E	11.	D	20.	B
3.	B	12.	D	21.	C
4.	E	13.	A	22.	A
5.	A	14.	C	23.	D
6.	E	15.	E	24.	C
7.	E	16.	D	25.	E
8.	C	17.	B		
9.	E	18.	C		

PRACTICE TEST 1: ANALYSIS SHEET

SECTION I

	Possible	Completed	Right	Wrong
VERBAL ABILITY				
Sentence completion				
Analogies				
Antonyms				
Reading comprehension				
OVERALL VERBAL				

SECTION II

QUANTITATIVE ABILITY				
Quantitative comparison				
Math ability				
OVERALL QUANTITATIVE				

SECTIONS III & IV

ANALYTICAL ABILITY				
Analysis of Explanations				
Logical Diagrams				
Analytical Reasoning				
OVERALL ANALYTICAL				

SECTION V

MATH ABILITY				

RAW SCORE = NUMBER RIGHT $- \frac{1}{4}$ (number attempted but missed)

OVERALL SCORES SHOULD BE RAW SCORES

SCORE APPROXIMATOR

Verbal Ability

Raw score	Scaled score
74–80	850–900
69–73	800–849
65–68	750–799
63–64	700–749
61–62	650–699
59–60	600–649
56–58	550–599
52–55	500–549
48–51	450–499
40–47	400–449
32–39	350–399
24–31	300–349
Below 24	Below 300

Quantitative Ability

Raw score	Scaled score	Raw score
51–55	850–900	73–80
47–50	800–849	68–72
44–46	750–799	63–67
40–43	700–749	58–62
37–39	650–699	53–57
34–36	600–649	48–52
32–33	550–599	45–47
30–31	500–549	42–44
27–29	450–499	37–41
23–26	400–449	32–36
17–22	350–399	23–31
12–16	300–349	17–22
Below 12 (without Section V)	Below 300	Below 16 (with Section V)

PRACTICE TEST I: PROBLEM EXPLANATIONS

SECTION I: VERBAL ABILITY

Sentence Completion

1. **D**   *distinguish*.
   You are looking for a word which *sets apart* "great civilizations from mere groups of communities." The word must be able to be used with "from." Choice (D) *distinguish* (differentiate) is the correct choice here. (C) *extricate* refers to physically setting apart or removing, not the meaning required in this sentence.

2. **C**   *incorrect-lie*.
   The key to this question is understanding the meaning of the word "tenet" (a principle, doctrine, or dogma firmly believed to be true). Choices (A), (B), and (D) do not make sense. Choice (E) is untrue, as a tenet *is* a *doctrine* by definition. Therefore the correct answer is (C) *incorrect-lie,* which makes sense because the basis of a tenet is the fact that it is believed in, not that it is necessarily true.

3. **B**   *exuded-stifling*.
   This sentence requires a verb for the word "closet" and an adjective modifying "fumes." The words "reprehensible odor" suggest that the fumes will need a strongly negative adjective. Therefore you can eliminate choices (C) and (D). Choice (E) is inapplicable since *grimaced* is inappropriate. Finally, choice (B) is better than (A) *enclosed-noxious,* because a closet cannot fully enclose or contain fumes without leaking (exuding) them. Also, noxious (poisonous) fumes do not necessarily have bad odors.

4. **A**   *plausible*.
   This sentence requires an adjective to modify "suppositions" (theories, hypotheses). The missing word should mean "credible" or "reasonable," since it should set up a contrast to the phrase "although there are few written records or definite evidences of their conquests." Only choice (A) *plausible* fits in this context.

5. **B** *national.*
The key phrases here are "cut across colonial boundary lines" and "breaking down local customs." The sentence calls for a word meaning the opposite of "local"—one that implies a broad, wholistic point of view. The answer clearly is (B) *national.*

6. **E** *ukase-rescinded.*
The context of the sentence suggests that the "restrictions against freedom of worship" were lifted or repealed. However, the first word of the missing pair must be some type of proclamation to make logical sense. Therefore, (B), (C), and (D) can be eliminated. In choice (A) *will-abrogated,* the first word does not make sense, since a will does not deal with far-reaching public issues. Therefore, only choice (E) is correct (*ukase* means an edict of the emperor and *rescind* means to repeal.)

7. **B** *stubborn-plaudits.*
There is a strong negative connotation to this sentence so you are looking for a pair of words to describe a negative attitude which will *not* bring something positive in return. The only choice containing this negative-positive combination is choice (B) *stubborn-plaudits* (enthusiastic approval).

8. **D** *persuasive.*
In this sentence the key words "success in converting . . . to his way of thinking" define the correct answer. Choice (D) *persuasive* (convincing) is the best possible choice.

Analogies

9. **B**
prosperous is to *prodigal* in the same way as *poor* is to *frugal.* A "prosperous" person tends to be a spendthrift (prodigal), just as a "poor" person tends to be thrifty (frugal). This is a cause-effect relationship, and is the most probable of the several cause-effect choices offered.

10. **A**
condone is to *error* in the same way as *extenuate* is to *crime.* To "condone" an "error" diminishes its seriousness, as does "extenuating" (excusing) a "crime." Note also the verb-noun relationship in both pairs.

11. **D**
terse is to *turgid* in the same way as *slim* is to *obese.* The terms in each pair are *opposites,* and the relationship in each case is between small (terse, slim) and large (turgid, obese).

12. A

failure is to *timorousness* in the same way as *sagacity* is to *experience*. This is an *effect-cause relationship*. "Failure" results from "timorousness" (fear) just as "sagacity" (sound judgment) results from "experience." Several of the other choices are cause-effect rather than effect-cause.

13. E

single is to *protean* in the same way as *unvarying* is to *transient*. The terms in each pair are opposites, and the relationship in each case is between the changeless (*single, unvarying*) and the changing (*protean, transient*).

14. C

acid is to *carboy* in the same way as *water* is to *jug*. Here is a *liquid-container relationship*: a "carboy" holds corrosive liquids such as "acid," just like a "jug" holds "water."

15. C

peremptory is to *positive* in the same way as *ancient* is to *old*. The terms in each pair are *synonyms*: "peremptory" means absolute or "positive," just as "ancient" means "old."

16. E

zeal is to *assiduously* in the same way as *indolence* is to *cursorily*. "Zeal" (enthusiastic devotion) is characterized by work done "assiduously" (with constant and careful attention), just as "indolence" (laziness) is characterized by work done "cursorily" (hastily, carelessly). (C) is a possible choice, but the types of words are not the same as those in the original analogy.

17. D

virtuoso is to *tyro* in the same way as *knowledge* is to *rudiments*. A "tyro" is a beginner in learning something, and a "virtuoso" is a learned master. Similarly, "rudiments" are basic skills, the beginnings of a mastery of "knowledge." Both pairs are *nouns* that have to do with *learning;* no other choice corresponds this closely.

Antonyms

18. *Salubrious*—healthful. Correct answer: (A) *pernicious*—harmful or fatal.

19. *Famine*—starvation. Correct answer: (B) *satiety*—state of overabundance.

20. Wary—careful, guarded. Correct answer: (C) *audacious*—bold, daring.

21. *Melancholy*—depressed. Correct answer: (D) *debonair*—sprightly.

22. *Disavow*—disclaim knowledge of; deny. Correct answer: (C) *asseverate*—to affirm positively.

23. *Contentious*—full of conflict or strife. Correct answer: (C) *amicable*—friendly.

24. *Ignominy*—disgrace, dishonor. Correct answer: (B) *nobility*—quality, distinction.

25. *Germane*—pertinent. Correct answer: (B) *irrelevant*.

26. *Querulous*—complaining. Correct answer: (E) *amenable*—agreeable.

27. *Exiguous*—scanty. Correct answer: (A) *copious*—plentiful, profuse.

Reading Comprehension

28. **B**
The other choices do not require you to *assume* anything; each is explicitly stated in the passage. (B) is *implied* in the last paragraph, and requires an assumption by the reader.

29. **C**
(A) and (D) are ideas developed later in the passage. (B) complements the correct answer, but does not mention "infallibility," as (C) does ("no more opportunity for error"). (E) completely contradicts the second sentence.

30. **C**
Mistakes about censorship are compared with mistakes about taxes and wars. (B) and (D) require that style neither demonstrates rhetorical skill nor a clear syllogistic construction.

31. **B**
This choice is supported by the second, central sentence of the second paragraph, which argues *against* the assumptive censorship in the first paragraph, and is followed by the sentence excerpted in (C) which argues *for* censorship based upon the careful disproving of opinions, not upon mere assumption.

32. B

"Enduring force" is *explicitly* connected with "a strong and self-assertive character." (D) is also true, but is not developed as strongly as (B) in the paragraph.

33. C

Schiller is a popularizer, addressing all social strata. The emphasis upon this achievement implies that only the rich and well-born had been addressed by previous, less-courageous dramatists.

34. D

The "difference between the two cases" is rephrased in the next sentence as the "dissimilarities between the poets themselves," clearly referring specifically to Ibsen and Schiller. "Themselves" signals this personal reference.

35. B

The author approves Schiller as popularizer, thereby implying disapproval of the compact and powerful upper class. But he does not clearly oppose the aristocracy, choice (D); stating that a high-minded, vigorous despot or tyrant (aristocrat) is better than a "pliant time-server."

36. D

The quote marks surrounding "popularizer" in line 9 signal its ambiguous meaning.

37. B

The passage is clearly about the search for meaning, but although Freud and Frankl are distinguished from one another, there is no statement or implication that Frankl considers the Pleasure Principle unimportant. In fact, it is implied that meaning brings pleasure.

38. B

Power may mean many things besides what a. states. No definition for it is implied in the passage. The last sentence in the first paragraph supports b.

39. C

The last sentence of the first paragraph supports b. It is lack of meaning which causes boredom, not lack of busyness, so busy people may become bored; therefore a. is incorrect.

40. **D**

According to the author, people *should* spend their lives trying to eradicate meaninglessness, so a. is incorrect. Sunday Neurotics become conscious of a "lack of content," not a lack of work or activity, so b. is incorrect.

41. **C**

a. paraphrases Nietzsche correctly. b. is incorrect because it merely speaks of "working" hours rather than "meaningful" hours.

42. **D**

a. is incorrect because "misunderstanding" is a minor point in the fourth paragraph. b. is incorrect because experience-curriculum is the *most important* trend in education, according to the author.

43. **A**

a. refers to the "departmentalization" of reading, and b. is correct according to the implications of "individualized" reading.

44. **C**

Sputnik served to "point up" new ideas, not to cause them, so a. is incorrect. In the third paragraph, the author supports "accrued knowledge" and continuous experiences, so b. is incorrect.

45. **D**

In paragraph 4, the author writes about physical and mental experience, but does not suggest a progression from concrete to abstract. In the same paragraph, he emphasizes the importance of critical thinking ("thinking through") in experiential learning.

46. **D**

The author speaks of reading briefly in relationship to other programs, not necessarily part of the experience-curriculum. And in the fourth paragraph he states that the curriculum offers equal opportunities regardless of IQ.

47. **A**

All five choices are possible characteristics of money, but (A) is treated most extensively in the paragraph.

48. **B**

"Alienable" means "capable of being transferred or sold."

49. D

The paragraph emphasizes money as the "metamorphosed shape of other commodities." It is therefore a sign or symbol (*token*) for commodities.

50. A

A price is the expression of a *quantity* of money; the commodity realizes *value;* thus, (E) is eliminated. In this paragraph, the price woos the money rather than the purchaser; thus (B) is eliminated.

51. E

(D) is also correct, but (E) is more precise because it is a direct quote.

52. E

All the other choices are subordinate to (E), because they are each treated in terms of (E) in the paragraph.

Sentence Completion

53. D *abridge—modify*.

The context of this sentence requires a pair of words which means "to shorten, edit or revise." The two words should be somewhat synonymous. Choices (B) and (D) both contain appropriate *first* words but only in (D) *abridge—modify* are both words applicable.

54. B *grumbles—querulous*.

The first word missing in this sentence will define the second. You are looking for a pair of words in which the first is a verb which is characteristic of a quality (adjective) described by the second word. Since there is no article (a, an) before the second blank, you cannot use a noun in that spot. The correct answer therefore is (B), as *querulous* means "constantly complaining or grumbling."

55. A *emphasis*.

This two-part sentence makes a contrast. The word missing in the second half must be the opposite of "indifference" (lack of interest). Choice (A) *emphasis* is the best answer, as it means deliberate accentuation or stress.

56. C *vengeance*.

The first exclamation in this question tells you that the speaker is in a position to destroy others. He is going to *get even* for humiliation he once suffered. Choice (A) *reprisal* is commonly used in reference to war, therefore the only correct choice is (C) *vengeance*, which means retaliation or retribution.

57. B *mitigate—temporary insanity.*
A lawyer would want to *lessen* the gravity of a client's offense. To do that he would try to show that the client was *not responsible*. Only choice (B) *mitigate—temporary insanity* contains two words which have the proper connotations.

58. B *winter—old age.*
The words missing in this sentence must complete an axiom which says that one single element does not make a whole. An axiom is usually metaphoric—it uses simple images to stand for larger, more complex ideas. The key to this axiom is the word "consolation." This signals that the axiom must offer hope for a situation that could be gloomy. Only choice (B) *winter—old age* fits this mood.

59. E *gnarled—mute.*
The key here is the word "antiquity." The missing words must contain an adjective for the word "base" that implies age. Therefore, you don't need to look beyond the first word in each pair. Choice (E) *gnarled* (old and weather-beaten)—*mute* (silent) is the correct choice.

60. A *servitude.*
The key to this question is the idea in the first sentence that liberty and slavery differ only slightly. Therefore the second sentence is going to conclude that "freedom can be easily perverted into" another word for slavery. This word is (A) *servitude.*

61. C *raze.*
The key words here are "opposed plans to" and "replace . . . with modern 'projects.'" Notice the negative connotation—you are looking for a word that implies *destroying* existing structures so that they may be *replaced*. Choice (A) *reconstruct* is incorrect since it implies duplicating the slums. (B) and (E) are not adequately negative. (D) *alleviate* could fit the sentence but the stronger word, *raze* (demolish, obliterate) best explains why there would be opposition to the plan.

Analogies

62. C
gossip is to *hamlet* in the same way as *press* is to *nation*. In both cases, an appropriate *medium of communication* (gossip, press) is paired with its *locale* (hamlet, nation).

63. B

character is to *dissipation* in the same way as *rock* is to *erosion*. One's "character" suffers "dissipation" (harmful waste) by the excessive energy of drinking, gambling, etc., just as a "rock" shows "erosion" (wasting away) from the excessive energy of wind and water.

64. D

pilot is to *sextant* in the same way as *woodman* is to *axe*. The relationship here is between the worker and his *essential* tool: the "pilot" depends upon his "sextant" to navigate, just as the "woodman" depends upon his "axe" to chop wood.

65. E

lagoon is to *bay* in the same way as *brook* is to *river*. The relationship in each pair is *between a smaller and larger body of water*. In the first pair both are saltwater terms and in the second both are freshwater; this characteristic rules out (C) as a choice, because it combines saltwater and freshwater terms.

66. E

caricature is to *portrait* in the same way as *paraphrase* is to *verbatim*. A "portrait" represents its subject more completely and truly than a "caricature," just as a story repeated "verbatim" (word for word) represents its subject more completely and truly than a "paraphrase" (summary).

67. D

phlegmatic is to *stolidity* in the same way as *headlong* is to *impetuosity*. One who is "phlegmatic" (sluggish, dull) is characterized by "stolidity" (an unexcited state), just as one who is "headlong" (reckless, moving with uncontrolled speed) is characterized by "impetuosity" (rashness, impulsiveness). Note the adjective-noun relationship in each pair.

68. E

contiguous is to *close* in the same way as *next* is to *by*. "Contiguous" denotes a direct, touching relationship between two things; whereas "close" denotes a less specific relationship. Similarly, "next" denotes a direct alignment of two things; whereas "by" denotes a less specific relationship.

69. C

martial is to *halcyon* in the same way as *warlike* is to *peaceful*. "Martial" is synonymous with "warlike," and "halcyon" is synonymous with "peaceful."

70. A

> *wheat* is to *chaff* in the same way as *wine* is to *dregs*. "Chaff" is the worthless remains of thrashed "wheat," just as "dregs" are the worthless remains after making "wine." The "dregs of humanity" (B) is a common expression, but too metaphorical to coincide with the initial analogy here.

Antonyms

71. *Parsimonious*—stingy, miserly. Correct answer: (D) *open-handed*—generous.

72. *Mellifluous*—sweetly flowing. Correct answer: (C) *raucous*—harsh, grating.

73. *Pariah*—outcast. Correct answer: (B) *cynosure*—something that attracts attention by its brilliance.

74. *Intransigent*—uncompromising. Correct answer: (D) *acquiescent*—yielding.

75. *Profligate*—recklessly extravagant. Correct answer: (E) *parsimonious*—miserly.

76. *Perspicacious*—perceptive, discerning. Correct answer: (B) *dull*.

77. *Recondite*—abstract, obscure. Correct answer: (C) *concise*.

78. *Aversion*—strong dislike. Correct answer: (D) *penchant*—inclination.

79. *Disclose*—reveal. Correct answer: (D) *dissimulate*—conceal.

80. *Equanimity*—tranquillity. Correct answer: (D) *perturbation*—uneasiness.

SECTION II: QUANTITATIVE ABILITY

Quantitative Comparison

1. C   Circumference of circle O $= \frac{1}{2}$ area of circle.
Using the proper formulas and substituting 4 for the radius gives

$$2\pi r \qquad (\tfrac{1}{2})\pi r^2 \text{ [Notice: 2 is not in the formula]}$$

$$2\pi(4) \qquad (\tfrac{1}{2})\pi(4)^2$$

$$\tfrac{1}{2}\,\pi(16)$$

$$8\pi \;=\; 8\pi$$

2. B $r^3 < r^2$
Substituting -1 for r gives

$$-1 < 1$$

It is evident that if $r < 0$, then r^3 will always be negative and r^2 will always be positive.

3. A   The average of

$$62, 64, 65, 67 \;>\; 64.3$$

A little math insight determines that the average in Column A is 64.5, since the 62 and 67 can be canceled.
Alternate method: Actually find the average and compare:

$$\frac{62 + 64 + 65 + 67}{4}$$

$$\frac{258}{4} = 64.5$$

4. B $3^{-3} < 4^{-2}$
Changing each to a fraction by removing the negative leaves $\frac{1}{3^3}$ and $\frac{1}{4^2}$ or $\frac{1}{27} < \frac{1}{16}$

5. D $x \,?\, y$
Trying different values for the inequalities results in different answers; for example, if $x = 3$ and $y = 3$, then $x = y$, and if $x = 3$ and $y = 4$ $x < y$. Therefore no comparison is possible.

6. **A** $3\sqrt{6} > \sqrt{18}$
Best method: Change $3\sqrt{6}$ to $\sqrt{54}$ by squaring 3 to get 9, then multiplying by 6. Now comparison is simple $\sqrt{54} > \sqrt{18}$

Alternate method: Simplifying:

$$\sqrt{18}$$
$$\sqrt{9 \times 2}$$
$$\sqrt{9} \times \sqrt{2}$$
$$3\sqrt{2}$$
$$3\sqrt{6} > 3\sqrt{2}$$
because
$$\sqrt{6} > \sqrt{2}$$

Alternate method: Approximate $3\sqrt{6}$:

$$3 \times 2.5 = 7.5$$

Approximate $\sqrt{18}$:

$$4.2$$
$$7.5 > 4.2$$

7. **B** $x + y < z$
The triangle in the diagram

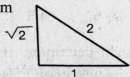

is not a right triangle because a right triangle would be of the

dimensions . Since one side is shorter than the

right triangle ratios, z is greater than 90°; therefore $x + y$ is less than 90°.

8. **B** $x < y$
In any triangle, angle size corresponds directly to the opposite side. x is opposite 1, and y is opposite $\sqrt{2}$, or 1.4.

9. **A** $m > -2$
Solving $m^3 = -1$ gives $m = -1$ and $-1 > -2$.

10. C

$$\frac{5}{\sqrt{5}} \times \frac{1}{3} \times \frac{4}{7} = \frac{1}{3} \times \sqrt{5} \times \frac{4}{7}$$

Canceling the same quantities from both sides leaves $\frac{5}{\sqrt{5}}$ to be compared to $\sqrt{5}$. Multiplying both by $\sqrt{5}$ results in $5 = 5$.

11. D $x - y ? y - x$

Substituting as follows gives two different outcomes:
If $x = 2$ and $y = 1$

$$\begin{array}{cc} (2) - (1) & (1) - (2) \\ 1 > & -1 \end{array}$$

If $x = 0$ and $y = 0$

$$\begin{array}{cc} 0 - 0 & 0 - 0 \\ & 0 = 0 \end{array}$$

Therefore no comparison is possible.

12. C $x = w + y$

An exterior angle of a triangle formed by extending one side is equal to the sum of the opposite two angles.

13. A $\frac{1}{2}\overset{\frown}{BD} > z$

If z were an inscribed angle, then z would equal $\frac{1}{2}\overset{\frown}{BD}$. But since z is outside the circle it must be smaller.

14. D BF ? FC

No dimensions given, cannot be determined.

15. C $2V = \overset{\frown}{DF}$

An inscribed angle is equal to $\frac{1}{2}$ the intercepted arc. Therefore $V = \frac{1}{2}\overset{\frown}{DF}$ or $2V = \overset{\frown}{DF}$.

16. A $180° > \overset{\frown}{BD}$

If line segment BD were a diameter passing through E, then $180°$ would equal $\overset{\frown}{BD}$. But BD is to the left of E, therefore $\overset{\frown}{BD}$ is less than $180°$.

17. C $\dfrac{\dfrac{1}{x} + \dfrac{1}{y}}{xy} = \dfrac{x+y}{x^2y^2}$

Simplifying $\dfrac{\dfrac{1}{x} + \dfrac{1}{y}}{xy}$:

$$\dfrac{\dfrac{y+x}{xy}}{xy}$$

$$\dfrac{y+x}{xy} \times \dfrac{1}{xy}$$

$$\dfrac{y+x}{x^2y^2} \text{ or } \dfrac{x+y}{x^2y^2}$$

18. B $\dfrac{13 \times 17}{48 \times 721} < \dfrac{15 \times 17}{48 \times 722}$

Canceling 17 and 48 from both columns leaves $\dfrac{13}{721}$ and $\dfrac{15}{722}$. Either cross-multiplying or using common reasoning (much faster) will give the correct answer.

19. B $x < y$
Solving $x^2 + 2x + 1 = 0$

$$(x + 1)(x + 1) = 0$$
$$x + 1 = 0$$

Therefore $x = -1$
Solving $4y^2 + 4y + 1 = 0$

$$(2y + 1)(2y + 1) = 0$$
$$2y + 1 = 0$$
$$2y = -1$$
$$y = -\dfrac{1}{2}$$

Since $-1 < -\dfrac{1}{2}$
Then $x < y$

20. D $p \; ? \; q$
Since p can range from 5 to 7 and q can be somewhere between 3 and 11, only one comparison cannot be determined.

21. **A** $g > h$

   g must be positive and h must be negative in the 4th quadrant. (Remember: 1st letter stands for across and 2nd letter means up or down.)

22. **A** $d > c$

   Point R is farther up than across because it is above the equal line.

23. **B** $b < d$

   Point Q lies on the x-axis, therefore $b = 0$. d is above the x-axis so it must be greater than zero.

24. **A** $h > -3$

   Point S is above $(-3, -3)$ and h refers to the distance up or down.

25. **A** $x > y$

   Solving these simultaneous equations by inspection results in $x = 4$ and $y = 1$.
   Alternate Method:

$$2x + 3y = 11$$
$$5x + 2y = 22$$

   Multiplying:

$$2(2x + 3y = 11)$$
$$3(5x + 2y = 22)$$

$$4x + 6y = 22$$
$$\underline{15x + 6y = 66}$$

   Subtracting $-11x \quad = -44$
$$x = 4$$

   Substituting into the original equation and solving:

$$2(4) + 3y = 11$$
$$8 + 3y = 11$$
$$3y = 3$$
$$y = 1$$

26. **A** The largest figure by which the number of Republican governors has exceeded Democratic governors is 12.

$$12 > 10$$

27. A % increase of   % decrease of
Democratic governors   Republican governors
from 1952–54   from 1952–54

Figuring % increase for each column:

$$\frac{27 - 18}{18} \qquad\qquad \frac{30 - 21}{30}$$

$$\frac{9}{18} \qquad\qquad\qquad \frac{9}{30}$$

$$50\% > 30\%$$

28. B The ratio of   The ratio of
Democratic governors   Democratic governors
to Republican governors   to Republican governors
in 1940   in 1956

$$\frac{28}{20} \qquad\qquad\qquad\qquad \frac{29}{19}$$

$$1\frac{8}{20} < 1\frac{9}{19}$$

By inspection—or cross-multiply fractions.

29. D Republican governors   ?   Re-elected Democratic
in 1960 is 16   governors in 1938
                                            cannot be determined

The graph does not give sufficient information to answer this
question.

30. D $a \times b$? $a + b$
Trying the values $a = 1$ and $b = 2$ results in

$$1 \times 2 \qquad\qquad\qquad 1 + 2$$

$$2 < 3$$

Using the values $a = 4$ and $b = 2$ results in

$$4 \times 2 \qquad\qquad\qquad 4 + 2$$

$$8 > 6$$

Since different values give different results, no comparison can
be determined.

Math Ability

31.   C   360

$C = \pi D$

$C = \frac{22}{7} \times 28 = 88$ inches

1 revolution of wheel covers 88 inches

$\frac{1}{2} \times 5280 \times \frac{12}{1} =$ traveling distance in inches

$6 \times 5{,}280 = 31{,}680$ inches

$$\begin{array}{r} 360 \text{ revolutions} \\ 88 \overline{)\,31{,}680} \\ \underline{264} \\ 528 \\ \underline{528} \end{array}$$

32.   C   6.3

In 42.10, discard for practical purposes the .10 and perform as follows:

$$\frac{42 \times .0003}{.002} = \frac{.0126}{.002} = \frac{12.6}{2} = 6.3$$

33.   D $\dfrac{rh + st}{h + t}$

Formula: Distance = rate × time

first distance traveled: $rh = r \times h$

second distance traveled: $st = s \times t$

total distance traveled: $rh + st$

total time traveled: $h + t$

Formula: Distance ÷ time = rate or

$\dfrac{rh + st}{h + t} =$ average rate in miles per hr.

34.   D   4

Given: $\dfrac{2a + 3b}{c}$, with

$a = \dfrac{1}{2}, b = \dfrac{2}{3}$, and $c = \dfrac{3}{4}$

By substitution, $\dfrac{2 \times \dfrac{1}{2} + 3 \times \dfrac{2}{3}}{\dfrac{3}{4}} = 4$

35.   A   50%

By geometry, we can prove that the area of each shaded-corner isosceles right triangle $= \frac{1}{4}$ the area of one of the squares or that the area of the four shaded corner isosceles right triangles $=$ the area of one square. We can also prove that the area of each shaded-side isosceles right triangle $= \frac{1}{2}$ the area of one square or that the area of the four shaded-side isosceles right triangles $=$ two squares in area.

By inspection, we count four unshaded squares and 1 shaded square. Adding together the areas of the shaded triangles, we have the equivalent of 1 square (the corner shaded triangles) and the equivalent of 2 squares (the side shaded triangles), plus the 1 shaded square, giving us four shaded squares. Since there are four unshaded squares, making a total of 8 squares, the area of the shaded part is 50% of the entire figure.

36.   E   83.

Suggestions for Series Problems

Find the differences between the numbers (or squares of differences). In this series, each difference is multiplied by 3 and added to the succeeding number.

3, 5: the difference is 2; this difference was multiplied by 3, giving 6, which was then added to 5, to make the next number in the series 11.

5, 11: the difference is 6; this difference was multiplied by 3, giving 18, which was then added to 11, to make the next number in the series 29.

11, 29: the difference is 18; this difference should be multiplied by 3, giving 54, which, when added to 29, will give the next number in the series, 83.

37.   B   35%

cost = $36

overhead = 10% of cost, or $3.60   profit = $9.00 (given)

∴ selling price = $48.60 from (36 + 3.60 + 9)

markup = $12.60 from ($48.60 selling price − $36 cost)

finally, $\dfrac{\$12.60 \text{ (markup)}}{\$36.00 \text{ (cost)}} = 35\%$

38. C 8 : 3

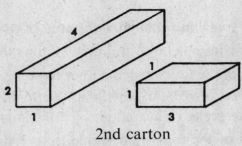

1st carton   2nd carton
V = 8   V = 3

$$\frac{V1}{V2} = \frac{8}{3} \text{ (or 8:3)}$$

39. A   increases in value
By increasing the value of m (by substituting numbers for letters) it is obvious that d increases in value.

40. E   41
$$9x + 5 = 23$$
$$9x = 23 - 5 \text{ or } 9x = 18$$
$$x = 2$$
$$18x + 5 = 36 + 5 \text{ or } 41$$

41. A   8 seconds
First we must figure the number of feet that the man walks diagonally (AC in the diagram). Then find the number of feet he

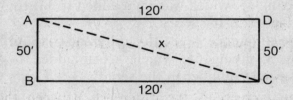

will walk by going along the perimeter of the lot (from C to A by way of D, or CD + AD).

Since the diagonal represented by x forms a right triangle, we have the equation $x^2 = 50^2 + 120^2$ or $x^2 = 16,900$, $x = 130$ feet (AC).

CD + AD (walking along the perimeter) = 170 feet (50 + 120).

∴ the man saves 40 feet by walking diagonally (170 − 130); and since he walks at the rate of 5 feet a second, he saves 8 seconds (40 ÷ 5).

42. **D** 44

If the auto is traveling 30 miles an hour, this means that the auto covers 30 miles in one hour or $\frac{1}{2}$ mile in one minute (30 miles $\div$ 60 min.).

To convert to seconds, as the answer calls for, divide $\frac{1}{2}$ by 60 seconds, viz., $\frac{\frac{1}{2}}{60} = \frac{1}{120}$ mile in one second. Then $\frac{1}{120} \times 5,280$ feet ($= 1$ mile) $= 44$ feet in one second

43. **E** none of these
By inspection

44. **C** $xy = 5$

Assume that $x = 5$ and $y = 1$ or that $x = 2$ and $y = 2\frac{1}{2}$. We can see that as x increases y decreases and vice versa.

The other possibilities are incorrect by inspection in a similar way (statements (A), (B), (D), and (E)).

45. **A** 1
Since the graphing line only slopes downward once.

46. **E** 5 years
In 1955 the GNP was just under 400 billion dollars. In 1960, the GNP was about 500 billion dollars.

47. **A** 1958–59
The sharpest upward angle appears from 1958–59.

48. **D** Eleven percent
Percentage increase is the difference between the two years' values divided by the first year's value.

$$1958 - \$450 \text{ billion}$$
$$1960 - \$500 \text{ billion}$$
$$\frac{500 - 450}{450} = \frac{50}{450}$$
$$\frac{1}{9} = 11\frac{1}{9}\%$$

or approximately 11%

49.   C   72 inches

Since the figure consists of 5 equal squares and the area of the figure is given as 180 sq. in., the area of each square = 36 sq. in., and the side of each square = 6 inches [area of a square = $(side)^2$]. Since there are 12 sides in the perimeter, the answer is arrived at by multiplying $12 \times 6 = 72$ inches.

50.   E $\dfrac{ry + sx}{sy}$

Dividing each denominator into sy and multiplying the result by the respective numerators, we get

$$\frac{r}{s} + \frac{x}{y} = \frac{ry + sx}{sy}$$

51.   D   8

Males arrested—3,417,863 or about 3,400,000
Females arrested—433,962 or about 430,000

$$\frac{3,400,000}{430,000} = \frac{340}{43} = 7.8 \text{ or } 8$$

52.   D   is false

More women were arrested for prostitution and commercialized vice than men.

53.   E   Disorderly conduct

By inspection

54.   B   Disorderly conduct

Disorderly conduct

$$\text{men} \quad \frac{373,760}{3,417,863} = 11\%$$

$$\text{women} \quad \frac{61,126}{433,962} = 14\%$$

Women's percent is greater than men's percent.

55.   A   Offenses against family and children

$$\text{Men} \frac{31,099}{3,407,893} \text{ or } \frac{31,000}{3,400,000} = \frac{31}{3,400} = .009 = .9\%$$

$$\text{Women} \frac{3,918}{433,962} \text{ or } \frac{4,000}{430,000} = \frac{4}{430} = .009 = .9\%$$

SECTION III: ANALYTICAL ABILITY

Analysis of Explanations

Set I.

1. **B**

   There is no inconsistency here, and the statement is a quite adequate explanation of the result.

2. **D**

   Although the statement is not inconsistent with the fact situation (Tom's visits to out-of-state schools imply their appeal), it is not an adequate explanation of his choice of a local college, nor is it directly deducible from the fact situation. The statement *weakens* a possible explanation of the result, so (D) is the correct choice.

3. **B**

   There is no inconsistency here, and the statement is a possible explanation of the result.

4. **A**

   Tom's equal consideration of colleges offering partial scholarships, full scholarships, and no scholarships, and his choice of a school which may or may not have offered a scholarship, indicates that financial need was *not* a factor in his choice, so the statement is contradictory.

5. **A**

   Tom visited many out-of-state colleges, presumably to acquire information, so this statement is inconsistent with the fact situation.

6. **E**

   There is nothing in the fact situation or the result which either supports, weakens, or contradicts this statement; it is therefore irrelevant to any explanation.

7. **C**

   This statement is not inconsistent with the facts; nor does it explain the result. But it is deducible from the fact that so many colleges did accept Tom.

8. **B**

   There is nothing inconsistent or contradictory about this statement, and since it presents a valid criterion for Tom's choice, (B) is correct.

9. **A**

Mrs. Snyder recommended that Tom apply to a number of *different* colleges.

10. **E**

There is nothing in the fact situation which either supports, weakens, or contradicts this statement; it is therefore irrelevant to any explanation.

Set II.

11. **B**

There is nothing inconsistent or contradictory about this statement, and since such a firing might result in programming changes (B) is a possible explanation.

12. **C**

Mr. Bell's reluctance is consistent with the facts, but his agreement to air the show does not explain the result. Therefore (A) and (B) are incorrect, but the statement *is* deducible from something in the fact situation.

13. **B**

There is nothing inconsistent about this statement, and it is a possible explanation of the result.

14. **A**

A discussion with the staff changed Mr. Bell's mind. They were therefore *not* in agreement with him.

15. **D**

The statement is neither inconsistent with nor deducible from the fact situation, and is too indirectly linked to the result to be a possible explanation. However, since ratings affect programming, it might support or weaken a possible explanation, so (D) is correct.

16. **D**

The statement is neither inconsistent with nor deducible from the fact situation, and is too indirectly linked to the result to be a possible explanation. However, given Mr. Dinkle's enthusiasm, a family tie is not out of the question, so the statement could support or weaken a possible explanation of the result.

17. **B**

This statement is not inconsistent, and does provide a possible explanation of the result.

18. **D**

This statement is neither inconsistent with nor deducible from anything in the fact situation, nor does it explain the result. However, the statement does *weaken* a possible explanation of the result, so (D) is correct.

19. **A**

Mr. Bell initially rejected the show because of his concern about controversial issues.

20. **E**

There is nothing in the fact situation or result which either supports, weakens, or contradicts this statement; it is therefore irrelevant to any explanation.

Set III.

21. **B**

The statement is not inconsistent with the facts, and does provide a possible—in fact probable—explanation.

22. **A**

The statement contradicts the fact of the workers' return to work.

23. **B**

The statement is not inconsistent with the facts, and does provide a possible explanation.

24. **D**

The statement weakens a possible explanation. But it is not inconsistent with the fact situation, nor is it deducible from the facts or the result.

25. **D**

This statement is neither inconsistent with nor deducible from anything in the fact situation, nor does it explain the result. However, the statement *supports* a possible explanation, namely that the workers agreed to continue receiving their already high wages.

26. **C**

The statement is not inconsistent; neither is it an explanation, but it is deducible from the fact that the workers reurned on August 29.

27. E

There is nothing in the fact situation or result which either supports, weakens, or contradicts this statement; it is therefore irrelevant to any explanation.

28. D

This statement is neither inconsistent with nor deducible from anything in the fact situation, nor does it explain the result. However, the statement does *weaken* a possible explanation, namely that the workers received a wage increase.

29. A

The strike was over wages; benefits are not mentioned.

30. C

This statement is not inconsistent; neither is it an explanation, but it is deducible from the fact that the strike lasted almost until the deadline.

Set IV.

31. B

This statement is not inconsistent, and does provide an adequate explanation.

32. A

Mrs. Mendez invited Mrs. Tucker, so she obviously *does* like her.

33. C

This statement is not inconsistent, nor is it an explanation, but it is deducible from the result.

34. D

This statement is neither inconsistent with nor deducible from anything in the fact situation, nor does it explain the result. However, the statement does weaken a possible explanation.

35. B

This statement is not inconsistent, and does provide a possible explanation; obligations to a boss are likely to take precedence over an evening of reminiscing with the Tuckers.

36. B

This statement is not inconsistent, and does provide a possible explanation.

37. **C**

This statement is not inconsistent, but it is a *possible* (though quite imaginative) explanation.

38. **E**

There is nothing in the fact situation or result which either supports, weakens, or contradicts this statement; it is therefore irrelevant to any explanation.

39. **B**

This statement is not inconsistent, and does provide a possible explanation, namely that the Handlers might not be available again for a dinner date.

40. **B**

This statement is not inconsistent, and does provide a possible explanation.

SECTION IV: ANALYTICAL ABILITY

Logical Diagrams

1. **D**

Roses are completely within the set of flowers, and cats are unrelated.

2. **C**

Plumbers and electricians have no members in common, but are both within the greater set of people.

3. **B**

All three sets—bowlers, trumpet players, and doctors—can have a or some members in common, but not necessarily all.

4. **B**

All three sets—housewives, tall women, and slender women—can have a or some members in common, but not necessarily all.

5. **B**

All three sets—adults, smokers, and women—can have a or some members in common, but not necessarily all.

6. **E**

Dancers are completely within the set of people who dance, and men can be in both sets, but not completely.

7. A

Sportswriters and television watchers can have members in common, but bluejays are unrelated.

8. D

Carrots and lettuce have no members in common, but are both within the set of salad ingredients.

9. B

Waiters and aunts have no members in common, but each can have members in common with song lovers.

10. B

Paper and metal have no members in common, but each can have members in common with, or be a type of, money.

11. E

Boys are completely within the set of males, and joggers can be within both sets, but not completely.

12. A

Wines are completely within the set of alcoholic beverages, and soaps are unrelated.

13. D

Glue and gum have no members in common, but are both known to be sticky substances.

14. C

Timex is within the set of watches, which are within the set of timepieces.

15. A

Cats are within the set of felines, and birds are unrelated.

Analytical Reasoning

Problems 16, 17, and 18 can be solved more easily if you diagram the given information. Carefully following statements (1)–(5) gives this diagram:

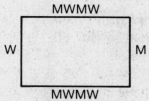

16. C

Women are seated across from men all around the table. By inspecting the diagram, you see that this statement is not true and therefore cannot be deduced.

17. D

He cannot be seated. Using the diagram and attempting to seat one more man will contradict statement (4), because two men would then have to be seated next to each other.

18. D   III.

They can be one man and one woman. Inserting one man and one woman into the diagram will not break any of the rules.

Questions 19–22 are best solved by first carefully charting the information given as follows:

	Mon.	Tues.	Wed.	Thurs.	Fri.
Florist	All Day	Morning			
Caterer	Afternoon	All Day			
Dressmaker	All Day			All Day	
Printer	Evening		Morning		Afternoon

19. B

She would have to see the caterer on Tuesday and the printer on Wednesday. Your chart shows that this is the only way she could see them all in one week.

20.   A

She could meet with the caterer and the printer at the same time. This could *not* occur because they are never available at the same time.

21.   C

She would have to see either the florist or caterer on Tuesday. Since the florist and caterer are the only ones available on Tuesday, and she would have to see four people in the two days (no more than three per day), she has to see the florist or caterer on Tuesday.

22.   C

Meet with the florist on Monday morning, the caterer on Tuesday afternoon, and the dressmaker on Monday afternoon. By making the proper adjustment on the chart, this answer is easily deducible.

23.   D   I & II.

The rate of price increase will continue and families will turn to renting instead of buying. These two can be assumed because the argument states that apartment living will increase noticeably in the near future.

24.   D   I & III.

That many inexpensive single-family dwellings are presently being built and that apartment living is also becoming very expensive are both facts that give possible reasons why people would *not* rent apartments, therefore weakening the argument.

25.   D

Home costs are increasing more rapidly than average family incomes. Because single-family dwellings will be unaffordable by the average family and apartment living will increase noticeably in the near future, the answer is deducible.

Questions 26–30 are best answered by first making the following chart, although many of the questions can be answered without completing the chart.

	Baseball Player	Football Player	Basketball Player	Sports-writer
Morton	No	Yes	No	No
Hiller	No	No	No	Yes
Nelson	No	No	Yes	No
Wood	Yes	No	No	No

The chart can be filled in by eliminating what each person *cannot* be.

1. Since Morton and Hiller were spectators when the baseball player pitched his first game (sentence 3), then they cannot be baseball players.

2. Both Wood and the football player have been interviewed by the writer at the same time (4); therefore Wood cannot be the football player or the writer.

3. The writer has written articles on Morton and Wood after separate interviews (5); therefore Morton is not the writer.

4. Since Wood doesn't know Nelson (6), then Nelson cannot be the football player or the writer as Wood has met them both.

5. Because the basketball player has never been interviewed (7), Wood and Morton cannot be basketball players.

Finally, careful inspection of the chart shows that Morton is the football player and Wood is the baseball player. Therefore Nelson is the basketball player and Hiller is the writer.

   This diagram has been completed to give you an overall perspective of the situation, but notice that many of the questions will be answerable by referring back to the statements directly; therefore, *you need not always take the time to complete the chart before you start answering the questions.*

26. D
Nelson is not the football player. This is not true by the chart, or deducible from statements (4) and (6). Since Wood doesn't know Nelson, and Wood and the football player have been interviewed together, then Nelson cannot be the football player.

27. A   I.
Wood knows the writer since he has been interviewed by him (4 or 5). II & III say the same thing, because Hiller is the writer, and both are false because Nelson, the basketball player, has never been interviewed.

28. **C** Nelson.
Nelson is the basketball player and has never been interviewed.

29. **E** None of the above.
The chart reveals this answer.

30. **D** I & III.
Morton will have been interviewed at least twice and the basketball player will never have been interviewed, since Morton is not the basketball player.

SECTION V: MATH ABILITY

1. **D** $\dfrac{mb}{h}$
Let $x =$ the number of miles the boy will walk in h hours.
Then $m : h = x : b$, or $hx = mb$, and $x = \dfrac{mb}{h}$

2. **E** $\dfrac{1}{6}$
$$\dfrac{4 \quad \text{(games won)}}{24 \text{ (total no. games played)}} = \dfrac{1}{6}$$

3. **B** 20 pints
Formula: Quantity of solution times the percentage of solution yields the quantity in solution.
Therefore, 60 pints $\times$ 20% $=$ 12 pints of pure alcohol in the original solution. Let $x =$ the number of pints of pure alcohol to be added.
$60 + x =$ total quantity of the new solution and $(60 + x) \times 40\% =$ the amount of pure alcohol in the new solution.
By adding the quantity of alcohol in the original solution to the quantity of alcohol in the new solution, viz., $12 + x = (60 + x)$ $(.4)$, or $60x = 1200$, $x = 20$ pints.

4. **E** 12 minutes
The problem may be answered as follows:
Formula: $\dfrac{\text{Time worked}}{\text{Time required}} =$ Part of job completed
Let $x =$ time that John and Frank will work together.
Then $\dfrac{x}{20} + \dfrac{x}{30} = 1$ (complete job)
or $5x = 60$, $x = 12$ minutes.

5. **A** $T = 50 + (n - 1)c$

Let n = the group of persons. Therefore, $n - 1$ = the group minus the driver.

If c cents is the charge for every person except the driver, then the group (exclusive of the driver) pays $c(n - 1)$ cents.

Given: 50 cents as the charge for the car and driver.

∴ the total cost $T = 50 + (n - 1)c$.

6. **E** is approximately $12\frac{1}{2}$ cubic inches

Formula:

1. Volume of a solid = volume of displaced water;
2. Volume of displaced water = $\pi \times r^2 \times$ length

By substitution,

volume = $\frac{22}{7} \times 4 \times 1 = \frac{88}{7}$

or 12.57 cubic inches = (approx.) $12\frac{1}{2}$ cubic inches

7. **E** The enclosed area is greatest when $x = y$

Each statement must be tested individually. We will find that statement (E) is false.

Proof: If $x = y$, the perimeter = $3x$. Since the perimeter is given as 60 feet, $3x = 60$, and $x = 20$. Therefore, $y = 20$. The area would be computed by multiplying 20×20 or 400 sq. ft. But in statement (D) we found that when $x = 15$, the enclosed area is 450 sq. ft. Therefore, statement (E) is FALSE.

8. **C** $3,750

Since the salesman's monthly salary is $50 and his total income is to be $200, his total monthly commission will be $150.

If x = the amount of his sales each month, then .04 times x = his monthly commission. We then form the equation $.04x = \$150$, $x = \$3,750$

9. **E** 6 rectangles

$(a + b)^2 = a^2 + 2ab + b^2$

Squares are represented by a^2 and b^2.

Two rectangles are represented by $2ab$.

$(a + b + c)^2 = a^2 + 2ab + b^2 + 2bc + c^2 + 2ac$

Three squares are represented by a^2, b^2, and c^2.

Two rectangles are represented by $2ab$, two by $2ac$, and two by $2bc$—a total of 6 rectangles.

10.   **C** $400.00

Net price = Marked price — Discount

Let x = Marked price

$x - .15x = .85x$ (price after first discount of 15%)

$.85x \times .10 = .085x$ (second discount of 10%)

$$\$306 = .85x - .085x \text{ or}$$
$$\$306,000 = 850x - 85x$$
$$\$306,000 = 765x$$
$$x = \$400.00$$

11.   **D**   If r is divided by 3 and h is multiplied by 9, V remains the same.

Initial volume $V = \dfrac{\pi r^2 h}{3}$

Volume after change $V_1 = \dfrac{\pi r_1^2 h_1}{3}$

$$V_1 = \frac{\pi \left(\dfrac{r}{3}\right)^2 (9h)}{3} = \frac{\pi \dfrac{r^2}{9} 9h}{3} = \frac{\pi r^2 h}{3}$$

$$V = \frac{\pi r^2 h}{3}$$

12.   **D**   225%, .225

Taking each alternative in turn:

(A) $.021\% = .00021$

(B) $1.5\% = .015 + \dfrac{15}{1000} = \dfrac{3}{200}$

(C) $\frac{1}{4}\% = \dfrac{1}{400} = .0025$

(D) $225\% = 2.25$

13.   **A** πab^2

Given: $r = b$ and $h = a$; also,

$$V = \pi \times b^2 \times a \text{ or } V = \pi ab^2$$

14.   **C** $2.50

Marked price − 20% = Selling price; 20% of Selling price = Profit; Cost = $1.60; Formula: Cost + Profit = Selling price.

Let x = Marked price.

Then $x - .20x$ = Selling price and

$.20 (x - .20x)$ or $.20x - .04x$ = Profit.

$\therefore 1.60 + .20x - .04x = x - .20x$

or $-64x = -160$ or $x = \$2.50$.

15. E none of these
The correct answer is 30 million.

16. D 60 million

17. B 3
60 million motor vehicles were registered in 1955.
20 million motor vehicles were registered in 1925.
$\frac{60}{20} = 3$ times as many motor vehicles were registered in 1955 as in 1925

18. C 20 million
80 million motor vehicles were registered in 1965.
60 million motor vehicles were registered in 1955.

$$\begin{array}{r} 80 \text{ million} \\ -60 \text{ million} \\ \hline 20 \text{ million} \end{array}$$

19. D $33\frac{1}{3}\%$
$\dfrac{20 \text{ million}}{60 \text{ million}} = \dfrac{1}{3} = 33\frac{1}{3}\%$

20. B $180.00
First contractor:
$$7 \times 3 = 21 \text{ man-days}$$
Second contractor:
$$4 \times 5 = 20 \text{ man-days}$$
Third contractor:
$$5 \times 9 = \underline{45 \text{ man-days}}$$
$774 \text{ or } \quad 86 \text{ man-days}$
1 man-day = $9
$\therefore$ Second contractor = $20 \times \$9 = \$180.00$

21. C $6\frac{3}{5}$ hours
Rate $\times$ Time = Distance
Walking: $y \times 4 = 4y$ (distance covered)
Returning: rate by means of auto = $5y$; distance traveled by auto = $8y$; time it took to return = $\dfrac{8y}{5y}$
$= 1\frac{3}{5}$ hours $\left(\text{Time} = \dfrac{\text{Distance}}{\text{Rate}}\right)$.
$\therefore$ 4 hours (going) + 1 hour (for lunch) + $1\frac{3}{5}$ hours (returning)
$= 6\frac{3}{5}$ hours (total time spent on trip)

22. **A**   70 cubic inches
     Volume $= l \times w \times h$ ($l =$ length; $w =$ width; $h =$ height)
     Volume $= 7$ inches $\times 4$ inches $\times \frac{5}{2}$ inches $= 70$ cubic inches

23. **D**   right
     Let $2x$, $3x$, and $5x$ represent the angles in accordance with the ratio given
     $\therefore 2x + 3x + 5x = 180°$ or $10x = 180$; $x = 18°$
     The angles then are respectively $36°$, $54°$, and $90°$
     The triangle must be a right triangle since it contains a right angle $(90°)$

24. **C**   900 sq. in.
     Let the side of one of the equal squares be represented by x.
     $\therefore 12x$ represents the perimeter or the sum of the sides of the rectangle formed.
     $12x = 360$ in.; $x = 30$ in.
     Since area $= x^2$, area $= 900$ sq. in.

25. **E**   10.
     $4a + 2c^2 - 3d^2$
     $4 \times 2 + 2 \times 1^2 - 3 \times 0^2 = 8 + 2 - 0 = 10$

PRACTICE TEST II

Tear out Answer Sheet for Practice Test II, pages xiii and xiv.

SECTION I: VERBAL ABILITY

TIME—50 MINUTES
80 QUESTIONS

Directions: Each question in this test consists of a sentence in which one or two words are missing. Beneath the sentence are five words or word sets. Choose the word or word set that *best* completes the sentence. Then mark the appropriate space in the answer column.

---

1.   The greatest of men have honestly admitted in their autobiographies that they were not _____ of virtue; that, merely, some of their abilities had received a striking _____.
   (A)   exemplars—emphasis
   (B)   paragons—aggravation
   (C)   destructive—reaction
   (D)   contemptuous—rejection
   (E)   unmindful—upturn

2.   While it may appear at the present time that the Soviets exceed us in missile production, I am certain that this _____ will _____ in due course.
   (A)   superiority—increase
   (B)   advantage—decline
   (C)   inferiority—diminish
   (D)   situation—defeat itself
   (E)   propaganda—develop

3.   The crowded cities and the concentration of industry in our country make us a _____ target of any _____ who can take us by surprise.
   (A)   difficult—enemy
   (B)   hostile—dictator
   (C)   easy—opponent
   (D)   vulnerable—adversary
   (E)   bristling—planes

4.   Though he was romantic and sensual in his outlook, his life was one of _____.
   (A)   profligacy
   (B)   naivete
   (C)   austerity
   (D)   virtuosity
   (E)   maturity

5. As long as learning is made continually repugnant, so long will there be a predisposition to _____ it when one is free from the authority of parents and teachers.

(A) master
(B) reject
(C) minimize
(D) inculcate
(E) enjoy

6. In economics, scarcity is defined as _____ of amount or supply in _____ to demands or wants.

(A) copiosity—regard
(B) puerility—respect
(C) plethora—respect
(D) satiety—proportion
(E) paucity—relation

7. Newton's picture of the universe was not one in which there was _____, and, in accordance with his teaching, the universe might very likely have been created out of one piece.

(A) examination
(B) verification
(C) inevitability
(D) development
(E) uniformity

8. This teacher has little regard for factual learning on the part of his students; his goal is to build men, not to make _____.

(A) dilettantes
(B) thinkers
(C) encyclopedias
(D) theorists
(E) martinets

9. Although our country is a land of plenty, we still have much to do to assure to all of our people _____ to develop their _____ for personal, group, and community usefulness.

(A) obligations—interests
(B) caprices—interests
(C) resources—impartiality
(D) opportunities—ambitions
(E) opportunities—capacities

10. There is much justification for the _____ forecast made by the officers of the corporation: compared with the earnings of the past three years, the income of the corporation was _____ than ever before.

(A) casual—less
(B) pessimistic—larger
(C) studied—more
(D) sanguine—greater
(E) long-term—far more

Directions: In each of the following questions select the lettered pair which best expresses a relationship similar to that expressed in the original pair.

---

11. COOLIE : RICKSHAW : :
(A) teacher : prodigy
(B) Shetland : pony
(C) horse : carriage
(D) hen : egg
(E) ass : Ford

12. COLLAPSE : REGIME : :
(A) fame : disgrace
(B) incarcerate : criminal
(C) illness : woman
(D) holocaust : earthquake
(E) founder : ship

13. REMOTE : PONDEROUS : :
(A) recondite : bulky
(B) hence : pensive
(C) protracted : laden
(D) yonder : onerous
(E) distant : momentous

14. BULL : PICADOR : :
(A) song : vocalist
(B) victim : executioner
(C) cow : matador
(D) eye : mote
(E) speaker : heckler

15. WHIG : TORY : :
   (A) Socialist : Monarchist
   (B) Democrat : Republican
   (C) Republican : Conservative
   (D) Liberal : Conservative
   (E) patriot : traitor

16. ARCTIC : GELID : :
   (A) penicillin : cure
   (B) tropical : luxuriant
   (C) invigoration : exhilaration
   (D) cold : muddy
   (E) disturbed : halcyon

17. BIGOTRY : TOLERANCE : :
   (A) urgency : exigency
   (B) profession : avocation
   (C) ribaldry : prodigality
   (D) unselfish : selfish
   (E) parsimony : magnanimity

18. ENCORE : CATCALL : :
   (A) amnesia : oblivion
   (B) applause : ridicule
   (C) felon : miscreant
   (D) generosity : lechery
   (E) constantly : bow

19. PRECIPITOUS : DISCONSOLATE : :
   (A) melancholy : unhappy
   (B) intrinsic : fatuous
   (C) askew : explicit
   (D) headlong : dejected
   (E) nebulous : credulous

Directions: Each question in this test consists of a word printed in capital letters followed by five words lettered (A) through (E). Choose the word that has most nearly the OPPOSITE meaning from the word in capital letters. Mark the appropriate space in the answer column. Consider all choices before deciding which one is best, since some choices are very close in meaning.

20. QUONDAM
    (A) sick
    (B) moribund
    (C) extant
    (D) near
    (E) remote

21. BENEVOLENT
    (A) inviolable
    (B) dishonorable
    (C) invidious
    (D) public
    (E) commonplace

22. WAVERING
    (A) bent
    (B) calm
    (C) peremptory
    (D) inviting
    (E) carping

23. PLATITUDE
    (A) banal
    (B) trite
    (C) epigram
    (D) wisdom
    (E) sorrow

24. REDOLENT
    (A) malodorous
    (B) sweet
    (C) fey
    (D) pellucid
    (E) clear

25. REPELLING
    (A) shy
    (B) diffident
    (C) contemptible
    (D) prepossessing
    (E) rebelling

26. DIRECT
    (A) surreptitious
    (B) naive
    (C) open
    (D) guide
    (E) express

27. ALLURING
    (A) facetious
    (B) dull
    (C) stern
    (D) wary
    (E) loathsome

28. TEMERITY
    (A) hard
    (B) image
    (C) tip
    (D) panic
    (E) circumspection

Directions: Each passage is followed by a group of questions. Read each passage and choose the *best* answer to each question. Then mark the appropriate space in the answer column. Answers should be chosen on the basis of what is stated and implied.

1   For the ease and pleasure of treading the old road, accepting
2 the fashions, the education, the religion of society, he takes the
3 cross of making his own, and, of course, the self-accusation, the faint
4 heart, the frequent uncertainty and loss of time, which are the net-
5 tles and tangling vines in the way of the self-relying and self-directed,
6 and the state of virtual hostility in which he seems to stand to society,
7 and especially to educated society. For all this loss and scorn, what
8 offset? He is to find consolation in exercising the highest functions
9 of human nature. He is one who raises himself from private consid-
10 eration and breathes and lives on public and illustrious thoughts.
11 He is the world's eye. He is the world's heart. He is to resist the
12 vulgar prosperity that retrogrades ever to barbarism, by preserving
13 and communicating heroic sentiments, noble biographies, melodious
14 verse, and the conclusions of history. Whatsoever oracles the human
15 heart, in all emergencies, in all solemn hours, has uttered as its com-
16 mentary on the world of actions—these he shall receive and impart.
17 And whatsoever new verdict Reason from her inviolable seat pro-
18 nounces on the passing men and events of today—this he shall hear
19 and promulgate.
20   These being his functions, it becomes him to feel all confidence
21 in himself, and to defer never to the popular cry. He and he only
22 knows the world. The world of any moment is the merest appear-
23 ance. Some great decorum, some fetish of a government, some
24 ephemeral trade, or war, or man, is cried up by half mankind and
25 cried down by the other half, as if all depended on this particular up
26 or down. The odds are that the whole question is not worth the
27 poorest thought which the scholar has lost in listening to the con-
28 troversy. Let him not quit his belief that a popgun is a popgun,
29 though the ancient and honorable of the earth affirm it to be the
30 crack of doom. In silence, in steadiness, in severe abstraction, let
31 him hold by himself; add observation to observation, patient of
32 neglect, patient of reproach, and bide his own time—happy enough
33 if he can satisfy himself alone that this day he has seen something
34 truly. Success treads on every right step. For the instinct is sure,
35 that prompts him to tell his brother what he thinks. He then learns
36 that in going down into the secrets of his own mind he has descended
37 into the secrets of all minds. He learns that he who has mastered any
38 law in his private thoughts, is master to that extent of all translated.
39 The poet, in utter solitude remembering his spontaneous thoughts

40 and recording them, is found to have recorded that which men in
41 crowded cities find true for them also. The orator distrusts at first
42 the fitness of his frank confessions, his want of knowledge of the
43 persons he addresses, until he finds that he is the complement of his
44 hearers—that they drink his words because he fulfills for them their
45 own nature; the deeper he dives into his privatest, secretest presenti-
46 ment, to his wonder he finds this is the most acceptable, most pub-
47 lic, and universally true. The people delight in it; the better part of
48 every man feels. This is my music; this is myself.

29. It is a frequent criticism of the scholar that he lives by himself, in
    an "ivory tower," remote from the problems and business of the
    world. Which of these below constitutes the best refutation by the
    writer of the passage to the criticism here noted?
    (A) the world's concerns being ephemeral, the scholar does
         well to renounce them and the world
    (B) the scholar lives in the past to interpret the present
    (C) the scholar at his truest is the spokesman of the people
    (D) the scholar is not concerned with the world's doings be-
         cause he is not selfish and therefore not engrossed in mat-
         ters of importance to himself and neighbors
    (E) the scholar's academic researches of today are the business-
         man's practical products of tomorrow

30. The scholar's road is rough, according to the passage read. Which
    of these is his greatest difficulty?
    (A) he must renounce religion
    (B) he must pioneer new approaches
    (C) he must express scorn for, and hostility to, society
    (D) he is uncertain of his course
    (E) there is a pleasure in the main-traveled roads in education,
         religion, and all social fashions

31. When the writer speaks of the "world's eye" and the "world's
    heart" he means
    (A) the same thing
    (B) culture and conscience
    (C) culture and wisdom
    (D) a scanning of all the world's geography and a deep sym-
         pathy for every living thing
    (E) mind and love

32. By the phrase "nettles and tangling vines" the author probably refers to
(A)   "self-accusation" and "loss of time"
(B)   "faint heart" and "self-accusation"
(C)   "the slings and arrows of outrageous fortune"
(D)   a general term for the difficulties of a scholar's life
(E)   "self-accusation" and "uncertainty"

33. The various ideas in the passage are best summarized in which of these groups?
1.   _____ truth versus society
     _____ the scholar and books
     _____ the world and the scholar
2.   _____ the ease of living traditionally
     _____ the glory of a scholar's life
     _____ true knowledge versus trivia
3.   _____ the hardships of the scholar
     _____ the scholar's functions
     _____ the scholar's justifications for disregarding the world's business
(A)   1 and 3 together
(B)   1 only
(C)   3 only
(D)   1, 2, and 3 together
(E)   1 and 2 together

34. "seems to stand" (line 6) means
(A)   is
(B)   ends probably in becoming
(C)   gives the false impression of being
(D)   is seen to be
(E)   the quicksands of time

35. "public and illustrious thoughts" (line 10) means
(A)   what the people think
(B)   thoughts in the open
(C)   thoughts for the good of mankind
(D)   thoughts transmitted by the people
(E)   the conclusions of history

Actually, politics and economics cannot be separated in the life of a nation, for they are two sides of the same life. But they stand to each other in the capacity of the navigation of a vessel and the destination of its freight. On board, it is the captain, not the merchant, whose goods are carried, who has priority. If the impression prevails today that economic leadership is the more powerful element, this is because political leadership has degenerated into partisan anarchy and hardly deserves the name of leadership at all, so that by contrast the economic leadership appears to tower above it. But when one house is left standing amid the ruins after an earthquake, it is not necessarily the most important one. In history, when it is moving on "in good form" and is not tumultuous or revolutionary, the economic leader has never been the one to make decisions. He adapts himself to the political considerations and serves them with the means that are in his hands. Without a strong policy there has never and nowhere been a healthy economic system, although materialistic theories teach the contrary. Adam Smith, the founder of political economy, treated economic existence as the true human life, money-making as the meaning of history, and was wont to describe statesmen as dangerous animals; yet this very England became what it became—the foremost country, economically speaking, in the world—owing, not to merchants and factory-owners, but to genuine politicians like the two Pitts, whose grandiose foreign policy was carried through often in the teeth of violent opposition from the short-sighted economists.

36. The captain represents
   - (A)   the traders
   - (B)   partisanship
   - (C)   the nation
   - (D)   the economists
   - (E)   statesmanship

37. The destination of the vessel's freight
   - (A)   determines the course the navigator will take
   - (B)   is left up to the merchant
   - (C)   is predetermined by the type of freight
   - (D)   is ultimately in the hands of the navigator
   - (E)   depends upon the nature of the vessel

38. The author was writing in a period of
   - (A)   great prosperity
   - (B)   political corruption
   - (C)   geological upheaval
   - (D)   economic depression
   - (E)   brilliant diplomacy

39. Adam Smith

(A) preferred politicians to statesmen

(B) was a materialist

(C) was a student of economics

(D) advanced a strong foreign policy

(E) was anti-English

40. Economic leaders in England

(A) were powerful in spite of the two Pitts

(B) were constantly abused by statesmen

(C) profited by the foreign policy of the Pitts

(D) were usually political leaders as well

(E) disapproved of Adam Smith's theories

Against the rising tide of worldliness an opposition, however, now began to appear. It was led by what may be called the spiritual noblesse of Islam, which, as distinguished from the hereditary nobility of Mecca, might also be designated as the nobility of merit, consisting of the "Defenders" (Ansar), and especially of the Emigrants who had lent themselves to the elevation of the Koreish, but by no means with the intention of allowing themselves thereby to be effaced. The opposition was headed by Ali, Zobair, Talha, both as leading men among the Emigrants and as disappointed candidates for the Caliphate. Their motives were purely selfish: not God's cause but their own, not religion but power and preferment, was what they sought. Their party was a mixed one. To it belonged the men of real piety, who saw with displeasure the promotion to the first places in the commonwealth of the great lords who had actually done nothing for Islam and had joined themselves to it only at the last moment. But the majority were merely a band of men without views, whose aim was a change not of system but of persons in their own interest. The movement was most energetic in Iraq and in Egypt. Its ultimate aim was the deposition of Othman in favor of Ali, whose own services as well as his close relationship to the Prophet seemed to give him the best claim to the Caliphate.

41. Did the party of the opposition contain men who were working impersonally for the welfare of Islam?

(A) yes

(B) no

(C) hard to tell from the passage

42. What two sorts of nobles are contrasted?
- (A)   men of real piety and men without views
- (B)   the "Defenders" and the Emigrants
- (C)   men of real piety and men working for selfish ambition
- (D)   of Islam and of Mecca
- (E)   spiritual and hereditary

43. What apparent inconsistency is there in the two statements about the leadership of the opposition?
- (A)   opposition was against worldliness but was itself selfish
- (B)   the leaders were men of real piety, but they were selfish
- (C)   the nobility were spiritual but purely selfish
- (D)   worked for selfish aims, later for Ali
- (E)   the majority were without views but wanted persons in their own interest

44. What claims had Ali to the Caliphate?
- a. a disappointed candidate
- b. hereditary nobility
- c. his own services
- d. his relation to Mahomet
- e. the disposition of Othman
- (A)   a, c
- (B)   c, d
- (C)   d, e
- (D)   c, e,
- (E)   a, d

In any country the wages commanded by laborers who have comparable skills but who work in various industries are determined by the productivity of the least productive unit of labor, i.e., that unit of labor which works in the industry which has the greatest economic disadvantage. We will represent the various opportunities of employment in a country like the United States by symbols: A, standing for a group of industries in which we have exceptional economic advantages over foreign countries; B, for a group in which our advantages are less; C, one in which they are still less; D, the group of industries in which they are least of all.

When our population is so small that all our labor can be engaged in the group represented by A, productivity of labor (and therefore wages) will be at their maximum. When our population increases so that some of the labor will have to be set to work in group B, the wages of all labor must decline to the level of the productivity in that group. But no employer, without government aid, will yet be able to afford to hire labor to exploit the opportunities represented by C and D, unless there is a further increase in population.

But suppose that the political party in power holds the belief that we should produce everything that we consume, that the opportunities represented by C and D should be exploited. The commodities that the industries composing C and D will produce have been hitherto obtained from abroad in exchange for commodities produced by A and B. The government now renders this difficult by placing high duties upon the former class of commodities. This means that workers in A and B must pay higher prices for what they buy, but do not receive higher prices for what they sell.

After the duty has gone into effect and the prices of commodities that can be produced by C and D have risen sufficiently, enterprisers will be able to hire labor at the wages prevailing in A and B, and establish industries in C and D. So far as the remaining laborers in A and B buy the products of C and D, the difference between the price which they pay for those products and the price that they would pay if they were permitted to import those products duty-free is a tax paid not to the government, but to the producers in C and D, to enable the latter to remain in business. It is an uncompensated deduction from the natural earnings of the laborers in A and B. Nor are the workers in C and D paid as much, estimated in purchasing power, as they would have received if they had been allowed to remain in A and B under the earlier conditions.

45.   When C and D are established, workers in these industries
    (A)   receive higher wages than do the workers in A and B.
    (B)   receive lower wages than do the workers in A and B.
    (C)   must be paid by government funds collected from the duties on imports.
    (D)   are not affected so adversely by the levying of duties as are workers in A and B.
    (E)   receive wages equal to those workers in A and B.

46.   We cannot exploit C and D unless
    (A)   the productivity of labor in all industries is increased.
    (B)   the prices of commodities produced by A and B are raised.
    (C)   we export large quantities of commodities produced by A and B.
    (D)   the producers in C and D are compensated for the disadvantages under which they operate.
    (E)   we allow duties to be paid to the producers in C and D rather than to the government.

47.   "No employer, without government aid, will yet be able to afford to hire labor to exploit the opportunities represented by C and D" because
   (A)   productivity of labor is not at the maximum.
   (B)   we cannot produce everything we consume.
   (C)   the population has increased.
   (D)   enterprisers would have to pay wages equivalent to those obtained by workers in A and B, while producing under greater economic disadvantages.
   (E)   productivity would drop correspondingly with the wages of labor.

48.   The government, when it places high duties on imported commodities of classes C and D,
   (A)   raises the price of commodities produced by A and B.
   (B)   is, in effect, taxing the workers in A and B.
   (C)   raises the wages of workers in C and D at the expense of the workers in A and B.
   (D)   does not affect the productivity of the workers in A and B, although the wages of these workers are reduced.
   (E)   is adopting a policy made necessary by the stability of the population.

49.   The author's main point is that
   (A)   it is impossible to attain national self-sufficiency.
   (B)   the varying productivity of the various industries leads to the inequalities in wages of workers in these industries.
   (C)   a policy that draws labor from the fields of greater natural productiveness to fields of lower natural productiveness tends to reduce purchasing power.
   (D)   wages ought to be independent of international trade.
   (E)   the government ought to subsidize C and D.

1   The second class of early French epics consists of the Arthurian
2 cycle, the *Matiere de Bretagne,* the earliest known compositions of
3 which are at least a century junior to the earliest *chanson de geste,*
4 but which soon succeeded the chansons in popular favor and ob-
5 tained a vogue both wider and far more enduring. It is not easy to
6 conceive a greater contrast in form, style, subject, and sentiment
7 than is presented by the two classes. In both, the religious sentiment
8 is prominent, but the religion of the chansons is of the simplest, not
9 to say of the most savage character. To pray to God and to kill his
10 enemies constitutes the whole duty of man. In the romances the
11 mystical element becomes, on the contrary, prominent, and fur-
12 nishes, in the Holy Grail, one of the most important features. In the

13 Carlovingian knight the courtesy and clemency which we have
14 learned to associate with chivalry are almost entirely absent. The
15 *gentix ber* contradicts, jeers at, and execrates his sovereign and his
16 fellows with the utmost freedom. He thinks nothing of striking his
17 *cortoise moullier* so that the blood runs down her *cler vis*. If a servant
18 or even an equal offends him, he will throw the offender into the fire,
19 knock his brains out, or set his whiskers ablaze. The Arthurian
20 knight is far more of the modern model in these respects.

50. The paragraph is in the main a contrast of two things. What are
they?
(A)   chivalry and the religious element
(B)   epic and romance
(C)   the Arthurian knight and the Carlovingian knight
(D)   the Arthurian romance and the chansons de geste
(E)   early French epics and the chansons

51. State the difference in respect to religion by checking the pair of
words which best fills the blank spaces. The religion of one was
_____; of the other, _____.
(A)   savage—elemental
(B)   savage—mystical
(C)   simple—prominent
(D)   savage—courteous
(E)   simple—complex

52. What word is paired with "Arthurian" in the contrast?
(A)   Carolovingian
(B)   geste
(C)   chansons
(D)   knight
(E)   chivalry

53. What does "execrates" mean as used in line 15 of the paragraph?
(A)   consecrates
(B)   reveres
(C)   detests
(D)   praises
(E)   appraises

Select the word or set of words which *best* completes each of the following sentences.

54. Some people lack a seasoning of _____; they embrace life eagerly and optimistically.
   (A) vacillation
   (B) vapidity
   (C) rancor
   (D) skepticism
   (E) consideration

55. These conditions are not _____ the nature of women but have grown up in spite of it.
   (A) intrinsic to
   (B) paramount in
   (C) compelling in
   (D) immutable in
   (E) extrinsic in

56. An impediment which makes _____ more difficult is _____.
   (A) achievement—a strike
   (B) efficiency—over-production
   (C) peace—the UN
   (D) accomplishment—a handicap
   (E) success—gambling

57. A _____ point is one that is _____.
   (A) subjective—objective
   (B) disputed—untenable
   (C) rejected—argumentative
   (D) valid—reliable
   (E) moot—disputable

58. History tells us that Demosthenes made several long speeches warning the Greeks against Philip of Macedon. Since these _____ were strongly worded, personal in nature, and full of abuse, a new word, _____, has passed over into our language.
   (A) speeches—demonstration
   (B) invectives—geriatrics
   (C) outbursts—genocide
   (D) paeans—acrimonious
   (E) declamations—philippics

59. The old actor lived in a world of his own, characterized by senility and garrulity. In particular, his speech pattern was affected. Whatever he said was marked by _____. One could not say that he was _____ in nature.
    (A) laconicism—rambling
    (B) inconsistency—incompetent
    (C) wisdom—foolish
    (D) circumlocution—disciplined
    (E) arrogance—concise

60. Words which are similar in sound but different in meaning are called _____.
    (A) homonyms
    (B) synonyms
    (C) logarithms
    (D) metaphors
    (E) antonyms

61. To succeed as an attorney, _____ abilities are needed for disputation and debate.
    (A) peripheral
    (B) grandiose
    (C) majestic
    (D) forensic
    (E) vocal

62. He may be deemed _____ who _____ considers the consequences before he acts.
    (A) impetuous—always
    (B) wary—generally
    (C) intrepid—casually
    (D) circumspect—occasionally
    (E) diffident—usually

Select the lettered pair which best expresses a relationship similar to that expressed in the original pair.

63. LETHARGIC : ABSTEMIOUS : :
    (A) torpid : temperate
    (B) dogmatic : truculent
    (C) pusillanimous : absent
    (D) latent : gregarious
    (E) militant : irascible

64. EXPEDITE : DEFER : :
- (A) dilatory : summary
- (B) catalyze : protract
- (C) procrastination : punctuality
- (D) extempore : temporize
- (E) retard : precocious

65. ASCETICISM : MODERATION : :
- (A) possibility : probability
- (B) conservatism : centrism
- (C) induction : deduction
- (D) contrition : attrition
- (E) coercion : persuasion

66. ESTIMATION : ADULATION : :
- (A) anathema : curse
- (B) amenable : agreeable
- (C) acme : vertex
- (D) deference : obsequiousness
- (E) acumen : perspicacity

67. DESTITUTE : DEVOID : :
- (A) politician : politics
- (B) obliteration : extirpation
- (C) private : sergeant
- (D) construction : building
- (E) affluent : forceful

68. CIRCLE : QUADRANT : :
- (A) polygon : hexagon
- (B) acute angle : obtuse angle
- (C) sphere : hemisphere
- (D) triangle : rectangle
- (E) duality : modality

69. NEUROSIS : PSYCHOSIS : :
- (A) fear : dread
- (B) demise : disease
- (C) aggression : war
- (D) illness : treatment
- (E) nervousness : reaction

70. POEM : PASTORAL : :
- (A)   science : curriculum
- (B)   miser : cupidity
- (C)   crystal ball : medium
- (D)   chauvinism : Pan-Slavism
- (E)   monastery : monk

71. SPECIES : HYBRID : :
- (A)   mixture : blend
- (B)   rock : metal
- (C)   metal : alloy
- (D)   block : chip
- (E)   plant : flower

The *opposite* of:

72. DISPUTABLE
- (A)   untrue
- (B)   incontrovertible
- (C)   unproven
- (D)   uncertain
- (E)   recondite

73. FELICITY
- (A)   calm
- (B)   peace
- (C)   drought
- (D)   inaptness
- (E)   luck

74. AVARICE
- (A)   munificence
- (B)   wastefulness
- (C)   kind
- (D)   self-seeking
- (E)   covetousness

75. UNSALABLE
- (A)   poor
- (B)   marketable
- (C)   sickly
- (D)   salutary
- (E)   junk

76. HELOT
- (A)   freeman
- (B)   peon
- (C)   universal
- (D)   Roman
- (E)   angel

77. SERPENTINE
- (A)   clever
- (B)   slippery
- (C)   straight
- (D)   alpine
- (E)   wiry

78. RITUALISTIC
- (A)   irreligious
- (B)   oratorical
- (C)   impolite
- (D)   ceremonious
- (E)   informal

79. REMISS
- (A)   remorseful
- (B)   attentive
- (C)   forgiving
- (D)   negligent
- (E)   permissive

80. EBB
- (A)   steep
- (B)   eke
- (C)   abate
- (D)   reactive
- (E)   flow

SECTION II: QUANTITATIVE ABILITY

TIME—50 MINUTES
55 QUESTIONS

Quantitative Comparison

(SUGGESTED TIME—20 MINUTES)
30 QUESTIONS

Directions: Each question in this section consists of two quantities, one in Column A and one in Column B. You are to compare the two quantities and on the answer sheet blacken space

A if the quantity in Column A is the greater;
B if the quantity in Column B is the greater;
C if the two quantities are equal;
D if the relationship cannot be determined from the information given.

All numbers used are real numbers.
Diagrams are not necessarily drawn to scale.

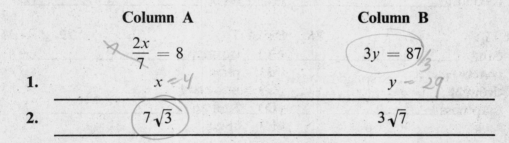

	Column A	**Column B**
1.	$\frac{2x}{7} = 8$	$3y = 87$
2.	$7\sqrt{3}$	$3\sqrt{7}$

Questions 3–6 refer to this diagram of a rectangular prism.

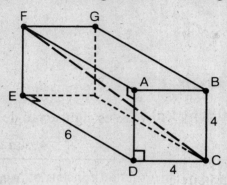

	Column A	**Column B**
3.	Volume	Surface Area
4.	AC	6
5.	7	CF
6.	FA + AD	$\frac{1}{3}$GB + 2BC
7.	$592 \times 21 \times 4$	$7 \times 592 \times 12$

$$x > y$$

8.	$x - 3$	$y + 4$
9.	The average speed of a car that travels 8 miles in 15 minutes	30

$$\frac{s}{r} > \frac{3}{5}$$

10.	s	r

x is a negative fraction

11.	$\frac{1}{x}$	$-x$

Questions 12–14 refer to this diagram:

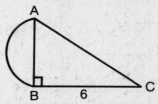

AB is a diameter   △ABC is isosceles right triangle

	Column A	Column B
12.	Area semicircle	Area triangle
13.	$\overset{\frown}{AB}$	AC
14.	$\angle A$	45°

x is a positive even integer

15.	$2x + 1$	6
16.	$-(r - s)$	$-r + s$

$$\sqrt{\frac{p + 4}{2}} = 8$$

17.	p	110
18.	$\dfrac{1}{8}$	15%

$x > 0$

19.	$\sqrt{x}$	$\sqrt[3]{x}$

Questions 20–24 refer to this graph.

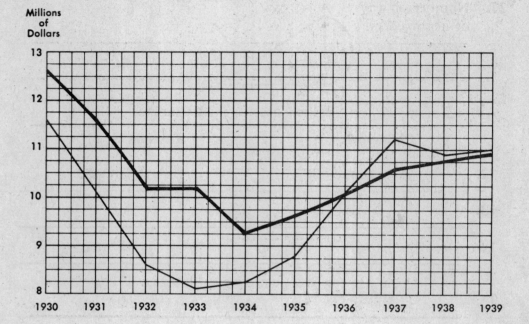

In the graph above the heavy curve represents postal receipts at St. Louis from 1930 to 1939. The light curve represents postal receipts at Detroit from 1930 to 1939.

	Column A	Column B
20.	Postal receipts in Detroit in 1937	$11,000,000
21.	The difference in receipts of St. Louis and Detroit in 1934	The difference in receipts of St. Louis and Detroit in 1932
22.	% decrease for St. Louis from 1932–1933	% decrease for St. Louis from 1933–1934
23.	Detroit receipts 1936	St. Louis receipts 1936
24.	Detroit's approximate % increase from 1935 to 1939	20%
25.	$\sqrt{26}$	5
26.	$9^5 - 9^4$	9^4

Column A	**Column B**
27. Number of ways 3 books can be arranged on a shelf	7

28. $(a^4 + b^3)^2$	$(a^3b^6)^3$

29. $\dfrac{1}{79} - \dfrac{1}{81}$	$\dfrac{1}{71} - \dfrac{1}{80}$

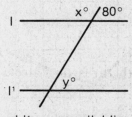

I and I¹ are parallel lines

30. x	y

Math Ability

(SUGGESTED TIME—20 MINUTES)
25 QUESTIONS

Directions: Solve each of the following problems and mark the *best* answer on your answer sheet. All scratch work should be done in the available space. All numbers used belong to the real number system. Diagrams are not necessarily drawn to scale.

---

31. The width of the ring (shaded portion of the figure) is exactly equal to the radius of the inner circle. What percent of the entire area is the area of the shaded portion?

(A) 25%
(B) 50%
(C) $66\frac{2}{3}$%
(D) 75%
(E) 90%

32. A baseball team won w games and lost l games. What fractional part of its games did it win?

(A) $\dfrac{l}{w}$

(B) $\dfrac{w}{l}$

(C) $\dfrac{w - l}{w}$

(D) $\dfrac{w + l}{w}$

(E) none of these

33. By what number is the area of a circle multiplied if its radius is doubled?
(A) $2\pi r$
(B) 2
(C) 3.1416
(D) 4
(E) 6

34. A motorist travels 120 miles to his destination at the average speed of 60 miles per hour and returns to the starting point at the average speed of 40 miles per hour. His average speed for the entire trip is
(A) 53 miles per hour
(B) 40 miles per hour
(C) 50 miles per hour
(D) 45 miles per hour
(E) 48 miles per hour

35. From the formula $K = \frac{1}{2}h(b + b_1)$, find the value of b_1 in terms of K, h, and b.

(A) $\dfrac{2K - b}{h}$

(B) $\dfrac{K}{2h} - b$

(C) $\dfrac{2K - hb}{h}$

(D) $\dfrac{Kh}{2} - b$

(E) $\dfrac{2b - K}{h}$

36. A woman bought a set of porch furniture at a 40 percent reduction sale held late in the summer. The furniture cost her $165. What was the original price of the furniture?
    (A) $66
    (B) $231
    (C) $275
    (D) $412.50
    (E) $510

37. The ratio of $\frac{1}{4}$ to $\frac{3}{8}$ is the same as the ratio of
    (A) 1 to 3
    (B) 1 to 4
    (C) 3 to 2
    (D) 3 to 4
    (E) 2 to 3

38. The figure below represents the end of a garage. Find, in feet, the length of one of the equal rafters AB or CB if each extends 12 inches beyond the eaves.

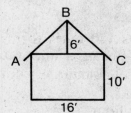

    (A) 10 feet
    (B) 11 feet
    (C) 13 feet
    (D) 22 feet
    (E) 33 feet

Questions 39–44 refer to this graph.

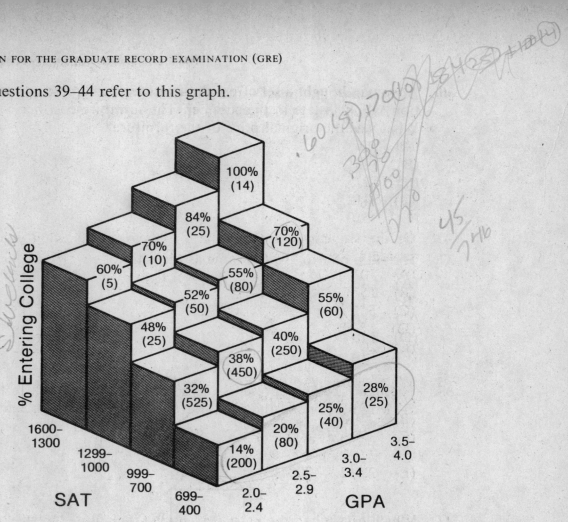

This graph illustrates a correlation between senior students attending 4 hypothetical high schools, SAT scores, GPA (Grade-Point Average), and percent entering college.

% refers to students actually entering college.

( ) indicates the total number of students graduating from high school in each category.

Total students graduating with GPA of 2.0 or better is 1,959.

Total students entering college is 746.

39. Approximately what percent of the students graduating entered college?
    (A)   20%
    (B)   28%
    (C)   34%
    (D)   40%
    (E)   70%

40. How many graduating students with a GPA of 3.5–4.0 and a SAT score of 1,000–1,299 did not enter college?
(A) 84
(B) 72
(C) 32
(D) 36
(E) 56

41. Of the students entering college, approximately what percent scored 1,300 (or about) on the SAT?
(A) 10%
(B) 15%
(C) 5%
(D) 1%
(E) 20%

42. Which group had the most students entering college?
(A) 3.0–3.4—700–999
(B) 2.0–2.4—700–999
(C) 3.5–4.0—400–699
(D) 2.0–2.4—400–699
(E) 2.5–2.9—700–999

43. Which group had the most students NOT entering college?
(A) 400–699
(B) 700–999
(C) 100–1,299
(D) 1,300–1,600
(E) Cannot be determined

44. Of the 1,959 students, approximately what percent scoring below 700 on the SAT did not enter college?
(A) 24%
(B) 12%
(C) 6%
(D) 48%
(E) Cannot be determined.

45. The expression a^x means that a is to be used as a factor x times. Therefore, if a^x is squared, the result is
(A) $a^{(x2)}$
(B) a^{2x}
(C) $2a^{2x}$
(D) $2a^x$
(E) none of these

46. A snapshot measures $1\frac{7}{8}$ inches $\times$ $2\frac{1}{2}$ inches. It is to be enlarged so that the longer dimension will be 4 inches. What will be the length of the shorter dimension?

(A) $2\frac{3}{8}$ inches

(B) $2\frac{1}{2}$ inches

(C) 3 inches

(D) $3\frac{3}{8}$ inches

(E) 5 inches

47. The difference between one half of a number and one fifth of it is 561. Find the number.

(A) 168
(B) 2805
(C) 1870
(D) 5610
(E) 1265

48. Successive discounts of 40 percent and 20 percent are equal to a single discount of

(A) 20%
(B) 30%
(C) 52%
(D) $\frac{1}{3}$%
(E) 60%

Questions 49–51 refer to the following diagram.

Key Contests in the Struggle for Control of Congress

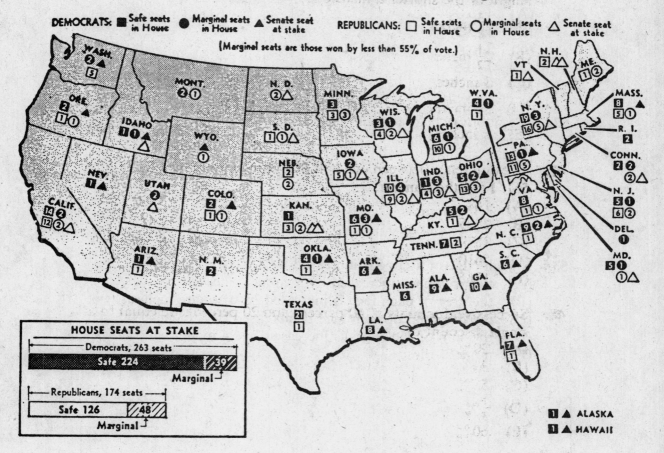

49. How many marginal seats in the House of Representatives do the Republicans control on the West Coast?
    (A) 1
    (B) 2
    (C) 3
    (D) 4
    (E) 5

50. How many safe seats in the House of Representatives do both parties have in Pennsylvania?
    (A) 14
    (B) 18
    (C) 12
    (D) 16
    (E) 24

51. The ratio between the total of Democratic seats and the total of Republican seats in the House of Representatives is approximately
(A)   4 to 3
(B)   3 to 2
(C)   5 to 4
(D)   7 to 5
(E)   9 to 5

52. If a cubic inch of a metal weighs 2 pounds, a cubic foot of the same metal weighs
(A)   8 pounds
(B)   24 pounds
(C)   288 pounds
(D)   3,454 pounds
(E)   3,456 pounds

53. If each edge of a cube is increased by 2 inches,
(A)   the volume is increased by 8 cubic inches
(B)   the area of each face is increased by 4 square inches
(C)   the diagonal of each face is increased by 2 inches
(D)   the sum of the edges is increased by 24 inches
(E)   none of these

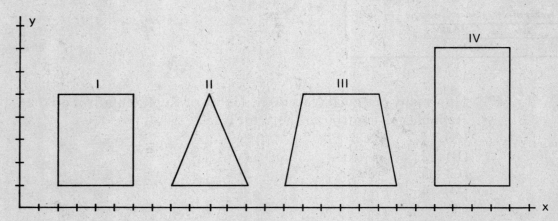

54. In the diagram above, each unit on the *x*-axis represents 4 inches and on the *y*-axis represents 5 inches.
    Which one of the diagrams has an area equal to the sum of two of the others?
(A)   I
(B)   II
(C)   III
(D)   IV
(E)   None of the above.

55. Approximate the value for:
.26 × .67 × .5 × .9

(A) .08
(B) .13
(C) .8
(D) .32
(E) .04

S T O P
IF YOU FINISH BEFORE TIME IS CALLED, CHECK YOUR WORK ON THIS SECTION ONLY. DO NOT WORK ON ANY OTHER SECTION IN THE TEST.

SECTION III: ANALYTICAL ABILITY

Analysis of Explanations

TIME—25 MINUTES
40 QUESTIONS

Directions: A fact and a result are presented. Following the result are several numbered statements. Evaluate each statement in relation to the fact situation and the result.

Each statement is to be considered separately from the other statements. The following sequence of A, B, C, D, and E is to be examined *in order* following each statement. The first choice that cannot be eliminated is the correct choice.

> *Choose A* if the statement is inconsistent with, or contradictory to, something in the fact situation, the result, or both together.
>
> *Choose B* if the statement presents a possible adequate explanation of the result.
>
> *Choose C* if the statement is deductible from something in the fact situation, the result, or both together.
>
> *Choose D* if the statement either supports or weakens a possible explanation of the result. It is then relevant to an explanation.
>
> *Choose E* if the statement is irrelevant to an explanation of the result.

Use common sense to make all decisions; no background in formal logic is necessary. Unlikely or remote possibilities should not be considered.

Set I.

FACT SITUATION: The North High School Panthers football team was well on its way to another league title, with one game left in the regular season. The Panthers had defeated all of their opponents by a wide margin, but this last game would be a tough one, as the Panthers were probably going to be without two of their star players, who were injured in practice.

Their opponent for this last game, the Madison High School Bulldogs, was an average team that was completing a catastrophic season. They had won only one game, with all of their losses being very close games.

RESULT: North High School defeated Madison High School by a score of 7–6.

1. North High School won the league title.

2. Two of the star players for North High School did not play.

3. Madison High School forfeited the game by not showing up.

4. The Panthers had never played the Bulldogs before.

5. Madison High School played their best game of the season.

6. The score was not indicative of the game.

7. North High School used an ineligible player.

8. This was Madison's only close game of the season.

9. The North High School fans were more enthusiastic than those from Madison.

10. Madison's best players were ejected late in the game.

Set II.

FACT SITUATION: Two former prison inmates had been planning to rob a local liquor store for four months. The robbery was carefully planned, with every detail noted, and was to take place on Friday the 13th at 10 P.M. The robbers approached the store at 9:45 P.M. and looked over the area. One of the men returned to the car to assure a fast getaway. When he was sure the store was empty, another robber pulled a nylon stocking over his face, entered the store, and pulled out a revolver, ordering the clerk to hand over the money. The clerk followed instructions and handed over the money, meanwhile pressing the silent alarm underneath the counter. After tying up the clerk, the robber left the store and jumped into the car, which was ready to go.

RESULT: The robbers were caught a few blocks from the store.

11.   The clerk remained very calm during the holdup.

12.   The police arrived late to the store.

13.   A customer in the store fainted when she saw the robber come in.

14.   A silent alarm system had been installed a few days before the robbery.

15.   The getaway car got a flat tire at the first stop sign.

16.   The alarm system failed to work.

17.   The robber's gun was not loaded.

18.   There was only $12 in the cash register.

19.   This was a first offense for the driver of the getaway car.

20.   The police had been tipped off about the robbery plan.

Set III.

FACT SITUATION: With his wife expecting a baby in the next week, Mr. Jones had a real dilemma. He had spent six months getting two tickets to the Rose Bowl game and his wife was due on that very same day. Being a football fanatic, Mr. Jones suggested to his wife that she check with the doctor about either inducing early labor or prolonging the time of birth. Mrs. Jones refused even to call the doctor. She felt that Mr. Jones was being ridiculously unreasonable and carefully outlined the consequences if he went to the game. Mr. Jones, coming to his senses, decided to sell the tickets at his office two days before the game.

RESULT: Mr. Jones attended the Rose Bowl game.

21.   Mrs. Jones's doctor refused to tamper with the expected birth date.

22.   The baby was born one day early.

23.   No one in the office bought the tickets.

24.   Mrs. Jones had a baby boy.

25.   Mr. Jones wanted too much money for the tickets.

26.   The game had been sold out for months.

27.   Mrs. Jones changed her mind before Mr. Jones sold the tickets.

28.   Mr. Jones was left with one ticket to the game for himself.

29.   Mrs. Jones gave birth on the day of the game.

30.   The doctor also attended the Rose Bowl game.

Set IV.

FACT SITUATION: In an attempt to win a local school board election, Jack Figby launched an all-out campaign against incumbent Roy Jamerson. Mr. Figby's campaign was based mainly on Mr. Jamerson's shortcomings rather than his own strengths. According to Mr. Figby, the incumbent had not lived up to his promises prior to the last election and was not representing the people. Figby said that Jamerson consistently voted against the rest of the school board on important issues and never proposed any positive legislation. Mr. Jamerson countered by presenting an administrative report commending him for his numerous proposal contributions to the school district and for his leadership during school board meetings. He supported this report with a documentation of his voting record and a long list of his achievements while serving the school district.

RESULT: Mr. Jamerson won the election.

31.   Mr. Figby ran a poor campaign.

32.   Mr. Jamerson was afraid to confront Figby's accusations.

33.   There was a third candidate running for the school board.

34.   Mr. Figby had never been on the school board.

35.   The voters preferred a man with experience.

36.   Jamerson thought that his voting record was significant.

37.   Figby strongly emphasized his own record.

38.   It rained heavily on election day.

39.   Jamerson ended the campaign with a majority of voters supporting him.

40.   Jamerson and Figby's wives were not good friends.

SECTION IV: ANALYTICAL ABILITY

TIME—25 MINUTES
30 QUESTIONS

Logical Diagrams

(SUGGESTED TIME—6 MINUTES)
15 QUESTIONS

Directions: In this section, five diagrams are presented that illustrate the relationship among three classes. You are to choose the one diagram that best illustrates the relationship among three given classes. There are three possible relationships between any *two* different classes:

One class completely within another class, but not vice versa, is represented by

When two classes have some, but not all, members in common, the relationship is represented by

When two classes have no members in common, the relationship is represented by

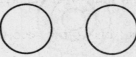

Note: The relative size of the circles does not represent the size of the class.

Questions 1–7 are based on the following diagrams.

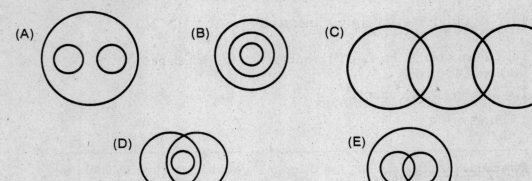

1. C Friends, enemies, adults

2. A Rake, hoe, gardening tools

3.   Alaska, Anchorage, United States

4. D Books, Bible, Holy scriptures

5.   Farmers, wheat farmers, young farmers

6.   Schools, colleges, state colleges

7.   Odd numbers, even numbers, counting numbers

Questions 8–15 are based on the following diagrams.

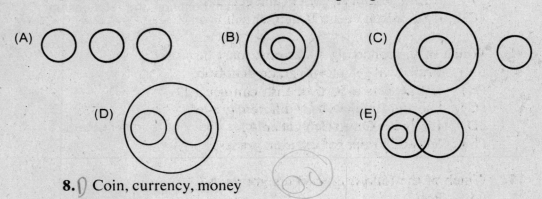

8. Coin, currency, money

9. Shoes, socks, feet

10.   Radio, television, color television

11.   Red fruit, strawberries, bananas

12. Sewing teachers, teachers, educators

13. Agrarian, manufacturing, mercantile

14. Forms of civil punishment, imprisonment, banishment

15. Cobra, snake, squirrel

Analytical Reasoning

(SUGGESTED TIME—19 MINUTES)
15 QUESTIONS

Directions: Each question or group of questions is based on a set of statements or a passage. You are required to choose the *best* answer to each question.

Questions 16–21

(1) Four students will get different passing grades.
(2) If Bob gets an A, then Lisa will get a D.
(3) If Lisa gets a C, then Bob will get a D.
(4) Bob will get a better grade than Frank.
(5) If Sue doesn't get an A, then Bob will get a C.
(6) If Lisa gets a B, then Frank won't get a D.
(7) If Lisa gets an A, then Frank gets a B.
(8) If Sue doesn't get a B, neither will Frank.

16. Which of the following statements must be *false?*
    (A) Frank will get a lower grade than Bob.
    (B) If Bob gets a B, then Lisa can get a D.
    (C) Sue and Frank will get different grades.
    (D) Lisa got a C and Bob got an A.
    (E) Sue and Frank got different grades.

17. Which of the following students got an A?
    (A) Bob
    (B) Sue
    (C) Lisa
    (D) Frank
    (E) None of the above

18. Which of the following students did not get a D?
 (A)   Bob, Sue, Lisa
 (B)   Sue, Bob, Frank
 (C)   Lisa, Frank, Sue
 (D)   Sue, Frank, Bob
 (E)   Lisa, Bob, Frank

19. Which statements let you deduce that Lisa cannot get an A?
 (A)   (1), (2), & (4)
 (B)   (3) & (5)
 (C)   (1), (4), & (7)
 (D)   (4) & (7)
 (E)   (2), (7), & (8)

20. Which of the eight statements repeats information available elsewhere in the set of statements?
 (A)   (2)
 (B)   (4)
 (C)   (5)
 (D)   (8)
 (E)   None of the above

21. The two lowest grades, C and D, were given respectively to
 (A)   a boy and a girl
 (B)   a girl and a boy
 (C)   two girls
 (D)   two boys
 (E)   Cannot be determined

Questions 22–24
 Recent studies show that aptitude test scores are declining because of lack of family stability and students' preoccupation with out-of-school activities. Therefore, not only the student's attitude but also his home environment must be changed to stop this downward trend.

22. The argument above fails to place any blame on
   I.   parents
  II.   schools
 III.   teachers
 (A)   I
 (B)   II
 (C)   III
 (D)   I & II
 (E)   II & III

23. The argument assumes that
    I.   the student's attitudes are of major importance in learning.
    II. heredity is more important than environment.
    III. this trend will be difficult to change.
    (A) I
    (B) I & II
    (C) II
    (D) I & III
    (E) II & III

24. The argument would be weakened if it was pointed out that
    I.   the aptitude tests are biased.
    II. basic skills are not emphasized at most schools.
    III. graduation requirements are lax.
    (A) I & II
    (B) I & III
    (C) I, II, III
    (D) II & III
    (E) None of the above.

Questions 25–30

    (1) Four men were seated at dinner.
    (2) Four different languages were spoken: German, French, English, and Italian.
    (3) Each man could speak two of the languages.
    (4) There was no language in common to all.
    (5) One language was common to three men.
    (6) Nobody spoke both French and German.
    (7) Robert couldn't speak English but could act as interpreter when Karl and Steve wanted to converse.
    (8) Steve spoke German and could also talk to Bill, who couldn't speak German.
    (9) Robert, Karl, and Bill could not all converse in the same language.
   (10) Karl spoke English and French.

25. Which of the following statements is *false?*
    I.   Nobody spoke both French and German.
    II. Nobody spoke both French and English.
    III. Everybody spoke English.
    (A) I
    (B) II
    (C) I & II
    (D) II & III
    (E) III

26. Which two statements let you deduce that Steve and Bill could not converse in French?

(A)   (9) & (10)
(B)   (5) & (7)
(C)   (6) & (8)
(D)   (4) & (9)
(E)   (3) & (7)

27. Which of the following statements is true?

I.   At least one language was common to two men.
II.   Robert, Karl, and Bill all spoke French.
III.   Steve could not converse with anyone in German.

(A)   I
(B)   I & II
(C)   I & III
(D)   II & III
(E)   I, II, & III

28. Which of the following languages was common to three men?

(A)   English
(B)   Italian
(C)   German
(D)   French
(E)   French and German

29. If another man joined the group at the dinner table, to converse with Karl and Bill he would have to speak

(A)   English
(B)   Italian
(C)   German
(D)   French
(E)   Could not occur

30. Which of the men spoke French?

I.   Karl
II.   Steve
III.   Robert
IV.   Bill

(A)   I
(B)   I & II
(C)   II & III
(D)   I & III
(E)   II, III, & IV

STOP
**IF YOU FINISH BEFORE TIME IS CALLED, CHECK YOUR
WORK ON THIS SECTION ONLY. DO NOT WORK
ON ANY OTHER SECTION IN THE TEST.**

SECTION V: MATH ABILITY

TIME—25 MINUTES
25 QUESTIONS

Directions: Solve each of the following problems and mark the *best* answer on your answer sheet. All scratch work should be done in the available space. All numbers used belong to the real number system. Diagrams are not necessarily drawn to scale.

---

1. A can do a piece of work in r days and B, who works faster, can do the same work in s days. Which of the following expressions, if any, represents the number of days it would take the two of them to do the work if they worked together?

   (A) $\dfrac{r + s}{2}$

   (B) $r - s$

   (C) $\dfrac{1}{r} + \dfrac{1}{s}$

   (D) $\dfrac{rs}{r + s}$

   (E) none of these

2. If y represents the tens digit and x the units digit of a two-digit number, then the number is represented by
   (A) $y + x$
   (B) yx
   (C) $10x + y$
   (D) $10y + x$
   (E) $10y + 10x$

3. A certain radio costs a merchant $72, which includes overhead and selling expenses. At what price must he sell it if he is to make a profit of 20 per cent of the selling price?
   (A) $86.40
   (B) $90
   (C) $92
   (D) $144
   (E) $100

4. A formula for infant feeding requires 13 ounces of evaporated milk and 18 ounces of water. If only 10 ounces of milk are available, how much water, to the nearest ounce, should be used?
   (A) 7 ounces
   (B) 14 ounces
   (C) 15 ounces
   (D) 21 ounces
   (E) 30 ounces

5. A 5-quart solution of sulfuric acid and water is 60 per cent acid. If a gallon of water is added, what per cent of the resulting solution is acid?
   (A) $33\frac{1}{3}\%$
   (B) 40%
   (C) 48%
   (D) 50%
   (E) $66\frac{2}{3}\%$

6. A wooden cone such as that shown in the figure at the right has its entire surface painted. Now suppose that it is cut into two parts with a saw, exposing a plane (flat) unpainted surface. All of the following figures could represent the cut (unpainted) surface EXCEPT

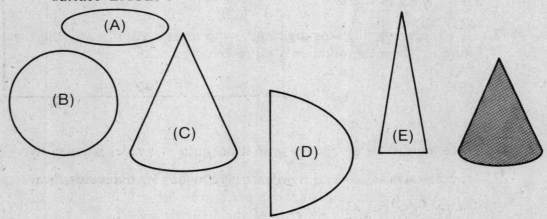

7. In a certain triangle ABC, the three angles are represented by $2x$, $3x - 10°$, and $3x + 30°$. What kind of triangle is ABC?
   (A) acute
   (B) isosceles
   (C) obtuse
   (D) right
   (E) none of these

8. Two triangles are each equilateral. Which of the following characteristics always belongs to these two triangles?
   (A) congruence
   (B) similarity
   (C) equal areas
   (D) equal perimeters
   (E) none of these

9. The base of an isosceles triangle is 16 and each of the equal sides is 10. Find the area of the triangle.
   (A) 160
   (B) 80
   (C) 36
   (D) 24
   (E) 48

10. Given a circle A whose diameter is 2 feet and a rectangular piece of tin B, 10 feet by 4 feet. Find, correct to the nearest square foot, the tin that will be left after the greatest possible number of circles of the size of A have been cut from B.
    (A) 0 sq. ft.
    (B) 2 sq. ft.
    (C) 9 sq. ft.
    (D) 20 sq. ft.
    (E) 18 sq. ft.

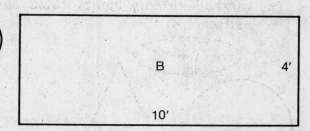

11. The number of diagonals, d, in a polygon of n sides is given by the formula $d = \dfrac{n^2 - 3n}{2}$. If a polygon has 90 diagonals, how many sides has it?
    (A) 8
    (B) 10
    (C) 12
    (D) 15
    (E) 20

12. A train left Albany for Buffalo, a distance of 290 miles, at 10:10 a.m. The train was scheduled to reach Buffalo at 3:45 p.m. If the average rate of the train on this trip was 50 miles per hour, it arrived in Buffalo
    (A) about 5 minutes ahead of schedule
    (B) on time
    (C) about 5 minutes late
    (D) about 13 minutes late
    (E) more than a quarter of an hour late

13. A box was made in the form of a cube. If a second cubical box has inside dimensions three times those of the first box, how many times as much does it contain?
    (A) 3
    (B) 9
    (C) 12
    (D) 27
    (E) 30

14. The number of telephones in Adelaide, Australia, is 48,000. If this represents 12.8 telephones per 100 of population, the population of Adelaide, to the nearest thousand, is
    (A) 128,000
    (B) 375,000
    (C) 378,000
    (D) 556,000
    (E) 700,000

Questions 15–20 refer to this graph.

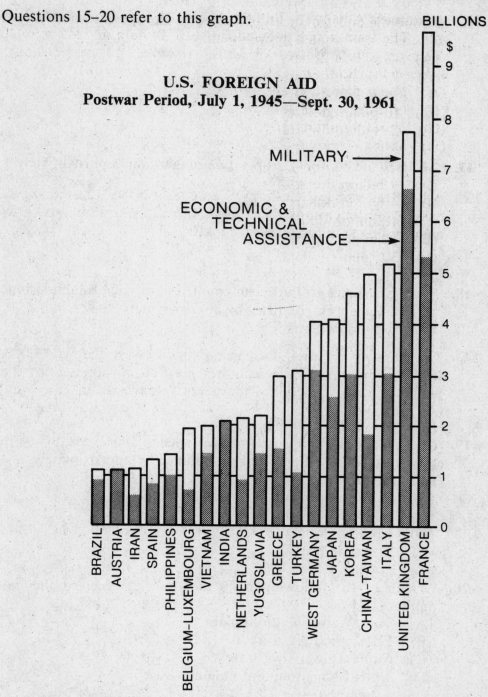

U.S. FOREIGN AID
Postwar Period, July 1, 1945—Sept. 30, 1961

MILITARY ⟶

ECONOMIC &
TECHNICAL
ASSISTANCE ⟶

BILLIONS
$
9
8
7
6
5
4
3
2
1
0

BRAZIL
AUSTRIA
IRAN
SPAIN
PHILIPPINES
BELGIUM-LUXEMBOURG
VIETNAM
INDIA
NETHERLANDS
YUGOSLAVIA
GREECE
TURKEY
WEST GERMANY
JAPAN
KOREA
CHINA-TAIWAN
ITALY
UNITED KINGDOM
FRANCE

15. Which of the following countries received the highest proportion
of economic and technical assistance, as compared with military
aid?
(A) France
(B) West Germany
(C) United Kingdom
(D) Brazil
(E) Austria

16. Economic and technical assistance to European nations shown on the graph totaled approximately
    (A) 18 billion dollars
    (B) 20 billion dollars
    (C) 34 billion dollars
    (D) 10 billion dollars
    (E) 26 billion dollars

17. Military aid to non-European nations totaled approximately
    (A) 9 billion dollars
    (B) 4 billion dollars
    (C) 18 billion dollars
    (D) 12 billion dollars
    (E) 30 billion dollars

18. Total assistance to European countries exceeded total assistance to non-European countries by approximately
    (A) 5 billion dollars
    (B) 20 billion dollars
    (C) 10 billion dollars
    (D) 25 billion dollars
    (E) 15 billion dollars

19. Total economic and technical assistance to all the nations on the graph exceeded total military assistance by approximately
    (A) 9 billion dollars
    (B) 30 billion dollars
    (C) 16 billion dollars
    (D) 3 billion dollars
    (E) 24 billion dollars

20. Which of the following pairs of countries received the most military aid?
    (A) Turkey and the Philippines
    (B) France and Austria
    (C) China-Taiwan and Italy
    (D) United Kingdom and Belgium-
        Luxembourg
    (E) Japan and Greece

21. Which fraction is the greatest of the following?

(A) $\dfrac{\sqrt{5}}{5}$

(B) $\dfrac{\sqrt{5}}{2\sqrt{5}}$

(C) $\dfrac{5}{\sqrt{5}}$

(D) $\dfrac{5}{2\sqrt{5}}$

(E) $\dfrac{2\sqrt{5}}{5}$

22. If a man walks 3 miles north, then 5 miles west, then 7 miles south and then 2 miles east, about how far is he from his starting point?
(A) 8 mi.
(B) 12 mi.
(C) 5 mi.
(D) 2 mi.
(E) 15 mi.

23. If $a = \dfrac{b}{c}$, where a, b, and c are non-zero rational numbers, then which is true?

(A) $\dfrac{a}{c} = b$

(B) $\dfrac{c}{b} = a$

(C) $ac = b$
(D) $bc = a$
(E) $ab = c$

24. If John has enough money to buy 3 hotdogs and 2 orders of fries or 2 hotdogs and 4 orders of fries, how many hotdogs could he buy if he bought no fries?
(A) 6
(B) 3
(C) 5
(D) 7
(E) 4

25. If b stands for the number of baseball players in the class and f stands for the number of football players and d stands for the athletes that play both, then how many total athletes are there in the class?
(A) $b - f - d$
(B) $b + f + d$
(C) $b - d - f$
(D) $b - d + f$
(E) $d - b - f$

PRACTICE TEST II: ANSWERS

SECTION I: VERBAL ABILITY

Sentence Completion

1.	A	5.	B	9.	E
2.	B	6.	E	10.	D
3.	D	7.	D		
4.	C	8.	C		

Analogies

11.	C	14.	E	17.	E
12.	E	15.	D	18.	B
13.	A	16.	B	19.	D

Antonyms

20.	C	23.	C	26.	A
21.	C	24.	A	27.	E
22.	C	25.	D	28.	E

Reading Comprehension

29.	C	38.	B	47.	D
30.	B	39.	C	48.	B
31.	C	40.	C	49.	C
32.	E	41.	A	50.	D
33.	C	42.	D	51.	B
34.	C	43.	B	52.	A
35.	C	44.	B	53.	C
36.	E	45.	E		
37.	D	46.	D		

Sentence Completion

54.	D	57.	E	60.	A
55.	A	58.	E	61.	D
56.	D	59.	D	62.	B

ANALOGIES

63.	A	66.	D	69.	C
64.	B	67.	B	70.	D
65.	B	68.	C	71.	C

ANTONYMS

72.	B	75.	B	78.	E
73.	D	76.	A	79.	B
74.	A	77.	C	80.	E

SECTION II: QUANTITATIVE ABILITY

QUANTITATIVE COMPARISON

1.	B	11.	B	21.	B
2.	A	12.	B	22.	B
3.	B	13.	A	23.	C
4.	B	14.	C	24.	A
5.	B	15.	D	25.	A
6.	C	16.	C	26.	A
7.	C	17.	A	27.	B
8.	D	18.	B	28.	D
9.	A	19.	D	29.	B
10.	D	20.	A	30.	A

MATH ABILITY

31.	D	40.	D	49.	C
32.	E	41.	C	50.	E
33.	D	42.	E	51.	B
34.	E	43.	B	52.	E
35.	C	44.	B	53.	D
36.	C	45.	B	54.	D
37.	E	46.	C	55.	A
38.	B	47.	C		
39.	D	48.	C		

SECTION III: ANALYSIS OF EXPLANATIONS

1.	C	15.	B	29.	D
2.	D	16.	D	30.	E
3.	A	17.	E	31.	B
4.	E	18.	E	32.	A
5.	D	19.	A	33.	D
6.	E	20.	B	34.	D
7.	D	21.	A	35.	B
8.	A	22.	B	36.	C
9.	B	23.	C	37.	A
10.	B	24.	E	38.	E
11.	C	25.	D	39.	B
12.	D	26.	E	40.	E
13.	A	27.	B		
14.	D	28.	C		

SECTION IV: ANALYTICAL ABILITY

Logical Diagrams

1.	C	6.	B	11.	C
2.	A	7.	A	12.	B
3.	B	8.	D	13.	A
4.	D	9.	A	14.	D
5.	E	10.	C	15.	C

Analytical Reasoning

16.	D	21.	A	26.	C
17.	B	22.	E	27.	C
18.	B	23.	D	28.	B
19.	C	24.	C	29.	A
20.	D	25.	D	30.	D

SECTION V: MATH ABILITY

1.	D	10.	C	19.	C
2.	D	11.	D	20.	C
3.	B	12.	D	21.	C
4.	B	13.	D	22.	C
5.	A	14.	B	23.	C
6.	C	15.	E	24.	E
7.	D	16.	E	25.	D
8.	B	17.	A		
9.	E	18.	B		

PRACTICE TEST II: ANALYSIS SHEET

SECTION I

	Possible	Completed	Right	Wrong

VERBAL ABILITY

	Possible	Completed	Right	Wrong
Sentence Completion				
Analogies				
Antonyms				
Reading Comprehension				
OVERALL VERBAL				

SECTION II

QUANTITATIVE ABILITY

	Possible	Completed	Right	Wrong
Quantitative Comparison				
Math Ability				
OVERALL QUANTITATIVE				

SECTION III & IV

ANALYTICAL ABILITY

	Possible	Completed	Right	Wrong
Analysis of Explanations				
Logical Diagrams				
Analytical Reasoning				
OVERALL ANALYTICAL				

SECTION V

MATH ABILITY

	Possible	Completed	Right	Wrong

RAW SCORE = NUMBER RIGHT $- \frac{1}{4}$ (number attempted but missed)

OVERALL SCORES SHOULD BE RAW SCORES

PRACTICE TEST II: EXPLANATIONS

SECTION I: VERBAL ABILITY

Sentence Completion

1. **A** exemplars—emphasis.
    The key words to note here are "greatest of men," "honestly admitted," and "abilities." The entire context of the sentence gives a positive connotation. You may therefore eliminate choices (B), (C), (D), and (E), which contain one or more negative words. Only Choice (A) lends the intended meaning to the sentence: that these great men deny being inherently great, their abilities were merely brought to public attention.

2. **B** advantage—decline.
    This sentence contains clues in its content and in its structure. The words "Soviets exceed us" give you the reference for the first word, which must mean being ahead. Structurally, the phrase "While it may appear at the present time," followed by the phrase "I am certain that," signals a shift in direction. Therefore, if the present state is one of *superiority*, you may expect this to *decrease*. Only Choice (B) *advantage—decline* has the proper combination of positive-negative words in the correct order.

3. **D** vulnerable—adversary.
    Thoughtful reading of this sentence clearly suggests that "crowded cities" and "concentrated industry" would make a country an easy target. Therefore choices (A), (B), and (E) may be eliminated. In the second blank, of course, you need a word meaning enemy. Both (C) and (D) meet these requirements; however, only (D) *vulnerable—adversary* is correct grammatically, since you cannot say "a easy target."

4. **C** austerity.
    Notice the signal word "though," which begins this sentence. This tells you that you are going to change connotations or see a contrast between the first and second parts of the sentence. The adjectives in the first section are "romantic and sensual." You want a word in direct contrast to these, an antonym. Only (C) *Austerity* (severity, denial of sensual pleasures) fits the bill.

5. B   reject.
The important words here are "repugnant," "predisposition" and "free from authority." The sentence requires a negative word that means to turn away from, or shun. Choices (A) and (E) are positive and therefore can be eliminated. (D) *inculcate* means a continuation of drummed-in learning, which does not suit the sentence, and (C) *minimize* is too bland a word, not showing enough action. (B) *Reject* is clearly the correct answer.

6. E   paucity—relation.
The word "scarcity" involves an *insufficient* supply in response to demand. Therefore, you are looking for a combination in which the first word means scanty or insufficient. (The second words in all choices are equally correct so they may be virtually ignored). Choices (A), (C), and (D) all mean plentiful, so they may be eliminated. Choice (B) *puerility* (childishness) has no relation; therefore the correct choice is (E) *paucity* (scantiness)—*relation*.

7. D   development.
The sentence tells you that Newton's picture of the universe *lacked* something. Due to this lack, his teachings could be taken to suggest that the universe was "created out of one piece." Choice (D) *development* best completes this sentence because it implies evolution or growth in contrast to the idea of "instant" creation.

8. C   encyclopedias.
This sentence sets up a contrast that is explained in its first half. The key phrase is "little regard for *factual* learning." As a result of this feeling, "his goal is to build *men*" as opposed to something concerned with the purely factual. Choice (B) *thinkers* and (D) *theorists* deal with theories and hypotheses as well as facts; therefore choice (C) *encyclopedias* is the best answer.

9. E   opportunities—capacities.
Two little words in this sentence are clues to the correct choice. The verbs "assure" and "develop" are important here because each of them will take a word in the answer as their object. Choices (A) and (B) can be eliminated, as the first word in each pair would not go well with "assure." Choice (C) can be eliminated because *impartiality* does not make sense in this context. In deciding between choices (D) and (E) you must examine the second word in each pair. Choice (E) is the best choice, as it makes better sense to speak of "developing their *capacities* for usefulness" than "developing their *ambitions* for usefulness."

10. **D** sanguine—greater.

You are looking for a pair of words with compatible connotations here. There is no indication of whether this connotation will be positive or negative, but the word describing the corporation's income must justify the use of the word describing "forecast." Choice (B) *pessimistic* is incorrect because it has mixed connotations. Choices (A), (C), and (E) are poor because their first words are too weak—they do not have any positive or negative connotations to match their second words. Choice (E), then, is the correct choice—*sanguine* (cheerful)—*greater*.

Analogies

11. **C**

COOLIE is to RICKSHAW in the same way as HORSE is to CARRIAGE. A "coolie" pulls a "rickshaw," just as a "horse" pulls a "carriage."

12. **E**

COLLAPSE is to REGIME in the same way as FOUNDER is to SHIP. To "founder" means to "collapse," or to fill with water and sink.

13. **A**

REMOTE is to PONDEROUS in the same way as RECONDITE is to BULKY. The same meaning relationship exists in both pairs: "remote" and "recondite" (beyond understanding) are synonyms, and so are "ponderous" and "bulky."

14. **E**

BULL is to PICADOR in the same way as SPEAKER is to HECKLER. The "picador" deliberately irritates the bull, just as a "heckler" deliberately irritates a "speaker." Choice (B) expresses killing rather than just irritation.

15. **D**

WHIG is to TORY in the same way as LIBERAL is to CONSERVATIVE. "Whig" and "Tory" were the terms denoting liberals and conservatives in England during the 18th and 19th centuries.

16. **B**

ARCTIC is to GELID in the same way as TROPICAL is to LUXURIANT. "Gelid" (frozen) describes the "arctic" climate, just as "luxuriant" (lush) describes a "tropical" climate.

17. E

BIGOTRY is to TOLERANCE in the same way as PARSIMONY is to MAGNANIMITY. The terms in each pair are *opposites*. (D) is an unacceptable choice because it uses a prefix to change meaning instead of the completely different word that is required.

18. B

ENCORE is to CATCALL in the same way as APPLAUSE is to RIDICULE. The terms in each pair are *opposite responses to a performance*. A good performance receives "applause" and cries of "encore," but a bad performance is subject to "ridicule" and "catcalls."

19. D

PRECIPITOUS is to DISCONSOLATE in the same way as HEADLONG is to DEJECTED. The same meaning relationship exists in both pairs, between "rash" or "hasty" (precipitous, headlong) and "depressed" (disconsolate, dejected).

Antonyms

20. Quondam—formerly existent. Correct answer: (C) extant—currently existing.

21. Benevolent—kindly, well-meaning. Correct answer: (C) invidious—meant to cause ill will.

22. Wavering—fluctuating. Correct answer: (C) peremptory—absolute, decisive.

23. Platitude—a trite remark. Correct answer: (C) epigram—witty saying.

24. Redolent—fragrant. Correct answer: (A) malodorous—bad-smelling.

25. Repelling—repulsing. Correct answer: (D) prepossessing—appealing.

26. Direct—straightforward. Correct answer: (A) surreptitious—secret, clandestine.

27. Alluring—attractive. Correct answer: (E) loathsome—abominable.

28. Temerity—boldness. Correct answer: (E) circumspection—caution.

Reading Comprehension

29.   C

The last section of the passage repeatedly emphasizes that the scholar's private thoughts turn out to be "most public, and universally true." The passage notes that many of the world's concerns are ephemeral, but does not suggest that the scholar renounce the world, rather that he seek its truths.

30.   B

The last sentence of the first paragraph summarizes the difficult efforts which that paragraph lists; the scholar's efforts are directed toward publishing "new verdicts" rather than traveling the "old road." He is not deliberately hostile, as (C) suggests, but may seem so.

31.   C

(A) is too simplistic. (E) is ambiguous and introduces "love" into a section which discusses matters of culture and wisdom exclusively. "Conscience" is implied by the sentence about "vulgar prosperity."

32.   E

(C) is from *Hamlet,* a play irrelevant to this passage. (D) presumes that the term is familiar, which it is not. "Nettles" are painful, as is self-accusation. "Uncertainty" is a more comprehensive, general term here than "loss of time," and is best associated with the equally general and comprehensive metaphor, "tangling vines."

33.   C

The passage does not equate scholarly work with either books or glory.

34.   C

The end of the passage states that the scholar's work finally delights every man; therefore, any "hostile" impression is indeed false.

35.   C

(A), (B), and (D) are the "old road" thought which the scholar avoids, and (E) is a mere fraction of what the scholar lives on.

36.   E

"Politics" = "Navigation"; therefore, the "Politician" (statesman) = "Navigator" (captain).

37. D

This is explicitly stated in the second and third sentences. (A) is also true, but irrelevant to the subject of this passage.

38. B

This is evident when the author states that "political leadership has degenerated into partisan anarchy."

39. C

All other choices are not supported by any evidence in the passage. Adam Smith, because he studied economics, was indeed a "student."

40. C

Because of the Pitts, England became "the foremost country, economically speaking, in the world."

41. A

This is stated in lines 15–17.

42. D

(E) is incorrect because "hereditary" is one of *several terms* for the nobility of Mecca; it is not *inclusive* enough.

43. B

(A), (C), and (E) do not specifically mention "leaders" and (D) is a vague fragment with no subject.

44. B

The passage notes Ali's "close relationship to the prophet."

45. E

This is stated in the first sentence of paragraph 4.

46. D

This is discussed in paragraphs 3 and 4; compensation is generated by "high duties" upon A and B commodities. The *prices* are not raised, so (B) is incorrect. The ambiguous subject "we" in (C) and (E) weakens them as choices.

47. D

A *supply* of workers is not abundant enough to make work in (C) and (D) attractive at necessarily lower wages because of lower productivity. Government aid ("high duties") allows equivalent wages to be paid in (C) and (D), and thereby attracts labor to these industries.

48. B
"It is an uncompensated deduction from the natural earnings of the laborers in (A) and (B)."

49. C
This is the conclusion reached in the last sentence of the passage, which describes the reduced purchasing power of C and D workers that occurs because C and D industries (fields of lower natural productiveness) enter the market.

50. D
This contrast is established in the first sentence. (A) and (C) are subordinate contrasts to (D), while (B) and (E) are beyond the scope of the passage.

51. B
The chansons are characterized by dutifully savage knights, whereas the Arthurian romances emphasize the knights' duty as the mystical search for the Holy Grail.

52. A
This is the only choice that, like "Arthurian," describes a type of knight.

53. C
Any other choice is inconsistent with the *unfriendly* connotations of "contradicts" and "jeers at."

Sentence Completion

54. D   skepticism.
This sentence sets up a contrast. The second part gives the antonyms of the word that you are looking for. You are seeking a word that means the opposite of "embracing life eagerly and optimistically." Choices (A), (B), and (E) may be eliminated. Choice (C) *rancor* (malevolence) has an effectively negative quality, but notice the key word "seasoning" in the first part of the sentence. This implies that a degree of this quality might be desirable in people. Therefore (D) *skepticism,* which is useful in limited quantities, is the better choice.

55. A   intrinsic to.
The key words in this sentence are "nature" and "grown up in spite of it." You are looking for words that mean the opposite of grown-up when used to describe "conditions." *Intrinsic to* is the correct choice, meaning inborn or basic to one's nature.

56. D accomplishment—a handicap.

This is a simple sentence of definition. The best answer in such a question is the choice that would necessarily be true in all instances. Choices (A), (B), (C), and (E) can all be eliminated because they either are not true or are not *necessarily* true (they would depend on circumstances).

57. E moot—disputable.

This is another sentence of definition requiring synonyms. Choices (A) and (B) are opposites, choice (C) is not properly related, and choice (D) is not necessarily so. *Moot* (subject to argument, debatable) and *disputable* are synonymous and therefore work best in the sentence.

58. E declamations—philippics.

What is required here is a pair of words in which the first is another word for speeches, and the second word is described by "strongly worded, personal in nature and full of abuse." Note that the second word should derive from one of the Greek names mentioned. Only (E) *declamation—philippics* works in this situation.

59. D circumlocution—disciplined.

The first word in the missing pair should relate to speech marked by "senility and garrulity." The second, in contrast, should be a positive adjective. Only two choices have this negative-positive relationship—(D) and (E). However, only *circumlocution* would be compatible with "senility and garrulity." Therefore, choice (D) is correct.

60. A homonyms.

This question is a simple case of straight definition. You must know that the word clearly defined by the sentence is choice (A) *homonyms*.

61. D forensic.

The key words here are "attorney," "disputation" and "debate." You need a very specific word that refers to abilities needed for disputation and debate as used by an attorney. Choice (D) *forensic* (pertaining to courts of law or public debate; argumentative) is the only appropriate choice.

62. B wary—generally.

A person who considers consequences before he acts is considered *cautious*. The term may vary in degree depending on how *often* a person thinks before acting. Therefore you are looking for an answer in which the proper relationship exists between the two words. Only answer (B) *wary—generally* fits this description.

Analogies

63. A

LETHARGIC is to ABSTEMIOUS in the same way as TORPID is to TEMPERATE. The same meaning relationship exists in both pairs, between "sluggish" (lethargic, abstemious) and "moderate" (abstemious, temperate).

64. B

EXPEDITE is to DEFER in the same way as CATALYZE is to PROTRACT. The same meaning relationship exists in both pairs, between "to complete quickly" (expedite, catalyze) and "to delay or prolong" (defer, protract).

65. B

ASCETICISM is to MODERATION in the same way as CONSERVATISM is to CENTRISM. "Ascetism" is extreme self-denial, as opposed to "moderation," which is neither self-denying nor self-indulgent. Similarly, "conservatism" is associated with ascetic political opinions, as opposed to "centrism," which is neither conservative nor liberal.

66. D

ESTIMATION is to ADULATION in the same way as DEFERENCE is to OBSEQUIOUSNESS. The same meaning relationship exists in both pairs, between "courteous regard or respect" (estimation, deference) and "excessive willingness to serve and obey" (adulation, obsequiousness).

67. B

DESTITUTE is to DEVOID in the same way as OBLITERATION is to EXTIRPATION. Each pair is a set of *synonyms:* the first pair are both adjectives, and the second pair are both nouns. The meaning of both "destitute" and "devoid" is "without anything," and "obliteration" and "extirpation" both mean "complete destruction."

68. C

CIRCLE is to QUADRANT in the same way as SPHERE is to HEMISPHERE. Here is a *whole-part relationship:* a "circle" may be divided into "quadrants," and a "sphere" may be divided into "hemispheres." (B) is unacceptable because it is a part-whole relationship.

69. C

NEUROSIS is to PSYCHOSIS in the same way as AGGRES-SION is to WAR. Here is a *lesser-greater relationship:* "neurosis" is a lesser form of mental illness and "psychosis" is the greater (more serious) form, just as "aggression" is a lesser form of violence than "war." (A) is a possible answer, but must be ruled out because "fear" and "dread" are not different enough in meaning.

70. D

POEM is to PASTORAL in the same way as CHAUVINISM is to PAN-SLAVISM. Here is a *general-particular relationship:* a "pastoral" is a particular type of "poem," just as "pan-Slavism" (a movement toward the unification of all Slavic countries) is a particular type of "chauvinism."

71. C

SPECIES is to HYBRID in the same way as METAL is to ALLOY. The relationship in each pair is between a "pure form" (species, metal) and a "combination or mixture" (hybrid, alloy).

Antonyms

72. Disputable—questionable. Correct answer: (B) incontrovertible —absolute.

73. Felicity—skillful faculty. Correct answer: (D) inaptness—without skill.

74. Avarice—greed. Correct answer: (A) munificence—generosity.

75. Unsalable—unsuitable for sale. Correct answer: (B) marketable —readily salable.

76. Helot—slave. Correct answer: (A) freeman—man who is free.

77. Serpentine—winding, like a snake. Correct answer: (C) Straight.

78. Ritualistic—strictly observing formal rites. Correct answer: (E) informal—unceremonious.

79. Remiss—careless. Correct answer: (B) attentive.

80. Ebb—recede. Correct answer: (E) flow—run, stream.

SECTION II: QUANTITATIVE ABILITY

Quantitative Comparison

1.   **B** $x < y$

Solving each equation:

$$\frac{2x}{7} = \qquad\qquad\qquad 3y = 87$$

$$\frac{7}{2} \times \frac{2x}{7} = \frac{8}{1} \times \frac{7}{2} \qquad\qquad \frac{3y}{3} = \frac{87}{3}$$

$$x = 28 \qquad\qquad\qquad\qquad y = 29$$

$$28 < 29$$

2.   **A** $7\sqrt{3} > 3\sqrt{7}$

Approximating $\sqrt{3}$ as 1.7 and $\sqrt{7}$ as 2.6

$$7(1.7) \qquad\qquad\qquad 3(2.6)$$
$$11.9 \qquad\qquad\qquad\quad 7.8$$

3.   **B**   Volume < Surface Area

Using the formula $L \times W \times H$ to solve for the volume,
$6 \times 4 \times 4 = 96$

Solving for the surface area is slightly more difficult. Area of the ends is $(4 \times 4) \times 2 = 32$. Area of the sides is $(4 \times 6) \times 4 = 96$. Total surface area is $32 + 96 = 128$.

$$96 < 128$$

4.   **B**   AC < 6

Using the Pythagorean Theorem to solve for AC:

$$(AD)^2 + (DC)^2 = (AC)^2$$
$$(4)^2 + \quad (4)^2 = (AC)^2$$
$$16 + \quad\quad 16 = AC^2$$
$$32 = AC^2$$
$$\sqrt{32} = AC$$

since the $\sqrt{32}$ is about 5.7

$$\sqrt{32} < 6$$

5. B $7 < CF$

This problem is probably best solved by inspection. With one side being 6 and another being 4, it is fairly evident that the diagonal of the rectangular prism will be greater than 7. Otherwise, the following longer method would work.

To find the length of CF, it is first necessary to find the length of diagonal EC. Using the Pythagorean Theorem:

$$(ED)^2 + (DC)^2 = (EC)^2,$$
$$(6)^2 + (4)^2 = (EC)^2$$
$$36 + 16 = EC^2$$
$$52 = EC^2$$
$$\sqrt{52} = EC$$

Now using the length of side EC as $\sqrt{52}$ and FE as 4, the Pythagorean Theorem gives the needed length.

$$(EC)^2 + (FE)^2 = (FC)^2$$
$$(\sqrt{52})^2 + (4)^2 = (FC)^2$$
$$52 + 16 = FC^2$$
$$68 = FC^2$$
$$\sqrt{68} = FC$$

since $\sqrt{68}$ is about 8.2

$$7 < \sqrt{68}$$

6. C $FA + AD = \frac{1}{3}GB + 2\,BC$

Substituting the proper values

$$6 + 4 \qquad\qquad \frac{1}{3}(6) + 2(4)$$
$$2 + 8$$
$$10 = 10$$

7. C $592 \times 21 \times 4 = 7 \times 592 \times 12$

Canceling the 592 from both columns leaves 21×4 and 7×12

$$84 = 84$$

8. **D** $x - 3$? $y + 4$

Following the given condition $x > y$, and substituting values such as $x = 4$, $y = 3$

$$(4) - 3 \qquad\qquad\qquad 3 + 4$$
$$1 < 7$$

Now trying the values $x = 12$, $y = 0$

$$(12) - 3 \qquad\qquad\qquad 0 + 4$$
$$9 > 7$$

Different values give different results: no comparison can be determined.

9. **A**

Cars average speed > 30. To find the average speed of the car in miles per hour multiply 8 miles by 4, since 15 minutes is $\frac{1}{4}$ of an hour.

$$8 \times 4 = 32$$

32 miles per hour is the average speed and $32 > 30$.

10. **D** $s \, ? \, r$

Trying some values in the equation $\frac{s}{r} > \frac{3}{5}$ gives different outcomes such as:

$$s = 4, r = 5 \qquad \frac{4}{5} > \frac{3}{5}$$
$$s < r$$

If $s = -4$ and $r = -5$, then

$$\frac{-4}{-5} \qquad \frac{3}{5}$$

and $s > r$

No determination possible.

11. B $\dfrac{1}{x} < -x$

Substituting a value for x, and considering the given condition (x is a negative fraction), makes it evident that column B will always be positive and column A negative, let $x = -\dfrac{1}{2}$

$$\dfrac{1}{-\dfrac{1}{2}} \qquad\qquad -\left(\dfrac{-1}{2}\right)$$

$$-2 < +\dfrac{1}{2}$$

12. B

Area semicircle $<$ Area triangle. $AB = 6$ because triangle ABE is isosceles. The radius of the semicircle is $\frac{1}{2}AB$ or 3. Using the area formula for the circle:

$$A = \pi r^2$$
$$A = \pi(3)^2$$
$$A = \pi(9)$$
$$A = 28$$

Taking $\dfrac{1}{2}$ of this leaves the area of the semicircle as 14.
Now using the area formula for the triangle:

$$A = \tfrac{1}{2}bh$$
$$A = \tfrac{1}{2}(6)\,(6)$$
$$A = \tfrac{1}{2}(36)$$
$$A = 18$$

and $14 < 18$

13. A $\overset{\frown}{AB} > AC$

Using the circumference formula for a circle of diameter 6:

$$C = \pi d$$
$$C = \pi(6)$$
$$C = 18$$

Taking $\frac{1}{2}$ of this leaves 9 as the length.

Now using the Pythagorean Theorem to find AC:

$$(AB)^2 + (BC)^2 = (AC)^2$$
$$(6)^2 + (6)^2 = (AC)^2$$
$$36 + 36 = AC^2$$
$$72 = AC^2$$
$$\sqrt{72} = AC$$

$\sqrt{72}$ is approximately 8.5
Therefore $9 > \sqrt{72}$

14. C $\angle A = 45°$

Since $\triangle ABC$ is an isosceles right triangle, $\angle A = \angle C$ and $\angle B = 90°$. This leaves $90°$ to be divided evenly between $\angle A$ and $\angle C$. Therefore $\angle A$ is $45°$.

15. D $2x + 1 ? 6$

Substituting 2 for x results in column A being

$$2(2) + 1 = 5$$
$$5 < 6$$

Now let x be 4

$$2(4) + 1 = 7$$
$$7 > 6$$

Different values give different results: therefore no determination is possible.

16. C $-(r - s) = -r + s$

This is really an example of the distributive property and can be solved by inspection.
Alternate method:

let $r = 3$ and $s = 2$
then $-(3 - 2)$ $-3 + 2$
$-(1)$
and $-1 = -1$

17.   **A** $p > 110$

Solve $\left(\sqrt{\dfrac{p+4}{2}}\right) = 8$ by squaring both sides $\left(\sqrt{\dfrac{p+4}{2}}\right)^2 = 8^2$.

$$\frac{p+4}{2} = 64$$
$$p + 4 = 128$$
$$p = 124$$

and $124 > 110$

Alternate method: Substituting 110 into the equation gives:

$$\sqrt{\frac{110+4}{2}} \overset{?}{=} 8$$
$$\sqrt{\frac{114}{2}} \overset{?}{=} 8$$
$$\sqrt{57} \overset{?}{=} 8$$

Since $\sqrt{57}$ is about 7.5, and $7.5 < 8$, p would have to be greater than 110 for the equation to be solved properly.

18.   **B** $\dfrac{1}{8} < 15\%$

Changing $\dfrac{1}{8}$ to a percent:

$$\frac{1}{8} = \frac{x}{100}$$
$$8x = 100$$
$$x = \frac{100}{8}$$
$$x = 12\frac{1}{2}\%$$
$$12\% < 15\%$$

19. D $\sqrt{x}$? $\sqrt[3]{x}$
Let $x = 1$

$$\begin{matrix} \sqrt{1} & & \sqrt[3]{1} \\ 1 & = & 1 \end{matrix}$$

Now let $x = 2$

$$\begin{matrix} \sqrt{2} & & \sqrt[3]{2} \\ 1.4 & > & 1.26 \end{matrix}$$

(The work on the second part of this problem is not necessary, as it is evident that $\sqrt{2} \neq \sqrt[3]{2}$ and that 1 was a unique situation.) More than one outcome possible means none can be determined.

20. A Postal receipts in Detroit in 1937 > $11,000.
By inspection the receipts for that year are a little greater.

21. B Difference in receipts in 1934 < Difference in receipts in 1932
By inspection, the lines are farther apart in 1932.

22. B % decrease 1932 to 1933 < % decrease 1933 to 1934
By inspection, the slope of the line shows a decrease from 1933 to 1934 and no decrease from 1932 to 1933.

23. C Detroit receipts 1936 = St. Louis receipts 1936.
Since the lines meet at the 1936 mark, they are equal.

24. A Detroit's approximate
    % increase from 1935 to 1939 > 20%
To find % increase put the difference of the receipts of the two years at the top of the fraction and the beginning year's value at the bottom:

$$\frac{11 - 8.75}{8.75} = \frac{2.25}{8.75} = \frac{2}{8}$$

or about 25%
and   25% > 20%

25. A $\sqrt{26} > 5$
Since $\sqrt{25} = 5$, $\sqrt{26}$ must be greater than 5.

26.   A $9^5 - 9^4 > 9^4$

9^5 is 9×9^4, so if 9^4 is subtracted from 9^5, the remainder is obviously much greater than 9^4.

Alternate method:

$$9^5 - 9^4 \qquad\qquad 9^4$$
$$(9 \times 9 \times 9 \times 9 \times 9) - (9 \times 9 \times 9 \times 9) \quad (9 \times 9 \times 9 \times 9)$$
$$59{,}049 - 6{,}561 \qquad\qquad 6{,}561$$
$$52{,}488 > 6{,}561$$

The long way!

27.   B   Number of ways
3 books can be $<$ 7
arranged on a shelf

Three books can be arranged 6 ways on a shelf:

ABC
ACB
BAC
BCA
CAB
CBA
or $3 \times 2 \times 1 = 6$

and $6 < 7$

28.   D $(a^4 + b^3)^2 \; ? \; (a^3 b^6)^3$

Let $a = 0$ and $b = 0$; then both columns are obviously equal. If $a = 1$ and $b = 0$, then column A is greater than column B; therefore the answer cannot be determined.

29.   B $\dfrac{1}{79} - \dfrac{1}{81} < \dfrac{1}{71} - \dfrac{1}{80}$

This problem is best solved by inspection. The difference between the two values in column B is obviously larger than the difference in Column A.

30.   A $x > y$

$y = 80°$ is evident by the diagram and rules of a transversal through parallel lines. $x = 100°$ because x and 80 must equal a straight line of $180°$, or $180° - 80° = x$. Therefore $100° > 80°$.

Math Ability

31. **D** 75%

Given: r = width of the ring (shaded portion) and r = radius of the inner circle; therefore, $2r$ = radius of the entire circle.

Formula:

1. area of circle = πr^2;
2. area of entire circle − area of inner circle = area of the shaded portion.

By substitution, for 2., above, $\pi(2r)^2$ or $4\pi r^2$ minus $\pi(r)^2$ or $\pi r^2 = 3\pi r^2$ (area of the shaded portion).

$$\frac{\text{Area of the shaded portion}}{\text{Area of the entire circle}} = \frac{3\pi r^2}{4\pi r^2} = \frac{3}{4} = 75\%.$$

32. **E** none of these

The correct answer is $\dfrac{w}{w+1}$.

Formula: $\dfrac{\text{won}}{\text{played}}$ = fractional part of games won

Games won = w; games played = $w + 1$

$\therefore \dfrac{w}{w+1}$ = fractional part of games won

33. **D** 4

Formula: Area of a circle = πr^2

If x = radius of original circle, then $2x$ = radius of new circle.
Area of original circle = πx^2; area of new circle = $\pi(2x)^2 = 4\pi x^2$.

$\therefore$ the area of the original circle has been multiplied by 4

34. **E** 48 mph.

$$\underline{120 \text{ miles} = 2 \text{ hours (60 mph)}}$$
$$\underline{120 \text{ miles} = 3 \text{ hours (40 mph)}}$$
$$240 \text{ miles} = 5 \text{ hours} = \text{average of 48 mph}$$

35. **C** $\dfrac{2K - hb}{h}$

$K = \frac{1}{2}h(b + b_1)$ or

$2K = h(b + b_1)$ or $2K = hb + hb_1$ or $2K - hb = hb_1$;

finally, $\dfrac{2K - hb}{h} = b_1$

36.   C $275

Formula: Selling price = original price − discount.

If x = the original price, we substitute $165 = x - .40x$ or $6x = 1650, $x = 275.

37.   E   2 to 3.

$$\frac{\frac{1}{4}}{\frac{3}{8}} = \frac{1}{4} \div \frac{3}{8} = \frac{1}{4} \times \frac{8}{3} = \frac{2}{3}$$

38.   B   11 feet

Since FG = 16 feet, EH = 16 feet (opposite sides of a parallelogram are =)

Since BD is an altitude, ED = DH = 8 feet (the altitude of an isosceles triangle is also the median)

$(EB)^2 = (BD)^2 + (ED)^2$ (right triangle)

$(EB)^2 = 6^2 + 8^2 = 100$; EB = 10 feet

AB = BE + EA (Given: EA = 1 ft.)

∴ AB = 11 feet

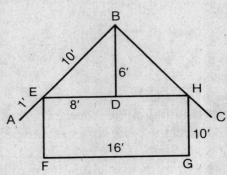

39.   D   40%

Total number of students graduating was 1,959 or about 2,000.

Total number of students entering college was 746 or about 750.

Changing to a percent $\frac{750}{2,000} = \frac{75}{200}$ or about 40%.

40.   D   36

120 students graduated with a GPA 3.5–4.0 and SAT scores of 1,000–1,299.

70% of these students entered college or junior college

70% × 120 = number entering college or junior college

70 × 120 = 84 students

$$\begin{array}{r} 120 \text{ students} \\ - \underline{84} \text{ entered college} \\ 36 \text{ students in this column did not enter college or} \end{array}$$

junior college.

Alternate method:

If 70% of the students went to college or junior college, then 30% did not go. 30% of 120 is 36 students.

41.   C   5%

Students entering college with scores of 1,300 or above is computed as follows:

$$\begin{array}{r} 60\% \text{ of } 5 = 3 \text{ with GPA } 2.0\text{–}2.4 \\ 70\% \text{ of } 10 = 7 \text{ with GPA } 2.5\text{–}2.9 \\ 84\% \text{ of } 25 = 21 \text{ with GPA } 3.0\text{–}3.4 \\ 100\% \text{ of } 14 = \underline{14} \text{ with GPA } 3.5\text{–}4.0 \\ \text{Total is } \overline{45} \end{array}$$

Students entering college is 746. Therefore, $\frac{45}{746}$ will give the percent requested. Approximating each value $\frac{50}{750} = \frac{5}{75} = \frac{1}{15} =$ .06-$\frac{2}{3}$ or just below 7% (Remember that the actual numbers were rounded up slightly.) This is closest to 5%.

42.   E   2.5–2.9—700–999

By inspection, only the 2.0–2.4—700–999 group and the 2.5–2.9—700–99 group should be considered, as they have easily the largest numbers graduating. Respectively

32% of 525 = 168

38% of 450 = 171

43.   B   700–999

This problem is most easily solved by inspection. Since the 700–999 group had by far the largest number of students and less than half entered college, this is the obvious answer.

44. **B**   12%
Students scoring below 700 and not entering college is computed as follows:

(2.0–2.4) $100\% - 14\% = 86\%$ (total % – % entering = % not entering)
$86\% \times 200 = 172$

(2.5–2.9) $100\% - 20\% = 80\%$
80% of $80 = 64$

(3.0–3.4) $100\% - 25\% = 75\%$
75% of $40 = 30$

(3.5–4.0) $100\% - 28\% = 72\%$
72% of $25 = \underline{\quad 18}$

Total   238 students not

entering college. Approximating and changing to a percent:
$$\frac{238}{1,959} = \frac{240}{1,960} = \frac{24}{196} = 12\%$$

45. **B** a^{2x}
$(a^x)^2 = a^{2x}$ (by inspection)

46. **C**   3 inches
Let $x =$ length of the shorter dimension
$\therefore 1\frac{7}{8} : x = 2\frac{1}{2} : 4$ or $\frac{5}{2}x = \frac{60}{8}$ or $40x = 120$, $x = 3$ inches

47. **C**   1870
If $x =$ the number, then the numbers are $\frac{x}{2}$ and $\frac{x}{5}$ (given).

$\therefore \frac{x}{2} - \frac{x}{5} = 561$ or $3x = 5610$, $x = 1870$

48. **C**   52%
SOLUTION
$\quad$ \$100 List Price
$\underline{\times \quad .40}$
$\quad$ \$40 1st Discount

$\quad$ \$60 1st Selling Price
$\underline{\times \quad .20}$
$\quad$ \$12.00 2nd Discount

$\quad$ \$60.00
$\underline{-12.00}$
$\quad$ \$48.00 2nd Selling Price

$\quad$ \$100 List
$\underline{- \quad 48}$ Selling Price
$\quad$ \$ 52 Total Discount $\qquad \frac{\$\ 52}{\$100} = 52\%$

49. **C** 3
By inspection of the chart and simple addition.

50. **E** 24
By inspection of the chart.

51. **B** 3 to 2
Total of Democratic seats is 263.
Total of Republican seats is 174.
263 to 174 is about 3 to 2.

52. **E** 3,456 pounds
1,728 cubic inches = 1 cubic foot
   1 cubic inch   = 2 pounds
1,728 cubic inches = 3,456 pounds

53. **D** the sum of the edges is increased by 24 inches
Since there are 12 edges to a cube and each edge is increased by
2 inches, the total increase is 24 inches.

54. **D** IV
Solve for the area of each figure:
I. $A = s \times s$ $A = (20) \times (16) = 320$

II. $A = \frac{1}{2}bh$ $A = \frac{1}{2}(16)\,(20) = \frac{1}{2}(320) = 160$

III. $A = h\,\dfrac{b + b}{2}$ $A = (20)\,\dfrac{16 + 24}{2} = 20\frac{40}{2} =$

$$20(20) = 400$$

IV. $A = L \times W$ $A = (30) \times (16) = 480$
Figure I = 320 plus figure II = 160 equals 480, which is figure
IV.

55. **A** .08
Changing the decimals to the nearest fraction gives $.26 \times .67 \times$
$.5 \times .9 = \frac{1}{4} \times \frac{2}{3} \times \frac{1}{2} \times \frac{9}{10}$.
Canceling leaves $\frac{1}{4} \times \frac{3}{10}$
OR $\frac{3}{40}$ = .075 or .08

SECTION III: ANALYSIS OF EXPLANATIONS

Set I.

1. C

This statement is not inconsistent, nor is it an explanation, but it is deducible from the fact that North High School was well on its way to the league title.

2. D

This statement is neither inconsistent with nor deducible from the fact situation, nor does it explain the result, but it does support or weaken a possible explanation.

3. A

North High School "defeated" Madison, so this statement is inconsistent.

4. E

There is nothing in the fact situation or result which either supports, weakens, or contradicts this statement; it is therefore irrelevant to any explanation.

5. D

This statement is neither inconsistent with nor deducible from the fact situation, nor does it explain the result, but it does support or weaken a possible explanation.

6. E

There is nothing in the fact situation or result which either supports, weakens, or contradicts this statement; therefore irrelevant (and ridiculous) to any explanation.

7. D

This statement is neither inconsistent with nor deducible from the fact situation, nor does it explain the result, but it does support a possible explanation, namely that North High School sent in an ineligible "star" player to strengthen their team.

8. A

All of Madison's games had been close.

9. B

This statement is not inconsistent, and does suggest the explanation that North's team spirit and playing ability were affected by their fans' enthusiasm.

10. B

This statement is not inconsistent and does suggest the explanation that Madison lost the game because it lost its best players.

Set II.

11. C

The statement is not inconsistent, nor does it directly explain the result, but it is deducible from the fact that the clerk pressed the alarm, followed instructions, and didn't panic.

12. D

This statement is neither inconsistent with nor deducible from the fact situation, nor does it directly explain the result, but it does support or weaken a possible explanation. Either the police arrived late but still caught the fleeing robbers minutes later [supports] or they arrived late and missed the robbers altogether [weakens].

13. A

This statement is inconsistent with the fact situation.

14. D

This statement is neither inconsistent with nor deducible from the fact situation, nor does it explain the result, but it does support the explanation that the police caught the robbers after hearing the alarm.

15. B

The statement is not inconsistent, and does provide an adequate explanation.

16. D

The statement is neither inconsistent with nor deducible from the fact situation, nor does it explain the result, but it does *weaken* an explanation of the resultant capture.

17. E

There is nothing in the fact situation or result which either supports, weakens, or contradicts this statement, and since no shots were fired it is irrelevant to any explanation.

18. E

There is nothing in the fact situation which either supports, weakens, or contradicts this statement; the amount of money is irrelevant to any explanation of the result.

19. A

The getaway driver was a former prison inmate.

20. B

This statement is not inconsistent, and does provide a possible explanation for the capture.

Set III.

21. A

Mrs. Jones refused to call the doctor, so this statement is inconsistent.

22. B

This statement is not inconsistent, and does explain Mr. Jones' attendance at the game.

23. C

This statement is not inconsistent, nor does it alone explain the result, but it is *deducible* from the result—that although Jones *tried* to sell the tickets, he didn't.

24. E

There is nothing in the fact situation or result which either supports, weakens, or contradicts this statement. The gender of the baby is plainly irrelevant to any explanation.

25. D

The statement is neither inconsistent with nor deducible from the fact situation, nor does it explain the result, but it does *support* the explanation that Jones was stuck with the tickets and decided to go.

26. E

There is nothing in the fact situation or result which either supports, weakens, or contradicts this statement; therefore the statement is irrelevant.

27. B

This statement is not inconsistent, and although improbable, is a possible explanation.

28. C

This statement is not inconsistent, nor does it alone explain the result, but it is deducible from the result.

29. **D**

The statement is neither inconsistent with nor deducible from the fact situation, nor does it explain the result, but it does *weaken* an explanation of why Jones would leave his wife to attend the game.

30. **E**

There is nothing in the fact situation or result which either supports, weakens, or contradicts this statement; therefore it is irrelevant.

Set IV.

31. **B**

The statement is not inconsistent, and is a possible explanation of the result.

32. **A**

Mr. Jamerson *did* directly confront Figby's accusations.

33. **D**

The statement is neither inconsistent with nor deducible from the fact situation, nor does it directly explain the result, but it does support the explanation that a three-way split vote tilted the election in Jamerson's favor.

34. **D**

The statement is neither inconsistent with nor deducible from the fact situation, nor does it directly explain the result, but it does support the explanation that the voters preferred a man with experience.

35. **B**

This statement is not inconsistent, and is a possible explanation of the result.

36. **C**

The statement is not inconsistent, nor does it alone explain the result, but it is deducible from Jamerson's presentation of his voting record during the campaign.

37. **A**

Figby emphasized Jamerson's weaknesses rather than his own strengths.

38. E

There is nothing in the fact situation or result which either supports, weakens, or contradicts this statement; therefore it is irrelevant.

39. B

This statement is not inconsistent, and is a clearly possible explanation.

40. E

There is nothing in the fact situation or result which either supports, weakens, or contradicts this statement; therefore it is irrelevant.

SECTION IV: ANALYTICAL ABILITY

Logical Diagrams

1. C

Friends and enemies have no members in common, but adults can have different members in common with both.

2. A

Rake and hoe have no members in common, but are both within the greater set of gardening tools.

3. B

Anchorage is in Alaska, and Alaska is in the United States.

4. D

Books and Holy scriptures have some members in common. The Bible is one of these members.

5. E

Wheat farmers and young farmers have members in common, and are both within the greater set of farmers.

6. B

State colleges are kinds of colleges, and colleges are kinds of schools.

7. A

Odd numbers and even numbers have no members in common, but are both within the set of counting numbers.

8. D

Coin and currency have no members in common, but are both within the greater set, money.

9. A

All of these sets have no members in common.

10. C

Color television is within the set of television, and radio is unrelated.

11. C

Strawberries are within the set of red fruit, and bananas are unrelated.

12. B

Sewing teachers are kinds of teachers, and teachers are kinds of educators.

13. A

Agrarian, manufacturing, and mercantile are three distinct categories with no members in common.

14. D

Imprisonment and banishment have no members in common, but are both forms of civil punishment.

15. C

Cobra is within the set of snakes, and squirrel is unrelated.

Questions 16–21 refer to statements that can be used to make a chart, as follows:

	A	B	C	D
Bob	X	O	X	X
Sue	O	X	X	X
Lisa	X	X	X	O
Frank	X	X	O	X

Keep in mind that the chart can be completed before starting the questions, or you may fill it in question by question.

This chart can be filled in by eliminating what grade each student could *not* get:

1. Since "Bob will get a better grade than Frank" (statement 4), and all four students received different passing grades, then Bob cannot get a D and Frank cannot get an A.

2. "If Lisa gets an A, then Frank gets a B" (7) is not possible, because Bob has to get a better grade than Frank, and if Frank gets a B, the only better grade is an A, which would be given to Lisa. Therefore Lisa cannot get an A and Frank cannot get a B.

3. "If Lisa gets a C, then Bob will get a D" (2) tells you that Lisa cannot get a C, because Bob cannot get a D.

4. "If Lisa gets a B, then Frank won't get a D" (6) is not possible because Frank would have to get a C and Bob would have to get an A. This contradicts statement (5). Therefore, Lisa got a D.

5. From statement (5), Sue must have gotten the A, as Bob cannot get a C because Lisa got a D. (Remember Bob has got to get a better grade than Frank.)

6. This chart leaves Bob getting the B and Frank getting the C.

16. D   Lisa got a C and Bob got an A.
By inspecting the chart, or by reading statement (3), you see that "If Lisa gets a C, then Bob will get a D."

17. B   Sue.
This question is best answered by using the chart.

18. B   Sue, Bob, Frank.
This is shown by the chart; since Lisa got the D, then Sue, Bob, and Frank didn't.

19. C   (1), (4), & (7).
According to (1), all four students got different passing grades. (4) says that Bob will get a better grade than Frank. (7) says that if Lisa gets an A, then Frank gets a B. But if Frank gets a B, then Bob must get an A.

20. D   (8).
If Sue doesn't get a B, neither will Frank. It can be established without this statement that Frank cannot get a B.

21. A   a boy and a girl.
This is shown by the chart.

22. E   II & III—schools and teachers.
These two are not mentioned in the argument.

23. D   I & III.
The student's attitudes are of major importance in learning; and this trend will be difficult to change. The argument notes that aptitude test scores are declining because of the student's attitudes. The wording of "not only" and "but also" . . . "must be" deliberately communicates the idea that this trend will be difficult to change.

24. C   I, II, III.
Pointing out that aptitude tests are biased, that basic skills are not emphasized at most schools, and that graduation requirements are lax, all weaken the argument.

Questions 25–30 refer to statements that can be used to complete the following chart, although the chart is not necessary for questions 25 and 26.

	English	French	German	Italian
Steve	X	X	O	O
Robert	X	O	X	O
Bill	O	X	X	O
Karl	O	O	X	X

This chart can be filled: with given information, by deduction, and by elimination. Since Karl spoke English and French (10), he cannot speak any other languages. Steve could not speak English or French because statement (7) tells you that Steve and Karl need an interpreter and Karl speaks English and French. Robert couldn't speak English, but had to be able to speak a common language with Steve and Karl (7), therefore Robert spoke French with Karl. Since Robert spoke French, he couldn't speak German because statement (6) says that nobody spoke both French and German; therefore, Robert could also speak Italian. Steve spoke German, and therefore could not speak French (6), but could converse with Bill, who couldn't speak German (8).

By looking at the partially completed chart, it is evident that Italian must be the language common to all, because statement (9) says Robert, Karl, and Bill could not all converse in the same language and one language is common to three (5). This eliminates the possibility of Bill's speaking French; therefore he must speak English and Italian.

Partially completed chart:

	English	French	German	Italian
Steve	X	X	O	O
Robert	X	O	X	O
Bill			X	
Karl	O	O	X	X

25. **D** II & III.
"Nobody spoke both French and English" is false because Karl spoke English and French (10). "Everybody spoke English" contradicts statement (4); there was no language common to all. "Nobody spoke both French and German" is statement (6).

26. C (6) & (8).

"Nobody spoke both French and German" and "Steve spoke German, and could also talk to Bill, who couldn't speak German." Therefore Steve and Bill could not converse in French.

27. C I & III.

From the chart, at least one language was common to two men and Steve could not converse with anyone in German because he was the only one who spoke German.

28. B Italian.

The chart reveals this.

29. A English.

The chart shows that Karl and Bill spoke English.

30. D I & III.

Karl and Robert spoke French.

SECTION V: MATH ABILITY

1. D $\dfrac{rs}{r+s}$

Formula: $\dfrac{\text{Time worked}}{\text{Time required}}$ = Part of job done

Let x = number of days needed when A and B work together.

Then $\dfrac{x}{r}$ (part of job completed by A when working with B) + $\dfrac{x}{s}$ (part of job completed by B when working with A) = 1 (the complete job). Then $sx + rx = rs$; $x(s + r) = rs$; $x = \dfrac{rs}{r+s}$

2. D $10y + x$

Let us assume that the number is 53. Then 5 is the tens digit (y) and 3 is the units digit (x).

$53 = 10(5) + (3) = 53$.

3. B $90

Formula: Selling price = Cost + Profit

Let x = selling price; therefore, $.20x$ = profit.

By substitution, $x = \$72 + .20x$ or $x - .20x = \$72$ or $80x = \$7,200$ or $x = \$90$

4. B 14 ounces

Let x = amount of water to be added. Then $13 : 18 = 10 : x$ or $13x = 180$ or $x = 13.8$ ounces or 14 ounces

5. **A** $33\frac{1}{3}\%$

Explanatory note: The quantity of solution $\times$ the percentage of solution yields the quantity in solution.

Therefore, 5 qts. $\times$ 60% = 3 qts. acid. Since 1 gallon of water or 4 quarts is added, the total quantity of solution is 9 qts., with 3 qts. of acid included. Using the formula,

$$\frac{\text{quantity of acid}}{\text{quantity of solution}} \times 100 = \text{percent of acid},\ \frac{3}{9} \times 100 = 33\frac{1}{3}\%$$

6. **C**

7. **D**   right

$2x + (3x - 10°) + (3x + 30°) = 180°$ or $8x + 20° = 180°$ or $x = 20°$.

Angle $2x = 40°$; angle $3x - 10° = 50°$; and angle $3x + 30° = 90°$.

Since the triangle contains a right angle, it must be a right triangle.

8. **B**   similarity

The triangles are similar since each angle of each triangle is equal to $60°$ ($a.a.a. = a.a.a.$).

9. **E**   48

In isosceles triangle ABC, draw altitude BD; now AD = DC = 8 (since the altitude of an isosceles triangle is also the median).

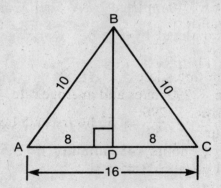

Let $x = BD$; then $(AB)^2 = (AD)^2 + (BD)^2$ (right triangle). By substitution, $10^2 = 8^2 + x^2$ or $x^2 = 36$, $x = 6$.

Since the area of a triangle $= \frac{1}{2}$ base $\times$ altitude, we have $\frac{1}{2} \times 16 \times 6 = 48$, which is the area of the triangle.

10.   C   9 sq. ft.

The largest number of circles that can be cut along the length of the rectangular piece of tin is 5, and the largest number of circles that can be cut along the width is 2, since the diameter of the given circle is 2 feet. Therefore, the maximum number of circles that can be cut is 10 (5 × 2).

To find the area of the tin that will be left, we must find the area of the rectangle and the area of the 10 circles. Then subtract the area of the 10 circles from the area of the rectangle. Or, briefly stated, area of tin = area of rectangle − area of 10 circles.

Formula: Area of circle = πr^2. By substitution, area of each circle = $\frac{22}{7} \times 1 \times 1 = 3.14$ sq. ft. The area of all 10 circles = 31.4 sq. ft.

Formula: Area of rectangle = base × altitude. By substitution, $10 \times 4 = 40$ sq. ft. (area of rectangle).

∴ 40 sq. ft. − 31.4 sq. ft. = 8.6 sq. ft. or 9 sq. ft. (area of tin left to the nearest sq. ft.)

11.   D   15

Given $d = 90$ and the formula $d = \dfrac{n^2 - 3n}{2}$

∴ $90 = \dfrac{n^2 - 3n}{2}$

$180 = n^2 - 3n$

or $n^2 - 3n - 180 = 0$

or $(n + 12)(n - 15) = 0$

$n = -12$ (invalid),

$n = 15$

12.   D   about 13 minutes late

Given distance = 290 miles and average rate = 50 miles per hour

Time = $\dfrac{\text{Distance}}{\text{Rate}} = \dfrac{290}{50} = 5\frac{4}{5}$ hours or 5 hours, 48 minutes

10:10 A.M. + 5 hours, 48 minutes = 3:58 P.M. Scheduled time of arrival given as 3:45 P.M.

∴ 13 minutes late

13.   D   27

Let x = side of first box and $3x$ = side of second box.

Volume of a cube = x^3; therefore, $(3x)^3$ or $27x^3$ = volume of second box.

14. B 375,000

$$\text{Ratio} = \frac{\text{Number}}{\text{Population}}$$

Given: Number = 48,000 and Ratio = $\frac{12.8}{100}$

$$\therefore \frac{12.8}{100} = \frac{48,000}{x}$$

or $12.8x = 48,000 \times 100$

$x = 375,000$

15. E Austria

By inspection, Austria received no military aid.

16. E 26 billion dollars

By approximating and totaling the shaded bars representing Europe:

Aus.	1
Bel.	1
Neth.	1
Yugosl.	1
Greece	2
Turkey	1
W. Ger.	3
Italy	3
U.K.	7
France	5
Total	25 billion, or about 26 billion

17. A 9 billion dollars

By approximating and totaling the unshaded bars representing non-European nations:

Brazil + Iran + Philippines	= $1\frac{1}{2}$
Vietnam + Japan	= 2
Korea	= $1\frac{1}{2}$
China-Taiwan	= 3

Total 8, or about 9 billion

18. **B** 20 billion dollars
Total assistance to European countries about 40 billion dollars.
Total assistance to non-European countries about 21 billion dollars.
The difference is 19, or about 20 billion dollars.

19. **C** 16 billion dollars
Total economic and technical assistance is about 39 billion dollars.
Total military assistance is about 23 billion dollars.
The difference is about 16 billion dollars.

20. **C** China-Taiwan and Italy
By inspection and addition, China-Taiwan and Italy received over 5 billion dollars, which is more than any of the other pairs.

21. **C** $\dfrac{5}{\sqrt{5}}$

By approximating and simple inspection:

$$\text{(A)} \quad \frac{\sqrt{5}}{5} = \frac{2.3}{5}$$

$$\text{(B)} \quad \frac{\sqrt{5}}{2\sqrt{5}} = \frac{2.3}{4.6} \text{ or } \frac{1}{2}$$

$$\text{(C)} \quad \frac{5}{\sqrt{5}} = \frac{5}{2.3}$$

$$\text{(D)} \quad \frac{5}{2\sqrt{5}} = \frac{5}{4.6}$$

$$\text{(E)} \quad \frac{2\sqrt{5}}{5} = \frac{4.6}{5}$$

$\dfrac{5}{2.3}$ is obviously the greatest.

22. C   5 miles

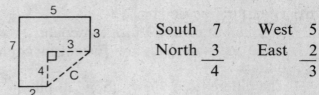

South	7	West	5
North	3	East	2
	4		3

Using the above diagram, subtracting to get the sides of the triangle, and remembering that all angles in the diagram are right angles, the Pythagorean Theorem will give the required distance.

$$a^2 + b^2 = c^2$$
$$3^2 + 4^2 = c^2$$
$$9 + 16 = c^2$$
$$25 = c^2$$
$$5 = c$$

Alternate method:
If you noticed that the sides of the triangle were 3 and 4, then the hypotenuse is 5 by the well-known 3:4:5 ratio of right triangles.

23. C $ac = b$

If $a = \dfrac{b}{c}$, then multiply both sides by c:

$$a \times c = \frac{b}{c} \times c$$

Canceling leaves $ac = b$.

24. E   4 hotdogs

Let h stand for hotdogs and f stand for fries; then $3h + 2f = 2h + 4f$
Solving for h

$$
\begin{array}{ccc}
3h + 2f = & & 2h + 4f \\
-2h - 2f & & -2h - 2f \\
\hline
1h & = & 2f
\end{array}
$$

Since $h = 2f$, and John can buy 3 hotdogs and 2 orders of fries, substituting 1 hotdog for the 2 fries gives a total of 4 hotdogs.

25. D $b - d + f$

To find the total you must add the football and baseball players, $b + f$, and subtract the both, d, since they have been counted twice. This leaves $b + f - d$, rearranged to $b - d + f$.

PRACTICE TEST III

Tear out Answer Sheet for Practice Test III, pages xv and xvi

SECTION I: VERBAL ABILITY

TIME—50 MINUTES
80 QUESTIONS

Directions: Each question in this test consists of a sentence in which one
or two words are missing. Beneath the sentence are five words or
word sets. Choose the word or word set that *best* completes the
sentence. Then mark the appropriate space in the answer column.

---

1. If oxygen were lacking, plants would die because oxygen
    _____ plant life.
    (A)   is dependent upon
    (B)   derives from
    (C)   is a by-product of
    (D)   is concerned with
    (E)   is basic to

2. One of the deleterious effects of failing to permit children to exer-
    cise _____ is the danger that they may remain so
    immature that they fail to successfully _____ school,
    home, and community.
    (A)   belligerence—overcome
    (B)   self-judgment—adjust to
    (C)   discipline—adjust to
    (D)   initiative—depreciate
    (E)   freedom of action—re-make

3. Many citizens objected vigorously to the _____ of
    the county offices, which, for the most part, could not be reached
    without traveling considerable distances.
    (A)   inaccessibility
    (B)   lack
    (C)   inefficiency
    (D)   corruption
    (E)   layout

4. After _____ has been removed, the _____
    is that which is left.
    (A)   one—residuum
    (B)   the interest—dividend
    (C)   the stain—evidence
    (D)   juice—fruit
    (E)   the obstruction—drawbridge

5. When the democratic principle shall have become firmly established in all nations, then we shall witness the _____ of prejudice, intolerance, and _____.
- (A) culmination—bigotry
- (B) nationalization—animosity
- (C) denunciation—crime
- (D) cessation—bigotry
- (E) condemnation—license

6. Since there was inadequate grazing area for the herds, the land was _____ populated.
- (A) inadequately
- (B) sparsely
- (C) rustically
- (D) unconditionally
- (E) disproportionately

7. The rights of citizens include the following: the right to life, liberty, the pursuit of happiness, and the free exercise of worship. _____ in these rights is the _____ to preserve and defend them to the best of their ability.
- (A) Extraneous—duty
- (B) Implicit—responsibility
- (C) Obligatory—opportunity
- (D) Precluded—principle
- (E) Inherent—privilege

8. International law _____ that a country _____ diplomatic representatives of countries with whom it maintains friendly relations.
- (A) suggests—emulate
- (B) states—scrutinize
- (C) includes—spurn
- (D) mandates—accredit
- (E) requires—welcome

9. One of the mistakes in our educational jargon is the common fault of stressing the interests of _____ and eliding over the interests of the _____.
- (A) the commonwealth—republic
- (B) the girls—boys
- (C) the aristocracy—oligarchy
- (D) society—individual
- (E) the community—state

10. The writers of mystery fiction who turn out several books a year may be considered _____.

(A) prolific

(B) stupendous

(C) artistic

(D) meticulous

(E) ambitious

Directions: In each of the following questions select the lettered pair which best expresses a relationship similar to that expressed in the original pair.

---

11.   TEPID : TORRID : :

(A)   turgid : horrid

(B)   pool : placid

(C)   cool : frigid

(D)   tumid : turbid

(E)   livid : lurid

12.   ALPHA : OMEGA : :

(A)   coda : prelude

(B)   prologue : epilogue

(C)   elephant : tail

(D)   plot : denouement

(E)   glossary : appendix

13.   CHRONOMETER : CALENDAR : :

(A)   pedometer : hydrometer

(B)   beat : measure

(C)   daylight saving : standard time

(D)   sun-dial : candle power

(E)   chronicle : anachronism

14.   MILLENNIUM : CENTURY : :

(A)   year : month

(B)   hour : minute

(C)   month : day

(D)   decade : year

(E)   minute : second

15. MERIDIAN : SETTING ::
    (A) start : finish
    (B) baptism : birth
    (C) pinnacle : climax
    (D) culminate : terminate
    (E) maturity : homestretch

16. HARBINGER : SPRING ::
    (A) fight : might
    (B) tail : comet
    (C) telegram : event
    (D) spring : winter
    (E) dawn : day

17. ART : CUBISM ::
    (A) scenery : play
    (B) setting : ring
    (C) mustache : face
    (D) poem : epic
    (E) drape : window

18. LITERAL : FREE ::
    (A) intrinsic : extrinsic
    (B) translate : paraphrase
    (C) communicate : express
    (D) simile : metaphor
    (E) news : hearsay

19. CITADEL : VAULT ::
    (A) virtue : disgrace
    (B) prop : cornice
    (C) building : foundation
    (D) head : foot
    (E) tower : dungeon

20. EXPOSITION : PRECIS ::
    (A) genuine : synthetic
    (B) volume : booklet
    (C) tome : epitaph
    (D) obese : slender
    (E) synopsis : compendium

Directions: Each question in this test consists of a word printed in capital letters followed by five words lettered (A) through (E). Choose the word that has most nearly the OPPOSITE meaning from the word in capital letters. Mark the appropriate space in the answer column. Consider all choices before deciding which one is best, since some choices are very close in meaning.

21. DISQUIETUDE
    (A) purity
    (B) fear
    (C) fortitude
    (D) ribaldry
    (E) field

22. HEINOUS
    (A) awful
    (B) apt
    (C) silly
    (D) creditable
    (E) venal

23. HERCULEAN
    (A) ponderous
    (B) deistic
    (C) big
    (D) puny
    (E) indecent

24. DAWDLE
    (A) hasten
    (B) sketch
    (C) parade
    (D) avoid
    (E) loiter

25. THRALLDOM
    (A) plebian
    (B) independence
    (C) prescience
    (D) allegiance
    (E) holding

26. INTEGRAL
    (A) shy
    (B) profane
    (C) fragmentary
    (D) lofty
    (E) wordy

27. MARTIAL
    (A) bachelor
    (B) thief
    (C) peaceful
    (D) solar
    (E) loud

28. LURE
    (A) refuse
    (B) repel
    (C) curb
    (D) decoy
    (E) misconstrue

29. MUNIFICENT
    (A) rare
    (B) cringing
    (C) unworldly
    (D) rich
    (E) stingy

30. PROFFER
    (A) return
    (B) tender
    (C) renege
    (D) spurn
    (E) cajole

31. ENTICE
    (A) frighten
    (B) disperse
    (C) exit
    (D) expunge
    (E) enjoy

Directions: Each passage is followed by a group of questions. Read each passage and choose the *best* answer to each question. Then mark the appropriate space in the answer column. Answers should be chosen on the basis of what is stated and implied.

According to Professor K's analysis, the next step to be negotiated among the states in order to eliminate war is the compulsory submission to international adjudication of all disputes between states. In this connection he asserts that courts of arbitration historically preceded legislatures in primitive society, that there is no substantial distinction between legal and political questions, and that international law, which has been said to cover only a small part of international relations, really covers the entire field, by permitting the states to regulate much of it municipally.

It would be splendid if the states were willing to subscribe to treaties agreeing to submit all their disputes to arbitration. But even though great advances have been made in persuading nations to submit disputes to judicial determination, governments have always made an exception of matters which they deemed of major importance. Because the first "courts" in primitive society may have had only the power to arbitrate, there is not much justification for the assumption that compulsory jurisdiction will develop out of voluntary arbitration, or that international legislative and executive bodies are probable later stages of organizational evolution. It is moreover doubted whether all conflicts originate in specific disputes, though they may originate in resentments, or in conflicting positions, policies and attitudes. Resentments over defeat or disadvantage in the competitive struggle may have to be borne municipally without effective complaint, but internationally the world is not so organized. There, resentments may find expression in diplomacy and forceful action, whether the cause be "legal" or not.

While Professor K is correct in maintaining that the distinction between legal and political questions, as an obstacle to or limitation on adjudication, is theoretically unsustainable or subjective only, since all questions between states are political and any question can be made "legal" by submitting it to judicial determination, the distinction representing a difference between willingness and unwillingness to submit. there is nevertheless much practical justification for the distinction. Had it not been for the endeavor of the nations in the first Hague Conference to segregate questions inherently susceptible of adjudication by the application of well-known principles of law from those more commonly regarded as falling within the sphere of political interests not based on law, we might not have had the submission of any but trifling issues. That the distinction serves a practical purpose may be inferred from the numerous treaties of arbitration concluded in the 20th century, and from Article 36 of the Statute of the Permanent Court of International Justice which, by naming certain types of "legal" issues over which compulsory jurisdiction might be exercised in cases involving those nations accepting the Optional Clause, gave a special inducement to numerous nations, even under reservations, to subscribe to Article 36. The fact that a court can have no independent existence, but must rest upon the willingness of states to maintain it, is indicated by resent history. For that reason, excessive demands must not be made upon it; to invoke it for the decision of a question more "political" than "legal" might do the court and the judicial process great injury. Then there are many matters of international import which the prevailing *mores,* in spite of analytical jurisprudence, actually consider as domestic. Would the United States submit to international arbitration such questions as how much subsidy shall be granted to American shipowners, and how high the tariff shall be on specified goods?

But Professor K's principal tenet rests on the theory that international law controls or governs not some, but all relations, between states. The provisions of the Covenant, Article 15, Section 8, and of the General Act of 1928, which refers to "questions which by international law are solely within the domestic jurisdiction of States," are said to be of doubtful validity since all questions are within the jurisdiction of international law. Why is that, since it is well known that commercial or immigration policy is a matter for states to decide, except as they might agree to international regulation? Because when "by international law" a matter is "left" to the domestic jurisdiction or not governed by any known rule of law, it is said that international law has "permitted" the state to regulate the matter as it chooses and has refrained from regulating the matter itself. Thus, "what is not forbidden is permitted." Hence what is not regulated is really regulated, by "providing" that international law will have nothing to do with the matter; and if it is to be regulated at all, this must be done by states municipally. Thus it is, so runs the argument, that international law is all-pervasive.

This will satisfy the monists, and the Hohfeldians have no difficulty in understanding what they say, but it is a matter of historical fact that states were known before international law had developed, even to its present primitive estate. Its very subjects, states, limit its scope. By custom and treaty the domain of international law was gradually extended, though often honored in the breach. It is thus a delegated body of law, covering only a limited number of topics and relations; powers not delegated have necessarily been reserved.

32. Apparently Professor K's primary object is to
    (A) distinguish between legal and political questions.
    (B) trace the development of international courts of arbitration.
    (C) eliminate the distinction between legal and political questions.
    (D) define the limits of international law.
    (E) eliminate war through compulsory international adjudication.

33. The writer believes that at the present time we must accept a system of international law which
   - (A) is completely divorced from any means of compulsion whatsoever.
   - (B) strengthens national sovereignty as opposed to international authority.
   - (C) has power to adjudicate all disputes of major importance.
   - (D) does not have the power to solve all problems which might lead to war.
   - (E) includes provision for those conflicts which do not arise from specific disputes.

34. The author believes that
   - (A) Professor K's assumptions based on historical precedent are valid.
   - (B) disadvantages ought not to be borne, municipally, without complaint.
   - (C) world peace is an impossible objective.
   - (D) at the present time the treatment of municipal problems is not really analogous to the treatment of international ones.
   - (E) a series of treaties binding nations to abide by decisions of an arbitrative court will secure world peace.

35. The writer implies that war could be eliminated if it were possible to
   - (A) make a practicable distinction between legal and political disputes, and have all legal disputes submitted to adjudication.
   - (B) eradicate the distinction between legal and political disputes.
   - (C) clearly delimit national from international problems.
   - (D) avoid making excessive demands of our international legal machinery.
   - (E) organize and govern the world like a municipality.

36. It is taken as axiomatic, by both Professor K and the author, that
   - (A) international law covers the entire field of international relationships.
   - (B) a court can exist only if the municipality is willing to maintain it.
   - (C) all international problems are political.
   - (D) there is justification for the distinction between political and legal disputes.
   - (E) power delegated is not necessarily power reserved.

37. The writer of the article believes that compulsory international adjudication of disputes

(A)   would create rather than reduce international friction.

(B)   will not eliminate the possibility of war, even if it is agreed to by all nations.

(C)   is a goal which will probably be achieved through gradual evolution of international law.

(D)   would be practical if all disputes between nations were considered "legal."

(E)   has been shown to be impractical by the experience of the Hague Conference.

38. The first Hague Conference

(A)   created some valuable new conceptions of international law.

(B)   reduced the scope of international law to a minimum.

(C)   organized a system of adjudication on a basis which was unlikely to be challenged by the member nations.

(D)   attempted to extend the scope of international law.

(E)   apparently did not believe that trouble could arise from purely political problems.

39. In Professor K's opinion, the size of subsidies granted to United States shipowners by the United States Government

(A)   should be regulated by the world court.

(B)   is more of a "political" question than a "legal" one.

(C)   should be submitted voluntarily for international adjudication.

(D)   may be regulated by the United States Government independent of international jurisdiction.

(E)   may be set by the U.S. Government, but only by delegated authority.

40. The author maintains that international law

(A)   makes the mistake of delegating powers without reservation.

(B)   is delimited by the sources of its authority.

(C)   in primitive society antedates nationalism.

(D)   can survive only with the voluntary submission of all states.

(E)   should apply itself to all political disputes between nations, as well as to political-legal disputes.

41. The writer and Professor K would NOT both agree that

(A)   there are some questions of international import which fall entirely outside the jurisdiction of international law.

(B)   there is no theoretical line demarcating "legal" from "political" questions.

(C)   the term "political question" is apt to be applied to a question of international import which nations are unwilling to submit to an international court.

(D)   international law, as it now stands, can be improved.

(E)   there are many matters of international import which are now considered to be domestic problems.

1   In the 17th century the religious orders and especially the
2 Jesuits absorbed even more of the activities and counted for more in
3 the public affairs of Portugal than in the preceding age. The pulpit
4 discharged some of the functions of the modern press, and men who
5 combined the gifts of oratory and writing filled it and distinguished
6 themselves, their order, and their country. The Jesuit Antonio
7 Vieira, missionary, diplomat, and voluminous writer, repeated the
8 triumphs he had gained in Bahia and Lisbon in Rome, which pro-
9 claimed him the prince of Catholic orators. His 200 sermons are a
10 mine of learning and experience, and they stand out from all others
11 by their imaginative power, originality of view, variety of treatment,
12 and audacity of expression. His letters are in a simple conversational
13 style, but they lack the popular locutions, humor, and individuality
14 of those of Mello. Vieira was a man of action, while the oratorian
15 Manoel Bernardes lived as a recluse, hence his sermons and devo-
16 tional works, especially *Luz e Calor* and the *Nova Floresta* breathe
17 a calm and sweetness alien to the other, while they are even richer
18 treasures of pure Portuguese. Perhaps the truest and most feeling
19 human documents of the century are the five epistles written by
20 Marianna Alcoforado, known to history as the *Letters of a Portu-
21 guese Nun*. Padre Ferreira de Almeida's translation of the Bible has
22 considerable linguistic importance, and philological studies had an
23 able exponent in Amaro de Roboredo.

42. Which of these is the best title for the paragraph?

(A)   Antonio Vieira

(B)   The Literature of Portugal in the 17th century

(C)   The Contribution of the Church to the Literature of Portugal

(D)   The Contribution of the Church to the Literature of Portugal in the 17th Century

(E)   Oratory in the 17th Century

43. Do you think Vieira was a typical priest?
  (A) yes
  (B) no
  (C) sometimes
  (D) don't know
  (E) probably

44. What evidence is given in the paragraph that Portugal in the 17th century stood well in comparison with other countries in respect to oratory?
  (A) the Portuguese distinguished themselves, their order, and their country
  (B) Portugal counted for more than in the preceding age
  (C) the truest documents of the century
  (D) Vieira was proclaimed the prince of Catholic orators at Rome
  (E) the pulpit discharged some of the functions of the modern press

45. What does "locutions" (line 13) mean as used in the paragraph?
  (A) elocutions
  (B) sermons
  (C) expressions
  (D) writings
  (E) recitals

46. What does "exponent" (line 23) mean as used in the paragraph?
  (A) leader
  (B) representative
  (C) part of
  (D) writer
  (E) paragon

It is a common belief that a thing is desirable because it is scarce and thereby has ostentation value. The notion that such a standard of value is an inescapable condition of settled social existence rests on one of two implicit assumptions. The first is that the attempt to educate the human race so that the desire to display one's possessions is not a significant feature of man's social behavior, is an infringement against personal freedom. The greatest obstacle to lucid discourse in these matters is the psychological anti-vaccinationist who uses the word freedom to signify the natural right of men and women to be unhappy and unhealthy through scientific ignorance instead of being healthy and happy through the knowledge which science confers. Haunted by a perpetual fear of the dark, the last lesson which man learns in the difficult process of growing up is "ye shall know the truth, and the truth shall make you free." The professional economist who is too sophisticated to retreat into the obscurities of this curious conception of liberty may prefer to adopt the second assumption, that the truth does not and cannot make us free because the need for ostentation is a universal species characteristic, and all attempts to eradicate the unconscionable nuisance and discord which arise from overdeveloped craving for personal distinction artificially fostered by advertisement, propaganda and so-called good breeding are therefore destined to failure. It may be earnestly hoped that those who entertain this view have divine guidance. No rational basis for it will be found in textbooks of economics. Whatever can be said with any plausibility in the existing state of knowledge rests on the laboratory materials supplied by anthropology and social history.

47. According to the writer, the second assumption
    (A) is fostered by propaganda and so-called good breeding.
    (B) is basically opposite to the view of the psychological anti-vaccinationist.
    (C) is not so curious a conception of liberty as is the first assumption.
    (D) is unsubstantiated.
    (E) is a religious explanation of an economic phenomenon.

48. The author's purpose in writing this paragraph is most probably to
    (A) denounce the psychological anti-vaccinationists.
    (B) demonstrate that the question under discussion is an economic rather than a psychological problem.
    (C) prove the maxim "ye shall know the truth, and the truth shall make you free."
    (D) prove that ostentation is not an inescapable phenomenon of settled social existence.
    (E) prove the inability of economics to account for ostentation.

49. In his reference to divine guidance, the writer is
    (A) being ironic.
    (B) implying that only divine guidance can solve the problem.
    (C) showing how the professional economist is opposing divine laws.
    (D) referring to opposition which exists between religion and science.
    (E) indicating that the problem is not a matter for divine guidance.

50. The writer believes that personal freedom
- (A)   is less important than is scientific knowledge.
- (B)   is a requisite for the attainment of truth.
- (C)   is attained by eradicating false beliefs.
- (D)   is no concern of the professional economist.
- (E)   is an unsophisticated concept.

51. The writer would consider as most comparable to the effect of a vaccination on the body, the effect of
- (A)   fear upon personality.
- (B)   science upon the supposed need for ostentation.
- (C)   truth upon the mind.
- (D)   knowledge upon ignorance.
- (E)   knowledge upon happiness.

In the terminology of the Domesday Inquest we find the villeins as the most numerous elements of the English population. Out of about 240,000 households enumerated in Domesday, 100,000 are marked as belonging to villeins. They are rustics performing, as a rule, work services for their lords. But not all the inhabitants of the villages were designated by that name. Villeins are opposed to socmen and freemen on one hand, to *bordarii,* cottagers, and slaves on the other. The distinction in regard to the first two of these groups was evidently derived from their greater freedom, although the difference is only one in degree and not in kind. In fact, the villein is assumed to be a person free by birth, but holding land of which he can not dispose freely. The distinction as against *bordarii* and cottagers is based on the size of the holding: the villeins are holders of regular shares in the village—that is, of the virgates, bovates, or half-hides which constitute the principal subdivisions in the fields and contribute to form the plough-teams—whereas the *bordarii* hold smaller plots of some five acres, more or less, and *cottarii* are connected with mere cottages and crofts. Thus the terminology of Domesday takes note of two kinds of differences in the status given to rustics: a legal one in connection with the right to dispose of property in land, and an economic one reflecting the opposition between the holders of shares in the fields and the holders of auxiliary tenements. The feature of personal serfdom is also noticeable, but it provides a basis only for the comparatively small group of *servi,* of whom only about 25,000 are enumerated in Domesday Book. The contrast between this exceptionally situated class and the rest of the population shows that personal slavery was rapidly disappearing in England about the time of the Conquest. It is also to be noticed that the Domesday Survey constantly mentions the *terra villanorum* as opposed to the demesne of the estates or manors of the time, and that the land of the rustics is taxed separately for the gold, so that distinction between the property of the lord and that of the peasant dependent on him is clearly marked and is by no means devoid of practical importance.

52. What would you choose as the best title for this paragraph?
    (A)   Serfdom in England
    (B)   The Domesday Inquest
    (C)   The Status of the Villein at the Time of the Norman Conquest
    (D)   Socman, Freeman, and Villein
    (E)   none of these

53. Were the villeins personal serfs?
    (A)   yes
    (B)   no
    (C)   sometimes
    (D)   never
    (E)   cannot tell from the passage

54. What is the largest measure of land mentioned in the paragraph?
    (A)   bovate
    (B)   half-hide
    (C)   five acres
    (D)   ploughteam
    (E)   virgate

55. Did a villein usually pay taxes on his land?
    (A)   yes
    (B)   no
    (C)   sometimes
    (D)   never
    (E)   cannot tell from the passage

56. Could a villein sell his land?
    (A)   yes
    (B)   no
    (C)   sometimes
    (D)   never
    (E)   cannot tell from the passage

Select the word or word set that *best* completes each of the following sentences.

57. The capable painter works in many media, including water color and _____.
  (A) sculpture
  (B) existentialism
  (C) modeling
  (D) embossing
  (E) tempera

58. To _____ means to explain in one's own words.
  (A) paraphrase
  (B) decipher
  (C) parody
  (D) translate
  (E) parabolize

59. The _____ of a person is officially called his _____.
  (A) face—countenance
  (B) speed—celerity
  (C) demeanor—regard
  (D) decease—termination
  (E) residence—domicile

60. Labor unions hold that capital is only the _____ of labor, and that its origin is subsequent to that of _____.
  (A) fruit—freedom
  (B) product—labor
  (C) machinery—labor
  (D) tool—wealth
  (E) slave—labor

61. The queen was the _____ of all eyes as she entered the room.
  (A) blight
  (B) misery
  (C) miracle
  (D) cynosure
  (E) tribulation

62. The student of human nature knows that its components are, for the most part, _____; but he is also aware that events —pleasant or unpleasant—do play a part in bringing to the fore at one time or another certain _____.
    (A) fixed—reactions
    (B) unstable—traits
    (C) immutable—characteristics
    (D) ephemeral—people
    (E) general—instincts

63. The school system hoped that the new plan would increase the _____ of its applicants by providing high salaries for beginning teachers.
    (A) discipline
    (B) number
    (C) independence
    (D) clamor
    (E) rostrum

64. The electrician put the parts of the television set together with the skill of the master craftsman for whom this was a(n) _____ occupation.
    (A) morbid
    (B) natural
    (C) peculiar
    (D) unnatural
    (E) avocational

65. At the trial, the defendant maintained a manner that could be best described as _____; but the revelations concerning his actions in the commission of the crime portrayed a personality that could only be described as _____.
    (A) sanctimonious—imperious
    (B) continent—self-possessed
    (C) suffering—emotional
    (D) impassive—impassioned
    (E) belligerent—jocose

Select the lettered pair which best expresses a relationship similar to that expressed in the original pair.

66. PHILOLOGIST : LANGUAGE : :
- (A) ornithologist : birds
- (B) botanist : animals
- (C) biologist : cells
- (D) etymologist : insects
- (E) pediatrician : feet

67. MYRIAD : SPARSE : :
- (A) many : few
- (B) plethora : innumerable
- (C) major : minor
- (D) predominant : sporadic
- (E) minority : plurality

68. DISSIPATION : DEPRAVITY : :
- (A) callowness : inexperience
- (B) repetition : monotony
- (C) attempt : achievement
- (D) familiarity : recognition
- (E) interest : boredom

69. TRIUMPH : EXULTATION : :
- (A) war : victory
- (B) emergency : desolation
- (C) calamity : distress
- (D) news : gratification
- (E) tidings : jubilation

70. WAIL : WHIMPER : :
- (A) lament : cry
- (B) chuckle : snicker
- (C) guffaw : laugh
- (D) smirk : simper
- (E) face : mouth

71. AIR : DIRIGIBLE : :
- (A) locomotive : steam
- (B) lion : tiger
- (C) wagon : horse
- (D) gasoline : taxi
- (E) water : boat

72. TRESPASS : WANDER : :
  (A) examine : glance
  (B) destroy : mar
  (C) sprawl : recline
  (D) perjure : relate
  (E) gorge : eat

73. CULMINATION : INCEPTION : :
  (A) lamb : cub
  (B) novice : fundamental
  (C) pod : seed
  (D) maturity : infancy
  (E) senility : puerility

The *opposite* of:

74. PACIFIC
  (A) tiff
  (B) quiet
  (C) Atlantic
  (D) warm
  (E) belligerent

75. PERPLEXITY
  (A) deadly
  (B) grand
  (C) pelf
  (D) acuity
  (E) certitude

76. DESICCATE
  (A) upgrade
  (B) collate
  (C) saturate
  (D) obfuscate
  (E) dry

77. FELICITOUS
  (A) effeminate
  (B) canine
  (C) sensuous
  (D) notorious
  (E) inappropriate

78. INVALUABLE
  (A) worthless
  (B) ponderable
  (C) valuable
  (D) cowardly
  (E) verifiable

79. FACILE
  (A) lazy
  (B) shallow
  (C) formidable
  (D) sound
  (E) easy

80. MANIFEST
  (A) explicit
  (B) latent
  (C) starboard
  (D) patent
  (E) unlisted

SECTION II: QUANTITATIVE COMPARISONS

TIME—50 MINUTES
55 QUESTIONS

Quantitative Comparison

(SUGGESTED TIME—20 MINUTES)
30 QUESTIONS

Directions: Each question in this section consists of two quantities, one in Column A and one in Column B. You are to compare the two quantities and on the answer sheet blacken space

    A if the quantity in Column A is the greater;
    B if the quantity in Column B is the greater;
    C if the two quantities are equal;
    D if the relationship cannot be determined from the information given.

All numbers used are real numbers.
Diagrams are not necessarily drawn to scale.

	Column A	Column B
1.	$\sqrt{.09}$	$(.09)^2$

$$y > 0$$

	Column A	Column B
2.	The average of: 3y, 5y, 3 and 5	The average of: 2y, 6y, 4 and 10

$$4 > x\text{-}y > 1$$

	Column A	Column B
3.	x	3

Questions 4–7 refer to this diagram

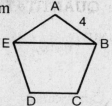

ABCDE is a regular pentagon

	Column A	Column B
4.	AB	EB
5.	Sum of interior angles of Pentagon ABCDE	$360°$
6.	$\angle$ AEB	$\angle$ ABE
7.	$\angle$ D + $\angle$ C	$180°$
8.	$\dfrac{13}{29}$	$\dfrac{14}{31}$

$$0 < y < x$$

9.	$(x + 2)(y + 3)$	$(x + 3)(y + 2)$

$$n > 1$$

10.	$(5n)^3$	$5n^3$

11.	$\dfrac{\frac{1}{3} + \frac{1}{2}}{\frac{1}{4} + \frac{1}{5}}$	2

15 is 30% of x
12 is 25% of y

12.	x	y

$$x > 0$$

13.	x^{-2}	x^{-3}

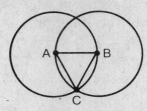

A and B are the centers of their respective circles.

Column A	Column B

14. AC | BC

$$m > 0$$

15. m^3 | $2m^2$

16. The perimeter of a square | The area of a square

$$a = 5, b = 3, c = -1$$

17. $\dfrac{a + c^2}{b}$ | $\dfrac{a^2 + c}{b^2}$

18. The percentage of increase from $400 to $500 | 20%

$$\frac{r}{3} = \frac{s}{5}$$

19. $5r$ | $3s$

Questions 20–24 refer to this diagram

Vertices of square ABCD lie on the circle.

20. $\angle$ DAC | $\angle$ BCA

21. $\overarc{AC}$ | $90°$

22. Radius of circle | $\dfrac{\sqrt{2}}{2}$

23. CD | $\overarc{AB}$

24. 2 × Area of Square ABCD | Area of circle

	Column A	**Column B**

$$x > 0 \qquad y > 0$$

25. $\sqrt{x + y}$ $\qquad\qquad\qquad$ $\sqrt{x} + \sqrt{y}$

$$x + 3y = 7$$
$$4x + 12y = 28$$

26. x $\qquad\qquad\qquad\qquad$ y

27. $\dfrac{1}{8} \times \dfrac{1}{4} \times \dfrac{1}{9}$ $\qquad\qquad$ $.125 \times .25 \times .1$

Questions 28–30 refer to this diagram

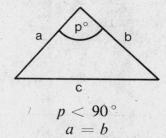

$$p < 90°$$
$$a = b$$

28. $b + c$ $\qquad\qquad\qquad\qquad$ a

29. c^2 $\qquad\qquad\qquad\qquad$ $a^2 + b^2$

30. a $\qquad\qquad\qquad\qquad$ $c - b$

Math Ability

(SUGGESTED TIME—30 MINUTES)
25 QUESTIONS

Directions: Solve each of the following problems and mark the *best* answer on your answer sheet. All scratch work should be done in the available space. All numbers used belong to the real number system. Diagrams are not necessarily drawn to scale.

---

31.   If p pencils cost c cents, n pencils at the same rate will cost

(A) $\dfrac{pc}{n}$ cents

(B) $\dfrac{cn}{p}$ cents

(C) npc cents

(D) $\dfrac{np}{c}$ cents

(E) $\dfrac{pc}{np}$ cents

32.   Find the value of a in the equation $5a - .5a = 9$.
(A)   0
(B)   2
(C)   9
(D)   4
(E)   6

33.   Of the following, the value of $\dfrac{\sqrt[3]{64.32}}{\sqrt{.041}}$ is closest to
(A)   400
(B)   200
(C)   20
(D)   16
(E)   8

34.   The difference between the area of a rectangle 6 feet by 4 feet and the area of a square having the same perimeter is
(A)   1 sq. ft.
(B)   2 sq. ft.
(C)   4 sq. ft.
(D)   6 sq. ft.
(E)   9 sq. ft.

35. If a boy has a number of dimes and quarters in his pocket adding
     up to $3.10, the largest possible number of dimes he can have is
     (A) 16
     (B) 28
     (C) 26
     (D) 21
     (E) 23

36. If x is less than 10, and y is less than 5, it follows that
     (A) x is greater than y
     (B) $x - y = 5$
     (C) $x = 2y$
     (D) $x + y$ is less than 15
     (E) none of these

37. The figure below represents a rectangle whose dimensions are
     l and w, surmounted by a semicircle whose radius is r.

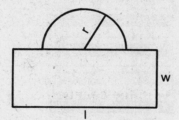

     Express the area of this figure in terms of l, w, r and π.
     (A) $wl + \dfrac{\pi r^2}{2}$
     (B) $lw + \pi r$
     (C) $lw + \pi r^2$
     (D) $\dfrac{\pi}{2} - r^2 lw$
     (E) wlr^2

38. A baseball team has won 50 games out of 75 played. It has 45
     games still to play. How many of these must the team win to
     make its record for the season 60 percent?
     (A) 20
     (B) 22
     (C) 25
     (D) 30
     (E) 32

Questions 39–43 refer to this graph.

**Employment of Production Workers
in Manufacturing**

1955 vs. 1947–1949 average

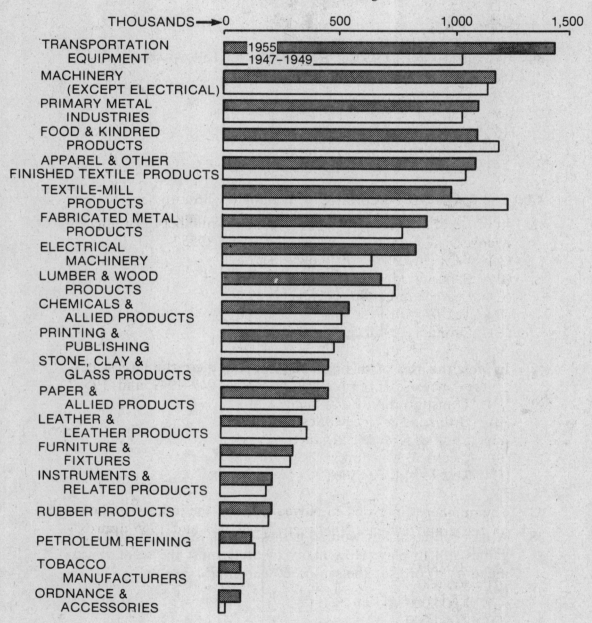

39. In how many industries did employment decline between 1947–1949 and 1955?
   (A) 2
   (B) 4
   (C) 6
   (D) 8
   (E) 10

40. Which of the following industries gained the most employees between 1947–1949 and 1955?
   (A) Textile-Mill Products
   (B) Fabricated Metal Products
   (C) Electrical Machinery
   (D) Ordnance & Accessories
   (E) Transportation Equipment

41. In which of the following industries did the number of employees decrease the most between 1947–1949 and 1955?
   (A) Fabricated Metal Products
   (B) Paper & Allied Products
   (C) Leather & Leather Products
   (D) Textile-Mill Products
   (E) Ordnance & Accessories

42. In which of the following industries was there the largest percentage increase in employees between 1947–1949 and 1955?
   (A) Transportation Equipment
   (B) Ordnance & Accessories
   (C) Food & Kindred Products
   (D) Electrical Machinery
   (E) Textile-Mill Products

43. The number of persons employed in all of the industries shown on the graph increased between 1947–1949 and 1955 approximately
   (A) 100,000
   (B) 500,000
   (C) 1,000,000
   (D) 2,000,000
   (E) 1,500,000

44. $N ! = N \times (N - 1) \times (N - 2) \ldots (2)(1)$

The value of $\dfrac{7!\,5!}{6!\,4!}$ is

(A) $\dfrac{35}{24}$

(B) 35

(C) 24

(D) 22

(E) 62

If x is positive then $|X| = X$ and $|-X| = X$

45. $|7| + |4 - 6| =$

(A) 17

(B) 5

(C) 9

(D) 7

(E) -2

46.

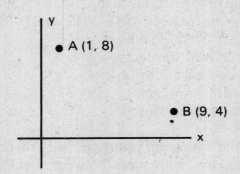

The midpoint of line segment AB is

(A) (8, 4)

(B) (3, 6)

(C) (6, 5)

(D) (5, 6)

(E) (4, 8)

47. If $x = -3$ and $y = (x + 5)(x - 5)$ then the value of y is:

(A) 16

(B) 64

(C) 9

(D) -9

(E) -16

48. If $\frac{1}{5} + \frac{1}{2} + \frac{1}{x} = 7$, then $x =$

(A) $\frac{10}{63}$

(B) $\frac{60}{7}$

(C) $\frac{63}{10}$

(D) $\frac{3}{19}$

(E) $\frac{7}{60}$

49. Suppose that # stands for a binary operation that divides the square of the first number by the square of the second number. Therefore,

$a \mathbin{\#} b = \dfrac{a^2}{b^2}$

The value of $4 \mathbin{\#} 6$ is

(A) $\frac{2}{3}$

(B) $\frac{2}{9}$

(C) $\frac{4}{9}$

(D) $\frac{6}{4}$

(E) $\frac{36}{16}$

50. The ratio of the shaded area of rectangle ABCD to the total area of the rectangle is:

(A) $\frac{1}{2}$

(B) $\frac{1}{4}$

(C) $\frac{1}{8}$

(D) $\frac{3}{16}$

(E) $\frac{9}{32}$

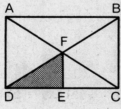

DE = EC

51. If $\dfrac{x^2yz + xyz^2}{xyz} = x + z$, then a necessary condition for this to

be true is:

I. $x + z < y$

II. $x^2 > z$

III. $xyz \neq 0$

(A)   I

(B)   I and II

(C)   I and III

(D)   III

(E)   II and III

Questions 52–55 refer to this graph.

DEFENSE AND SECURITY

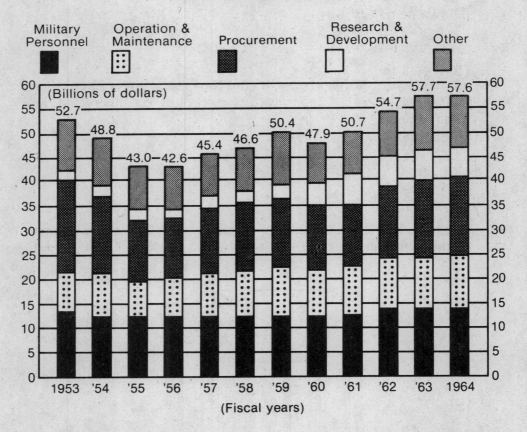

(Fiscal years)

52. Which of the following statements about the graph is true?
   (A) The federal government has never spent less than ten billion dollars a year on research and development.
   (B) Federal government expenditures for research and development have steadily declined.
   (C) Federal government expenditures on military personnel have risen steadily over the past ten years.
   (D) Federal government expenditures for military personnel have never been less than ten billion dollars.
   (E) Total military expenditures by the federal government have risen steadily over the past ten years.

53. Between which two years did total military expenditures by the federal government rise most sharply?
   (A) 1954–1955
   (B) 1961–1962
   (C) 1956–1957
   (D) 1959–1960
   (E) 1958–1959

54. In which of the following years did the federal government spend more on research and development than on operation and maintenance?
   (A) 1962
   (B) 1953
   (C) 1961
   (D) 1960
   (E) none of these

55. What was the approximate percentage decrease from 1954 to 1955?
   (A) 11%
   (B) 9%
   (C) 15%
   (D) 13%
   (E) 1%

SECTION III: ANALYSIS OF EXPLANATIONS

TIME—25 MINUTES
40 QUESTIONS

Directions: A fact situation and a result are presented. Following the result are several numbered statements. Evaluate each statement in relation to the fact situation and the result.

Each statement is to be considered separately from the other statements. The following sequence of A, B, C, D, and E is to be examined *in order* following each statement. The first choice that cannot be eliminated is the correct choice.

Choose A if the statement is inconsistent with, or contradictory to, something in the fact situation, the result, or both together.

Choose B if the statement presents a possible adequate explanation of the result.

Choose C if the statement is deducible from something in the fact situation, the result, or both together.

Choose D if the statement either supports or weakens a possible explanation of the result. It is then relevant to an explanation.

Choose E if the statement is irrelevant to an explanation of the result.

Use common sense to make all decisions; no background in formal logic is necessary. Unlikely or remote possibilities should not be considered.

Set I.

FACT SITUATION: While taking inventory at a specialty clothing store, assistant manager Sally Crandell noticed that an important shipment was missing. With the pre-school rush about to begin the next week, the shipment's whereabouts immediately became a major problem. Sally notified the store manager, Tim Rivers, who immediately had the store carefully searched by the entire staff. Tim instructed Sally to call the delivery service, the warehouse, and then the regional office.

RESULT: The shipment, worth over $1,000, could not be located.

1. The shipment was never ordered.

2. School apparel was included in the shipment.

3. Sally Crandell was fired before the pre-school rush began.

4. Tim Rivers was planning to take another job after the pre-school rush.

5. The assistant manager never called the delivery service, the warehouse, or the regional office.

6. The shortage became evident as Tim was closing the store one evening.

7. Considering the emergency, Tim Rivers reacted poorly as a store manager.

8. The delivery service had been shut down.

9. Sally Crandell did a thorough job of taking inventory.

10. Sally's maiden name was Rivers.

Set II.

FACT SITUATION: Mr. Robbins, a junior high math teacher, was training a student teacher for her first day of teaching. Jill Weber, the student teacher, had observed Mr. Robbins teach algebra for two weeks and was making final preparations for taking over his algebra class on Monday. Mr. Robbins felt that Jill had outstanding potential and would be a fine teacher, but could not decide how to let her break in. He debated whether to let Jill walk in on Monday and take over the complete class for two weeks, or to give her a 30-minute section each day, or whether it would be best to let her teach for a few days and then observe and evaluate her performance for a few days. Mr. Robbins discussed all of these possibilities with Jill to get her reaction. Jill wanted to teach a few days and then observe and evaluate for a few days, because she was a little nervous about taking the class.

RESULT: Mr. Robbins let Jill take the complete class for two weeks.

11.   Mr. Robbins had confidence in Jill's ability.

12.   Jill wanted to teach English.

13.   Mr. Robbins discussed all of the possibilities with Jill after his decision was already made.

14.   Student teaching can be a traumatic experience for the first few weeks.

15.   Mr. Robbins was taken ill for two weeks.

16.   Jill had relatives visiting from Idaho.

17.   Jill was not an overly confident teacher.

18.   The chairman of the math department stepped in and dictated Mr. Robbins' decision.

19.   The entire class expressed a vote of confidence in Jill.

20.   Mr. Robbins was worried about Jill's capabilities.

Set III.

FACT SITUATION: Sargeant, a German Shepherd, had been the Barkers' pet dog for 11 years and was considered part of the family. One evening when the Barkers returned from an early movie, Sargeant was not in the back yard. The Barkers frantically checked the neighborhood, but Sargeant was nowhere to be found. Mrs. Barker tried to calm the three young girls. After driving up and down the local streets for an hour, Mr. Barker and their oldest son, Ted, went to the animal shelter. Meanwhile, the Barkers' oldest daughter, June, called all of the neighbors, asking them if they had seen Sargeant. One of the neighbors thought he had seen Sergeant chasing a cat in the afternoon, but no one knew his present whereabouts.

RESULT: Mr. Barker and Ted returned home two hours later with a happy Sargeant, ruffled but unharmed.

21. The Barkers had at least 4 children.

22. Sargeant was intentionally let out by Ted.

23. Sargeant jumped the fence to chase a cat.

24. The youngest Barker son was staying with a friend.

25. Sargeant had been in a fight with another dog.

26. Sargeant was at the animal shelter.

27. The back yard gate was left unlocked.

28. Sargeant was too young to find his way home.

29. The Barkers' children liked Sargeant.

30. Sargeant was not at the animal shelter.

Set IV.

FACT SITUATION: Mr. Wilson had not had an accident or even a traf-. fic ticket in 24 years. Driving was an important part of his business and he drove over 100 miles each day. One day, as Mr. Wilson was leaving for work, his car was struck by another car before he left his driveway. Mrs. Mumple, a very poor driver, had driven over the curb and across the Wilson's lawn, trying to avoid an oncoming truck. Seeing the accident, the truck driver stopped to check on the damages and to give assistance. The truck driver could not understand why Mrs. Mumple reacted so erratically upon seeing the truck approach. Fortunately, Mr. Wilson's car was only slightly damaged and no one was injured.

RESULT: Mrs. Mumple was given a traffic ticket by a nearby police officer for reckless driving.

31. Mrs. Mumple was driving under 30 mph when she saw the truck.

32. Mr. Wilson was late for work.

33. Mr. Wilson was also given a traffic ticket.

34. Mrs. Mumple overreacted at the sight of the truck coming towards her.

35. A policeman saw the whole incident from the corner.

36. Mr. Wilson's traffic record was only slightly marred by Mrs. Mumple.

37. The truck driver was slightly intoxicated and his truck was too close to the center line.

38. Mr. Wilson could not go to his insurance office because he was late for a dental appointment.

39. Mrs. Mumple was very angry at the truck driver.

40. The truck driver used good judgment and common sense.

SECTION IV: ANALYTICAL ABILITY

TIME—25 MINUTES
30 QUESTIONS

Logical Diagrams

(SUGGESTED TIME—6 MINUTES)
15 QUESTIONS

Directions: In this section, five diagrams are presented that illustrate the relationship among three classes. You are to choose the one diagram that best illustrates the relationship among three given classes. There are three possible relationships between any *two* different classes:

One class completely within another class, but not vice versa, is represented by

When two classes have some, but not all members in common, the relationship is represented by

When two classes have no members in common, the relationship is represented by

Note: The relative size of the circles does not represent the size of the class.

Questions 1–7 are based on the following diagrams:

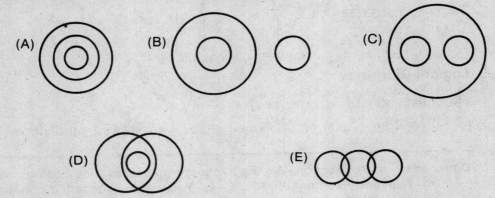

1. Water, liquid, alcohol

2. Pneumonia, infections, viral pneumonia

3. Racket sports, tennis, badminton

4. Beaver, mammal, rodent

5. Hat, headgear, socks

6. Gas, vapor, steam

7. Small cars, fast cars, miniature racers

Questions 8–15 are based on the following diagrams:

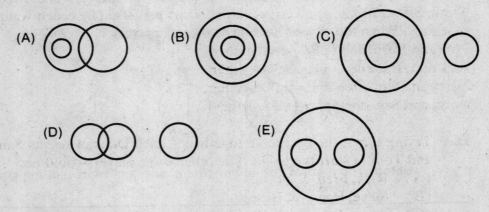

8. Comedian, actor, dentist

9. Substances, solids, metals

10. Bicycles, unicycles, cycles

11.   Mirror, fence, wooden objects

12.   Seat, chair, rocker

13.   Three-dimensional figures, spheres, squares

14.   Silverware, spoons, forks

15.   Long-sleeved shirts, checkered shirts, long-sleeved solid shirts

Analytical Reasoning

(SUGGESTED TIME—19 MINUTES)
15 QUESTIONS

Directions: Each question or group of questions is based on a set of statements or a passage. You are required to choose the *best* answer to each question.

Questions 16–19

Coach Duncan is selecting a starting lineup for his first basketball game of the season. Sam, Tom, and Rick are three tall players and Fred, Norm, Steve, Bruce, and Harry are five short players. The coach wants to start with two tall players and three shorter players.
Fred and Norm don't play well together.
Rick and Bruce don't play well together.
Harry and Steve don't play well together.
Norm and Sam don't play well together.

16.   Trying to put the best team together, Coach Duncan selects Sam and Tom to start the game. The other three players could be:
(A)   Rick, Fred, & Norm
(B)   Steve, Harry, & Bruce
(C)   Steve, Fred, & Norm
(D)   Fred, Bruce, & Harry
(E)   Steve, Bruce, & Norm

17. If the coach decides that Tom will not start the game, then which one of the following most likely will start?
    (A)   Fred
    (B)   Norm
    (C)   Steve
    (D)   Bruce
    (E)   Harry

18. If the coach decides that Sam will start the game and Steve will not start, then which of the following statements are probably true?
    I.   Harry will start the game.
    II. Bruce will start the game.
    (A)   I
    (B)   II
    (C)   I & II
    (D)   Either I or II, but not both
    (E)   Neither I nor II

19. To play their best, which of the following must be true?
    I.   Steve and Harry never play together.
    II.   Fred and Sam play together.
    III. Bruce and Tom never play together.
    (A)   I
    (B)   II
    (C)   III
    (D)   I & II
    (E)   I & III

Questions 20–22

The 55-mile-per-hour speed limit has not only lowered the number of accidents, it has also saved many lives. Yet, auto insurance rates have not reflected this decrease. Therefore, insurance companies are making profits rather than lowering premiums.

20. Considering the statements above, the best argument(s) for the insurance companies is (are) that
    I.   drivers don't follow posted speed limits.
    II.   slower traffic means more time on the road.
    III. company costs have increased drastically.
    (A)   I
    (B)   II
    (C)   III
    (D)   I & III
    (E)   II & III

21. This argument would be strengthened by pointing out that
 - I.   company costs have decreased in the last few years.
 - II. automobiles are more expensive now.
 - III. repair costs have increased.
 - (A) I
 - (B) II
 - (C) III
 - (D) I & II
 - (E) II & III

22. This argument implies that
 - (A) the 55-mph speed limit is unfair.
 - (B) auto manufacturers agree with insurance companies' policies.
 - (C) the driver is being taken advantage of by the insurance companies.
 - (D) saving lives is of more importance than lowering premiums.
 - (E) driving skills have improved greatly since the 55-mph limit has been in effect.

Questions 23–28

Professional sports (regular games and playoffs) are played during the following months:

Football is played from the beginning of September to the end of January.
Baseball is played from the beginning of April to the end of October.
Basketball is played from the beginning of October to the end of May.
Hockey is played from the beginning of October to the end of May.
Soccer is played from the beginning of April to the end of August.
Tennis is played from the beginning of April to the end of August.

23. During which two months could a sports fan watch five different sports on television in each month?
 - (A) April and October
 - (B) May and January
 - (C) April and May
 - (D) September and October
 - (E) November and February

24. During one month, all of the professional sports can be seen *except:*
   (A) Baseball
   (B) Football
   (C) Basketball
   (D) Hockey
   (E) Soccer

25. How many different sports can be seen in January, February, and March?
   (A) 5
   (B) 2
   (C) 4
   (D) 1
   (E) 3

26. If a fan enjoyed only baseball and football, he could enjoy television sports for how many months during the year?
   (A) 11
   (B) 12
   (C) 9
   (D) 10
   (E) 5

27. How many of the sports have a season longer than six months?
   (A) 2
   (B) 3
   (C) 4
   (D) 5
   (E) 6

28. If a fan wanted to watch television sports year-round, which two sports could he watch?
   (A) Football and baseball
   (B) Football and basketball
   (C) Soccer and hockey
   (D) Tennis and basketball
   (E) Hockey and baseball

Questions 29–30

It may be true that there are two sides to every question, but it is also true that there are two sides to a sheet of flypaper and it makes a big difference to the fly which side he chooses.

29. This statement assumes that
   (A)   every question has more than one answer.
   (B)   the choice of questions is very important.
   (C)   flypaper is not useful.
   (D)   every question may be interpreted more than one way.
   (E)   every question has an answer.

30. Which of the following is true?
   I.   The statement uses an analogy to make a point.
   II.   The statement emphasizes the importance of choice.
   III.   The statement points out the ways of getting stuck on a question.
   (A)   I
   (B)   II
   (C)   III
   (D)   I & III
   (E)   I & II

SECTION V: MATH ABILITY

TIME—25 MINUTES
25 QUESTIONS

Directions: Solve each of the following problems and mark the *best* answer on your answer sheet. All scratch work should be done in the available space. All numbers used belong to the real number system. Diagrams are not necessarily drawn to scale.

---

1. $2.5 \times 0.30 =$
   (A) $\frac{3}{4}$
   (B) $\frac{3}{5}$
   (C) 7.5
   (D) $\frac{1}{2}$
   (E) 2.8

2. If $\frac{3}{5} + \frac{1}{2} + x = 3$, then $x =$

(A) $\frac{10}{19}$

(B) $\frac{30}{11}$

(C) $\frac{19}{10}$

(D) $\frac{11}{10}$

(E) $\frac{10}{11}$

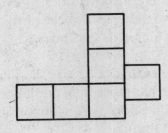

3. If the design above is made of squares measuring 2 on each side, what is the perimeter?

(A) 26

(B) 28

(C) 30

(D) 29

(E) 27

4. If the ratio of a to b is 9 times the ratio of b to a, then $\frac{b}{a}$ could be

(A) $\frac{9}{1}$

(B) $\frac{1}{2}$

(C) 3

(D) $\frac{1}{3}$

(E) 2

5. Multiply 5 times the number n. Add 10 to the result and divide by 5. Subtract 3 from this and you get:

(A) $n + 1$

(B) $n - 1$

(C) $n + 3$

(D) $5n + 1$

(E) $5n + 3$

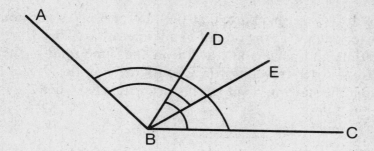

6. In the diagram ∠ ABC = 140°
   ∠ ABE = 90° and ∠ DBC = 70°
   How many degrees in ∠ DBE?
   (A)   40°
   (B)   70°
   (C)   50°
   (D)   20°
   (E)   80°

7. One end of a ladder 32 feet long is placed 10 feet from the outer
   wall of a building that stands on level ground. How far up the
   building, to the nearest foot, will the ladder reach?
   (A)   28 feet
   (B)   29 feet
   (C)   30 feet
   (D)   31 feet
   (E)   40 feet

8. The length of a rectangle is 3 inches greater than its width and
   its area is 88 square inches. An equation that may be used to find
   the width, w, of the rectangle is
   (A) $3w^2 = 88$
   (B) $w^2 - 3w = 88$
   (C) $w^2 + 3w - 88 = 0$
   (D) $\dfrac{w^2}{3} = 88$
   (E)   none of these

9. On a certain map the scale is given as 1 inch = 1 mile. A boy
   copies the map, making each dimension three times as large as
   the given dimensions. On his map how many miles will 6 inches
   represent?
   (A)   2 miles
   (B)   3 miles
   (C)   6 miles
   (D)   18 miles
   (E)   9 miles

10. A boy travels on his bicycle at the rate of 6 miles per hour and his sister on hers at the rate of 5 miles per hour. They start at the same time and place and travel over the same road in the same direction. After traveling for 3 hours the boy turns back. How far from the starting point has his sister traveled when they meet?
   (A)   16 miles
   (B)   17 miles
   (C)   about 16.4 miles
   (D)   about 16.9 miles
   (E)   23 miles

11. The equation $2x - y - 4 = 0$ is represented graphically below. Which, if any, of the following statements is false?
   (A)   As x increases, y increases.
   (B)   When $x = 0$, $y = -4$; when $y = 0$, $x = 2$.
   (C)   The angle marked θ is greater than $45°$.
   (D)   The graph, if continued, would pass through the point $x = 15$, $y = 26$.
   (E)   none of these

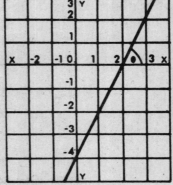

12. If an event can succeed in p ways (all equally probable) and fail in q ways, the probability that the event will succeed is $\dfrac{p}{p + q}$.

   Which, if any, of the following statements is true?
   (A)   The probability of drawing a glass marble in a single draw from a bag containing 8 glass marbles and 12 clay marbles is $\dfrac{2}{3}$.
   (B)   The letters x, y, and z can be arranged in 6 different orders: xyz, zyx, yxz, etc. If one of these arrangements is chosen at random, the probability that z will be the middle letter is $\dfrac{1}{6}$.
   (C)   If one of the integers from 8 to 15 inclusive is chosen at random, the probability that the integer is even is equal to the probability that it is odd.
   (D)   The probability that a man, aged 40, will live to reach the age of 70 is $\dfrac{4}{7}$.
   (E)   none of these.

13. Which of the following sets of numbers is arranged in order of value beginning with the smallest?

   (A) $53 : 125$, $3\sqrt{.0196}$, $.425$, $\frac{266}{625}$

   (B) $\frac{266}{625}$, $.425$, $3\sqrt{.0196}$, $53 : 125$

   (C) $3\sqrt{.0196}$, $\frac{266}{625}$, $.425$, 53.125

   (D) $3\sqrt{.0196}$, $53 : 125$, 425 $\frac{266}{625}$

   (E) none of these

14. How many pieces of cardboard 3 inches by 5 inches, laid in the same direction, can be cut from a sheet 17 inches by 22 inches with minimum waste?
   (A) 20
   (B) 21
   (C) 24
   (D) 25
   (E) 29

15. If in any two-digit number the tens digit is represented by x and the units digit by y, which, if any, of the following statements would be false?
   a. $10x + y$ represents the number.
   b. xy represents the number.
   c. yx represents the number formed by reversing the digits.
   d. The difference between the number and the number formed by reversing the digits is exactly divisible by 9.
   e. The sum of the number and the number formed by reversing the digits is exactly divisible by 11.
   (A) a.
   (B) b., c.
   (C) d., e.
   (D) b., c., d., e.
   (E) none of these

16. A man paid $44.10 in cash for an electric motor after receiving a discount of 10 per cent from the list price and than a discount of 2 per cent from the new price. Find the list price of the motor.
   (A) $38.90
   (B) $49.39
   (C) $49.48
   (D) $50.11
   (E) $50.00

17. Two stations, A and B, are located six miles apart on a railroad. The rates of cartage of coal are 50 cents per ton per mile from A and 75 cents per ton per mile from B. At a certain consumer's home, located on the railroad between A and B, the cost for cartage is the same whether the coal is delivered from A or from B. Find the distance from this home to A.

(A) 3 miles

(B) $3\frac{1}{2}$ miles

(C) $3\frac{3}{5}$ miles

(D) 4 miles

(E) 5 miles

Questions 18–22 refer to these graphs.

Some Key Indicators That Figure in Tax Cut Debate

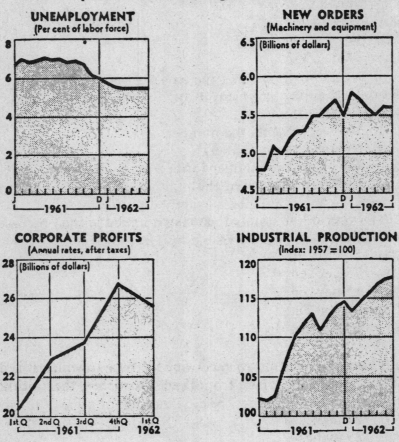

18. During the period illustrated, the level of unemployment
  (A)   remained fairly constant
  (B)   generally rose
  (C)   generally declined
  (D)   rose sharply and then declined
  (E)   declined sharply and then rose

19. During the period illustrated, corporate profits
  (A)   remained fairly constant
  (B)   rose steadily
  (C)   declined steadily
  (D)   declined and then rose
  (E)   rose and then declined

20. During the period illustrated, new orders were highest in (about)
  (A)   November, 1961
  (B)   January, 1962
  (C)   March, 1961
  (D)   April, 1962
  (E)   May, 1962

21. Corporate profits were lowest in
  (A)   the first quarter of 1962
  (B)   the last quarter of 1961
  (C)   the first quarter of 1961
  (D)   the second quarter of 1961
  (E)   the third quarter of 1961

22. In the period illustrated, industrial production increased approximately
  (A)   5 per cent
  (B)   75 per cent
  (C)   15 per cent
  (D)   91 per cent
  (E)   50 percent

23. An altitude h of a triangle is twice the base to which it is drawn. If the area of the triangle is 225 square inches, then altitude h is
  (A)   15 inches
  (B)   20 inches
  (C)   25 inches
  (D)   30 inches
  (E)   35 inches

24. The minimum temperatures at Jonesville for each day of one week were as follows:

$$+7°, \quad +13°, \quad +5°, \quad -4°, \quad -8°, \quad 0°, \quad +3°$$

Find, to the nearest degree, the average minimum temperature.
(A) 6°
(B) 2°
(C) 16°
(D) 4°
(E) 8°

x	7	11	15	19	23	27
y	2	10	18	26	34	42

25. In the chart above, x and y increase proportionately. When x is 47, y will be
(A) 80
(B) 82
(C) 70
(D) 94
(E) 102

PRACTICE TEST III: ANSWERS

SECTION I: VERBAL ABILITY

SENTENCE COMPLETION

1.	E	5.	D	9.	D
2.	B	6.	B	10.	A
3.	A	7.	B		
4.	A	8.	D		

ANALOGIES

11.	C	15.	D	19.	E
12.	B	16.	E	20.	B
13.	B	17.	D		
14.	D	18.	B		

ANTONYMS

21.	C	25.	B	29.	E
22.	D	26.	C	30.	C
23.	D	27.	C	31.	A
24.	A	28.	B		

READING COMPREHENSION

32.	E	41.	A	50.	C
33.	E	42.	D	51.	C
34.	D	43.	B	52.	C
35.	A	44.	D	53.	B
36.	B	45.	C	54.	D
37.	B	46.	B	55.	A
38.	A	47.	D	56.	B
39.	E	48.	D		
40.	B	49.	A		

SENTENCE COMPLETION

57.	E	60.	B	63.	B
58.	A	61.	D	64.	B
59.	E	62.	C	65.	D

ANALOGIES

66.	A	69.	C	72.	D
67.	A	70.	C	73.	D
68.	B	71.	E		

ANTONYMS

74.	E	77.	E	80.	B
75.	E	78.	A		
76.	C	79.	C		

SECTION II: QUANTITATIVE ABILITY

QUANTITATIVE COMPARISON

1.	A	11.	B	21.	A
2.	B	12.	A	22.	C
3.	D	13.	D	23.	B
4.	B	14.	C	24.	A
5.	A	15.	D	25.	B
6.	C	16.	D	26.	D
7.	A	17.	B	27.	A
8.	B	18.	A	28.	A
9.	A	19.	C	29.	B
10.	A	20.	C	30.	A

MATH ABILITY

31.	B	40.	E	49.	C
32.	B	41.	D	50.	C
33.	C	42.	D	51.	D
34.	A	43.	B	52.	D
35.	C	44.	B	53.	B
36.	D	45.	C	54.	E
37.	A	46.	D	55.	A
38.	B	47.	E		
39.	C	48.	A		

SECTION III: ANALYSIS OF EXPLANATIONS

1.	B	15.	B	29.	C
2.	C	16.	E	30.	D
3.	D	17.	C	31.	E
4.	E	18.	B	32.	C
5.	B	19.	B	33.	A
6.	A	20.	A	34.	B
7.	A	21.	C	35.	B
8.	B	22.	A	36.	C
9.	C	23.	B	37.	D
10.	E	24.	E	38.	A
11.	B	25.	D	39.	E
12.	A	26.	B	40.	C
13.	D	27.	D		
14.	D	28.	A		

SECTION IV: ANALYTICAL ABILITY

Logical Diagrams

1.	C	6.	A	11.	D
2.	A	7.	D	12.	B
3.	C	8.	C	13.	C
4.	A	9.	B	14.	E
5.	B	10.	E	15.	A

Analytical Reasoning

16.	D	21.	A	26.	D
17.	A	22.	C	27.	B
18.	C	23.	C	28.	E
19.	D	24.	B	29.	D
20.	B	25.	E	30.	E

SECTION V: MATH ABILITY

1.	A	10.	C	19.	E
2.	C	11.	E	20.	B
3.	B	12.	C	21.	C
4.	D	13.	D	22.	C
5.	B	14.	B	23.	D
6.	D	15.	B	24.	B
7.	C	16.	E	25.	B
8.	C	17.	C		
9.	A	18.	C		

PRACTICE TEST III: ANALYSIS SHEET

SECTION I

	Possible	Completed	Right	Wrong
VERBAL ABILITY				
Sentence Completion				
Analogies				
Antonyms				
Reading Comprehension				
OVERALL VERBAL				

SECTION II

QUANTITATIVE ABILITY

	Possible	Completed	Right	Wrong
Quantitative Comparison				
Math Ability				
OVERALL QUANTITATIVE				

SECTION III & IV

ANALYTICAL ABILITY

	Possible	Completed	Right	Wrong
Analysis of Explanations				
Logical Diagrams				
Analytical Reasoning				
OVERALL ANALYTICAL				

SECTION V

MATH ABILITY

	Possible	Completed	Right	Wrong

RAW SCORE = NUMBER RIGHT $- \frac{1}{4}$ (Number attempted but missed)

OVERALL SCORES SHOULD BE RAW SCORES

PRACTICE TEST III: EXPLANATIONS

SECTION I: VERBAL ABILITY

Sentence Completion

1. **E** is basic to.
   This sentence sets up a cause-effect pattern that leads to the conclusion that plant life is *dependent* upon oxygen. Therefore, oxygen is (E) *basic to* (necessary to) plant life.

2. **B** self-judgment—adjust to.
   This sentence requires a pair of *positive* words, the first of which is a noun exercised by children and the second being an action in relation to "school, home, and community." Choices (A), (D), and (E) can each be eliminated for containing words with negative connotations. (C) is incorrect because discipline is more often *received* by children than *exercised by* them. Choice (B) clearly is the best answer.

3. **A** inaccessibility.
   All of the choices here are things that could be vigorously objected to. However, the key words are: "could not be reached," which is a perfect definition of the correct answer: (A) *inaccessibility*.

4. **A** one—residuum.
   The key here is the relationship between two parts. The second word must be something that remains after something else is removed. Choices (C), (D), and (E) make no sense in this context. Choice (B) *the interest-dividend* would be correct if the second word were "principle." Therefore only (A) is correct (*residuum* means remainder).

5. **D** cessation—bigotry.
   The key words here are "democratic principle," "prejudice" and "intolerance." The first word of the answer should mean the *end* and the second word must be a negative word in keeping with prejudice and intolerance. Only choice (D) fits these requirements.

6. **B** Sparsely.
The signal word "since" tells us that this will be a cause-effect sentence again. The key words "inadequate grazing area for the herds" would lead to the conclusion that the population would be sparse (scanty or scattered).

7. **B** Implicit—responsibility.
The context of this sentence clearly demands a first word that means *implied* or *contained in* and a second word meaning *duty*. Only choice (B) meets both requirements. Choice (E) would be a reasonable second choice, as *inherent* would fit the sentence, but *privilege* does not carry the sense of obligation required by the phrase "to the best of their ability."

8. **D** mandates—accredit.
Key words here are "international law," "diplomatic representatives," and "friendly relations." The word "law" demands a strong first word in the answer, while "friendly" sets up a positive connotation. Therefore, we may eliminate choices (A), (B), and (C). Choice (D) *requires—welcome* would be understood—it doesn't rely on international *law,* rather it is customary. Therefore (D) *mandates* (orders)—*accredit* (give authority to) is the correct answer.

9. **D** society—individual.
The key words in this sentence are "in our educational jargon." Choices (A), (C), and (E) can be eliminated immediately as they are not commonly a part of our educational language. Choice (B) is not a reasonable selection as it is not true. Therefore the answer is (D) *society—individual,* an issue which is often a focal point of educational debate.

10. **A** prolific.
The key words are "turn out several books a year." We need a word that expresses productivity. Choices (B), (C), and (D) may be quickly eliminated, as they are irrelevant here. While (E) *ambitious* is a possible choice, it implies a desire or striving for success, whereas the *best* choice (A) *prolific* means fruitful or productive.

Analogies

11. C

TEPID is to TORRID in the same way as COOL is to FRIGID. "Tepid" means slightly warm and "torrid" means very hot, just as "cool" means slightly cold and "frigid" means very cold.

12. B

ALPHA is to OMEGA in the same way as PROLOGUE is to EPILOGUE. "Alpha" is the first letter of the Greek alphabet and "Omega" is the last letter, just as a "prologue" is the first part or introduction to a poem, play, or story and an "epilogue" is the last part or conclusion.

13. B

CHRONOMETER is to CALENDAR in the same way as BEAT is to MEASURE. The "chronometer" and the "calendar" are both used to measure time of day, just as the "beat" and the "measure" are both used to measure time in music.

14. D

MILLENNIUM is to CENTURY in the same way as DECADE is to YEAR. A millennium is ten centuries long, and a decade is ten years long. (A) is incorrect because the year : month ratio is 12 : 1.

15. D

MERIDIAN is to SETTING in the same way as CULMINATE is to TERMINATE. "Meridian" and "culminate" both denote the highest altitude of a celestial body, and "setting" and "terminate" are both associated with the conclusion or end point of something.

16. E

HARBINGER is to SPRING in the same way as DAWN is to DAY. A "harbinger" (often a robin) is the sign that spring is beginning, just as "dawn" is the sign that "day" is beginning.

17. D

ART is to CUBISM in the same way as POEM is to EPIC. Here is a *general-particular relationship:* "Cubism" is a type of "art," just as an "epic" is a type of "poem."

18.   **B**

LITERAL is to FREE in the same way as TRANSLATE is to PARAPHRASE. A "literal" interpretation does not alter the actual facts or words, but a "free" interpretation may. Similarly, to "translate" requires sticking to the actual facts or words, whereas a "paraphrase" may alter or summarize them. (E) is incorrect because "news" is itself a paraphrase rather than an unaltered reproduction of events.

19.   **E**

CITADEL is to VAULT in the same way as TOWER is to DUNGEON. The same meaning relationship exists in both pairs, between a "fortress at a commanding height" (citadel, tower) and a "locked cellar room" (vault, dungeon).

20.   **B**

EXPOSITION is to PRECIS in the same way as VOLUME is to BOOKLET. A "precis" is a short exposition or summary, just as a "booklet" is a short volume. (D) is incorrect because the words are adjectives, not nouns.

Antonyms

21.   Disquietude—uneasiness. Correct answer: (C) *fortitude*—patient endurance.

22.   Heinous—atrocious. Correct answer: (D) *creditable*—honorable.

23.   Herculean—possessing or requiring enormous strength. Correct answer: (D) *puny*—tiny.

24.   Dawdle—to waste time. Correct answer: (A) *hasten*—to hurry.

25.   Thralldom—slavery. Correct answer: (B) *independence*—freedom.

26.   Integral—entire or complete. Correct answer: (C) *fragmentary*—incomplete.

27.   Martial—warlike. Correct answer: (C) *peaceful.*

28.   Lure—attract. Correct answer: (B) *repel*—revolt.

29.   Munificent—generous. Correct answer: (E) *stingy*—greedy.

30. Proffer—to offer. Correct answer: (C) *renege*—to go back on one's word.

31. Entice—allure. Correct answer: (A) *frighten*—scare.

Reading Comprehension

32. E

This object is stated in the first sentence. All other choices are issues or aspects of "compulsory international adjudication."

33. E

The second paragraph states that conflicts which do not arise from specific disputes may lead to war ("forceful action"), unless provided for by international law.

34. D

This municipal-international comparison is applied to the matter of conflicts not arising from specific disputes (second paragraph). In this paragraph, the writer questions Professor K's use of primitive courts as historical precedents, and claims that worldwide submission to arbitration treaties is wishful thinking; therefore (A) and (E) are incorrect.

35. A

The writer cites the "numerous treaties of arbitration concluded in the 20th century" (third paragraph) that are based on a distinction between legal and political disputes.

36. B

This choice is stated almost verbatim in the second paragraph; it is called "fact" (axiom) by the author. All other choices are issues under discussion in the passage, and therefore not axiomatic.

37. B

This is a possibility implicit in conflicts that do not arise from specific disputes (second paragraph). This question draws from the same information as does question No. 2.

38. A

The Hague conference distinguished legal questions from political questions, resulting in "numerous treaties or arbitration conducted in the 20th century." This question draws from the same information as does question No. 4.

39.   E

The final, rhetorical question of paragraph three evokes the answer, "No, because the subsidy question is not a *legal* issue requiring a court decision." But *it is an international political issue,* and is therefore not independent of international jurisdiction.

40.   B

"its very subjects, states, limit its scope" (last paragraph). "Limit" and "Delimit" mean the same thing in this case.

41.   A

Professor K's "principal tenet" is that international law governs all relations (paragraph 4). The writer contends that the states existed before the law existed; they delegate it and limit its scope. This question draws from the same information as does question No. 9.

42.   D

(A) and (B) are not specific enough, and (C) is beyond the scope of the paragraph.

43.   B

His many accomplishments beyond priestly duties and his title as "prince of Catholic orators" portray him as far from typical.

44.   D

(A) is not a specific piece of *evidence* from the paragraph, as is (D).

45.   C

A "locution" is a word, phrase, or expression.

46.   B

An "exponent," as used here, is "a person or thing which is an example or symbol of something."

47.   D

The notion that "the need for ostentation is a universal species characteristic" has "no rational basis." (A) is an answer that relies on information extraneous to the paragraph.

48.   D

All other choices are minor aspects or issues all related to the author's single purpose. Therefore (D) is correct because it *contains* the other choices.

49. A

Ironic terms mean the opposite of what is expressed; here the writer goes on to argue for rational proof, demonstrating his actual disbelief in anything like divine guidance.

50. C

A difficult and important lesson, he says, is "ye shall know the truth, and the truth shall make you free."

51. C

The anti-vaccinationist who avoids health out of ignorance is compared to anyone who ignores the truth of knowledge.

52. C

(A) and (B) are beyond the scope of the paragraph, and (D) gives equal weight to terms treated quite unequally. Since all the information in the paragraph is related to the lives and status of rustics (villeins), (C) is correct.

53. B

The villeins were "free by birth," as distinguished from the *servi*.

54. D

(A), (B), and (E) contribute to form "ploughteams," and five acres is a smaller plot held by the *bordarii*.

55. A

"The land of the rustics is taxed separately for the gold."

56. B

An important characteristic of villeins is that they hold land of which they cannot dispose freely.

Sentence Completion

57. E *Tempera.*

The key words are "painter" and "media," meaning an artist's creative materials. The word "including" tells you that the missing word must be a medium. Choice (B) is a philosophy and (A), (C), and (D) are all *processes* (which, incidentally, are not related to painting anyway). Only (E) *tempera* (a type of water-base paint) is applicable.

58. A *Paraphrase.*

This is another case of pure definition. The sentence defines choice (A) *paraphrase*.

59.   E   *residence—domicile*.

The key word here is "officially." You are looking for two words that are synonyms. The second word, however, must be used in official circumstances. Only choice (E) *residence-domicile* meets this requirement, as domicile is a legal term meaning permanent legal residence.

60.   B   *product—labor*.

The point of view in this sentence is that of the *labor unions*. In this context capital would be seen as a result of labor, coming *after* labor in origin and dependent upon it. Clearly, only choice (B) *product—labor* gives the sentence this meaning.

61.   D   *Cynosure*.

The drift of this sentence clearly requires a word having a positive connotation, since it is assumed that the sight of the queen would be a pleasing one. Only (C) and (D) are positive, and (C) *miracle* sounds awkward in this sentence. Therefore (D) *cynosure* (something that attracts attention by its brilliance) is the correct answer.

62.   C   *immutable—characteristics*.

The key words in this sentence are "human nature" and "components." Also the word "but" following the semicolon signals a change in direction or contrast. The first part of the sentence must be intended to say that the components of human nature are unchanging, since the second half of the sentence implies that events may bring about variations. Only choices (A) and (C) are logical possibilities; however, the word *immutable* better fits the context of human nature than the word *fixed,* which more often applies to mechanical objects. Finally, the sentence contains the phrase "bringing to the fore," which implies bringing to the surface things that are already present. *Reactions* occur in response to stimuli and then are gone. *Characteristics* are always present and come to the surface when the situation is correct. Therefore, choice (C) is the correct answer.

63.   B   *Number*.

The key words here are "increase," "applicants," and "by providing high salaries." The lure of more money to applicants would have no effect on their characters or quality—it would only increase their *number,* choice (B).

64. B *Natural.*

The clue to the correct answer here is found in the words "skill of the master craftsman." The sentence requires a strongly *positive* word that implies ease. Therefore, choices (A), (C), and (D) can be eliminated quickly. Choice E) *avocational* (relating to a hobby) is a good possibility except that it suggests "just for fun," which would clash with the key words "master craftsman." Therefore, choice (B) *natural* is the best possible answer.

65. D *impassive—impassioned.*

The word "but" in this sentence signals a shift in direction. Therefore you are looking for a pair of words of opposite meaning: one describing the defendant's courtroom behavior and one describing his personality during the crime. Choice (D) *impassive— impassioned* makes logical sense by describing undemonstrative behavior in court and heated behavior during the crime.

Analogies

66. A

PHILOLOGIST is to LANGUAGE in the same way as ORNITHOLOGIST is to BIRDS. A "philologist" studies "language," just as an "ornithologist" studies "birds." A biologist studies life, not just cells.

67. A

MYRIAD is to SPARSE in the same way as MANY is to FEW. "Myriad" means "many," and "sparse" means "few."

68. B

DISSIPATION is to DEPRAVITY in the same way as REPETITION is to MONOTONY. Here is a *cause-effect relationship:* "dissipation" (harmful waste of time and energy) contributes to "depravity" (corruptness), just as "repetition" contributes to "monotony" (boredom).

69. C

TRIUMPH is to EXALTATION in the same way as CALAMITY is to DISTRESS. Here is a cause-effect relationship: A "triumph" results in "exaltation" (great joy), just as a "calamity" results in "distress."

70. C

WAIL is to WHIMPER in the same way as GUFFAW is to LAUGH. A "wail" is a loud, prolonged "whimper," just as a "guffaw" is a loud, prolonged "laugh." (A) is incorrect because a lament may be silent; it is not necessarily a prolonged cry.

71. E

AIR is to DIRIGIBLE as WATER is to BOAT. A "dirigible" flies through the "air," just as a "boat" sails through the "water." A taxi does not run *through* gasoline.

72. D

TRESPASS is to WANDER as PERJURE is to RELATE. "Trespassing" is illegal "wandering," just as to "perjure" is to "relate" an event illegally and untruthfully.

73. D

CULMINATION is to INCEPTION in the same way as MATURITY is to INFANCY. The same meaning relationship exists in both pairs, between the "high point" (culmination, maturity) and the "beginning" (inception, infancy).

Antonyms

74. Pacific—peaceful. Correct answer: (E) *belligerent*—quarrelsome.

75. Perplexity—confusion. Correct answer: (E) *certitude*—sureness.

76. Desiccate—to dry up. Correct answer: (C) *saturate*—to soak.

77. Felicitous—appropriate, well-suited. Correct answer: (E) *inappropriate*—not fitting.

78. Invaluable—priceless. Correct answer: (A) *worthless*—having no value.

79. Facile—easily done. Correct answer: (C) *formidable*—tremendously difficult.

80. Manifest—obvious, evident. Correct answer: (B) *latent*—concealed.

SECTION II: QUANTITATIVE ABILITY

Quantitative Comparison

1. **A** $\sqrt{.09} > (.09)^2$

   Simplifying $\sqrt{.3 \times .3}$ $.09 \times .09$

   $.3 > .0081$

2. **B**   The average of   The average of
   $3y$, $5y$, 3 and 5 $2y$, $6y$, 4, and 10

   Simplifying, $\dfrac{3y + 5y + 3 + 5}{4}$ $\dfrac{2y + 6y + 4 + 10}{4}$

   $\dfrac{8y + 8}{4}$ $\dfrac{8y + 14}{4}$

   $\dfrac{8y}{4} + \dfrac{8}{4}$ $\dfrac{8y}{4} + \dfrac{14}{4}$

   $2y + 2$ $2y + \dfrac{14}{4}$

   Subtracting $2y$ from both leaves

   $$2 < \frac{14}{4}$$

3. **D** $x\ ?\ 3$

   To satisfy this compound inequality $4 > x - y > 1$, there are many possible values for x and y. If $x = 5$ then y could be 2; or if $x = 12$, then y could be 0. Therefore x could be either greater than, less than, or equal to 3 and the answer cannot be determined.

4. **B** $AB < EB$

   Any diagonal of a regular pentagon is greater than any of the sides.

   Alternate method:
   Using the following formula for finding the interior degrees of a polygon $180(N - 2)$ and subtracting 5 for N (Number of sides of a pentagon) gives:

   180 (N — 2)
   180 (5 — 2)
   180 (3)
   540

   There are 540° in the interior of the pentagon. Dividing this by 5 for the number of equal angles leaves 108° in each angle. Angle A is 108° in triangle ABE, and therefore is the greatest angle in the triangle. The longest side of a triangle is across from the largest angle, so $AB < EB$.

5. **A**   Sum of interior angles $> 360°$
of Pentagon ABCDE
From the previous problem $540° > 360°$

Alternate method:
The sum of the interior degrees of a pentagon can be derived by dividing the pentagon into triangles as shown. Since there are 3 triangles and $180°$ in a triangle, there are $3 \times 180°$ or $540°$ in the pentagon.

6. **C** $\angle AEB = \angle ABE$
Since the pentagon is equilateral, side $AB =$ side AE, and therefore $\angle AEB = \angle ABE$ as angles opposite equal sides in a triangle are equal.

7. **A** $\angle D + \angle C > 180°$
From the previous problems, each angle of the pentagon is $108°$, therefore

$$108° + 108° = 216°$$
$$216° \quad > \quad 180°$$

8. **B** $\dfrac{13}{29} < \dfrac{14}{31}$
Using the method of cross-multiplying gives

Since $403 < 406$
Then $\dfrac{13}{29} < \dfrac{14}{31}$

9. **A** $(x + 2)(y + 3) > (x + 3)(y + 2)$

Simplifying each column leaves

$$xy + 3x + 2y + 6 \qquad xy + 2x + 3y + 6$$

Subtracting xy, $2x$, $2y$, and 6 from both sides leaves

$$x > y$$

from the condition given $0 < y < x$.

10. **A** $(5n)^3 > 5n^3$

Simplify Column A

$$(5n)(5n)(5n) = 125n^3$$

Now dividing both columns by $5n^3$

$$\frac{125n^3}{5n^3} \qquad \frac{5n^3}{5n^3}$$

leaves $25 > 1$

Alternate method:

Substituting into each column let $n = 2$

$$\begin{array}{cc} (5 \times 2)^3 & 5(2)^3 \\ (10)^3 & 5(8) \end{array}$$

Therefore $1{,}000 > 40$

11. **B** $\dfrac{\frac{1}{3} + \frac{1}{2}}{\frac{1}{4} + \frac{1}{5}} < 2$

Simplifying column A

$$\frac{\frac{5}{6}}{\frac{9}{20}} = \frac{5}{6} \times \frac{20}{9} = \frac{100}{54} = 1\frac{46}{54}$$

and $1\frac{46}{54} < 2$

12. **A** $x > y$

Solving each problem, first for x: 15 is 30% of x

$$\frac{30}{100} = \frac{15}{x}$$
$$\frac{3}{10} = \frac{15}{x}$$

Cross-multiplying:

$$3x = 150$$
$$x = 50$$

Solving for y: 12 is 25% y

$$\frac{25}{100} = \frac{12}{y}$$
$$\frac{1}{4} = \frac{12}{y}$$

Cross-multiplying: $y = 48$
and $50 > 48$

13. **D** $x^{-2} ? x^{-3}$

Substituting for x

let $x = 1$

$$(1)^{-2} \qquad\qquad (1)^{-3}$$
$$\frac{1}{(1)^2} \qquad\qquad \frac{1}{(1)^3}$$
$$\frac{1}{1} \quad = \quad \frac{1}{1}$$

Now let $x = 2$

$$(2)^{-2} \qquad\qquad (2)^{-3}$$
$$\frac{1}{(2)^2} \qquad\qquad \frac{1}{(2)^3}$$
$$\frac{1}{4} \quad > \quad \frac{1}{8}$$

Since different values give different outcomes, no answer can be determined.

14.   C   AC = BC

Since A and B are the centers of their respective circles, AB is a radius of each. By inspection, AB = AC = BC as they are all radii of equal circles.

15.   D m^3 ? $2m^2$

Trying the value $m = 1$ gives

$$(1)^3 \qquad\qquad 2(1)^2$$
$$1 \qquad < \qquad 2$$

Now letting $m = 2$ gives

$$(2)^3 \qquad\qquad 2(2)^2$$
$$8 \qquad = \qquad 8$$

Solution cannot be determined because different values give different answers.

16.   D   Perimeter of square ? Area of square
Using the appropriate formulas

$$4s \ ? \ s^2$$

and substituting different values for s will give different answers.

If $s = 1$

$$4(1) \qquad\qquad (1)^2$$
$$4 \qquad > \qquad 1$$

If $s = 4$

$$4(4) \qquad\qquad (4)^2$$
$$16 \qquad = \qquad 16$$

Therefore the relationship cannot be determined.

17. B $\dfrac{a + c^2}{b} < \dfrac{a^2 + c}{b^2}$

Substituting the given values $a = 5$, $b = 3$, $c = -1$

$$\dfrac{(5) + (-1)^2}{3} \qquad \dfrac{(5)^2 + (-1)}{(3)^2}$$

Simplifying:

$$\dfrac{5 + 1}{3} \qquad \dfrac{25 - 1}{9}$$

$$\dfrac{6}{3} \qquad \dfrac{24}{9}$$

And $\qquad 2 \;<\; 2\frac{2}{3}$

18. A Percent increase from \$400 to \$500 > 20%
To find percent increase subtract the smaller amount from the larger and divide by the smaller:

$$\dfrac{500 - 400}{400} = \dfrac{100}{400} = \dfrac{1}{4} = 25\%$$

and $25\% > 20\%$

19. C $5r = 3s$
Cross-multiply the given equation

$$\dfrac{r}{3} = \dfrac{s}{5}$$

Leaves $5r = 3s$

20. C $\angle\,\mathrm{DAC} = \angle\,\mathrm{BCA}$
Since all sides of a square are equal, $\mathrm{AD} = \mathrm{DC}$. Angles opposite equal sides in a triangle are equal.
Therefore, $\angle\,\mathrm{DAC} = \angle\,\mathrm{BCA}$

21.   A $\overset{\frown}{AC} > 90°$

B is an inscribed right angle that subtends arc AC. The formula for finding the arc of an inscribed angle is Arc $= 2x$ (inscribed angle)

Substituting

$$\overset{\frown}{AC} = 2 \times (90°)$$
$$\overset{\frown}{AC} = 180°$$

Therefore $\overset{\frown}{AC} > 90°$

Alternate method:

By inspection, AC is a diameter making $\overset{\frown}{AC}$ a semicircle. A circle is composed of 360° and a semicircle is 180°

$$180° > 90°$$

22.   C   Radius of circle $= \dfrac{\sqrt{2}}{2}$

Using the Pythagorean Theorem to find the length of diameter AC gives

$$(AB)^2 + (BC)^2 = (AC)^2$$
$$(1)^2 + \quad (1)^2 = (AC)^2$$
$$1 + 1 = (AC)^2$$
$$2 = (AC)^2$$
$$\sqrt{2} = AC$$

Since the radius is $\frac{1}{2}$ of the diameter

$$\tfrac{1}{2} \text{ of } \sqrt{2} \text{ is } \dfrac{\sqrt{2}}{2}$$
$$\text{and } \dfrac{\sqrt{2}}{2} = \dfrac{\sqrt{2}}{2}$$

23.   B $CD < \overset{\frown}{AB}$

$CD = AB$ because ABCD is a square. $AB < \overset{\frown}{AB}$ because the shortest distance between two points is a straight line. Following some simple logic, since

$$AB = CD \text{ and } AB < \overset{\frown}{AB}, \text{ therefore}$$
$$CD < \overset{\frown}{AB}$$

24. A $2 \times$ Area of square $>$ Area of circle
Using the proper formulas

$$A = s \times s \qquad\qquad A = \pi r^2$$

and substituting $s = 1$ and $r = \dfrac{\sqrt{2}}{2}$

from an earlier problem

$$A = (1) \times (1) \qquad\qquad A = \pi\left(\frac{\sqrt{2}}{2}\right)^2$$

$$2(1) \qquad\qquad\qquad \pi\frac{2}{4}$$

$$3.14 \times \frac{1}{2}$$

Therefore $2 > 1.57$

25. B $\sqrt{x + y} < \sqrt{x} + \sqrt{y}$
Substituting $x = 1$, $y = 1$

gives $\qquad \sqrt{1 + 1} \qquad \sqrt{1} + \sqrt{1}$

$$\sqrt{2} \qquad\qquad 1 + \quad 1$$

$$1.4 \quad < \quad 2$$

Trying other values gives the same result.

26. D $x \, ? \, y$
By inspection, the two given equations are the same: $x + 3y = 7$ and $4x + 12y = 28$ if the second equation is simplified by dividing by 4. Since the two equations are equivalent, no definite values for x and y can be determined.

27. A $\dfrac{1}{8} \times \dfrac{1}{4} \times \dfrac{1}{9} > .125 \times .25 \times .1$

Changing the decimals in Column B to fractions:

$$\frac{125}{1,000} \times \frac{25}{100} \times \frac{1}{10}$$

and reducing to simplest form gives this comparison:

$$\frac{1}{8} \times \frac{1}{4} \times \frac{1}{9} \qquad \frac{1}{8} \times \frac{1}{4} \times \frac{1}{10}$$

Canceling out the $\dfrac{1}{8}$ and $\dfrac{1}{4}$ from each side leaves

$$\frac{1}{9} > \frac{1}{10}$$

28. **A** $b + c > a$
The sum of any two sides of a triangle is greater than the third side.

29. **B** $c^2 < a^2 + b^2$
If $p = 90°$ then $c^2 = a^2 + b^2$, but since $p < 90°$, the opposite side C gets smaller. Therefore, $c^2 < a^2 + b^2$.

30. **A** $A > C - B$
The sum of any two sides of a triangle is greater than the third side, therefore the difference of any two sides of a triangle is less than the third side. Solving algebraically:

$$a + b > c$$

Subtracting b from both sides leaves $a > c - b$

Math Ability

31. **B** $\dfrac{cn}{p}$ cents

Formula: $\dfrac{\text{Number}}{\text{Cost}} = \dfrac{\text{Number}}{\text{Cost}}$

If x represents the cost of n pencils, we have, by substitution,

$\dfrac{p}{c} = \dfrac{n}{x}$ or $px = cn$ or $x = \dfrac{cn}{p}$ cents

32. **B** 2
$5a - .5a = 9$ or $4.5a = 9$ or $45a = 90$, $a = 2$

33. **C** 20
$$\sqrt[3]{64.32} = 4.01$$
$$\sqrt[2]{.041} = .202$$
$$\frac{4}{.2} = 4 \times \frac{10}{2} = 20$$

34. **A** 1 sq. ft.
P = 20 ft.   P = 20 ft.
A = 24 sq. ft.   A = 25 sq. ft.

$$\begin{array}{r} 25 \\ -24 \\ \hline 1 \text{ sq. ft.} \end{array}$$

35. **C** 26
26 × \$.10 = \$2.60 + .50 = \$3.10

36. **D** $x + y$ is less than 15
If x is less than 10 and y is less than 5, then $x + y$ MUST be less than 15. None of the others is possible.

37. **A** $wl + \dfrac{\pi r^2}{2}$

This figure represents both a rectangle and a semicircle.
Formulas:
Area of rectangle = l (length) × w (width) or lw or wl

Area of semicircle = $\dfrac{\pi r^2}{2}$

Area of this figure = $wl + \dfrac{\pi r^2}{2}$

38. **B** 22
$\dfrac{\text{Won}}{\text{Played}}$ = Percent; Let x = no. of games the team must win

$$\frac{50 + x}{75 + 45} = 60\% \text{ or } \frac{50 + x}{120} = \frac{60}{100}$$
or 100 (50 + x) = 120 × 60
100x = 2,200; x = 22

39. **C** 6
By inspection, total the number of white columns that are longer than black columns.

40. **E** Transportation equipment
By observation, and by comparing the two columns for each industry. Actual subtraction of values is not necessary in this case, as the answer is obvious.

41. **D** Textile-Mill
By observation, and by comparing the two columns for each industry.

42. D Ordinance and Accessories
In this case, observing how *many* times greater the black column is than the white column gives the answer. Ordinance and Accessories about 4 times greater in 1955 than 1947–1949.

43. B 500,000
By approximating the amounts gained and lost by each industry for the years compared, the answer is roughly 500,000. Using numbers is not necessary here; approximating lengths is simpler and quicker.

44. B 35

$$7! = 7 \times 6 \times 5 \times 4 \times 3 \times 2 \times 1$$
$$5! = 5 \times 4 \times 3 \times 2 \times 1$$
$$6! = 6 \times 5 \times 4 \times 3 \times 2 \times 1$$
$$4! = 4 \times 3 \times 2 \times 1$$

Substituting

$$\frac{(7 \times 6 \times 5 \times 4 \times 3 \times 2 \times 1)(5 \times 4 \times 3 \times 2 \times 1)}{(6 \times 5 \times 4 \times 3 \times 2 \times 1)(4 \times 3 \times 2 \times 1)}$$

Canceling leaves $\dfrac{(7)(5)}{(1)(1)}$ or 35

Alternate method:

$$7! = 7(6!)$$
$$5! = 5(4!)$$

Substituting

$$\frac{7(6!)\ 5(4!)}{6!\ 4!}$$

and canceling gives $7 \times 5 = 35$

45. C 9

$$|7| = 7$$
$$|4 - 6| = |-2| = 2$$
$$7 + 2 = 9$$

46. D (5,6)

Adding the x values together and y values together of points

A and B (1,8)
          + (9,4)
          ————
          10,12

dividing each by 2 to find the midpoint leaves (5,6)

47. E −16

Substituting $x = -3$ leaves

$$y = (-3 + 5)(-3 - 5)$$
and $\quad y = (2)(-8)$
finally, $\quad y = -16$

48. A $\dfrac{10}{63}$

Multiplying the equation $\dfrac{1}{5} + \dfrac{1}{2} + \dfrac{1}{x} = 7$ by the common denominator $10x$ gives

$$\frac{10x}{5} + \frac{10x}{2} + \frac{10x}{x} = 7(10x)$$

reduced down to: $2x + 5x + 10 = 70x$
simplifying to: $7x + 10 = 70x$
Subtracting $7x$: $10 = 63x$
Dividing by 63: $\dfrac{10}{63} = x$

49. C $\dfrac{4}{9}$

$$a \,\#\, b = \frac{a^2}{b^2}$$

Substituting $a = 4$ and $b = 6$

$$4 \,\#\, 6 = \frac{(4)^2}{(6)^2} = \frac{16}{36} = \frac{8}{18} = \frac{4}{9}$$

50. C $\dfrac{1}{8}$

The area of the rectangle is divided into 4 equal areas. The shaded area is $\dfrac{1}{2}$ of one of the areas; therefore,

$$\frac{1}{2} \times \frac{1}{4} = \frac{1}{8}$$

51. D   III

The necessary condition refers to the denominator not equalling 0, as you cannot divide by 0. Therefore $xyz \neq 0$.

52. D

Federal government expenditures for military personnel have never been less than ten billion dollars. By inspection of the graph.

53. B   1961–1962

The rise from 1961 to 1962 was about 4 billion, which is greater than that of any two successive years.

54. E   None of these

The government never spent more on research and development than on operation and maintenance.

55. A   11%

To figure percentage decrease:

$$\frac{(\text{Fiscal year 1954}) - (\text{Fiscal year 1955})}{(\text{Fiscal year 1954})}$$

replacing values:

$$\frac{(48.8) - (43.0)}{48.8}$$

$$\frac{5.5}{48.8} = .11 \text{ or } 11\%$$

SECTION III: ANALYTICAL ABILITY

Analysis of Explanations

Set I.

1. B

The statement is not contradictory and does present a possible explanation of the result.

2. C

The statement is not contradictory and does not explain the result, but is deducible from the fact that the shipment was important for the pre-school rush.

3. **D**

The statement is not inconsistent, does not explain the result, and is not deducible from the fact situation, but it does *support* a possible explanation, namely that without Sally's experienced assistance, no one else could locate the shipment.

4. **E**

The statement does not contradict, explain, support, or weaken the fact situation or the result; it is therefore irrelevant.

5. **B**

The statement is not contradictory, and does present a possible explanation of the result.

6. **A**

The shortage became evident as Sally was taking inventory.

7. **A**

Tim immediately had the store searched, thereby reacting quite well.

8. **B**

The statement is not contradictory, and does present a possible explanation of the result.

9. **C**

The statement is not contradictory and does not explain the result, but is deducible from the fact that Sally discovered that a shipment was missing.

10. **E**

The statement does not contradict, explain, support, or weaken the fact situation or the result; it is therefore irrelevant.

Set II.

11. **B**

The statement is not contradictory, and does present a possible explanation of the result.

12. **A**

We are told that Jill is an algebra teacher.

13. D

The statement is not inconsistent, does not explain the result, and is not deducible from the fact situation, but it does *support* a possible explanation, namely that Robbins' mind was already made up.

14. D

The statement is not inconsistent, does not explain the result, and is not deducible from the fact situation, but it does weaken a possible explanation of the fact that Robbins had Jill take the complete class for two weeks.

15. B

The statement is not contradictory, and does present a possible explanation of the result.

16. E

The statement does not contradict, explain, support, or weaken the fact situation or the result; it is therefore irrelevant.

17. C

The statement is not inconsistent, nor is it an explanation, but it is deducible from the fact that Jill was nervous about teaching.

18. B

The statement is not contradictory, and does present a possible explanation of the paradoxical result.

19. B

The statement is not contradictory, and does present a possible explanation of the result.

20. A

We are told that Mr. Robbins felt that Jill would be a fine teacher.

Set III.

21. C

The statement is not inconsistent, nor is it an explanation, but it is deducible from the reference in the fact situation to 3 younger girls and a son.

22. A

Sargeant had disappeared before Ted arrived home.

23.   B

The statement is not inconsistent, and presents a possible explanation of the result.

24.   E

The statement does not contradict, explain, support, or weaken the fact situation or the result; it is therefore irrelevant.

25.   D

The statement is not inconsistent, does not explain the result, and is not deducible from the fact situation, but it does *support* a possible explanation, especially since Sargeant was "ruffled."

26.   B

The statement is not inconsistent, and since Mr. Barker and Ted did go to the animal shelter, it presents a possible explanation of the result.

27.   D

The statement is not inconsistent, and does not explain the result, but is deducible from the fact that Sargeant escaped.

28.   A

Sargeant was at least 11 years old.

29.   C

The statement is not inconsistent, nor is it an explanation, but it is deducible from the fact that the children became upset at Sargeant's disappearance.

30.   D

The statement is not contradictory, does not explain the result, and is not deducible from the fact situation, but it does either support or weaken a possible explanation, since Sargeant may or may not have been found at the shelter.

Set IV.

31.   E

The statement does not contradict, explain, support, or weaken the fact situation or the result; it is therefore irrelevant.

32.   C

This statement is not inconsistent with the fact that Mr. Wilson was delayed, and does not explain the result. You may deduce that the accident delay made Mr. Wilson late for work.

33. A

The fact situation and the result contradict this statement.

34. B

This statement is not inconsistent, and does provide a possible explanation for Mrs. Mumple's apparently "reckless" driving.

35. B

This statement is not inconsistent, and is a possible explanation of the result.

36. C

The statement is not contradictory and does not explain the result, but is deducible from the fact that Mr. Wilson's innocent involvement would nevertheless become part of his driving record.

37. D

The statement is not inconsistent, does not explain the result, and is not deducible from the fact situation, but it does *weaken* a possible explanation, namely that Mrs. Mumple's erratic reaction was unwarranted.

38. A

We are told that Mr. Wilson was on his way to work.

39. E

The statement does not contradict, explain, support, or weaken the fact situation or the result; it is therefore irrelevant.

40. C

The statement is not inconsistent, nor does it explain the result, but it is deducible from the fact that the truck driver stopped to give assistance.

SECTION IV: ANALYTICAL ABILITY

Logical Diagrams

1. C

Water and alcohol have no members in common, but are both within the set of liquids.

2. A

Viral pneumonia is a kind of pneumonia, and pneumonia is a kind of infection.

3. C

Tennis and badminton are different games, but are both within the set of racket sports.

4. A

Beaver is a kind of rodent, and rodent is a kind of mammal.

5. B

Hat is a kind of headgear, and socks are unrelated.

6. A

Steam is a kind of vapor, and vapor is a kind of gas.

7. D

Small cars and fast cars have some members in common. Miniature racers is within this intersection or overlap.

8. C

Comedian is within the greater set of actors, and dentist is unrelated.

9. B

Metal is a kind of solid, and solids are kinds of substances.

10. E

Bicycles and unicycles are different, but are both within the set of cycles.

11. D

Fence and wooden objects can have some members in common, mirror is unrelated.

12. B

Rocker is a kind of chair, and chair is a kind of seat.

13. C

Spheres are within the set of three-dimensional figures, and squares are unrelated.

14. E

Spoons and forks have no elements in common, but are both within the set of silverware.

15. A

Long-sleeved solid shirts are within the set of long-sleeved shirts, but checkered shirts has members in common only with long-sleeved shirts.

Questions 16–19 can be solved much more easily by the use of the following diagram (lines connect players that do not play well together according to the statements given):

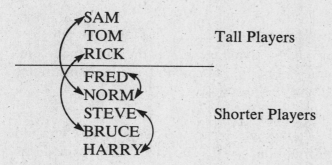

SAM
TOM   Tall Players
RICK
FRED
NORM
STEVE   Shorter Players
BRUCE
HARRY

16. **D** Fred, Bruce, & Harry.
With Sam starting, Norm will not start, because they do not play well together. With Tom starting, Rick will not start because only two tall players are needed. This leaves Fred, Steve, Bruce, and Harry, but Steve and Harry do not play well together; therefore either Fred, Bruce, & Harry or Fred, Bruce, & Steve will start the game.

17. **A** Fred.
If Tom does not start the game, then Sam and Rick will start. If Sam and Rick start the game, then Norm and Bruce will not start. This leaves Fred, Steve, and Harry; but Steve and Harry do not play well together, therefore Fred is the most likely to start the game.

18. **C** I & II.
Harry and Bruce will start the game. If Sam starts the game, then Norm will not. If Steve will not start the game then Harry probably will. Harry, Bruce, and Fred will have to start the game because they are the only shorter players left. Fred is not one of the choices.

19. **D** I & II.
Steve and Harry never play together and Fred and Sam do play together. Steve and Harry don't play well together. If Sam plays, then Norm doesn't, and Fred does. (Check the diagram for the best combination.)

20. **B** II.
Slower traffic means more time on the road. This is the only possibility, as more time on the road could mean more accidents. I and III are not good arguments for the insurance companies, as both are negated by the original statements.

21.   A   I.
Company costs have decreased in the last few years. This would be one more reason why the companies should lower their premium rates.

22.   C
The driver is being taken advantage of by the insurance companies. This is pointed out by the statement, "Yet, auto insurance rates have not reflected this decrease."

Questions 23–28 should definitely be charted to give a more clear and concise picture of the information given. The chart can be made as follows:

	Jan.	Feb.	Mar.	Apr.	May	Jun.	Jul.	Aug.	Sep.	Oct.	Nov.	Dec.
Football	✓								✓	✓	✓	✓
Baseball				✓	✓	✓	✓	✓	✓	✓		
Basketball	✓	✓	✓	✓	✓					✓	✓	✓
Hockey	✓	✓	✓	✓	✓					✓	✓	✓
Soccer				✓	✓	✓	✓	✓				
Tennis				✓	✓	✓	✓	✓				

23.   C   April and May.
The chart shows this.

24.   B   Football.
The chart shows this.

25.   E   3.
Football, basketball, and hockey can be seen in January. Hockey and basketball can be seen in February and March. The question asks for the number of different sports—football, basketball, hockey.

26.   D   10.
These two sports, one or both, are played during every month except for February and March.

27.   B   3.
Baseball, basketball, and hockey have seasons longer than six months.

28. E   Hockey and baseball.
The chart shows this.

29. D
Every question may be interpreted more than one way. It is stated that there are two sides to every question.

30. E   I & II.
This statement uses an analogy to make a point (equating questions to flypaper). This statement emphasizes the importance of choice by stating that it is a big difference to the fly which side he chooses.

SECTION V: MATH ABILITY

1. A $\frac{3}{4}$

$$2.5 = 2\frac{1}{2} = \frac{5}{2}$$
$$0.30 = \frac{30}{100} = \frac{3}{10}$$
$$\frac{5}{2} \times \frac{3}{10} = \frac{15}{20} = \frac{3}{4}$$

2. C $\frac{19}{10}$
Solving for x:

$$\frac{3}{5} + \frac{1}{2} + x = 3$$
$$\frac{6}{10} + \frac{5}{10} + x = 3$$
$$\frac{11}{10} + x = 3$$

Subtracting $\frac{11}{10}$ from both sides leaves

$$x = 1\frac{9}{10} \text{ or } \frac{19}{10}$$

3. B 28
By carefully counting the number of sides around the outside of the figure and multiplying by two. (Don't let the square on the right of the figure bother you; use some common sense.)

4. D $\frac{1}{3}$

Setting up the ratio

$$\frac{a}{b} = \frac{9b}{a}$$

and solving

$$a^2 = 9b^2$$
$$a = 3b$$

then $\dfrac{a}{b} = \dfrac{3}{1}$ and $\dfrac{b}{a} = \dfrac{1}{3}$

5. B $n - 1$

The complete expression by following instructions is

$$\frac{5n + 10}{5} - 3$$

Simplifying by dividing the 5 into $5n + 10$ leaves

$$n + 2 - 3 \text{ or } n - 1.$$

6. D $20°$

The complete angle ABC is $140°$, and the two angles inside the complete angle are $90°$ and $70°$, totaling $160°$. Therefore $20°$ must be overlapping or in angle DBE.

7. C 30 feet

The area of a right triangle is formed. $x^2 + 10^2 = 32^2$ or $x^2 + 100 = 1,024$ or $x^2 = 924$
$x = 30.3$ or 30 feet (to the nearest foot)

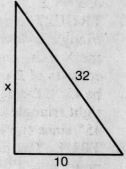

8. C $w^2 + 3w - 88 = 0$

w = width of rectangle
$w + 3$ = length of rectangle
Area = length $\times$ width or $(w + 3)(w)$
$\therefore w^2 + 3w = 88$ or $w^2 + 3w - 88 = 0$

9. **A**   2 miles
    $3 : 1 = 6 : x$ or $3x = 6$ or $x = 2$ miles

10. **C**   about 16.4 miles

    $$\text{Time} = \frac{\text{Distance}}{\text{Rate}}$$

    <u>Distance covered after 3 hours</u>
    Boy—$6 \times 3 = 18$ miles
    Girl—$5 \times 3 = 15$ miles

    Distance between them $= 3$ miles

    $x =$ distance traveled by the girl after first 3 hours
    $3 - x =$ distance traveled by the boy during this time
    $$\therefore \frac{x}{5} = \frac{3 - x}{6}$$
    (the element of Time is eliminated here since it is the same for both the girl and the boy)
    $6x = 15 - 5x$ or $11x = 15$
    $x = 1.4$ miles
    $\therefore$ the girl (sister) traveled $15 + 1.4$ or 16.4 miles

11. **E**   none of these
    The following coordinates of x and y may be obtained from the graph:

x	0	1	2	3
y	−4	−2	0	2

    (A)   TRUE (by inspection). As x increases, y increases.
    (B)   TRUE (by inspection). When $x = 0$, $y = 4$; when $y = 0$, $x = 2$.
    (C)   TRUE. The angle marked ⊖ is greater than 45°. A right triangle is formed by the straight line $2x - y - 4 = 0$, the X axis, and the line $x = 3$. The leg opposite angle ⊖ consists of 2 units and the adjacent leg of 1 unit. ⊖ would be 45° if the legs were equal (the acute angles of an isosceles right triangle are each 45°). The angle must be more than 45° since the leg opposite the angle ⊖ is the greater.
    (D)   TRUE. The graph, if continued, would pass through the point $x = 15$, $y = 26$.
    The coordinates of a point which lies on a graph will satisfy the equation of the graph.
    $2x - y - 4 = 0$ or
    $2(15) - (26) - 4 = 0$ or
    $30 - 30 = 0$
    $0 = 0$

12.   C   If one of the integers from 8 to 15 inclusive is chosen at random, the probability that the integer is even is equal to the probability that it is odd.

$$P_{even} = 4 = 8, 10, 12, 14;$$
$$q_{even} = 4 = 9, 11, 13, 15$$
$$\frac{p}{p + q} = \frac{4}{4 + 4} = \frac{1}{2}$$
$$P_{odd} = 4 = 9, 11, 13, 15;$$
$$q_{odd} = 4 = 8, 10, 12, 14$$
$$\frac{p}{p + q} = \frac{4}{4 + 4} = \frac{1}{2}$$

$\therefore$ (C) is true inasmuch as $\frac{1}{2} = \frac{1}{2}$

13.   D $3\sqrt{.0916}$, 53 : 125, .425, $\frac{266}{625}$

The expressions should be converted to decimal form.

Expression (A)
$$53 : 125 = \frac{53}{125} = \frac{424}{1000} = .424$$

Expression (B) $3\sqrt{.0916} =$
$$3\sqrt{\frac{196}{10,000}} = \frac{3 \times 14}{100} = \frac{42}{100} = .42$$

Expression (C)
.425 = .425 (no change required)

Expression (D) $\frac{266}{625} = .4256$

14.   B   21

Diagram (1)
17-inch side: 3-inch cuts; 22-inch side: 5-inch cuts = total 20

Diagram (2)
17-inch side: 5-inch cuts; 22-inch side: 3-inch cuts = total 21

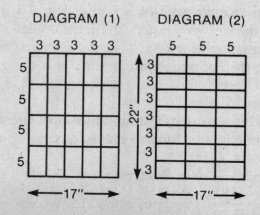

15. B b, c.
Each statement must be tested individually. Let us assume that the number is 35; 3 would be the tens digit and 5 would be the units digit. Or $x = 3$, $y = 5$.

> a. $10(3) + 5 = 35$ (True)
> b. $3 \times 5 = 15$ (False)
> c. $5 \times 3 = 15$ (not 53) (False)
> d. $53 - 35 = 18$ (which is exactly divisible by 9) (True)
> e. $35 + 53 = 88$ (which is exactly divisible by 11) (True)

16. E $50.
The problem may be solved as follows: Let x = list price
Then $x - .1x = .9x$ (price after first discount of 10%)
$.9x - .02(.9x) = \$44.10$ (price after both discounts 10% and 2%)
$.9x - .018x = \$44.10$; $x = \$50$

17. C $3\frac{3}{5}$ miles
Given: distance between A and B = 6 miles.
Then x = number of miles from A and $6 - x$ = number of miles from B. Cost of cartage from A = $.50(x)$; cost of cartage from B = $.75(6 - x)$.
$\therefore .50(x) = .75(6 - x)$ or
$.50x = 4.5 - .75x$; $x = 3\frac{3}{5}$ miles

18. C generally declined
By inspection.

19. E rose and then declined
By inspection.

20. B January, 1962
By inspection and comparison.

21. C the first quarter of 1961
By inspection and comparison.

22. C 15 percent
In January, 1961, industrial production was about 103 and in the last month indicated, June, 1962, industrial production was about 118.
To find the percent of increase
$$\frac{118 - 103}{103} = \frac{15}{103} \text{ or about 15 percent.}$$

23. D   30 inches

If h = altitude, then $\frac{1}{2}h$ = base

Area of a triangle = $\frac{1}{2}$ base × altitude

$225 = \frac{1}{2}h \times h = \frac{1}{4}h^2$ or $900 = h^2$

$h = 30$ inches

24. B   2°

The sum of the temperatures given = 16°; the number of readings is 7

∴ $16° \div 7 = 2\frac{2}{7}°$ or 2° (to the nearest degree)

25. B   82

As x increases 4, y increases 8; therefore the chart can be continued as follows:

x	31	35	39	43	47
y	50	58	66	74	82

Therefore when $x = 47$, $y = 82$.

Alternate method:

Since y is increasing twice as fast as x, and to get to 47, x will be increased by 20, then y will have to be increased by 40.

$40 + 42 = 82$.

6

Basic Skills Review

A Comprehensive Review of Arithmetic, Algebra, Geometry, Word Problems, and Graph Reading.

The second part of the GRE consists of a series of problems that measure mathematical ability and insight. The subject matter of these problems is based on standard high school mathematical courses, including elementary algebra and geometry. The questions are designed to measure (1) your knowledge of elementary mathematics, (2) your ability to apply your mathematical knowledge to new situations, and (3) the extent of your mathematical insight when presented with nonroutine concepts and problems.

The following review section is designed to sharpen your skills and refresh your memory for handling a great variety of mathematical problems. First, take the diagnostic self-tests at the beginning of the sections on arithmetic, algebra, and geometry. Second, correct each self-test and check the problems you missed with the corresponding encircled numbers in each section. These sections are keyed to give you a careful explanation of the type of problem you missed. Finally, each section provides extra practice problems and complete explanations to help you strengthen your skills.

The diagnostic tests are on the following pages:

Arithmetic—page 380
Algebra—page 425
Geometry—page 456

A basic skills review checklist follows to help you review systematically.

BASIC SKILLS CHECKLIST

AREAS COVERED:

Arithmetic

- _____Fractions
- _____Decimals
- _____Percent
- _____Properties of numbers
- _____Squares and square roots
- _____Number series
- _____Signed numbers

Algebra

- _____Algebraic equations
- _____Literal equations
- _____Evaluation of expressions
- _____Simultaneous equations
- _____Monomials and polynomials
- _____Factoring
- _____Solving quadratic equations
- _____Inequalities

Geometry

Angles

- _____Types of angles
- _____Pairs of angles
- _____Parallel lines, perpendicular lines and their angles

Triangles

- _____Types of triangles
- _____The Pythagorean Theorem

Plane and Solid Figures

- _____Polygons
- _____Circles
- _____Perimeter and area

Word Problems

————Key words and phrases
————Guidelines for solving word problems
————Number problems
————Age problems
————Motion problems
————Perimeter problems
————Ratio and proportion problems
————Interest problems
————Mixture problems
————Work problems

Graphs

————Bar graphs
————Circle graph or pie chart
————Line graphs
————Horizontal bar graph
————Circle graph
————Vertical bar graph
————Combination circle graphs
————Multiple line graph
————Cumulative bar graph
————Number charts
————Triangular graphs
————Mapping chart
————Flow chart

ARITHMETIC DIAGNOSTIC SELF-TEST

(1.) Reduce $\frac{14}{35} = \frac{2}{5}$

(2.) $\frac{3}{11} + \frac{6}{11} = \frac{9}{11}$

(3.) $\frac{1}{3} + 1\frac{2}{5} + 4\frac{2}{15} = \frac{5}{15} + \frac{21}{15} + \frac{62}{15} = \frac{88}{15} = 5\frac{13}{15}$

(4.) $3\frac{1}{5} + 4\frac{3}{8} = 7\frac{23}{40}$

(5.) $\frac{11}{18} - \frac{4}{9} = \frac{11}{18} - \frac{8}{18} = \frac{3}{18} = \frac{1}{6}$

(6.) $6\frac{1}{4} - 3\frac{2}{3} = 2\frac{7}{12}$

(7.) $\frac{3}{8} \times \frac{2}{7} = \frac{6}{56} = \frac{3}{28}$

(8.) $5 \times \frac{3}{7} = \frac{15}{7} = 2\frac{1}{7}$

(9.) Change to improper fraction: $4\frac{3}{8} = \frac{35}{8}$

(10.) $6\frac{1}{5} \times 3\frac{2}{3} = \frac{31}{5} \times \frac{11}{3} = \frac{341}{15} = 22\frac{11}{15}$

(11.) $\frac{5}{9} \times \frac{3}{7} = \frac{35}{63} \times \frac{21}{63} = \frac{56}{63} = \frac{8}{9}$ $\frac{35}{63} \times \frac{27}{63}$

(12.) $7\frac{11}{12} \div 4\frac{1}{6}$ $\frac{95}{12} \times \frac{6}{25}$

(13.) $\dfrac{\frac{1}{7} + \frac{3}{5}}{9 + 1} =$ $\dfrac{\frac{5}{35} + \frac{21}{35}}{9+1} = \dfrac{\frac{26}{35}}{10} = \frac{26}{35} \times \frac{1}{10} = \frac{13}{35} \times \frac{1}{35} = \frac{91}{35}$

$\frac{91}{35} = 2\frac{21}{35}$

(14.) $\dfrac{\frac{1}{5} + \frac{1}{6}}{\frac{1}{4} + \frac{2}{3}} =$

(15.)   3.7 + 2.9 + 14.136 = *20.736*

(16.)   8.2 − 2.176 =

(17.)   5.351 − 4.8 = *.551*

(18.)   6.3 × 4.1 = *25.83*

(19.)   91.32 ÷ .04 = *2283*

(20.) $\frac{3}{5}$ is *60*%

(21.)   45% is what fraction? *$\frac{45}{100} = \frac{9}{20}$*

(22.)   What is 27% of 53? *14.31*

(23.)   7 is what percent of 25? *28 %*

(24.)   12 is 30% of what number? *40*

(25.)   Bob's wages increased from $150 to $200 last week. What was his percentage increase? *25 %*

(26.)   Is 99 prime? *no*

(27.)   What is the mean or average of 78, 91, 64, 82, 50? *73*

(28.)   Give an approximation for $\sqrt{30}$ *= 5.4*

(29.)   Simplify $\sqrt{50}$ *~ $\sqrt{49}$ ~ 7*   *5.5*

(30.)   −8 + 5 = *−3*

(31.)   −6 − 5 = *−11*

(32.)   −5 − (−12) = *−17*

(33.)   (−18) (5) = *−13*

(34.)   −12 ÷ +4 = *−3*

(35.) $\frac{−18}{−3}$ *= −6*

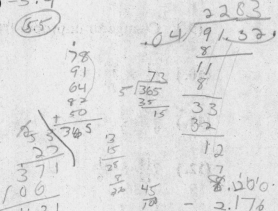

ANSWERS TO ARITHMETIC DIAGNOSTIC SELF-TEST

1. $\frac{2}{5}$

2. $\frac{9}{11}$

3. $5\frac{13}{15}$

4. $7\frac{23}{40}$

5. $\frac{3}{18} = \frac{1}{6}$

6. $2\frac{7}{12}$

7. $\frac{3}{28}$

8. $\frac{15}{7} = 2\frac{1}{7}$

9. $\frac{35}{8}$

10. $\frac{341}{15} = 22\frac{11}{15}$

11. $\frac{5}{21}$

12. $\frac{19}{10} = 1\frac{9}{10}$

13. $\frac{13}{175}$

14. $\frac{2}{5}$

15. 20.736

16. 6.024

17. .551

18. 25.83

19. 2,283

20. 60%

21. $\frac{9}{20}$

22. 14.31

23. 28%

24. 40

25. $33\frac{1}{3}\%$

26. No

27. 73

28. 5.5

29. $5\sqrt{2}$

30. -3

31. -11

32. $+7$

33. -90

34. -3

35. $+6$

ARITHMETIC

FRACTIONS

A fraction is a piece of something. In arithmetic, a fraction is made up of two parts—one part above a line and the other part under the line. The number below the line in a fraction is called the *denominator*, and the number above the line is called the *numerator*. The *denominator* tells the number of equal pieces into which something has been divided. For example, if the denominator is 4, it tells you that something has been divided into 4 equal pieces. The *numerator* tells how many of the pieces are in the fraction.

$$\frac{3}{4} \quad \text{numerator} \atop \text{denominator}$$

You read this fraction as three-fourths. The 4 in the denominator tells you that something has been divided into 4 equal parts. The 3 in the numerator means the fraction represents 3 of these parts. For example, if you have $\frac{3}{4}$ of a pie, it means the pie has been cut into four equal pieces and you have three of these pieces. This type of fraction is called a *common fraction*.

If a number includes both a whole number and a fraction, it is called a *mixed number*. Thus, $3\frac{1}{2}$ is a mixed number. If a fraction's numerator is larger than its denominator, it is called an *improper fraction*: $\frac{8}{3}$, $\frac{17}{4}$, and $\frac{89}{67}$ are all improper fractions.

Reducing Fractions

All solutions to fraction problems must be reduced to *lowest terms*. This may be done by dividing the numerator and the denominator by the *highest* number that will go into both evenly.

① EXAMPLES:

(1) $\frac{8}{32}$ may be reduced by dividing the numerator and denominator both by 8. Thus, $\frac{8}{32} = \frac{1}{4}$, since $8 \div 8 = 1$ and $32 \div 8 = 4$.

(2) $\frac{12}{28}$ may be reduced by dividing both the numerator and denominator by 4. Thus, $\frac{12}{28} = \frac{3}{7}$, since $12 \div 4 = 3$ and $28 \div 4 = 7$. Notice that if we divided both the numerator and denominator in this problem by 2 we would get $\frac{6}{14}$, which could again be reduced, by dividing by 2, to $\frac{3}{7}$. For this reason it is important when reducing fractions to try to find the *highest* number that will divide into the numerator and denominator to avoid having to reduce more than one time.

PRACTICE EXERCISES 1:
Reduce the following fractions to lowest terms. (Answers to Practice Exercises appear at end of chapter.)

1. $\frac{4}{36}$ = $\frac{1}{9}$

2. $\frac{7}{42}$ = $\frac{1}{6}$

3. $\frac{12}{90}$ = $\frac{4}{30}$ = $\frac{2}{15}$

4. $\frac{51}{85}$ = $\frac{3}{5}$

Addition of Fractions

To add fractions it is necessary to find the *lowest common denominator*, or L.C.D. This is the *smallest* number that can be divided evenly by all the denominators in the problem. Sometimes the L.C.D. will be one of the denominators in the problem and sometimes it will be an entirely new number. All problems in addition of fractions fall into one of the following three categories.

TYPE I: All the Denominators Are the Same

To get the answer, simply add the numerators and place the sum over the common denominator.

② EXAMPLES:

(1)
$$\begin{array}{r} \frac{2}{13} \\ +\frac{7}{13} \\ \hline \frac{9}{13} \end{array}$$

(2)
$$\begin{array}{r} \frac{3}{20} \\ \frac{7}{20} \\ +\frac{5}{20} \\ \hline \frac{15}{20} = \frac{3}{4} \end{array}$$

TYPE II: One of the Denominators Is the L.C.D.

To get the answer, use the denominator of the fraction that all the other denominators will divide into evenly as the L.C.D. Then change all the other fractions to fractions with this denominator. This can be done by dividing the L.C.D. by each denominator of each fraction and multiplying this answer by the respective numerators of the fractions. Although this may sound complicated, the following example shows that it is easier than it sounds.

③ EXAMPLE: *Add*

(1) $4\frac{3}{8}$

$1\frac{1}{4}$

$5\frac{5}{24}$

The smallest number that can be divided evenly by all the denominators is 24, which is the L.C.D. Dividing 24 by each denominator and multiplying the answer by the numerator, we have:

$$\frac{3}{8} = \frac{9}{24}$$

$$\frac{1}{4} = \frac{6}{24}$$

$$\frac{5}{24} = \frac{5}{24}; \text{ then adding:}$$

$$\begin{array}{r} 4\frac{9}{24} \\ 1\frac{6}{24} \\ 5\frac{5}{24} \\ \hline 10\frac{20}{24}, \end{array}$$

and reducing the fraction: $10\frac{5}{6}$ is the answer.

TYPE III: *None of the Denominators Is the L.C.D.*

To get the answer, it is usually sufficient to find the L.C.D. by multiplying all the denominators together and then proceeding as in Type II problems.

(4) EXAMPLES:

(1) *Add*

$$2\frac{3}{4}$$

$$+5\frac{1}{9}$$

We use 36 as the L.C.D., since it is the product of the denominators, 4 and 9. Then,

$$2\frac{27}{36}$$

$$+5\frac{4}{36}$$

$$7\frac{31}{36} \text{ Ans.}$$

(2)

$$\frac{1}{3}$$

$$\frac{1}{4}$$

$$+\frac{1}{5}$$

We use 60 as the L.C.D., since it is the product of the denominators, 3, 4, and 5 ($3 \times 4 \times 5 = 60$). Then,

$$\frac{20}{60}$$

$$\frac{15}{60}$$

$$+\frac{12}{60}$$

$$\frac{47}{60} \text{ Ans.}$$

Multiplying all the denominators together, however, sometimes gives a common denominator larger than the *lowest* common denominator.

EXAMPLE:

$$\frac{3}{12} + \frac{4}{18}$$

Multiplying the denominators, $12 \times 18 = 216$; but the L.C.D. is 36, not 216. In such a case the L.C.D. can be found by inspection or by trial and error. When you look at the problem, think of multiples of 12 that might be divisible by 18. $2 \times 12 = 24$ is not divisible, but $3 \times 12 = 36$ is.

Note: If fractions add up to more than 1 (i.e., the answer is an improper fraction), change the answer to a mixed number by (1) dividing the numerator by the denominator, and (2) writing the remainder as a fraction:

EXAMPLE:

$$\frac{1}{3} = \frac{2}{6}$$
$$+\frac{5}{6} = \frac{5}{6}$$

$$\frac{7}{6} = 6\overline{)7} = 1\frac{1}{6}$$
$$\underline{6}$$
$$1$$

PRACTICE EXERCISES 2:
(Answers to Practice Exercises appear at end of chapter.)

(1) If Marie adds $3\frac{3}{5}$ cups of sugar to $2\frac{7}{15}$ cups of sugar, how many cups of sugar will she have altogether?

(2) Emmanuel has cut three pieces of wood of lengths $\frac{1}{3}$ ft., $\frac{2}{6}$ ft., $\frac{5}{18}$ ft., which he intends to use to make a coffee table. What is the total length of the three pieces?

(3) What is the sum of $\frac{5}{6}$ and $\frac{6}{7}$?

(4) The number of inches of rainfall on three successive days was $4\frac{1}{5}''$, $3\frac{2}{7}''$, and $1\frac{1}{2}''$. What was the total number of inches of rainfall for the three days?

Subtraction of Fractions

To subtract one fraction from another, you use the same general procedure as in addition of fractions.

(5) EXAMPLES:

(1)

$$\begin{array}{r} \frac{11}{12} \\ -\frac{7}{12} \\ \hline \frac{4}{12} = \frac{1}{3} \end{array}$$

(2)

$$\begin{array}{rl} 5\frac{5}{18} = & 5\frac{5}{18} \\ -2\frac{1}{6} = & -2\frac{3}{18} \\ \hline & 3\frac{2}{18} = 3\frac{1}{9} \end{array}$$

In the subtraction of mixed numbers, if the number you are subtracting (lower) has a fraction in it larger than the fraction that is in the number you are subtracting from (upper), you must: (1) find the L.C.D., (2) borrow 1 from the upper whole number, (3) change 1 to a fraction with the L.C.D., (4) add it to the upper fraction. Then, proceed as in previous examples. Thus,

(6)

$$\begin{array}{r} 7\frac{1}{3} \\ -3\frac{5}{6} \\ \hline \end{array}$$

The L.C.D. is 6. Borrow 1 $\left(=\frac{6}{6}\right)$ from 7, and to $\frac{1}{3}\left(=\frac{2}{6}\right)$ add $\frac{6}{6}$, thus: $\frac{2}{6} + \frac{6}{6} = \frac{8}{6}$. Now, the upper mixed number is $6\frac{8}{6}$ (that is, $7\frac{1}{3} = 6\frac{8}{6}$). Then,

$$\begin{array}{r} 6\frac{8}{6} \\ -3\frac{5}{6} \\ \hline 3\frac{3}{6} = 3\frac{1}{2}. \end{array}$$

PRACTICE EXERCISES 3:
(Answers to Practice Exercises appear at end of chapter.)

(1) Find the difference between $\frac{7}{8}$ and $\frac{3}{16}$.

(2) What is the remainder, if from a piece of cloth $3\frac{3}{4}$ feet long, a piece $1\frac{1}{3}$ feet long has been cut away?

(3) Subtract: $6\frac{3}{8}$
$\qquad\qquad -2\frac{3}{4}$

(4) If a job takes $4\frac{2}{9}$ days to do and the men on the job have already worked $2\frac{3}{5}$ days, how many days of work remain to complete the job?

(5) Subtract $3\frac{3}{4}$ from 8.

Multiplication of Fractions

To multiply fractions, simply find the products of their numerators and denominators.

⑦ EXAMPLES:

(1) $\frac{4}{7} \times \frac{3}{5} = \frac{12}{35}$

(2) $\frac{3}{8} \times \frac{5}{6} = \frac{15}{48} = \frac{5}{16}$

⑧ (3) $3 \times \frac{5}{8} = \frac{3}{1} \times \frac{5}{8} = \frac{15}{8} = 1\frac{7}{8}$

To change a mixed number to an improper fraction, (1) multiply the whole number part of the mixed number by the denominator of the fraction, (2) add the product to the fraction's numerator, and (3) place the sum over the denominator.

(9) EXAMPLE:

Change $7\frac{5}{6}$ to an improper fraction.

(1) $6 \times 7 = 42$

(2) $42 + 5 = 47$

(3) $\frac{47}{6}$

Thus, $7\frac{5}{6} = \frac{47}{6}$.

To multiply mixed numbers, change each mixed number to an improper fraction and proceed as indicated above.

(10) EXAMPLES:

(1) $4\frac{2}{3} \times \frac{2}{7} = \frac{14}{3} \times \frac{2}{7} = \frac{28}{21} = 1\frac{7}{21} = 1\frac{1}{3}$

(2) $3\frac{1}{2} \times 2\frac{2}{3} = \frac{7}{2} \times \frac{8}{3} = \frac{56}{6} = 9\frac{2}{6} = 9\frac{1}{3}$

PRACTICE EXERCISES 4:
(Answers to Practice Exercises appear at end of chapter.)

(1)   Find the product of $\frac{4}{9}$ and $\frac{5}{8}$.

(2)   If Carlos cuts off $\frac{1}{3}$ of a metal pipe $12\frac{3}{4}''$ long, how much has he cut off?

(3)   Multiply $6\frac{3}{5}$ by $2\frac{3}{11}$.

(4)   Raymond was absent from school $\frac{1}{6}$ of the total number of school days in November. If there were 21 school days that month, how many days was he absent?

Division of Fractions

To divide fractions, simply *invert* (turn upside down) the *divisor* (the fraction to be divided into the given fraction) and then proceed as in multiplication. Convert mixed numbers to fractions and proceed in the same way.

(11) EXAMPLES:

(1) $\dfrac{2}{3} \div \dfrac{1}{4} = \dfrac{2}{3} \times \dfrac{4}{1} = \dfrac{8}{3} = 2\dfrac{2}{3}$

(2) $\dfrac{2}{9} \div 8 = \dfrac{2}{9} \div \dfrac{8}{1} = \dfrac{2}{9} \times \dfrac{1}{8} = \dfrac{2}{72} = \dfrac{1}{36}$

(3) $7 \div 5\dfrac{5}{6} = \dfrac{7}{1} \div \dfrac{35}{6} = \dfrac{7}{1} \times \dfrac{6}{35} = \dfrac{42}{35} = 1\dfrac{7}{35} = 1\dfrac{1}{5}$

(12)

(4) $3\dfrac{7}{8} \div 1\dfrac{11}{20} = \dfrac{31}{8} \div \dfrac{31}{20} = \dfrac{31}{8} \times \dfrac{20}{31} = \dfrac{20}{8} = 2\dfrac{4}{8} = 2\dfrac{1}{2}$

PRACTICE EXERCISES 5:
(Answers to Practice Exercises appear at end of chapter.)

(1) Divide $\dfrac{9}{10}$ by $\dfrac{1}{5}$.

(2) If 9 is divided by $\dfrac{3}{4}$, what is the result?

(3) What is the quotient of $2\dfrac{1}{6} \div 26$?

(4) How many times can $6\dfrac{2}{3}$ fit into 60?

Simplifying Complex Fractions

When the numerator or denominator of a fraction consists of the sum or difference of two numbers, the two numbers should be combined into one number in the interest of simplification.

(13) EXAMPLES:

(1) $\dfrac{25 + 3}{4 + 3} = \dfrac{28}{7} = 4$

(2) $\dfrac{\frac{1}{3} + \frac{1}{2}}{8 + 4} = \dfrac{\frac{2 + 3}{6}}{12} = \dfrac{\frac{5}{6}}{12} = \dfrac{5}{6} \times \dfrac{1}{12} = \dfrac{5}{72}$

(14)

(3)

$\dfrac{\frac{1}{3} + \frac{3}{4}}{\frac{2}{5} + \frac{1}{2}} = \dfrac{\frac{4 + 9}{12}}{\frac{4 + 5}{10}} = \dfrac{\frac{13}{12}}{\frac{9}{10}} = \dfrac{13}{12} \times \dfrac{\cancel{10}^{5}}{9} = \dfrac{65}{54} = 1\dfrac{11}{54}$

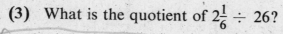
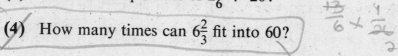
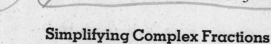

PRACTICE EXERCISES 6:
(Answers to Practice Exercises appear at end of chapter.)

(1) Reduce to lowest terms: $\dfrac{2+24}{100}$ $= \dfrac{26}{100} = \dfrac{13}{50}$

(2) Reduce to lowest terms: $\dfrac{\frac{1}{2}-\frac{1}{4}}{\frac{5}{8}}$ $= \dfrac{\frac{4}{8}-\frac{2}{8}}{\frac{5}{8}} = \dfrac{2}{8} \times \dfrac{8}{5} = \dfrac{2}{5}$

ok now

(3) Simplify: $\dfrac{3+\frac{1}{2}+2}{3+\frac{1}{3}}$ $= \dfrac{5\frac{1}{2}}{3\frac{1}{3}} = \dfrac{\frac{11}{2}}{\frac{10}{3}} = \dfrac{11}{2} \times \dfrac{3}{10} = \dfrac{33}{20} = 1\dfrac{13}{20}$

ok now

(4) Simplify: $\dfrac{\frac{1}{2}+\frac{1}{8}}{5}$ $= \dfrac{\frac{8+2}{16}}{5} = \dfrac{10}{16} \times \dfrac{1}{5} = \dfrac{2}{16} = \dfrac{1}{8}$

Answers and Solutions

PRACTICE EXERCISES 1:

(1) $\dfrac{1}{9}$

(2) $\dfrac{1}{6}$

(3) $\dfrac{2}{15}$

(4) $\dfrac{3}{5}$

PRACTICE EXERCISES 2:

(1) $6\dfrac{1}{15}$

$$3\tfrac{3}{5} = 3\tfrac{9}{15}$$
$$+2\tfrac{7}{15} = 2\tfrac{7}{15}$$
$$5\tfrac{16}{15} = 5 + 1\tfrac{1}{15} = 6\tfrac{1}{15}$$

(2) $\dfrac{17}{18}$

$$\tfrac{1}{3} = \tfrac{6}{18}$$
$$\tfrac{2}{6} = \tfrac{6}{18}$$
$$+\tfrac{5}{18} = \tfrac{5}{18}$$
$$\tfrac{17}{18}$$

(3) $1\dfrac{29}{42}$

$$\tfrac{5}{6} = \tfrac{35}{42}$$
$$+\tfrac{6}{7} = \tfrac{36}{42}$$
$$\tfrac{71}{42} = 1\tfrac{29}{42}$$

(4) $8\dfrac{69}{70}$

$$4\tfrac{1}{5} = 4\tfrac{14}{70}$$
$$3\tfrac{2}{7} = 3\tfrac{20}{70}$$
$$1\tfrac{1}{2} = 1\tfrac{35}{70}$$
$$8\tfrac{69}{70}$$

PRACTICE EXERCISES 3:

(1) $\dfrac{11}{16}$

$$\dfrac{7}{8} = \dfrac{14}{16}$$
$$-\dfrac{3}{16} = -\dfrac{3}{16}$$
$$\dfrac{11}{16}$$

(2) $2\dfrac{5}{12}$

$$3\dfrac{3}{4} = 3\dfrac{9}{12}$$
$$-1\dfrac{1}{3} = -1\dfrac{4}{12}$$
$$2\dfrac{5}{12}$$

(3) $3\dfrac{5}{8}$

$$6\dfrac{3}{8} = 5\dfrac{3}{8} + \dfrac{8}{8} = 5\dfrac{11}{8}$$
$$-2\dfrac{3}{4} \qquad = -2\dfrac{6}{8}$$
$$3\dfrac{5}{8}$$

(4) $1\dfrac{28}{45}$

$$4\dfrac{2}{9} = 4\dfrac{10}{45} = 3\dfrac{10}{45} + \dfrac{45}{45} = 3\dfrac{55}{45}$$
$$-2\dfrac{3}{5} = -2\dfrac{27}{45} \qquad\qquad = -2\dfrac{27}{45}$$
$$1\dfrac{28}{45}$$

(5) $4\dfrac{1}{4}$

$$8 = \dfrac{8}{1} = \dfrac{32}{4}$$
$$-3\dfrac{3}{4} \qquad = -\dfrac{15}{4}$$
$$\dfrac{17}{4} = 4\dfrac{1}{4}$$

PRACTICE EXERCISES 4:

(1) $\dfrac{5}{18}$

$$\dfrac{4}{9} \times \dfrac{5}{8} = \dfrac{20}{72} = \dfrac{5}{18}$$

(2) $4\dfrac{1}{4}$

$$\dfrac{1}{3} \times 12\dfrac{3}{4} = \dfrac{1}{3} \times \dfrac{51}{4} = \dfrac{51}{12} = 4\dfrac{1}{4}$$

(3) 15

$$6\dfrac{3}{5} \times 2\dfrac{3}{11} = \dfrac{\cancel{33}^{3}}{\cancel{5}_{1}} \times \dfrac{\cancel{25}^{5}}{\cancel{11}_{1}} = 15$$

(4) $3\dfrac{1}{2}$

$$\dfrac{1}{6} \times \dfrac{21}{1} = \dfrac{21}{6} = 3\dfrac{1}{2}$$

PRACTICE EXERCISES 5:

(1) $4\frac{1}{2}$

$$\frac{9}{10} \div \frac{1}{5} = \frac{9}{10} \times \frac{5}{1} = \frac{45}{10} = 4\frac{1}{2}$$

(2) 12

$$9 \div \frac{3}{4} = \frac{9}{1} \div \frac{3}{4} = \frac{\cancel{9}^{3}}{1} \times \frac{4}{\cancel{3}_{1}} = 12$$

(3) $\frac{1}{12}$

$$2\frac{1}{6} \div 26 = \frac{\cancel{13}^{1}}{6} \times \frac{1}{\cancel{26}_{2}} = \frac{1}{12}$$

(4) 9

$$60 \div 6\frac{2}{3} = \frac{60}{1} \div \frac{20}{3} = \frac{\cancel{60}^{3}}{1} \times \frac{3}{\cancel{20}_{1}} = 9$$

PRACTICE EXERCISES 6:

(1) $\frac{13}{50}$

$$\frac{2 + 24}{100} = \frac{26}{100} = \frac{13}{50}$$

(2) $\frac{2}{5}$

$$\frac{\frac{1}{2} - \frac{1}{4}}{\frac{5}{8}} = \frac{\frac{2-1}{4}}{\frac{5}{8}} = \frac{\frac{1}{4}}{\frac{5}{8}} = \frac{1}{\cancel{4}_{1}} \times \frac{\cancel{8}^{2}}{5} = \frac{2}{5}$$

(3) $1\frac{13}{20}$

$$\frac{3 + \frac{1}{2} + 2}{3 + \frac{1}{3}} = \frac{5\frac{1}{2}}{3\frac{1}{3}} = \frac{11}{2} \times \frac{3}{10} = \frac{33}{20} = 1\frac{13}{20}$$

(4) $\frac{1}{8}$

$$\frac{\frac{1}{2} + \frac{1}{8}}{5} = \frac{\frac{4+1}{8}}{5} = \frac{\frac{5}{8}}{5} = \frac{\cancel{5}}{8} \times \frac{1}{\cancel{5}_{1}} = \frac{1}{8}$$

DECIMAL FRACTIONS

Another way of writing fractions is to use *decimal fractions*. Using a symbol called a *decimal point* before a number makes that number a fraction. The number of places to the right of the decimal point tells the size of the fraction. Whole numbers appear to the left of the decimal point. Below are the place units for decimal fractions up to a millionth.

.3	*tenths*
.03	*hundredths*
.003	*thousandths*
.0003	*ten thousandths*
.00003	*hundred thousandths*
.000003	*millionths*

Decimal fractions are based on the *decimal system*, a place-value system based on tens. In this system, each place is worth one-tenth of the value of the place to its left. For example, in the number 8.93, the 3 stands for $\frac{3}{100}$, the 9 stands for $\frac{9}{10}$, and the 8 stands for 8 ones.

Decimal fractions are related to common fractions in this way:

$$.3 = \frac{3}{10} \qquad .03 = \frac{3}{100}$$

$$.003 = \frac{3}{1,000} \qquad .0003 = \frac{3}{10,000}$$

Remember that .01 is smaller than .1 and that .001 is smaller still. (One-hundredth of an inch is smaller than one-tenth of an inch, and one-thousandth of an inch is even smaller.)

By the decimal's position, or place, you know what size unit it stands for. Use the unit's name in reading or writing the numbers. For example:

.137 is one hundred thirty-seven *thousandths*, or $\frac{137}{1,000}$

.43 is forty-three *hundredths*, or $\frac{43}{100}$

.9034 is nine thousand thirty-four *ten thousandths*, or $\frac{9,034}{10,000}$

A *decimal mixed number* (both a whole number and a decimal fraction) is read or written by substituting the word "and" for the decimal point, and adding the proper decimal term at the end. For example:

5.07 is five *and* seven hundredths, or $5\frac{7}{100}$

14.107 is fourteen *and* one hundred seven thousandths, or $14\frac{107}{1,000}$

325.0065 is three hundred twenty-five *and* sixty-five ten thousandths, or $325\frac{65}{10,000}$

Rounding Off Decimals

To round off a decimal to a given place, look at the number in the place immediately to the right of the given place. If this number is less than 5, leave the numbers before it as they are. If this number is 5 or more, increase the number just before it by one.

4.438   rounds off to the nearest hundredth as 4.44
11.104   rounds off to the nearest hundredth as 11.10
.2178   rounds off to the nearest thousandth as .218
.4399   rounds off to the nearest tenth as .4
7.04   rounds off to the nearest tenth as 7.0

PRACTICE EXERCISES 1:
(Answers to Practice Exercises appear at end of chapter.)

(1) Round off 4.76 to the nearest tenth.

(2) Round off 3.893 to the nearest hundredth.

(3) Round off 5.1198 to the nearest thousandth.

Addition of Decimals

Arrange the numbers of a problem so that decimals that stand for the same unit size are in the same column. Carelessness in writing the problem can lead to incorrect answers.

⑮ EXAMPLE 1: $4.5 + .58 + 72.134 =$

Written correctly:	*Incorrectly*:
4.5	4.5
.58	.58
+72.134	+72.134
77.214	

Line up the decimal points in all the numbers. Remember to put the decimal point in the proper place in the sum.

If the sum of any column is more than ten, remember to put the carry number above the next column to the left before adding that column.

EXAMPLE 2: $15.68 + 8.4 =$

$$
\begin{array}{r}
11 \\
15.68 \\
+\ 8.4 \\
\hline
24.08
\end{array}
$$

PRACTICE EXERCISES 2: *Add*
(Answers to Practice Exercises appear at end of chapter.)

(1) $9.4 + .09 + 14.2 =$ 23.69

(2) $514.6 + 36.43 + .074 =$ 551.104

(3) $2.4 + 11.03 + 7.56 =$ 20.99

Subtraction of Decimals

Here again, decimals of the same unit size must be put in the same column and the decimal points lined up. In order to solve some problems, you may have to add zeros to a decimal. Any number of zeros may be added to the right of a decimal fraction. They do not change the value of the fraction. For example:

$$.5 = .50 = .500 = .5000$$
$$.02 = .020 = .0200$$

(16) EXAMPLE 1:
Two zeros are added to the minuend 5.7.

$$5.7 - 3.241 = \quad \overset{69}{5.7\cancel{0}0} \\ \underline{-3.241} \\ 2.459$$

(17) EXAMPLE 2:
Zeros need not be added to the bottom number.

$$5.234 - 3.1 = \quad 5.234 \\ \underline{-3.1} \\ 2.134$$

The method of borrowing or regrouping decimals is the same as in subtraction of whole numbers.

EXAMPLE 3:
$$9.2 - .7$$
$$\overset{8}{\cancel{9}.2} \\ \underline{- .7} \\ 8.5$$

EXAMPLE 4:
$$7.14 - 2.36$$

$$\overset{6\ \ 10}{\cancel{7}.\ \cancel{1}\ 4} \\ \underline{-2.\ 3\ 6} \\ 4.\ 7\ 8$$

PRACTICE EXERCISES 3: SUBTRACT
(Answers to Practice Exercises appear at end of chapter.)

(1)   9.008
      −3.334
      _____
      5.674

(2)   121.7
      −106.2
      _____
      15.5

(3)   18.730
      − 9.006
      _____
      9.724

Multiplication of Decimals

You work out problems in decimal multiplication the same way as you do in whole-number multiplication. The only difference is placing the decimal point in the final product. The number of decimal places in the answer must be equal to the sum of the decimal places in both numbers, the one you multiply and the one you multiply by.

(18) EXAMPLE 1:

        1.3   one decimal place in the multiplicand
     ×   .4   one decimal place in the multiplier
        .52   there must be two decimal places in the product.

EXAMPLE 2:

        .003   three decimal places in the multiplicand
     ×   .02   two decimal places in the multiplier
     .00006   five decimal places are needed in the product.

PRACTICE EXERCISES 4: MULTIPLY
(Answers to Practice Exercises appear at end of chapter.)

(1)   12.4
        × 3.6

(2)   .0003
        × .005

(3)   14.81
        × .906

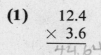

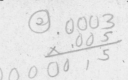
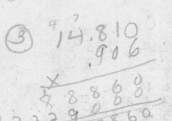

Division of Decimals

You solve decimal division problems in the same way as whole-number division problems. The only difference is remembering to put the decimal point in the proper place in the quotient. This is done by moving the decimal point of the divisor (the number you are dividing by) to the right as many places as are necessary to make it a whole number. Then move the decimal point of the dividend (the number being divided) the same number of places and put the decimal point of the quotient directly above this new place. If necessary, add zeros to the dividend.

(19) EXAMPLES:

(1) $2.4\overline{)72.48}$ Moving the decimal point one place to the right in both divisor and dividend gives $24\overline{)724.8}$, and dividing gives

$$\begin{array}{r} 30.2 \\ 24\overline{)724.8} \end{array}$$

(2) $.314\overline{)1.570} = 314\overline{)1,570.} \quad \begin{array}{r}5.\end{array}$

(3) $.006\overline{)72.600} = 6\overline{)72,600.} \quad \begin{array}{r}12,100.\end{array}$

PRACTICE EXERCISES 5: DIVIDE
(Answers to Practice Exercises appear at end of chapter.)

(1) $3.6\overline{)1.0836}$

(2) $.07\overline{)2.849}$

(3) $.08\overline{)265.6}$

Answers and Solutions

PRACTICE EXERCISES 1:

(1) 4.8

(2) 3.89

(3) 5.120

PRACTICE EXERCISES 2:

(1)	23.69	**(3)**	20.99
	9.4		2.4
	.09		11.03
	14.2		7.56
	23.69		20.99

(2)	551.104
	514.6
	36.43
	.074
	551.104

PRACTICE EXERCISES 3:

(1)   5.674
       9.008
    —3.334
       5.674

(2) 15.5
     121.7
   —106.2
      15.5

(3) 9.724
    18.730
  — 9.006
     9.724

PRACTICE EXERCISES 4:

(1)   44.64
      12.4
       3.6
      744
   372
   44.64

(2) .0000015
     .0003
      .005
   .0000015

(3) 13.41786
    14.81
     .906
    8886
  13329
  13.41786

PRACTICE EXERCISES 5:

(1) .301

$$\begin{array}{r} .301 \\ 3.6\overline{)\,1.0836} \\ 108 \\ \hline 3 \\ 0 \\ \hline 36 \\ 36 \end{array}$$

(2) 40.7

$$\begin{array}{r} 40.7 \\ .07\overline{)\,2.849} \end{array}$$

(3) 3320

$$\begin{array}{r} 3,320. \\ .08\overline{)\,265.60} \\ 24 \\ \hline 25 \\ 24 \\ \hline 16 \\ 16 \\ \hline 00 \end{array}$$

PERCENTAGE

Changing Decimals to Percents

To change a *decimal to a percent*, move the decimal point two places to the *right* of its original location, and add the percent sign.

EXAMPLES:

(1)   .03 = 3%

(2)   .094 = 9.4%

(3)   4.37 = 437%

Changing Fractions to Percents

To change a *fraction to a percent*, multiply the fraction by 100, and add the percent sign.

⑳ EXAMPLES:

(1) $\dfrac{2}{5} = \dfrac{2}{5} \times \overset{20}{\cancel{100}} = 40\%$

(2) $\dfrac{3}{8} = \dfrac{3}{\underset{2}{\cancel{8}}} \times \overset{25}{\cancel{100}} = \dfrac{3}{2} \times 25 = \dfrac{75}{2} = 37\tfrac{1}{2}\%$

 PRACTICE EXERCISES 1:
(Answers to Practice Exercises appear at end of chapter.)

Change the following decimals or fractions to percents.

(1) .64

(2) 1.96

(3) .003

(4) $\dfrac{7}{20}$

(5) $\dfrac{17}{25}$

(6) $\dfrac{5}{6}$

Changing Percents to Decimals

To change *a percent to a decimal*, move the decimal point two places to the *left* of its original location.

EXAMPLES:

(1) $53\% = .53$

(2) $9\% = .09$

(3) $42.6\% = .426$

Changing Percents to Fractions

To change *a percent to a fraction*, place the percent over 100 and reduce to lowest terms.

(21) EXAMPLES:

(1) $75\% = \dfrac{75}{100} = \dfrac{3}{4}$

(2) $33\frac{1}{3}\% = \dfrac{33\frac{1}{3}}{100} = \dfrac{\frac{100}{3}}{\frac{100}{1}} = \dfrac{100}{3} \times \dfrac{1}{100} = \dfrac{1}{3}$

PRACTICE EXERCISES 2:
(Answers to Practice Exercises appear at end of chapter.)

Change the following percents to decimals.

(1) $48\% = .48$

(2) $1\% = .01$

(3) $263\% \quad 2.63$

Change the following percents to fractions.

(4) $65\% \quad \frac{65}{100} = \frac{13}{20}$

(5) $16\frac{2}{3}\% \quad \dfrac{\frac{50}{3}}{\frac{100}{1}} = \frac{50}{3} \times \frac{1}{100} = \frac{1}{6}$

(6) $120\% \quad \dfrac{\frac{120}{1}}{\frac{100}{1}} \quad 1\frac{1}{2} \quad \frac{120}{100} = \frac{60}{50} = \frac{6}{5} = 1\frac{1}{5}$

SOME MATHEMATICS TO REMEMBER

Remembering important equivalents can be very helpful in simplifying problems and eliminating unnecessary computations. The following table will aid you in memorizing the important equivalents:

$$1\% = .01 = \frac{1}{100} \qquad 33\tfrac{1}{3}\% = .33\tfrac{1}{3} = \frac{1}{3}$$

$$10\% = .10 = \frac{1}{10} \qquad 66\tfrac{2}{3}\% = .66\tfrac{2}{3} = \frac{2}{3}$$

$$20\% = .20 = \frac{1}{5} \qquad 12\tfrac{1}{2}\% = .12\tfrac{1}{2} \text{ or } .125 = \frac{1}{8}$$

$$30\% = .30 = \frac{3}{10} \qquad 37\tfrac{1}{2}\% = .37\tfrac{1}{2} \text{ or } .375 = \frac{3}{8}$$

$$40\% = .40 = \frac{2}{5} \qquad 62\tfrac{1}{2}\% = .62\tfrac{1}{2} \text{ or } .625 = \frac{5}{8}$$

$$50\% = .50 = \frac{1}{2} \qquad 87\tfrac{1}{2}\% = .87\tfrac{1}{2} \text{ or } .875 = \frac{7}{8}$$

$$60\% = .60 = \frac{3}{5} \qquad 16\tfrac{2}{3}\% = .16\tfrac{2}{3} = \frac{1}{6}$$

$$70\% = .70 = \frac{7}{10} \qquad 83\tfrac{1}{3}\% = .83\tfrac{1}{3} = \frac{5}{6}$$

$$80\% = .80 = \frac{4}{5} \qquad 100\% = 1.00 = 1$$

$$90\% = .90 = \frac{9}{10} \qquad 200\% = 2.00 = 2$$

$$25\% = .25 = \frac{1}{4} \qquad 250\% = 2.50 = 2\tfrac{1}{2}$$

$$75\% = .75 = \frac{3}{4}$$

Finding the Percent of a Quantity

1. Change the percent to a decimal (or fraction, if necessary).
2. Multiply the decimal (fraction) by the number in the problem.

(22) EXAMPLE 1:

What is 35% of 108?

```
     108
   × .35
   -----
     540
     324
   -----
   37.80    Thus, 37.8 is 35% of 108.
```

EXAMPLE 2:

29% of 340 is how much?

```
     340
   × .29
   -----
    3060
     680
   -----
   98.60    Thus, 29% of 340 is 98.60.
```

Pᴿᴬᴄᴛɪᴄᴇ Exᴇʀᴄɪꜱᴇꜱ 3:
(Answers to Practice Exercises appear at end of chapter.)

(1) What is 30% of 160?

(2) 4% of 903 is?

(3) 512% of 300 is how much?

Finding What Percent One Quantity Is of Another

1. Decide which of the numbers is the *base* quantity in the problem; that is, the quantity *of* which you are to find the percent.
2. Decide which number is *part* of the base quantity; that is, which number is the percent *to be found*.
3. Make a fraction of the two numbers with the *part* as the numerator and the *base* as the denominator.
4. Multiply this fraction by 100 to get the final answer.

(23) Exᴀᴍᴘʟᴇꜱ:

(1) 8 is what percent of 20?
The base quantity is 20, and the part is 8; thus we make the fraction $\frac{8}{20}$.

$$\frac{8}{\underset{1}{\cancel{20}}} \times \frac{\overset{5}{\cancel{100}}}{1} = 8 \times 5 = 40\%$$

(2) What percent of 720 is 180?

$$\frac{\overset{18}{\cancel{180}}}{\underset{72}{\cancel{720}}} \times \frac{100}{1} = \frac{18}{72} \times \frac{100}{1} = \frac{1,800}{72} = 72 \overline{)\,1,800}^{\,25\%}$$
$$\underline{144}$$
$$360$$

Pᴿᴬᴄᴛɪᴄᴇ Exᴇʀᴄɪꜱᴇꜱ 4:
(Answers to Practice Exercises appear at end of chapter.)

(1) 25 is what percent of 200?

(2) What percent of 900 is 150?

(3) $60 is what percent of $180?

(4) What % of 510 is 370?

Finding the Base Quantity

1. Change the percent to a decimal (or fraction, if necessary)
2. Make a ratio of the unknown and the number. The unknown goes on the bottom.
3. Set up a proportion.
4. Solve the proportion.

(24) EXAMPLE:
20 is 40% of what number?

$$40\% = \frac{40}{100} = \frac{4}{10} = \frac{2}{5}$$

Let x stand for the unknown,

$$\frac{2}{5} = \frac{20}{x}$$

Cross-multiply to get

$$2x = 5(20)$$
$$2x = 100$$
$$x = 50$$

Thus, 20 is 40% of 50.

PRACTICE EXERCISES 5:
(Answers to Practice Exercises appear at end of chapter.)

(1) 40 is 25% of what number?

(2) 56 is 64% of what number?

(3) 45% of what number is 135?

Percent of Gain or Loss

These problems may be solved by using the following general formula:

$$\%\text{ Gain or Loss} = \frac{\text{difference between the two amounts}}{\text{original amount}} \times 100$$

This is a common type of percentage problem.

㉕ EXAMPLES:

(1) If a union contract increased John's weekly wage from $80 to $112 a week, what was the percent of increase in his wages?

$$\% \text{ Gain} = \frac{112-80}{80} \times \frac{100}{1} = \frac{32}{\cancel{80}_4} \times \frac{\cancel{100}^5}{1} = \frac{160}{4} = 40\%$$

(2) Mr. Garcia bought some stocks for $3,000. A year later they were worth $1,200. What was his percent of loss?

$$\% \text{ Loss} = \frac{3,000-1,200}{3,000} \times \frac{100}{1} =$$

$$\frac{\cancel{1,800}^3}{\cancel{3,000}_5} \times \frac{100}{1} = \frac{3}{\cancel{5}_1} \times \frac{\cancel{100}^{20}}{1} = 60\%$$

MISCELLANEOUS PROBLEMS

(1) The alcoholic content of a particular bottle of wine is 12%. If the bottle contains 32 ounces, how many ounces are alcohol?

$$\begin{array}{r} 32 \\ .12 \\ \hline 64 \\ 32 \\ \hline 3.84 \text{ ounces} \end{array}$$

(2) What percent of the boxes below is shaded?

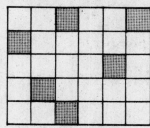

$$\frac{6 \text{ (Shaded)}}{30 \text{ (Total)}} = \frac{1}{\cancel{5}_1} \times \frac{\cancel{100}^{20}}{1} = 20\%$$

(3) If on a test containing 45 questions Clara got 30 correct, what percent did she answer correctly?

$$\frac{30 \text{ (Correct)}}{45 \text{ (Total)}} = \frac{2}{3} \times \frac{100}{1} = \frac{200}{3} = 66\frac{2}{3}\%$$

PRACTICE EXERCISES 6:
(Answers to Practice Exercises appear at end of chapter.)

(1) There are 300 enrollees in a job training program. If 85% of them are women, how many men are in the program?

(2) What percent of the boxes below is *unshaded*?

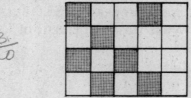

(3) If Gloria got 3 problems wrong out of 24 on a mathematics test, what percent of the problems did she answer incorrectly?

(4) If a color TV set cost $600 when it was first available on the market, and it can now be bought for $480, what is the percent of decrease (loss) in price?

Answers and Solutions

PRACTICE EXERCISES 1:

(1) 64%

(2) 196%

(3) .3%

(4) 35%

$$\frac{7}{20} \times \frac{\overset{5}{\cancel{100}}}{1} = 35\%$$

(5) 68%

$$\frac{17}{25} \times \frac{\overset{4}{\cancel{100}}}{1} = 68\%$$

(6) $83\frac{1}{3}\%$

$$\frac{5}{6} \times \frac{100}{1} = \frac{500}{6} = 83\frac{1}{3}\%$$

PRACTICE EXERCISES 2:

(1) .48

(2) .01

(3) 2.63

(4) $\frac{13}{20}$

(5) $\frac{1}{6}$

(6) $1\frac{1}{5}$

PRACTICE EXERCISES 3:

(1) 48
    160
    .30
    ―――
  48.00

(2) 36.12
   903
   .04
   ―――
  36.12

(3) 1536
    5.12
    300
  ―――――
  1,536.00

PRACTICE EXERCISES 4:

(1) $\frac{25}{200} = 12\frac{1}{2}\%$

(2) $\frac{150}{900} = 16\frac{2}{3}\%$

(3) $\frac{60}{180} = 33\frac{1}{3}\%$

(4) $\frac{370}{510} = 72\frac{28}{51}\%$

PRACTICE EXERCISES 5:

(1) 160
40 is 25% of what number?
$$25\% = \frac{25}{100} = \frac{1}{4}$$
$$\frac{1}{4} = \frac{40}{x}$$
$$x = 4(40)$$
$$x = 160$$

(2) $87\frac{1}{2}$ or 87.5
56 is 64% of what number?
$$67\% = \frac{64}{100} = \frac{32}{50} = \frac{16}{25}$$
$$\frac{16}{25} = \frac{56}{x}$$
$$16x = 56(25)$$
$$16x = 1,400$$
$$x = \frac{1,400}{16}$$
$$x = 87\frac{1}{2}$$

(3) 300
45% of what number is 135?
$$45\% = \frac{45}{100} = \frac{9}{20}$$
$$\frac{9}{20} = \frac{135}{x}$$
$$9x = 20(135)$$
$$9x = 2,700$$
$$x = \frac{2,700}{9}$$
$$x = 300$$

PRACTICE EXERCISES 6:

(1) 45
$$\begin{array}{r} 300 \\ \underline{.85} \\ 1500 \\ 2400 \\ \hline 255.00 \text{ are women} \\ 300 - 255 = 45 \end{array}$$

(2) 65%

$$\frac{7}{\cancel{20}} \times \frac{\cancel{100}^{5}}{1} = 35\% \text{ shaded}$$

So $100\% - 35\% = 65\%$ unshaded

(3) $12\frac{1}{2}\%$

$$\frac{3}{24} = \frac{1}{8} \times \frac{100}{1} = \frac{100}{8} = 12\frac{1}{2}\%$$

(4) 20%

$$\% \text{ loss} = \frac{600 - 480}{600} \times \frac{100}{1} = \frac{\cancel{120}^{1}}{\cancel{600}_{5}} \times \frac{100}{1} = \frac{1}{5} \times \frac{100}{1} = 20\%$$

PROPERTIES OF NUMBERS

Prime Numbers

Prime numbers are numbers that can be divided evenly only by themselves and the number 1. Thus 13 is a prime because there is no number (factor) except 1 that will go into it without a remainder. The number 21 is *not* a prime since it is easily divisible by 3 and by 7. Below is a list of all the prime numbers from 1 to 50:

Table of Prime Numbers

3, 5, 7, 11, 13, 17, 19, 23, 29, 31, 37, 41, 43, 47

(26) EXAMPLES:
Which of the following numbers are prime?

(1)   91

(2)   57

(3)   87

(4)   71

57 and 71 are prime
91 is divisible by 7 and 13
87 is divisible by 3 and 29

PRACTICE EXERCISES 1:
(Answers to Practice Exercises appear at end of chapter.)
Which is the prime number in each of the following groups of numbers?

(1) 49, 51, 61, 93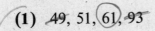

(2) 63, 78, 117, 79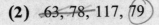

(3) 101, 105, 123, 119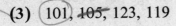

Divisibility Rules

The following set of rules can help you save time in trying to check the divisibility of numbers:
2—A number is divisible by 2 if it ends in 0, 2, 4, 6, or 8.
3—A number is divisible by 3 if the total of its digits is divisible by 3.

EXAMPLE:
126   total of digits = 9   since 9 is divisible by 3,
126 is divisible by 3
4—A number is divisible by 4 if the number formed by the last two
digits is divisible by 4.

EXAMPLE:
648   since 48 is divisible by 4, then 648 is divisible by 4

5—A number is divisible by 5 if it ends in 0 or 5.

6—A number is divisible by 6 if it is divisible by 2 and 3.
(Use the rules for both.)

EXAMPLE:
186   since 186 ends in 6, it is divisible by 2
total of digits = 15, since 15 is divisible by 3,
186 is divisible by 3.
186 is divisible by 2 and 3, therefore it is divisible by 6.

7—No simple rule.

8—A number is divisible by 8 if the number formed by the last 3 digits is divisible by 8.

EXAMPLE:
2,488   since 488 is divisible by 8, then 2,488 is divisible by 8

9—A number is divisible by 9 if the total of its digits is divisible by 9.

EXAMPLE:
2,853   total of digits = 18   since 18 is divisible by 9, 2,853 is divisible by 9.

Average of Numbers

There are two common types of average, the *mean* and the *median*. The mean of a number of figures is obtained by adding up all the figures and dividing the sum by the number of figures. When we speak of an *average*, we generally are speaking of a *mean*.

(27) EXAMPLES:

(1)   Mr. Calderon is a commercial artist who works on a free-lance basis. If his income for five successive weeks was $150, $175, $220, $160, and $185, find his mean earnings per week for that period.

Mean: $\dfrac{150 + 175 + 220 + 160 + 185}{5} = \dfrac{890}{5} = \$178$

(2)   On three consecutive days in January it snowed $3\frac{1}{2}''$, $12\frac{1}{4}''$, and $4\frac{1}{2}''$.

What was the mean number of inches of snowfall per day?

$$\frac{3\frac{1}{2} + 12\frac{1}{4} + 4\frac{1}{2}}{3} = \frac{20\frac{1}{4}}{3} = \frac{81}{4} \div \frac{3}{1} = \frac{81}{4} \times \frac{1}{3} = \frac{81}{12} = 6\frac{3}{4}''$$

The *median* is an average obtained by counting. First you rearrange the numbers in rank order. It is most convenient to list them in a column with the largest number at the top. The median is defined as the number that divides the half of the numbers with the larger values from the half with the smaller values.

EXAMPLES:

(1)   Values
        39
        35
        33
        30   ← Median is 30 (7 is an *odd* number of values)
        26
        24
        22

(2)   Values
        21
        19
        16
        15
        14   ← Median is 14.5 (8 is an *even* number of values)
        11
        9
        8

PRACTICE EXERCISES 2:
(Answers to Practice Exercises appear at end of chapter.)

(1) What is the mean of 14.3, 6.5, 7.8, and 3.4?

(2) On five examinations Lisa scored 60, 80, 95, 75, and 90. What was her median score?

(3) Stacy's weight has varied from September through February as follows: 105 lbs, 118 lbs, 110 lbs, 115 lbs, 112 lbs, and 106 lbs. What was her mean weight for this period of time?

Squares and Square Roots of Numbers

The *square* of a number is the result of multiplying the number by itself. For instance, the square of 7 is $7 \times 7 = 49$. It is useful to memorize the squares of the numbers from 1 to 20.

Table of Squares

Number	Square	Number	Square
1	1	11	121
2	4	12	144
3	9	13	169
4	16	14	196
5	25	15	225
6	36	16	256
7	49	17	289
8	64	18	324
9	81	19	361
10	100	20	400

The symbol for the squaring operation is a small 2 written above and just to the right of the number to be squared. Thus for "eight squared equals 64" we write $8^2 = 64$.

The square root of a number is the number which, when multiplied by itself, will give the number under the square sign. Thus $\sqrt{16} = 4$ since $4 \times 4 = 16$. It is useful to memorize the exact squares for the numbers from 1 to 20.

Table of Square Roots

$$\sqrt{1} = 1 \qquad \sqrt{121} = 11$$
$$\sqrt{4} = 2 \qquad \sqrt{144} = 12$$
$$\sqrt{9} = 3 \qquad \sqrt{169} = 13$$
$$\sqrt{16} = 4 \qquad \sqrt{196} = 14$$
$$\sqrt{25} = 5 \qquad \sqrt{225} = 15$$
$$\sqrt{36} = 6 \qquad \sqrt{256} = 16$$
$$\sqrt{49} = 7 \qquad \sqrt{289} = 17$$
$$\sqrt{64} = 8 \qquad \sqrt{324} = 18$$
$$\sqrt{81} = 9 \qquad \sqrt{361} = 19$$
$$\sqrt{100} = 10 \qquad \sqrt{400} = 20$$

Approximating Square Roots

Sometimes you will be asked to find the square root of a number that is not an exact square. In such a case it will be necessary to find an approximate answer by using the procedure explained below.

(28) EXAMPLE:

Approximate $\sqrt{42}$

The $\sqrt{42}$ is between $\sqrt{36}$ and $\sqrt{49}$. $\sqrt{36} < \sqrt{42} < \sqrt{49}$

$\sqrt{36} = 6$

$\sqrt{49} = 7$

Therefore $6 < \sqrt{42} < 7$

and since $\sqrt{42}$ is about halfway between $\sqrt{36}$ and $\sqrt{49}$, $\sqrt{42}$ is about 6.5.

To check, multiply $6.5 \times 6.5 = 42.25$ or about 42.

PRACTICE EXERCISES 3:
(Answers to Practice Exercises appear at end of chapter.)

(1) Approximate: $\sqrt{22}$

(2) Approximate: $\sqrt{71}$

(3) Approximate: $\sqrt{\dfrac{400}{24}}$

Simplifying Square Roots

Sometimes you will have to simplify square roots or write them in simplest form. In fractions, $\frac{2}{4}$ can be reduced to $\frac{1}{2}$. In square roots, $\sqrt{32}$ can be simplified to $4\sqrt{2}$.

(29)

To simplify a square root, first factor the number under the $\sqrt{}$ into a counting number times a perfect square number. (Perfect square numbers are 1, 4, 9, 16, 25, 36, 49, . . .)

$$\sqrt{32} = \sqrt{16 \times 2}$$

Then take the square root of the perfect square number

$$\sqrt{16 \times 2} = \sqrt{16} \times \sqrt{2} = 4 \times \sqrt{2}$$

and finally write as a single expression: $4\sqrt{2}$

Remember that most square roots cannot be simplified, as they are already in simplest form, such as $\sqrt{7}$, $\sqrt{10}$, $\sqrt{15}$.

PRACTICE EXERCISES 4:
(Answers to Practice Exercises appear at end of chapter.)

(1) Simplify: $\sqrt{18}$ = $\sqrt{9 \cdot 2}$ = $3\sqrt{2}$

(2) Simplify: $\sqrt{75}$ = $\sqrt{25 \cdot 3}$ = $5\sqrt{3}$

(3) Simplify: $\sqrt{96}$ $\sqrt{16 \cdot 6}$ $4\sqrt{6}$

Number Series

Number series (sometimes called *progressions*) are sequences of numbers having some regular pattern.

Arithmetic series are number series having a *common difference*. An example of such a series would be 3, 6, 9, 12, 15, . . . since each successive number may be obtained by adding 3 to the one before it. Hence 3 is the common difference. The common difference may be found by subtracting any number in the series from the one immediately after it.

Geometric series are number series having a *common ratio*. An example of such a series would be 2, 8, 32, 128, . . . since each successive number may be obtained by multiplying the one before it by 4. Hence, 4 is the common ratio. The common ratio may be found by dividing any number in the series by the one immediately preceding it.

EXAMPLES:

(1) Find the eighth term in the series 27, 31, 35, 39, . . .
The common difference is 4, so we add 4 to 39 in order to get the next term and continue to add 4 to each number until we get to the eighth term: 27, 31, 35, 39, 43, 47, 51, 55. So *55* is the eighth term.

(2) Find the sixth term in the series 1, 3, 9, 27, . . .
The common ratio is 3. If we continue the series we have 1, 3, 9, 27, 81, 243. So *243* is the sixth term.

PRACTICE EXERCISES 5:
(Answers to Practice Exercises appear at end of chapter.)

(1) Find the seventh term in the series 9, 14, 19, 24, . . .

(2) Find the ninth term in the series 2, 11, 20, 29, . . .

(3) Find the eighth term in the series 13, 26, 52, 104, . . .

(4) Find the sixth term in the series 1, 6, 36, 216, . . .

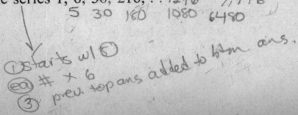

Answers and Solutions

Practice Exercises 1:

(1) 61

(2) 79

(3) 101

Practice Exercises 2:

(1) 8

$$\frac{14.3 + 6.5 + 7.8 + 3.4}{4} = \frac{32}{4} = 8$$

(2) 80

60   75   80   90   95

(3) 111 lbs.

$$\frac{105 + 118 + 110 + 115 + 112 + 106}{6} = \frac{666}{6} = 111 \text{ lbs.}$$

Practice Exercises 3:

(1) 4.7

$\sqrt{16} < \sqrt{22} < \sqrt{25}$
$4 < \sqrt{22} < 5$
$4 < 4.7 < 5$

Check: 4.7
          $\times$ 4.7
          $\overline{329}$
          $\underline{188}$
          $\overline{22.09} = 22$

(2) 8.4

$\sqrt{64} < \sqrt{71} < \sqrt{81}$
$8 < \sqrt{71} < 9$
$8 < 8.4 < 9$

Check: 8.4
          $\times$ 8.4
          $\overline{33\ 6}$
          $\underline{672}$
          $\overline{70.56} = 71$

(3) 4.1

$\sqrt{\dfrac{400}{24}} = \sqrt{16.7}$

$\sqrt{16} < \sqrt{16.7} < \sqrt{25}$
$4 < \sqrt{16.7} < 5$
$4 < 4.1 < 5$

Check: 4.1
          $\times$ 4.1
          $\overline{41}$
          $\underline{164}$
          $\overline{16.81} = 16.7$, approximately

PRACTICE EXERCISES 4:

(1) $3\sqrt{2}$

$$\sqrt{18} = \sqrt{9 \times 2}$$
$$= \sqrt{9} \times \sqrt{2}$$
$$= 3 \times \sqrt{2}$$
$$= 3\sqrt{2}$$

(2) $5\sqrt{3}$

$$\sqrt{75} = \sqrt{25 \times 3}$$
$$= \sqrt{25} \times \sqrt{3}$$
$$= 5 \times \sqrt{3}$$
$$= 5\sqrt{3}$$

(3) $4\sqrt{6}$

$$\sqrt{96} = \sqrt{16 \times 6}$$
$$= \sqrt{16} \times \sqrt{6}$$
$$= 4 \times \sqrt{6}$$
$$= 4\sqrt{6}$$

PRACTICE EXERCISES 5:

(1) 39
9, 14, 19, 24, 29, 34, *39*

(2) 74
2, 11, 20, 29, 38, 47, 56, 65, *74*

(3) 1,664
13, 26, 52, 104, 208, 416, 832, *1,664*

(4) 7,776
1, 6, 36, 216, 1,296, *7,776*

SIGNED NUMBERS

For all of the arithmetic problems in the preceding chapters it was sufficient for us to use *positive* numbers such as 8, 15, $12\frac{1}{2}$, 9.4, etc. However, when we consider the difference between (say) having $50 and owing $50, or a temperature of 31 degrees above zero and 31 degrees below zero, or throwing a ball 25 feet up from the roof of a house and having it fall 25 feet below the roof, we begin to see the need for having to enlarge our concepts of numbers to include numbers less than zero—*negative numbers*. If we do this with the situations just mentioned, then they may be represented numerically as follows.

1. Having $50: +50
   Owing $50: −50
2. 31° above zero: +31°
   31° below zero: −31°
3. Throwing a ball 25 feet above the roof: +25
   A ball falling 25 feet below the roof: −25

In order to deal with problems involving considerations such as those illustrated above it will be necessary to know how to perform operations including both positive and negative numbers. All of the positive and negative numbers together are referred to as *signed numbers*.

A positive number has a *plus* sign before it, while a negative number has a *minus* sign before it. Any number without a sign is assumed to be *positive*. *Zero* is represented at all times as 0 without any sign.

Addition of Signed Numbers

When adding two signed numbers whose signs are the same (i.e., both are positive or both are negative) simply *add* the numbers and place the common sign in front of the answer.

✰ When adding two signed numbers whose signs are different (i.e., one sign is positive and one sign is negative) find the *difference* between the two numbers and place the *sign of the larger number* in front of the answer.

(30) EXAMPLES:

(1) $\begin{array}{r} +\ 9 \\ +\ 5 \\ \hline +14 \end{array}$

(2) $\begin{array}{r} -12 \\ -27 \\ \hline -39 \end{array}$

(3) $\begin{array}{r} +16 \\ -\ 7 \\ \hline +\ 9 \end{array}$

(4) $\begin{array}{r} +15 \\ -40 \\ \hline -25 \end{array}$

✰ You may be asked to add more than two signed numbers together. In these cases first add the positive numbers and the negative numbers separately; then add the respective sums.

EXAMPLES:

(1) *Add*
$\begin{array}{r} +24 \\ -12 \\ +13 \\ -10 \end{array}$

(a) $\begin{array}{r} +24 \\ +13 \\ \hline +37 \end{array}$ $\begin{array}{r} -12 \\ -10 \\ \hline -22 \end{array}$

(b) $\begin{array}{r} +37 \\ -22 \\ \hline +15 \end{array}$

(2) *Add*
$\begin{array}{r} -45 \\ +13 \\ -41 \\ +18 \\ -63 \end{array}$

(a) $\begin{array}{r} +13 \\ +18 \\ \hline +31 \end{array}$ $\begin{array}{r} -\ 45 \\ -\ 41 \\ -\ 63 \\ \hline -149 \end{array}$

(b) $\begin{array}{r} -149 \\ +\ 31 \\ \hline -118 \end{array}$

PRACTICE EXERCISES 1: ADD
(Answers to Practice Exercises appear at end of chapter.)

(1) +8
     +4
     12

(2) − 9
     −14
     −23

(3) +48
     −63
     −15

(4) +12
     −10
     +2

(5) +49
     +13
     +62

(6) −12
     −12
     −24

(7) −70
     +85
     +15

(8) −63
     +49
     −14

(9) +1
     +2
     −3
     −4
     −4

(10) +12   *8/4*   *31*
     −13   *−26*   *13*
     +14   *18*   *44*
     −15
     −16
     −18

Subtraction of Signed Numbers

To subtract signed numbers change the sign of the *subtrahend* (bottom number) after circling the original sign, and follow the rules of addition.

(31) (32) EXAMPLES:
Subtract

(1)   + 12
     − ⊕ 17
     ─────
       − 5

(2)   − 50
     + ⊖ 27
     ─────
       − 23

(3)   + 40
     + ⊖ 65
     ─────
       + 105

(4)   − 20
     − ⊕ 13
     ─────
       − 33

PRACTICE EXERCISES 2: SUBTRACT
(Answers to Practice Exercises appear at end of chapter.)

(1)   +30
   + −14
        44

(2)   −16
   −   + 9
       −25

(3)   −28
      +28
        0

(4)   +34
      +44
       70

(5)   0
      +14
       74

(6)   +17
        0
      +17

(7)   −63
     − +19
      −82

(8)   +72
   + −69
      +141

(9)   −16
      +15
      − 1

(10) +58
      +31
      + 27

Multiplication and Division of Signed Numbers

If the two signed numbers to be multiplied or divided have the *same sign*, perform the indicated operation and place a *plus sign* in front of the answer.

If the two signed numbers to be multiplied or divided have *different signs*, perform the indicated operation and place a *minus sign* in front of the answer.

same signs = pos.
dif. signs = neg.

(33) EXAMPLES:
Multiply
(1) $(+14)(+3) = +42$
(2) $(-15)(-5) = +75$
(3) $(+10)(-3) = -30$
(4) $(-18)(+4) = -72$

(34) EXAMPLES:
Divide
(1) $+14 \div +2 = +7$
(2) $\dfrac{-20}{-5} = +4$

(35)
(3) $+100 \div -4 = -25$
(4) $\dfrac{-50}{+5} = -10$

PRACTICE EXERCISES 3:
(Answers to Practice Exercises appear at end of chapter.)

Perform the indicated operation on the signed numbers below.

(1) $(+3)(+7)$ = +21

(2) $(-8)(-5)$ + 40

(3) $(+5)(-6)$ -30

(4) $(-10)(+7)$ -70

(5) $(-9)(0)$ 0

(6) $\dfrac{+35}{+5}$ + 7

(7) $-9 \div -9$ +1

(8) $\dfrac{40}{-8}$ -5

(9) $\dfrac{-65}{+13}$ - 5

(10) $\dfrac{0}{-6}$ 0

Parentheses

Parentheses are used to group terms (numbers or symbols) into a larger unit. If you wish to show addition of the group of terms, you precede the parentheses with a plus sign.

EXAMPLE:
$$4 + 5 + 7 = 4 + (5 + 7)$$

Preceding parentheses by a minus sign changes the sign of every term inside the parentheses when you remove the parentheses. You can think of the minus sign as being a minus 1 multiplied by the numbers in parentheses.

EXAMPLE:
$$4 - (-5 - 7) = 4 + 5 + 7$$
4 + 5 + 7

PRACTICE EXERCISES 4:
(Answers to Practice Exercises appear at end of chapter.)

Remove the parentheses from each expression below.

(1) 3 + (1 − 4)   3 + 1 + 4   ⑦

(2) 5 − (3 + 7)   5 − 3 − 7

(3) 3 − (−4 + 6)   3 + 4 − 6

(4) 9 + (10 + 1)   9 + 10 + 1

(5) 10 − (−3 − 6)   10 + 3 + 6

(6) 2 − (1 − 16)   2 − 1 + 16

Answers and Solutions

PRACTICE EXERCISES 1:		PRACTICE EXERCISES 2:
(1) +12		(1) +44
(2) −23		(2) −25
(3) −15		(3) 0
(4) +2		(4) −10
(5) +62		(5) +14
(6) −24		(6) +17
(7) +15		(7) −82
(8) −14		(8) +141
(9) −4		(9) −1
(10) −18		(10) +27

PRACTICE EXERCISES 3:

(1) +21

(2) +40

(3) −30

(4) −70

(5) 0

(6) +7

(7) +1

(8) −5

(9) −5

(10) 0

PRACTICE EXERCISES 4:

(1) $3 + 1 - 4$

(2) $5 - 3 - 7$

(3) $3 + 4 - 6$

(4) $9 + 10 + 1$

(5) $10 + 3 + 6$

(6) $2 - 1 + 16$

ALGEBRA DIAGNOSTIC SELF-TEST

(1.) Solve for x: $x - 32 = 53$ 85

(2.) Solve for x: $4x = 68$ 17

(3.) Solve for y: $3y + 8 = 32$ 8

(4.) Solve for x: $7x + 9 = 5x + 17$

(5.) Solve for x: $wx + r = t$

(6.) Solve for y: $\dfrac{a}{y} = \dfrac{c}{m}$

(7.) If $a = 3$ and $b = 7$, evaluate $\dfrac{a + 2}{b} + \dfrac{b}{a + b}$

(8.) If $x = 2$, $y = 5$, evaluate $3x^2 y^2$

(9.) Solve for a and b:
$$3a + 2b = 1$$
$$2a - 3b = -8$$

(10.) Add: $-5xy + 3xy =$

(11.) Multiply: $7^3 \times 7^5 =$ 49 15

(12.) Simplify: $(-9xy)(-4x^2y^3) =$ 36 x³ y⁴

(13.) Simplify: $(x^5y^6)^3 =$ x 15 y 18

(14.) $9^8 \div 9^5 =$ 9³

(15.) Simplify: $\dfrac{-35a^7b^3}{7a^3b^2}$

(16.) Simplify: $(3x + 7y) + (6x - 2y)$ 9x + 5y

(17.) Simplify: $(3s^2 + 4st + 13t^2) - (2s^2 + 2st + 3t^2)$

(18.) Multiply: $(2x + 4)(3x - 1)$

(19.) Multiply: $(a^2 + 3ab + 4)(2a + b)$

(20.) Divide: $(12a^8 - 8a^7) \div 2a^3$

(21.) Divide: $(x^2 + 3x - 18) \div (x + 6)$

(22.) Factor: $n^2 - 9$

(23.) Factor: $4x^2 + 2x$

(24.) Factor: $x^2 + 3x + 2$

(25.) Factor: $x^2 - 5x - 6$

(26.) Factor: $x^2 - 9x + 8$

(27.) Solve for x: $x^2 - 25 = 0$

(28.) Solve for y: $y^2 - 5y = 0$

(29.) Solve for r: $r^2 - 10r + 24 = 0$

(30.) Solve for t: $t^2 + 24t = 81$

(31.) Solve for x: $5x + 2 > 17$

(32.) Solve for x: $-4x - 8 < 12$

ANSWERS TO ALGEBRA DIAGNOSTIC SELF-TEST

1. $x = 85$

2. $x = 17$

3. $y = 8$

4. $x = 4$

5. $x = \dfrac{t - r}{w}$

6. $y = \dfrac{am}{c}$

7. $\dfrac{99}{70} = 1\dfrac{29}{70}$

8. 300

9. $a = -1, b = 2$

10. $-2xy$

11. 7^8

12. $36x^3y^4$

13. $x^{15}y^{18}$

14. 9^3

15. $-5a^4b$

16. $9x + 5y$

17. $s^2 + 2st + 10t^2$

18. $6x^2 + 10x - 4$

19. $2a^3 + 7a^2b + 8a + 3ab^2 + 4b$

20. $6a^5 - 4a^4$

21. $x - 3$

22. $(n + 3)(n - 3)$

23. $2x(2x + 1)$

24. $(x + 1)(x + 2)$

25. $(x + 1)(x - 6)$

26. $(x - 1)(x - 8)$

27. $x = +5, -5$

28. $y = 0, 5$

29. $r = 4, 6$

30. $t = 3, -27$

31. $x > 3$

32. $x > -5$

ALGEBRA

Algebra is that branch of mathematics that deals with the relationship of known and unknown quantities. Letters are used in algebra problems to stand for unknown quantities or numbers.

ALGEBRAIC EQUATIONS

The relationship of numbers or symbols in an algebra problem is expressed in a statement called an *equation*.

An example of an equation would be $y - 5 = 11$. This equation says that when you subtract 5 from the unknown number y, you will have 11 left. Therefore, you know that $y = 16$, because $16 - 5 = 11$.

You should remember that an equation in algebra is like a balance scale.

When a number and a letter are written together without any operation sign between them $(+, -, \times, \div)$, multiplication is understood. For example, $5x$ means 5 times x.

If you add, subtract, multiply, or divide on one side of an equation, then you must do the same thing on the other side of the equation.

Solution of Equations

You solve an equation by finding a value for the unknown quantity or quantities represented by letters or symbols. To solve an equation, you change it around (restructure it) so that all the known parts are on one side and the unknown is on the opposite side. By applying opposite operations we can isolate the unknown and obtain the answer.

(1) EXAMPLE 1:
What can you do to eliminate the -6 from the left? Use signed numbers.

$$
\begin{aligned}
t - 6 &= 8 \\
+6 &= +6 \\
\hline
t &= 14
\end{aligned}
$$

Step 1: Add $+6$ to -6.

Step 2: However, you cannot change one side without doing the same to the other side, so add $+6$ to the other side.

Step 3: Solution is complete. The value of the equation is not changed because the same amount (6) was added to both sides of the $=$ sign.

EXAMPLE 2:

What can you do to eliminate the $+7$ from the left side of the equation?

$$
\begin{array}{rcr}
r + 7 &=& 9 \\
-7 &=& -7 \\
\hline
r &=& 2
\end{array}
$$

Step 1: Add -7 to $+7$ to eliminate that term on the left.

Step 2: You must add the same quantity (-7) to the opposite side.

Step 3: Solution is complete. Remember, you added -7 to both sides.

Notice how, in the next two examples, that when the unknown is multiplied by a number we divide to get the solution, and when the unknown is divided by a number we multiply to get the answer.

Note: In algebra a raised dot is used to indicate multiplication.

(2) **EXAMPLE 3:**

Step 1:

$$7t = 84$$

Step 2:

$$\frac{7t}{7} = \frac{84}{7}$$

Step 3:

$$t = 12$$

EXAMPLE 4:

Step 1:

$$\frac{g}{-4} = 13$$

Step 2:

$$-4 \cdot \frac{g}{-4} = 13 \cdot (-4)$$

Step 3:

$$g = -52$$

Sometimes it is necessary to use two steps of opposite operations in order to solve for the unknown in an equation. This may be done as follows:

③ EXAMPLE 5:

Step 1: Subtract 9 from each side of the equation.

$$
\begin{aligned}
2a + 9 &= 15 \\
-9 &= -9 \\
\hline
2a &= 6
\end{aligned}
$$

Step 2: Divide each side by 2.

$$
\frac{\cancel{2}a}{\cancel{2}} = \frac{\overset{3}{\cancel{6}}}{\cancel{2}}
$$
$$
a = 3
$$

EXAMPLE 6:

Step 1: Add $+2$ to each side.

$$
\begin{aligned}
14t - 2 &= 5 \\
+2 &= +2 \\
\hline
14t &= 7
\end{aligned}
$$

Step 2: Divide each side by 14.

$$
\frac{14t}{14} = \frac{7}{14}
$$
$$
t = \frac{1}{2}
$$

④ EXAMPLE 7:

Step 1: Subtract 5 from each side.

$$
\begin{aligned}
6x + 5 &= 4x + 15 \\
-5 & -5 \\
\hline
6x &= 4x + 10
\end{aligned}
$$

Step 2: Subtract $4x$ from each side.

$$
\begin{aligned}
6x &= 4x + 10 \\
-4x & -4x \\
\hline
2x &= 10
\end{aligned}
$$

Step 3: Divide each side by 2.

$$
\frac{2x}{2} = \frac{10}{2}
$$
$$
x = 5
$$

EXAMPLE 8:

Step 1: Add 6 to each side.

$$\left(\tfrac{3}{5}\right)x - 6 = 12$$
$$\underline{\phantom{\left(\tfrac{3}{5}\right)x-}+6 \qquad +6}$$
$$\left(\tfrac{3}{5}\right)x \qquad = 18$$

Step 2: Multiply each side by $\tfrac{5}{3}$.

$$\left(\tfrac{5}{3}\right)\left(\tfrac{3}{5}\right)x = 18\left(\tfrac{5}{3}\right)$$
$$x = 30$$

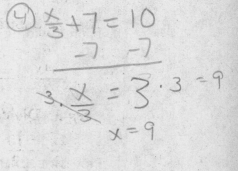

PRACTICE EXERCISES 1:
(Answers to Practice Exercises appear at end of chapter.)

Solve for the unknown in each of the following equations.

(1) $x + 7 = 15$

(2) $6y = 78$

(3) $2m - 5 = 37$

(4) $\dfrac{x}{3} + 7 = 10$

(5) $7x - 2 = 4x + 7$

(6) $\tfrac{5}{7}x + 6 = 26$

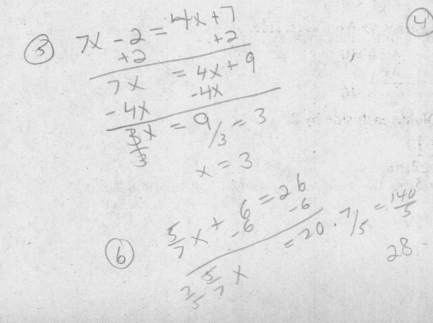

Literal Equations

Sometimes equations have only letters, and you will be asked to solve for a particular letter. The procedure is exactly the same as that outlined above.

(5) EXAMPLES:

(1) Solve for x, if $rx - c = t$.
Add c to both sides:

$$rx - c = t$$
$$\underline{+ c = +c}$$
$$rx \quad = t + c$$

Divide each side by r, solving for x:

$$\frac{rx}{r} = \frac{t + c}{r}$$
$$x = \frac{t + c}{r}$$

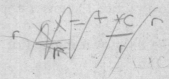

(6) (2) Solve for y, if $\dfrac{a}{y} = \dfrac{b}{c}$.

Note: To solve this problem you must first *cross-multiply* the numerators and denominators of the fractions. This means that you (1) multiply the denominator of the fraction on the left side of the equation by the numerator of the fraction on the right side of the equation, and (2) multiply the numerator of the fraction on the left by the denominator of the fraction on the right. Thus,

$$\text{if } \frac{a}{y} = \frac{b}{c}, \text{ then}$$
$$yb = ac$$

Then, dividing both sides by b,

$$\frac{yb}{b} = \frac{ac}{b}$$
$$y = \frac{ac}{b}$$

PRACTICE EXERCISES 2:
(Answers to Practice Exercises appear at end of chapter.)

(1) Solve for t if $st + m = q - r$.

(2) Solve for z if $\dfrac{b}{z} = \dfrac{d}{e}$.

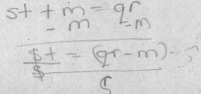

Answers and Solutions

PRACTICE EXERCISES 1:

(1) $x = 8$

$$x + 7 = 15$$
$$\underline{ - 7 = -7}$$
$$x = 8$$

(2) $y = 13$

$$\frac{6y}{6} = \frac{78}{6}$$
$$y = 13$$

(3) $m = 21$

$$2m - 5 = 37$$
$$\underline{ + 5 = +5}$$
$$\frac{\cancel{2}m}{\cancel{2}} = \frac{42}{2}$$
$$m = 21$$

(4) $x = 9$

$$\frac{x}{3} + 7 = 10$$
$$\underline{\phantom{\frac{x}{3}} - 7 = -7}$$
$$\cancel{3} \cdot \frac{x}{\cancel{3}} = 3 \,(3)$$
$$x = 9$$

(5) $x = 3$

$$7x - 2 = 4x + 7$$
$$\underline{ + 2 + 2}$$
$$7x = 4x + 9$$

$$7x = 4x + 9$$
$$\underline{-4x -4x}$$
$$3x = 9$$

$$\frac{3x}{3} = \frac{9}{3}$$
$$x = 3$$

(6) $x = 28$

$$\frac{5}{7}x + 6 = 26$$
$$\underline{\phantom{\frac{5}{7}x} - 6 -6}$$
$$\frac{5}{7}x = 20$$
$$\left(\frac{7}{5}\right)\frac{5}{7}x = 20\left(\frac{7}{5}\right)$$
$$x = 28$$

PRACTICE EXERCISES 2:

(1) $\dfrac{q - r - m}{s}$

$$st + m = q - r$$
$$\underline{\quad - m = \quad - m}$$
$$\frac{st}{s} = \frac{q - r - m}{s}$$
$$t = \frac{q - r - m}{s}$$

(2) $z = \dfrac{be}{d}$

$$\frac{b}{z} = \frac{d}{e}$$
$$\frac{zd}{d} = \frac{be}{d}$$
$$z = \frac{be}{d}$$

EVALUATION OF ALGEBRAIC EXPRESSIONS AND FORMULAS

Evaluation means "finding the value of." Problems in evaluation may concern obtaining the value of (1) algebraic expressions or (2) expressions that set forth a general fact, rule, or principle that deals with such things as finding roots of equations, converting temperatures, finding areas and volumes, and calculating interest. The latter type of expressions are called *formulas*. In both of these types, in order to carry out the evaluation, simply substitute the numerical values given for the letters in the problem and then perform the indicated operations.

EXAMPLES:

(1) If $t = 7$ and $b = 4$, simplify $3t + 5bt$.
    Note: "Simplify" will sometimes be used instead of "evaluate."
    $3t + 5bt = 3(7) + 5(4)(7) = 21 + 140 = 161$

(2) If $a = 5$ and $b = 3$, evaluate
$$\frac{1}{b} + \frac{3}{a - b} - \frac{2}{a + b} = \frac{1}{3} + \frac{3}{2} - \frac{2}{8} = 1\frac{5}{6} - \frac{1}{4} = 1\frac{7}{12}$$

PRACTICE EXERCISES 1:
(Answers to Practice Exercises appear at end of chapter.)

(1) If $a = 4$ and $b = 2$, find the value of $6ab + 5b - a$.

(2) If $x = 5$ and $c = 3$, simplify $\dfrac{6}{x + c} - \dfrac{2}{x - c} + \dfrac{8}{c}$.

EXAMPLE:

If $F = \frac{9}{5}(C + 32)$, find F when $C = 45°$.

$F = \frac{9}{5}C + 32$

$F = \frac{9}{5}(45) + 32$

$F = 81 + 32$

$F = 113°$

EXAMPLE:

If $S = \frac{1}{2}gt^2$, find S when $g = 32$ and $t = 4$.

$S = \frac{1}{2}gt^2$

$S = \frac{1}{2}(32)(4)^2$

$S = 16 \cdot 16$

$S = 256$

PRACTICE EXERCISES 2:
(Answers to Practice Exercises appear at end of chapter.)

(1) If $C = \frac{5}{9}(F - 32)$, find C when $F = 77°$

(2) If $I = prt$, find I when $p = \$400$, $r = 5\%$, and $t = 3$ yrs.

Answers and Solutions

PRACTICE EXERCISES 1:

(1) 54

$6ab + 5b - a$, when $a = 4$, $b = 2$

$= 6 \cdot 8 + (5 \cdot 2) - 4 = 48 + 10 - 4 = 54$

(2) $2\frac{5}{12}$

$\frac{6}{x + c} - \frac{2}{x - c} + \frac{8}{c}$, when $x = 5$, $c = 3$

$= \frac{6}{8} - \frac{2}{2} + \frac{8}{3} = \frac{18}{24} - \frac{24}{24} + \frac{64}{24} = \frac{58}{24} = 2\frac{10}{24} = 2\frac{5}{12}$

PRACTICE EXERCISES 2:

(1) $25°$

$C = \frac{5}{9}(F - 32)$

$C = \frac{5}{9}(77 - 32)$

$C = \frac{5}{\cancel{9}}(\cancel{45})^{5}$

$C = 25°$

(2) $\$60$

$I = prt$

$I = \$\cancel{400}^{4} \times \frac{5}{\cancel{100}_{1}} \times \frac{3}{1}$

$I = 4 \times 5 \times 3$

$I = \$60$

SOLVING FOR TWO UNKNOWNS

When you are given *two* equations with the same two unknowns, you can solve for both unknowns.

(9) **EXAMPLE 1:**
$$3a + 4b = 24$$
$$2a + b = 11$$
Solve for a and b.

Step 1: To solve the equations, you must change one or both of the equations in such a way that you can eliminate one of the unknowns by adding or subtracting the equations. In this problem, you can multiply the bottom equation through by -4.
$$3a + 4b = 24$$
$$-8a - 4b = -44$$

Step 2: Add the equations.
$$3a + 4b = 24$$
$$\underline{-8a - 4b = -44}$$
$$-5a \qquad = -20$$

Step 3: Solve for a.
$$-5a = -20$$
$$5a = 20$$
$$a = 4$$

Step 4: Substitute the value of a in one of the equations to solve for b.
$$3a + 4b = 24$$
$$3(4) + 4b = 24$$
$$12 + 4b = 24$$
$$4b = 12$$
$$b = 3$$

You can eliminate *either* unknown in order to solve a problem of this kind. Here is the same problem, worked by eliminating a.

EXAMPLE 2:

$3a + 4b = 24$
$2a + \ b = 11$

Step 1: Eliminate a by multiplying the first equation by 2 and the second by -3.

$$6a + 8b = \ \ \ 48$$
$$-6a - 3b = -33$$

Step 2: Add the equations.

$$6a + 8b = \ \ \ 48$$
$$-6a - 3b = -33$$
$$\overline{ 5b = \ \ \ 15}$$

Step 3: Solve for b.

$$5b = 15$$
$$\ b = \ 3$$

Step 4: Substitute to find the value of a.

$$2a + \ b = 11$$
$$2a + 3 \ \ = 11$$
$$2a = \ 8$$
$$a = \ 4$$

PRACTICE EXERCISES
(Answers to Practice Exercises appear at end of chapter.)

Solve for a and b or x and y in each problem.

(1) $6a - 2b = 32$
     $3a + 2b = 22$

(2) $3a + 3b = 24$
     $2a + \ b = 13$

(3) $4x + 2y = 16$
     $2x + 3y = 14$

(4) $6x + 2y = 24$
     $\ x + \ y = 5$

Answers and Solutions

PRACTICE EXERCISES

(1) $a = 6, b = 2$

$$6a - 2b = 32$$
$$\underline{3a + 2b = 22}$$
$$9a = 54$$
$$a = 6$$

Substitute to find b:

$$6a - 2b = 32$$
$$6(6) - 2b = 32$$
$$36 - 2b = 32$$
$$- 2b = -4$$
$$b = 2$$

(2) $a = 5, b = 3$

$$3a + 3b = 24$$
$$2a + b = 13$$
$$3a + 3b = 24$$
$$\underline{-6a - 3b = -39}$$
$$-3a = -15$$
$$a = 5$$

Substitute to find b:

$$2a + b = 13$$
$$2(5) + b = 13$$
$$10 + b = 13$$
$$b = 3$$

(3) $x = 2\frac{1}{2}, y = 3$

$$4x + 2y = 16$$
$$2x + 3y = 14$$
$$4x + 2y = 16$$
$$\underline{-4x - 6y = -28}$$
$$- 4y = -12$$
$$y = 3$$

Substitute to find x:

$$4x + 2y = 16$$
$$4x + 2(3) = 16$$
$$4x + 6 = 16$$
$$4x = 10$$
$$x = 2\frac{1}{2}$$

(4) $x = 3.5, y = 1.5$

$$6x + 2y = 24$$
$$x + y = 5$$
$$6x + 2y = 24$$
$$\underline{-2x - 2y = -10}$$
$$4x = 14$$
$$x = 3.5$$

Substitute to find y:

$$x + y = 5$$
$$3.5 + y = 5$$
$$y = 1.5$$

MONOMIALS AND POLYNOMIALS

Monomials

Monomials are algebraic expressions consisting of only one term. Examples of monomials are $8t$, $-3b$, $4xy^2$, and $.7r^3$.

Adding and Subtracting Monomials

To add or subtract monomials simply follow the rules of signed numbers in order to determine which number to place in front of the particular monomial in the problem.

⑩ EXAMPLES:
Add

(1) $\begin{array}{r} -9m^2t \\ +5m^2t \\ \hline -4m^2t \end{array}$

(2) $\begin{array}{r} +\ 5rmx \\ -\ 9rmx \\ +14rmx \\ \hline 10rmx \end{array}$

EXAMPLES:
Subtract

(1) $\begin{array}{r} -\ 7x^2y \\ +\ominus\ 5x^2y \\ \hline -\ 2x^2y \end{array}$

(2) $\begin{array}{r} +\ 18ab^3c^2 \\ +\ominus 12ab^3c^2 \\ \hline 30ab^3c^2 \end{array}$

Multiplying Monomials

To multiply monomials of the same base (letter or letters), find the exponent of the product by *adding* the exponents of the monomials involved. An exponent tells how many times a number is multiplied by itself. Thus $2^3 = 2 \times 2 \times 2$. The ^{3} is the exponent. If the monomials are preceded by factors, multiply the factors as in arithmetic.

(11) **EXAMPLES:**

(1) $e^4 \cdot e^5 = e^{4+5} = e^9$

(2) $5^2 \cdot 5^3 = 5^5 = 5 \times 5 \times 5 \times 5 \times 5 = 3,125$

(3) $m^6 \cdot m^8 \cdot m^{12} = m^{26}$

(12) (4) $(-7a^3b)(+5a^2b^2) = -35a^5b^3$

Note that in example (4) the product of -7 and $+5$ is -35, the product of a^3 and a^2 is a^5, and the product of b and b^2 is b^3 since any monomial having no exponent indicated is assumed to have an exponent of one.

When monomials are being *raised to a power* the answer is obtained by multiplying the exponents of each part of the monomial by the power to which it is being raised.

(13) **EXAMPLES:**

(1) $(a^7)^3 = a^{21}$

(2) $(x^3y^2)^4 = x^{12}y^8$

Dividing Monomials

To divide monomials of the same base, divide any factor as in arithmetic, then find the exponent of the quotient by taking the difference of the exponents of the monomials involved.

(14) **EXAMPLES:**

(1) $\dfrac{m^{10}}{m^3} = m^7$

(2) $\dfrac{7^4}{7^3} = 7^1 = 7$

(15) (3) $\dfrac{-20t^9b^8}{+4t^7b^5} = -5t^2b^3$

Note that in (3) the quotient of -20 and $+4$ is -5, the quotient of t^9 and t^7 is t^2, and the quotient of b^8 and b^5 is b^3.

PRACTICE EXERCISES: MONOMIALS
(Answers to Practice Exercises appear at end of chapter.)

(1)   *Add* $-8m^2bt$
$-4m^2bt$
$\underline{+5m^2bt}$

(2)   *Subtract* $-17abcd$
$\underline{-17abcd}$

(3)   *Multiply* $(b^2cd^4)^5$

(4)   *Multiply* $(-8b^2c^4)(+2b^2c)$

(5)   *Divide* $\dfrac{-30ab^3d^4}{-15b^2d}$

Polynomials

A *polynomial* is an algebraic expression consisting of two or more terms; that is, two or more monomials. Examples of polynomials are $7b + 8$, $X^2 + Y^2 + Z^2$, and $9c^2 + 4c - 3$.

Adding and Subtracting Polynomials

To add or subtract polynomials, arrange like monomials in columns Then, simply add or subtract the columns of monomials.

⑯ EXAMPLES:
Add

(1) $5X - 7Y$
$\underline{9X + 4Y}$
$14X - 3Y$

(2) $a^2 + 5b + 7$
$2a^2 - 6b - 3$
$\underline{-5a^2 + 4b + 6}$
$-2a^2 + 3b + 10$

Subtract

(1) $3cd \quad - 6mt$
$+ \ominus 2cd - \oplus 9mt$
$\overline{\qquad cd \qquad - 15mt}$

(2) $8s^2 \qquad - 5st \qquad + 4t^3$

⑰ $+ \ominus \ 5s^2 + \ominus 3st - \oplus 2t^3$
$\overline{13s^2 \qquad - 2st \qquad + 2t^3}$

Multiplying Polynomials

To multiply polynomials place the smaller polynomial beneath the larger polynomial. Then multiply each term in the larger polynomial by each term in the smaller polynomial. Arrange the results of these successive multiplications in columns containing the same type of monomials. Add up each column for the final answer.

⑱ EXAMPLES:
Multiply

(1) $(3m + 6)$ by $(2m - 4)$

$$3m + 6$$
$$\underline{2m - 4} \qquad\qquad \text{(multiplying)}$$
$$6m^2 + 12m$$
$$\underline{\qquad -12m - 24} \qquad \text{(adding)}$$
$$6m^2 \qquad\quad - 24$$

⑲ (2) $(a^2 + 2ab - 3)\,(a + 4b)$

$$a^2 + 2ab - 3$$
$$\underline{a + 4b}$$
$$a^3 + 2a^2b - 3a$$
$$\underline{\quad + 4a^2b \qquad + 8ab^2 - 12b}$$
$$a^3 + 6a^2b - 3a + 8ab^2 - 12b$$

Dividing Polynomials

To divide a *polynomial by a monomial* simply divide each term in the polynomial by the monomial.

To divide a *polynomial by a polynomial* the procedure to be used is comparable to long division of whole numbers.

⑳ EXAMPLE 1:
Divide
$(16a^7 - 12a^5) \div 4a^2$

$$\frac{\overset{4}{\cancel{16}}a^7 - \overset{3}{\cancel{12}}a^5}{\cancel{4}a^2} = 4a^5 - 3a^3$$

㉑ **EXAMPLE 2:**
Divide
$(x^2 + 18x + 45)$ by $(x + 3)$

(Note similarity to long division.)

$$24 \overline{)1512} \qquad\qquad x + 3 \overline{)x^2 + 18x + 45}$$

$$\begin{array}{r} 6 \\ 24 \overline{)1512} \end{array} \qquad\qquad \begin{array}{r} x \\ x + 3 \overline{)x^2 + 18x + 45} \end{array}$$

$$\begin{array}{r} 6 \\ 24 \overline{)1512} \\ \underline{144} \\ 72 \end{array} \qquad\qquad \begin{array}{r} x \\ x + 3 \overline{)x^2 + 18x + 45} \\ \underline{x^2 + 3x} \\ + 15x + 45 \end{array}$$

$$\begin{array}{r} 63 \\ 24 \overline{)1512} \\ \underline{144} \\ 72 \end{array} \qquad\qquad \begin{array}{r} x + 15 \\ x + 3 \overline{)x^2 + 18x + 45} \\ \underline{x^2 + 3x} \\ 15x + 45 \end{array}$$

$$\begin{array}{r} 63 \\ 24 \overline{)1512} \\ \underline{144} \\ 72 \\ \underline{72} \end{array} \qquad\qquad \begin{array}{r} x + 15 \\ x + 3 \overline{)x^2 + 18x + 45} \\ \underline{x^2 + 3x} \\ 15x + 45 \\ \underline{15x + 45} \end{array}$$

PRACTICE EXERCISES: POLYNOMIALS
(Answers to Practice Exercises appear at end of chapter.)

(1) *Add*
$$5x^2y^2 - 4ab$$
$$-6x^2y^2 + 3ab$$
$$+2x^2y^2 - ab$$

(2) *Subtract*
$$5x^2 - 3xy - 2y^2$$
$$-3x^2 - 3xy + 2y^2$$

(3) *Multiply*
$(a^2 + m)(a - 2)$

(4) Find the product of $(x^2 + 3x - 9)$ and $(x - 2)$.

(5) Find the quotient of $(20x^3b^2 - 10x^2b^3) \div 10x^2b^2$.

(6) *Divide*
$(x^2 + 22x + 85)$ by $(x + 17)$

Answers and Solutions

PRACTICE EXERCISES: MONOMIALS

(1) $-7m^2bt$

(2) 0

(3) $b^{10}c^5d^{20}$

(4) $-16b^4c^5$

(5) $2abd^3$

PRACTICE EXERCISES: POLYNOMIALS

(1) $x^2y^2 - 2ab$

(2) $8x^2 - 4y^2$

$$
\begin{array}{r}
5x^2 \quad\; - 3xy \quad\; - 2y^2 \\
\underline{+ \ominus 3x^2 + \ominus 3yx - \oplus 2y^2} \\
8x^2 \qquad\qquad\qquad - 4y^2
\end{array}
$$

(3) $a^3 + ma - 2a^2 - 2m$

$$
\begin{array}{l}
a^2 + m \\
\underline{a\; - 2} \\
a^3 + am \\
\underline{\qquad\quad - 2a^2 - 2m} \\
a^3 + am - 2a^2 - 2m
\end{array}
$$

(4) $x^3 + x^2 - 15x + 18$

$$
\begin{array}{r}
x^2 + 3x\; - 9 \\
\underline{x\; - 2} \\
x^3 + 3x^2 - \; 9x \\
\underline{- 2x^2 - \; 6x + 18} \\
x^3 + \; x^2 - 15x + 18
\end{array}
$$

(5) $-2x + b$

(6) $x + 5$

$$
\begin{array}{r}
x\; + 5 \\
x + 17 \overline{\smash{)}\; x^2 + \quad 22x + 85} \\
\underline{x^2 - \oplus 17x} \\
5x + 85 \\
\underline{5x + 85}
\end{array}
$$

FACTORING

To *factor* an algebraic expression means to find the two or more quantities whose product will give the original quantity. There are three basic types of expressions you ought to be able to factor. These, and the methods for factoring each, are outlined below.

Type I: The Difference Between Two Squares

1. Determine the square roots of the letter term and the perfect numerical square.
2. Place these square roots within the brackets of the factors, one with a *plus* sign and one with a *minus* sign.

(22) EXAMPLES:
Factor

(1) $m^2 - 64 = (m + 8)(m - 8)$

(2) $a^4 - 144 = (a^2 + 12)(a^2 - 12)$

Type II: Expressions Containing Common Unknown Factor

1. The unknown in the expression is one factor.
2. Find the remaining factor by dividing the expression by the first factor.

(23) EXAMPLES:
Factor

(1) $b^2 - 13b = b(b - 13)$

(2) $x^4 - 25x^2 = x^2(x^2 - 25) = x^2(x + 5)(x - 5)$

Note: Since $(x^2 - 25)$ can be factored further, the result is *three* rather than the usual *two* factors.

3. In expressions of more than two terms, any coefficient held in common by all terms can be factored.

EXAMPLE:
Factor

$4b^3 + 2b^2 - 3b = b(4b^2 + 2b - 3)$

Type III: Quadratic Expressions Containing Three Terms

Quadratic expressions are expressions containing an unknown whose highest degree is 2. Such expressions as $4x^2 + 3$, $x^2 - 7$, and $2x^2 + 3x - 5$ are all examples of quadratic expressions. It is particularly important to be able to factor these expressions since this is a necessary step in solving quadratic equations.

Procedure

1. If the sign of the last number of the expression is *positive:*
   (a) Find two numbers whose *product* is the last number of the expression, and whose *sum* is the coefficient (number) in the middle term.
   (b) Give *both* factors the sign of the *middle* term of the expression.

2. If the sign of the last number of the expression is *negative:*
   (a) Find two numbers whose *product* is the last number of the expression, and whose *difference* is the coefficient (number) in the middle term.
   (b) Give the larger of these two numerical factors the sign of the middle term. Give the remaining numerical factor the opposite sign.

EXAMPLES:
Factor

(24) (1) $x^2 + 8x + 15$
$(x + 3)(x + 5)$

Notice that $3 \times 5 = 15$ and $3 + 5 = 8$, the coefficient of the middle term. Also note that the signs of both factors are $+$, the sign of the middle term.

(25) (2) $x^2 - 5x - 14$
$(x - 7)(x + 2)$

Notice that $7 \times 2 = 14$, and $7 - 2 = 5$, the coefficient of the middle term. Also note that the sign of the larger factor 7 is $-$ while the other factor 2 has a $+$ sign.

(3) $x^2 + 2x - 24$
$(x - 4)(x + 6)$

(26) (4) $x^2 - 17x + 72$
$(x - 8)(x - 9)$

PRACTICE EXERCISES:

(Answers to Practice Exercises appear at end of chapter).

Factor the following quadratic expressions.

(1) $a^2 + 26a$

(2) $x^2 - 121$

(3) $c^4 - 49$

(4) $t^2 - 35t$

(5) $x^2 - x - 30$

(6) $r^2 + 14r + 45$

(7) $t^2 + 5t - 24$

(8) $m^2 - 16m + 48$

Answers and Solutions

PRACTICE EXERCISES:

(1) $a(a + 26)$

(2) $(x + 11)(x - 11)$

(3) $(c^2 + 7)(c^2 - 7)$

(4) $t(t - 35)$

(5) $(x + 5)(x - 6)$

(6) $(r + 9)(r + 5)$

(7) $(t + 8)(t - 3)$

(8) $(m - 4)(m - 12)$

SOLVING QUADRATIC EQUATIONS

Quadratic equations are equations in which the highest degree of the unknown is 2. Examples of such equations are:

(a) $x^2 + 4x - 5 = 0$
(b) $m^2 - 3m = 0$
(c) $t^2 - 81 = 0$
(d) $y^2 - 3y = 28$

In all the examples above, with the exception of (d), the equation is set equal to zero. When this is the case the equation is considered to be in *standard form*. If the equation is not set equal to zero we re-arrange the terms by the method of opposite operations so that the equation will equal zero.

Below you will see how this can be done for example (d) by subtracting 28 from both sides of the equation.

$$
\begin{array}{r}
y^2 - 3y = 28 \\
- 28 = -28 \\
\hline
y^2 - 3y - 28 = 0
\end{array}
$$

Now equation (d) is in standard form. Notice that when an equation is in standard form, the square term is written first (y^2), the first degree term is written second ($-3y$), and the number is written last (-28).

The equations you solved in the chapter on algebraic equations were first degree, or *linear*, equations and had one, and only one, solution. Quadratic equations are second degree equations, and therefore they each have *two* solutions.

Procedure for Solving Quadratic Equations

1. Factor the equation.
2. Set each factor equal to zero.
3. Solve each of the resulting first degree equations by the method outlined in "Solving Equations."
4. Check your solution by substituting your answers in the original equation.

EXAMPLES:

Solve the following quadratic equations:

(27) (1) $m^2 - 256 = 0$

(Factor into two linear equations. The only way for the whole expression to equal zero is for *at least* one of the factors to be zero. So set *both* equal to zero to obtain both possible answers [roots].)

$$
\begin{array}{cc}
(m + 16) & (m - 16) = \quad 0 \\
m + 16 = \quad 0 & m - 16 = \quad 0 \\
\underline{-16 = -16} & \underline{+16 = +16} \\
m \qquad = -16 & m \qquad = +16 \\
\end{array}
$$
$$m = +16, -16$$

CHECK:

$$
\begin{array}{cc}
m^2 - 256 = 0 & m^2 - 256 = 0 \\
(-16)^2 - 256 = 0 & (+16)^2 - 256 = 0 \\
256 - 256 = 0 & 256 - 256 = 0 \\
0 = 0 & 0 = 0 \\
\end{array}
$$

(28) (2) $q^2 - 8q = 0$
$q(q - 8) = 0$
$$q = 0, \text{ and}$$
$(q - 8) = \quad 0$
$$\underline{+8 = +8}$$
$$q = 8$$
$$q = 0, 8$$

CHECK:

$$
\begin{array}{ccc}
q^2 - 8q = 0 & & q^2 - 8q = 0 \\
(0)^2 - 8(0) = 0 & & (8)^2 - 8(8) = 0 \\
& \text{and} & \\
0 - 0 = 0 & & 64 - 64 = 0 \\
0 = 0 & & 0 = 0 \\
\end{array}
$$

(29) (3) $d^2 - 13d + 36 = 0$
$(d - 9)(d - 4) = 0$
$$
\begin{array}{ccc}
d - 9 = \quad 0 & & d - 4 = \quad 0 \\
\underline{+9 = +9} & \text{and} & \underline{+4 = +4} \\
d = +9 & & d = +4 \\
\end{array}
$$
$$d = 9, 4$$

CHECK:
$$d^2 - 13d + 36 = 0$$
$$(9)^2 - 13(9) + 36 = 0$$
$$81 - 117 + 36 = 0$$
$$117 - 117 = 0$$
$$0 = 0$$
$$d^2 - 13d + 36 = 0$$
$$(4)^2 - 13(4) + 36 = 0$$
$$16 - 52 + 36 = 0$$
$$52 - 52 = 0$$
$$0 = 0$$

㉚ (4) $x^2 + 5x = 84$

First put the equation in standard form:
$$x^2 + 5x - 84 = 0$$
$$(x + 12)(x - 7) = 0$$

$$\begin{array}{ll} x + 12 = 0 & \qquad x - 7 = 0 \\ \underline{- 12 = -12} & \qquad \underline{+ 7 = +7} \\ x = -12 & \qquad x = 7 \\ x = -12, 7 \end{array}$$

CHECK:
$$x^2 + 5x = 84$$
$$(7)^2 + 5(7) = 84$$
$$49 + 35 = 84$$
$$84 = 84$$
$$x^2 + 5x = 84$$
$$(-12)^2 + 5(-12) = 84$$
$$144 - 60 = 84$$
$$84 = 84$$

PRACTICE EXERCISES:
(Answers to Practice Exercises appear at end of chapter.)

(1) $t^2 - 289 = 0$

(2) $m^2 + 47m = 0$

(3) $y^2 - 18y + 45 = 0$

(4) $x^2 + 13x = -40$

Answers and Solutions

PRACTICE EXERCISES:

(1) $t = +17, -17$

$$t^2 - 289 = 0$$

$(t + 17) = 0$	$(t - 17) = 0$
$t + 17 = 0$	$t - 17 = 0$
$\underline{\quad -17 = -17}$	$\underline{\quad +17 = +17}$
$t \quad = -17$	$t \quad = 17$

(2) $m = 0, -47$

$$m^2 - 47m = 0$$
$$m(m + 47) = 0$$

$m \quad = 0$	$m + 47 = 0$
	$\underline{\quad -47 = -47}$
	$m \quad = -47$

(3) $y = 3, 15$

$$y^2 - 18y + 45 = 0$$

$y - 15 = 0$	$y - 3 = 0$
$\underline{\quad +15 = +15}$	$\underline{\quad +3 = +3}$
$y \quad = 15$	$y \quad = 3$

(4) $x = -5, -8$

$$x^2 + 13x = -40$$
$$x^2 + 13x + 40 = 0$$
$$(x + 8)(x + 5) = 0$$

$x + 8 = 0$	$x + 5 = 0$
$\underline{\quad -8 = -8}$	$\underline{\quad -5 = -5}$
$x \quad = -8$	$x \quad = -5$

INEQUALITIES

The relationship of numbers or symbols can be expressed with "$=$" for equations or "$>$" and "$<$" signs designating inequalities.

The symbol "$>$" stands for "is greater than." Example $5 > 4$ or $-3 > -4$.

The symbol "$<$" stands for "is less than." Example $4 < 5$ or $-4 < -3$.

Inequalities can be solved very similarly to equations.

③1 EXAMPLE 1:

Step 1: Subtract 3 from each side of the inequality:

$$2x + 3 > 9$$
$$\underline{ - 3 \qquad -3}$$
$$2x \qquad > \qquad 6$$

Step 2: Divide each side by 2:

$$\frac{2x}{2} > \frac{6}{2}$$
$$x > 3$$

Therefore x is some value greater than 3, such as 3.1, 4, 5, . . .

The only difference in solving inequalities (as compared to equations) occurs when you *multiply* or *divide* through the inequality by a negative number. *When multiplying* or *dividing though an inequality by a negative number, change the direction of the inequality sign.*

③2 EXAMPLE 2:

Step 1: Subtract 5 from each side of the inequality:

$$-3x + 5 < 20$$
$$\underline{ - 5 \qquad -5}$$
$$-3x \qquad < \qquad 15$$

Step 2: Divide both sides by -3 and change direction of the inequality:

$$\frac{-3x}{-3} < \frac{15}{-3}$$
$$x > -5$$

PRACTICE EXERCISES 1:
(Answer to Practice Exercises appear at end of chapter. Solve each of the following inequalities.)

(1) $4x - 3 < 13$

(2) $3 - 2x > 7$

(3) $5x + 6 > 2x + 21$

The symbol "$\geq$" stands for "is greater than *or* equal to." Examples, $5 \geq 4$ and $5 \geq 5$ are both true.

The symbol "$\leq$" stands for "is less than *or* equal to." Examples, $4 \leq 5$ and $4 \leq 4$ are both true.

Equations involving these symbols can be solved exactly the same as inequalities.

EXAMPLE:

Step 1: Add 7 to both sides
$$3x - 7 \geq 14$$
$$\underline{+7 +7}$$
$$3x \geq 21$$

Step 2: Divide each side by 3
$$\frac{3x}{3} \geq \frac{21}{3}$$
$$x \geq 7$$

Therefore x is a value equal to or greater than 7.

PRACTICE EXERCISES 2:
(Answers to Practice Exercises appear at end of chapter.)

(1) $7x + 4 \geq 32$

(2) $\frac{2}{3}x + 5 \leq 17$

Answers and Solutions

PRACTICE EXERCISES 1:

(1) $x < 4$

$$
\begin{array}{rcr}
4x - 3 &<& 13 \\
+\,3 && +\,3 \\
\hline
4x &<& 16 \\
\dfrac{4x}{4} &<& \dfrac{16}{4} \\
x &<& 4
\end{array}
$$

(2) $x < -2$

$$
\begin{array}{rcr}
3 - 2x &>& 7 \\
-3 && -3 \\
\hline
-2x &>& 4 \\
\dfrac{-2x}{-2} &>& \dfrac{4}{-2} \\
x &<& -2
\end{array}
$$

(3) $x > 5$

$$
\begin{array}{rcr}
5x + 6 &>& 2x + 21 \\
-6 && -6 \\
\hline
5x &>& 2x + 15 \\
-2x && -2x \\
\hline
3x &>& 15 \\
\dfrac{3x}{3} &>& \dfrac{15}{3} \\
x &>& 5
\end{array}
$$

PRACTICE EXERCISES 2:

(1) $x \geq 4$

$$
\begin{array}{rcr}
7x + 4 &\geq& 32 \\
-4 && -4 \\
\hline
7x &\geq& 28 \\
\dfrac{7x}{7} &\geq& \dfrac{28}{7} \\
x &\geq& 4
\end{array}
$$

(2) $x \leq 18$

$$
\begin{array}{rcr}
\frac{2}{3}x + 5 &\leq& 17 \\
-5 && -5 \\
\hline
\frac{2}{3}x &\leq& 12 \\
\left(\frac{3}{2}\right)\frac{2}{3}x &\leq& 12\left(\frac{3}{2}\right) \\
x &\leq& 18
\end{array}
$$

GEOMETRY DIAGNOSTIC SELF-TEST

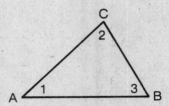

(1.)   Which of the following name the same angle?
(A) $\angle$ A, $\angle$ ACD, $\angle$ CAB
(B) $\angle$ ACB, & $\angle$ CAB
(C) $\angle$ A, $\angle$ 1, & $\angle$ B
(D) $\angle$ A, $\angle$ CAB, & $\angle$ 1
(E) $\angle$ ACB, $\angle$ 1, & $\angle$ B

(2.)   An acute angle measures_____.

(3.)   An obtuse angle measures_____.

(4.)   A straight angle measures_____.

(5.)   A right angle measures_____.

(6.)

In the diagram:
(A) $\angle$ 1 = $\angle$ 3
(B) $\angle$ 1 = $\angle$ 2 & $\angle$ 3 = $\angle$ 4
(C) $\angle$ 2 = $\angle$ 4 & $\angle$ 2 = $\angle$ 3
(D) $\angle$ 1 = $\angle$ 2 & $\angle$ 3 = $\angle$ 2
(E) $\angle$ 1 = $\angle$ 4 & $\angle$ 2 = $\angle$ 3

(7.)   Two angles whose sum is 90° are said to be_____ to each other.

(8.)   Two angles whose sum is 180° are said to be_____ to each other.

(9.)   Two angles next to each other, sharing a common side and vertex, are called_____.

(10.)   An angle bisector_____.

(11.)

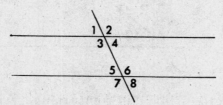

In the diagram:
  I. $\angle 1 = \angle 2 = \angle 4 = \angle 5$
  II. $\angle 1 = \angle 4 = \angle 5 = \angle 8$
  III. $\angle 2 = \angle 3 = \angle 6 = \angle 7$
  IV. $\angle 5 = \angle 8$ only
  V. $\angle 5 = \angle 6 = \angle 8$
  (A)   I & V
  (B)   II
  (C)   III
  (D)   II & III
  (E)   II & IV

(12.)   Two lines that meet at right angles are_____ to each other.

(13.)   The sum of the angles of any triangle is_____.

(14.)   A triangle whose three sides are of different lengths is called _____.

(15.)   A triangle that has 2 equal sides is called_____.

(16.)   If all sides of a triangle are equal, the triangle is_____.

(17.)   If two angles of a triangle measure 43° each, what is the measure of the third angle?

(18.)   The longest side of triangle ABC is_____.

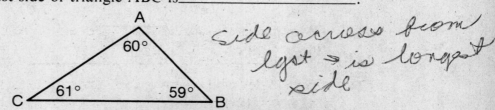

side across from lgst ⇒ is longest side

(19.) A triangle can have sides of length 2, 2, and 5. True or false?

(20.) Find angle z in the diagram below:

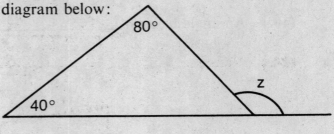

$z =$ _____.

(21.) Find the length of side c in right triangle ABC:

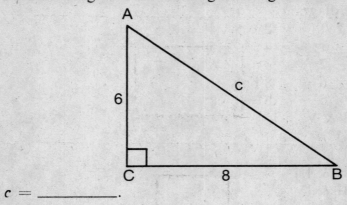

$c =$ _____.

(22.) Find the length of side r in right triangle QRS:

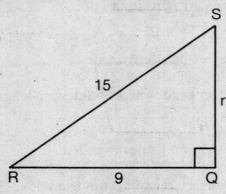

$r =$ _____.

(23.) Name:_____

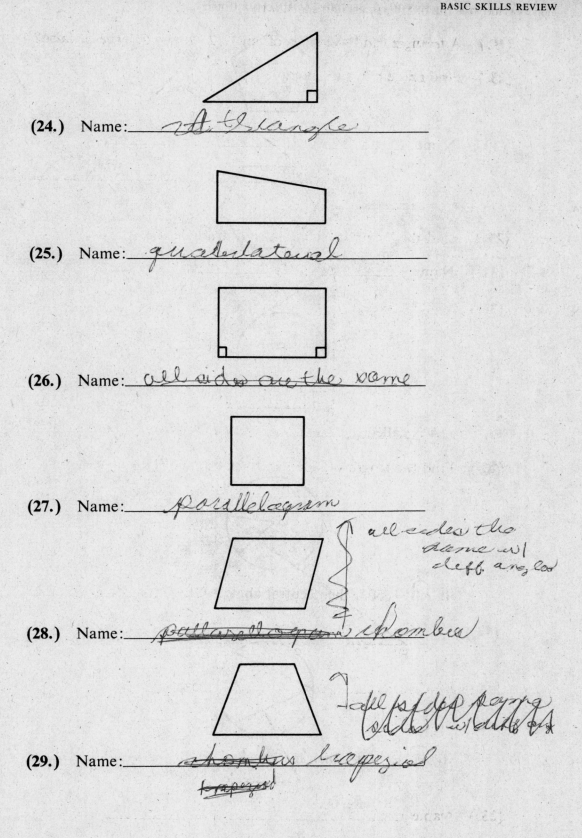

(24.) Name: _rt. triangle_

(25.) Name: _quaderlateral_

(26.) Name: _all sides are the same_

(27.) Name: _parallelogram_

all sides the same w/ deff. angles

(28.) Name: ~~Pallarellogram~~ rhombus

all sides parng sides w/ sides w

(29.) Name: ~~rhombus~~ trapezied
~~trapezied~~

go from vertices to vertices — don't cross lines

*Interior of pentagon.
→ break into triangles
18 × 3 = 540*

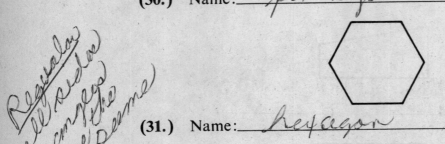

(30.)   Name:___*pentagon*_____

*Regular
all sides)
× angles
are same)*

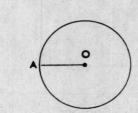

(31.)   Name:___*hexagon*_____

(32.)

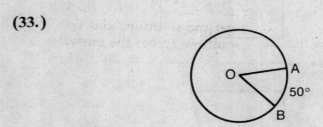

OA is called the ___*radius*___ of Circle O.

(33.)

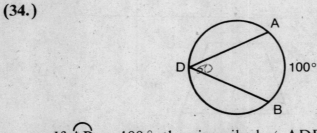

If $\overset{\frown}{AB} = 50°$, then central angle AOB = ___*equal*___.

(34.)

If $\overset{\frown}{AB} = 100°$, then inscribed $\angle$ ADB = ___*50°*___.

*vertix
on
circle*

*inscribed angle
is ½*

(35.)   Find the perimeter of square ABCD

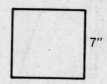

7"

$P =$ ___2×4=28___ .

(36.)   Find the perimeter of rectangle ABCD:

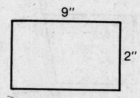

9"

2"

$P =$ ___(9+2)2 = 22___ .

$2\frac{2}{7}$

3.14

(37.)   Find the circumference of circle O:

$C = 2\pi r = \pi D$

If they say approx. use 3

7"

$C =$ _____ .

(38.)   Find the area of triangle ABC:

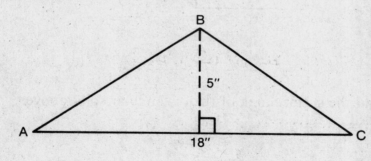

B

5"

A

18"

C

$A =$ ___$\frac{1}{2}bh$___ .

9×5=45

(39.)   Find the area of trapezoid ABCD:

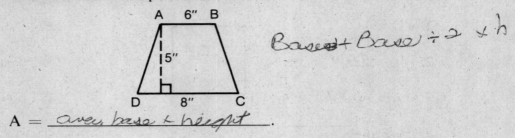

Base + Base ÷ 2 × h

A = *area, base × height* .

(40.)   Find the area of parallelogram ABCD:

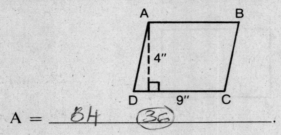

A = *BH*   (36) .

(41.)   Find the volume of the rectangular solid below:

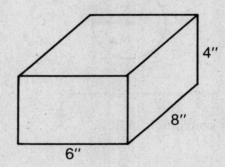

V = *length × width × height*.

(42.)   Find the surface area of the rectangular solid above.

SA = _____.

32 64

mutiply ea. side and double it
Then add

ANSWERS TO GEOMETRY DIAGNOSTIC SELF-TEST

1. D

2. less than 90 degrees

3. greater than 90 degrees

4. 180 degrees

5. 90 degrees

6. B

7. complementary

8. supplementary

9. adjacent angles

10. divides an angle equally in two

11. D

12. perpendicular

13. 180 degrees

14. scalene

15. isosceles

16. equilateral

17. 94 degrees

18. AB

19. False

20. $z = 120$ degrees

21. $c = 10$

22. $r = 12$

23. triangle

24. right triangle

25. quadrilateral

26. rectangle

27. square

28. parallelogram

29. trapezoid

30. pentagon

31. hexagon

32. radius

33. 50 degrees

34. 50 degrees

35. $P = 28$ in.

36. $P = 22$ in.

37. $C =$ about 44 square in.

38. $A = 45$ sq. in.

39. $A = 35$ sq. in.

40. $A = 36$ sq. in.

41. $V = 192$ cu. in.

42. $SA = 208$ sq. in.

GEOMETRY

Geometry is the study of solid and plane shapes and figures. *Solid figures* have length, width, and thickness. They occupy space in three dimensions. *Plane figures* have only length and width. For example, a square is a plane figure and a cereal box is a solid figure.

This section on geometry will be divided into three chapters:

(1) Angles
(2) Triangles
(3) Plane and solid figures

ANGLES

An *angle* is formed by two straight lines that have the same endpoint, called the *vertex*. The side that is horizontal is called the *initial side*. The side that rotates to form the size of the angle is called the *terminal side*. Thus an angle may be represented as follows:

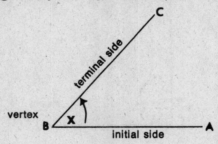

When the terminal side rotates once completely about the vertex, it has passed through 360 degrees. Thus the sizes of all angles range from 0° to 360°.

Angles can be named in three different ways, as in the angle above:

1. By the interior marking, $\angle x$
2. By the vertex, $\angle B$
3. By the three points determining the intersecting lines, with the middle point being the vertex, $\angle CBA$ ($\angle ABC$ is the same.)

Types of Angles

(2) 1. *Acute angle*—any angle measuring more than 0° and less than 90°.

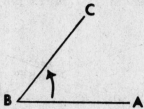

(3) 2. *Obtuse angle*—Any angle measuring more than 90° and less than 180°.

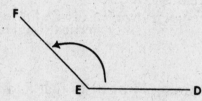

(4) 3. *Straight angle*—Any angle measuring exactly 180°.

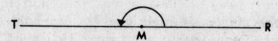

(5) 4. *Right angle*—Any angle measuring exactly 90°.

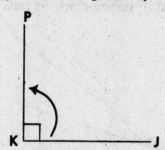

PRACTICE EXERCISES 1: TYPES OF ANGLES
(Answers to Practice Exercises appear at end of chapter.)

(1) What kind of angle is formed between the hands of a clock when it is
   (a) 6 o'clock?
   (b) 2 o'clock?
   (c) 3 o'clock?
   (d) 8 o'clock?

Pairs of Angles

1. *Vertical Angles*—The opposite pair of angles formed by two intersecting lines are called *vertical angles*. Vertical angles are equal.

⑥

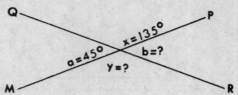

In the diagram above, lines QR and MP intersect, forming two pairs of angles, *x* and *y*, and *a* and *b*. If $a = 45°$ then $b = 45°$ and if $x = 135°$ then $y = 135°$, since vertical angles are equal to each other.

2. *Complementary angles*—Two angles that add up to $90°$ are *complementary* angles. If angle $x = 60°$ and angle $y = 30°$ then x and y are complementary angles since $60° + 30° = 90°$.

⑦

3. *Supplementary angles*—Two angles that add up to $180°$ are *supplementary* angles. If angle $s = 73°$ and angle $t = 107°$ then s and t are supplementary angles since $73° + 107° = 180°$.

⑧

4. *Adjacent angles*—Two angles next to each other that share a common side and have the same vertex.

⑨

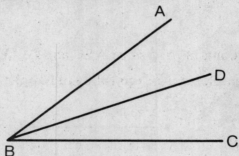

In the diagram above, $\angle$ ABD and $\angle$ DBC are adjacent.

⑩ 5. *Angle Bisector*—Divides an angle into two equal angles.

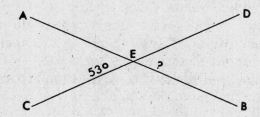

In the diagram above, YW is an angle bisector, therefore $\angle$ XYW = $\angle$ WYZ.

EXAMPLES:

(1)   If lines AB and CD intersect at E, and if angle AEC measures 53°, then how many degrees are there in angle BED?

Angle BED contains 53° since AEC and BED are vertical angles.

(2)   Find the complement of the following angles.
      (a) 17°   (b) t°

      (a) $90 - 17 = 73°$
      (b) $(90 - t)°$

(3)   Find the supplement of the following angles.
      (a) 124°   (b) $(x + 9)°$

      (a) $180 - 124 = 56°$
      (b) $180 - (x + 9)$
         $= 180 - x - 9$
         $= (171 - x)°$

PRACTICE EXERCISES 2: PAIRS OF ANGLES
(Answers to Practice Exercises appear at end of chapter.)

(1) In the diagram below, angle XTM and angle _____ are
vertical with respect to each other.

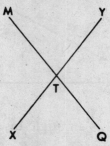

(2) Find the complement of
(a) $74\frac{1}{2}°$
(b) $(q - 5)°$

(3) Find the supplement of
(a) $180°$
(b) $(m - 30)°$

Parallel Lines, Perpendicular Lines, and Their Angles

Two or more lines are said to be *parallel* if they never meet no matter
how far they are extended. A line drawn cutting across parallel lines
is called a *transversal*. In the diagram below, lines AB and CD are
⑪ parallel, and are cut by transversal T.

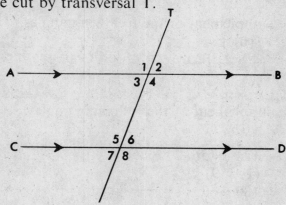

You can see that a transversal cutting through two parallel lines
causes eight angles to be formed. These angles are related to each
other in several ways, as follows.

1. *Corresponding Angles* (matching angles)

$\angle\,2 = \angle\,6$

$\angle\,4 = \angle\,8$

$\angle\,1 = \angle\,5$

$\angle\,3 = \angle\,7$

2. *Alternate Interior Angles*

$\angle\,3 = \angle\,6$

$\angle\,4 = \angle\,5$

3. *Consecutive Interior Angles*

$\angle\,4 + \angle\,6 = 180°$

$\angle\,3 + \angle\,5 = 180°$

You will notice that corresponding and alternate interior angles are *equal*, while consecutive interior angles are *supplementary*.

⑫ Two lines are said to be perpendicular to each other if they meet at 90° angles, as in the diagram below.

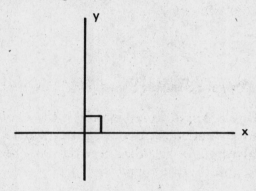

PRACTICE EXERCISES 3:
(Answers to Practice Exercises appear at end of chapter.)

(1) In the figure, name all the pairs of the following types of angles.

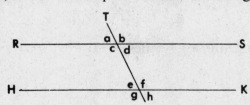

(a) Vertical angles
(b) Consecutive interior angles
(c) Corresponding angles
(d) Alternate interior angles

Answers and Solutions

PRACTICE EXERCISES 1: TYPES OF ANGLES

(1) (a) Straight angle
     (b) Acute angle
     (c) Right angle
     (d) Obtuse angle

PRACTICE EXERCISES 2: PAIRS OF ANGLES

(1) Angle QTY

(2) (a) $15\frac{1}{2}^{\circ}$

$$90 - 74\frac{1}{2} = 15\frac{1}{2}^{\circ}$$

  (b) $(95 - q)^{\circ}$

$$90^{\circ} - (q - 5)^{\circ} = 90^{\circ} - q + 5 = (95 - q)^{\circ}$$

(3) (a) 0°

$$180 - 180 = 0^{\circ}$$

  (b) $(210 - m)^{\circ}$

$$180 - (m - 30) = 180 - m + 30 = (210 - m)^{\circ}$$

PRACTICE EXERCISES 3:

(1) (a) Vertical Angles

$\angle a = \angle d$ $\angle e = \angle h$

$\angle b = \angle c$ $\angle f = \angle g$

  (b) Consecutive Interior Angles

$\angle d + \angle f = 180^{\circ}$

$\angle c + \angle e = 180^{\circ}$

  (c) Corresponding Angles

$\angle b = \angle f$ $\angle a = \angle e$

$\angle d = \angle h$ $\angle c = \angle g$

  (d) Alternate Interior Angles

$\angle d = \angle e$

$\angle c = \angle f$

TRIANGLES

⑬ A triangle is a flat, closed, three-sided figure. The sum of the angles of any triangle is 180°.

Types of Triangles

⑭ 1. A *scalene* triangle is a triangle whose *three* sides are of different lengths.
⑮ 2. An *isosceles* triangle is a triangle that has *two* equal sides.
⑯ 3. An *equilateral* triangle is a triangle that has *three* equal sides.
 4. A *right* triangle is a triangle that has a right angle (90°).

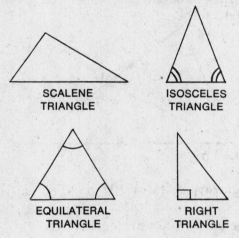

SCALENE TRIANGLE   ISOSCELES TRIANGLE

EQUILATERAL TRIANGLE   RIGHT TRIANGLE

⑰ EXAMPLE 1:
Two angles of a triangle measure 45° and 85°. How many degrees are there in the third angle?

The angles of a triangle add up to 180°. The sum of 45° and 85° is 130°. Therefore, the remaining angle must be 180° − 130° = *50°*

EXAMPLE 2:
In triangle ABC below, angle C is three times angle A and angle B is five times angle A. Find the number of degrees in each angle of the triangle.

Let y = the number of degrees in angle A
Then $3y$ = the number of degrees in angle C
Then $5y$ = the number of degrees in angle B

Since the sum of the angles of the triangle is $180°$ we can say

$$y + 3y + 5y = 180$$
$$\frac{9y}{9} = \frac{180}{9}$$
$$y = 20° \ (\angle\,A)$$
$$3y = 60° \ (\angle\,C)$$
$$5y = 100° \ (\angle\,B)$$

Notice that $20 + 60 + 100 = 180°$.

A line joining the vertex and the midpoint of the opposite side of a triangle is called the median.

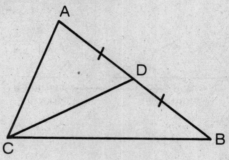

CD is a median, therefore $AD = DB$

Angles opposite equal sides are equal.
Sides opposite equal angles are equal.
In the diagram:

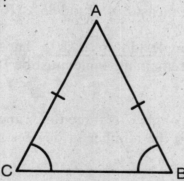

Since side $AC = AB$, then $\angle\,C = \angle\,B$, and if $\angle\,C = \angle\,B$ then $AC = AB$.

The side opposite the largest angle is the longest side.
The side opposite the smallest angle is the smallest side.

⑱ In the diagram:

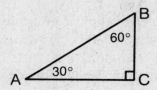

AB is the longest side and BC is the shortest side—by their opposite angles.

⑲ The sum of any two sides of a triangle is greater than the third side.

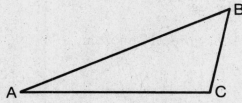

$$AB + BC > AC$$
$$AC + BC > AB$$
$$AB + AC > BC$$

The exterior angles of any triangle are formed by continuing one side. This exterior angle is equal to the sum of the opposite two angles.

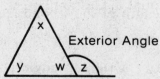

⑳ Exterior Angle Z equals $x + y$.

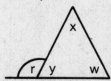

Exterior Angle r equals $x + w$.

PRACTICE EXERCISES 1: ANGLES OF A TRIANGLE
(Answers to Practice Exercises appear at end of chapter.)

(1) If two angles of a triangle are $23\frac{1}{2}°$ and $143\frac{1}{2}°$, find the third angle.

(2) One angle of a triangle is $44°$. The second angle is $4°$ larger than the third angle. Determine the number of degrees in the second and third angles.

The Pythagorean Theorem

In any right-angle triangle (triangle containing a 90° angle) the side opposite the 90° angle is called the *hypotenuse*. The other two sides are called the *legs* of the triangle.

The Greek mathematician Pythagoras discovered that a particular relation exists among the three sides of *all* right triangles. This relation is known as the Pythagorean theorem.

Statement of the Pythagorean Theorem

In any right triangle the square of the hypotenuse is equal to the sum of the squares of the legs.

Formula of the Pythagorean Theorem

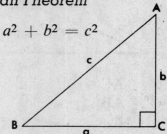

$$a^2 + b^2 = c^2$$

Thus, if we are told the lengths of the two legs of a right triangle it is possible to find the length of the hypotenuse.

Also, if the lengths of the hypotenuse and one leg are given, it is possible to find the length of the second leg.

(21) EXAMPLE 1:

Find the hypotenuse of a right triangle whose legs are 8″ and 15″ respectively.

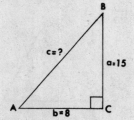

$$a^2 + b^2 = c^2$$
$$15^2 + 8^2 = c^2$$
$$225 + 64 = c^2$$
$$289 = c^2$$
$$\sqrt{289} = c$$

Therefore, $c = 17″$

(22) EXAMPLE 2:

Find the third side of a right triangle whose hypotenuse is 20″ and one of whose legs is 16″ long.

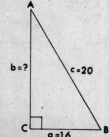

$$a^2 + b^2 = c^2$$
$$16^2 + b^2 = 20^2$$
$$256 + b^2 = 400$$
$$-256 \qquad = -256$$
$$b^2 = 144$$
$$b = \sqrt{144}$$
$$b = 12″$$

PRACTICE EXERCISES 2: PYTHAGOREAN THEOREM
(Answers to Practice Exercises appear at end of chapter.)

(1) Find the diagonal of a rectangle whose width is 5″ and whose length is 12″.

(2) A ladder 25 feet long rests against the wall of a building at a point 24 feet above the ground. How far from the wall is the bottom of the ladder?

Answers and Solutions

PRACTICE EXERCISES 1: ANGLES OF A TRIANGLE

(1) $13°$

$$180 - \left(143\tfrac{1}{2} + 23\tfrac{1}{2}\right) = 180 - 167 = 13°$$

(2) $66°, 70°$

Let x = the third angle
Let $x + 4$ = the second angle
Then $x + x + 4 + 44 = 180$

$$
\begin{aligned}
2x + 48 &= 180 \\
-48 &= -48 \\
\hline
\frac{2x}{2} &= \frac{132}{2} \\
x &= 66° \\
\text{and } x + 4 &= 70°
\end{aligned}
$$

PRACTICE EXERCISES 2: PYTHAGOREAN THEOREM

(1)   13 ″

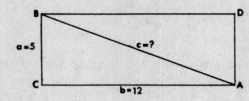

$$a^2 + b^2 = c^2$$
$$25 + 144 = c^2$$
$$169 = c^2$$
$$\sqrt{169} = c$$
$$13'' = c$$

(2)   7 feet

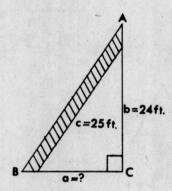

$$a^2 + \quad b^2 = \quad c^2$$
$$a^2 + \quad 24^2 = \quad 25^2$$
$$a^2 + 576 = \quad 625$$
$$\underline{-\ 576 = -576}$$
$$a^2 \qquad\quad = \quad 49$$
$$a = \sqrt{49}$$
$$a = 7 \text{ ft.}$$

PLANE AND SOLID FIGURES

Plane figures have only two dimensions: length and width. They have no thickness. They are not three-dimensional. The most common plane figures and their characteristics are:

Polygons (many-sided figures)

Triangle—a three-sided figure. The sum of the interior angles (angles (23) inside the triangle) = 180°.

(24) *Right Triangle*—a triangle that has one interior right angle and two acute angles.

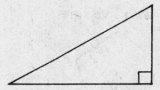

(25)   *Quadrilateral*—any four-sided figure.

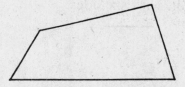

Rectangle—a four-sided figure. The opposite sides are parallel and equal in length. Each interior angle = 90°. The sum of the (26) interior angles = 360°.

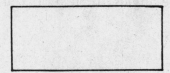

Square—a four-sided figure. The opposite sides are parallel and all sides are equal in length. Each interior angle = 90°. The sum of (27) the interior angles = 360°.

Parallelogram—a four-sided figure. The opposite sides are parallel and equal in length. No interior right angles. Opposite angles are equal in size. The sum of interior angles = 360°.

(28)

Trapezoid—a four-sided figure. The bases only are parallel. No sides necessarily equal in length. The sum of the interior angles = 360°.

(29)

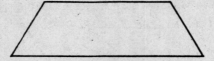

(30)   *Pentagon*—a polygon with five sides.

(31)   *Hexagon*—a polygon with six sides.

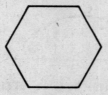

The term "regular" means that all sides of the figure are of the same length. Example: A *regular pentagon* is a five-sided polygon with sides of equal length; the angles are also of equal measure.

Circles

Circle—a figure formed by a single curved line. Every point is of equal distance from the center point of the figure.

A circle is named by its center point.

Radius—a line segment drawn from the center of the circle and
(32) ending on the circle. (Plural—*radii*.)

OM is the radius of circle O

Chord—a line segment that has both endpoints on the circle.
Diameter—a line segment (chord) with both endpoints on the circle and passing through the center of the circle. (2 *radii* = diameter)
Arc—a section or part of the circle. Measured in degrees or radians.

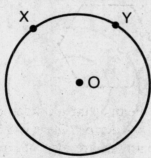

Notice minor arc XY, the shorter arc, and major arc XY, the longer arc. Arcs are written $\overgroup{XY}$. In most cases $\overgroup{XY}$ would refer to the minor arc.

Central angle—an angle with its vertex on the center of the circle. The measure of the central angle is the same as the measure of its corresponding arc.

(33)

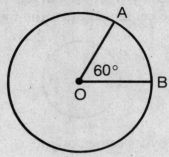

$\angle$ AOB = 60°; therefore $\overset{\frown}{AB}$ = 60°

Inscribed angle—an angle with all three vertices on the circle. The measure of an inscribed angle is half the measure of the corresponding arc.

(34)

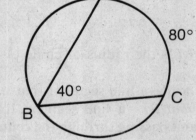

If $\overset{\frown}{AC}$ = 80° then $\angle$ ABC = 40°

Concentric circles—two circles of different size with a common center.

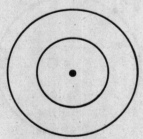

Perimeter and Area

You now have some idea of what the most elementary plane figures look like. Most often you will be asked to find either the *perimeter* or the *area* of one of these figures. The *perimeter* means the sum of the distances around the outside (edge) of any plane figure. The *area* is the number of square units of space contained within a plane figure.

Below is a table of formulas for the perimeters and areas of the most common plane figures. The letters used in these formulas, and what they represent, are: l = length, w = width, s = side, b = base, h = height, r = radius, and d = diameter. The symbol π (pi) is a Greek letter and is a *mathematical constant*; that is, its value never changes. It is always equal to the fraction $\frac{22}{7}$ $\left(\text{or } 3\frac{1}{7}\right)$ or in decimal form, 3.14 +. Its value is obtained from the ratio of the circumference (perimeter) of a circle to its diameter. This means that the circumference of *any* circle is about $3\frac{1}{7}$ times its diameter.

Perimeters and Areas of Plane Figures		
Figure	*Perimeter*	*Area*
Square	$P = 4s$	$A = s^2$
Rectangle	$P = 2l + 2w$	$A = lw$
Triangle	$P = s_1 + s_2 + s_3$	$A = \frac{1}{2}bh$
Parallelogram	$P = 2l + 2w$	$A = bh$
Circle	$C = 2\pi r$ or πd	$A = \pi r^2$
Trapezoid	$P = b_1 + b_2 + s_1 + s_2$	$A = \frac{1}{2}h(b_1 + b_2)$

EXAMPLES:

Find the *perimeters* of the figures below:

(*Note:* Parentheses and the multiplication signs are used interchangeably, as they are on the examination.)

㉟ (1) *Square*
$P = 4s = 4(5) = 20''$

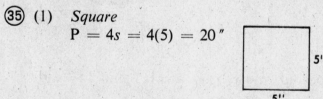

㊱ (2) *Rectangle*
$P = 2l + 2w = 2(8) + 2(3) = 16 + 6 = 22''$

㊲ (3)   *Circle*
$$C = 2\pi r = \frac{2}{1} \times \frac{22}{7} \times \frac{14}{1} = 88''$$

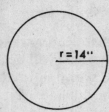

Find the *areas* of the figures below.

㊳ (4)   *Triangle*
$$A = \tfrac{1}{2}bh = \frac{1}{2} \times \frac{12}{1} \times \frac{4}{1} = 24 \text{ square inches}$$

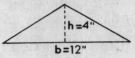

㊴ (5)   *Trapezoid*
$$A = \tfrac{1}{2}h(b_1 + b_2)$$

(*h* is the perpendicular distance between bases) $= \frac{1}{2}(6)\,(9 + 7) =$

$$\frac{1}{2} \times \frac{6}{1} \times \frac{16}{1} = 48 \text{ square inches}$$

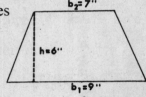

㊵ (6)   *Parallelogram*
$$A = bh = 6(5) = 30 \text{ square inches}$$

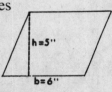

PRACTICE EXERCISES 1: PERIMETERS AND AREAS
(Answers to Practice Exercises appear at end of chapter.)

(1)   Find the area of a square whose side is $6\frac{1}{2}''$.

(2)   Find the perimeter of a triangle whose sides are $2\frac{1}{2}''$, $3\frac{3}{4}''$, and $5\frac{1}{6}''$ long.

(3)   Find the area of a trapezoid whose bases are $11''$ and $14''$ and whose height is $5''$.

(4)   Find the perimeter of a rectangle whose length is $8''$ and whose width is $2\frac{1}{2}''$.

(5)   Find the area of a circle whose radius is $10''$.

Congruence and Similarity

Two plane geometric figures are said to be *congruent* if they are identical in size and shape. They are said to be *similar* if they have the same shape but are not identical in size.

EXAMPLES:
All squares are similar.

These triangles are congruent.

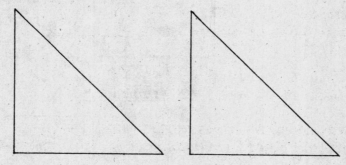

Volumes of Solid Figures

Three of the most common solid geometric figures are the cube, the rectangular solid, and the cylinder. Each of these figures may be thought of as the three-dimensional extensions of three flat two-dimensional figures, namely the square, rectangle, and circle.

The table below indicates the formulas to be used to find the volumes of these figures. The volume of a solid is the amount of cubic units of space the figure contains.

Formulas for Volumes of Solid Figures

Figure	Volume
Cube	$V = s^3 = s \times s \times s$
Rectangular Solid	$V = lwh$
Cylinder	$V = \pi r^2 h$

EXAMPLES:
Find the volumes of the solid figures below whose dimensions are

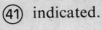 indicated.

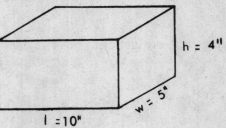

(1) *Rectangular Solid*
     $V = lwh = 10(5)\,(4) = 200$ cubic inches

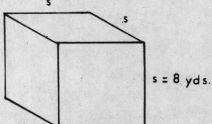

(2) *Cube*
     $V = s^3 = 8 \times 8 \times 8 = 512$ cubic yards

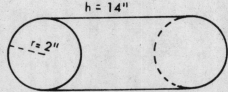

(3) *Cylinder*
     $V = \pi r^2 h = \dfrac{22}{7} \times \dfrac{2}{1} \times \dfrac{2}{1} \times \dfrac{\overset{2}{\cancel{14}}}{1} = 22(8) = 176$ cubic inches

(42) **(4)**   *Surface Area of a rectangular solid*

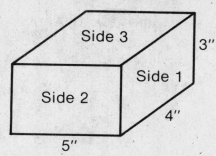

Area of Side 1 = 3″ × 4″ = 12 square″
Area of Side 2 = 5″ × 3″ = 15 square″
Area of Side 3 = 5″ × 4″ = 20 square″
Since there are 2 of each of these sides
Surface Area = 2(12) + 2(15) + 2(20)
                = 24 + 30 + 40
                = 94 square″

PRACTICE EXERCISES 2: VOLUMES OF SOLID FIGURES
(Answers to Practice Exercises appear at end of chapter.)

(1)   What is the volume of a cube whose side is $5\frac{1}{2}$″?

(2)   If a rectangular solid has a length of 4 inches, a width of 3 inches, and a height of 2 feet, find its volume.

(3)   Given that a cylinder's height is 42″ and its radius is 3″, determine its volume.

(4)   Find the surface area of a rectangular solid that measures 4″ by 7″ by 6″.

Answers and Solutions

PRACTICE EXERCISES 1: PERIMETERS AND AREAS

(1) $42\frac{1}{4}$ square inches

$$A = s^2 = \left(6\frac{1}{2}\right)\left(6\frac{1}{2}\right) = \frac{13}{2} \times \frac{13}{2} = \frac{169}{4} = 42\frac{1}{4} \text{ sq. in.}$$

(2) $11\frac{5}{12}''$

$$P = s_1 + s_2 + s_3 = 2\frac{1}{2} + 3\frac{3}{4} + 5\frac{1}{6} = 11\frac{5}{12}''$$

(3) $62\frac{1}{2}$ square inches

$$A = \frac{1}{2}h\,(b_1 + b_2) = \frac{1}{2}(5)\,(14 + 11) = \frac{1}{2} \times \frac{5}{1} \times \frac{25}{1} =$$
$$\frac{125}{2} = 62\frac{1}{2} \text{ sq. in.}$$

(4) $21''$

$$P = 2l + 2w = 2(8) + 2\left(2\frac{1}{2}\right) = 16 + 5 = 21''$$

(5) 314 square inches

$$A = \pi r^2 = 3.14 \times 10 \times 10 = 3.14 \times 100 = 314 \text{ sq. in.}$$

Note: Here 3.14 is more convenient than $\frac{22}{7}$ as a value of pi.

PRACTICE EXERCISES 2: VOLUMES OF SOLID FIGURES

(1) $166\frac{3}{8}$ cubic inches

$$V = s^3 = 5\frac{1}{2} \times 5\frac{1}{2} \times 5\frac{1}{2} = \frac{11}{2} \times \frac{11}{2} \times \frac{11}{2} = \frac{1331}{8} =$$
$$166\frac{3}{8} \text{ cubic inches}$$

(2) 288 cubic inches

$$V = l \times w \times h = 4 \times 3 \times 24 = 288 \text{ cu. in.}$$

Notice that 2 feet had to be converted to 24 inches so that all dimensions would be expressed in the same units.

(3) 1,188 cubic inches

$$V = \pi r^2 h = \frac{22}{\cancel{7}} \times \frac{3}{1} \times \frac{3}{1} \times \frac{\cancel{42}^{\,6}}{1} = 1,188 \text{ cu. in.}$$

(4) 188 square inches

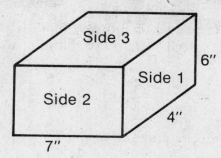

Area of side 1 = 4 × 6 = 24 square inches
Area of side 2 = 6 × 7 = 42 square inches
Area of side 3 = 4 × 7 = 28 square inches
Surface Area = 2(24) + 2(42) + 2(28)
            = 24 + 84 + 56
            = 188 square inches

WORD PROBLEMS

To solve word problems using basic arithmetic, you must remember to read and interpret carefully all the information that is given in the problem. Here is a basic step-by-step guide that you can follow in preparing to solve all word problems.

Step 1: What are you told? List on the paper on which you are doing your work all numbers discussed in the problem, and what they stand for. This allows you to refer to them at any time while solving the problem.

Step 2: What are you asked? Read the problem carefully to find out what you are being asked to do. Otherwise, you may do a lot of work correctly and still come up with the wrong answer.

Step 3: Which information do you need? All the information given may not be needed to solve the problem. Choose the necessary information and ignore the rest.

Step 4: Are there any key words in the problem? They tell you what method of solution is needed. Learn the key words that usually mean add, subtract, multiply, or divide.

Step 5: How can you organize the information for solution? For example, do you have to change all measurements in the problem to the same unit? (All in feet, hours, miles, etc.)

Key Words and Phrases

Many word problems use words or phrases that give clues as to how the problem should be solved. The most common words or phrases are:

Add

Sum—as in, the sum of 3, 6, and 10

Total—as in, the total of three payments

Addition—as in, if a recipe calls for the addition of 3 lbs.

Plus—as in, 3 lbs. plus 6 lbs.

Increase—as in, his rent was increased by $10

More than—as in, this week the attendance was 5 more than last week

Added to—as in, if you added $16 to the cost

Successive—as in, the total of five successive payments

Subtract

Difference—as in, what is the difference between, or the difference of

Fewer—as in, there were 16 fewer apples left

Remainder—as in, what quantity remains, or is left

Less—as in, if there are now 3 apples less than there were an hour ago

Reduced—as in, the rent was reduced by

Decreased—as in, if he decreased his car's speed by

Multiply

Total—as in, if you spend $8 a week on cigarettes, what is the total for a four-week period

Of—as in, $\frac{1}{8}$ of the class

Times—as in, 3 times as many boys came to football practice today

At—as in, the cost of 12 yds. of cloth at 85¢ a yd. is

Product—as in, the product of 4 and 3 is

Divide

Ratio—as in, what is the ratio of

Divide—as in, if the class was divided into 4 sections

Quotient—as in, the final quotient is

All of the word problems below will require you to make use of your knowledge of algebra. The steps above indicate how you can mentally *prepare* to solve the problem. The following simple set of instructions will enable you to actually *solve* word problems.

Guideline for Solving Word Problems

1. Represent all unknown quantities algebraically (with letters) based on the information provided about them in the problem.
2. Write down an equation expressing the relationship between the unknowns in the problem. This step is equivalent to changing some statement(s) in the problem into mathematical language.
3. Solve the equation to determine the value of the unknowns.

Number Problems

EXAMPLE 1:

If one number is three times as large as another and the smaller number is increased by 19 the result is 6 less than twice the larger. Find the two numbers.

Let t = the smaller number
Let $3t$ = the larger number
Then $t + 19 = 2(3t) - 6$

$$t + 19 = 6t - 6$$
$$\underline{-t \qquad\quad = -t}$$
$$19 = 5t - 6$$
$$\underline{+\ 6 = \qquad +6}$$
$$25 = 5t$$
$$\frac{25}{5} = \frac{5t}{5}$$
$$5 = t$$

Since $t = 5$, $3t = 15$, so the two numbers are *5* and *15*.

EXAMPLE 2:

One number exceeds another number by 5, If the sum of the two numbers is 39 find the numbers.

Let m = the smaller number
Let $m + 5$ = the larger number
Then $m + m + 5 = 39$

$$2m + 5 = 39$$
$$\underline{\quad - 5 = -5}$$
$$2m = 34$$
$$\frac{2m}{2} = \frac{34}{2}$$
$$m = 17$$

So, $m + 5 = 22$, and the two numbers are *17* and *22*.

Age Problems

EXAMPLE 1:

Lisa is 16 years younger than Kathy. If the sum of their ages is 30 years, how old is Lisa?

Let x = Kathy's age
Let $x - 16$ = Lisa's age
Then $x + x - 16 = 30$

$$2x - 16 = 30$$
$$\underline{\quad + 16 = +16}$$
$$2x = 46$$
$$\frac{2x}{2} = \frac{46}{2}$$
$$x = 23$$

But Lisa is $x - 16$, so Lisa is $23 - 16 = 7$ yrs. old.

EXAMPLE 2:

Clyde is four times as old as Douglas. If the difference between their ages is 39 years find out how old Clyde is.

Let b = Douglas' age
Let $4b$ = Clyde's age
Then $4b - b = 39$

$$3b = 39$$
$$\frac{3b}{3} = \frac{39}{3}$$
$$b = 13$$

But Clyde is $4b$, so Clyde's age = $4(13) = 52$ yrs. old.

Motion Problems

These problems on the examination usually require you to represent some quantity like rate, distance, or time algebraically rather than actually solving an entire problem.

EXAMPLE 1:

Madelaine left her home and walked a distance of d miles at the rate of 5 mph. She then turned around and walked back home at the rate of 3 mph. Represent in terms of d the total time Madelaine spent walking.

Since Rate $\times$ Time = Distance, or $r \times t = d$, if we divide both sides of the equation by Rate we get

$$\text{Time} = \frac{\text{Distance}}{\text{Rate}} \text{ or } t = \frac{d}{r}$$

Therefore, the time Madelaine spent walking away from her house is $\frac{d}{5}$, while the time she spent walking back is $\frac{d}{3}$. Hence, the total time is $\frac{d}{5} + \frac{d}{3}$ or $\frac{8d}{15}$.

EXAMPLE 2:

If Carl rows a boat upstream at the rate of 6 mph and the stream flows at the rate of b mph, represent the net rate at which Carl moves upstream.

Carl moves upstream at 6 mph but the stream pushes back against his efforts at b mph. Therefore, his net speed upstream must be $(6 - b)$ mph.

Perimeter Problems

EXAMPLE 1:

The length of a rectangle is 6 less than four times the width. If the perimeter of the rectangle is 28 inches, find its length and width.

Let w = the width
Let $4w - 6$ = the length
Then $w + w + 4w - 6 + 4w - 6 = 28$

$$10w - 12 = 28$$
$$\underline{+ 12 = +12}$$
$$10w = 40$$
$$\frac{10w}{10} = \frac{40}{10}$$
$$w = 4''$$

$4w - 6 = 4(4) - 6 = 16 - 6 = 10''$

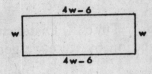

EXAMPLE 2:

Each of the equal sides of an isosceles triangle (a triangle with two equal sides) is 5 more than twice the third side. If the perimeter of the triangle is 45 inches, find the sides of the triangle.

Let m = the base of the triangle
Let $2m + 5$ = each of the two equal sides
Then $m + 2m + 5 + 2m + 5 = 45$

$$5m + 10 = 45$$
$$\underline{- 10 = -10}$$
$$5m = 35$$
$$\frac{5m}{5} = \frac{35}{5}$$
$$m = 7$$

$2m + 5 = 2(7) + 5 = 19$

So the base is 7 and each equal side is 19.

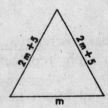

Ratio and Proportion Problems

A *ratio* is one kind of comparison between two numbers. It may be written as a fraction as in $\frac{4}{7}$ or with a colon as in 4 : 7.

A *proportion* is a statement that two ratios are equal. For instance, $\frac{5}{10} = \frac{1}{2}$ or 5 : 10 = 1 : 2 and 3 : 4 = 6 : 8 or $\frac{3}{4} = \frac{6}{8}$.

EXAMPLE 1:

A blueprint for a new high school is drawn to a scale of $\frac{1}{27}'' = 1''$. If the height of one of the windows is to be 6 ft., by what length will the window be represented on the blueprint?

Note: Bear in mind that all numbers should be represented in the same units; that is, in either inches or feet, but not both in the same problem.

Blueprint	Actual Size
$\frac{1}{27}''$	$1''$
x''	6 ft. = 72 $''$

We must change the following English sentence into an equation expressing a proportion: 'If $\frac{1}{27}''$ represents $1''$ of actual size, then x'' represents $72''$ of actual size.'

This may be done as follows:

$$\frac{\frac{1}{27}}{1} = \frac{x}{72}$$

Then cross-multiply to get:

$$x = \frac{1}{27} \cdot \frac{72}{1}$$
$$x = \frac{72}{27} = 2\frac{18}{27} = 2\frac{2}{3}''$$

EXAMPLE 2:

The following proportion, $\dfrac{a}{b} = \dfrac{d}{d}$ is equivalent to which equation below?

(a) $\dfrac{d}{c} = \dfrac{a}{b}$

(b) $c = \dfrac{ba}{d}$

(c) $\dfrac{c}{d} = \dfrac{a}{b}$

(d) $cb = \dfrac{a}{d}$

If we cross-multiply the given proportion we get $ad = bc$. We then look at the choices given to see which one will give the same products when cross-multiplied. Inspecting the four possibilities, we see that the only one which will do this is choice (c), which is the answer.

PRACTICE EXERCISES 1:
(Answers to Practice Exercises appear at end of chapter.)

(1) Michael is three years older than twice Carol's age. If their ages added together total 42 years, how old is Michael?

(2) The difference between two numbers is 16 less than twice their sum. If the larger number is one more than twice the smaller, find the numbers.

(3) If on a map $\frac{1}{5}'' = 1''$, then a distance of 6 ft. would be represented by what distance on the map?

(4) If an airplane travels for 17 hours and goes a distance of $(e + 8)$ miles, represent its rate in terms of e.

(5) The perimeter of a rectangle is 54 inches. If the width is 3 inches less than half the length, find the dimensions of the rectangle.

(6) If Sharlene is three times as old as Maurice, and their ages total 50 years, find out how old Sharlene is.

(7) Which of the following is an alternative way of writing the proportion $\frac{m}{t} = \frac{f}{s}$?

(a) $mf = ts$

(b) $\frac{s}{t} = \frac{f}{m}$

(c) $\frac{st}{m}$

(d) $\frac{m}{t} = \frac{s}{f}$

(8) A boat in still water travels at K mph, but a 9 mph wind pushes it in the opposite direction. With what net rate does it move forward?

Interest Problems

EXAMPLE 1:

What yearly interest would be earned on $500 at a rate of 5% interest?

Change 5% to a fraction by placing the 5 over 100, and multiply by the amount invested.

$$\frac{5}{\cancel{100}} \times \frac{\cancel{500}}{1} = \$25$$

EXAMPLE 2:

How much money would be needed in a savings account to earn $100 per month at 6% interest per year?

$100 per month would be $1200 per year. Let M be the amount of money needed.

$$.06M = \$1200$$
$$M = \frac{\$1200}{.06} = \$20,000$$

Mixture Problems

A mixture problem gives a percentage or fractional composition of a substance in terms of its ingredients and asks questions about the composition of the substance. There are two basic relationships to remember about mixtures:

1. The percentage of a certain ingredient in a mixture times the amount of the mixture equals the amount of the ingredient.

2. When two mixtures are added together, the amount of one ingredient in the final mixture equals the sum of the amounts of that ingredient in the parts.

EXAMPLE:

A chemist has 2 quarts of 25% acid solution and 1 quart of 40% acid solution. If he mixes these, what will be the concentration of acid in the final mixture?

To understand this kind of problem, it is helpful to organize the information on a table. Enter the information you know and systematically fill in the missing information.

	rate $\times$ $\dfrac{qt\ (acid)}{qt\ (sol)}$	amount of sol $=$ qts (sol)	amount of acid qts (acid)
25% solution	0.25	2	0.50
40% solution	0.40	1	0.40
mixture	x	3	$3x$

Applying basic relationship number 2 above,

$$3x = 0.50 + 0.40$$
$$3x = 0.90$$
$$x = 0.30, \quad \text{a } 30\% \text{ concentration of acid in the final mixture}$$

Work Problems

Work problems are based on the following relationship:

$$\text{rate} \times \text{time} = \text{work}$$

EXAMPLE:

Jack can chop down 20 trees in 1 hour. Ted can chop down 18 trees in $1\frac{1}{2}$ hours. If the two men work together, how long will it take them to chop down 48 trees?

    As in the mixture problem, it is helpful to organize your work in a table. Let x be the length of time required for the two men together to chop down 48 trees. The x is entered under *time* for both Jack and Ted on lines 3 and 4, since each man works the same amount of time.

	rate $\times$	time $=$	work
	trees/hr	*hours*	*trees*
1. Jack	20	1	20
2. Ted	12	$1\frac{1}{2}$	18
3. Jack	20	x	$20x$
4. Ted	12	x	$12x$

$$20x + 12x = 48$$
$$32x = 48$$
$$x = 1\frac{1}{2} \text{ hours}$$

PRACTICE EXERCISES 2:
(Answers to Practice Exercises appear at end of chapter.)

(1) Jack invested $1500 at $4\frac{1}{2}\%$ a year. How much interest will he earn in two years?

(2) If a chemist mixes 2 pints of 40% acid solution with 1 pint of pure acid, what will be the acid concentration of the final solution?

(3) Mary can complete 50 order forms in an hour. Jean can complete 60 in $1\frac{1}{2}$ hours. How long will it take them together to complete 180 forms?

Answers and Solutions

PRACTICE EXERCISES 1:

(1) 29 yrs. old

$$\text{Let } x = \text{Carol's age}$$
$$\text{Let } 2x + 3 = \text{Michael's age}$$
$$x + 2x + 3 = 42$$
$$3x + 3 = 42$$
$$-3 = -3$$
$$3x = 39$$
$$\frac{3x}{3} = \frac{39}{3}$$
$$x = 13$$

So $2x + 3 = 2(13) + 3 = 26 + 3 = 29$

(2) 7 and 3

$$\text{Let } q = \text{the smaller number}$$
$$\text{Let } 2q + 1 = \text{the larger number}$$
$$(2q + 1) - q = 2(q + 2q + 1) - 16$$
$$q + 1 = 2(3q + 1) - 16$$
$$q + 1 = 6q + 2 - 16$$
$$q + 1 = 6q - 14$$
$$\underline{-q \qquad = -q}$$
$$1 = 5q - 14$$
$$\underline{+ 14 = \qquad + 14}$$
$$15 = 5q$$

$$\frac{\overset{3}{\cancel{15}}}{\cancel{5}} = \frac{\cancel{5}q}{\cancel{5}}$$
$$q = 3$$
$$2q + 1 = 7$$

(3) $14\frac{2}{5}''$

6 ft. = 72 in.

$$\frac{\frac{1}{5}}{1} = \frac{x}{72}$$
$$x = \frac{1}{5} \cdot \frac{72}{1}$$
$$x = \frac{72}{5} = 14\frac{2}{5}''$$

(4) $\dfrac{e + 8}{17}$

$$\text{Rate} = \frac{\text{Distance}}{\text{Time}} = \frac{e + 8}{17}$$

(5) Length $= 20''$, width $= 7''$

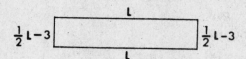

$$L + L + \frac{1}{2}L - 3 + \frac{1}{2}L - 3 = 54$$

$$3L - 6 = 54$$
$$\underline{+\,6 = +\,6}$$
$$3L = 60$$

$$\frac{\cancel{3}L}{\cancel{3}} = \frac{\overset{20}{\cancel{60}}}{\cancel{3}}$$

$$L = 20''$$

$$\frac{1}{2}L - 3 = \frac{1}{2}(20) - 3 = 10 - 3 = 7'' = \text{width}$$

(6) $37\frac{1}{2}$ yrs. old

Let m = Maurice's age
Let $3m$ = Sharlene's age

$$3m + m = 50$$
$$4m = 50$$
$$\frac{4m}{4} = \frac{50}{4}$$
$$m = 12\frac{1}{2}$$

So $3m = 3(12\frac{1}{2}) = 37\frac{1}{2}$

(7) (b)

If we cross-multiply in (b) $\dfrac{s}{t} \times \dfrac{f}{m}$ we get $sm = tf$, which is the same set of products which results from cross-multiplying the given proportion $\dfrac{m}{t} \times \dfrac{f}{s}$.

(8) $(K - 9)$ mph

PRACTICE EXERCISES 2:

(1) $135

Let I equal the interest.

$I = 4\frac{1}{2}\% \times \$1500 \times 2 \text{ years}$

$I = .045 \times \$1500 \times 2$

$I = .045 \times \$3000$

$I = \$135$

(2) 60%

Set up a table:

	rate $\times$	amount of sol $=$	amount of acid
	pt (acid) / pt (sol)	pts (sol)	pts (acid)
40% solution	0.40	2	0.80
100% solution	1.00	1	1.00
mixture	x	3	$3x$

$3x = 1.80$

$x = .60$, a 60% concentration

(3) 2 hours

Let $x =$ the time it will take the two women together, and set up a table:

	rate $\times$	time $=$	work
	forms/hr	hours	forms
1. Mary	50	1	50
2. Jean	40	$1\frac{1}{2}$	60
3. Mary	50	x	$50x$
4. Jean	40	x	$40x$

$50x + 40x = 180$

$90x = 180$

$x = 2 \text{ hours}$

GRAPHS

Graphs and charts show the relationship of numbers or quantities in visual form. By looking at a graph, you can see the relationship between two or more sets of information at a glance. If such information were presented in written form, it would be hard to read and understand.

To read a graph, you must know what *scale* the graph has been drawn to. Somewhere on the face of the graph there will be an explanation of what each division of the graph means. Sometimes the divisions will be labeled. At other times, this information will be given in a small box called a *scale* or *legend*. For instance, a map, which is a specialized kind of graph, will always carry a scale or legend on its face telling you such information as $1'' = 100$ miles or $\frac{1}{4}'' = 2$ miles.

Bar Graphs

The bar graph shows how the information is compared by using broad lines, called bars, of varying lengths. Sometimes single lines are used as well. Bar graphs are good for showing a quick comparison of the information involved; however, the bars are difficult to read accurately unless the end of the bar falls exactly on one of the divisions of the scale. If the end of the bar falls between divisions of the scale, it is not easy to arrive at the precise figure represented by the bar. In bar graphs, the bars can run either vertically or horizontally. The sample bar graph below is a horizontal graph.

Expenditures Per Pupil—1964

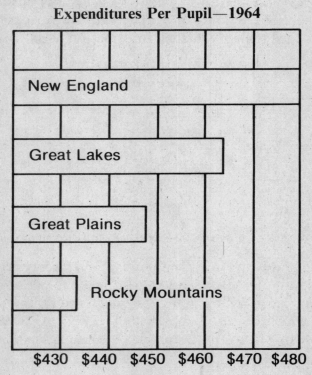

The individual bars in this kind of graph may carry a label within the bar, as in this example. The label may also appear alongside each bar. The scale used on the bars may appear along one axis as in the example, or it may be noted somewhere on the face of the graph. Each numbered space on the x- (or horizontal) axis represents an expenditure of $10 per pupil. A wide variety of questions may be answered by a bar graph, such as:

(1) Which area of the country spends least per pupil? Rocky Mountains.

(2) How much does the New England area spend per pupil? $480.

(3) How much less does the Great Plains spend per pupil than the Great Lakes? 464 − 447 = 17 $17/pupil.

(4) How much more does New England spend on a pupil than the Rocky Mountain area? $480 − 433 = $47/pupil.

Circle Graph or Pie Chart

A circle graph shows how an entire quantity has been divided or apportioned. The circle represents 100% of the quantity; the different parts into which the whole has been divided are shown by sections, or wedges, of the circle. Circle graphs are good for showing how money is distributed or collected, and for this reason they are widely used in financial graphing. The information is usually presented on the face of each section, telling you exactly what the section stands for and the value of that section in comparison to the other parts of the graph.

Sources of Income—Public Colleges of U.S.

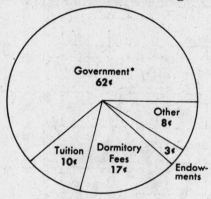

*Government refers to all levels of government—not exclusively the federal government.

The circle graph above indicates where the money originates that is used to maintain public colleges in the U.S. The size of the sections tells you at a glance which source is most important (GOVERNMENT) and which is least important (ENDOWMENTS). The sections total 100¢ or $1.00. This graph may be used to answer the following questions:

(1) What is the most important source of income to the public colleges? Government

(2) What part of the revenue dollar comes from tuition? 10¢

(3) Dormitory fees bring in how many times the money that endowments bring in? $5\frac{2}{3}$ times $\left(\frac{17}{3} = 5\frac{2}{3}\right)$

(4) What is the least important source of revenue to public colleges? Endowments

Line Graphs

Graphs that have information running both across (horizontally) and up and down (vertically) can be considered to be laid out on a grid having a *y*-axis and an *x*-axis. One of the two quantities being compared will be placed along the *y*-axis, and the other quantity will be placed along the *x*-axis. When we are asked to compare two values, we subtract the smaller from the larger.

Shares of Stock Sold
New York Stock Exchange

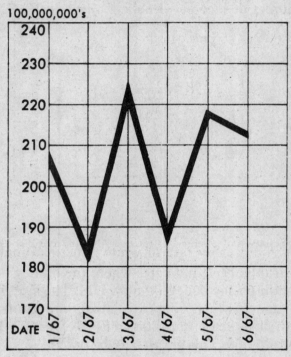

Our sample line graph represents the total shares of stock sold on the New York Stock Exchange between January and June. The months are placed along the *x*-axis, while the sales, in units of 100,000,000 shares, are placed along the *y*-axis.

(1) How many shares were sold in March? 225,000,000

(2) What is the trend of stock sales between April and May? The volume of sales rose.

(3) Compare the share sales in January and February. 25,000,000 fewer shares were sold in February.

(4) During which months of the period was the increase in sales largest? February to March

PRACTICE EXERCISES
(Answers to Practice Exercises appear at end of chapter.)

Mortality Rate of Americans by Race

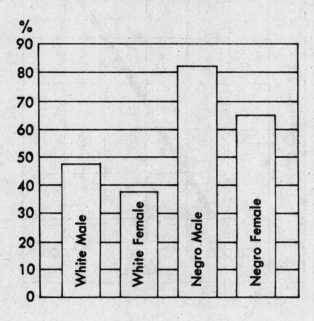

(1) What is the mortality rate of white American males?

(2) What is the mortality rate of black American females?

(3) Approximately how many times greater is the black male mortality rate than the white male mortality rate?

(4) Which group has the lowest mortality rate?

Teacher Salary
Master's Degree Scale

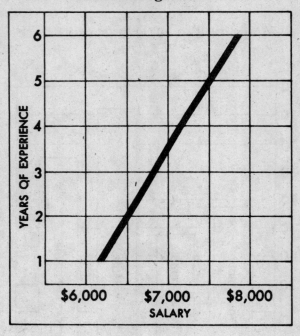

(1)   A person with one year's teaching experience and a Master's degree will be earning how much?

(2)   Compare the salaries of a person with one year's experience and six years' experience on this salary guide.

(3)   If the same pattern holds, what should a person with seven year's experience be earning?

(4)   If a teacher with a Master's degree is earning $7,200, how many years of experience does he have?

Belafonte Associates
Business Costs

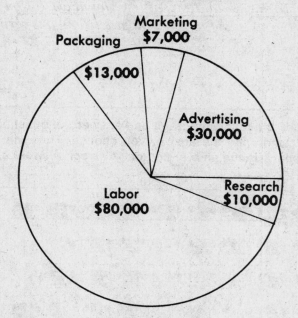

(1) What fraction of the advertising budget is the research budget?

(2) What is their largest single cost of doing business?

(3) What was their total cost of doing business?

(4) What fraction of their total cost was the cost of marketing?

Answers and Solutions

(1) Bar Graph

(1) 48%

(2) 65%

(3) About two times as great

(4) White females

(2) Line Graph

(1) About $6200

(2) $1650 more by six years

(3) About $8200

(4) 4 years

(3) Circle Graph

(1) $\frac{1}{3}$

(2) labor

(3) $140,000

(4) $\frac{1}{20}$

GRAPHIC DATA TESTS

The following graphic data tests are to familiarize you with many different types of graphs and to give you practice in answering questions from each type.

Graphic Data Test 1

Directions: Study the following graph and answer the questions that come after it. Underline the answer you choose. Then mark the appropriate space in the answer column. *Correct answers appear at end of test.*

1930

1935

1940

1945

1950

The pictograph above represents the number of telephones in use in a certain city. Each complete symbol represents 20,000 telephones.

1. How many telephones were in use in this city in 1945?
   (A)   110,000
   (B)   220,000
   (C)   200,000
   (D)   120,000
   (E)   none of these

2. How many more telephones were in use in this city in 1945 than in 1935?
   (A)   50,000
   (B)   25,000
   (C)   70,000
   (D)   75,000
   (E)   none of these

3. Find the percent of increase in the number of telephones in use in 1950 over the number in use in 1930.
   (A)   50%
   (B)   10%
   (C)   20%
   (D)   25%
   (E)   none of these

4. If it is estimated that 280,000 telephones were in use in 1955, how many symbols should be used to picture this on the graph?
(A) 18
(B) 15
(C) 14
(D) 16
(E) none of these

5. During what year were there 190,000 telephones in use?
(A) 1930
(B) 1935
(C) 1940
(D) 1945
(E) none of these

Correct Answers and Solutions Graphic Data Test 1

1. B 220,000
$20,000 \times 11 = 220,000$

2. A 50,000
220,000 (telephones in use in 1945)
$-170,000$ (telephones in use in 1935)
50,000 (more telephones in use in 1945)

3. D 25%
1950—$12\frac{1}{2}$ symbols
1930—10 symbols
$2\frac{1}{2}$ symbol increase
$2\frac{1}{2} = \frac{1}{4}$ of 10 = 25%

4. C 14
14 symbols
$20,000\overline{)280,000}$

5. C 1940
9.5
$20,000\overline{)190,000.0}$
$9.5 = 9\frac{1}{2}$
$9\frac{1}{2}$ symbols in 1940

Graphic Data Test 2

Directions: Study the following graph and answer the questions that come after it. Underline the answer you choose. Then mark the appropriate space in the answer column. *Correct answers appear at end of test.*

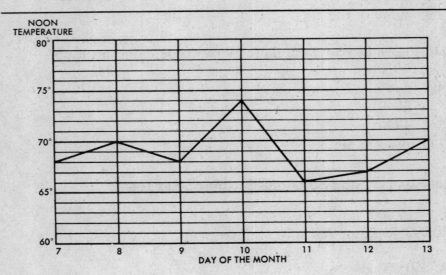

The graph above shows the noon temperature at a weather station on seven consecutive days in June.

1. On what day was the noon temperature the highest?
   (A) 5th
   (B) 10th
   (C) 13th
   (D) 11th
   (E) none of these

2. For what two consecutive days was the change in noon temperature the least?
   (A) 7th and 8th
   (B) 8th and 9th
   (C) 11th and 12th
   (D) 12th and 13th
   (E) none of these

3. For what two consecutive days was the change in noon temperature the greatest?
   (A) 8th and 9th
   (B) 9th and 10th
   (C) 11th and 12th
   (D) 12th and 13th
   (E) none of these

4. What was the average noon temperature for the week?
   (A)   68°
   (B)   69°
   (C)   70°
   (D)   71°
   (E)   none of these

5. How many degrees warmer was it at noon on June 9 than at noon on June 12?
   (A)   2°
   (B)   10°
   (C)   1°
   (D)   4°
   (E)   none of these

Correct Answers and Solutions Graphic Data Test 2

1. **B**   10th
   On the 10th day the noon temperature was 74°.

2. **C**   11th and 12th
   On the 11th and 12th days the temperature rose from 66° to 67°, a change of 1°.

3. **E**   none of these
   The correct answer is the 10th and the 11th days.

4. **B**   69°

   $$
   \begin{array}{r}
   68° \text{ (7th day temperature)} \\
   70° \text{ (8th day temperature)} \\
   68° \text{ (9th day temperature)} \\
   74° \text{ (10th day temperature)} \\
   66° \text{ (11th day temperature)} \\
   67° \text{ (12th day temperature)} \\
   70° \text{ (13th day temperature)}
   \end{array}
   $$

   7 (days)) 483°
   69° (Average noon day temperature)

5. **C**   1°

   68° (noon temperature, June 9)
   −67° (noon temperature, June 12)
   1° (warmer)

Graphic Data Test 3

Directions: Study the following graph and answer the questions that come after it. Underline the answer you choose. Then mark the appropriate space in the answer column. *Correct answers appear at end of test.*

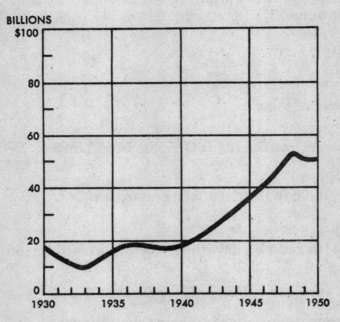

The graph above shows food expenditures in the United States for each of the years 1930 to 1950 inclusive.

1.   During what year were expenditures for food the lowest?
    (A)   1932
    (B)   1933
    (C)   1940
    (D)   1939
    (E)   none of these

2.   During what year were expenditures for food the highest?
    (A)   1945
    (B)   1930
    (C)   1950
    (D)   1947
    (E)   none of these

3. Approximately how many billions of dollars were spent for food in 1950?
   (A)   50
   (B)   45
   (C)   55
   (D)   40
   (E)   none of these

4. In what year did expenditures for food first reach 40 billion?
   (A)   1945
   (B)   1946
   (C)   1940
   (D)   1947
   (E)   none of these

5. During which one of these five-year periods did expenditures for food remain about the same?
   (A)   1930–1935
   (B)   1935–1940
   (C)   1940–1945
   (D)   1945–1950
   (E)   none of these

Correct Answers and Solutions Graphic Data Test 3

1. **B**   1933
   Food expenditure dropped to a low point of about $8 billion during 1933.

2. **E**   none of these
   The correct answer is 1948. A high point of approximately $52 billion was reached during 1948.

3. **A**   50
   Approximately $50 billion was spent on food during 1950.

4. **B**   1946
   The graph crosses the $40 billion line in year 1946.

5. **B**   1935–1940
   The graph line remained relatively stable between the five-year period, 1935–1940.

Graphic Data Test 4

Directions: Study the following graph and answer the questions that come after it. Underline the answer you choose. Then mark the appropriate space in the answer column. *Correct answers appear at end of test.*

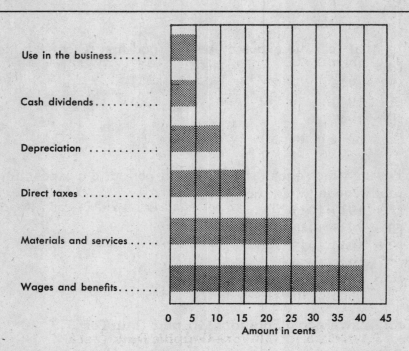

In a recent year a large industrial concern used each dollar of its sales income as shown in the graph above.

1.   How many cents of each dollar of sales income did the company use to pay wages and benefits?
(A)   35
(B)   40
(C)   45
(D)   50
(E)   none of these

2.   How many more cents out of each sales dollar was spent on wages and benefits than on materials and services?
(A)   15
(B)   25
(C)   10
(D)   20
(E)   none of these

3. What was the total number of cents out of each sales dollar that the company set aside for depreciation and for use in the business?
    (A)   5
    (B)   10
    (C)   15
    (D)   20
    (E)   none of these

4. The amount the company paid in direct taxes was how many times the amount it paid in cash dividends?
    (A)   10
    (B)   5
    (C)   2
    (D)   3
    (E)   none of these

5. What percent of each sales dollar was paid in cash dividends?
    (A)   11%
    (B)   2%
    (C)   10%
    (D)   5%
    (E)   none of these

Correct Answers and Solutions Graphic Data Test 4

1. **B**   40
    The bottom bar, which represents wages and benefits, reaches the 40-cent line.

2. **A**   15
    　　40 cents (spent on wages and benefits)
    　−25 cents (spent on materials and services)
    　　15 cents more was spent on wages and benefits

3. **C**   15
    　　　5 cents (set aside for use in business)
    　+10 cents (set aside for depreciation)
    　　15 cents is the total amount set aside for use in business and for depreciation

4. **D**   3
    (spent on direct taxes)　$\dfrac{15}{5} = 3$
    (spent on cash dividends)

5. **D**   5%
    $\dfrac{\$.05}{\$1.00}$ (spent on cash dividends) $= \dfrac{5}{100}$

    $\dfrac{.05}{\overline{)5.00}} = 5\%$

Graphic Data Test 5

Directions: Study the following graph and answer the questions that come after it. Underline the answer you choose. Then mark the appropriate space in the answer column. *Correct answers appear at end of test.*

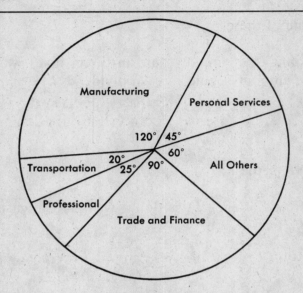

The circle graph above shows how the wage earners in a certain city earned their living one year. The number of degrees required for each angle is given on the graph and should be used in solving these problems.

1. Find the fractional part of the graph that represents the number of wage earners earning their living in the area of trade and finance.

   (A) $\frac{1}{9}$

   (B) $\frac{1}{4}$

   (C) $\frac{1}{5}$

   (D) $\frac{1}{10}$

   (E) none of these

2. Find the fractional part of the graph that represents the number of wage earners working in the area of personal services.

(A) $\frac{4}{5}$

(B) $\frac{1}{2}$

(C) $\frac{1}{8}$

(D) $\frac{1}{7}$

(E) none of these

3. How many times as many persons worked in the area of trade and finance as in the area of personal services?

(A) 50

(B) $\frac{1}{2}$

(C) 45

(D) 2

(E) none of these

4. What fractional part of the graph represents the number of wage earners working in the field of manufacturing?

(A) $\frac{1}{3}$

(B) $\frac{1}{12}$

(C) $\frac{1}{6}$

(D) $\frac{2}{3}$

(E) none of these

5. If there were 180,000 wage earners in the city that year, how many persons were engaged in transportation?

(A) 20,000

(B) 18,000

(C) 9,000

(D) 36,000

(E) none of these

Correct Answers and Solutions Graphic Data Test 5

1. **B** $\frac{1}{4}$

$$\frac{\text{(Workers in trade and finance) } 90°}{\text{(degrees in a circle) } 360°} = \frac{1}{4}$$

2. **C** $\frac{1}{8}$

$$\frac{\text{(those in personal services) } 45°}{\text{(degrees in a circle) } 360°} = \frac{1}{8}$$

3. **D** 2

$$\frac{\text{(those in trade and finance) } 90°}{\text{(those in personal services) } 45°} = 2$$

4. **A** $\frac{1}{3}$

$$\frac{\text{(workers in manufacturing) } 120°}{\text{(degrees in a circle) } 360°} = \frac{1}{3}$$

5. **E** none of these

The correct answer is 10,000.

$$\frac{\text{(workers in transportation) } 20°}{\text{(degrees in a circle) } 360°} = \frac{1}{18}$$

$$\frac{1}{\cancel{18}_1} \times \cancel{180,000}^{10,000} = 10,000 \text{ wage earners engaged in transportation}$$

Graphic Data Test 6

Directions: Study the following graph and answer the questions that come after it. Underline the answer you choose. Then mark the appropriate space in the answer column. *Correct answers appear at end of test.*

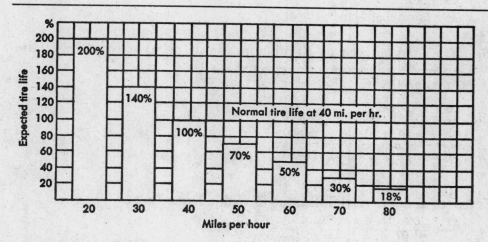

The graph above shows the life expectancy of a tire moving at various speeds.

1. At what speed is the normal life of a tire determined?
    (A)   100 mph
    (B)   50 mph
    (C)   40 mph
    (D)   20 mph
    (E)   none of these

2. The life of a tire on a car driven at 20 miles per hour is how many times greater than the life of a tire on a car driven at 40 miles per hour?
    (A) $\frac{1}{2}$
    (B)   1
    (C) $1\frac{1}{2}$
    (D)   2
    (E)   none of these

3. What car speed will result in tires lasting only half of their normal tire life?
    (A)   20
    (B)   60
    (C)   40
    (D)   80
    (E)   none of these

4. If a car is driven at 30 miles per hour, what percent more than normal tire life may be expected?
    (A)   140%
    (B)   100%
    (C)   40%
    (D)   20%
    (E)   none of these

5. If a car is driven at 70 miles per hour, what percent less than normal tire life may be expected?
    (A)   70%
    (B)   30%
    (C)   40%
    (D)   90%
    (E)   none of these

Correct Answers and Solutions Graphic Data Test 6

1. **C**   40 mph

2. **D**   2
    Driving 20 mph, expected tire life is 200%.
    Driving 40 mph, expected tire life is 100%.
    $$\frac{200\%}{100\%} = \frac{2}{1} \text{ or 2 times greater}$$

3. **B**   60
    Driving 60 mph, expected tire life is 50%.
    $$50\% = \frac{1}{2}$$

4. **C**   40%
    Driving 30 mph, expected tire life is 140%.
    Normal tire life is 100%.
    $$\begin{array}{r} 140\% \\ -100\% \\ \hline 40\% \end{array}$$ more than normal tire life may be expected

5. **A**   70%
    Normal tire life is 100%.
    Driving 70 mph, expected tire life is 30%.
    $$\begin{array}{r} 100\% \\ - 30\% \\ \hline 70\% \end{array}$$ less than normal tire life may be expected

Graphic Data Test 7

Directions: Study the following graph and answer the questions that come after it. Underline the answer you choose. Then mark the appropriate space in the answer column. *Correct answers appear at end of test.*

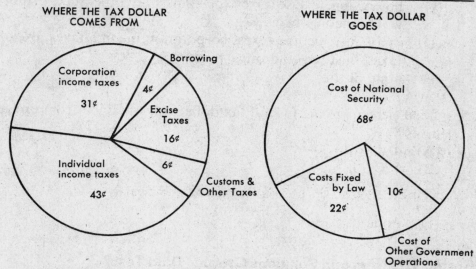

WHERE THE TAX DOLLAR
COMES FROM

Corporation income taxes
31¢

Borrowing
4¢

Excise Taxes
16¢

6¢

Individual income taxes
43¢

Customs & Other Taxes

WHERE THE TAX DOLLAR
GOES

Cost of National Security
68¢

Costs Fixed by Law
22¢

10¢

Cost of Other Government Operations

The graphs above were published by the federal government to show where the tax dollar comes from and where it goes.

1. What percent of the federal tax dollar was spent on national security?
    (A) 34%
    (B) 24%
    (C) 68%
    (D) 6.8%
    (E) none of these

2. What percent more money was obtained from individual income taxes than from corporation income taxes?
    (A) 11%
    (B) 12%
    (C) 31%
    (D) 43%
    (E) none of these

3. How many dollars, of every million dollars collected in taxes, were obtained from excise taxes?
    (A) $16
    (B) $16,000
    (C) $160,000
    (D) $1,600
    (E) none of these

4. List the four sources of income whose total approximately equals the amount spent for national security.
   (A) corporation income taxes, individual income taxes, borrowing, excise taxes
   (B) corporation income taxes, excise taxes, customs and other taxes, borrowing
   (C) borrowing, excise taxes, customs and other taxes, individual income taxes
   (D) individual income taxes, corporation income taxes, excise taxes, customs and other taxes
   (E) none of these

5. What percent of the federal tax dollar was obtained from excise taxes?
   (A) 4%
   (B) 1.6%
   (C) 16%
   (D) 6%
   (E) none of these

Correct Answers and Solutions Graphic Data Test 7

1. **C** 68%
   $\frac{68}{100} = 68\%$

2. **B** 12%
   $\frac{43}{100} = 43\%$ (obtained from individual income taxes)

   $\frac{31}{100} = 31\%$ (obtained from corporation income taxes)

   $\begin{array}{r} 43\% \\ -31\% \\ \hline \end{array}$
   12% more was obtained from corporation income taxes

3. **C** $160,000
   $1,000,000 × .16 = $160,000

4. **C** Borrowing, excise taxes, customs and other taxes, individual income taxes
(borrowing)	$.04
(excise taxes)	.16
(customs and other taxes)	.06
(individual income taxes)	.43
	$.69 or 69¢

   (which approximately equals the amount spent on national security, 68¢)

5. **C** 16%
   $\frac{16}{100} = 16\%$

Graphic Data Test 8

Directions: Study the following graph and answer the questions that come after it. Underline the answer you choose. Then mark the appropriate space in the answer column. *Correct answers appear at end of test.*

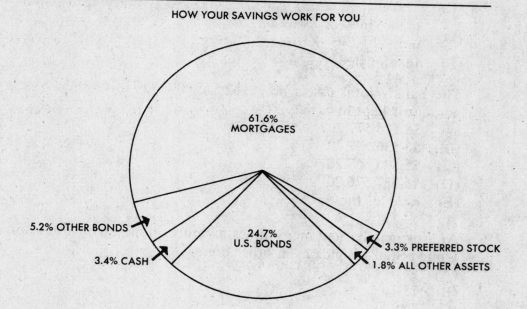

HOW YOUR SAVINGS WORK FOR YOU

61.6%
MORTGAGES

5.2% OTHER BONDS

3.4% CASH

24.7%
U.S. BONDS

3.3% PREFERRED STOCK

1.8% ALL OTHER ASSETS

The graph above was published by a bank in a large city to show its depositors how it invests their savings.

1. What percent of the bank's assets are invested in preferred stock?
   (A)   33%
   (B)   3.4%
   (C)   3.3%
   (D)   1.8%
   (E)   none of these

2. In what one way is approximately one fourth of the bank's assets invested?
   (A)   Other bonds
   (B)   Preferred stock
   (C)   Cash
   (D)   United States Bonds
   (E)   none of these

3. Which fraction is nearest to the bank's total investment in mortgages:

(A) $\frac{1}{2}$

(B) $\frac{3}{4}$

(C) $\frac{5}{8}$

(D) $\frac{3}{5}$

(E)   none of these

4. The bank's total assets are $162,575,800. Of this total, what amount is kept in cash?
   (A) $5,526,577.20
   (B) $5,536,577.20
   (C) $5,526,567.20
   (D) $5,537,576.20
   (E)   none of these

5. Approximately how many times as much money is invested in United States Bonds as in other bonds?
   (A)   5
   (B)   25
   (C)   7
   (D)   6
   (E)   none of these

Correct Answers and Solutions Graphic Data Test 8

1. **C**   3.3%

2. **D**   United States Bonds
   24.7% (United States Bonds) is approximately one-fourth of 100%.

3. **C** $\frac{5}{8}$
   61.6% (mortgages) is close to 62.5% or $\frac{5}{8}$.

4. **E**   none of these
   The correct answer is $5,527,577.20.
   $162,575,800 × .034 = $5,527,577.20

5. **A** 5
   24.7% was invested in United States Bonds.
    5.2% was invested in other bonds.
   $\frac{24.7\%}{5.2\%}$ 4.75 or about 5 times as much was invested in
            $52.\overline{)247.}$ United States Bonds

Graphic Data Test 9

Directions: Study the following graph and answer the questions that come after it. Underline the answer you choose. Then mark the appropriate space in the answer column. *Correct answers appear at end of test.*

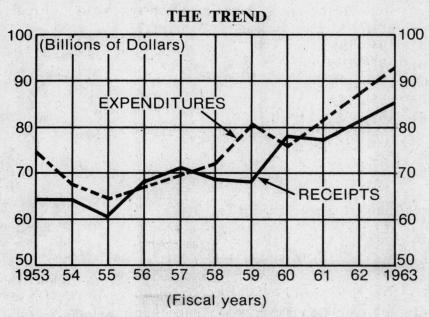

THE TREND

(Billions of Dollars)

EXPENDITURES

RECEIPTS

(Fiscal years)

1. In which of the following years did federal government revenue exceed expenditures?
   (A)   1954
   (B)   1957
   (C)   1962
   (D)   1959
   (E)   1953

2. In which of the following years was federal government revenue greatest?
   (A)   1960
   (B)   1953
   (C)   1962
   (D)   1959
   (E)   1955

3. As shown on the graph, what was the largest differential between federal government expenditures and income in any one year?
   (A)   approximately five billion dollars
   (B)   approximately seven billion dollars
   (C)   approximately eight and a half billion dollars
   (D)   approximately eleven and a half billion dollars
   (E)   approximately three billion dollars

4. As shown on the graph, between which two years did federal government expenditures rise most sharply?
   (A) 1961–1962
   (B) 1955–1956
   (C) 1958–1959
   (D) 1961–1962
   (E) 1959–1960

5. As shown on the graph, between which two years did federal government revenue decline most sharply?
   (A) 1954–1955
   (B) 1959–1960
   (C) 1960–1961
   (D) 1955–1956
   (E) 1957–1958

Correct Answers Graphic Data Test 9

1. **B** 1957

2. **C** 1962

3. **D** approximately eleven and a half billion dollars

4. **C** 1958–1959

5. **A** 1954–1955

Graphic Data Test 10

Directions: Study the following graph and answer the questions that come after it. Underline the answer you choose. Then mark the appropriate space in the answer column. *Correct answers appear at end of test.*

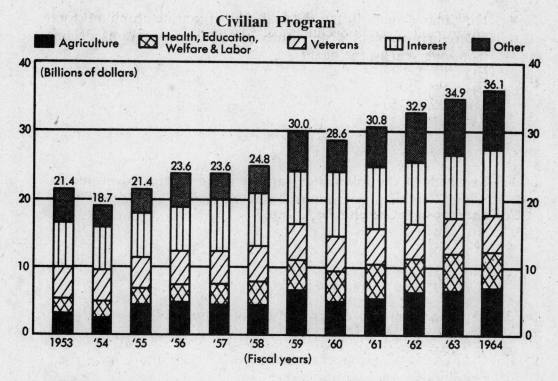

Civilian Program

■ Agriculture   ⊠ Health, Education, Welfare & Labor   ▨ Veterans   ⊞ Interest   ■ Other

(Billions of dollars)

1953: 21.4 '54: 18.7 '55: 21.4 '56: 23.6 '57: 23.6 '58: 24.8 '59: 30.0 '60: 28.6 '61: 30.8 '62: 32.9 '63: 34.9 1964: 36.1

(Fiscal years)

1. Which of the following statements about the graph is false?
    (A)   Federal government expenditures on interest have always exceeded expenditures on health, education and welfare.
    (B)   Federal government expenditures on veterans have never exceeded ten billion dollars a year.
    (C)   Federal government expenditures on agriculture have risen steadily over the last ten years.
    (D)   Total federal expenditures on civilian programs have not risen steadily over the last ten years.
    (E)   The federal government spent more on civilian programs in 1964 than in any other year.

2. Between which two years did federal government expenditures on civilian programs rise most sharply?
    (A)   1954–1955
    (B)   1958–1959
    (C)   1961–1962
    (D)   1955–1956
    (E)   1960–1961

3. In which of the following years were government expenditures on agriculture the highest?
    (A) 1958
    (B) 1959
    (C) 1955
    (D) 1961
    (E) 1960

4. How many times during the years shown on the graph did total federal government expenditures on civilian programs decline from one year to the next?
    (A) 1
    (B) 2
    (C) 3
    (D) 4
    (E) 5

5. In which of the following years were the federal government's "other" civilian program expenses the highest?
    (A) 1956
    (B) 1953
    (C) 1960
    (D) 1962
    (E) 1954

Correct Answers Data Interpretation Test 10

1. **C** Federal government expenditures on agriculture have risen steadily over the last ten years.

2. **B** 1958–1959

3. **B** 1959

4. **B** 2

5. **D** 1962

Graphic Data Test 11

Directions: Study the following graph and answer the questions that come after it. Underline the answer you choose. Then mark the appropriate space in the answer column. *Correct answers appear at end of test.*

Employment in Factories in New England 1920–1936

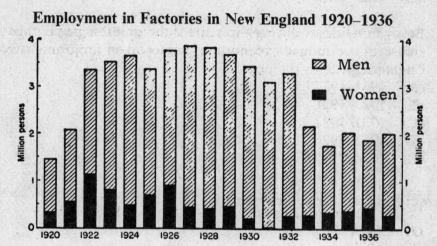

1. Between which of the following two-year periods did the number of women employed in factories in New England rise most sharply?
    (A)   1924–1925
    (B)   1925–1926
    (C)   1926–1927
    (D)   1921–1922
    (E)   1920–1921

2. In which of the following years were the fewest men employed in factories in New England?
    (A)   1934
    (B)   1920
    (C)   1936
    (D)   1931
    (E)   1922

3. In 1926, approximately how many times more men than women were employed in factories in New England?
    (A)   2
    (B)   3
    (C)   4
    (D)   5
    (E)   6

4. Between which two years was there the sharpest decline in the number of persons employed in factories in New England?
   (A) 1930–1931
   (B) 1924–1925
   (C) 1932–1933
   (D) 1935–1936
   (E) 1933–1934

5. Between which two years was there the greatest percentage increase in the number of women employed in factories in New England?
   (A) 1931–1932
   (B) 1920–1921
   (C) 1921–1922
   (D) 1925–1926
   (E) 1924–1925

Correct Answers Graphic Data Test 11

1. **D** 1921–1922

2. **B** 1920

3. **B** 3

4. **C** 1932–1933

5. **A** 1931–1932

Graphic Data Test 12

Directions: Study the following graph and answer the questions that come after it. Underline the answer you choose. Then mark the appropriate space in the answer column. *Correct answers appear at end of test.*

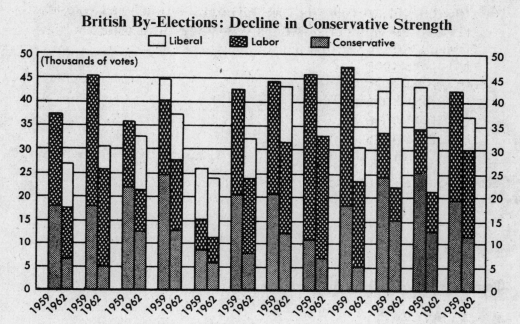

British By-Elections: Decline in Conservative Strength

☐ Liberal   ▨ Labor   ▨ Conservative

(Thousands of votes)

The twelve by-elections which are shown on the chart are spotted throughout England and Scotland. The constituencies involved were, from left to right, Leicester Northeast, West Lothian, Derbyshire West, Middlesbrough West, Montgomery, Derby North, Stockton-on-Tees, Pontefract, Middlesbrough East, Orpington, Blackpool and Lincoln.

1. In how many districts was the Labor vote 5000 or more larger in 1962 than in 1959?
   (A) 0
   (B) 1
   (C) 2
   (D) 3
   (E) 4

2. In how many districts was the total vote larger in 1962 than in 1959?
   (A) 0
   (B) 1
   (C) 2
   (D) 3
   (E) 4

3. In how many districts in which there was a Liberal vote in 1959 was the Liberal vote larger in 1962?
   (A) 1
   (B) 2
   (C) 3
   (D) 4
   (E) 5

4. In which of the following districts did the total 1962 vote most closely approximate in size the total 1959 vote?
   (A) Leicester Northeast
   (B) Blackpool
   (C) Derby North
   (D) Stockton-on-Tees
   (E) Lincoln

5. How many of the districts did the Conservatives win in 1959?
   (A) 2
   (B) 4
   (C) 6
   (D) 8
   (E) 10

Correct Answers Graphic Data Test 12

1. **A** 0

2. **B** 1

3. **D** 4

4. **D** Stockton-on-Tees

5. **B** 4

Graphic Data Test 13

Directions: Study the following table and answer the questions that come after it. Underline the answer you choose. Then mark the appropriate space in the answer column. *Correct answers appear at end of test.*

English Language Daily and Sunday U.S. Newspapers
(as of Sept. 30, 1961)

State	Morning papers & circulation		Evening papers & circulation		Total M & E & circulation		Sunday papers & circulation	
Alabama	4	211,795	16	475,130	20	686,925	14	569,646
Alaska	—	—	6	53,514	6	53,514	1	4,102
Arizona	3	174,445	11	214,667	14	389,112	6	314,401
Arkansas	5	145,650	29	237,395	34	383,045	10	311,962
California	17	1,703,395	113	2,859,565	130	4,562,960	30	4,109,024
Colorado	3	215,664	21	424,383	24	640,047	8	640,701
Connecticut	6	225,318	19	581,487	25	806,805	6	472,853
Delaware	1	34,518	2	87,934	3	122,452	—	—
District of Columbia	1	407,089	2	454,747	3	861,836	2	787,480
Florida	15	1,025,441	30	689,925	45	1,715,366	30	1,541,024
Georgia	6	394,854	23	522,285	29	917,139	11	824,233
Hawaii	1	70,097	4	137,558	5	207,655	3	208,274
Idaho[1]	4	70,080	12	81,905	15	151,985	5	115,918
Illinois	9	1,858,502	73	1,982,819	82	3,841,321	18	2,968,730
Indiana	10	446,928	80	1,195,272	90	1,642,220	18	1,095,571
Iowa[1]	4	292,665	41	655,009	44	947,674	9	841,827
Kansas[1]	5	232,428	47	427,714	51	660,142	14	413,565
Kentucky[1]	5	290,732	22	408,948	26	699,680	12	502,161
Louisiana	4	347,503	15	384,317	19	731,820	8	585,912
Maine	5	197,460	4	54,765	9	252,225	1	101,421
Maryland	4	224,967	8	524,332	12	749,299	3	658,952
Massachusetts[1]	6	904,594	45	1,481,978	50	2,386,572	8	1,492,880
Michigan	1	550,000	52	1,769,599	53	2,319,599	11	2,021,405
Minnesota	5	388,118	25	691,395	30	1,079,513	6	952,619
Mississippi	4	81,283	14	184,727	18	266,010	6	151,935

English Language Daily and Sunday U.S. Newspapers (Cont.)

State	Morning papers & circulation		Evening papers & circulation		Total M & E & circulation		Sunday papers & circulation	
Missouri	7	762,909	47	1,063,583	54	1,826,492	13	1,461,555
Montana	4	106,559	12	62,952	16	169,511	9	154,169
Nebraska	3	167,697	17	304,312	20	472,009	5	349,462
Nevada	2	38,147	6	58,291	8	96,438	3	79,154
New Hampshire[1]	1	25,007	9	102,378	9	127,385	1	43,004
New Jersey	5	409,753	22	1,078,478	27	1,488,231	9	977,717
New Mexico	1	47,720	18	140,352	19	188,072	13	159,632
New York	22	5,033,688	66	3,711,276	88	8,744,964	20	9,198,327
North Carolina	9	548,473	38	562,890	47	1,111,363	15	743,038
North Dakota	2	35,481	9	127,046	11	162,527	2	88,600
Ohio	8	840,173	88	2,473,971	96	3,314,144	19	2,083,904
Oklahoma	7	319,374	44	430,476	51	749,850	41	669,934
Oregon	4	248,608	20	397,664	24	646,272	5	472,819
Pennsylvania[1]	28	1,415,099	95	2,785,703	120	4,200,802	12	2,866,417
Rhode Island	1	61,910	6	237,326	7	299,236	2	199,904
South Carolina	8	346,595	9	149,348	17	495,943	7	378,076
South Dakota	2	6,755	11	164,514	13	171,269	4	116,440
Tennessee	7	497,545	23	573,733	30	1,071,278	11	784,155
Texas	26	1,251,207	91	1,708,992	117	2,960,199	79	2,601,166
Utah	1	101,201	4	141,201	5	242,402	4	239,139
Vermont	2	53,659	6	36,643	8	90,302	1	11,744
Virginia	9	410,129	22	493,243	31	903,372	12	601,824
Washington	6	337,231	21	640,658	27	977,889	10	842,684
West Virginia	10	233,010	21	250,151	31	483,161	9	364,540
Wisconsin	3	265,451	35	907,778	38	1,173,229	8	983,681
Wyoming	6	37,454	4	37,502	10	74,956	4	38,818

English Language Daily and Sunday U.S. Newspapers (Cont.)

State	Morning papers & circulation		Evening papers & circulation		Total M & E & circulation		Sunday papers & circulation	
Total U.S., Sept. 30, 1961	312	24,094,361	1,458	35,167,103	1,761	59,261,464	558	48,216,499
Total U.S., Sept. 30, 1960	312	24,028,788	1,459	34,852,958	1,763	58,831,746	563	47,698,651
Total U.S., Sept. 30, 1959	306	23,547,046	1,455	34,752,677	1,755	58,299,723	564	47,848,477
Total U.S., Sept. 30, 1958	308	23,206,964	1,460	34,387,490	1,756	57,594,454	558	47,041,223
Total U.S., Sept. 30, 1957[2]	309	23,170,552	1,453	34,634,893	1,755	57,805,445	544	47,044,349
Total U.S., Sept. 30, 1956[2]	314	22,491,500	1,454	34,610,010	1,761	57,101,510	546	47,162,246
Total U.S., Sept. 30, 1955[2]	316	22,183,408	1,454	33,963,951	1,760	56,147,359	541	46,447,658

Source: Editor & Publisher

[1]"All-day" newspapers are listed in morning and evening columns, and their circulations are divided between morning and evening figures. Adjustments have been made in state and U.S. total figures.   [2]Excludes newspapers and circulations for Alaska and Hawaii.

1. The circulation of morning newspapers is greater than that of evening newspapers in
   - (A) Massachusetts
   - (B) Pennsylvania
   - (C) Wyoming
   - (D) Florida
   - (E) North Carolina

2. The circulation of Sunday newspapers is greater than that of the combined morning and evening newspapers in
   - (A) Alabama
   - (B) Virginia
   - (C) Connecticut
   - (D) West Virginia
   - (E) New York

3. The smallest number of combined morning and evening newspapers are circulated in
   - (A) New Jersey and North Carolina
   - (B) Tennessee and Wisconsin
   - (C) Idaho and Nebraska
   - (D) Rhode Island and South Carolina
   - (E) Maryland and Nevada

4. Which of the following statements is true?
   - (A) Total morning newspaper circulation has increased steadily since 1955.
   - (B) Total evening newspaper circulation has increased steadily since 1955.
   - (C) Total combined morning and evening newspaper circulation has increased steadily since 1955.
   - (D) Total Sunday newspaper circulation has increased steadily since 1955.
   - (E) Fewer evening newspapers are circulated in California than in Pennsylvania.

5. The largest increase in total Sunday newspaper circulation occurred between
   - (A) 1960 and 1961
   - (B) 1959 and 1960
   - (C) 1958 and 1959
   - (D) 1957 and 1958
   - (E) 1956 and 1957

Correct Answers Graphic Data Test 13

1. **D**   Florida

2. **E**   New York

3. **C**   Idaho and Nebraska

4. **A**   Total morning newspaper circulation has increased steadily since 1955.

5. **C**   1958 and 1959

Graphic Data Test 14

Directions: Study the following table and answer the questions that come after it. Underline the answer you choose. Then mark the appropriate space in the answer column. *Correct answers appear at end of test.*

Marriage and Divorce

(New statutory enactments and recent judicial decisions or interpretation may affect the following summary, therefore Government officials or an attorney should be consulted for advice.)

Marriages and Divorces in the United States, 1890–1961

Year	Marriage Number	Marriage Rate[1]	Divorce Number	Divorce Rate[1]	Year	Marriage Number	Marriage Rate[1]	Divorce Number	Divorce Rate[1]
1890	570,000	9.0	33,461	.5	1932	981,903	7.9	164,241	1.3
1895	620,000	8.9	40,387	.6	1933	1,098,000	8.7	165,000	1.3
1900	709,000	9.3	55,751	.7	1934	1,302,000	10.3	204,000	1.6
1905	842,000	10.0	67,976	.8	1935	1,327,000	10.4	218,000	1.7
1910	948,166	10.3	83,045	.9	1936	1,369,000	10.7	236,000	1.8
1915	1,007,595	10.0	104,298	1.0	1937	1,451,296	11.3	249,000	1.9
1916	1,075,775	10.6	114,000	1.1	1938	1,330,780	10.3	244,000	1.9
1917	1,144,200	11.1	121,564	1.2	1939	1,403,633	10.7	251,000	1.9
1918	1,000,109	9.7	116,254	1.1	1940	1,595,879	12.1	264,000	2.0
1919	1,150,186	11.0	141,527	1.3	1941	1,695,999	12.7	293,000	2.2
1920	1,274,476	12.0	170,505	1.6	1942	1,772,132	13.2	321,000	2.4
1921	1,163,863	10.7	159,580	1.5	1943	1,577,050	11.7	359,000	2.6
1922	1,134,151	10.3	148,815	1.4	1944	1,452,394	10.9	400,000	2.9
1923	1,229,784	11.0	165,096	1.5	1945	1,612,992	12.2	485,000	3.5
1924	1,184,574	10.4	170,952	1.5	1946	2,291,045	16.4	610,000	4.3
1925	1,188,334	10.3	175,449	1.5	1947	1,991,878	13.9	483,000	3.4
1926	1,202,574	10.2	184,678	1.6	1948	1,811,155	12.4	408,000	2.8
1927	1,201,053	10.1	196,292	1.6	1949	1,579,798	10.6	397,000	2.7
1928	1,182,497	9.8	200,176	1.7	1950	1,667,231	11.1	385,144	2.6
1929	1,232,559	10.1	205,876	1.7	1951	1,594,694	10.4	381,000	2.5
1930	1,126,856	9.2	195,961	1.6	1952	1,539,318	9.9	392,000	2.5
1931	1,060,914	8.6	188,003	1.5	1953	1,546,000	9.8	390,000	2.5

Marriage and Divorce (Cont.)

Year	Marriage Number	Marriage Rate[1]	Divorce[2] Number	Divorce[2] Rate[1]
1954	1,490,000	9.2	379,000	2.4
1955	1,531,000	9.3	377,000	2.3
1956	1,585,000	9.5	382,000	2.3
1957	1,518,000	8.9	381,000	2.2

Year	Marriage Number	Marriage Rate[1]	Divorce[2] Number	Divorce[2] Rate[1]
1958	1,451,000	8.4	368,000	2.1
1959	1,494,000	8.5	395,000	2.2
1960[3]	1,527,000	8.5	391,000	2.2
1961[3]	1,547,000	8.5	(4)	2.2

Source: Public Health Service, U.S. Department of Health, Education and Welfare

[1]Per 1,000 population. Divorce rates for 1917–19 and 1941–46 are based on population including armed forces overseas. Marriage rates are based on population excluding armed forces overseas.   [2]Includes annulments.   [3]Provisional.   [4]Not available.

NOTE: Figures for marriages for all years include partial or complete estimates for some states; figures for divorces are estimated, except for 1900, 1905 and 1922–32. Alaska is included beginning 1959, Hawaii beginning 1960.

1. In 1947, there was one divorce in the United States for approximately every _____ marriage(s)?
   (A) 1
   (B) 2
   (C) 3
   (D) 4
   (E) 5

2. In 1895, there was one divorce in the United States for approximately every _____ marriages?
   (A) 5
   (B) 10
   (C) 15
   (D) 20
   (E) 25

3. Approximately how many times higher than the divorce rate in 1890 was the divorce rate in 1945?
   (A) 6
   (B) 11
   (C) 5
   (D) 15
   (E) 7

4. According to the table, in which year was there the second largest number of divorces in the United States?
   (A) 1945
   (B) 1946
   (C) 1960
   (D) 1947
   (E) none of these

5. According to the table, in which year was there the second largest number of marriages in the United States?
   (A) 1946
   (B) 1948
   (C) 1941
   (D) 1942
   (E) none of these

Correct Answers Graphic Data Test 14

1. **D** 4

2. **C** 15

3. **E** 7

4. **A** 1945

5. **E** none of these.
   The correct answer is 1947.

Graphic Data Test 15

Directions: Study the following table and answer the questions that come after it. Underline the answer you choose. Then mark the appropriate space in the answer column. *Correct answers appear at end of test.*

Distribution of U.S. Population by Race, 1850–1960

Year	White	Black	Indian	Japanese	Chinese	All other	Total nonwhite
						Nonwhite	
1850	19,553,068	3,638,808	—	—	—	—	3,638,808
1860	26,922,537	4,441,830	44,021	—	34,933	—	4,520,784
1870	33,589,377	4,880,009	25,731	55	63,199	—	4,968,994
1880	43,402,970	6,580,793	66,407	148	105,465	—	6,752,813
1890	55,101,258	7,488,676	248,253	2,039	107,488	—	7,846,456
1900	66,809,196	8,833,994	237,196	24,326	89,863	—	9,185,379
1910	81,731,957	9,827,763	265,683	72,157	71,531	3,175	10,240,309
1920	94,820,915	10,463,131	244,437	111,010	61,639	9,488	10,889,705
1930	110,286,740	11,891,143	332,397	138,834	74,954	50,978	12,488,306
1940	118,214,870	12,865,518	333,969	126,947	77,504	50,467	13,454,405
1950	134,942,028	15,042,286	343,410	131,768	117,629	110,240	15,755,333
1960	158,831,732	18,871,831	523,591	464,332	237,292	374,397	20,491,443
Urban	110,428,332	13,807,640	145,593	381,114	226,577	280,000	14,840,418
Rural	48,403,400	5,064,191	377,998	83,218	10,715	68,299	5,651,025

1. Approximately how many times more white persons were there than non-whites in the United States in 1960?
   (A) 2
   (B) 4
   (C) 6
   (D) 8
   (E) 10

2. Between which two years was there the greatest increase in the number of non-whites in the United States?
   (A) 1850 and 1860
   (B) 1860 and 1890
   (C) 1890 and 1920
   (D) 1940 and 1950
   (E) 1950 and 1960

3. Between which two years was there the greatest percentage increase of Japanese in the United States?
    (A) 1870 and 1880
    (B) 1910 and 1920
    (C) 1950 and 1960
    (D) 1900 and 1950
    (E) 1890 and 1900

4. Between which two years was there the greatest increase in the number of whites in the United States?
    (A) 1880 and 1890
    (B) 1910 and 1930
    (C) 1850 and 1870
    (D) 1890 and 1910
    (E) 1950 and 1960

5. During how many decades has the Chinese population of the United States declined?
    (A) 1
    (B) 2
    (C) 3
    (D) 4
    (E) 5

Correct Answers Graphic Data Test 15

1. **D** 8

2. **E** 1950 and 1960

3. **E** 1890 and 1900

4. **B** 1910 and 1930

5. **C** 3

Directions: Study the following table and answer the questions that come after it. Underline the answer you choose. Then mark the appropriate space in the answer column. *Correct answers appear at end of test.*

How Consumers Spend Their Dollars
(in millions of dollars)

Group	1929	1932	1939	1945	1947	1949	1958	1959	1961
Food and tobacco	21,374	12,719	21,072	45,924	58,274	58,384	82,999	85,027	88,738
Clothing, accessories, and jewelry	11,018	5,973	8,299	20,247	22,952	23,451	31,046	33,053	34,502
Personal care	1,116	817	1,004	2,077	2,253	2,324	4,425	4,877	5,790
Housing	11,421	8,964	8,940	12,205	15,567	19,295	37,656	39,924	43,928
Household operation	10,509	6,675	9,461	14,865	23,949	25,651	41,278	44,060	47,315
Medical care and death expenses	3,620	2,575	3,386	5,902	7,685	9,003	18,082	19,697	22,426
Personal business	5,221	3,111	3,725	4,787	5,707	7,015	17,046	18,872	21,615
Transportation	7,496	3,924	6,250	6,694	15,390	20,864	33,565	38,998	40,093
Recreation	4,327	2,439	3,446	6,314	9,352	10,122	16,842	18,356	20,638
Private education and research	664	571	628	871	1,411	1,683	3,641	4,053	5,106
Religious and welfare activities	1,196	973	938	1,572	2,032	2,235	3,997	4,281	4,971
Foreign travel and remittances—net	799	467	317	1,621	837	1,131	2,621	2,798	2,936
Total personal consumption expenditures	78,761	49,208	67,466	123,079	165,409	181,158	293,198	313,996	338,058

Source: U.S. Department of Commerce

1. As shown in the table, how many times has total consumer expenditure declined?
   (A) 1
   (B) 2
   (C) 3
   (D) 4
   (E) 5

2. As shown in the table, how many times has consumer expenditure for housing declined?
   (A) 1
   (B) 2
   (C) 3
   (D) 4
   (E) 5

3. How many times greater was consumer expenditure for food and tobacco in 1959 than in 1939?
   (A) 1
   (B) 2
   (C) 3
   (D) 4
   (E) 5

4. For which two items was consumer expenditure most nearly the same in 1961?
   (A) food and tobacco and housing
   (B) private education and research; religious and welfare activities
   (C) housing and household operation
   (D) housing and transportation
   (E) recreation and personal business

5. Which of the following items of expenditure shows the largest percentage increase between 1929 and 1961?
   (A) food and tobacco
   (B) medical care and death expenses
   (C) religious and welfare activities
   (D) household operation
   (E) personal care

Correct Answers Graphic Data Test 16

1. **A** 1

2. **B** 2

3. **D** 4

4. **B** private education and research; religious and welfare activities

5. **B** medical care and death expenses

Graphic Data Test 17

Directions: Study the following graph and answer the questions that come after it. Underline the answer you choose. Then mark the appropriate space in the answer column. *Correct answers appear at end of test.*

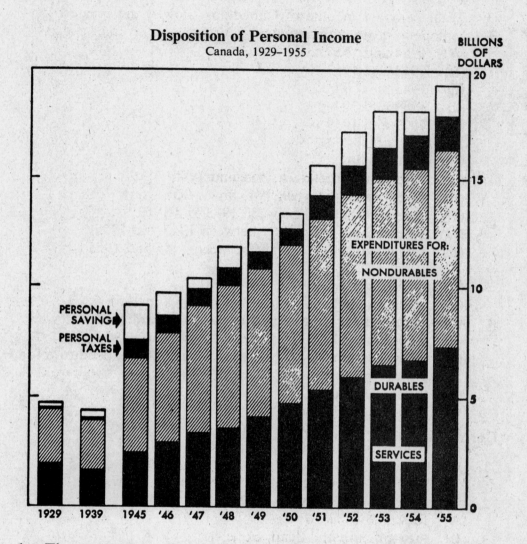

Disposition of Personal Income
Canada, 1929–1955

BILLINGS OF DOLLARS

PERSONAL SAVING
PERSONAL TAXES

EXPENDITURES FOR:
NONDURABLES
DURABLES
SERVICES

1929 1939 1945 '46 '47 '48 '49 '50 '51 '52 '53 '54 '55

1. The percentage of total personal income paid in personal taxes by Canadians
   (A) increased steadily between 1945 and 1955
   (B) decreased and then increased between 1945 and 1955
   (C) remained fairly constant between 1945 and 1955
   (D) increased and then declined between 1945 and 1955
   (E) decreased steadily between 1945 and 1955

2. Expenditures for services by Canadians
   (A)   increased steadily between 1945 and 1955
   (B)   decreased and then increased between 1945 and 1955
   (C)   remained fairly constant between 1945 and 1955
   (D)   increased and then declined between 1945 and 1955
   (E)   decreased steadily between 1945 and 1955

3. Total personal income of Canadians showed the greatest percentage increase between
   (A)   1954 and 1955
   (B)   1948 and 1953
   (C)   1945 and 1948
   (D)   1939 and 1945
   (E)   1929 and 1939

4. Canadians' savings
   (A)   rose steadily between 1929 and 1955
   (B)   rose steadily between 1946 and 1955
   (C)   rose and then fell between 1945 and 1955
   (D)   rose and fell irregularly between 1945 and 1955
   (E)   remained fairly constant between 1945 and 1955

5. Canadians' total income
   (A)   approximately tripled between 1945 and 1955
   (B)   rose and fell irregularly between 1945 and 1955
   (C)   approximately doubled between 1945 and 1955
   (D)   increased at a faster rate than Canadians' expenditure for durables
   (E)   none of these

Correct Answers Graphic Data Test 17

1.   B   decreased and then increased between 1945 and 1955

2.   A   increased steadily between 1945 and 1955

3.   D   1939 and 1945

4.   D   rose and fell irregularly between 1945 and 1955

5.   C   approximately doubled between 1945 and 1955

Graphic Data Test 18

Directions: Study the following graph and answer the questions that come after it. Underline the answer you choose. Then mark the appropriate space in the answer column. *Correct answers appear at end of test.*

WORLD MOTOR VEHICLES

PERSONS PER REGISTERED
PASSENGER CAR, 1960

U.S.	2.9
CANADA	4.3
AUSTRALIA	5.1
SWEDEN	6.2
FRANCE	8.1
U.K.	9.4
SWITZERLAND	10.3
BELGIUM	12.0
WEST GERMANY	12.1
SOUTH AFRICA	16.8
VENEZUELA	21.8
FINLAND	23.8
ITALY	24.6
ARGENTINA	51.2
MEXICO	69.9
CZECHOSLOVAKIA	77.5
EAST GERMANY	108.5
BRAZIL	116.8
COLOMBIA	188.8
JAPAN	220.8
PHILIPPINES	299.7
YUGOSLAVIA	339.2
U.S.S.R.	348.0
EGYPT	367.5

1. Considering all countries as having equal populations, approximately how many persons are there per registered car in the European countries (excluding the U.S.S.R.) listed on the graph?
   (A)   33
   (B)   68
   (C)   57
   (D)   92
   (E)   104

2. Considering all countries as having equal populations, approximately how many persons per car are there in the Latin American countries listed on the graph?
(A) 62
(B) 89
(C) 95
(D) 34
(E) 98

3. Considering populations as equal, in which of the following pairs of countries are there the fewest persons per car?
(A) France and Japan
(B) Sweden and Colombia
(C) The United States and Egypt
(D) South Africa and East Germany
(E) Canada and Yugoslavia

4. In which of the following pairs are there the most persons per car?
(A) France and Japan
(B) Sweden and Colombia
(C) The United States and Egypt
(D) South Africa and East Germany
(E) Canada and Yugoslavia

5. As shown by the graph, on which continent are the countries with the fewest persons per car?
(A) North America
(B) South America
(C) Asia
(D) Africa
(E) Europe

Correct Answers Graphic Data Test 18

1. C 57

2. B 89

3. D South Africa and East Germany

4. C The United States and Egypt

5. A North America

Graphic Data Test 19

Directions: Study the following graph and answer the questions that come after it. Underline the answer you choose. Then mark the appropriate space in the answer column. *Correct answers appear at end of test.*

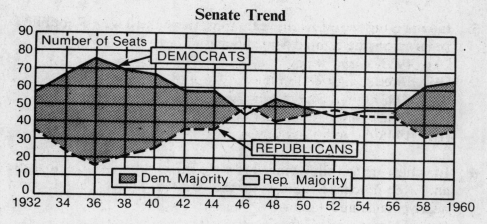

Senate Trend

1. In which year were there the most Democratic Senators in the United States Senate?
   (A) 1958
   (B) 1940
   (C) 1936
   (D) 1946
   (E) 1960

2. In which of the following years were there more Republican than Democratic Senators in the United States Senate?
   (A) 1944
   (B) 1946
   (C) 1948
   (D) 1932
   (E) 1960

3. Approximately how many Democratic Senators were there in the United States Senate in 1958?
   (A) 30
   (B) 40
   (C) 50
   (D) 60
   (E) 70

4. What was the approximate ratio of Democratic Senators to Republican Senators in the United States Senate in 1938?
   (A) 3:2
   (B) 4:3
   (C) 5:1
   (D) 7:2
   (E) 7:4

5. In which of the following years were there the fewest Republican Senators in the United States Senate?
   (A) 1938
   (B) 1958
   (C) 1948
   (D) 1932
   (E) 1944

6. In which of the following years were the numbers of Democratic and Republican Senators in the United States Senate most nearly the same?
   (A) 1944
   (B) 1960
   (C) 1936
   (D) 1958
   (E) 1954

Correct Answers Graphic Data Test 19

1. **C** 1936

2. **B** 1946

3. **D** 60

4. **D** 7:2

5. **A** 1938

6. **E** 1954

Graphic Data Test 20

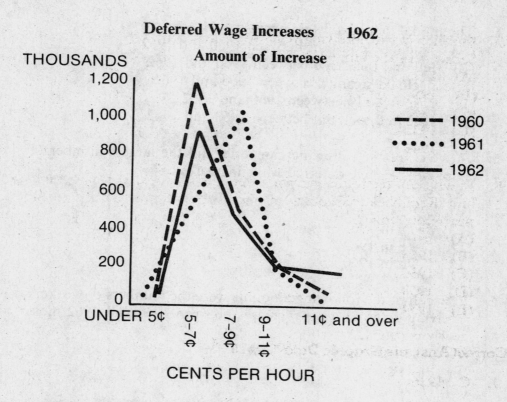

Deferred Wage Increases   1962

Amount of Increase

1. The total number of persons receiving deferred wage increases in 1962 approximated
   - (A)   one million
   - (B)   two and a half million
   - (C)   one and a half million
   - (D)   three million
   - (E)   two million

2. In 1961, more employees received wage increases in the following amount than in any other
   - (A)   under 5¢
   - (B)   5–7¢
   - (C)   7–9¢
   - (D)   9–11¢
   - (E)   11¢ and over

3. In which of the following categories did the fewest employees receive a deferred wage increase?
   (A) under 5¢ in 1961
   (B) under 5¢ in 1962
   (C) 9–11¢ in 1962
   (D) 11¢ and over in 1960
   (E) 11¢ and over in 1962

4. The modal deferred wage increase
   (A) remained constant between 1960 and 1962
   (B) fell and then rose between 1960 and 1962
   (C) declined steadily between 1960 and 1962
   (D) rose steadily between 1960 and 1962
   (E) rose and then fell between 1960 and 1962

5. In which of the following categories did the largest number of employees receive deferred wage increases?
   (A) 9–11¢ in 1962
   (B) 7–9¢ in 1962
   (C) 5–7¢ in 1961
   (D) 5–7¢ in 1962
   (E) 7–9¢ in 1960

6. In which of the following amounts were the numbers of workers receiving deferred wage increases between 1960 and 1962 most nearly constant?
   (A) 11¢ and over
   (B) 9–11¢
   (C) 7–9¢
   (D) 5–7¢
   (E) under 5¢

Correct Answers Graphic Data Test 20

1. E two million

2. C 7–9¢

3. B under 5¢ in 1962

4. E rose and then fell between 1960 and 1962

5. D 5–7¢ in 1962

6. B 9–11¢

Graphic Data Test 21

Directions: Study the following graph and answer the questions that come after it. Underline the answer you choose. Then mark the appropriate space in the answer column. *Correct answers appear at end of test.*

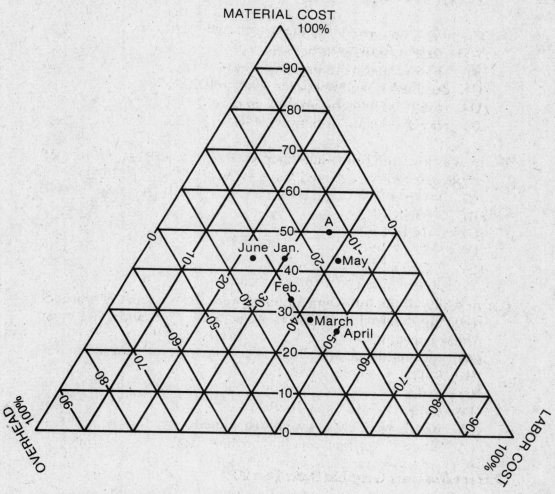

In the graph above, point A gives the ideal proportions of manufacturing cost to be devoted to material cost, labor cost, and overhead. The other points show how these items were proportioned for the first six months of one year. For each item percentages read from the base of the triangle to the vertex. In the statements which follow, select the phrase which best completes the statement.

1.   During the first four months, the percentage spent for material
   (A)   increased
   (B)   increased and then decreased
   (C)   decreased
   (D)   remained constant
   (E)   decreased gradually, then increased rapidly

2. The percentage spent for material and labor together in January was
  (A) ideal
  (B) twice that spent for overhead
  (C) four times that spent for overhead
  (D) more than in June
  (E) excessive

3. From February to May, the percentage spent for
  (A) overhead decreased steadily
  (B) material decreased steadily
  (C) material increased, then decreased
  (D) labor remained constant
  (E) labor increased

4. The most nearly ideal month was
  (A) January
  (B) February
  (C) March
  (D) April
  (E) May

5. The percentages spent for overhead
  (A) fluctuate most widely
  (B) do not vary more than 10%
  (C) are consistently higher than ideal
  (D) do not depend on those spent for material and labor
  (E) are consistently lower than ideal

6. In considering May and June:
  (A) Costs were equally well distributed
  (B) June's overhead was higher than ideal
  (C) May's labor costs were too low
  (D) May was ideal
  (E) June's material cost was too high

7. The average percentage spent on labor was
  (A) between 30 and 35
  (B) one-fourth the total cost
  (C) higher than that spent for overhead
  (D) half the total cost
  (E) under 30

Correct Answers Graphic Data Test 21

1. **C**   decreased

2. **D**   more than in June

3. **A**   overhead decreased steadily

4. **E**   May

5. **C**   are consistently higher than ideal

6. **B**   June's overhead was higher than ideal

7. **C**   higher than that spent for overhead

Graphic Data Test 22

Directions: Study the following graph and answer the questions that come after it. Underline the answer you choose. Then mark the appropriate space in the answer column. *Correct answers appear at end of test.*

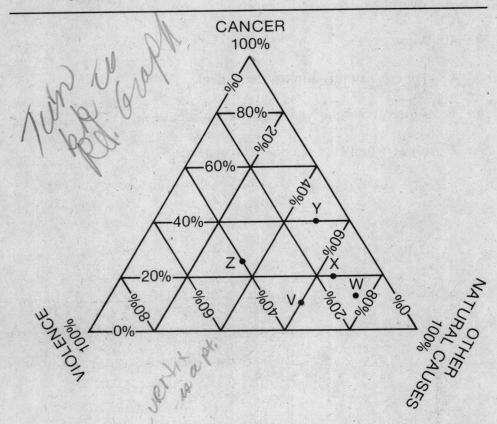

The triangular graph above compares, for five countries, V, W, X, Y, and Z, percentages of deaths due to cancer, other natural causes, and violence. Each vertex represents 100% of deaths due to the given cause, and the base opposite represents 0% due to that cause. For example, in country V, approximately 10% of the deaths were caused by cancer, 60% by other natural causes, and approximately 30% by violence.

1. In which country or countries were more than 35 percent of the deaths due to violence?
   (A) W only
   (B) Y only
   (C) Z only
   (D) none of the countries
   (E) all of the countries

2. In which country was the percentage of deaths due to cancer the highest?
    (A) V
    (B) W
    (C) X
    (D) Y
    (E) Z

3. Approximately what percentage of deaths in country Y was due to violence?
    (A) 10
    (B) 40
    (C) 50
    (D) 80
    (E) 90

4. In which country were the number of deaths caused by violence and the number of deaths caused by cancer most nearly equal?
    (A) V
    (B) W
    (C) X
    (D) Y
    (E) cannot be determined from the data

    don't have #'s – not enough info.

5. For which country was the ratio of the percentage of deaths caused by violence to the percentage of those caused by cancer the greatest?
    (A) V
    (B) W
    (C) X
    (D) Y
    (E) Z

    poorly wded skip

6. In which country was the number of deaths due to cancer the greatest?
    (A) V
    (B) W
    (C) Y
    (D) Z
    (E) cannot be determined from the data

7. In which country was the smallest percentage of all natural deaths due to cancer?
    (A) V
    (B) W
    (C) X
    (D) Y
    (E) Z

Correct Answers Graphic Data Test 22

1. **C**   Z only

2. **D**   Y

3. **A**   10

4. **E**   cannot be determined from the data

5. **A**   V

6. **E**   cannot be determined from the data

7. **A**   V

Graphic Data Test 23

Directions: Study the following map and answer the questions that come after it. Underline the answer you choose. Then mark the appropriate space in the answer column. *Correct answers appear at end of test.*

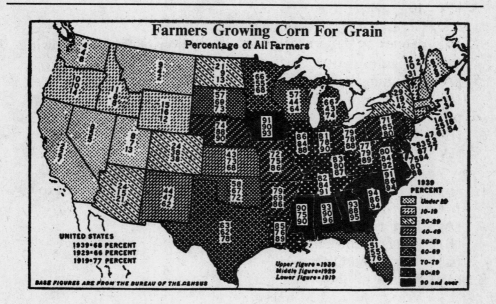

1. In what state(s) west of the Mississippi did 90 percent or more of the farmers raise corn for grain in 1919?
   (A) Minnesota and Kansas
   (B) Missouri and Kansas
   (C) Iowa
   (D) Kansas and Nebraska
   (E) Nebraska and Iowa

2. In 1939, how many states had the same percentage of farmers growing corn for grain as Colorado had in 1919?
   (A) 0
   (B) 1
   (C) 2
   (D) 3
   (E) not answerable

3. What was the average percentage of Illinois farmers raising corn for grain for the three years referred to on the map?
   (A) 77.7
   (B) 83.0
   (C) 86.0
   (D) 91.25
   (E) 129.0

4. The quantity of corn produced for grain was the same in Mississippi and Missouri in what year?
   (A) 1919
   (B) 1929
   (C) 1935 (approx.)
   (D) 1939
   (E) not answerable

5. What two states had the lowest proportion of farmers growing corn for grain in 1929?
   (A) Washington and Montana
   (B) Maine and California
   (C) Montana and Nevada
   (D) Washington and California
   (E) Montana and Maine

6. In what two states east of the Missouri River did 60 percent to 69 percent of the farmers raise corn for grain in 1939?
   (A) Illinois and Wisconsin
   (B) Texas and Michigan
   (C) Texas and Oklahoma
   (D) Michigan and Minnesota
   (E) Wisconsin and Minnesota

7. In Washington, Oregon, and California combined, the percentage of farmers growing corn for grain in 1919 exceeded the percentage in 1939 by what percent?
   (A) 0
   (B) 6
   (C) 8
   (D) 13
   (E) not answerable

8. The proportion of farmers in New York growing corn for grain in 1919 was what percent greater than the proportion in North Dakota in 1939?
   (A) 21
   (B) 50
   (C) 100
   (D) 200
   (E) not answerable

9. The number of farmers in Vermont in 1939 was approximately 24,000 and in 1929 approximately 25,000. The number of farmers growing corn for grain in 1939 was an increase of approximately what percent over those in 1929?
    (A) 2.0
    (B) 13.2
    (C) 15.2
    (D) 20.0
    (E) not answerable

10. Based on the map and the following table, in which of the three states given was there an increase in farmers growing corn for grain between the 1929 and 1939 figures?

TOTAL NUMBER OF FARMERS

	1929	1939
New Mexico..........	31,000	34,000
Oregon.............	55,000	62,000
Texas..............	495,000	418,000

    (A) Oregon
    (B) Oregon and New Mexico
    (C) Oregon and Texas
    (D) Texas and New Mexico
    (E) All three

11. Assuming that the number of farmers in the United States increased by 8 percent from 1919 to 1929, the number of farmers growing corn for grain decreased by what percent from 1919 to 1929?
    (A) 3.0
    (B) 7.4
    (C) 10.1
    (D) 11.9
    (E) not answerable

12. In general, the states in which the highest percentage of farmers grow corn for grain are the states which lead in the production of
    (A) citrus fruits
    (B) cotton
    (C) potatoes
    (D) sugar beets
    (E) wheat

Correct Answers Graphic Data Test 23

1. **E** Nebraska and Iowa

2. **A** 0

3. **C** 86.0

4. **B** 1929

5. **B** Maine and California

6. **D** Michigan and Minnesota

7. **D** 13

8. **A** 21

9. **B** 13.2

10. **B** Oregon and New Mexico

11. **B** 7.4

12. **B** cotton

Graphic Data Test 24

Directions: Study the following graph and answer the questions that come after it. Underline the answer you choose. Then mark the appropriate space in the answer column. *Correct answers appear at end of test.*

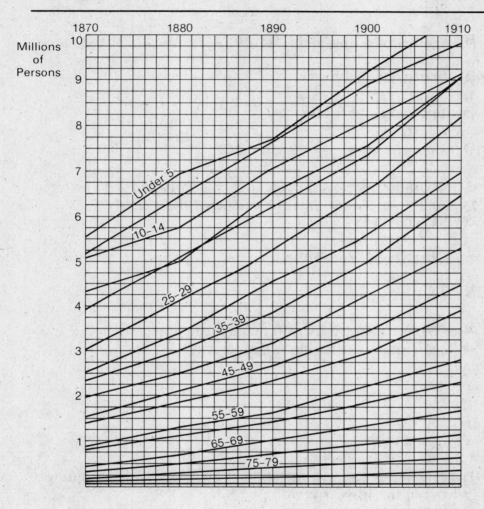

The graph above shows the population of the United States by age groups from 1870 to 1910. (Assume that there is immigration and emigration, and that the death rate and birth rate are the same.)

1. In 1890, the population of the "65–69" age group was most nearly
   (A)   500,000
   (B)   750,000
   (C)   1,000,000
   (D)   1,500,000
   (E)   none of these

2. The population of the "Under 5" age group was most nearly 6,000,000 in
    (A)   1870
    (B)   1872
    (C)   1882
    (D)   1880
    (E)   1874

3. The number of people in the "15–19" age group in 1910 was most nearly
    (A)   8,750,000
    (B)   9,000,000
    (C)   9,050,000
    (D)   9,250,000
    (E)   none of these

4. In 1880, those people who were in this country and were between 25 and 29 years of age in 1870 numbered most nearly
    (A)   3,000,000
    (B)   3,375,000
    (C)   4,100,000
    (D)   4,450,000
    (E)   not answerable

5. Over the period 1870 to 1910 the number of people in the "80–84" age group increased by what percent?
    (A)   1%
    (B)   50%
    (C)   100%
    (D)   300%
    (E)   none of these

6. The rate of increase in population in the "35–39" age group was greatest in the 10-year period
    (A)   1870–1880
    (B)   1890–1900
    (C)   1900–1910
    (D)   1880–1890
    (E)   not answerable

7. The excess of immigration over emigration in the "5–9" age group was greatest in the 10-year period
    (A)   1870–1880
    (B)   1890–1900
    (C)   1900–1910
    (D)   1880–1890
    (E)   not answerable

8. In 1910 the difference in population between the "15–19" and the "20–24" age groups was most nearly
   (A)   500
   (B)   50,000
   (C)   120,000
   (D)   250,000
   (E)   none of these

9. The difference between the population of the "35–44" age group and that of the "15–19" age group in 1870 was most nearly
   (A)   250,000
   (B)   430,000
   (C)   1,700,000
   (D)   2,100,000
   (E)   none of these

10. Assuming no immigration or emigration, those in the "40–44" age group in 1870 who were alive in 1910 numbered approximately
   (A)   25,000
   (B)   375,000
   (C)   2,250,000
   (D)   5,275,000
   (E)   none of these

11. In comparing the "15–19" and the "20–24" age groups, the graph shows that:
   (A)   Immigration into the "15–19" age group was greater than that into the "20–24" age group from 1880 to 1890.
   (B)   From 1900 to 1910 immigration into the "20–24" age group was greater than that into the "15–19" age group.
   (C)   In the "15–19" and the "20–24" age groups, immigration was the same from 1890 to 1900.
   (D)   Between 1890 and 1900, immigration into the "15–19" age group was the same as that into the "20–24" age group.
   (E)   None of the above conclusions may be drawn.

12. Assume that the birth rate during the period 1880–1890 is double that during the period 1870–1880. In the "50–54" age group, the excess of immigration over emigration for the period 1870–1880 is how many times as large as the excess for the period 1880–1890?
   (A) $\frac{1}{2}$
   (B)   1
   (C)   2
   (D) $2\frac{1}{2}$
   (E)   not answerable

13. Which of the following age groups had the greatest percentage increase in the ten-year period 1870–1880?
(A) "Under 5"
(B) "5–9"
(C) "10–14"
(D) "65–69"
(E) none of these

14. If the birth rate and the death rate of the "Under 5" age group are the same for the two periods 1870–1880 and 1880–1890, then the excess of immigration over emigration in the "Under 5" age group for the period 1870–1880 is greater than the excess for the period 1880–1890 by approximately
(A) 500,000
(B) 750,000
(C) 2,130,000
(D) 3,200,000
(E) not answerable

15. The population difference between the "25–29" age group and the "40–44" age group in 1900 numbered approximately
(A) 1,750,000
(B) 2,000,000
(C) 2,250,000
(D) 3,500,000
(E) none of these

Correct Answers and Solutions Graphic Data Test 24

1. **C**   1,000,000

2. **E**   1874

3. **C**   9,050,000

4. **A**   3,000,000

5. **D**   300%

6. **C**   1900–1910

7. **A**   1870–1880

8. **A**   500

9. **A**   250,000

10. **D**   5,275,000

11. **E**   None of the above conclusions may be drawn.

12. **A** $\frac{1}{2}$

13. **B**   "5–9"

14. **A**   500,000

15. **C**   2,250,000

Graphic Data Test 25

Directions: Study the following graphs and answer the questions that come after them. Underline the answer you choose. Then mark the appropriate space in the answer column. *Correct answers appear at end of test.*

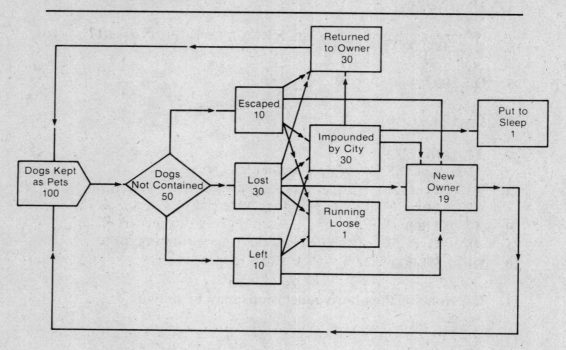

This chart shows the fate of 100 pet dogs. 50 of the 100 were not contained. 10 escaped, 30 were lost, 10 were left intentionally, and so on. Answer the following questions based on the chart above.

1. What percent of the original 100 dogs were impounded by the city?
    (A) 24%
    (B) 60%
    (C) 30%
    (D) 15%
    (E) Cannot be determined.

2. How many of the original 100 dogs were ultimately kept as pets?
    (A) 100
    (B) 2
    (C) 30
    (D) 98
    (E) 81

3. Of the dogs not contained, what percent went to new owners?
  (A) 19%
  (B) 38%
  (C) 60%
  (D) 49%
  (E) Cannot be determined.

4. What was the ratio of dogs lost to dogs escaped or left?
  (A) 3:1
  (B) 1:3
  (C) 5:3
  (D) 5:4
  (E) 3:2

5. Which of the following statements is true?
  (A) Less than 10% of the original dogs were lost.
  (B) None of the escaped dogs were put to sleep.
  (C) None of the dogs left were returned to owners.
  (D) Over 5% of the original dogs were running loose.
  (E) None of the above answers is true.

Correct Answers Graphic Data Test 25

1. C

2. D

3. B

4. E

5. E

Verbal Ability Review

ETYMOLOGIES, WORD LISTS

The Verbal Ability section of the GRE includes antonyms (words that have opposite meanings), sentence completions (word fill-ins), analogies (word relationships), and reading comprehension. All of these areas test your vocabulary to some extent. Developing your vocabulary is a lengthy process, but since verbal ability tests require that you understand the meanings of words, it is important for you to have a strong vocabulary. In high school and college, you have doubtless learned the meanings of many words, and you have probably learned to figure out the meanings of words you do not know.

The following pages provide aids to vocabulary building. First, you will find lists of prefixes, suffixes, and common roots and their meanings. Knowing these word elements will help you work out the meanings of unfamiliar words. Next is a list of over 2,300 words to help you review many words that generally appear in college course work. You probably know the meanings of many of the words, so use the list to help yourself recall the ones you know and learn the ones you do not know.

After you have gone over the vocabulary material, you may wish to take the extra practice verbal ability tests that begin afterward.

COMMON PREFIXES

Prefix	Meaning	Examples
ab, a-, abs-	away from	*abhor*—to withdraw from in fear or disgust *abscond*—to run away
ad- (also a-, ac-, af-, ag-, an-, ap-, ar-, as-, at-)	to; toward	*adapt*—to fit to *accede*—to attain to
ambi-	both	*ambivalent*—having two feelings
amphi-	on both sides; around	*amphibian*—an animal that lives first in the water and then adapts to land life *amphitheater*—a theater with seats on all sides
ante-	before	*antebellum*—before the war
anti-	against	*antifreeze*—a substance added to a liquid to prevent freezing
auto-	self	*automobile*—a self-propelled vehicle
bi-	two	*bifocals*—glasses with lenses for two focuses
circum-	around	*circumscribe*—to draw around
com-, con-, co-, col-	with; together	*combine*—to bring together *conjoin*—to join together *co-worker*—one who works with
contra,- contro-, counter	against	*contradict*—to say the opposite *counteract*—to act against
de-	away from; down; the opposite of	*depart*—to go away from *decline*—to turn down *deactivate*—to make inactive
di-	twice	*dioxide*—an oxide with two atoms of oxygen in a molecule
dia-	across; through	*diagonal*—across or through a figure *diagnose*—to determine what is wrong through knowledge
dis-	apart; not	*disperse*—to scatter widely *dishonest*—not honest
dys-	bad; ill	*dysfunction*—a poor functioning
epi-	upon	*epitaph*—an inscription on a tombstone (upon burial)
equi-	equal; equally	*equitable*—fair
ex-, e-, ef-	out; from	*excavate*—to hollow out *eject*—to throw out *effuse*—to pour out
extra-	outside; beyond	*extraordinary*—outside the usual
fore-	before; in front of	*foresee*—to anticipate
geo-	earth	*geology*—the study of the earth
homo-	same; equal; like	*homonym*—a word with the same pronunciation as another word
hyper-	over; too much	*hypertension*—unusually high tension

Prefix	Meaning	Examples
hypo-	under; too little	*hypodermic*—under the skin
in-, il-, ig-, ir-, im-	not	*inactive*—not active
		illegal—not legal
		ignoble—not noble
		irreverent—not reverent
		improbable—not probable
in-, il-, ir-, im-	in; into	*inject*—to put in
		illuminate—to light up
		irradiate—to shine light on
		implant—to fix firmly (in)
inter-	between; among	*interurban*—between cities
intra-, intro-	within; inside of	*intravenous*—directly into a vein
		introvert—one who looks inside himself
mal-, male-	bad; wrong; ill	*malfunction*—to fail to function correctly
		malevolent—wishing harm to others
mis-	wrong; badly	*mistreat*—to treat badly
mis-, miso-	hatred	*misanthrope*—one who hates men
mono-	one; alone	*monologue*—a speech by one person
neo-	new	*neologism*—a new word or a new meaning for an old word
non-	not; the reverse of	*nonsense*—something that makes no sense
omni-	all; everywhere	*omnipresent*—present everywhere
pan-	all	*pandemic*—existing over a whole area
per-	by; through; throughout	*pervade*—to be present throughout
poly-	many	*polyglot*—speaking or writing several languages
post-	after	*postwar*—after the war
pre-	before; earlier than	*preview*—a preliminary viewing
		prehistorical—before written history
pro-	forward; going ahead of; supporting	*proceed*—to go forward
		proboscis—a snout
		prowar—supporting the war
re-	again; back	*retell*—to tell again
		recall—to call back
retro-	backward	*retroactive*—applying to things that have already taken place
se-	apart	*secede*—to withdraw
semi-	half; partly	*semicircle*—half a circle
		semiliterate—able to read and write a little
sub-	under; less than	*submarine*—underwater
		subconscious—beneath the consciousness

Prefix	Meaning	Examples
super-	over; above; greater	*superimpose*—to put something over something else
		superstar—a star greater than the others
syn-, sym-, syl-, sys-	with; at the same time	*synchronize*—to make things agree
		symmetry—balance on two sides of a dividing line
tele-	far	*telepathy*—communication by thoughts alone
trans-	across	*transcontinental*—across the continent
un-	not	*unhelpful*—not helpful

COMMON SUFFIXES

Suffix	Meaning	Examples
-able, -ible, -ble	able to; capable of being	*viable*—able to live
		edible—capable of being eaten
-acious, -cious	having the quality of	*tenacious*—holding firmly
-al	of; like	*nocturnal*—of the night
-ance, -ancy	the act of; a state of being	*performance*—the act of performing
		truancy—the act of being truant
-ant, -ent	one who	*occupant*—one who occupies
		respondent—one who responds
-ar, -ary	connected with; concerning	*ocular*—pertaining to the eye
		beneficiary—one who receives benefits
-ence	the act, fact, or quality of	*existence*—the quality of being
-er, -or	one who does	*teacher*—one who teaches
		visitor—one who visits
-ful	full of; having qualities of	*fearful*—full of fear
		masterful—having the qualities of a master
-fy	to make	*deify*—to make into a god
-ic, -ac	of; like; pertaining to	*cryptic*—hidden
		cardiac—pertaining to the heart
-il, -ile	pertaining to	*civil*—pertaining to citizens
		infantile—pertaining to infants or infancy
-ion	the act or condition of	*correction*—the act of correcting
-ism	the philosophy, act, or practice of	*patriotism*—support of one's country

Suffix	Meaning	Examples
-ist	one who does, makes, or is occupied with	*artist*—one who is occupied with art
ity, -ty, -y	the state or character	*unity*—the state of being one *novelty*—the quality of being novel or new
-ive	containing the nature of; giving or leaning toward	*pensive*—thoughtful
-less	without; lacking	*heartless*—cruel; without a heart
-logue	a particular kind of speaking or writing	*dialogue*—a conversation or interchange
-logy	a kind of speaking; a study or science	*eulogy*—a speech or writing in praise of someone *theology*—the study of God and related matters
-ment	the act of; the state of	*alignment*—the act of aligning *retirement*—the state of being retired
-ness	the quality of	*eagerness*—the quality of being eager
-ory	having the nature of; a place or thing for	*laudatory*—showing praise *laboratory*—a place where work is done
-ous, -ose	full of; having	*dangerous*—full of danger *verbose*—wordy
-ship	the art or skill of; the state or quality of being	*leadership*—the ability to lead
-some	full of; like	*troublesome*—full of trouble
-tude	the state or quality of	*servitude*—slavery or bondage
-y	full of; somewhat; somewhat like	*musty*—having a stale odor *chilly*—somewhat cold *willowy*—like a willow

COMMON ROOTS

Root	Meaning	Examples
acr	sharp; bitter	*acrid*—sharp; bitter
act, ag	to do; to act	*activity*—action *agent*—one who does
acu	sharp; keen	*acuity*—keenness
alt	high	*exalt*—to raise or lift up
anim	life; mind	*animate*—to make alive
ann	year	*annual*—yearly
anthrop	man, mankind	*misanthrope*—one who hates people
apt	fit	*adapt*—to fit to
arch	to rule	*patriarch*—a father and ruler
aud	to hear	*audience*—those who hear
bas	low	*debase*—to make lower
belli	war	*bellicose*—hostile; warlike

Root	Meaning	Examples
ben, bene	well; good	*benevolent*—doing or wishing good
bio	life	*biology*—the study of living things
brev	short	*abbreviate*—to shorten
cad, cas	to fall	*cadence*—the fall of the voice in speaking; movement in sound
		cascade—a small waterfall
cap, capt, cip, cept, ceive, ceit	to take or hold	*captive*—one who is caught and held
		receive—to take
cav	hollow	*excavate*—to hollow out
cede, ceed, cess	to go; to give in	*precede*—to go before
		access—a means of going to
chrom	color	*chromatic*—having color
chron, chrono	time	*synchronize*—to make agree in time
		chronology—the order of events
cid, cis	to cut; to kill	*incisive*—cutting into; sharp
		homicide—the killing of a man by another
clin	to lean; to bend	*decline*—to bend or turn downward
clud, clus, clos, claud, claus	to close; to shut	*exclude*—to shut out
		claustrophobia—fear of closed places
cogn, cognit	to know; to learn	*cognizant*—aware
		recognition—knowing on sight
cor, cord	heart	*accord*—agreement
corp, corpor	body	*corporal*—bodily
cred, credit	to believe	*credible*—believable
crypt	hidden	*cryptic*—with hidden meaning
cum	to heap up	*cumulative*—increasing by additions
cur	to care	*accurate*—careful and precise
curr, curs, cours	to run	*current*—the flow of running water
		cursory—hastily done
da, date	to give	*date*—a given time
dem, demo	people	*demography*—a statistical study of population
di	day	*diary*—a daily record
dic, dict	to say	*diction*—wording; verbal expression
		indict—to make a formal accusation
doc, doct	to teach	*doctrine*—something taught
dol	grief; pain	*doleful*—sorrowful
domin	to rule; to master	*dominion*—rule; a ruled territory
dorm	to sleep	*dormant*—sleeping; inactive
duc, duct	to lead	*induce*—to lead to action
		aqueduct—a pipe or waterway

Root	*Meaning*	*Examples*
dynam	power	*dynamite*—a powerful explosive
ego	I	*egocentric*—seeing everything in relation to oneself
eu	good; beautiful	*euphonious*—having pleasant sound
fac, fact, fic, fec, fect	to make; to do	*facile*—easy to do
		artifact—an object made by man
		fiction—something that has been made up
fer, ferr, lat	to carry, bring, or bear	*refer*—to carry to something or somebody else
		translate—to bring from one language to another
fid	faith; trust	*confide*—to tell a trusted person
fin	end; limit	*final*—coming at the end
fort, force	strong	*fortitude*—strength
		enforce—to give strength to
frag, fract	to break	*fragment*—a part broken from the whole
		fracture—a break
gen	birth	*generate*—to give birth to
gen, gener	kind; race	*general*—applying to a whole class or kind
		gender—classification of words by sex
gnos	to know	*agnostic*—one who believes people cannot know whether God exists
grad, gress	to step; to go	*graduate*—to go from one state to another
		progress—to move forward
graph, gram	writing	*graphic*—relating to writing
		telegram—a written message sent over a distance
helio	sun	*heliolatry*—sun worship
hydro	water	*hydrant*—a pipe from which one draws water
jac, jact, jec, ject	to throw	*trajectory*—the path of an object that has been thrown or shot
		project—to propose; to put forward
junct	to join	*junction*—a joining
jur	to swear	*perjure*—to lie under oath
labor	to work	*elaborate*—worked out carefully
leg, lect	to gather; to choose	*legion*—a large number gathered together
		elect—to choose
leg	law	*legislate*—to make laws
liber	book	*library*—a book collection
liber	free	*liberation*—freedom
loc	place	*dislocate*—to displace
loqu, locut	to talk	*loquacious*—talkative
		elocution—style of speaking

Root	*Meaning*	*Examples*
luc	light	*elucidate*—to clarify ("throw light on")
magn	great	*magnanimous*—of noble mind; generous
		magnate—an important person
man, mani, manu	hand	*manipulate*—to work with the hands
		manuscript—a document written by hand
mar	the sea	*maritime*—having to do with the sea
medi	middle	*intermediate*—in the middle
meter, metr, mens	to measure	*thermometer*—an instrument to measure temperature
		symmetry—similarity of measurement on both sides
		immense—very large (unmeasureable)
micro	small	*microbe*—an organism too small to be seen with the naked eye
min, mini	small	*minute*—very tiny
		miniature—a small copy of something
mit, mitt, miss	to send	*admit*—to allow in
		missile—a projectile
mon, monit	to advise, warn, remind	*monument*—a plaque, statue, building, etc., set up to remind of someone or something
		premonition—an advance warning
mort, mori	to die	*mortal*—destined to die
		moribund—dying
mov, mot, mob	to move	*remove*—to move away
		emotion—strong (moving) feelings
		immobile—not movable
mut	to change	*immutable*—never changing
nat, nasc	born	*prenatal*—before birth
		nascent—coming into being; being born
nav	ship	*circumnavigate*—to sail around
nocturn	night	*nocturnal*—taking place at night
nomy	law; arranged order	*astronomy*—the science of the stars
nov, novus	new	*innovation*—something new
onym	name	*anonymous*—without a name
oper	to work	*operative*—capable of working
pac	peace	*pacify*—to calm
par	equal	*disparate*—not alike; distinct
pars, part	part	*parse*—to separate into parts
		depart—to go away from

Root	Meaning	Examples
pater, patr	father	*paternal*—fatherly *patriarch*—a father and ruler
path, pat, pas	feeling, suffering	*empathy*—"feeling with" another person *patient*—suffering without complaint *passion*—strong emotion
ped, pede, pod	foot	*pedestal*—the bottom of a statue, column, etc. *impede*—to hinder *podium*—a platform on which to stand
pel, puls	to drive	*expel*—to drive out *repulse*—to drive back
pend, pens	to hang; to weigh; to pay	*pendulous*—hanging loosely *pensive*—thoughtful *pension*—a payment to a person after a certain age
pet, petit	to seek	*impetus*—a motive *petition*—to request
phil, philo	loving	*philanthropy*—a desire to help mankind *philosophy*—love of knowledge
phobia	fear	*hydrophobia*—fear of water
phon, phone	sound	*symphony*—harmony of sounds *telephone*—an instrument for sending sound over a distance
plac	to please	*placate*—to stop from being angry
polis	city	*metropolis*—a major city
pon, pos, posit, pose	to place	*proponent*—a person who makes a suggestion or supports a cause *deposit*—to place
port, portat	to carry	*porter*—one who carries *transportation*—a means of carrying
psych, psycho	mind	*psychology*—the science of the mind
quer, quisit	to ask	*query*—a question *inquisition*—a questioning
quies	quiet	*acquiesce*—to agree without protest
radi	ray	*irradiate*—to shine light on
rap, rapt	to seize	*rapine*—the act of seizing others' property by force *rapture*—being seized or carried away by emotion
rid, ris	to laugh	*ridiculous*—laughable *risible*—causing laughter
rog, rogate	to ask	*prerogative*—a prior right *interrogate*—to question

Root	*Meaning*	*Examples*
rupt	break	*disrupt*—to break up
sat, satis	enough	*satiate*—to provide with enough or more than enough
		satisfy—to meet the needs of
schis, schiz	to cut	*schism*—a split or division
		schizophrenia—a mental disorder characterized by a separation of the thoughts and emotions
sci	to know	*science*—knowledge
scop	to watch; to view	*telescope*—an instrument for seeing things from a distance
scrib, script	to write	*describe*—to tell or write about
		transcript—a written copy
sec, sect	to cut	*sectile*—cutable with a knife
		bisect—to cut in two
sed, sess, sid	to sit	*sediment*—material that settles to the bottom (in liquid)
		session—a meeting
		preside—to have authority
sent, sens	to feel; to think	*sentiment*—feeling
		sensitive—responding to stimuli
sequ, secu, secut	to follow	*sequence*—order
		consecutive—one following another
solv, solut	to loosen	*absolve*—to free from guilt
		solution—the method of working out an answer
soph	wise; wisdom	*sophisticate*—a worldly-wise person
spec, spect, spic	to look; to appear	*specimen*—an example
		inspect—to look over
		perspicacious—having sharp judgment
spir, spirit	to breathe	*expire*—to exhale; to die
		spirit—life
sta, stat	to stand	*stable*—steady
		stationary—fixed; unmoving
stru, struct	to build	*construe*—to explain or deduce the meaning
		structure—a building
suas, suad	to urge	*persuasive*—having the power to cause something to change
		dissuade—to change someone's course
sum, sumpt	to take	*assume*—to take on
		resumption—taking up again
tact, tang	to touch	*tactile*—able to be touched or felt
		intangible—unable to be touched
tempor	time	*temporal*—lasting only for a time; temporary

Root	Meaning	Examples
ten, tent, tain	to hold	*untenable*—unable to be held
		retentive—holding
		maintain—to keep or keep up
tend, tens	to stretch	*extend*—to stretch out or draw out
		tension—tautness
terr	land	*territory*—a portion of land
the, theo	god	*atheist*—one who believes there is no God
		theocracy—rule by God or by persons claiming to represent Him
thermo	heat	*thermal*—having to do with heat
tract	to draw	*attract*—to draw
trud, trus	to thrust	*protrude*—to stick out
		intrusive—pushing into or upon something
un, uni	one	*unanimous*—of one opinion
		uniform—of one form
urb	city	*suburb*—a district near a city
ut, util	to use; useful	*utile*—useful
		utility—the quality of being useful
vac	empty	*vacuum*—empty space
ven, vent	to come	*convene*—to meet together
		advent—an arrival
ver	true	*verify*—to prove to be true
verd	green	*verdant*—green
vert, vers	to turn	*avert*—to turn away
vi, via	way	*deviate*—to turn off the prescribed way
		via—by way of
vid, vis	to see	*evident*—apparent; obvious
		invisible—unable to be seen
vinc, vict	to conquer	*convince*—to overcome the doubts of
		victory—an overcoming
vit, viv	to live	*vital*—alive
		vivacious—lively
voc, voke, vocat	to call	*vocal*—spoken or uttered aloud
		invoke—to call on
		vocation—a calling
void	empty	*devoid*—without
volv, volut	to roll or turn around	*evolve*—to develop by stages; to unfold
		convoluted—coiled
vol	to fly	*volatile*—vaporizing quickly

VOCABULARY REVIEW LIST
A

abase—to degrade
abash—to embarrass
abate—to decrease
abattoir—a slaughterhouse
abdicate—to give up
aberration—a deviation
abet—to aid
abeyance—temporary suspension
abhor—to detest
abject—miserable
abjure—to give up on oath
ablution—washing the body
abnegate—to renounce
abominate—to loathe
aboriginal—first; existing someplace
    since the beginning
abort—to cut short
abrade—to rub off
abridge—to shorten
abrogate—to cancel by authority
abscond—to run away
absolve—to free of guilt
abstemious—moderate in eating and
    drinking
abstract—a summary
abstruse—hard to understand
abut—to border on
abysmal—bottomless; wretched
accede—to take on the duties (of); to
    attain (to)
acclivity—an upward slope
accolade—a demonstration of honor
accouterments—one's clothes
accretion—accumulation
accrue—to accumulate
acerbity—sharpness
acme—a peak
acquiesce—to yield
acquit—to clear of a charge
acrid—sharp
acrimony—bitterness
actuate—to put into motion
acumen—keenness
adage—an old saying
adamant—unyielding
adduce—to give as proof
adept—skilled; expert
adhere—to stay fast
adipose—fatty
adjudicate—to judge
adjunct—something added
adjure—to charge under oath

admonish—to warn
adroit—skillful
adulation—flattery
adulterate—to make impure
adumbration—a foreshadowing; an
    outlining
advent—an arrival
adventitious—accidental
adversity—misfortune
advocate—to support
aesthetic—pertaining to beauty
affable—friendly
affected—artificial
affidavit—a sworn statement in writing
affinity—a close relationship
affirmation—assertion
affluent—wealthy
affray—a noisy quarrel
affront—an insult
agenda—a program
agglomerate—to gather into a mass
aggrandize—to make greater
aggravate—to make worse
aggregate—a group of things together
aggrieved—wronged
aghast—horrified
agile—nimble
agnostic—one who doesn't know
agrarian—agricultural
akimbo—with hands on hips
alacrity—eagerness
albeit—although
alchemy—early chemistry
alienate—to make unfriendly
allay—to calm
allege—to declare
allegory—a symbolic story
alleviate—to relieve
alocate—to distribute
allude—to refer indirectly
alluvial—pertaining to soil deposits left
    by water
altercation—an angry argument
altruism—unselfish concern for others
amass—to accumulate
amatory—showing love
ambidextrous—skillful; able to use both
    hands equally well
ambrosia—the food of the gods
ambulant—moving about
ameliorate—to improve
amenable—easily led

amenity—a pleasant quality
amiable—friendly
amity—friendship
amnesty—pardon
amorphous—shapeless
amplify—to increase
amulet—a charm
anachronism—something misplaced in time
analgesic—a pain-reliever
analogous—comparable
anarchy—absence of government
anathema—a curse
anchorite—a recluse
ancillary—serving as an aid
animadversion—a critical comment
animate—to bring to life
animosity—hatred
annals—yearly records
anneal—to heat and then cool; to strengthen
annuity—a yearly payment
annul—to invalidate
anomoly—an abnormality
antediluvian—before the Biblical Flood; very old
anterior—toward the front
anthropoid—resembling man
antipathy—a strong dislike
antipodes—exact opposites
antithesis—opposite
apathetic—indifferent
aperture—an opening
apex—a peak
aphorism—an adage
aplomb—self-possession; poise
apocryphal—of doubtful authenticity
apogee—the highest point
apoplexy—sudden paralysis
apostate—one who abandons his faith or cause
apothecary—druggist
apothegm—a saying
apotheosis—deification
appall—to shock or dismay
apparition—a ghost
appease—to pacify
appellation—a name or title
append—to attach
apposite—apt
apprise—to notify
appurtenance—an accessory or possession

aquiline—curved or hooked
arabesque—an elaborate architectural design
arable—plowable (land)
arbiter—a judge or umpire
arbitrary—left to one's judgment; despotic
arboreal—pertaining to trees
archaic—ancient or old-fashioned
archetype—an original model or perfect example
archipelago—a group of islands
archives—a place where records are kept; records
ardor—passion
arduous—laborious
argot—jargon
armada—a fleet of warships
arraign—to bring to court to answer charges
arrant—complete; out-and-out
arrears—unpaid debts
arrogate—to appropriate
articulate—to join; to speak clearly
artifact—a manmade object, particularly a primitive one
artifice—ingenuity; trickery
artisan—a skilled craftsman
ascendant—rising
ascetic—self-denying
ascribe—to assign or attribute
aseptic—free of bacteria
askance—with a sideways look; suspiciously
askew—crookedly
asperity—harshness
aspersion—a slanderous remark
assail—to assault
assay—to test or analyze; to try
asseverate—to assert
assiduous—diligent
assimilate—to incorporate
assuage—to lessen
astral—pertaining to the stars
astute—clever; shrewd
atavism—a throwback to an earlier state; a reappearance of a characteristic from an earlier generation
atheist—one who believes there is no God
athwart—across
atrophy—to waste away
attenuate—to weaken

attest—to confirm
attribute—a characteristic
attrition—wearing away
atypical—abnormal
audacious—bold
audible—loud enough to be heard
augment—to enlarge
augur—to foretell
august—inspiring reverence and respect
aural—pertaining to the ear or hearing
auspices—sponsorship
auspicious—favorable
austerity—severity; the condition of denying oneself
autocrat—a dictator
autonomy—self-government; independence
auxiliary—a thing or person that gives aid
avarice—greed
aver—to affirm
averse—opposed
avid—greedy
avocation—a hobby
avoirdupois—weight
avow—to acknowledge
avuncular—pertaining to an uncle; like an uncle
awry—not straight

B

bacchanal—a drunken party
badger—to tease or annoy
badinage—playful talk; banter
baffle—to perplex
baleful—harmful
balk—to obstruct; to refuse to move
balm—something that soothes or heals
banal—trite; commonplace
bandy—to toss back and forth; exchange
baneful—deadly
barbaric—uncivilized
baroque—very ornate
barrage—a prolonged attack of artillery fire or words
barrister—a man of the legal profession
bastion—a fortification or defense
bate—to lessen
bathos—sentimentality
batten—to thrive
bayou—a marshy body of water
beatific—blissful
beatitude—perfect happiness

bedizen—to dress in a showy way
bedlam—a madhouse; a place of chaos
beguile—to charm or deceive
behemoth—a large and powerful animal or thing
behoof—behalf; interest
belabor—to beat; to scold or criticize
beleaguer—to besiege
belie—to contradict
bellicose—warlike
belligerent—warlike
benediction—a blessing
benefactor—one who provides benefits
benevolent—kindly
benighted—surrounded by darkness; unenlightened
benign—kindly; harmless
benison—a blessing
berate—to scold
berserk—frenzied
beset—to attack
bestial—like a beast; brutish
bestow—to present (as a gift); to confer
bestride—to mount with one leg on each side
bête noire—something or someone hated or feared
bibliophile—one who loves books
bibulous—inclined to drink alcoholic beverages
biennial—every two years
bigot—an intolerant person
bilious—bad-tempered
billingsgate—vulgar, abusive talk
binate—paired
bivouac—a temporary encampment
bizarre—odd; eccentric
blanch—to make white; to bleach; (a person) to turn white
bland—mild
blandishment—flattery
blasphemy—profanity
blatant—unpleasantly loud
blazon—to make known; to adorn or decorate
bleak—unsheltered; bare
blight—anything that kills, withers, or stunts
blithe—gay
bloated—swollen
bludgeon—a club
bluster—to act in a noisy manner
bode—to foreshadow
boisterous—rowdy

bolster—to support

bombastic—using unnecessarily pompous language

bondage—slavery

boor—a rude person

bootless—useless

bounty—generosity

bourgeois—pertaining to the middle class

bovine—cowlike

bowdlerize—to remove offensive passages (from a book)

braggadocio—a braggart

brandish—to shake or wave (something) in a menacing way

brash—impudent

bravado—a show of bravery

brazen—shameless

breach—a violation

brevity—briefness

brigand—a bandit

broach—to open or introduce

bromidic—dull

bruit—to rumor

brusque—abrupt in manner

bucolic—rural; pastoral

buffoonery—clowning

bullion—gold or silver bars

bulwark—a defense

bumptious—conceited or forward

burgeon—to grow

burlesque—to imitate in order to ridicule

burnish—to polish

buttress—a support

buxom—healthy; plump

C

cabal—a small group of conspirators

cache—a hiding place; hidden things

cacophony—harsh sound

cadaver—a corpse

cadence—rhythm

cadre—a basic structure; a nucleus or framework

caitiff—a mean person

cajole—to coax or wheedle

caliber—quality or value

calk, caulk—to fill cracks or seams

calligraphy—penmanship

callous—unfeeling

callow—immature

calumny—slander

camaraderie—fellowship

canaille—rabble; mob

canard—a false, often malicious report

candor—frankness

canny—shrewd

cant—slang or argot

canvass—to go through for opinions, votes, etc.

capacious—roomy

capitulate—to surrender

capricious—erratic, changeable

captious—quick to find fault

captivate—to fascinate

careen—to lean to the side or from side to side

caricature—an imitation or drawing that exaggerates certain features of the subject

carmine—red

carnage—slaughter

carnal—bodily

carousal—a rowdy drinking party

carp—to make petty complaints

carrion—decaying flesh

carte blanche—a free hand; unlimited authority

castigate—to punish

casualty—a mishap

casuistry—false reasoning

cataclysm—an upheaval

catalyst—an agent or change

catapult—to shoot or launch; to leap

catastrophe—a calamity

categorical—absolute

catholic—universal

causerie—a chat

caustic—corrosive

cauterize—to burn

cavalcade—a procession

caveat—a warning

cavil—to quibble

cede—to give up one's rights to (something); to transfer ownership of

celerity—speed

celestial—heavenly

celibate—unmarried

censure—to blame or criticize

cerebration—thought; thinking

cessation—stopping

cession—the giving up (of something) to another

chafe—to rub for warmth; to irritate

chaff—husks of grain; anything worthless

chagrin—embarrassment

chaotic—totally disorderly

charatan—imposter; quack

charnel—a place where corpses or bones are put

chary—watchful

chaste—pure

chastise—to punish

chattel—personal property

chauvinism—fanatical patriotism or partisanship

checkered—characterized by diverse experiences

chicanery—trickery or deception

chide—to rebuke

chimerical—imaginary

choleric—quick-tempered

chronic—long-lasting or perpetual

chronicle—a historical record arranged in order of time

churlish—rude

circuitous—roundabout

circumlocution—an indirect or lengthy way of saying something

circumscribe—to encircle

circumspect—cautious

circumvent—to surround; to prevent (something) by cleverness

citadel—a fortress

cite—to quote

civility—politeness

clandestine—secret

clarion—clear (sound) like a trumpet

cleave—to split

cleft—a split

clemency—leniency

cliché—an overworked expression

climacteric—a crucial period or event

climactic—pertaining to the climax, or high point

clique—an exclusive group of people

cloister—a monastery or convent

cloy—to satiate

coadjutor—an assistant

coalesce—to unite or merge

codicil—an addition or supplement

coerce—to force

coffer—a strongbox

cogent—forceful

cogitate—to think over

cognate—related

cognizant—aware

cognomen—a name

cohesion—tendency to stick together

cohort—a group or band; an associate

coincident—happening at the same time

collaborate—to work together

collateral—side by side; parallel

collocation—an arrangement

colloquial—conversational; informal (speech)

colloquy—a formal discussion or conference

collusion—conspiracy

colossal—huge

comatose—pertaining to a coma

comely—attractive

comestible—edible

comity—politeness

commensurate—equal in size or measure

comminuted—powdered

commiseration—sympathy or sorrow

commodious—spacious

commutation—an exchange or substitution

compassion—deep sympathy

compatible—able to get along well together

compendious—brief but comprehensive

compile—to gather in an orderly form

complacent—self-satisfied

complaisant—obliging; agreeable

complement—that which completes something

compliant—submissive

component—a part of the whole

comport—to behave or conduct (oneself)

compunction—guilt; remorse

concatenate—linked together; connected

concede—to acknowledge or admit as true

conciliate—to make up with

concise—brief and clear

conclave—a private or secret meeting

conclusive—decisive

concoct—to devise

concomitant—accompanying

concordat—an agreement

concourse—a crowd; a space for crowds to gather

concupiscent—having strong appetites

concurrent—running together or at the same time

condescend—to deal with someone beneath oneself on his own level, sometimes patronizingly

condign—deserved or suitable

condolence—expression of sympathy
condone—to pardon or overlook
conducive—tending or leading
conduit—a pipe or channel for liquids
configuration—an arrangement
confiscate—to seize by authority
conflagration—a large fire
confute—to prove wrong
congeal—to solidify
congenital—existing from birth
conglomerate—a mass or cluster
congruent—corresponding
congruous—suitable, fitting
conjecture—a guess
conjoin—to unite
conjugal—pertaining to marriage
conjure—to produce by magic
connive—to pretend not to see another's wrongdoing; to cooperate or conspire in wrongdoing
connoisseur—one with expert knowledge and taste in an area
connotation—an idea suggested by a word or phrase that is different from the literal meaning of the word or phrase
consanguinity—blood relationship; close relationship
conscript—to draft (as for military service)
consecrate—to dedicate
consensus—general agreement
consign—to hand over; to put in the care of another
consonance—agreement
consort—a spouse, particularly of a king or queen; a traveling companion
consternation—great emotion that leaves one helpless and confused
constituency—the people served by an elected official
constrain—to confine or hold back
constrict—to make smaller by applying pressure; to restrict
construe—to interpret
consummate—to bring to completion; to finish
contaminate—to pollute
contemn—to scorn
contentious—quarrelsome; controversial
context—the words around a particular portion of a speech or passage; surroundings and background

contiguous—touching along one side; adjacent
continence—self-restraint; moderation
contingent—possible; accidental; depending on something else
contortion—a twisting
contraband—smuggled merchandise
contravene—to oppose; to dispute
contrition—remorse or repentance
contrivance—something that is thought up or devised; an invention
controvert—to contradict; to debate
contumacious—insubordinate; disobedient
contumely—humiliating rudeness
contusion—bruise
conundrum—a puzzling question or problem
convene—to assemble
conversant—familiar (with)
conveyance—a vehicle or other means of carrying
convivial—pertaining to festivity; sociable
convoke—to call together
convolution—a twisting together; a twist or coil
copious—plentiful
corollary—a proposition that follows from another that has been proved
corporeal—bodily
corpulent—very fat
correlation—a mutual relationship; a correspondence
corroborate—to confirm
corrosive—capable of eating or wearing away; sarcastic; biting
corsair—a pirate or pirate ship
cortege—a procession
coterie—a clique
countermand—to revoke (an order)
coup d'état—an overthrow of a government
covenant—an agreement
covert—hidden
covetous—envious
cower—to shrink in fear
coy—bashful; reserved; coquettish
cozen—to cheat or deceive
crabbed—ill-tempered
crass—grossly stupid or dull
craven—cowardly
credence—belief
credulous—easily or too easily convinced

creed—a statement of belief, religious or otherwise

crepitate—to crackle

criterion—a standard for judging

crone—a hag

crony—a close companion

crux—a problem; the deciding point

cryptic—hidden

cudgel—a stick or club

culinary—pertaining to the kitchen or cooking

cull—to pick out or select

culmination—the highest point

culpable—blameworthy

cumbersome—burdensome; clumsy

cuneate—wedge-shaped

cupidity—greed

curmudgeon—a bad-tempered person

curry—to try to obtain favor by flattery

cursory—superficial

curtail—to cut short

cynic—a person who believes all actions are motivated by selfishness

D

dais—a platform in a hall or room

dally—to play or trifle; to waste time

dank—damp

dastard—a mean coward

daunt—to intimidate

dauntless—bold

dearth—scarcity

debacle—an overwhelming defeat or failure

debase—to lower in dignity, quality, or value

debauch—to corrupt

debilitate—to weaken

debonair—courteous; gay

decadence—decay

decamp—to break camp; to run away

deciduous—falling off at a certain time or yearly (as leaves from trees)

decimate—to kill a large part of

declivity—a downgrade; a slope

decorous—proper

decoy—a lure or bait

decrepit—weak from age

decry—to speak against publicly

deduce—to reason out logically; to conclude from known facts

de facto—actual

defalcate—to misuse money left in one's care; to embezzle

defamation—slander

default—neglect; failure to do what is required

defection—desertion

deference—regard for another's wishes

defile—to make dirty or pollute; to dishonor

definitive—conclusive; distinguishing

deflect—to turn aside; to deviate

defunct—dead; no longer operating

deign—to condescend

delete—to strike out or erase

deleterious—harmful

delineate—to sketch or design; to portray

delude—to mislead

delusion—a false belief

demagogue—one who stirs people up by emotional appeal in order to gain power

demarcate—to mark the limits of

demean—to degrade

demeanor—bearing or behavior

demise—death

demolition—destruction

demonic—pertaining to a demon or demons

demur—to delay; to object

demure—serious; prim

denizen—an inhabitant

denouement—the outcome or solution of a plot

depict—to portray

depilate—to rid of hair

deplete—to reduce or exhaust

deplore—to lament or feel sorry about

deploy—to station forces or troops in a planned way

depravity—corruption

deprecate—to express disapproval of

depreciate—to lessen in value

depredate—to plunder or despoil

deranged—insane

derelict—abandoned

deride—to mock; to laugh at

derogatory—expressing a low opinion

descant—to discuss at length

descry—to detect (something distant or obscure)

desecrate—to make profane

desiccate—to dry up

desist—to stop

despicable—contemptible

despoil—to strip; to pillage

despotism—tyranny

destitute—lacking; in extreme need of things

desuetude—state of disuse

desultory—aimless; random

deterrent—something that discourages (someone) from an action

detonate—to explode

detraction—belittling the worth of something or someone

detriment—injury; hurt

deviate—to turn aside

devious—winding; going astray

devoid—lacking

devolve—to transfer to another person

devout—pious

dexterous, dextrous—skillful

diabolical—devilish

diadem—a crown

diapason—the entire range of musical sounds

diaphanous—transparent or translucent

diatribe—a bitter denunciation

dichotomy—a division into two parts

dictum—an authoritative statement

didactic—instructive

diffident—unconfident; timid

diffusion—the act of spreading (something) out in all directions

digress—to turn aside or deviate, especially in writing or speaking

dilapidation—a state of disrepair

dilate—to expand

dilatory—tending to delay; tardy

dilemma—a choice of two unsatisfactory alternatives

dilettante—one who involves himself in the arts as a pastime

diligent—hard-working

diminution—a lessening

dint—means

dire—terrible; fatal; extreme

dirge—funereal music

disavowal—a denial

discernible—able to be seen or distinguished

discerning—having good judgment; astute

disclaim—to disown

discomfit—to frustrate the plans of

disconcert—to upset or confuse

disconsolate—sad; dejected

discordant—not harmonious

discountenance—to make ashamed; to discourage

discreet—showing good judgment in conduct; prudent

discrete—separate; not connected

discretion—individual judgment; quality of being discreet

discursive—passing from one subject to another

disdain—to think (someone or something) unworthy

disheveled—messy

disingenuous—insincere

disinterested—not influenced by personal advantage

disjointed—disconnected

disparage—to belittle

disparity—inequality

disperse—to scatter or distribute

disport—to amuse or divert

disputatious—inclined to dispute

disquisition—a formal inquiry; an elaborate essay

dissemble—to disguise or pretend

disseminate—to scatter

dissimulate—to dissemble; to pretend

dissident—not agreeing

dissipate—to scatter or disperse

dissolute—loose in morals

dissonance—discord

dissaude—to advise against; to divert by persuasion

distend—to expand

distrait—absent-minded; preoccupied

distraught—troubled; confused; harassed

diurnal—daily

diverge—to extend from one point in separate directions

diverse—differing; various

divest—to strip or deprive

divination—the act of foreseeing or foretelling

divulge—to reveal

docile—easy to teach or discipline

doff—to take off

doggerel—poorly written verse

dogma—a belief or doctrine; a positive statement of opinion

dogmatic—positive in manner or in what one says

doldrums—low spirits

dolorous—sorrowful

dolt—a stupid fellow

domicile—a home

dormant—sleeping; inactive

dorsal—pertaining to the back

dossier—collected documents on a person

dotage—senility

doughty—valiant

dour—stern; sullen

dregs—sediment; the most worthless part of something

drivel—silly talk

droll—amusing and strange

dross—waste or refuse

drudgery—tiresome work

dubious—doubtful

ductile—able to be drawn or hammered thin without breaking

dulcet—sweet-sounding

duplicity—deception; double-dealing

durance—imprisonment

duress—compulsion; forcible restraint

E

ebullient—enthusiastic

eccentricity—oddity

éclat—brilliant success; acclaim

eclectic—made up of material collected from many sources

ecumenical—universal; intended to bring together the Christian churches

edict—a decree

edifice—a (usually large) building

edify—to instruct and improve

educe—to elicit or draw forth

efface—to rub out

effectual—efficient

effervesce—to bubble; to be lively or boisterous

effete—exhausted; worn out

efficacy—power to have effect

effigy—an image or figure that represents a disliked person

effluence—a flowing forth

effrontery—shameless boldness

effulgent—radiant

effusive—pouring out; gushing

egotism—constant reference to oneself

egregious—flagrant

egress—emergence; exit

elation—high spirits

eleemosynary—pertaining to charity

elegy—a poem, particularly a lament for the dead

elicit—to draw out

elucidate—to explain; to throw light on

elusive—hard to grasp

emaciated—very thin

emanate—to flow forth

embellish—to ornament or beautify

embody—to give bodily form to; to make concrete

embroil—to confuse by discord; to involve in confusion

embryonic—undeveloped

emend—to correct

eminent—lofty; distinguished

emollient—something that soothes or softens (the body)

emolument—one's fees or salary

empirical—based on observation or experience

empyreal—heavenly

emulate—to imitate with the hope of equaling or surpassing

enclave—an area enclosed inside a foreign territory

encomium—high praise

encompass—to encircle; to contain

encroach—to trespass

encumber—to impede or burden

endemic—native to a particular area

endue—to invest or endow

enervate—to weaken

engender—to cause or produce

engrossed—absorbed; fully occupied

engulf—to swallow up or overwhelm

enhance—to make greater; to heighten

enigma—a puzzle

enjoin—to order; to prohibit

ennui—boredom

enormity—great wickedness

ensconce—to shelter; to settle comfortably

ensue—to follow right after

enthrall—to captivate

entity—a being or thing

entourage—a group of associates or attendants

entreaty—a serious request

entrepreneur—a man of business

envenom—to make poisonous; to embitter

environs—surroundings; vicinity

ephemeral—short-lived

epicure—a connoisseur of food and drink

epigram—a short, pointed poem or saying

epistle—a long, formal letter

epithet—a descriptive phrase; an uncomplimentary name

epitome—an abstract; a part that represents the whole

epoch—a period of time

equable—uniform; tranquil

equanimity—even temper

equestrian—pertaining to horses

equilibrium—a state of balance between various forces or factors

equity—fairness

equivocal—ambiguous; doubtful

equivocate—to deceive; to lie

erode—to eat away

errant—wandering

erudite—scholarly

escarpment—a steep slope

eschew—to avoid

esculent—edible

esoteric—for a limited, specially initiated group

esprit de corps—group spirit

espouse—to marry; to advocate (a cause)

estimable—worthy of respect or esteem

estival—pertaining to summer

estranged—separated

ethereal—celestial; spiritual

ethnic—pertaining to races or cultures

eugenic—pertaining to the bearing of genetically healthy offspring

eulogy—high praise

euphemism—an inoffensive expression substituted for an unpleasant one

euphoria—a feeling of well-being

euthanasia—painless death

evanescent—fleeting

evasive—not frank or straightforward

evince—to make evident; to display

eviscerate—to disembowel

evoke—to call forth

evolve—to develop gradually; to unfold

exacerbate—to make more intense; to aggravate

exact—to call for; to require

exasperate—to vex

excise—to cut away

excoriate—to strip of skin; to denounce harshly

exculpate—to free from blame

execrable—detestable

exemplary—serving as a good example

exhort—to urge

exigency—an emergency

exiguous—meager

exonerate—to acquit

exorbitant—excessive; extravagant

exorcise—to drive out (an evil spirit)

expatiate—to talk freely and at length

expedite—to speed up or make easy

expedient—advantageous

expeditious—efficient and quick

expiate—to atone for

expound—to set forth

expunge—to blot out; to erase

expurgate—to rid (a book) of offensive material

extant—in existence

extemporaneous—not planned

extenuate—to make thin; to diminish

extirpate—to pluck out

extol—to praise

extort—to take from a person by force

extradition—the surrender by one state to another of an alleged criminal

extraneous—not essential

extricate—to free

extrinsic—unessential; extraneous

extrovert—one whose interest is directed outside himself

extrude—to force or push out

exuberant—profuse; effusive

exude—to discharge or ooze; to radiate; to diffuse

F

fabricate—to build; to lie

façade—the front of a building

facet—a small plane of a gem; an aspect

facetious—humorous; joking

facile—easy; expert

facilitate—to make easier

faction—a clique or party

factious—producing or tending to dissension

factitious—artificial

factotum—an employee with many duties

faculty—an ability; a sense

fain—gladly

fallacious—misleading; containing a fallacy

fallible—capable of error

fallow—(land) left unplanted during a growing season

falter—to move unsteadily; to stumble or stammer

fanaticism—excessive enthusiasm

fastidious—hard to please; easy to offend

fatalism—the belief that all events are ruled by fate

fatuous—foolish

fauna—animal life

faux pas—an error in social behavior

fawn—to seek favor by demeaning oneself

fealty—loyalty

feasible—practical

feckless—weak; careless

feculent—filthy; foul

fecundity—fertility; productiveness

feign—to pretend

feint—a move intended to throw one's opponent off guard

felicitous—apt; happy in expression

fell—cruel; fierce

felonious—wicked

ferment—a state of unrest

ferret—to search out

fervent, fervid—hot; ardent

fete—a lavish entertainment, often in someone's honor

fetid—stinking

fetish—an object supposed to have magical power; any object of special devotion

fetter—to shackle or restrain

fettle—state of the body and mind

fiasco—a complete failure

fiat—a command

fickle—changeable

fidelity—faithfulness

fiduciary—pertaining to one who holds something in trust for another

figment—an invention; a fiction

filch—to steal

filial—pertaining to a son or daughter

finale—a conclusion

finesse—skill; cunning

finite—limited

fissure—a narrow opening or cleft

flaccid—flabby

flag—to droop or lose vigor

flagellate—to whip or flog

flagitious—wicked and vile

flagrant—glaring (as an error)

flail—to beat

flamboyant—ornate; showy

flatulent—gas-producing; windy in speech

flaunt—to show off; to display

flay—to skin; to pillage; to censure harshly

fledgling—a young bird that has his feathers; an immature person

flippant—pert

florid—flowery; ornate

flotsam—ship wreckage floating on the sea; drifting persons or things

flout—to reject

fluctuate—to waver

fluent—fluid; easy with words

flux—a moving; a flowing

foible—a failing or weakness

foist—to pass off fraudulently

foment—to stir up

foppish—like a dandy

foray—a raid

forbearance—patience

foreboding—a feeling of coming evil

formidable—threatening

forswear—to renounce

forte—strong point

fortitude—strength; courage

fortuitous—accidental

foster—to rear; to promote

fractious—unruly

fraught—filled

fray—a commotion or fight

freebooter—a plunderer; a pirate

frenetic—frantic; frenzied

frenzy—violent emotional excitement

fresco—a painting done on fresh plaster

freshet—a stream or rush of water

frigid—very cold

fritter—to waste

frivolous—of little importance or value; trivial

froward—obstinate

fructify—to bear fruit

frugal—thrifty

fruition—use or realization; enjoyment

frustrate—to counteract; to prevent from achieving something

fulminate—to explode suddenly; to thunder forth verbally

fulsome—offensive, particularly because of insincerity

funereal—appropriate to funerals

furor—a fury or frenzy

furtive—stealthy

fusion—union

futile—useless

G

gadfly—a fly that attacks livestock; a person who annoys people or moves them to action

gainsay—to deny

gambol—to skip and frolic

gamut—the whole range

gape—to open wide

Gargantuan—gigantic

garish—gaudy

garner—to gather or store

garnish—to decorate

garrulous—talkative

gasconade—boastful talk

gelid—icy; frozen

generality—a broad, vague statement

generic—pertaining to a whole class, kind, or group

genial—favorable to growth; kindly

genre—a kind or category

gentility—of the upper classes; having taste and refinement

gentry—people of education and good birth

germane—relevant and pertinent to the case at hand

germinal—in the first stage of growth

gesticulation—gesture

ghastly—horrible

gibbet—gallows

gibe—to scoff at; to deride

gist—the main point in a debate or question

glaucous—bluish- or yellowish-green

glean—to gather what has been left in a field after reaping; to pick up, little by little

glib—fluent

gloaming—dusk

gloat—to look at with evil satisfaction or greed

glut—to overfill

glutinous—gluey

gluttony—excess in eating

gnarled—twisted

gnomic—wise and pithy

goad—to urge; to drive

gorge—to stuff

gouge—to scoop out; to tear out

gradation—arrangement by grades or steps

gradient—a slope; the degree of a slope

graphic—vivid; pertaining to writing

granary—a storehouse for grain

grandiloquent—using pompous language

grandiose—imposing; splendid

gratis—free

gratuitous—given freely; unwarranted

gregarious—tending to flock together

grimace—an expression that twists the face

grotesque—distorted; bizarre; absurd

grotto—a cave

grovel—to lie prone; to act humble or abject

grueling—punishing

gudgeon—a person who is easy to trick

guerdon—a reward

guile—deceit

guileless—innocent

gullible—easily tricked

gustatory—pertaining to tasting

gusto—liking; great appreciation or relish

guttural—pertaining to the throat

H

habiliments—clothing; equipment

habitable—able or fit to be lived in

hackneyed—trite

haggard—unruly; looking worn and wasted from exertion or emotion

haggle—to bargain

halcyon—peaceful

hale—healthy and sound

hallucination—a perception of something imaginary

hamper—to obstruct or hinder

haphazard—random

hapless—unlucky

harangue—a long speech; a tirade

harass—to worry or torment

harbinger—a forerunner

harp—to persist in talking or writing (about something)

harridan—a shrewish old woman

harrow—to rob or plunder

harry—to raid; to torment or worry

haughty—showing scorn for others; proud

hauteur—haughtiness

hawser—a large rope or cable for mooring or anchoring a ship

hector—to bully

hedonism—the pursuit of pleasure as the primary goal of life

heedless—careless; unmindful

hegemony—leadership; dominance

heinous—abominable

herbaceous—pertaining to herbs or leaves

herculean—of great size, strength, or courage

heresy—a religious belief opposed by the church

heterodox—unorthodox; inclining toward heresy

heterogeneous—dissimilar; varied

hiatus—a gap or break

hibernal—pertaining to winter

hierarchy—an arrangement in order of rank

hieratic—priestly

hieroglyphic—written in symbols; hard to read or understand

hilarity—mirth

hinder—to restrain or hold back

hirsute—hairy

histrionic—theatrical

hoary—white; white-haired

holocaust—destruction by fire

homage—allegiance or honor

homicide—the killing of one person by another

homily—a long, dull sermon

homogeneous—similar; uniform

hone—to sharpen

hortatory—encouraging; giving advice

horticulture—the growing of plants

hybrid—of mixed or unlike parts

hydrous—containing water

hyperbole—exaggeration

hypercritical—too critical

hypochondriac—one who constantly believes he is ill

hypocritical—pretending to be what one is not

hypothetical—assumed; supposed

I

iconoclast—one who attacks traditional ideas

ideology—a body of ideas

idiom—a language or dialect; a particular phrasing that is accepted in use, although its meaning may be different from the literal meaning of the words

idiosyncrasy—a personal pecularity

idolatry—worship

idyll—a poem based on a simple scene

igneous—pertaining to or produced by fire

ignoble—dishonorable; base

ignominious—shameful; degrading

illicit—unlawful; prohibited

illusory—unreal; deceptive

imbibe—to drink, drink in, or absorb

imbroglio—a confusion; a misunderstanding

imbue—to color; to inspire (with ideas)

immaculate—spotless; clean

immanent—existing within

imminent—about to happen

immolate—to sacrifice

immutable—unchangeable

impair—to make worse or weaker; to reduce

impale—to fix on a pointed object

impalpable—not capable of being felt; not capable of being grasped by the mind

impasse—a situation with no escape or solution

impassive—not feeling pain; calm

impeccable—faultless

impecunious—poor; penniless

impede—to obstruct or delay

impending—about to happen

impenitent—without regret

imperious—domineering

impermeable—unable to be penetrated

impertinent—irrelevant; impudent

imperturbable—unable to be disturbed; impassive

impervious—impenetrable; not affected (by something)

impetuous—rushing; rash or impulsive

impetus—a force; a driving force

impiety—lack of reverence (for God or parents)

implacable—incapable of being pacified

implicate—to involve; to imply

implicit—implied; absolute

impolitic—unwise

import—meaning; significance

importune—to urge persistently

impotent—weak; powerless

imprecate—to pray for (evil)

impregnable—unable to be conquered or entered

impresario—a manager in the performing arts

impromptu—offhand

impropriety—being improper

improvident—not providing for the future

impugn—to oppose or challenge

impunity—freedom from punishment or harm

impute—to charge another (with a negative trait)

inadvertent—heedless; unintentional

inane—empty; foolish

inarticulate—unable to speak understandably or at all

incantation—a chant supposed to work magic

incapacitate—to disable

incarcerate—to imprison

incendiary—pertaining to destruction by fire

inception—beginning

incessant—never-ending

inchoate—just begun; incipient

incipient—in the first stage of existence

incisive—keen, sharp

inclement—stormy; harsh

incognito—disguised

incongruous—incompatible; inappropriate

inconsequential—unimportant

incontrovertible—undeniable

incorrigible—unreformable

increment—increase; the amount of increase

incriminate—to accuse of a crime; to involve in a crime

incubus—a nightmare; an oppressive burden

inculcate—to instill

inculpate—to incriminate

incursion—an inroad; a brief raid

indefatigable—untiring

indemnify—to insure; to reimburse

indict—to charge formally with

indigenous—growing or living in a particular area

indite—to compose and write

indolent—lazy; idle

indomitable—hard to discourage or defeat

indubitable—unquestionable

indulgent—giving in to one's own desires; kind or lenient

indurate—hardened

ineffable—inexpressible

ineluctable—unavoidable

inept—unfit; clumsy

inert—powerless to move; slow

inexorable—unrelenting; unalterable

infallible—incapable of error

infamous—notorious

inference—something that is drawn as a conclusion

infernal—pertaining to hell; diabolical

infidel—one who doesn't believe in a particular doctrine or religion

infinite—limitless; vast

infirmity—weakness

influx—a flowing in

infringe—to violate

ingenious—having genius; clever; original

ingenuous—candid; frank

ingrate—an ungrateful person

ingratiate—to win another's favor by efforts

inherent—innate; characteristic

inhibit—to hold back or repress

inimical—hostile; in opposition

iniquitous—wicked

injunction—a command; an order enjoining, or prohibiting, (someone) from doing something

innate—existing in someone from birth or in something by its nature

innocuous—harmless; noncontroversial

innuendo—an indirect remark or reference

inordinate—unregulated; immoderate

inscrutable—obscure; not easily understood

insensate—not feeling; inanimate; insensitive

insidious—crafty

insinuate—to work gradually into a state; to hint

insipid—tasteless; dull

insolent—impudent; disrespectful

insolvent—bankrupt; unable to pay debts

insouciant—carefree; indifferent

instigate—to urge on to some action; to incite

insular—like an island; isolated; narrow-minded

insuperable—unable to be overcome

insurgent—a person who rises up against (political) authority

intangible—unable to be touched; impalpable

integrity—wholeness; soundness; honesty

intelligentsia—intellectuals as a group

inter—to bury

interdict—to prohibit; to restrain or impede

interim—meantime

interjection—something thrown in or interrupted with; an exclamation

intermittent—periodic; starting and stopping

internecine—mutually harmful or destructive

interpolate—to insert

interregnum—a break, as between governments or regimes

intestate—without a (legal) will to distribute one's property after death

intimate—to hint

intractable—unruly or stubborn

intransigent—refusing to agree or compromise

intrepid—fearless

intrinsic—inherent; of the nature of a thing

introvert—a person who looks inside himself more than outside

intuition—immediate understanding

inundate—to flood

inured—habituated (to something unpleasant)

invective—a violent verbal attack

inveigh—to talk or write strongly (against)

inveigle—to trick or entice

inverse—opposite

investiture—the giving of office to someone

inveterate—of long standing

invidious—offensive

inviolable—not to be violated; unable to be violated

invulnerable—unable to be injured or wounded

iota—a tiny amount

irascible—quick-tempered

irksome—tiresome; annoying

irony—humor in which one says the opposite of what he means; an occurrence that is the opposite of what is expected

irremediable—incurable or irreparable

irrevocable—unable to be called back or undone

iterate—to repeat

itinerant—traveling

J

jaded—tired; satiated

jargon—incoherent speech; a mixed language; the particular vocabulary of one group

jaundiced—yellow; prejudiced

jeopardy—peril

jettison—to throw overboard

jetty—a wall built out into the water

jocose—humorous

jocular—joking

jocund—cheerful

journeyman—a worker who has learned a trade

judicious—wise

juggernaut—any extremely strong and irresistible force

juncture—a point of joining; a critical point in the development of events

junket—a feast or picnic; a pleasure excursion

junta—men engaged in political intrigue

juxtapose—to place side by side

K

ken—understanding

kinetic—pertaining to motion

kith—friends

knavery—dishonesty; deceit

knell—to ring solemnly

knoll—a small hill

L

labyrinth—a maze

lacerate—to tear or mangle

lachrymose—tearful

lackadaisical—spiritless; listless

laconic—brief; using few words

lacuna—a gap where something is missing

laggard—one who is slow

laity—all the people who are not clergy

lambent—flickering; glowing

lampoon—to attack or ridicule

languid—weak; listless

languish—to lose vigor; to droop

larceny—theft

largess, largesse—generosity

lascivious—lewd; lustful

lassitude—weariness

latent—hidden or undeveloped

lateral—pertaining to the side or sides
latitude—freedom to act
laudatory—praising
leaven—to spread something throughout something else to bring about a gradual change
lecherous—lustful
legerdemain—trickery
lesion—an injury
lethal—deadly
lethargic—dull; sluggish
levity—gaiety
liaison—a linking up
libel—false printed material intended to harm a person's reputation
libertine—one who lives a morally unrestrained life
libidinous—lustful; lewd
licentious—morally unrestrained
liege—a name for a feudal lord or his subject
lieu—place (in lieu of)
limn—to paint or draw; to describe in words
limpid—clear
literal—word-for-word; actual
lithe—flexible; limber
litigation—carrying out a lawsuit
littoral—pertaining to the shore or coast
livid—black-and-blue; lead-colored
loath—reluctant
loathe—to detest
locution—a word or phrase; a style of speech
logistics—the part of military science having to do with obtaining and moving men and materials
longevity—long life
loquacious—talkative
lout—a stupid person
lubricity—smoothness; trickiness
lucent—shining; giving off light
lucid—transparent; clear
lucrative—profitable
lucre—money
ludicrous—absurd
lugubrious—mournful
luminary—a body that sheds light; a person who enlightens; any famous person
lurid—sensational
lustrous—shining
luxuriant—lush; rich

M

macabre—gruesome; horrible
macerate—to soften by soaking; to break or tear into small pieces
Machiavellian—crafty and deceitful
machination—a secret plot or scheme
magnanimous—generous; not petty
magnate—an important person, often in a business
magniloquent—lofty or pompous
maim—to disable or mutilate (a person)
maladroit—clumsy
malaise—a vague feeling of illness
malcontent—discontented
malediction—a curse
malefactor—one who does evil
malevolent—wishing ill to others
malfeasance—a wrongdoing
malicious—spiteful
malign—to slander
malignant—evil; harmful
malinger—to pretend to be ill to avoid doing something
malleable—able to be hammered; pliable
mammoth—enormous
mandate—an official order or command
mandatory—required
maniacal—insane; raving
manifest—apparent or evident
manipulate—to work with the hands; to control by unfair means
manumission—liberation from slavery
marauder—a raider
maritime—pertaining to the sea
martial—pertaining to war or the military; warlike
martinet—a strict disciplinarian
masochist—one who enjoys suffering
masticate—to chew up
maternal—pertaining to a mother or motherhood
matrix—a die or mold
maudlin—foolishly sentimental
maunder—to act dreamily or vaguely
mauve—purple
maverick—one who refuses to go along with his group
mawkish—sickeningly sweet
maxim—a principle or truth precisely stated; a saying
mayhem—maiming another person; violence or destruction
meander—to wind or wander

mecca—a place where many people visit

mediate—to help two opposing sides come to agreement

mediocre—ordinary; average

mélange—a mixture

melee—a noisy fight among a lot of people

meliorate—to improve

mellifluous—sweet and smooth

mendacious—lying

mendicant—a beggar

menial—pertaining to servants; servile

mentor—a wise advisor or teacher

mercantile—pertaining to merchants or trade

mercenary—motivated by money; greedy

mercurial—like mercury; quick; changeable

meretricious—superficially alluring

mesa—a high, flat land with steep sides

metamorphosis—a change or transformation

metaphysical—pertaining to the nature of being or reality

mete—to distribute

meticulous—very careful about details

mettle—quality of character, especially good character

miasma—a vapor rising from a swamp; an unwholesome atmosphere

mien—manner or bearing

migrant—a person or an animal that moves from place to place

militate—to work (against)

mimetic—imitative

mimic—to imitate

minatory—threatening

mincing—acting overly dainty or elegant

minion—a favorite (follower); a subordinate

ministration—the carrying out of a minister's duties; service

minutiae—minor details

misadventure—a bit of bad luck

misanthrope—one who dislikes other people

misapprehension—misunderstanding

miscegenation—marriage between a man and a woman of different races

miscellany—a collection of varied things

misconstrue—to misinterpret

miscreant—an evil person

misdemeanor—a minor offense

misgiving—a doubt or fear

mishap—an unfortunate accident

misnomer—the wrong name applied to something

misogynist—one who hates women

mitigate—to make less painful

mnemonic—helping the memory

mobile—capable of moving or being moved

mode—a manner or style

modicum—a bit

modish—in style

modulate—to adjust or regulate

moiety—a share

mollify—to pacify

molt—to shed skin or other outer parts

molten—melted

momentous—very important

monetary—pertaining to money

monolith—a large piece of stone

moot—debatable

morbid—pertaining to disease; gruesome

mordant—biting; sarcastic

mores—ways or customs that are quite important to a culture

moribund—dying

morose—gloomy

mortify—to punish (oneself) by self-denial; to make (someone) feel ashamed

mote—a speck

motif—a main feature or theme

motility—ability to move by itself

motley—of many colors; made up of many unlike parts

mountebank—a quack

mufti—civilian clothes

mulct—to fine; to get money from someone by deceit

multiplicity—a great number (of various things)

mundane—worldly; commonplace

munificent—generous; lavish

muse—to ponder

mutable—changeable

mute—silent

mutilate—to damage by cutting off or injuring vital parts

mutinous—inclined to rebel or revolt

myopia—nearsightedness

myriad—a great number

N

nadir—the lowest point

naiad—a water nymph; a female swimmer

naiveté—simplicity; lack of sophistication

narcissism—love for and interest in the self

nascent—being born; starting to develop

natal—pertaining to one's birth

nauseous—sickening

nebulous—vague; indefinite

necromancy—black magic

nefarious—wicked

negation—denial; the absence of a positive quality

negligible—so unimportant that it can be neglected

nemesis—fair punishment; something that seems to defeat a person constantly

neolithic—pertaining to the Stone Age

neophyte—a beginner

nepotism—special consideration to relatives, particularly in assignment to offices or positions

nettle—to sting; to irritate or annoy

neurosis—a mental disorder

nexus—a connection

nicety—exactness and delicacy

niggardly—stingy

nihilist—one who believes there is no basis for knowledge; one who rejects common religious beliefs

nocturnal—pertaining to night

noisome—harmful; offensive

nomadic—moving from place to place

nomenclature—a system for naming

nominal—pertaining to names; slight

nonchalant—cool; indifferent

noncommittal—not aligning oneself with any side or point of view

nondescript—having few distinguishing qualities; hard to classify

nonentity—something that exists only in the mind; something or someone of little importance

nonpareil—without equal

nonplus—to perplex

non sequitur—something that does not follow logically from what went before

nostalgia—homesickness

notorious—well-known (often unfavorably)

novice—a beginner

noxious—harmful; unwholesome

nuance—a slight variation of color, tone, etc.

nugatory—worthless

nullify—to make invalid or useless

nurture—to feed and/or raise (a child)

nutrient—a food

O

oaf—a clumsy, stupid person

obdurate—hardhearted; hardened; inflexible

obeisance—a motion of reverence

obese—very fat

obfuscate—to make unclear; to confuse

objurgate—to rebuke

oblation—an offering

oblique—slanting; indirect

obliquity—the state of being oblique

obliterate—to wipe out

oblivion—forgetfulness

obloquy—verbal abuse or the disgrace that results from it

obnoxious—offensive

obscure—dim; unclear

obsequious—too servile or submissive

obsession—an idea that persists in the mind

obsolete—out-of-date; no longer used

obstreperous—unruly

obtrude—to push out

obtrusive—pushy in calling attention to oneself

obtuse—blunt; dull

obviate—to make unnecessary

occlude—to close; to shut in or out

occult—hidden; secret; mysterious

odious—offensive

odoriferous—having a (pleasant) odor

odyssey—a long journey

officious—providing help that is not wanted

ogle—to look at openly and with desire

oleaginous—oily

olfactory—pertaining to the sense of smell

oligarchy—a state ruled by a few persons

ominous—threatening

omnipotent—all-powerful

omniscient—all-knowing

omnivorous—eating both animals and vegetables

onerous—burdensome

onslaught—an attack

opaque—letting no light through

opiate—a medicine or anything else that quiets and deadens

opportune—at the right time

opprobrium—disgrace

optimum—best

opulence—wealth; abundance

oracular—wise; prophetic

ordure—filth

orifice—a mouth or opening

ornate—heavily decorated; showy

ornithologist—one who studies birds

orthodox—holding the accepted beliefs of a particular group

oscillate—to move back and forth

osculate—to kiss

ossify—to harden into bone; to settle into a habit

ostensible—apparent

ostentatious—showy; pretentious

ostracize—to banish or exclude

overt—open; observable

overweening—extremely proud

P

pacifist—one who opposes war

paean—a song of joy or praise

palatable—suitable for eating

palatial—like a palace

palaver—idle talk

pall—to become boring or otherwise bothersome

palliate—to lessen or ease (pain); to excuse

pallid—pale

palpable—able to be felt or to be grasped by the senses

paltry—insignificant

panacea—a cure-all

pander—to cater to another's unworthy desires, especially sexual

panegyric—a formal tribute

panoply—a suit of armor; a protective or showy covering

paradigm—an example or model

paradox—a statement that appears false but may be true; a statement that contradicts itself and is false

paragon—a model of perfection

paramount—chief; dominant

paranoia—a state in which one believes that others are against him or that he is a great or famous person

paraphernalia—personal possessions; equipment or gear

parasite—one who lives off another without giving anything in return

paregoric—a medicine

pariah—an outcast

parity—equality

parlance—a manner of speaking or writing

paroxysm—an attack or convulsion

parricide—the killing of a parent

parry—to ward off (a blow); to evade

parsimony—stinginess

partiality—bias; prejudice

parvenu—one who has risen in wealth or power quickly

passive—yielding; nonresisting

pastoral—pertaining to shepherds or rural life in general

patent—obvious

pathetic—pitiful

pathos—a feeling of pity or sorrow

patriarch—a father and ruler

patricide—the killing of one's father

patrimony—an inheritance

paucity—scarcity

pecadillo—a minor fault

peculate—to embezzle

pecuniary—pertaining to money

pedagogue—a teacher, often a narrow-minded one

pedantic—narrow-minded in teaching

pedestrian—ordinary and uninteresting

pejorative—derogatory

pellucid—clear; easy to understand

penance—voluntary self-punishment

penchant—a taste or liking

pendant—something that hangs

pendent—hanging

penitent—sorry or ashamed

pensive—thoughtful

penurious—stingy; poverty-stricken

penury—poverty

percussion—the impact of one thing against another

perdition—damnation; hell

peregrinations—travels

peremptory—final; undeniable or unopposable; dictatorial

perennial—lasting all through the year; lasting a long time

perfidious—treacherous

perforce—necessarily

perfunctory—without care; superficial

perigee—the point nearest the earth in an orbit

peripatetic—moving or walking about

periphery—the boundary of something; the perimeter

perjury—telling a lie under oath

permeable—able to be passed through

permeate—to pass through; to spread through

permutation—a complete change

pernicious—deadly

perpetrate—to do (something bad)

perpetual—eternal

perquisite—a benefit in addition to one's regular pay; prerogative

persiflage—a light style of talking; banter

perspective—the appearance of things caused by their positions and distances; a way of seeing things in their true relation to each other

perspicacious—keen; acute in judgment

pertinacious—persistent

pertinent—relevant

perturb—to upset or alarm

peruse—to study; to read casually

pervade—to spread throughout

perverse—wrong or corrupt; perverted; stubborn

perversion—an abnormal form; a twisting or distortion

pervious—able to be passed through or penetrated; open-minded

pessimist—one who looks on the dark side and expects the worst

pestilence—an epidemic; anything harmful

petrify—to turn to stone; to harden; to stun with fear

petulant—pert; irritable

phalanx—military ranks in close formation; a group of individuals

philander—to carry on light love affairs

philanthropist—one who gives money to help others

philistine—a narrow and conventional person who ignores the arts and culture

phlegmatic—sluggish; calm

phobia—an irrational, unwarranted fear (of something)

physiognomy—one's face and facial expressions

pied—spotted

piety—faithfulness to religious duties; devotion to family

pillage—to loot or plunder

pinion—to cut or tie a bird's wings to keep it from flying; to bind a man's arms; to shackle

pious—devout

piquant—sharp or biting to the taste; stimulating

pique—to offend or provoke

pithy—meaningful; concise

pittance—a meager amount

placate—to pacify

placid—calm; quiet

plaintive—mournful

plait—to pleat or braid

platitude—a dull or commonplace remark

platonic—intellectual or spiritual but not sexual (relationship)

plaudit—applause; an expression of approval

plausible—apparently true

plebeian—a common man

plebiscite—a vote by the people on a political issue

plenary—full; complete

plenipotentiary—a man who has full power as a governmental representative

plethora—excess

plutocracy—government by the wealthy

poach—to trespass; to steal

pogrom—a systematic persecution or killing of a group

poignant—sharply affecting the senses or feelings

politic—prudent; crafty

poltroon—a coward

polygamy—having more than one husband or wife

polyglot—speaking or writing several languages

pommel—the knob on the end of a sword or on a saddle

pompous—stately; self-important

ponder—to consider carefully

portend—to foreshadow

portent—an omen

posit—to place in position; to set forth as fact

posterity—all future generations

portly—stout

posthumous—born after one's father is dead; published after the writer's death; happening after death

postprandial—after-dinner

potable—drinkable

potentate—a ruler

potential—possible; latent

potpourri—a collection of varied things

poultice—a hot, soft mass, sometimes put on sore parts of the body

practicable—feasible; usable

pragmatic—practical; dealing with daily matters

prate—to chatter

precarious—uncertain; risky

precedent—a legal occurrence that is an example for future ones

precept—a rule of conduct

precipitate—to throw downward; to bring on

precipitous—like a precipice; abrupt

preclude—to make impossible; to prevent

precocious—developing earlier than usual

precursor—a forerunner

predatory—living by robbing or exploiting others; feeding on other animals

predicate—to state as a quality of someone or something; to affirm

predilection—a preference

predispose—to make receptive

preeminent—better than others in a particular quality

prefatory—introductory

prelude—opening

premeditate—to think out ahead of time

premise—a statement on which an argument is based

premonition—a forewarning; a foreboding

preponderate—to sink downward; to predominate

preposterous—absurd

prerogative—a right or privilege

presage—to warn; to predict

prescience—foreknowledge

presentiment—a premonition or foreboding

presumption—taking something upon oneself without permission; forwardness

pretentious—claiming greatness; showing off

preternatural—abnormal; supernatural

prevaricate—to avoid the truth; to lie

primordial—existing from the beginning; original

pristine—in original condition; pure and unspoiled

privy (to)—told about (something) in secret

probity—honesty

proboscis—a long snout; a nose

proclivity—a slope; a tendency

procrastinate—to delay or postpone

prodigal—wasteful; generous

prodigious—wonderful; huge

profane—nonreligious; irreverent

proffer—to offer

proficient—skilled

profligate—immoral; wasteful

profound—very deep

profusion—a great abundance

progenitor—a forefather

progeny—children or descendants

prognosis—a forecast

proletarian—a worker

prolific—producing a lot (of children, fruit, or ideas)

prolix—wordy; long-winded

promiscuous—containing many various elements; engaging in indiscriminate sexual affairs

promontory—a headland

promulgate—to make known

prone—lying face downward; disposed (to do something)

propagate—to breed or reproduce

propensity—a natural tendency

propinquity—nearness; kinship

propitiate—to appease

propitious—gracious; boding well; advantageous

proponent—one who puts forth an idea

propound—to propose

propriety—suitability

prosaic—commonplace

proscribe—to outlaw or forbid

prosody—the study or the art of verse or versification

prostrate—lying face downward; overcome

protégé—one who is helped in his career by another

protocol—a document outlining points of agreement; a system of proper conduct in diplomatic encounters

prototype—a model

protract—to prolong

protrude—to stick out

protuberant—sticking out

provident—providing for future needs

proviso—a condition (that one must meet)

provoke—to excite; to anger

prowess—boldness; skill

proximity—nearness

proxy—a person who acts for another

prudent—careful; wise

puerile—childish

pugnacious—quarrelsome

puissant—powerful

pulchritude—beauty

pulmonary—pertaining to the lungs

punctilious—careful about detail; exact

pungent—sharp; biting

punitive—pertaining to punishment

purloin—to steal

purport—to claim

purveyor—one who supplies

purview—scope; range

pusillanimous—timid; uncourageous

putative—reputed

putrid—rotten; stinking

Q

quack—one who practices medicine without training; a charlatan

quaff—to drink

quagmire—a bog; a difficult situation

quail—to lose courage

qualm—a sudden ill feeling; a sudden misgiving

quandary—a dilemma

queasy—nauseous; uneasy

quell—to subdue; to quiet

querulous—complaining

query—a question

quibble—to object to something for petty reasons

quiescent—inactive

quietude—quiet; rest

quintessence—the most perfect example

quip—a witty remark

quirk—a twist (as of luck); an evasion; a peculiarity

quixotic—like Don Quixote; romantic and idealistic

quizzical—comical; teasing; questioning

R

rabble—a mob; the masses

rabid—violent; fanatical

raillery—satire; teasing

raiment—clothing

ramification—a branching; a consequence or result of something

rampant—growing or spreading richly; wild and uncontrollable in behavior

rancid—spoiled, as stale fat

rancor—hate

rankle—to provoke anger or rancor

rant—to rave

rapacious—greedy; predatory

rapine—taking away people's property by force; plunder

rapprochement—a bringing together

rarefied—thin; refined

ratiocination—reasoning

rationalize—to explain rationally; to find motives for one's behavior that are not the true ones

raucous—loud and rowdy

ravage—to ruin

ravening—look greedily for prey

ravenous—extremely hungry

rebate—to return (part of money paid); to deduct (from a bill)

rebuke—to scold sharply

recalcitrant—stubborn; hard to handle

recant—to take back (a belief or statement)

recapitulate—to summarize

recidivist—one who falls back into crime or other bad behavior; a repeater

reciprocal—done in return; occurring on both sides

recluse—one who lives apart from others

reconcile—to bring together again; to make consistent

recondite—not understandable by most people; obscure

reconnaissance—looking over a situation to get information

recourse—turning to (someone or something) for help

recreant—cowardly; disloyal

recrimination—answering an attack by attacking in return

rectify—to make right

rectitude—moral uprightness

recumbent—lying down; resting

recurrent—happening again one or more times

redeem—to get back; to save from sin; to make (oneself) worthy again by making amends

redolent—sweet-smelling

redoubtable—fearful

redress—to rectify

redundant—more than enough; wordy

refection—refreshment

refraction—the bending of a light ray or sound wave

refractory—stubborn

refulgent—shining

refutation—disproof

regale—to entertain with a feast

regeneration—renewal; rebirth

regime—a system or period of government

regimen—a system of diet and other physical care designed to aid the health

regressive—going backward

reimburse—to pay back

reiterate—to repeat over and over

rejuvenate—to make seem young again

relegate—to send away (to someplace)

relevant—pertaining to the matter in question

relinquish—to give (something) up

relish—to enjoy

remediable—curable; correctable

reminisce—to remember

remiss—careless in one's duty

remission—foregiveness; a letting up

remnant—remainder

remonstrate—to protest

remunerative—profitable

render—to give over; to give up; to cause to become

renegade—one who gives up his religion or cause and joins the opposition

renounce—to give up (a right, for example)

renovate—to renew

reparable—able to be repaired

reparation—a repairing; making up for a wrong

repartee—a clever reply; clever conversation back and forth

repast—a meal

repercussion—an effect of an event

repertoire—the selection of works a performer or group is prepared to perform

replenish—to refill

replete—full; stuffed

repository—a place where things are kept

reprehensible—deserving criticism

reprieve—a postponement of punishment

reprimand—a formal rebuke

reprisal—force used in retaliation for an act by another country

reproach—to make (someone) feel ashamed

reprobate—a person of no principles

reprove—to rebuke or disapprove

repudiate—to disown; to deny

repugnant—contradictory; offensive

requiem—a Mass or music for the dead

requisite—required

requite—to return or repay

rescind—to repeal (an order)

recision—the act of rescinding

resilient—elastic; buoyant

respite—a delay; a letup

resplendent—splendid

restitution—restoration; reimbursement

restive—balky; unruly; restless

resurgent—rising again

resuscitate—to revive

retaliate—to return injury or evil in kind

retentive—holding; able to remember

reticent—speaking very little

retinue—a group of followers or attendants

retort—to answer in kind; to reply sharply or cleverly

retract—to take back

retribution—just punishment or reward

retrieve—to recover (something); to save

retroactive—applying to the past

retrograde—going backward

retrospective—looking backward

revelry—merrymaking

reverberate—to reecho

reverie—a daydream

revert—to go back to a former state
revile—to abuse; to scold
revoke—to withdraw; to rescind
revulsion—a sudden change in feeling; disgust
rheumy—watery
ribald—vulgar; coarse
rife—occurring everywhere; plentiful
rigor—strictness; exactness
risible—laughable
risqué—daring
robust—healthy and strong
rococo—an elaborate architectural style
roseate—rosy; cheerful
rote—routine
rotund—rounded; stout
rubicund—reddish
rudiment—a basic principle; a first stage
rueful—pitiable; mournful
ruminate—to ponder
rummage—to search through
ruse—a trick
ruthless—cruel

S

sable—black
saccharine—pertaining to sugar; too sweet
sacerdotal—priestly
sacrilegious—in violation of something sacred
sacrosanct—holy; not to be violated
sadist—one who gets pleasure from hurting others
sagacious—perceptive; shrewd
sage—wise
salacious—lecherous; pornographic
salient—leaping; standing out; prominent
saline—salty
sallow—having a sickly, yellowish coloring
salubrious—healthful
salutary—conducive to good health
sanctity—holiness
sang-froid—coolness; calmness
sanguine—blood-colored; cheerful and optimistic
sapient—wise
sardonic—sarcastic
sartorial—pertaining to tailors or clothing
sate—to satisfy completely
satiate—to glut

saturate—to soak
saturnine—gloomy
savant—a scholar
savoir-faire—tact
savor—to season; to taste or smell appreciatively
scabrous—scaly; improper
scapegoat—one who is blamed for the wrongs of another
scathing—harsh; biting
schism—a split
scintilla—a tiny bit
scintillate—to sparkle; show verbal brilliance
scion—an offspring
scoff—to jeer (at)
scourge—a whip; a punishment
scruple—a qualm or doubt
scrupulous—very careful in doing what is correct
scrutiny—close inspection
scurrilous—coarse; vulgar
scuttle—to scurry; to sink (a ship); to abandon (a plan)
sebaceous—pertaining to fat
secede—to withdraw
secular—worldly
sedate—calm; serious
sedentary—sitting much of the time
seditious—pertaining to revolt against the government
sedulous—diligent
seethe—to boil; to foam
seine—a fishing net
seismic—pertaining to earthquakes
semantic—pertaining to meaning
semblance—appearance
senile—showing mental deterioration due to old age
sensual—pertaining to the body or the senses
sententious—pointed; full of trite wordings
sentient—feeling; conscious
sepulcher—a tomb
sequester—to set apart; to withdraw
serene—calm
serrated—having notches along the edge
servile—slavelike
sever—to separate; to cut in two
shackle—to hold back; to restrain
shambles—a slaughterhouse; a place of disorder
shard—a broken piece (of pottery)

sheathe—to put (a knife or sword) into its covering

shibboleth—a phrase or a practice that is observed by a particular group

shoddy—cheap; poorly made

shunt—to turn aside

sidereal—pertaining to the stars or constellations

simian—pertaining to monkeys

simile—a figure of speech that compares things by using *like* or *as*

simper—to smile in a silly way

simulate—to pretend or fake

sinecure—a job that requires little work

sinister—threatening; evil

sinuous—winding; devious

skeptical—doubting

skittish—playful; jumpy

skulk—to slink

slake—to satisfy

slatternly—dirty; untidy

sleazy—flimsy (as a fabric); cheap or shoddy

slothful—lazy

slough—to shed; a swamp

slovenly—careless or untidy

sluggard—a lazy person

sobriety—soberness

sojourn—a temporary stay

solecism—a misuse of grammar; a breach of manners

solicitous—expressing care; eager

soliloquy—a talking to oneself

solstice—the point at which the sun is farthest north or south of the equator

solvent—able to pay one's debts

somatic—pertaining to the body

somnambulism—sleepwalking

somnolent—sleepy; making one sleepy

sonorous—rich and full (sound)

soothsayer—one who predicts the future

sophisticated—urbane; not naive

sordid—dirty; ignoble

soupçon—a trace or hint

spasmodic—intermittent

specious—appearing correct but not really so

specter—a ghost

spectral—ghostly

splenetic—bad-tempered

spontaneous—arising naturally or by its own force

sporadic—occasional

sportive—playful

spurious—false; not real

squalid—filthy; sordid

squander—to waste

staid—sober

stalwart—sturdy; brave; firm

stamina—endurance

stark—prominent; barren; blunt

status—position or state

staunch, stanch—to stop (blood) flowing from a wound; to stop or check

stellar—pertaining to the stars

stentorian—very loud

stigma—a sign of disgrace

stilted—elevated; pompous

stint—to hold back in distributing or using

stipend—a salary or allowance

stoical—showing no reaction to various emotions or events

stolid—unexcitable

strait—a narrow waterway; a difficult situation

strategem—a scheme or trick

striated—striped or furrowed

stricture—censure; a limitation

strident—having a harsh or shrill sound

stringent—strict

stultify—to make stupid, dull, or worthless

suave—urbane; polished

subaltern—a subordinate

subjugate—to conquer

sublimate—to purify

sublime—exhalted; grand

suborn—to get someone to do something illegal

sub rosa—in private

subsequent—coming later

subservient—servile

subsidiary—supplementary; secondary

subsidy—a grant of money

subsistence—a means of providing one's basic needs

substantiate—to confirm

subterfuge—any means by which one conceals his intentions

subtle—thin; characterized by slight differences and qualities; not obvious

subversive—inclined to overthrow or harm the government

succinct—clear and brief
succor—to aid
succulent—juicy
suffuse—to spread throughout
sully—to soil
sultry—hot and close
summation—adding up
sumptuous—lavish
sunder—to split apart
sundry—miscellaneous
superannuated—too old to be of use; outdated
supercilious—haughty
superficial—pertaining to the surface aspects of something
superfluous—more than the amount needed
superlative—of the best kind; supreme
supersede—to take the place of
supine—lying on the back
supple—flexible
supplicant—one who prays for or asks for (something)
surcease—an end
surfeit—to provide too much of something; to satiate
surly—rude and ill-tempered
surmise—a guess made on the basis of little evidence
surreptitious—secret
surrogate—a substitute
surveillance—a watch over someone
sustenance—maintenance
sybaritic—loving luxury
sycophant—one who flatters to gain favor of important people
sylvan—pertaining to the woods
symmetry—balance
symposium—a meeting for the exchange of ideas
synchronize—to regulate several things so they will correspond in time
synopsis—a summary
synthesis—a putting together
synthetic—not natural; artificial

T

tacit—unspoken; understood rather than declared
taciturn—reluctant to speak
tactful—saying and doing the appropriate thing when people's feelings are involved
tactile—pertaining to the sense of touch

taint—to infect or spoil
talisman—a charm supposed to have magic power
tangible—touchable; objective
tantamount—equal (to)
tantalize—to tempt (someone) with something he cannot have
tautological—employing needless repetition of an idea
tawdry—cheap and gaudy
tawny—tan in color
tedious—tiresome
temerity—foolish boldness
temperate—moderate
template—a pattern
temporal—temporary; worldly
tenacious—holding fast
tenet—a principle
tentative—proposed but not final; hesitant
tenuous—thin; slight
tenure—the period of time for which something is held; a permanent status in a job based on length of service
tepid—lukewarm
termagant—a shrewish old woman
terminal—pertaining to the end
terrestrial—earthly; pertaining to land
terse—concise
tertiary—third
testy—irritable
theocracy—rule of a state by God or by God's authority
therapeutic—curing
thermal—pertaining to heat
thespian—pertaining to drama; an actor
thralldom—slavery
throes—pangs
thwart—to obstruct or prevent
tirade—a lengthy, violent speech
titanic—huge
tithe—a tenth of something
titular—pertaining to a title; in name only
toady—one who tries to gain another's favor; sycophant
tome—a book, especially a large one
torpid—dormant; slow-moving
tortuous—twisting; devious
toxic—poisonous
tract—a stretch of land
tractable—easy to manage or control

traduce—to slander

trammel—to confine or entangle

tranquil—calm; peaceful

transcend—to go beyond

transcribe—to write out in one form from another

transgression—a breaking of a rule; a violation of a limit

transient—not permanent

transition—a change from one thing to another

transitory—fleeting

translucent—allowing light through

transmute—to change from one form to another

transpire—to become known

trappings—one's clothes and equipment

transverse—lying across

trauma—a severe injury or shock

travail—hard work; pain

traverse—to go across

travesty—a burlesque; a distortion (of something)

treatise—a formal, written presentation of a subject

trek—to travel slowly

tremor—a trembling; a vibration

tremulous—trembling; afraid

trenchant—keen; forceful

trepidation—uncertainty and anxiety

tribulation—great unhappiness; a trying circumstance

tribunal—a law court

trite—overworked; no longer novel

troth—truth; one's word, as a promise

truckle—to submit and be servile

truculent—cruel; rude

truism—a statement that is known to be true

trumpery—something pretentious but not worth anything

truncate—to cut off part of

truncheon—a club

tryst—a meeting

tumid—swollen; inflated

turbid—muddy; dense

turbulence—a state of commotion or agitation

turgid—swollen; pompous

turncoat—a renegade; a traitor

turnkey—a jailer

turpitude—vileness

tutelage—care; guardianship

tyro—a beginner

U

ubiquitous—omnipresent

ulterior—on the far side; later; beyond what is said

ultimate—the farthest, final, or highest

ultimatum—a nonnegotiable demand

umbrage—offense

unadulterated—pure

unanimity—agreement

unassuming—modest

unbridled—uncontrolled; free

uncanny—strange; weird

unconscionable—done without applying one's conscience

uncouth—clumsy; not having culture or polish

unction—ointment; an intense manner of behavior; unctuousness

unctuous—oily; displaying fake religious feeling

undulate—to move in waves

unearth—to dig up

unequivocal—clear

unfaltering—unhesitating

unfathomable—not understandable

ungainly—awkward

unguent—an ointment

unimpeachable—undoubtable; above reproach

unique—unlike any other

unkempt—untidy

unmitigated—unrelieved

unprecedented—never having occurred before

unremitting—not letting up

unruly—unmanageable

unseemly—not proper

untenable—unable to be held

unwitting—unconscious; unaware

unwonted—rare

upbraid—to rebuke

urbane—polished and refined

usurp—to take by force

usury—lending money at outrageously high interest rates

utilitarian—useful

utopian—idealistic; perfect

uxorious—overly fond of one's wife

V

vacillate—to move one way and then the other; to waver

vacuous—empty; stupid

vagary—a peculiarity

vainglorious—vain and boastful

valiant—brave

validate—to confirm legally

vanguard—the group in front

vapid—dull

variegated—having a variety of colors in splotches; diverse

vaunt—a boast

veer—to change direction

vegetate—to have a dull, inactive existence

vehement—having great force or passion

venal—bribable

vendetta—a feud

vendor—a seller

vengeance—punishment; revenge

veneer—a thin covering of fine wood over cheaper wood; a thin and superficial display of a noble quality

venerable—old and honorable

venerate—to respect deeply

venial—forgivable

vent—to allow (steam or feelings) to escape

veracious—truthful

verbatim—word-for-word

verbiage—wordiness

verbose—wordy

verdant—green

verily—truly

verisimilar—appearing to be true

verity—truth

vernacular—the common speech of an area or its people

versatile—changeable; adaptable

vertigo—dizziness

vestige—a trace

viable—able or likely to live

viand—something to eat

vicarious—substitute; done or experienced by one person through another

vicissitudes—changes

victuals—food

vie—to compete

vigilant—watchful

vilify—to slander

vindicate—to free of blame

vindictive—seeking revenge

virile—manly; masculine

virtuoso—a skilled performer

virulent—deadly

visage—one's face

viscid—sticky; viscous

viscous—sticky; viscid

visionary—like a vision; unrealistic

vitiate—to spoil or debase

vitriolic—bitter

vituperation—harsh language

vivacious—lively

vivid—lively; intense

vociferous—loud

volatile—turning to vapor quickly; changeable

volition—employing one's will

voluble—talkative

voluptuous—sensual; inclined toward luxury

voracious—greedy

votary—one who has taken a vow; a follower or supporter of a cause

vouchsafe—to grant

vulnerable—in a position to be attacked or injured

W

waggish—playful

waive—to give up (a right, etc.)

wan—pale

wane—to decrease

wanton—morally loose; unwarranted

warranty—a guarantee

wary—cautious

wastrel—one who wastes (money)

weal—welfare

wheedle—to coax

whet—to sharpen

whimsical—fanciful

whit—(the) least bit

wily—sly

windfall—a surprising bit of good luck

winnow—to pick out the good elements or parts of something

winsome—charming

witless—foolish

witticism—a clever remark

wizened—withered; dried up

wont—accustomed

wraith—a ghost

wreak—to allow to be expressed;
   to inflict
wrest—to take away by force
wry—twisted; stubborn

X

xenophobia—dislike of foreigners

Y

yeoman—a man who has a small
   amount of land

Z

zany—clownish; crazy
zealot—one who is extremely devoted
   to his cause
zenith—the highest point
zephyr—a breeze

8

Extra Practice in Verbal Ability

SENTENCE COMPLETION

EXTRA PRACTICE TEST

Directions: Each question in this test consists of a sentence in which one or two words are missing. Beneath the sentence are five words or word sets. Choose the word or word set that *best* completes the sentence. Then mark the appropriate space in the answer column.

1. The _____ demeanor of the crowd influenced the sheriff to _____.
   - (A) disciplined—arrest them
   - (B) enthusiastic—commend them
   - (C) wild—threaten them
   - (D) belligerent—pacify them
   - (E) destructive—reason with them

2. Early in the 19th century, in the South, it had become the fashion to raise only one stable crop, whereas in the North the crops were _____.
   - (A) staple
   - (B) unstable
   - (C) fallow
   - (D) diversified
   - (E) wild

3. The writers of mystery fiction who turn out several books a year may be considered _____.
- (A) prolific
- (B) stupendous
- (C) artistic
- (D) meticulous
- (E) ambitious

4. A(n) _____ may be defined as the perpetration of (a) _____.
- (A) maxim—saw
- (B) witticism—banality
- (C) murder—assault
- (D) cliche—conspiracy
- (E) offense—calumny

5. Certain community groups on the East Side have opposed plans to _____ its slums and replace them with modern "projects."
- (A) reconstruct
- (B) resurrect
- (C) raze
- (D) alleviate
- (E) alter

6. A strike is usually resorted to only when less _____ measures fail.
- (A) mercenary
- (B) drastic
- (C) urgent
- (D) meaningful
- (E) preferable

7. "I am as strong as a lion" is an example of _____.
- (A) oxymoron
- (B) simile
- (C) personification
- (D) metaphor
- (E) alliteration

8. The man with the cut asked the druggist for a bottle of
_____ of iodine.
- (A)   concoction
- (B)   melange
- (C)   mixture
- (D)   tincture
- (E)   solution

9. A _____ is a minute particle of a(n) _____.
- (A)   second—matter
- (B)   protozoa—fish
- (C)   molecule—substance
- (D)   millimeter—ammeter
- (E)   dyne—energy

10. Many of our pioneer American writers were confronted with the
choice of striving for originality or emulating the masters of the
old world with _____ skill and technique.
- (A)   consummate
- (B)   individual
- (C)   pecuniary
- (D)   sustained
- (E)   innate

11. Only the fear of immediate massive _____ prevents
the enemy from launching an attack upon us.
- (A)   destruction
- (B)   retaliation
- (C)   terror
- (D)   revenge
- (E)   condemnation

12. The electrician put the parts of the television set together with
the skill of the master craftsman for whom this was a(n)
_____ occupation.
- (A)   morbid
- (B)   natural
- (C)   peculiar
- (D)   unnatural
- (E)   avocational

13. As often happens with those who rule by emotion rather than by reason, their discussion soon retrogressed from _____ to _____.
    - (A) argument—controversy
    - (B) consideration—rationalization
    - (C) disagreement—altercation
    - (D) dispute—disagreement
    - (E) squabbling—wrangling

14. It is a custom in France on July 14th for the President of the Republic to offer _____ to certain prisoners in full _____.
    - (A) acquittal—amnesty
    - (B) amnesty—pardon
    - (C) parole—acquittal
    - (D) restitution—clemency
    - (E) clemency—amnesty

15. Today, although we are witnessing a period of _____ employment, we still find that many people are unemployed, particularly, since labor is relatively _____.
    - (A) high scale—high priced
    - (B) high level—scarce
    - (C) optimum—immobile
    - (D) industrial—rural
    - (E) continuing—unskilled

16. When he saw his brother approach, he _____; he was sorry to have made such a show of his true feelings. He would have given much to have been able to suppress the _____ at the same moment.
    - (A) shouted—reaction
    - (B) sighed—fervor
    - (C) grimaced—action
    - (D) laughed—jeer
    - (E) exulted—distortion

17. If a young man calls and he says that he is a _____ the young lady should not be offended because he is _____.
    - (A) doctor—reliable
    - (B) philanthropist—parsimonious
    - (C) teacher—scholarly
    - (D) celibate—a hermit
    - (E) celibate—a bachelor

18. Only the rich can save money without _____.
  (A) distinction
  (B) shame
  (C) compulsion
  (D) privation
  (E) argument

19. The syndicalists who would introduce anarchy are unconcerned about the _____ such a form of government will bring with it.
  (A) plutocracy
  (B) republicanism
  (C) chaos
  (D) dictatorship
  (E) democracy

20. During the post-war period, _____ firms met with great difficulty in maintaining their business as soon as the standard brands of _____ companies became generally available.
  (A) foreign—established
  (B) newer—established
  (C) specialized—rationalized
  (D) manufacturing—agricultural
  (E) ordinance—missile

21. Man has added much to the science of horticulture. In particular, he has accomplished a great deal in the selection and breeding of flowers through _____ and _____.
  (A) protection—incision
  (B) modification—adaptation
  (C) sheltering—pruning
  (D) grafting—restriction
  (E) colonizing—selection

22. Since the judge feels that the defendant's offense is _____, he will, probably, give him a light sentence.
  (A) vindictive
  (B) venal
  (C) militant
  (D) vindicable
  (E) heinous

23. In this game he was an amateur, not an expert, and thus, for the first time, became a(n) _____ instead of a man of action.
(A) connoisseur
(B) spectator
(C) lawyer
(D) pragmatist
(E) authority

24. The tornado left all the buildings a(n) _____ mass of destruction.
(A) massive
(B) motley
(C) destitute
(D) unrecognizable
(E) incomparable

25. Unlike his cousin, the artist, who was colorful, whimsical, and erratic, the teacher was prosaic, _____, and consistent.
(A) infallible
(B) commonplace
(C) objective
(D) disorganized
(E) subtle

SENTENCE COMPLETION EXTRA PRACTICE TEST ANSWERS

1.	D	10.	A	19.	C
2.	D	11.	B	20.	B
3.	A	12.	B	21.	B
4.	B	13.	C	22.	D
5.	C	14.	B	23.	B
6.	B	15.	C	24.	D
7.	B	16.	C	25.	C
8.	D	17.	E		
9.	C	18.	D		

ANALOGIES

EXTRA PRACTICE TEST 1

Directions: In each of the following, select the lettered pair that best expresses a relationship similar to that expressed in the original pair.

1. SAILOR : PIRATE ::
   (A) transient : permanent
   (B) plant : fungus
   (C) mate : captain
   (D) police : thief
   (E) wolf : prey

2. SPRINTER : GUN ::
   (A) butterfly hunter : net
   (B) dog : whistle
   (C) fencer : sword
   (D) fighter : bell
   (E) writer : pen

3. WRINKLE : FOLD ::
   (A) tear : cut
   (B) steal : lose
   (C) paper : refuse
   (D) sprinkle : rub
   (E) wrinkle : smooth

4. WIND : GALE ::
   (A) storm : sea
   (B) atmospheric pressure : clear day
   (C) affection : passion
   (D) contraction : dilation
   (E) breeze : gale

5. FRAME : PICTURE ::
   (A) sash : window
   (B) painting : canvas
   (C) setting : diamond
   (D) border : exile
   (E) shell : egg

6. TRAIN : WHISTLE ::
   (A) air raid : siren
   (B) car : horn
   (C) swimmer : bell buoy
   (D) ship : anchor
   (E) singer : tune

7. REFUGEE : HAVEN ::
   (A) child : bed
   (B) fish : bowl
   (C) exile : sanctuary
   (D) prisoner : dungeon
   (E) berth : stowaway

8. WAIT : LOITER ::
   (A) bum : thief
   (B) diligent : tardy
   (C) late : laggard
   (D) work : putter
   (E) regress : ingress

9. SHRUB : PRUNE ::
(A) beard : shave
(B) hair : trim
(C) lawn : mow
(D) scissors : cut
(E) wool : shear

10. FACADE : BUILDING ::
(A) personality : qualities
(B) vestibule : apartment
(C) aspect : appearance
(D) demeanor : character
(E) front : affront

11. PARCHED : DESERT ::
(A) captive : jail
(B) inundated : flood
(C) penurious : slum
(D) glum : outlook
(E) withered : plant

12. PARAGRAPH : GIST ::
(A) play : outcome
(B) matter : essence
(C) matter : particle
(D) epitome : paraphrase
(E) molecule : atom

13. BUOY : DETOUR ::
(A) ship : hurricane
(B) ocean : road
(C) canal : road
(D) warning : signal
(E) storm : accident

14. MOTORIST : ROAD SIGN ::
(A) telegraph operator : Morse code
(B) English : pronunciation
(C) vocabulary : alphabet
(D) bicyclist : roadblock
(E) reader : punctuation

15. SYNONYM : SAME ::
(A) antonym : unlike
(B) antonym : opposite
(C) metaphor : poetry
(D) metonymy : versification
(E) triangle : pyramid

16. LEG : KNEE ::
(A) angle : elbow
(B) hand : wrist
(C) compound sentence : conjunction
(D) ribs : breastbone
(E) simile : metaphor

17. SUPPLENESS : ACROBAT ::
(A) paint : artist
(B) fleetness : runner
(C) imagination : artist
(D) strength : detective
(E) grace : chess-player

18. LAUGH : SMILE ::
(A) grumble : scowl
(B) lament : condole
(C) express : restrain
(D) entice : endow
(E) cry : sigh

19. ANARCHY : CHAOS ::
(A) hierarchy : peace
(B) oppression : confusion
(C) disturbance : problem
(D) dictator : democrat
(E) government : order

20. CEILING : PILLAR ::
(A) steel : girder
(B) society : law
(C) apex : climax
(D) prices : subsidy
(E) tree : trunk

21. EMOTION : REASON : :
    (A) deference : thought
    (B) devotion : fondness
    (C) anger : spite
    (D) fulmination : recrimination
    (E) intemperate : critical

22. FISH : MERMAID : :
    (A) horse : centaur
    (B) crocodile : dragon
    (C) fish : nymph
    (D) shark : whale
    (E) horse : man

23. SOLDIER : KHAKI : :
    (A) sum : gold
    (B) grass : green
    (C) soldier : whisper
    (D) cork : bottle
    (E) king : purple

24. WEIGHT : PAPER : :
    (A) stopper : door
    (B) anchor : ship
    (C) sound : whisper
    (D) cork : bottle
    (E) length : inch

25. PACT : FEUD : :
    (A) alliance : organization
    (B) conciliation : revolution
    (C) treaty : covenant
    (D) entreaty : parity
    (E) concord : discord

ANALOGIES EXTRA PRACTICE TEST 1 ANSWERS

1.	B	10.	D	19.	E
2.	D	11.	C	20.	D
3.	A	12.	B	21.	E
4.	C	13.	B	22.	A
5.	C	14.	E	23.	E
6.	B	15.	B	24.	B
7.	C	16.	B	25.	E
8.	D	17.	B		
9.	B	18.	A		

EXTRA PRACTICE TEST 2

Directions: In each of the following, select the lettered pair that best expresses a relationship similar to that expressed in the original pair.

1. FEATHERS : PLUMAGE : :
    (A)   skin : leather
    (B)   drawers : cupboard
    (C)   New York State : The United States
    (D)   pillows : bed
    (E)   fur : hair

2. EAST : ORIENT : :
    (A)   mysterious : orient
    (B)   south : tropic
    (C)   north : polar
    (D)   equator : latitude
    (E)   west : occident

3. DEFTNESS : PIANIST : :
    (A)   thought : teacher
    (B)   grace : ballplayer
    (C)   easel : artist
    (D)   skill : boxer
    (E)   fleetness : runner

4. UNIFORM : SOLDIER : :
    (A)   dungarees : child
    (B)   clothing : man
    (C)   screen : fireplace
    (D)   domino : masquerader
    (E)   wings : airman

5. WOOD : LATTICE : :
    (A)   metal : auto radiator
    (B)   iron : grille
    (C)   tile : fireplace
    (D)   steel : building
    (E)   wood : door

6. UMBRELLA : RAIN : :
    (A)   roof : snow
    (B)   aspirin : cold
    (C)   screen : insects
    (D)   hood : coat
    (E)   sewer : water

7. RELAX : BODY : :
    (A)   slacken : rope
    (B)   sleep : fatigue
    (C)   empty : ballast
    (D)   knockout : boxer
    (E)   conciliation : strike

8. MUSIC : SCORE : :
    (A)   music : anthology
    (B)   paper : portfolio
    (C)   penmanship : handwriting
    (D)   poetry : verse
    (E)   song : paean

9. STORM : SUBSIDE : :
    (A)   snow : rain
    (B)   attack : die
    (C)   revolution : quell
    (D)   degree : cool
    (E)   fight : rumpus

10. NORTH STAR : VANE : :
    (A)   air pressure : barometer
    (B)   constancy : capriciousness
    (C)   sun : sextant
    (D)   mirror : mirage
    (E)   honesty : hypocrisy

11. AGNOSTIC : ATHEIST : :
    (A)   orthodox : heterodox
    (B)   heretic : pagan
    (C)   unbeliever : iconoclast
    (D)   questionable : definite
    (E)   vague : defiant

12. SMITH : SMITHY : :
    (A)   druggist : drug store
    (B)   sickly : sickliness
    (C)   chemist : laboratory
    (D)   miser : miserliness
    (E)   captain : ship

13. SECOND : TIME ::
- (A) inch : space
- (B) point : line
- (C) pound : weight
- (D) steak : potatoes
- (E) minute : day

14. DESIST : CONTINUE ::
- (A) supply : produce
- (B) lose : possess
- (C) advance : hesitate
- (D) recur : cease
- (E) perform : undertake

15. DESTINATION : VOYAGE ::
- (A) success : talent
- (B) consequence : misdeed
- (C) goal : motivation
- (D) objective : campaign
- (E) triumph : victory

16. OAK : ACORN ::
- (A) vegetable : earth
- (B) flight : motion
- (C) bird : egg
- (D) crime : implication
- (E) muscle : cell

17. POUND : PIERCE ::
- (A) club : sword
- (B) cut : break
- (C) cut : parry
- (D) break : crack
- (E) thrust : pierce

18. PAW : CAT ::
- (A) wing : robin
- (B) hole : chipmunk
- (C) egg : chicken
- (D) purr : kitten
- (E) hoof : horse

19. CLOCK : HOURGLASS ::
- (A) matter : mind
- (B) cannon : catapult
- (C) church : temple
- (D) temple : foundation
- (E) oak : scorn

20. LETTER : TELEGRAM ::
- (A) tortoise : hare
- (B) word : number
- (C) truth : lie
- (D) modesty : egotism
- (E) essay : thesis

21. LAW : SOCIETY ::
- (A) law : jury
- (B) prisoner : cell
- (C) rules : baseball
- (D) prisoner : law
- (E) jury : sentence

22. PRAISE : DEJECTION ::
- (A) relaxation : recreation
- (B) laziness : obesity
- (C) precipice : mountain
- (D) diploma : graduate
- (E) rest : fatigue

23. MEMBER : LEAGUE ::
- (A) appurtenance : object
- (B) leverage : aggregate
- (C) obstinate : deadlock
- (D) fiber : fabric
- (E) nucleus : cell

24. BLACKMAIL : VICTIM ::
- (A) death : suffer
- (B) money : kidnapper
- (C) money : prisoner
- (D) ransom : captive
- (E) war : prisoner

25. TREASON : STATE ::
- (A) treason : institution
- (B) orthodoxy : atheism
- (C) institution : state
- (D) atheism : agnosticism
- (E) heresy : church

ANALOGIES EXTRA PRACTICE TEST 2 ANSWERS

1.	E	10.	B	19.	B
2.	E	11.	D	20.	A
3.	D	12.	C	21.	C
4.	D	13.	A	22.	E
5.	B	14.	D	23.	D
6.	C	15.	D	24.	D
7.	A	16.	C	25.	E
8.	D	17.	A		
9.	C	18.	E		

EXTRA PRACTICE TEST 3

Directions: In each of the following, select the lettered pair that best expresses a relationship similar to that expressed in the original pair.

1. CHARCOAL : WOOD ::
    - (A) steel : iron
    - (B) coke : coal
    - (C) oxygen : nitrogen
    - (D) skeleton : body
    - (E) bread : yeast

2. TRIANGLE : SQUARE ::
    - (A) pyramid : cube
    - (B) hexagon : pentagon
    - (C) square : parallelogram
    - (D) cone : cylinder
    - (E) triangle : cone

3. APRICOT : FIG ::
    - (A) raisin : prune
    - (B) privet : barberry
    - (C) grape : raisin
    - (D) cherry : wine
    - (E) wine : alcohol

4. NATIONALIZATION : SOCIALISM ::
    - (A) taxation : totalitarianism
    - (B) entrepreneur : laissez-faire
    - (C) freedom : dictatorship
    - (D) independence : agriculture
    - (E) serfdom : feudalism

5. ICHTHYOLOGIST : MARINE LIFE ::
    - (A) philologist : stamps
    - (B) ornithologist : horticulture
    - (C) entomologist : words
    - (D) archeologist : antiquity
    - (E) theologian : astronomy

6. POTATO : PECK ::
    - (A) bullion : silver
    - (B) diamond : carat
    - (C) ring : gold
    - (D) bushel : oat
    - (E) gold : ore

7. INTRODUCTION : CONCLUSION ::
    - (A) motor : housing
    - (B) power : freight
    - (C) engine : caboose
    - (D) beginning : commencement
    - (E) cabin : train

8. PEWTER : LEAD ::
    - (A) brass : copper
    - (B) zinc : iron
    - (C) tin : foil
    - (D) coin : silver
    - (E) urn : copper

9. BICARBONATE : GASTRIC ACIDITY ::
    - (A) steam : engine
    - (B) praise : depression
    - (C) apathy : despair
    - (D) hope : despair
    - (E) ulcer : cancer

10. DEAN : STUDENTS ::
    - (A) guide : tourists
    - (B) minister : congregation
    - (C) doctor : patients
    - (D) leader : paratroop team
    - (E) scientists : knowledge

11. HOMICIDE : MURDER ::
    - (A) weakness : act
    - (B) accident : assault
    - (C) prevaricate : deny
    - (D) hallucination : nightmare
    - (E) untruth : lie

12. EGOTISM : SELFISH ::
    - (A) hardihood : hardy
    - (B) friendship : friend
    - (C) fortitude : force
    - (D) great : greater
    - (E) solitude : indifference

13. CERTAINLY : SURELY : :
(A) rarely : generally
(B) surely : accidentally
(C) necessity : invention
(D) incidentally : fortuitous
(E) probably : perhaps

14. LUXURY : LETHARGY : :
(A) because : out
(B) hardship : luck
(C) emergency : effect
(D) opulence : affluence
(E) necessity : invention

15. THAT IS : SUCH AS : :
(A) like : i. e.
(B) to wit : thus
(C) namely : for example
(D) viz. : ibid.
(E) for instance : especially

16. PROVIDED THAT : AGREEMENT : :
(A) granted that : nevertheless
(B) relying upon : enmity
(C) in accordance with : depending
(D) except : consent
(E) on condition that : acceptance

17. RESPECTED : RESPECTFUL : :
(A) intend : pretend
(B) kneeling : pious
(C) proud : haughty
(D) sycophant : king
(E) reverend : reverent

18. OVERDOSE : HEAPING MEASURE : :
(A) potion : beverage
(B) too : very
(C) of : off
(D) copious : scanty
(E) approach : accost

19. SOLO : ENSEMBLE : :
(A) each : everybody
(B) spool : thread
(C) ocean : wave
(D) house : beams
(E) ball of wool : skein

20. DISEASE : IMMUNITY : :
(A) obligation : debt
(B) change : adaptation
(C) custom : conformity
(D) transgression : pardon
(E) tax : exemption

21. GLANCE : SCRUTINIZE : :
(A) watch : search
(B) eye : sight
(C) look : see
(D) touch : grasp
(E) ponder : examine

22. MUSCLE : CRAMP : :
(A) stone : crack
(B) machine : jam
(C) pain : throb
(D) lightning : flash
(E) order : cancel

23. PLATEAU : PLAIN : :
(A) lake : river
(B) peak : crevice
(C) country : state
(D) mountain : valley
(E) order : cancel

24. POODLE : KENNEL : :
(A) pugilist : ring
(B) bird : nest
(C) canary : cage
(D) fish : tackle
(E) tiger : zoo

25. PROBLEM : SOLUTION : :
(A) crossword puzzle : design
(B) suitcase : handle
(C) frame : window
(D) password : sentry
(E) door : key

ANALOGIES EXTRA PRACTICE TEST 3 ANSWERS

1.	B	10.	B	19.	A
2.	A	11.	E	20.	E
3.	A	12.	A	21.	D
4.	E	13.	E	22.	B
5.	D	14.	E	23.	D
6.	B	15.	C	24.	C
7.	C	16.	E	25.	E
8.	A	17.	E		
9.	B	18.	B		

ANTONYMS

EXTRA PRACTICE TEST 1

Directions: Each question in this test consists of a word printed in capital letters followed by five words lettered (A) through (E). Choose the word that has most nearly the OPPOSITE meaning from the word in capital letters. Underline the word you choose. Then mark the appropriate space in the answer column. *Correct answers appear at end of test.*

1. AGGREGATE
   (A) portion
   (B) bulk
   (C) ensemble
   (D) integrity
   (E) sum

2. AILING
   (A) healthy
   (B) affected
   (C) declining
   (D) disordered
   (E) worn

3. ALARMED
   (A) terrified
   (B) shrinking
   (C) fearful
   (D) cowardly
   (E) valiant

4. ALERT
   (A) vivacious
   (B) enterprising
   (C) brisk
   (D) alive
   (E) apathetic

5. ALIEN
   (A) impertinent
   (B) heterogeneous
   (C) dissimilar
   (D) conflicting
   (E) similar

6. RECONDITE
   (A) obvious
   (B) hidden
   (C) deep
   (D) emerging
   (E) valiant

7. TORPID
   (A) torpor
   (B) dull
   (C) keen
   (D) generous
   (E) molar

8. PUERILE
   (A) immature
   (B) mature
   (C) plain
   (D) lone
   (E) gay

9. ERRATIC
(A) consistent
(B) enraged
(C) latent
(D) comic
(E) tall

10. REFRACTORY
(A) disobedient
(B) obedient
(C) willful
(D) dilatory
(E) cruel

11. ALIENATE
(A) mingle
(B) detach
(C) dissever
(D) put asunder
(E) unravel

12. ALIGHT
(A) settle
(B) ascend
(C) descend
(D) dismount
(E) pitch

13. ALLEGE
(A) impute
(B) dogmatize
(C) confess
(D) retract
(E) bow

14. ALLOY
(A) mar
(B) debauch
(C) debase
(D) purify
(E) pollute

15. ALTERATION
(A) gap
(B) fracture
(C) break
(D) continuity
(E) change

16. CALLOW
(A) candle
(B) sophisticated
(C) gentle
(D) wise
(E) heroic

17. AUSTERE
(A) mad
(B) odd
(C) pure
(D) gentle
(E) pretense

18. PERFIDIOUS
(A) coy
(B) liberal
(C) faithful
(D) continual
(E) absent

19. INDOLENT
(A) doleful
(B) lazy
(C) clumsy
(D) industrious
(E) brusque

20. BLAND
(A) delicious
(B) grand
(C) odd
(D) brusque
(E) unhappy

21. GARRULOUS
(A) prolix
(B) winded
(C) verbose
(D) loud
(E) concise

22. GENERATE
(A) quicken
(B) revive
(C) live
(D) grow
(E) die

23. **GENIAL**
    (A) sullen
    (B) agreeable
    (C) chatty
    (D) happy
    (E) pleasing

24. **GENTLE**
    (A) arrogant
    (B) altruistic
    (C) considerate
    (D) patient
    (E) unselfish

25. **GHASTLY**
    (A) nasty
    (B) beautiful
    (C) disgusting
    (D) eerie
    (E) foul

ANTONYMS EXTRA PRACTICE TEST 1 ANSWERS

1.	A	10.	B	19.	D
2.	A	11.	A	20.	D
3.	E	12.	B	21.	E
4.	E	13.	D	22.	E
5.	E	14.	D	23.	A
6.	A	15.	D	24.	A
7.	C	16.	B	25.	B
8.	B	17.	D		
9.	A	18.	C		

EXTRA PRACTICE TEST 2

Directions: Each question in this test consists of a word printed in capital letters followed by five words lettered (A) through (E). Choose the word that has most nearly the OPPOSITE meaning from the word in capital letters. Underline the word you choose. Then mark the appropriate space in the answer column. *Correct answers appear at end of test.*

1. NOBLE
    (A) base
    (B) born
    (C) patrician
    (D) regal
    (E) kingly

2. INNOCUOUS
    (A) harmful
    (B) innocent
    (C) guilty
    (D) tender
    (E) unruly

3. PRECOCIOUS
    (A) forward
    (B) slow
    (C) backward
    (D) cute
    (E) ferocious

4. IMPOTENT
    (A) powerful
    (B) weak
    (C) dull
    (D) mighty
    (E) congenial

5. INDUBITABLE
    (A) questionable
    (B) definite
    (C) sure
    (D) obliged
    (E) deny

6. GLORY
    (A) satisfaction
    (B) humiliation
    (C) delight
    (D) exultation
    (E) gratification

7. GRACEFUL
    (A) awkward
    (B) deft
    (C) facile
    (D) handy
    (E) skillful

8. GRAVITATE
    (A) ascend
    (B) alight
    (C) descend
    (D) dismount
    (E) settle

9. GRUDGING
    (A) angry
    (B) mean
    (C) illiberal
    (D) liberal
    (E) pinched

10. GUILE
    (A) legend
    (B) imposture
    (C) dissimulation
    (D) truth
    (E) myth

11. ARDUOUS
- (A) ardent
- (B) easy
- (C) able
- (D) real
- (E) raw

12. OBSOLETE
- (A) novel
- (B) outworn
- (C) urban
- (D) stranger
- (E) wrong

13. FASTIDIOUS
- (A) mysterious
- (B) clean
- (C) negligent
- (D) outmoded
- (E) real

14. VAGUE
- (A) definite
- (B) unsure
- (C) dutiful
- (D) wan
- (E) reckless

15. DIMINUTIVE
- (A) small
- (B) large
- (C) plump
- (D) verbose
- (E) ranting

16. WROUGHT
- (A) undone
- (B) mild
- (C) cooked
- (D) roasted
- (E) broiled

17. UNCOUTH
- (A) boor
- (B) refined
- (C) buffoon
- (D) clown
- (E) sneak

18. STINGY
- (A) ludicrous
- (B) generous
- (C) indolent
- (D) allied
- (E) torpid

19. BARBAROUS
- (A) savage
- (B) stupid
- (C) cultured
- (D) enraged
- (E) willful

20. SEVERE
- (A) strong
- (B) lax
- (C) haughty
- (D) genial
- (E) harmful

21. ALTRUISTIC
- (A) unambitious
- (B) tolerant
- (C) meek
- (D) considerate
- (E) arrogant

22. AMBIGUOUS
- (A) obtuse
- (B) foggy
- (C) cloudy
- (D) obscure
- (E) clear

23. AMBITIOUS
   (A) rich
   (B) busy
   (C) active
   (D) slothful
   (E) vigorous

24. AMIABLE
   (A) intractable
   (B) complaisant
   (C) diffident
   (D) pliable
   (E) tractable

25. AMITY
   (A) aversion
   (B) fondness
   (C) friendship
   (D) love
   (E) comity

ANTONYMS EXTRA PRACTICE TEST 2 ANSWERS

1.	A	10.	D	19.	C
2.	A	11.	B	20.	B
3.	C	12.	A	21.	E
4.	A	13.	C	22.	E
5.	A	14.	A	23.	D
6.	B	15.	B	24.	A
7.	A	16.	A	25.	A
8.	A	17.	B		
9.	D	18.	B		

EXTRA PRACTICE TEST 3

Directions: The following questions consist of a word printed in capital letters followed by five words lettered (A) through (E). Choose the word that has most nearly the OPPOSITE meaning from the word in capital letters. Underline the word you choose. Then mark the appropriate space in the answer column. *Correct answers appear at end of test.*

1. BREAK
   (A) continuity
   (B) alteration
   (C) fracture
   (D) intermission
   (E) interruption

2. PURIFY
   (A) defile
   (B) deft
   (C) gifted
   (D) posted
   (E) scholarly

3. BROAD
   (A) grand
   (B) bulky
   (C) small
   (D) spacious
   (E) massive

4. BRUSH
   (A) disinfect
   (B) cleanse
   (C) contaminate
   (D) flush
   (E) lave

5. BRUTALITY
   (A) kindness
   (B) acrimoniousness
   (C) truculence
   (D) churlishness
   (E) ferocity

6. BUILD
   (A) wreck
   (B) cause
   (C) establish
   (D) fashion
   (E) shape

7. BULK
   (A) whole
   (B) portion
   (C) all
   (D) entirety
   (E) unity

8. BUNGLING
   (A) sluggish
   (B) clever
   (C) clumsy
   (D) empty
   (E) imbecile

9. MENDACIOUS
   (A) liar
   (B) truthful
   (C) physical
   (D) stubborn
   (E) naive

10. CLEMENT
    (A) pleasant
    (B) clear
    (C) cruel
    (D) practical
    (E) gentle

11. NIGGARDLY
(A) lavish
(B) vapid
(C) stingy
(D) surly
(E) bold

12. DILATORY
(A) easy
(B) dilate
(C) prompt
(D) motivate
(E) violent

13. OBDURATE
(A) tenuous
(B) turbulent
(C) brisk
(D) yielding
(E) stubborn

14. HETEROGENEOUS
(A) able
(B) opposite
(C) uniform
(D) simulate
(E) putrid

15. TERSE
(A) verbose
(B) abrupt
(C) arrogant
(D) hungry
(E) brave

16. ADMIT
(A) refute
(B) accept
(C) pocket
(D) seize
(E) catch

17. ADORATION
(A) hatred
(B) amity
(C) fondness
(D) liking
(E) love

18. ADROIT
(A) workmanlike
(B) fey
(C) facile
(D) deft
(E) awkward

19. ADVANCE
(A) move ahead
(B) revert
(C) keep abreast
(D) press forward
(E) proceed

20. ADVANTAGEOUS
(A) righteous
(B) beneficial
(C) agreeable
(D) bad
(E) wholesome

21. SAGACIOUS
(A) brilliant
(B) stupid
(C) gifted
(D) talented
(E) wise

22. AUTONOMOUS
(A) dependent
(B) autonomy
(C) tasty
(D) puerile
(E) horrible

23. **FEASIBLE**
    (A) practical
    (B) impractical
    (C) helpful
    (D) advisable
    (E) tenacious

24. **DEVOUT**
    (A) religious
    (B) adored
    (C) impious
    (D) revered
    (E) timid

25. **STAID**
    (A) frivolous
    (B) solid
    (C) cunning
    (D) lofty
    (E) angry

ANTONYMS EXTRA PRACTICE TEST 3 ANSWERS

1.	A	10.	C	19.	B
2.	A	11.	A	20.	D
3.	C	12.	C	21.	B
4.	C	13.	D	22.	A
5.	A	14.	C	23.	B
6.	A	15.	A	24.	C
7.	B	16.	A	25.	A
8.	B	17.	A		
9.	B	18.	E		

READING COMPREHENSION

EXTRA PRACTICE TEST 1

Directions: Read the following passage and answer each of the questions that come after it. Choose the *best* answer. Underline the answer you choose. Then mark the appropriate space in the answer column. *Correct answers appear at end of test.*

The blood levels resulting from the injection of a new penicillin were of a shorter duration than those obtained under the same conditions from a commercial penicillin. This new penicillin (No. 128) had an activity of 3,500 units/mg. as compared with 2,300, 1,667, and 900 units/mg. for penicillins K, G, and X, respectively. An experiment was set up to determine whether the rate of excretion of a pure pencillin is a function of its potency in terms of units/mg., or, in other words, of the number of molecules injected. The penicillins used were analytically pure, and were dissolved in normal saline at a concentration of 5,000 units/ml.

Each penicillin, on different days, was injected into each of the same four subjects. Twenty-five thousand units were injected intravenously into one arm, and blood samples withdrawn from the other arm at suitable intervals. Urinary excretion of the penicillins was measured at half-hourly intervals during the first two hours and hourly thereafter. The urine was assayed by the usual cylinder-plate method against *Staphylococcus aureus* 209P, and the blood levels were determined. A penicillin G standard was used in each case.

The duration of penicillin blood levels of at least 0.03 unit/ml. for each of the penicillins was as follows: penicillin G, 2–2.5 hours; penicillin 128, 1–1.25 hours; penicillin K, .5–.75 hour; and penicillin X, 4–4.5 hours. During the first two hours, the various penicillins were excreted in the following percentages: penicillin G, 83; penicillin 128, 58; penicillin K, 28; and penicillin X, 78. Penicillins G and X were excreted in the amount of approximately 80 percent, the difference between them being within experimental error. Penicillin K, however, was excreted to the extent of only about 30 percent.

1. At the concentrations in which penicillin G occurs in the blood, voiding by the kidneys in the first two hours
    (A)   almost completely removes it
    (B)   decreases its potency slightly
    (C)   has practically no effect on it
    (D)   increases its concentration
    (E)   decreases its potency greatly

2. It would seem that penicillin K is
    (A)   destroyed rapidly in the body, and is therapeutically effective
    (B)   destroyed rapidly in the body, and is not therapeutically effective
    (C)   fairly stable in the body, and is therapeutically effective
    (D)   fairly stable in the body, and is not therapeutically effective
    (E)   harmful to the stability of the body

3. Apparently penicillins G and X are sufficiently stable that their excretion by the kidneys represents the limiting factor in the maintenance of
    (A)   a high rate of inactivation
    (B)   the number of molecules injected
    (C)   their sensitivity
    (D)   therapeutic blood levels
    (E)   a low rate of inactivation

4. The experimental dosage of each of the penicillins was
    (A)   inversely proportional to the molecular weights of the penicillins used
    (B)   proportional to the body weights of the subjects
    (C)   proportional to the molecular weights of the penicillins used
    (D)   the same for all subjects
    (E)   varied slightly in each subject

READING COMPREHENSION TEST 1 ANSWERS

1.	A	3.	D
2.	B	4.	D

EXTRA PRACTICE TEST 2

Directions: Read the following passage and answer each of the questions that come after it. Choose the *best* answer. Underline the answer you choose. Then mark the appropriate space in the answer column. *Correct answers appear at end of test.*

"Good personnel relations of an organization depend upon mutual confidence, trust, and good will. The basis of confidence is understanding. Most troubles start with people who do not understand each other. When the organization's intentions or motives are misunderstood, or when reasons for actions, practices, or policies are misconstrued, complete cooperation from individuals is not forthcoming. If management expects full cooperation from employees, it has a responsibility of sharing with them the information which is the foundation of proper understanding, confidence, and trust. Personnel management has long since outgrown the days when it was the vogue to 'treat them rough and tell them nothing.' Up-to-date personnel management provides all possible information about the activities, aims, and purposes of the organization. It seems altogether creditable that a desire should exist among employees for such information which the best-intentioned executive might think would not interest them and which the worst-intentioned would think was none of their business."

1.   The above paragraph implies that one of the causes of the difficulty which an organization might have with its personnel relations is that its employees
    (A)   have not expressed interest in the activities, aims, and purposes of the organization
    (B)   do not believe in the good faith of the organization
    (C)   have not been able to give full cooperation to the organization
    (D)   do not recommend improvements in the practices and policies of the organization
    (E)   can afford little time to establish good relations with their organization

2.   According to the above paragraph, in order for an organization to have good personnel relations, it is NOT essential that
    (A)   employees have confidence in the organization
    (B)   the purposes of the organization be understood by the employees
    (C)   employees have a desire for information about the organization
    (D)   information about the organization be communicated to employees
    (E)   the basis of confidence be mutual understanding

3. According to the paragraph, an organization which provides full information about itself to its employees
(A) understands the intentions of its employees
(B) satisfies a praiseworthy desire among its employees
(C) is managed by executives who have the best intentions toward its employees
(D) is confident that its employees understand its motives
(E) is acting foolishly

4. The one of the following which is the most suitable title for the paragraph is
(A) The Foundations of Personnel Relations
(B) The Consequences of Employee Misunderstanding
(C) The Development of Personnel Management Practices
(D) The Acceptance of Organizational Objectives
(E) The Goals of Big Business

READING COMPREHENSION TEST 2 ANSWERS

1. B   3. B
2. C   4. A

EXTRA PRACTICE TEST 3

Directions: Read the following passage and answer each of the questions that come after it. Choose the *best* answer. Underline the answer you choose. Then mark the appropriate space in the answer column. *Correct answers appear at end of test.*

"A standard comprises characteristics attached to an aspect of a process or product by which it can be evaluated. Standardization is the development and adoption of standards. When they are formulated, standards are not usually the product of a single person, but represent the thoughts and ideas of a group, leavened with the knowledge and information which are currently available. Standards which do not meet certain basic requirements become a hindrance rather than an aid to progress. Standards must not only be correct, accurate, and precise in requiring no more and no less than what is needed for satisfactory results, but they must also be workable in the sense that their usefulness is not nullified by external conditions. Standards should also be acceptable to the people who use them. If they are not acceptable, they cannot be considered to be satisfactory, although they may possess all the other essential characteristics."

1. According to the above paragraph, a processing standard that requires the use of materials that cannot be procured, is most likely to be
  (A) incomplete
  (B) inaccurate
  (C) unworkable
  (D) unacceptable
  (E) unnatural

2. According to the above paragraph, the construction of standards to which the performance of job duties should conform is most often
  (A) the work of the people responsible for seeing that the duties are properly performed
  (B) accomplished by the person who is best informed about the functions involved
  (C) the responsibility of the people who are to apply them
  (D) attributable to the efforts of various informed persons
  (E) the result of someone's haphazard direction

3. According to the above paragraph, when standards call for finer tolerances than those essential to the conduct of successful production operations, the effect of the standards on the improvement of production operations is
  (A) negative
  (B) nullified
  (C) negligible
  (D) beneficial
  (E) lessened

4. The one of the following which is the most suitable title for the above paragraph is
  (A) The Evaluation of Formulated Standards
  (B) The Attributes of Satisfactory Standards
  (C) The Adoption of Acceptable Standards
  (D) The Use of Process or Product Standards
  (E) The Origins of Standards

READING COMPREHENSION TEST 3 ANSWERS

1.	C	3.	A
2.	D	4.	B

EXTRA PRACTICE TEST 4

Directions: Read the following passage and answer each of the questions that come after it. Choose the *best* answer. Underline the answer you choose. Then mark the appropriate space in the answer column. *Correct answers appear at end of test.*

Semanticists point out that words and phrases often acquire connotations tinged with emotions. Such significances are attached because of the context, the history of the usage of the expression, or the background of the person reading or listening. Thus, "the hills of home" may evoke a feeling of nostalgia or a pleasant sensation; but "Bolshevik" may arouse derision or disgust in the minds of many people.

The term "progressive education" has gone through several stages in the connotative process. At one time progressive education was hailed as the harbinger of all that was wise and wholesome in classroom practice, such as the recognition of individual differences and the revolution against formalized dictatorial procedures. However, partly because of abuses on the fanatical fringe of the movement, many people began to associate progressive schools with frills, fads, and follies. What had been discovered and developed by Froebel in Germany, by Pestalozzi in Switzerland, by Montessori in Italy, and by men like Parker and Dewey in the United States was muddled in a melange of mockery and misunderstanding and submerged in satirical quips. As a result, many educators have recently avoided the expression and have chosen to call present educational practices "new" or "modern" rather than "progressive."

Actually "progressive" ideas in any field are as ancient as the history of mankind. As long as individuals question the old ways of doing things and use their intelligence to experiment, advancement will take place. But since every new action produces a reaction, periods of confusion and criticism are to be expected. What we need is a method for distinguishing fact from fancy and arriving at judgments through a consideration of the average rather than of the extreme. If such a method were applied to "progressive education," the term would probably enjoy a better reputation than it has today.

1.   The title which best fits the sense of the passage is
   (A)   The Influence of Progressive Education
   (B)   The Misinterpretation of Progressive Education
   (C)   The Progress of Mankind in Education
   (D)   The History of Progressive Education
   (E)   Progressive vs. Traditional Education

2. A conspicuous feature of the style of this passage is
    (A) alliteration
    (B) metaphors
    (C) satire
    (D) oxymoron
    (E) similes

3. The author implies that
    (A) progressive education is full of silly activities
    (B) progressive ideas in any field are associated with the present era
    (C) periods of confusion and criticism are a natural result of the introduction of a new idea
    (D) inherent in progressive education is a method of distinguishing fact from fancy
    (E) progressive education has reached its greatest popularity in the schools today

4. All of the following are explanations of the acquisition by a word of additional connotations, according to the author, *except*
    (A) the context in which the word appears
    (B) the use to which the word has been put over a period of time
    (C) a desire on the part of the user to feel a pleasant sensation
    (D) the experience of the user
    (E) the events of the period

5. All of the following are offered by the author as reasons for the avoidance by many educators of the term "progressive education" *except* the fact that
    (A) progressive education is confused because its origin stemmed from many countries
    (B) extremists who called themselves "progressives" engaged in distorted practices
    (C) it was widely ridiculed
    (D) it was judged incorrectly
    (E) it was associated with extravagant and foolish notions

READING COMPREHENSION TEST 4 ANSWERS

1. B	3. C	5. A
2. A	4. C	

EXTRA PRACTICE TEST 5

Directions: Read the following passage and answer each of the questions that come after it. Choose the *best* answer. Underline the answer you choose. Then mark the appropriate space in the answer column. *Correct answers appear at end of test.*

Of all the areas of learning the most important is the development of attitudes. Emotional reactions as well as logical thought processes affect the behavior of most people. "The burnt child fears the fire" is one instance; another is the rise of despots like Hitler. Both these examples also point up the fact that attitudes stem from experience. In the one case the experience was direct and impressive; in the other it was indirect and cumulative. The Nazis were indoctrinated largely by the speeches they heard and the books they read.

The classroom teacher in the elementary school is in a strategic position to influence attitudes. This is true partly because children acquire attitudes from these adults whose word they respect. Another reason it is true is that pupils often delve somewhat deeply into a subject in school that has only been touched upon at home or has possibly never occurred to them before. To a child who had previously acquired little knowledge of Mexico, his teacher's method of handling such a unit would greatly affect his attitude toward Mexicans.

The media through which the teacher can develop wholesome attitudes are innumerable. Social studies (with special reference to races, creeds and nationalities), science, matters of health and safety, the very atmosphere of the classroom . . . these are a few of the fertile fields for the inculcation of proper emotional reactions.

However, when children come to school with undesirable attitudes, it is unwise for the teacher to attempt to change their feelings by cajoling or scolding them. She can achieve the proper effect by helping them obtain constructive experiences. To illustrate, first-grade pupils afraid of policemen will probably alter their attitudes after a classroom chat with the neighborhood officer in which he explains how he protects them. In the same way, a class of older children can develop attitudes through discussion, research, outside reading and all-day trips.

Finally, a teacher must constantly evaluate her own attitude because her influence can be deleterious if she has personal prejudices. This is especially true in respect to controversial issues and questions on which children should be encouraged to reach their own decisions as a result of objective analysis of all the facts.

1. The central idea conveyed in the above passage is that
    (A)   attitudes affect our actions
    (B)   teachers play a significant role in developing or changing pupils' attitudes
    (C)   by their attitudes, teachers inadvertently affect pupils' attitudes
    (D)   attitudes can be changed by some classroom experiences
    (E)   attitudes are affected by experience

2. The author implies that
    (A)   children's attitudes often come from those of other children
    (B)   in some aspects of social studies a greater variety of methods can be used in the upper grades than in the lower grades
    (C)   the teacher should guide all discussions by revealing her own attitude
    (D)   people usually act on the basis of reasoning rather than on emotion
    (E)   parents' and teachers' attitudes are more often in harmony than in conflict

3. A statement *not* made or implied in the passage is that
    (A)   attitudes cannot easily be changed by rewards and lectures
    (B)   a child can develop in the classroom an attitude about the importance of brushing his teeth
    (C)   attitudes can be based on the learning of falsehoods
    (D)   the attitudes of children are influenced by all the adults in their environment
    (E)   the children will be influenced by the teacher's judgment in controversial matters

4. The passage specifically states that
    (A)   teachers should always conceal their own attitudes
    (B)   whatever attitudes a child learns in school have already been introduced at home
    (C)   direct experiences are more valuable than indirect ones
    (D)   teachers can sometimes have an unwholesome influence on children
    (E)   it is unwise for the teacher to attempt to change children's attitudes

5. The first and fourth paragraphs have all the following points in common *except*
    (A)   how reading affects attitudes
    (B)   the importance of experience in building attitudes
    (C)   how attitudes can be changed in the classroom
    (D)   how fear sometimes governs attitudes
    (E)   how differences in approach change attitudes

READING COMPREHENSION TEST 5 ANSWERS

1.	B	3.	D	5.	C
2.	B	4.	D		

EXTRA PRACTICE TEST 6

Directions: Read the following passage and answer each of the questions that come after it. Choose the *best* answer. Underline the answer you choose. Then mark the appropriate space in the answer column. *Correct answers appear at end of test.*

The conservative of today hardly knows what to conserve. His bargain with destiny seems broken, and instead of consciousness of achievement and contentment with what is, he is more likely to be filled with a sense of frustration. This frustration is an uncertain quantity with which to deal, since it is characteristically explosive and negative. Under its guidance, conservatism may become a driving force to suppress the inconsequential; it may be a force that is forgetful at the same time of fundamental changes that will undermine a way of political existence. The conservative is happiest when he is unconscious of politics, when the essential propositions of social organization do not have to be defended. But the weakness of conservatism appears in not knowing always what are the fundamental propositions supporting its manner of living, and in inability to judge the consequences of political and economic mutation. Conservatism, however, is at least that body of social thought which does not have to be defended. Conflict, struggle, and protest must be conscious and filled with a sense of purpose. In conflict, there is always the conscious defense of what is presumed to be an interest, and there is an attack on what others deem to be their interest. Likewise, radicalism can never be unconscious or merely habitual, for it is a protest against something that is. But it must not be forgotten that in no state of society have all interests reached an equilibrium which permits of complete cooperation and no struggle. In this sense, conservatism represents a functional value in existence, since the stability of a conservative society is a situation in which the conflict of interest and wills is muted and restricted.

1. The conservative of today
   (A) is typical of all conservatives.
   (B) is unconscious of politics.
   (C) has no place in society.
   (D) is unpredictable in his reactions.
   (E) is a failure.

2. Frustration in the conservative
   (A) is a result of his conflict with radicalism.
   (B) prevents his recognizing changes dangerous to his interests.
   (C) is caused by his failure to defend conservatism.
   (D) becomes a strong guiding force in society.
   (E) is a stabilizing influence.

3. A strong conservatism
   (A) is the only hope of the world today.
   (B) can, like radicalism, never be unconscious or merely habitual.
   (C) is a dangerous force in the rapidly changing modern world.
   (D) always carries with it an element of frustration.
   (E) must comprehend the basis of the way of life it upholds.

4. Radicalism escapes the pitfalls facing conservatism because
   (A) it is characteristically explosive.
   (B) it is always clearly aware of the ultimate results of political and economic changes.
   (C) the protest inherent in radicalism necessarily carries with it a conscious purpose.
   (D) from its very nature it can never be frustrated.
   (E) it is never concerned with inconsequentials.

5. The conservative outlook is of value to the world because
   (A) it preserves all that is best.
   (B) it rises above politics and inconsequential bickerings.
   (C) its lack of conflict is an indication of what we may hope for in a cooperative society.
   (D) such a social attitude constantly produces political and economic mutations.
   (E) its body of social thought does not need to be defended.

6. An essential for any intelligent social attitude is
   (A) a clear perception of the results of social changes and trends.
   (B) a proper balance between the stability of the conservative and the explosiveness of the radical.
   (C) satisfaction with the status quo.
   (D) an unbroken bargain with destiny.
   (E) a conscious effort to change existing conditions.

READING COMPREHENSION TEST 6 ANSWERS

1. D	3. E	5. E
2. B	4. C	6. A

EXTRA PRACTICE TEST 7

Directions: Read the following passage and answer each of the questions that come after it. Choose the *best* answer. Underline the answer you choose. Then mark the appropriate space in the answer column. *Correct answers appear at end of test.*

The study of village communities has become one of the fundamental methods of discussing the ancient history of institutions. It would be out of the question here to range over the whole field of human society in search for communal arrangements of rural life. It will be sufficient to confine the present inquiry to the varieties presented by nations of Aryan race, not because greater importance is to be attached to these nations than to other branches of humankind, although this view might also be reasonably urged, but principally because the Aryan race in its history has gone through all sorts of experiences, and the data gathered from its historical life can be tolerably well ascertained. Should the road be sufficiently cleared in this particular direction, it will not be difficult to connect the results with similar researches in other racial surroundings.

The best way seems to be to select some typical examples, chiefly from the domain of Celtic, Slavonic, and Germanic social history, and to try to interpret them in regard to the general conditions in which communal institutions originate, grow, and decay. As the principal problem will consist in ascertaining how far land was held in common instead of being held, as is usual at present, by individuals, it is advisable to look out for instances in which this element of holding in common is very clearly expressed. We ought to get, as it were, acclimatized to the mental atmosphere of such social arrangement in order to counteract a very natural but most pernicious bent prompting one to apply to the conditions of the past the key of our modern views and habitual notions. A certain acquaintance with the structure of Celtic society, more especially the society of ancient Wales, is likely to make it clear from the outset to what extent the husbandry and law of an Aryan race may depend on institutions in which the individual factor is greatly reduced, while the union first of kinsmen and then of neighbors plays a most decisive part.

1. Do you think that these paragraphs come at the beginning, the middle, or the end of an article?
    (A)   beginning
    (B)   middle
    (C)   end

2. What do you think is the best title for the article?
- (A) The Aryan race
- (B) Celtic, Slavonic, and Germanic history
- (C) Village communities
- (D) The ancient history of institutions
- (E) The fundamental methods of discussing mankind

3. To what sort of nations does the author restrict his inquiry?
- (A) Aryan
- (B) nations with early civilization
- (C) nations which have passed through many experiences
- (D) European
- (E) monarchial

4. According to the paragraph, would it be reasonable to assert that greater importance is to be attached to the Aryan nations than to others?
- (A) yes
- (B) no
- (C) sometimes
- (D) usually
- (E) never

5. According to the paragraph, is it desirable to try to explain the social conditions of the past by the ideas of the present time?
- (A) yes
- (B) no
- (C) sometimes
- (D) usually
- (E) never

6. What two reasons are given in justification of the author's limitation of his inquiry?
- a. greater importance is attached to them
- b. must get mental atmosphere
- c. selection of typical examples
- d. the Aryan race has gone through all sorts of experiences
- e. the data about the Aryans are fairly exact
- f. the road is sufficiently cleared
- (A) a, d
- (B) c, e
- (C) b, a
- (D) e, f
- (E) d, e

7. Who were the common owners in cases where land was held in common?

    (A)   all the people

    (B)   relatives or neighbors

    (C)   Celtic, Slavonic, and Germanic

    (D)   the first owners

    (E)   groups of people

READING COMPREHENSION TEST 7 ANSWERS

1.	A	4.	B	7.	B
2.	C	5.	B		
3.	C	6.	E		

EXTRA PRACTICE TEST 8

Directions: Read the following passage and answer each of the questions that come after it. Choose the *best* answer. Underline the answer you choose. Then mark the appropriate space in the answer column. *Correct answers appear at end of test.*

In the Federal Convention of 1787, the members were fairly well agreed as to the desirability of some check on state laws; but there was sharp difference of opinion whether this check should be political in character as in the form of a congressional veto, or whether the principle of judicial review should be adopted.

Madison was one of the most persistent advocates of the congressional veto and in his discussion of the subject he referred several times to the former imperial prerogative of disallowing provincial statutes. In March, 1787, he wrote to Jefferson, urging the necessity of a federal negative upon state laws. He referred to previous colonial experience in the suggestion that there should be "some emanation" of the federal prerogative "within the several states, so far as to enable them to give a temporary sanction to laws of immediate necessity." This had been provided for in the imperial system through the action of the royal governor in giving immediate effect to statutes, which nevertheless remained subject to royal disallowance. In a letter to Randolph a few weeks later, Madison referred more explicitly to the British practice, urging that the national government be given "a negative, in all cases whatsoever, on the Legislative acts of the States, as the King of Great Britain heretofore had." Jefferson did not agree with Madison; on practical grounds rather than as a matter of principle, he expressed his preference for some form of judicial control.

On July 17, Madison came forward with a speech in support of the congressional veto, again supporting his contention by reference to the royal disallowance of colonial laws: "Its utility is sufficiently displayed in the British System. Nothing could maintain the harmony and subordination of the various parts of the empire, but the prerogative by which the Crown stifles in the birth every Act of every part tending to discord or encroachment. It is true the prerogative is sometimes misapplied thro' ignorance or a partiality to one particular part of the empire: but we have not the same reason to fear such misapplications in our System." This is almost precisely Jefferson's theory of the legitimate function of an imperial veto.

This whole issue shows that the leaders who wrestled with confederation problems during and after the war understood, in some measure at least, the attitude of British administrators when confronted with the stubborn localism of a provincial assembly.

1. Madison was advocating
    (A)   royal disallowance of state legislation.
    (B)   a political check on state laws.
    (C)   the supremacy of the states over the federal government.
    (D)   the maintenance of a royal governor to give immediate effect to statutes.
    (E)   discord and encroachment among the states.

2. From this passage there is no indication
    (A)   of what the British System entailed.
    (B)   of Jefferson's stand on the question of a check on state laws.
    (C)   that the royal negative had been misapplied in the past.
    (D)   that Jefferson understood the attitude of British administrators.
    (E)   of what judicial review would entail.

3. According to this passage, Madison believed that the federal government
    (A)   ought to legislate for the states.
    (B)   should recognize the sovereignty of the several states.
    (C)   ought to exercise judicial control over state legislation.
    (D)   should assume the king's former veto power.
    (E)   was equivalent to a provincial assembly.

4. Madison's conception of a congressional veto

   (A) was opposed to Jefferson's conception of a congressional veto.

   (B) developed from fear that the imperial negative might be misused.

   (C) was that the federal prerogative should be exercised in disallowing state laws.

   (D) was that its primary function was to give temporary sanction to laws of immediate necessity.

   (E) was that its primary function was to prevent such injustices as "taxation without representation."

5. Madison believed that

   (A) the congressional veto would not be abused.

   (B) the royal prerogative ought to have some form of check to correct misapplications.

   (C) the review of state legislation by the federal government ought to remain subject to a higher veto.

   (D) the imperial veto had not been misused.

   (E) utility rather than freedom is the criterion for governmental institutions.

6. Jefferson believed that

   (A) the congressional veto would interfere with states' rights.

   (B) Madison's proposal smacked of imperialism.

   (C) the veto of state legislation was outside the limits of the federal prerogative.

   (D) the British System would be harmful if applied in the United States.

   (E) an imperial veto should include the disallowance of all legislation leading to discord.

7. Madison's main principle was that

   (A) the national interest is more important than the interests of any one state.

   (B) the national government should have compulsive power over the states.

   (C) the king can do no wrong.

   (D) the United States should follow the English pattern of government.

   (E) the veto power of the royal governor should be included in the federal prerogative.

8.   Madison thought of the states as
(A)   emanations of the federal government.
(B)   comparable to provinces of a colonial empire.
(C)   incapable of creating sound legislation.
(D)   having no rights specifically delegated to them.
(E)   incapable of applying judicial review of their legislation.

9.   Which of the following is the best argument which could be made against Madison's proposition?
(A)   the United States has no king.
(B)   the federal government is an entity outside the jurisdiction of the states.
(C)   each state has local problems concerning which representatives from other states are not equipped to pass judgment.
(D)   the federal prerogative had been misused in the past.
(E)   it provides no means of dealing with stubborn localism.

READING COMPREHENSION TEST 8 ANSWERS

1. B	4. C	7. B
2. E	5. A	8. B
3. D	6. D	9. C

9

Extra Practice in Quantitative Ability

MATH ABILITY

EXTRA PRACTICE TEST 1

Directions: Each question in this test is followed by five possible answers lettered (A) through (E). Underline the correct answer. Then mark the appropriate space in the answer column. *Correct answers and solutions appear at end of test.*

1. The part of the total quantity represented by a 24 degree sector of a circle graph is

(A) $6\frac{2}{3}\%$

(B) 12%

(C) $13\frac{1}{3}\%$

(D) 24%

(E) none of these

2. If the shipping charges to a certain point are 62 cents for the first 5 ounces and 8 cents for each additional ounce, the weight of a package for which the charges are $1.66 is

(A) 13 ounces

(B) $1\frac{1}{8}$ pounds

(C) $1\frac{1}{4}$ pounds

(D) $1\frac{1}{2}$ pounds

(E) none of these

3. If 15 cans of food are needed for 7 men for 2 days, the number of cans needed for 4 men for 7 days is
   - (A)   15
   - (B)   20
   - (C)   25
   - (D)   30
   - (E)   none of these

4. The total saving in purchasing thirty 13-cent ice cream pops for a class party at a reduced rate of $1.38 per dozen is
   - (A)   35 cents
   - (B)   40 cents
   - (C)   45 cents
   - (D)   50 cents
   - (E)   none of these

5. The quotient for the division of 36 apples among 4 children may be correctly found by thinking
   - (A) $36 \div \frac{1}{4}$
   - (B) $36 \overline{)4.0}$
   - (C) $\frac{1}{4}$ of 36
   - (D) $\frac{4}{36}$
   - (E)   none of these

6. The missing term in the equation: $\frac{1}{3}$ of ? $= \frac{1}{2}$ of 90 is
   - (A)   45
   - (B)   30
   - (C)   15
   - (D)   35
   - (E)   none of these

7. The fraction closest to $\frac{4}{5}$ is
   - (A) $\frac{2}{3}$
   - (B) $\frac{7}{9}$
   - (C) $\frac{8}{11}$
   - (D) $\frac{5}{8}$
   - (E) $\frac{3}{4}$

8. Of the following, the one which may be used correctly to compute the value of $4 \times 22\frac{1}{2}$ is

(A) $(4 \times 45) + \left(4 \times \frac{1}{2}\right)$

(B) $\left(\frac{1}{2} \text{ of } 4\right) + (2 \times 4) + (2 \times 4)$

(C) $\left(4 \times \frac{1}{2}\right) + (4 \times 2) + (4 \times 2)$

(D) $(4 \times 20) + (4 \times 2) + \left(4 \times \frac{1}{2}\right)$

(E) none of these

9. $16\frac{1}{2} \div \frac{1}{4}$ may correctly be expressed as

(A) $\left(\frac{1}{4} \times 16\right) + \left(\frac{1}{4} \times \frac{1}{2}\right)$

(B) $4 \overline{)16.5}$

(C) $(4 \times 16) + \left(4 \times \frac{1}{2}\right)$

(D) $\frac{1}{4}$ times $\frac{33}{2}$

(E) none of these

10. In computation, $\frac{3}{4}$ may be correctly transformed into $\frac{6}{8}$ for the same reason that
(A) $7(3 + 4) = 21 + 28$
(B) $.2 \overline{)\,.34} = 2 \overline{)34}$
(C) 3 apples + 5 apples = 8
(D) $3 + 4 = 4 + 3$
(E) none of these

11. With a tax rate of .0200, a tax bill of $1050 corresponds to an assessed valuation of
(A) $21,000
(B) $52,500
(C) $21
(D) $1029
(E) none of these

12. A sales agent after deducting his commission of 6 percent, remits $2491 to his principal. The sale amounted to
(A) $2809
(B) $2640
(C) $2650
(D) $2341.54
(E) none of these

13. The percent equivalent of .0295 is
- (A) 2.95%
- (B) 29.5%
- (C) .295%
- (D) 295%
- (E) none of these

14. An angle of 105 degrees is a
- (A) straight angle
- (B) obtuse angle
- (C) acute angle
- (D) reflex angle
- (E) none of these

15. A quart is approximately 60 cubic inches. A cubic foot of water weighs approximately 60 pounds. Therefore, a quart of water weighs approximately
- (A) 2 pounds
- (B) 3 pounds
- (C) 4 pounds
- (D) 5 pounds
- (E) none of these

16. If the same number is added to both the numerator and the denominator of a proper fraction
- (A) the value of the fraction is decreased
- (B) the value of the fraction is increased
- (C) the value of the fraction is unchanged
- (D) the effect of the operation depends on the original fraction
- (E) none of these

17. The least common multiple of 3, 8, 9, 12 is
- (A) 36
- (B) 72
- (C) 108
- (D) 144
- (E) none of these

18. On a bill of $100, the difference between a discount of 30% and 20% and a discount of 40% and 10% is
- (A) nothing
- (B) $2
- (C) $20
- (D) 20%
- (E) none of these

19. $\frac{1}{3}$ percent of a number is 24. The number is

(A) 8
(B) 72
(C) 800
(D) 720
(E) none of these

20. The cost of importing five dozen china dinner sets, billed at $32 per set and paying a duty of 40 percent is

(A) $224
(B) $2688
(C) $768
(D) $1344
(E) none of these

21. The population of a city is 7.85 million. The area is approximately 200 square miles. The number of thousand persons per square mile is

(A) 3.925
(B) 39.25
(C) 392.5
(D) 39,250
(E) none of these

22. The longest straight line that can be drawn to connect two points on the circumference of a circle whose radius is 9 inches is

(A) 9 inches
(B) 18 inches
(C) 282,753 inches
(D) 4.5 inches
(E) none of these

23. It is believed that every even number is the sum of two prime numbers. Two prime numbers whose sum is 32 are

(A) 7, 25
(B) 11, 21
(C) 13, 19
(D) 17, 15
(E) none of these

24. If $7\frac{1}{2}$ is divided by $1\frac{1}{5}$, the quotient is

(A) $6\frac{1}{4}$

(B) 9

(C) $7\frac{1}{10}$

(D) $6\frac{3}{5}$

(E) none of these

25. A farmer has a cylindrical metal tank for watering his stock. It is 10 feet in diameter and 3 feet deep. If one cubic foot contains about 7.5 gallons, the approximate capacity of the tank in gallons is

(A) 12

(B) 225

(C) 4

(D) 1700

(E) none of these

MATH ABILITY EXTRA PRACTICE TEST 1 ANSWERS

1.	A	10.	B	19.	E
2.	B	11.	B	20.	B
3.	D	12.	C	21.	B
4.	C	13.	A	22.	B
5.	C	14.	B	23.	C
6.	E	15.	A	24.	A
7.	B	16.	B	25.	D
8.	D	17.	B		
9.	C	18.	B		

PRACTICE TEST 1 EXPLANATIONS

1. A $6\frac{2}{3}\%$

$$\frac{24}{360} = \frac{2}{30} = \frac{1}{15} = .06\frac{2}{3} = 6\frac{2}{3}\%$$

2. B $1\frac{1}{8}$ lbs.

Total charges   = $1.66
Charge for 1st 5 oz. =   .62

$1.04 (remaining charges at rate of .08 an oz.)

$1.04 ÷ .08 oz. = 13 oz.

∴ 5 oz. + 13 oz. = 18 oz. (Total number of oz. in weight of package.) or $\frac{18}{16} = 1\frac{1}{8}$ lbs.

3. D 30

If 15 cans of food are needed for 7 men for 2 days, $7\frac{1}{2}$ cans are needed for these same 7 men for 1 day.

$7\frac{1}{2} \div 7 = \frac{15}{14}$, the number of cans needed by 1 man for 1 day.

$\therefore 4 \times 7 \times \frac{15}{14} = 30$, the number of cans needed by 4 men for 7 days.

4. C 45 cents

$\$.13 \times 30 = \$3.90$ (regular rate)

$30 = 2\frac{1}{2}$ dozen; $\$1.38 \times 2\frac{1}{2} = \$3.45$ (reduced rate)

Total saving $= \$.45$ ($\$3.90 - \$3.45$)

5. C $\frac{1}{4}$ of 36

$\frac{36}{4} = 9$

6. E none of these

The correct answer is 135.

$\frac{1}{3}$ of ? $= \frac{1}{2}$ of 90

$\frac{1}{3}x = 45$

$x = 3 \times 45$

$x = 135$

7. B $\frac{7}{9}$

$\frac{4}{5} = .80$

$\frac{2}{3} = .66$

$\frac{7}{9} = .78$

$\frac{8}{11} = .73$

$\frac{5}{8} = .63$

$\frac{3}{4} = .75$

8. D $(4 \times 20) + (4 \times 2) + \left(4 \times \frac{1}{2}\right)$

$(4 \times 20) + (4 \times 2) + \left(4 \times \frac{1}{2}\right) = 80 + 8 + 2 = 90$

(This is an example of the Distributive Law, which links the operations of addition and multiplication.)

9. C $(4 \times 16) + \left(4 \times \frac{1}{2}\right)$

$$16\frac{1}{2} \div \frac{1}{4} = \frac{16\frac{1}{2}}{4} = 16\frac{1}{2} \times \frac{4}{1} = (4 \times 16) + \left(4 \times \frac{1}{2}\right)$$

10. B $.2\,\overline{)\,3.4} = 2\,\overline{)\,34}$

$$\frac{(3 \times 2)}{(4 \times 2)} = \frac{6}{8}$$

$$\frac{.2 \times 10}{3.4 \times 10} = \frac{2}{34}$$

11. B $52,500
$$.0200x = \$1050$$
$$200x = \$10,500,000$$
$$2x = \$105,000$$
$$x = \$52,500 \text{ (assessed valuation)}$$

12. C $2650
$$\$2491 + .06x = x$$
$$x = 2491 + .06x$$
$$1.00x - .06x = 2491$$
$$94x = 2491$$
$$94x = 249,100$$
$$94\,\overline{)\,249,100\,}\;\;\$2,650$$

Proof

$2650	$2491
× .06	+ 159
$159.00	$2650

13. A 2.95%
$$.0295 = 2.95\%$$

14. B obtuse angle
An obtuse angle is an angle greater than $90°$.

15. A 2 pounds
A quart $= 60$ cu. in.
60 lbs. $= 1$ cu. ft. (or 1728 cu. in.) $(12 \times 12 \times 12)$
       (Keep like units of measure together)
60 lbs. $= 1728$ cu. in.
 1 lb. $= \frac{1728}{60} =$ approximately .29 cu. in.

   If 29 cu. in. weigh 1 lb., then 60 cu. in. weigh 2 lbs. (approx.). Therefore, a quart weighs 2 lbs. (approx.).

16. **B** the value of the fraction is increased

(1) Start with the fraction $\frac{2}{3}$

(2) $\dfrac{2+2}{3+2} = \dfrac{4}{5}$

(3) $\dfrac{2}{3} = \dfrac{10}{15}$ $\dfrac{4}{5} = \dfrac{12}{15}$

17. **B** 72

Common multiple: can be evenly divided by all the numbers.
Least common multiple: the lowest of these numbers.

18. **B** $2
Formula

Step 1: Express percentages as decimals

Step 2: Subtract each discount from *one*

Step 3: Multiply all the results

Step 4: Subtract the product from *one*

Step 1: .3, .2 and .4, .1

Step 2: .7, .8 and .6, .9

Step 3: $.7 \times .8 = .56$ (represents percent remaining after the discounts are taken) $.6 \times .9 = .54$

Step 4:
$$\begin{array}{cc} 1.00 & 1.00 \\ -\ .56 & -\ .54 \\ \hline .44 & .46 \end{array}$$

The difference is 2%
Then $100 \times .02 = $2

19. **E** none of these
The correct answer is 7200.

$$\frac{1}{300}x = 24$$
$$x = 24 \times 300$$
$$x = 7200$$

20. **B** $2688

$$\begin{array}{r} \$\ 32 \\ \times\ \ \ 60 \\ \hline \$1920 \end{array}$$ Cost of dinner sets before paying duty

$$\begin{array}{r} \$1920 \\ \times\ \ \ \ .40 \\ \hline \$\ \ 768.00 \end{array}$$ Duty

$$\begin{array}{r} \$1920 \\ +\ \ \ 768 \\ \hline \$2688 \end{array}$$ Cost of dinner sets *after* paying duty

21. B 39.25

$$\underset{200\,\overline{)\,7850.00}}{39.25}\text{ (per square mile)}$$
(population in thousands)

The answer is 39.25.

22. B 18 inches

9 inches + 9 inches = 18 inches

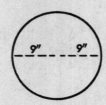

23. C 13, 19

A prime number is an integer which cannot be divided except by itself and one integer; a whole number as opposed to a fraction or a decimal.

24. A $6\frac{1}{4}$

$$\frac{7\frac{1}{2}}{1\frac{1}{5}} = \frac{15}{2} \div \frac{6}{5} = \frac{15}{2} \times \frac{5}{6} = \frac{25}{4} = 6\frac{1}{4}$$

or

$$6.25 = 6\frac{1}{4}$$
$$1.2\,\overline{)\,7.5}$$

25. D 1700

$$A = \pi r^2$$
$$= 3(5)^2$$
$$= 75 \text{ sq. ft.}$$

$$\pi = \frac{22}{7} = 3 \text{ (approx.)}$$

Volume of tank = 75 × 3 = 225 cubic feet

$$\begin{array}{r} 225 \\ \times\quad 7.5 \\ \hline 1125 \\ 1575 \\ \hline 1687.5 \text{ gallons or approx. 1700} \end{array}$$

EXTRA PRACTICE TEST 2

Directions: Each question in this test is followed by five possible answers lettered (A) through (E). Underline the correct answer. Then mark the appropriate space in the answer column. *Correct answers and solutions appear at end of test.*

1. One cube has an edge that is 6 inches long, and another has an edge 2 inches long. How many of the 2-inch cubes will be needed to equal the volume of one 6-inch cube?
   (A) 3
   (B) 9
   (C) 18
   (D) 27
   (E) none of these

2. Which of the following sets of numbers is arranged in order of size beginning with the largest?

   (A) $1^5; \sqrt[3]{8}; \dfrac{3.5}{5}; (.4)^2$

   (B) $\sqrt[3]{8}; 1^5; (.4)^2; \dfrac{3.5}{5}$

   (C) $\sqrt[3]{8}; (.4)^2; 1^5; \dfrac{3.5}{5}$

   (D) $\sqrt[3]{8}; 1^5; \dfrac{3.5}{5}; (.4)^2$

   (E) none of these

3. A candy recipe calls for $\frac{1}{2}$ cup each of milk, maple syrup and butter to every 3 cups of sugar used. What fractional part of the recipe is maple syrup?

   (A) $\dfrac{1}{9}$

   (B) $\dfrac{1}{4}$

   (C) $\dfrac{1}{6}$

   (D) $\dfrac{1}{3}$

   (E) none of these

4. If the base of a parallelogram is doubled, but the altitude is kept constant, the area will be
   (A)   one half as large
   (B)   four times as large
   (C)   twice as large
   (D)   one fourth as large
   (E)   none of these

5. The corresponding sides of two similar right triangles are in the ratio 1:2. Which of the following statements is false?
   (A)   An altitude of the smaller triangle is to the corresponding altitude of the larger triangle as 1 is to 2.
   (B)   The perimeter of the larger triangle is twice the perimeter of the smaller.
   (C)   The angles of one triangle are equal to the corresponding angles of the other.
   (D)   The area of the larger triangle is twice the area of the smaller.
   (E)   The triangles have the same shape but do not have the same size.

6. On a 3-hour examination of 200 questions there are 50 mathematics problems. If twice as much time should be allowed for each mathematics problem as for each of the other questions, how many minutes should be spent on the mathematics problems?
   (A)   60 minutes
   (B)   72 minutes
   (C)   90 minutes
   (D)   120 minutes
   (E)   none of these

7. What is the radius of the largest circular disc that can be cut from a strip of metal 15 inches by 21 inches?
   (A) $7\frac{1}{2}$ inches
   (B)   15 inches
   (C) $157\frac{1}{2}$ inches
   (D)   315 inches
   (E)   none of these

8. Jane paid $2.50 to have a new cover put on her old umbrella, instead of buying a new umbrella for $4. What percent of the cost of a new umbrella did she save?
    (A) 1.5%
    (B) $37\frac{1}{2}$%
    (C) 60%
    (D) $62\frac{1}{2}$%
    (E) none of these

9. An airplane is flying in still air at 200 miles an hour. How many seconds are required for it to travel a mile?
    (A) $3\frac{1}{3}$ seconds
    (B) 18 seconds
    (C) 60 seconds
    (D) 3600 seconds
    (E) none of these

10. The accompanying figure represents a cross section of a tunnel. ABCD is a rectangle 20.0 feet by 10.0 feet, surmounted by a semicircle.
    Find the area of the cross section to the nearest square foot. (Use $\pi = 3.14$)
    (A) 231 sq. ft.
    (B) 357 sq. ft.
    (C) 514 sq. ft.
    (D) 628 sq. ft.
    (E) none of these

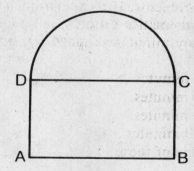

11. If $8x$ represents the perimeter of a rectangle and $2x + 3$ represents its length, what is its width?
    (A) $10x + 3$
    (B) $2x - 3$
    (C) 3
    (D) $6x - 3$
    (E) none of these

12. The base of a rectangular bin is 8 feet by 5 feet. To what level depth will 200 bushels of grain fill the bin? (1 cubic foot = .8 bushel)
   (A) 5 feet
   (B) $6\frac{1}{4}$ feet
   (C) 25 feet
   (D) 4 feet
   (E) none of these

13. Mr. Brown owned a house, which he rented for $100 a month. The house was assessed for $9000. In 1961 the rate of taxation was increased from $25 to $28 per $1000 assessed valuation. By what amount was Mr. Brown's monthly income reduced as a result of the increase in that year's taxes?
   (A) $2.25
   (B) $21
   (C) $25
   (D) $27
   (E) none of these

14. In making a State income-tax return for the calendar year 1955, a single person was allowed to take an exemption of $1000 and a married person, $2500. If the status of the taxpayer changed during the year, the exemption had to be apportioned in accordance with the number of months (to the nearest month) before and after the change. To how great an exemption was a man entitled who married on June 11, 1955?
   (A) $1250
   (B) $1500
   (C) $1750
   (D) $1875
   (E) none of these

15. A cube 4 inches on each edge is painted on all faces. If this cube is cut into 1-inch cubes, how many of the 1-inch cubes will have paint on *none* of their faces?
   (A) none
   (B) 2
   (C) 16
   (D) 4
   (E) none of these

16. Find the value of x in the equation $\sqrt{9} + \sqrt{16} = x$
   (A) 5
   (B) 7
   (C) 12
   (D) 25
   (E) none of these

17. If 3 children weigh a total of 152 lb. 4 oz., what is their average weight?

(A) $50\frac{1}{3}$ lb.

(B) 50 lb. 12 oz.

(C) 50 lb. 8 oz.

(D) 50 lb. $1\frac{1}{3}$ oz.

(E) none of these

18. A man has borrowed $4000 at 4 percent. How much additional money can he borrow at 6 percent if his total interest cost is not to exceed $250 a year?

(A) $80

(B) $90

(C) $1500

(D) $4000

(E) none of these

19. The area of a trapezoid is found by multiplying one half the sum of its bases by its altitude. If the bases are 2 ft. 3 in. and 3 ft. 9 in. and the altitude is 1 ft. 6 in., find the number of square feet in the area of the figure.

(A) $4\frac{1}{2}$ sq. ft.

(B) 9 sq. ft.

(C) 54 sq. ft.

(D) 648 sq. ft.

(E) none of these

20. In order to hold a telegraph pole vertical, a wire was stretched from a point on the pole 24 feet above the ground to a stake 18 feet from the foot of the pole. How long was the wire between these two points?

(A) 6 feet

(B) 30 feet

(C) 42 feet

(D) 432 feet

(E) none of these

21. The radius of a circle is 6 inches. The ratio of the number of square inches in its area to the number of inches in its circumference is

(A) 1:1

(B) 2:1

(C) 3:1

(D) 6:1

(E) none of these

22. An automobile travels m miles in h hours. At this rate, how far will it travel in x hours?

(A) $\dfrac{m}{x}$

(B) $\dfrac{mx}{h}$

(C) $x = \dfrac{m}{h}$

(D) $\dfrac{mh}{x}$

(E) none of these

23. In a 3-hour examination of 350 questions, there are 50 mathematics problems. If twice as much time should be allowed for each problem as for each of the other questions, how many minutes should be spent on the mathematical problems?
(A) 45 minutes
(B) 52 minutes
(C) 60 minutes
(D) 72 minutes
(E) none of these

24. A rectangular picture measures $4\frac{1}{2}$ in. by $6\frac{3}{4}$ in. If the picture is proportionally enlarged so that the shorter side is $7\frac{1}{2}$ inches, what will be the length of the longer side?

(A) $9\frac{3}{4}$ inches

(B) $11\frac{1}{4}$ inches

(C) $13\frac{1}{2}$ inches

(D) $20\frac{1}{4}$ inches

(E) none of these

25. A typewriter was listed at $120.00 and was bought for $96.00. What was the rate of discount?

(A) $16\frac{2}{3}\%$
(B) 20%
(C) 24%
(D) 25%
(E) none of these

MATH ABILITY EXTRA PRACTICE TEST 2 ANSWERS

1.	D	10.	B	19.	A
2.	D	11.	B	20.	B
3.	A	12.	B	21.	C
4.	C	13.	A	22.	B
5.	D	14.	D	23.	A
6.	B	15.	E	24.	B
7.	A	16.	B	25.	B
8.	B	17.	B		
9.	B	18.	C		

PRACTICE TEST 2 EXPLANATIONS

1. D 27

$$V1 = 6^3 = \overset{3}{\cancel{6}} \times \overset{3}{\cancel{6}} \times \overset{3}{\cancel{6}} = 27$$
$$V2 = 2^3 = \underset{1}{\cancel{2}} \times \underset{1}{\cancel{2}} \times \underset{1}{\cancel{2}}$$

2. D $\sqrt[3]{8}$; 1^5; $\dfrac{3.5}{5}$; $(.4)^2$

$$\sqrt[3]{8} = 2 \qquad\qquad \frac{3.5}{5} = .7$$
$$1^5 = 1 \qquad\qquad (.4)^2 = .16$$

3. A $\dfrac{1}{9}$

The recipe consists of $4\frac{1}{2}$ cups of the various items.

$$\therefore \frac{1}{2} \div 4\frac{1}{2} = \frac{1}{2} \times \frac{2}{9} = \frac{1}{9} \text{ maple syrup}$$

4. C twice as large
Area of a parallelogram $= b \times h$
Let $b = 6$, $h = 4$; therefore, area $= 24$.
Let $b = 12$, $h = 4$; therefore, area $= 48$ (twice as large)

5. D The area of the larger triangle is twice the area of the smaller. Formula: The areas of two similar triangles are in the same ratio as the squares of two corresponding sides. It is given that the sides are in the ratio 1:2. Therefore, the areas are in the ratio 1^2:2^2, which $= 1$:4. It is, therefore, apparent that the larger triangle is four times, not twice, the area of the smaller. By similar analysis, statements (A), (B), (C), and (E) will be found to be true.

6. **B**   72 minutes

Let x = time for question other than mathematics and $2x$ = time for each mathematics problem.

Then $150x$ = time for all questions other than mathematics and $50(2x)$ or $100x$ = total time for all mathematics problems. ∴ $150x + 100x = 180$ minutes (3 hours) or $250x = 180$, $x = .72$ minutes and $2x = 1.44$ minutes (time for each mathematics problem). ∴ $50 \times 1.44 = 72$ minutes

7. **A** $7\frac{1}{2}$ inches

The diameter of the largest circular disc = 15 inches; therefore, the radius (which is $\frac{1}{2}$ the diameter) = $7\frac{1}{2}$ inches.

8. **B** $37\frac{1}{2}\%$

$4 (cost of new umbrella) − $2.50 (paid by Jane) = $1.50 (saved by Jane).

∴ $\dfrac{\$1.50}{\$4.00} = 37\frac{1}{2}\%$.

9. **B**   18 seconds

Let x = number of seconds required for the airplane to travel a mile.

∴ $\dfrac{200 \text{ miles}}{3600 \text{ seconds } (= 1 \text{ hour})} = \dfrac{1 \text{ mile}}{x}$ or $200x = 3600$,

$x = 18$ seconds

10. **B**   357 sq. ft.

We have in the figure given a rectangle and a semicircle. Our plan is to obtain the area of the rectangle and the area of the semicircle and add them together for the answer.

Formula for area of rectangle: base $\times$ altitude

By substitution, area of rectangle = 20×10 or 200 sq. ft.

Formula for area of semicircle: $\dfrac{\pi r^2}{2}$

(Since diameter = 20, $r = 10$.)

By substitution, area of semicircle = $\dfrac{3.14 \text{ (given)} \times 10^2}{2} =$

$\dfrac{314}{2} = 157$ sq. ft.

The area of the cross section = $200 + 157 = 357$ sq. ft.

11. B $2x - 3$

Given the length $(2x + 3)$ and the perimeter $(8x)$, we are to find the width. Let w = width.

Formula:

perimeter = 2 (length + width)

By substitution, $8x = 2 (2x + 3 + w)$ or $8x = 4x + 6 + 2w$ or $4x - 6 = 2w$; $w = 2x - 3$

12. B $6\frac{1}{4}$ feet

It is first necessary to find the volume of the rectangular bin before we can ascertain the level depth or height. Let x = the volume or number of cubic feet that will contain the 200 bushels of grain. We then form the proportion, 1 cubic foot : .8 bushel = x : 200; x = 250 cubic feet.

Now we use the formula: Volume = length × width × height

Let h = height or level depth.

By substitution, 250 cubic feet = 8 feet × 5 feet × h or $40h = 250$; $h = 6\frac{1}{4}$ feet

13. A $2.25

The increase in taxes for Mr. Brown in 1961 was $3 per $1000 ($28 minus $25).

The total increase on the $9000 assessment was $27 (9 × 3).

$27 ÷ 12 = $2.25 (decrease in Mr. Brown's monthly income as a result of increased taxation)

14. D $1875

Allowance as a single person: $\frac{5}{12}$ × $1000

Allowance as a married person: $\frac{7}{12}$ × $2500

Total allowance or exemption: $\frac{5}{12}$ × $1000 + $\frac{7}{12}$ × $2500 = $\frac{22500}{12}$ = $1875

15. E   none of these

The 4 inch cube, when cut into 1 inch cubes, will contain 64 cubes (4 × 4 × 4).

8 of the 1 inch cubes will have paint on none of their faces, 4 cubes in the second layer and 4 cubes in the third layer which are not visible or exposed. To answer this question fully, one would have to construct and examine a working model.

16. B   7

$\sqrt{9} = 3 + \sqrt{16} = 4 = 7$; $x = 7$

17. B 50 lbs. 12 oz.
Change 152 lb. 4 oz. to 150 lb. 36 oz. and divide by 3.

18. C $1500
Formula: Interest = Principal × Rate
  By substitution, $4000 × .04 = $160 (interest)
  Since the man's total interest cost is not to exceed $250 a year, $90 is the extent of the additional interest cost that he may undertake ($250 − $160 = $90). Let x represent the amount of the additional money that he can borrow at 6%. We then form the equation, $(x) (.06) = \$90$ or $6x = \$9000$, $x = \$1500$

19. A $4\frac{1}{2}$ sq. ft.

Area of trapezoid $= \frac{1}{2}$ (base$_1$ + base$_2$) × altitude

  By substitution, $= \frac{1}{2}$ (2 ft. 3 in. + 3 ft. 9 in.) × 1 ft. 6 in. $=$

$\frac{1}{2}$ × 6 feet × $1\frac{1}{2}$ feet or $\frac{1}{2}$ × 6 feet × $\frac{3}{2}$ feet $= \frac{18}{4}$ feet $= 4\frac{1}{2}$ sq. ft.

20. B 30 feet
A right triangle is formed as in the diagram.

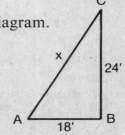

Let x = AC, the length of the wire; CB = 24; AB = 18.
$\therefore x^2 = 24^2 + 18^2$ or $x^2 = 900$, $x = 30$ feet

21. C 3:1

$\dfrac{A}{C} = \dfrac{\pi r^2}{2\pi r} = \dfrac{r}{2} = \dfrac{6}{2} = \dfrac{3}{1}$ (3:1) or

$A = \pi r^2 \quad C = 2\pi r \quad \dfrac{36\pi}{12\pi} = \dfrac{3}{1}$ (3:1)
$\quad = \pi 36 \qquad = \pi 12$

22. B $\dfrac{mx}{h}$

Distance = Rate × Time

$m = \dfrac{m}{h} \times h$ (substituting)

Let y = distance traveled in x hours

$y = \dfrac{m}{h} \times x = \dfrac{mx}{h}$

23. A 45 minutes
Given
　　1 mathematics problem equivalent to 2 other questions in time to be spent
　　50 mathematics problems equivalent to 100 regular questions in time to be spent
　　350 questions (including mathematics problems) equivalent to 400 regular questions in time to be spent
　　3 hours for 400 (regular) questions
Solving
　　100 of the 400 is mathematics $(2 \times 50) \frac{100}{400} =$ time devoted to 50 mathematics problems
　　$\frac{1}{4}$ of 3 hours $= 45$ minutes

24. B $11\frac{1}{4}$ inches
Proportion
$$\frac{4\frac{1}{2}}{7\frac{1}{2}} = \frac{6\frac{3}{4}}{x}$$

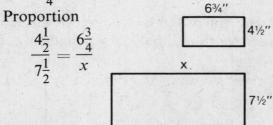

Solving
$$4\frac{1}{2}x = 6\frac{3}{4} \times 7\frac{1}{2}; \quad \frac{9}{2}x = \frac{27}{4} \times \frac{15}{2};$$

$$x = \frac{\frac{27}{4} \times \frac{15}{2}}{\frac{9}{2}}; \quad x = \frac{27}{4} \times \frac{15}{2} \times \frac{2}{9} = \frac{45}{4} = 11\frac{1}{4} \text{ inches}$$

25. B 20%
Cost $=$ \$96, Listed Price $=$ \$120, Discount $=$ \$24
$$\frac{24}{120} = \frac{2}{10} = 20\%$$

EXTRA PRACTICE TEST 3

Directions: Each question in this test is followed by five possible answers lettered (A) through (E). Underline the correct answer. Then mark the appropriate space in the answer column. *Correct answers and solutions appear at end of test.*

1. On a $9840 bill for equipment, what is the difference between a discount of 30 percent and a discount series of 20 percent and 10 percent?
   (A) no difference
   (B) $196.80
   (C) $787.20
   (D) $2755.20
   (E) none of these

2. If the fuel consumption of a 110-horsepower engine is 0.75 pounds per horsepower per hour, how many pounds of fuel will be used in 40 minutes?
   (A) 0.50 pounds
   (B) 30 pounds
   (C) 50 pounds
   (D) 55 pounds
   (E) none of these

3. A clock that loses 4 minutes every 24 hours was set right at 6 a. m. on January 1. What was the time indicated by this clock when the right time was 12 o'clock noon on January 6?
   (A) 11:36
   (B) 11:38
   (C) 11:39
   (D) 11:40
   (E) none of these

4. The sides of a church spire are four congruent triangles, each with an altitude of 40 feet and a base of 10 feet. Find the area of the spire.
   (A) 200 sq. ft.
   (B) 600 sq. ft.
   (C) 400 sq. ft.
   (D) 1600 sq. ft.
   (E) none of these

5. If a man's salary is $b per month and if during a certain month he spends $c, what fractional part of his salary does he save?

(A) $b - c$

(B) $\dfrac{c}{b}$

(C) $\dfrac{b - c}{b}$

(D) $\dfrac{b}{c}$

(E) none of these

6. A bowler has an average of 150 points a game for 12 games. If he bowls 6 more games, how high an average must he make in these games to raise his average for the 18 games to 160?

(A) 170
(B) 180
(C) 210
(D) 225
(E) none of these

7. A store offers for sale 5 packages of cereal, all of the same kind and quality but manufactured by different firms and containing different amounts. Determine which of the following is most economical.

(A) 6 oz. for 5 cents
(B) 11 oz. for 9 cents
(C) 1 lb. for $12\frac{1}{2}$ cents
(D) 14 oz. for 11 cents
(E) 1 lb. 3 oz. for 16 cents

8. A plane leaves Denver, Colorado on June 1st at 1 p.m. Mountain Standard Time and arrives at New York City at 8 p.m. Eastern Daylight Time. The actual time of flight was

(A) 3 hours
(B) 4 hours
(C) 5 hours
(D) 6 hours
(E) none of these

9. In measuring a distance of 1 mile, an error of 11 feet was made. Which of the following correctly represents the size of the error?

(A) 1 inch in 40 feet
(B) 0.2%
(C) 1 foot in 150 yards
(D) 1:500
(E) none of these

10. A coffee shop blends two kinds of coffee, putting in 2 parts of the 33 cents a pound grade to 1 of the 24 cents grade. If the mixture is changed to 1 part of the 33-cent kind and 2 parts of the 24-cent kind, how much will the shop save in blending 100 pounds?
    (A) $1
    (B) $0.90
    (C) $3
    (D) $9
    (E) none of these

11. What is the largest integer that is a factor of all three of the following numbers: 2160, 1344, 1440?
    (A) 6
    (B) 8
    (C) 12
    (D) 16
    (E) none of these

12. Divide 49 by .035
    (A) 1.4
    (B) 14
    (C) 140
    (D) 1400
    (E) none of these

13. Find the value of $\left(4\frac{5}{8} - 2\frac{3}{4}\right) \div \frac{5}{4}$
    (A) 1
    (B) 2
    (C) $1\frac{7}{10}$
    (D) $2\frac{3}{10}$
    (E) none of these

14. Express .3% as a common fraction.
    (A) $\frac{1}{3}$
    (B) $\frac{3}{10}$
    (C) $\frac{3}{100}$
    (D) $\frac{3}{1000}$
    (E) none of these

15. The annual income of a family is budgeted as follows: $\frac{1}{10}$ for clothing, $\frac{1}{3}$ for food and $\frac{1}{5}$ for rent. This leaves $1320 for other expenses and savings. Find the annual income.
(A) $2156
(B) $3600
(C) $23,760
(D) $39,600
(E) none of these

16. Mr. Smith's tax on his house for 1956 was $283.79. If the tax rate for that year was $3.835 per $100 of assessed valuation, for what amount was Mr. Smith's house assessed?
(A) $10.88
(B) $74
(C) $1088.33
(D) $7400
(E) none of these

17. A furniture dealer has put a chair on sale with discounts of 25 percent and 10 percent from $60, the marked price. How much will it cost to buy the chair?
(A) $13.50
(B) $21
(C) $39
(D) $40.50
(E) none of these

18. The distance between Chicago and Cleveland is 354 miles. If a person leaves Chicago at 9:50 a.m. Central Time and arrives in Cleveland at 5:30 p.m. the same day Eastern Standard Time, at what average speed does he travel, correct to the nearest mile?
(A) 46 mph
(B) 50 mph
(C) 53 mph
(D) 55 mph
(E) none of these

19. The oil burner in a certain house is used to heat the house and to heat the hot water. During the seven cold months when the house is heated, an average of 200 gallons of oil a month is used. In the remaining five months, when the house is not heated, a total of 200 gallons of oil is used. What percentage of the year's oil supply is required to heat water during these five months?

(A) $\frac{1}{8}\%$

(B) 7%

(C) $12\frac{1}{2}\%$

(D) 14%

(E) none of these

20. The distance, s, in feet that a body falls in t seconds is given by the formula $s = 16t^2$. If a body has been falling for 5 seconds, how far will it fall during the 6th second?

(A) 16 feet

(B) 80 feet

(C) 176 feet

(D) 576 feet

(E) none of these

21. The cost of 63 inches of ribbon at 12 cents per yard is

(A) $.20

(B) $.21

(C) $.22

(D) $.23

(E) none of these

22. If $1\frac{1}{2}$ cups of cereal are used with $4\frac{1}{2}$ cups of water, the amount of water needed with $\frac{3}{4}$ of a cup of cereal is

(A) 2 cups

(B) $2\frac{1}{8}$ cups

(C) $1\frac{1}{4}$ cups

(D) $2\frac{1}{2}$ cups

(E) none of these

23. Under certain conditions, sound travels at about 1100 feet per second. If 88 feet per second is approximately equivalent to 60 miles per hour, the speed of sound, under the above conditions, is closest to
   (A)   730 miles per hour
   (B)   750 miles per hour
   (C)   740 miles per hour
   (D)   760 miles per hour
   (E)   none of these

24. If one angle of a triangle is three times a second angle and the third angle is 20 degrees more than the second angle, the second angle is
   (A)   32°
   (B)   34°
   (C)   40°
   (D)   50°
   (E)   none of these

25. Assuming that on a blueprint $\frac{1}{4}$ inch equals 12 inches, the actual length in feet of a steel bar represented on the blueprint by a line $3\frac{3}{8}$ inches long is
   (A) $3\frac{3}{8}$ feet
   (B) $6\frac{3}{4}$ feet
   (C) $12\frac{1}{2}$ feet
   (D) $13\frac{1}{2}$ feet
   (E)   none of these

MATH ABILITY EXTRA PRACTICE TEST 3 ANSWERS

1.	B	10.	C	19.	C
2.	D	11.	E	20.	C
3.	C	12.	D	21.	B
4.	E	13.	E	22.	E
5.	C	14.	D	23.	B
6.	B	15.	B	24.	A
7.	C	16.	D	25.	D
8.	B	17.	D		
9.	B	18.	C		

PRACTICE TEST 3 EXPLANATIONS

1. **B** $196.80
   30% of $9840 = $2952; 20% of 9840 = $1968; $9840 − $1968 = $7872. 10% of $7872 = $787.20; $1968 = $787.20 = $2755.20. $2952 − $2755.20 = $196.80

2. **D** 55 pounds
   Since 0.75 pounds produces one horsepower per hour, .75 × 110 = 82.5 pounds (no. pounds of fuel used to produce 110 horsepower in 1 hour)
   $\therefore \frac{40}{60} \times 82.5$ or $\frac{2}{3} \times 82.5 = 55$ pounds

3. **C** 11:39
   Total time between the two given dates = 5 days + 6 hours or 5 × 24 + 6 = 126 hours
   The object is to find the total number of minutes lost by the clock during the 126 hours. Let us call this loss x.
   $\therefore \frac{4}{24} = \frac{x}{126}$ or $24x = 504$, $x = 21$ minutes lost
   $\therefore$ the time indicated by the clock at 12 o'clock noon on January 6 was 11:39 (12 o'clock − 21 minutes).

4. **E** none of these
   The correct answer is 800 sq. ft.
   Formula: Area of triangle $= \frac{1}{2}$ base × altitude
   Area of spire $= 4 \times \frac{1}{2}$ base × altitude
   By substitution $= 4 \times \frac{1}{2} \times 10 \times 40 = 800$ sq. ft.

5. **C** $\frac{b-c}{b}$
   If the man earns b and spends c, he saves $b − c$.
   Formula: $\dfrac{\text{amount saved}}{\text{amount earned}}$ = fractional part of salary saved
   By substitution, $\dfrac{b-c}{b}$ = fractional part of salary saved

6. **B** 180
   The bowler has achieved a total of 1800 points (150 × 12). His aim is to achieve 2880 points (160 × 18) in 6 more games, which means 1080 points more (2880 − 1800).
   $\therefore$ 1080 ÷ 6 = 180 points (the new average he must achieve)

7.   C   1 lb. for $12\frac{1}{2}$ cents

Method: find the cost per ounce in each of the five statements and compare.

(A) $.05 \div 6 = \$.0083$

(B) $.09 \div 11 = \$.0081$

(C) $\dfrac{.12\frac{1}{2}}{16} = \$.00781$ (most economical)

(D) $.11 \div 14 = \$.00785$

(E) $.16 \div 19 = \$.0084$

8.   B   4 hours actual flying time

In traveling eastward we set our clocks forward for each time zone.

TIME ZONES			
PACIFIC	MOUNTAIN	CENTRAL	EASTERN
4 A.M.	5 A.M.	6 A.M.	7 A.M. EST 8 A.M. EDT

Plane left at 1 p.m. Traveled 7 hours, arriving at 8 p.m. E.D.T. Subtract 2 hours' difference between Mountain Time and Eastern Standard Time (E.S.T.). Subtract another hour for Eastern Daylight Time (E.D.T.). That is, $7 - 3 = 4$ hours actual flying time.

9.   B   0.2%

$$\frac{11 \text{ feet}}{5280 \text{ feet}} = \frac{1 \text{ foot}}{480 \text{ feet}}$$

$$\frac{12 \times 1 \text{ inch}}{12 \times 40 \text{ feet}} = \frac{1 \text{ inch}}{40 \text{ feet}}$$

10.   C $3

Blend 1: 2 lbs. $\times$ .33 $+$ 1 lb. $\times$ .24 $=$ .90 per 3 lbs.

Blend 2: 1 lb. $\times$ .33 $+$ 2 lbs. $\times$ .24 $=$ .81 per 3 lbs.

Saving per lb., using blend 2 $=$ .09 per 3 lbs. (.90 $-$ .81), which is .03 per lb.

Saving per 100 lbs., using blend 2 $=$ \$3   (100 $\times$ .03)

11. **E** none of these
The correct answer is 48.
   2160: the factors are 2, 2, 2, 2, 3, 3, 3, 5
   1344: the factors are 2, 2, 2, 2, 2, 2, 3, 7
   1440: the factors are 2, 2, 2, 2, 2, 2, 3, 3, 5
   By inspection, we see that the factors are $2 \times 2 \times 2 \times 2 \times 3 = 48$

12. **D** 1400
$49 \div .035 = 49000 + 35$ (moving decimals 3 places to the right). Then solve by using the algorism
$$35 \overline{)49000} = 1400$$

13. **E** none of these
The correct answer is $1\frac{1}{2}$.
   The problem may be solved as follows:
$$\left(4\frac{5}{8} - 2\frac{3}{4}\right) \div \frac{5}{4} = \left(\frac{37}{8} - \frac{11}{4}\right) \div \frac{5}{4} = \left(\frac{37}{8} - \frac{22}{8}\right) \div$$
$$\frac{5}{4} = \frac{15}{8} \div \frac{5}{4} = \frac{15}{8} \times \frac{4}{5} = \frac{3}{2} = 1\frac{1}{2}$$

14. **D** $\frac{3}{1000}$
$$.3\% = \frac{.3}{100} = \frac{3}{1000}$$

15. **B** $3600
If x represents the annual income, then $\frac{x}{10}$ = amount spent for clothing, $\frac{x}{3}$ = amount spent for food, and $\frac{x}{5}$ = amount spent for rent.
$$\therefore \frac{x}{10} + \frac{x}{3} + \frac{x}{5} + \$1320 = x. \quad x = \$3600$$

16. **D** $7400
Let x = assessment of Mr. Smith's house.
   Since the tax rate was $3.835 per $100, this was = .03835.
   Formula: assessment $\times$ tax rate = tax paid.
   By substitution, $.03835x = \$283.79$.
   Solving, we find that $x = \$7400$.

17. **D** $40.50
Formula: marked price minus discounts = cost.
   $60 minus $15 (25% $\times$ $60) = $45 (price after first discount)
   $45 minus $4.50 (10% $\times$ $45, the second discount) = $40.50 (cost)

18. C   53 mph

Time interval = 6 hours 40 minutes or $6\frac{2}{3}$ hours. (Note: In converting Central Standard Time to Eastern Standard Time, add 1 hour.)

$$\text{Formula: Rate} = \frac{\text{distance}}{\text{time}} = \frac{354}{6\frac{2}{3}} = 354 \times \frac{3}{20} = \frac{1062}{20} =$$

53.1 mph or 53 mph (to the nearest mile)

19. C $12\frac{1}{2}\%$

Year's oil supply = 1600 gallons (200 × 7 = 1400 gallons + 200 for the remaining 5 months)

$$\therefore \frac{200}{1600} = \frac{1}{8} = 12\frac{1}{2}\% \text{ (percentage of the year's oil supply re-}$$

quired to heat water during the 5 months when the house is not heated)

20. C   176 feet

Formula: $s = 16t^2$

By substitution, $s = 16 \times 5^2 = 16 \times 25 = 400$ feet (distance covered in 5 seconds)

By substitution: $s = 16 \times 6^2 = 16 \times 36 = 576$ feet (distance covered in 6 seconds)

$\therefore 576 - 400 = 176$ feet (distance body will fall during the 6th second)

21. B $.21

SOLUTION

$$63 \text{ inches} = \frac{63}{36} \text{ yards}; \frac{\overset{21}{\cancel{63}}}{\underset{2}{\cancel{36}}} \times \overset{.01}{\cancel{12}} = 21 \text{ cents or } \$.21$$

ALTERNATE SOLUTION

12 cents per yard

$\frac{12}{36} = \frac{1}{3}$ cents per inch

$\frac{63}{1}$ inches $\times \frac{1}{3}$ cents $= \frac{63}{3} = 21$ cents or $.21

22. **E** none of these

The correct answer is $2\frac{1}{4}$ cups.

SOLUTION

Proportion

	Cereal	Water
1st mixture	$1\frac{1}{2}$ cups	$4\frac{1}{2}$ cups
2nd mixture	$\frac{3}{4}$ cups	x cups

$\frac{3}{4}$ is half of $1\frac{1}{2}$

Therefore, half of $4\frac{1}{2}$ is $2\frac{1}{4}$ cups

ALTERNATE SOLUTION

From the data given, we form the proportion, $1\frac{1}{2}$ (cups of cereal) : $4\frac{1}{2}$ (cups of water) $= \frac{3}{4}$ (cup of cereal) : x

$$\therefore \quad \frac{3}{2} : \frac{9}{2} = \frac{3}{4} : x$$
$$\frac{3}{2}x = \frac{27}{4}$$
$$x = \frac{9}{4} = 2\frac{1}{4} \text{ cups}$$

23. **B** 750 miles per hour

Speed of sound = 1100 feet per second

88 feet per second = 60 miles an hour

$\frac{1100}{88} = 12\frac{1}{2}$ (the number of times the speed of sound is greater than 60 miles an hour)

$\therefore \quad 60 \times 12\frac{1}{2} = 750$ miles per hour

24. A $32°$

Let x = second angle
Let $3x$ = first angle
Let $x + 20°$ = third angle
$\therefore 5x + 20° = 180°$
$\qquad\qquad x = 32°$

25. D $13\frac{1}{2}$

$$\frac{\frac{1}{4} \text{ inches}}{12} = \frac{3\frac{3}{8} \text{ inches}}{x}$$

$$\frac{1}{4} \div \frac{12}{1} = \frac{27}{8} \div \frac{x}{1}$$

$$\frac{1}{4} \times \frac{1}{12} = \frac{27}{8} \times \frac{1}{x}$$

$$\frac{1}{48} = \frac{27}{8x}$$

$$8x = 48 \times 27 = 1296$$

$$x = 162 \text{ inches}$$

$$= 13\frac{1}{2} \text{ feet}$$

QUANTITATIVE COMPARISON

EXTRA PRACTICE TEST

Directions: Each question in this section consists of two quantities, one in Column A and one in Column B. You are to compare the two quantities and on the answer sheet blacken space

    A if the quantity in Column A is the greater;
    B if the quantity in Column B is the greater;
    C if the two quantities are equal;
    D if the relationship cannot be determined from the information given.

All numbers used are real numbers.
Diagrams used are not necessarily drawn to scale.

	Column A	Column B
1.	2^4	8
2.	$y - 1$ ($x \neq y$)	$x + 1$
3.	$1 + \dfrac{x}{y}$ ($x \neq y$)	$\dfrac{x + y}{y}$
4.	.004	.04\%
5.	$\dfrac{4\sqrt{3}}{\sqrt{2}}$	$\sqrt{24}$

Column A	Column B

Questions 6–10 refer to this diagram:

$$AB \ || \ DE \qquad \angle C = 90°$$

	Column A	Column B
6.	$\angle A + \angle B$	$\angle CDE + \angle CED$
7.	$\angle ADE$	$\angle B + 85°$
8.	AD	BE
9.	DE	$EC + DC$
10.	$\dfrac{DC}{AC}$	$\dfrac{EC}{BC}$
11.	$\sqrt{7^2 - 6^2}$	$\sqrt{7^2} - \sqrt{6^2}$
12.	$3 + \dfrac{3 + \frac{1}{2}}{3}$	$3 + \dfrac{6 + \frac{1}{2}}{6}$
13.	The average of 12, 14, 16, 18, 20, 22	The average of 11, 13, 15, 17, 19, 21

$$x > 2$$

	Column A	Column B
14.	$3x + 2$	$2x + 3$
15.	4% interest on $2,000 for 1 year	8% interest on $1,000 for 2 years

$$x = 2, \ y = 3$$

	Column A	Column B
16.	$\dfrac{x^2 + 3x}{x(y^2 + y)}$	$\dfrac{y^2 + y}{y(x^2 + x)}$

Questions 17–19 refer to this diagram:

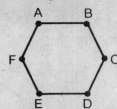

ABCDEF is a regular hexagon

	Column A	Column B
17.	$\angle$ A	$\angle$ D
18.	$\angle$ E	$90°$
19.	AB	$9''$
20.	$4\,!$	$3\,!\,2\,!$
21.	The price of 2 lbs. of candy at 42¢ a lb.	The price of 3 lbs. of candy at 32¢ a lb.
22.	$(x + y)^2$	$x^2 + y^2$

$$x < 4 < y$$

23.	$x + 4$	$y - 4$
24.	The circumference of a semi-circle with radius $4''$	The perimeter of a pentagon with each side $4''$ long.
25.	$\frac{2}{5} \times \frac{1}{9} \times \frac{3}{8}$	$\frac{2}{11} \times \frac{2}{5} \times \frac{3}{8}$

EXTRA PRACTICE TEST ANSWERS

1.	A	10.	C	19.	D
2.	D	11.	A	20.	A
3.	C	12.	A	21.	B
4.	A	13.	A	22.	D
5.	C	14.	A	23.	D
6.	C	15.	B	24.	B
7.	A	16.	B	25.	B
8.	D	17.	C		
9.	B	18.	A		

Putting It All Together!

SOME FINAL IMPORTANT TIPS

Arrive on time
Not to early → bring 2-3 pencils put them on table
walk, id, and
Eat. reg. meal
a→high protein breakfast
don't eat sugar, drink coffee
depresses you

THE WEEK BEFORE THE TEST:

1. Familiarize yourself with the location of your testing center. If necessary, visit the location, check parking facilities and exact room location. *Know where you are going*

2. Remember to carefully review the test directions and strategies for each area. *won't label ea. area — boil notes down to a few pts*

3. Don't make extreme changes in your daily routine. Take care of the physical you! *Do what you usually do.*

4. Get a good night's sleep before the exam. *normal*

5. Cramming the night before the exam will usually do *more harm than good*. Don't cram the night before! *It raise anxiety.*

go in w/ main pts → other pts. will come in

ON THE DAY OF THE EXAM:

1. Arrive on time and be ready.
2. Bring the necessary materials—identification, admission ticket, 3 or 4 sharpened No. 2 pencils, a good eraser, a watch.
3. Approach the exam confidently, using the Positive Systematic Approach.
4. Read the directions carefully, twice if necessary.
5. Start off crisply, stay with it, use every second effectively.
6. Work the ones you know first, then come back and do the others.
7. Make *educated* guesses when you can eliminate one or more choices. Don't guess blindly.
8. Use only the information given, don't complicate a problem.
9. Eliminate un-needed information in problems—simplify.
10. Underline key words, mark in diagrams, take advantage of being allowed to write on the actual exam booklet. *all the time*
11. Look at all choices before marking your answer. *except ana. of explan.*
12. Rephrase difficult questions for yourself.
13. Work calmly and carefully. *Make sure that your answer is reasonable*.
14. Make sure you are answering the *right* question.
15. The key to getting a good score on the GRE is in getting the ones right that you *know* how to do and *should* get right.

use a quick two ck system

Subjectlword

If you get nervous take 15 deep breaths muscle cram norm send release

689